The Blue Guides

	Albania		Rome
	Australia		Venice
			Tuscany
Austria	Austria		Umbria
	Vienna		Sicily
	Bali, Java and Lombok		Jordan
	Belgium and Luxembourg		Malaysia and Singapore
	Bulgaria		Malta and Gozo
			Mexico
	China		Morocco
	Cyprus		
		Netherlands	Netherlands
Czech & Slovak	Czech & Slovak Republics		Amsterdam
Republics	Prague		
			Poland
	Denmark		Portugal
	Egypt		
		Spain	Spain
France	France		Barcelona
	Paris and Versailles		Madrid
	Burgundy		
	Loire Valley		Sweden
	Midi-Pyrénées		Switzerland
	Normandy		Thailand
	Provence		Tunisia
	South West France		
	Corsica	**Turkey**	Turkey
			Istanbul
Germany	Berlin and eastern Germany		
		UK	England
Greece	Greece		Scotland
	Athens and environs		Wales
	Crete		Channel Islands
	Rhodes and the		London
	Dodecanese		Oxford and Cambridge
			Country Houses of
Hungary	Hungary		England
	Budapest		
		USA	New York
	Southern India		Museums and Galleries of
	Ireland		New York
			Boston and Cambridge
Italy	Northern Italy		
	Southern Italy		
	Florence		

We have done our very best to ensure that this guide is up-to-date and error free. However, things do change between editions. We should be delighted to hear from any of our readers who have comments, suggestions or corrections for the next edition of the Blue Guide. Writers of the most helpful letters will be awarded a free Blue Guide of their choice.

Poland

**Jasper Tilbury
and Paweł Turnau**

BLUE GUIDE

A&C Black • London
WW Norton • New York

1st edition © Jasper Tilbury and Paweł Turnau, January 2000
Published by A & C Black (Publishers) Limited
35 Bedford Row, London WC1R 4JH

Maps and plans drawn by RJS Associates, © A&C Black

Illustrations © Piotr Turnau

A CIP catalogue record of this book is available from the British Library.

ISBN 0–7136–3899–0

Published in the United States of America by
WW Norton and Company Inc.
500 Fifth Avenue, New York, NY 10110

Published simultaneously in Canada by
Penguin Books Canada Limited
10 Alcorn Avenue, Toronto
Ontario M4V 3B2

ISBN 0–393–31424–3 USA

The authors and the publishers have done their best to ensure the accuracy of all the information in Blue Guide Poland. However, they can accept no responsibility for any loss, injury or inconvenience sustained by any traveller as a result of information or advice contained in the guide.

Cover photograph: Wawel Cathedral Clock Tower, Kraków, by Phil Robinson, Robert Harding Picture Library. **Title page illustration**, Inowłodź. Church, Mazovia.

Jasper Tilbury was born in London. He graduated in modern history from the University of St Andrews. Since 1989 he has lived in Kraków, where he works as a freelance journalist and translator.

Paweł Turnau was born in Kraków. He graduated in philosophy from the Jagiellonian University. He lives in Kraków and works as a translator and researcher.

Printed and bound in Great Britain by Butler & Tanner Ltd., Frome and London.

Introduction

By European standards, Poland is a medium-sized country, with an area exceeding that of the UK by one third (312,700 sq. km). It is also a country of enormous variety, both in terms of geography and culture, offering the visitor a wealth of historic towns, pristine nature reserves and attractive resorts.

With the demise of Communism in 1989, the stereotype of permanent food shortages, atrocious services and general shoddiness is losing currency, though Western ignorance about Polish culture and society remains surprisingly high. Political stability and a growing free market economy have turned the country into a major holiday destination, with revenues from tourism reaching several billion dollars per year. Hardly a week passes without some feature story in the Western press extolling the virtues of 'fashionable Kraków' or hiking trips to the 'undiscovered' Bieszczady Mountains. For their part, agencies have been quick to explore the new possibilities afforded by tourism, offering, in addition to conventional sightseeing, holidays based around special interests.

Geographically, Poland can be divided into five distinct regions. Three of these—the Baltic coastline with its dunes and marshes, the post-glacial lake-lands in the north and northeast, and the fertile loess plain of central Poland—account for 75 per cent of the country's land mass. A belt of ancient uplands stretches further south, eroded over millions of years. The younger Carpathian and Sudeten mountain ranges mark the southern borders of Poland. Three quarters of the country's area is less than 200m above sea level, and most of it is part of the North European Plain.

From the historical point of view, the division of Poland into regions is less straightforward. The country's 1000 years of recorded history is ridden with conflict, turmoil and rapid reversals of fortune. The present borders of Poland are only 50 years old, and 100 years ago they did not exist at all. Another four centuries back, and Poland was the largest European state. Today, its 40-million population is ethnically and religiously one of the most homogenous in the world—90 per cent of Poles declare themselves to be Roman Catholic—but before the last war, national minorities comprised one third of the population. Waves of emigration in the 19C–20C have caused the Polish diaspora to rise to over 10 million. Today, for instance, more Poles live in Chicago than Gdańsk.

Poland is commonly seen as a bridge between east and west, between Europe and Asia. For some, it is a bulwark of Christianity; for others, a springboard for economic expansion into the vast markets of the former Soviet Union. Most visitors from western Europe or America will find Poland a relatively cheap holiday destination, one that is largely unspoilt by tourism, and yet much less hazardous than its eastern neighbours. Its architecture is a curious mixture of familiar Italian, German or Dutch styles with something exotic and oriental added. Its people and customs may sometimes engender a feeling that the clock has been set back a hundred years—churches full on Sundays, 'chivalrous' attitudes towards women.

Despite the rapid expansion of mass culture and western consumerism, the country's links to its past are very much alive. Diverse cultural legacies are evident in all the major cites: Gdańsk, with its burgher architecture and Hanseatic traditions; Kraków, with its unique version of Italian Renaissance; Poznań, initially the cradle of the Polish state, centuries later transformed into the prosperous capital of a Prussian province; Warsaw, with its magnificent Neo-classical palaces and bizarre Socialist Realist districts; and Wrocław, the boisterous life of its medieval market square contrasting with the meditative quiet of its ecclesiastical island.

Most visitors to Poland will begin their itineraries in one of these five cities, which certainly have most to offer in the way of sites and monuments. They have accordingly been given due prominence in this Guide. However, there is much more to the country than this, and visitors who venture out into the provinces are bound to find the experience rewarding. Connoisseurs of art and architecture should not miss Toruń, Malbork, Kazimierz Dolny or Zamość. Nature-lovers will be attracted to the Masurian lakes, the Tatra and Bieszczady mountains, the marshes of the Biebrza and Narew rivers, and the Białowieża primeval forest.

The Guide is divided into six parts, each dealing with one region, set apart from the others on historical and geographical grounds. Except for the least populated north-eastern corner of Poland (Warmia and Masuria), each region is best explored from one of the five cities mentioned above—capitals of their respective regions.

Acknowledgements

The publication of this, the first *Blue Guide to Poland*, would not have been possible without the help of many people. We cannot hope to mention them all by name, but we would like to thank, in particular, Gemma Davies, the Blue Guides series editor, for her patience and helpful comments, as well as Miranda Robson for her meticulous editorial work. A special word of gratitude is due to Jan Paweł Piotrowski of the now defunct Central Tourist Information Office (COIT) in Warsaw, who arranged a grant for the two introductory chapters by Prof. Zdzisław Żygulski and Krzysztof Myszkowski, and gave us access to the COIT database and numerous printed materials. Blanka A. Rosenstiel kindly offered financial assistance on behalf of the American Institute of Polish Culture in Miami.

Our extensive travels around Poland were made possible thanks to generous help with accommodation provided by the following people: Anna Andrejuk, Sabina Anna Borek, Leszek Buzantowicz, Waldemar Głuch, Maria Gacka, Lucyna Gurniewicz, Piotr Jankowski, Adam Jarema, Marian Klauze, Alex Kloszewski, Gabriela Kreft, Ryszard Kurowski, Ryszard Lewkowicz, Stanisław Litman, Waldemar Majewski, Witold Nol, Janina Nóżka, Elżbieta Pniewska, Wojciech Przybyłko, M. Różański, Henryk Skowron, Marek Stopczyk, Lucyna Szczygieł, Piotr Szewczuk, Elżbieta Szwarocha, Marek Wiącek, Henryk Wiśniewski, R. Wojciechowski, Danuta Zielińska, Feliks Zielnik, Zdzisław Ziomek, Mieczysław Zyner, and Halina Żelińska. We are grateful for the encouragement given to us by ambassadors Desmond Llewelyn-Smith (UK) and Thomas J. Simons (US), Bishop Bronisław Dembowski, William Faix, and especially the EU Ambassador to Poland, Alexander H. Dijckmeester. Our research into Polish art and culture was greatly facilitated by Adam Pirożyński, director of the Jagiellonian Library in Kraków. Jasper Tilbury would also like to thank Adam Karwowski, former director of the LOT Polish airlines office in London, for help with tickets.

The authors have taken every effort to ensure that the Guide is accurate, but the pace of change in Poland inevitably means that some of the information will already be outdated. Any comments or suggestions are most welcome, and can be sent to the publisher or directly to the authors at: uzturnau@cyf-kr.edu.pl or tilbury@kr.onet.pl.

Contents

Małopolska

Pomerania

Warmia and Masuria

Silesia

Maps and plans

Country map *inside front and back covers*

Regional maps

Town plans

Ground plans

Explanatory notes

The first **names of Polish monarchs and saints** have not been translated (thus avoiding clumsy anglicisations such as 'Laidslaus' or 'Boleslaus') but their epithets have. Thus, 'Kazimierz the Great' is preferred to 'Kazimierz Wielki' or 'Casimir the Great'. Where possible, names have been kept in the original. Exceptions include names of famous personages that have a conventional English (Latin) spelling. Thus, 'Copernicus' is preferred to 'Kopernik'.

Road distances are given in kilometres and are based on official publications.

Stars. One or two **stars** have been used in this guide to indicate places or buildings of special interest. Places and buildings prefixed by two stars are considered to be of major importance on a European or world scale.

Times are given according to the 24-hour clock, as is conventional in Poland.

Street names honouring famous communists have been abandoned in Poland since 1989 in favour of original pre-war names or, in some cases, wholly new ones. Thus, (older) city maps should be used with caution, as sometimes these changes will not have been incorporated.

Palaces are sometimes known under alternative names. This is usually because at various points in their history they were owned by different noble families. Thus, some maps will refer to the palace at No. 15 ul. Krakowskie Przedmieście in Warsaw as the Czartoryski Palace, while others will call it the Potocki Palace. In this guide we have given preference to the names most commonly used.

Abbreviations

c	circa	ha	hectare
C	century	ul. (ulica)	street
km	kilometre	pl. (plac)	square/plaza
m	metre	al. (aleja)	avenue

Acronyms

ORBIS Poland's largest national tourist agency and hotel chain
IT Tourist information office
PTTK Polish Tourist Association (hostel accommodation)
PAPT Polish Agency for the Promotion of Tourism

Practical Information

Planning your trip

When to go

Poland has a temperate climate which is more continental than Britain's, with colder winters and warmer summers. The average daytime temperature in July, the hottest month, is 23°C, though in recent years daily temperatures in excess of 30°C have been common. Summer (July–August) is not the best time to visit due to the large volume of tourist traffic. Accommodation is scarce, cities are hot and overcrowded, while coastal, lakeland and mountain resorts overflow with day-trippers and Polish families on their holidays. July and August also have the highest rainfall (75–100mm per month on average). Early autumn (September) is attractive due to the mild temperatures and the fabulous colours of the deciduous forests. This is the best time to visit mountain or lakeland regions; it is also the cultural season, with many festivals taking place in towns and cities. The first snowfalls usually come in November, and 'white Christmases are the rule. January and February are the coldest winter months, when average temperatures drop to below freezing. During exceptionally cold winters temperatures as low as -30°C (-22°F) have been recorded.

Winter tourism (December–March) is popular in Poland, and there is usually plenty of snow in the mountains for skiing enthusiasts, though, as in summer, the few resorts and inadequate infrastructure cannot cope with all the tourist traffic. Spring (April–June) is the best season for sightseeing and outdoor pursuits. May and June have many sunny days with clear skies, and there is usually much in the way of cultural events and entertainment.

Passports and formalities

Visas are no longer required of EU and US citizens to enter Poland. The maximum period of stay is six months for British nationals and three months for US and EU nationals. This period is not extendible within Poland, so if you wish to stay longer you must return to your country of origin and apply for a regular tourist visa at the Polish embassy or consulate. Canadian and Australian citizens must have tourist visas to enter Poland. These are issued for a maximum of ninety days, but may be extended in Poland at the Voivodship Office (Urząd Wojewódzki), Foreign Visitors Department (Oddział ds. Cudzoziemców), ul. Krucza 5/11, Warsaw, ☎ (0-22) 625-5904, or its counterpart in other Polish cities. Tourist visas are single-, double- or multiple-entry and may be used up to six months from their date of issue. Applicants must have a full (not temporary) passport that is valid for at least one month after the expiry date of the visa. Transit visas, which may be purchased at the border, are valid for 48 hours and are only issued if you can show a visa (if required) for your next country of destination; you must also enter and leave Poland through different border crossings.

Embassies and Consulates
Polish embassies and consulates abroad
- UK: 19 Weymouth St, London W1N 4EA, ☎ (020) 7580-0476; 73 New Cavendish St, London W1N 7RB, ☎ (020) 7580-0475.
- US: 2224 Wyoming Ave, NW, Washington DC 20008, ☎ (202) 232-4517; Madison Ave, New York, NY 10016, ☎ (212) 889-8360.
- **Australia**: 10 Trelawny St, Wollahara, Sydney, NSW 2025, ☎ (02) 9363-9816.
- **Canada**: 443 Daly St, Ottawa, Ontario , ☎ (613) 236-0468; 2603 Lakeshore Blvd West, Toronto, Ontario M8V 1G5, ☎ (416) 252-5471.
Embassies and consulates in Poland
- UK: al. Róż 1, Warsaw, ☎ (0-22) 628-1001 to 05.
- US: al. Ujazdowskie 29/31, Warsaw, ☎ (0-22) 628 3041 to 49.
- **Australia**: ul. Estońska 3/5, Warsaw, ☎ (0-22) 617-6081 to 85.
- **Canada**: ul. Matejki 1/5, Warsaw, ☎ (0-22) 629-8051 to 56.

Customs
Import regulations. Visitors can bring the following items into Poland duty free: articles for personal use connected with the length and purpose of stay, including one of each of the following: a personal computer, VCR, cassette player, radio, TVs etc., together with accessories such as cassettes/video tapes/CDs/diskettes (10 of each), a portable musical instrument, surfboard, kayak, bicycle, tent, binoculars and one pair of skis. Two still cameras and one cine/video camera together with accessories and ten rolls of film are allowed. Permits issued by a Polish consulate are needed for sporting or hunting guns, hand guns and air pistols. Visitors may import precious jewellery provided its total weight does not exceed 50g as well as gifts and souvenirs not exceeding $100 in total value. In addition, adults may bring in the following alcoholic beverages and tobacco products: .25 litre of spirits, .75 litre of wine, 1 litre of beer, 250 cigarettes or 50 cigars or 250g of tobacco.

Export regulations. Gifts and souvenirs not exceeding $100 in total value may be taken out of Poland duty free. The export regulations for alcoholic beverages and tobacco products are the same as for import. Special export licences are required for all items manufactured prior to 9 May 1945.

If you need further information concerning customs regulations, contact the **Main Customs Office** (Główny Urząd Ceł), pl. Powstanców Warszawy 1, Warsaw, ☎ (0-22) 694-3194; or the Customs Office, Okęcie International Airport, Warsaw, ☎ (0-22) 650-2873.

National tourist organisations
The **Polish Agency for the Promotion of Tourism** (Polska Agencja Promocji Turystyki, PAPT) is the main state-run tourist organisation in Poland. It has over 50 branch offices in towns and cities around the country (see the relevant chapters of this Guide for addresses). The quality of these offices varies, but most will at least sell information brochures, guide books, catalogues, maps and plans. In the better offices, visitors can get information about local places of interest, guides, travel agency services, transport, restaurants, accommodation, sports equipment rental, and cultural events. In smaller towns you may find that the office staff

speak no English—in these cases hotels are the best alternative. If you need additional information before arrival, contact the Polish National Tourist Association:
- UK: 1st floor, Remo House, 310–312 Regent St, London W1R 5AJ,
  ☎ (020) 7580-8811.
- US: 275 Madison Ave, Suite 1711, New York, NY 10016,
  ☎ (212) 338-9412.

The other major tourist organisation in Poland is **Orbis**, also known abroad as Polorbis. It, too, has branches in just about every Polish town and city and usually offers a broader range of services than PAPT, with special emphasis on travel. For instance, at Orbis offices you can buy domestic and international rail and coach tickets, thus avoiding the long queues at stations—an added convenience is that Orbis offices are usually located in town centres. Recently privatised, the company also runs a national chain of reliable, high standard hotels. Reservations can be made at any Orbis office. Staff will also give you information about guided tours and excursions, package deals, equipment hire, car rental, cultural and sporting events etc. Holidays can be booked direct through Orbis offices abroad (see below), which also supply a good selection of general information about the country. The addresses of Orbis offices in major Polish cities are given in the relevant sections of this Guide.

There are a number of other tourist organisations operating in Poland, the best known of which are: **PTTK** (The Polish Tourist Association), dealing mainly in hostel accommodation, countryside trips and outdoor pursuits; **Gromada**, which has its own hotel chain and specialises in spa holidays; and **Almatur**, the main student travel bureau, offering cheap holidays and accommodation for young people. Another good source of tourist information and services are private travel agencies.

Tour operators
Listed below are Polish-run tour operators with a proven track record in travel and tourism:
UK
- Fregata Travel, 100 Dean St, London W1, ☎ (020) 7734-5101.
- Polorbis, 82 Mortimer St, London W1, ☎ (020) 7636-2267.
- Tazab Travel, 273 Old Brompton Rd, London SW7, ☎ (020) 7373-1186.
- Travelines, 154 Cromwell Rd, London SW7, ☎ (020) 7370-6131.

US
- Fregata Travel, 250 West 57th St, Suite 1211, New York, NY 10107, ☎ (212) 541-5707; fax (212) 262-3220.
- Orbis, 342 Madison Ave, Suite 1512, New York, NY 10173, ☎ (212) 867-5011.

Disabled travellers
Poland is well behind Western countries in terms of provision for disabled travellers. In Warsaw, a few modern hotels have wheelchair access and the Fundacja TVS runs special services for the disabled (see Warsaw section), but elsewhere facilities are rare. For more information on travel abroad, contact the Royal Association for Disability and Rehabilitation, 12 City Forum, 250 City Road, London, ☎ (020) 7250-322.

Currency regulations ~ money

There is no compulsory currency exchange in Poland. You may bring in as much foreign currency as you wish, but you will not be able to (re)export more foreign currency than is specified on the currency declaration you fill out at the border. If you have money sent directly to you in Poland, you will need a bank certificate (equivalent to a customs declaration) to take it out of the country again. The export (or import) of Polish currency—the złoty (abbreviated to zł or PLN)—is prohibited, but as it is only internally convertible, there would be little point in exporting it anyway. Before you leave Poland, you should convert all your złoty into pounds/dollars or some other foreign currency. There are numerous places to do this (see below). It is a good idea to have a small amount of złotys on arrival in Poland as the exchange rates at airports and train stations are always bad. Most high-street banks will order Polish currency for you, though this may take a day or two.

The Polish złoty comes in the following denominations: banknotes: 200, 100, 50, 20, 10; coins: 5, 2, 1. One złoty contains 100 grosz (gr.), denominated as follows: 50, 20, 10, 5, 2, 1. You should be careful when handling Polish banknotes, and on no account accept any note that has three zeros or more—this is the old money that went out of circulation in January 1997. The best place to change cash is at a *kantor* (private exchange office), as they offer better rates than banks. *Kantor's* are easy to find—every town or city will have many—are often open at weekends and sometimes 24 hours (especially in main stations). If you arrive in Poland by road and need cash immediately, you can change money at the PZM (Polish Motoring Association) offices found at many border crossings. You should be careful not to bring any marked or damaged foreign notes, as banks and *kantors* will often refuse to accept them.

Nowadays, credit and debit cards are widely used in Polish towns and cities and indeed Polish banks offer Visa and Mastercards to their customers. Most large hotels and travel agencies, many supermarkets and some shops and restaurants now accept plastic. Transactions are basically secure. Selected banks and hotels will also give cash advances on most major cards. In case of **loss or theft of a credit card**, you should immediately contact PolCard Ltd., Warsaw, ☎ (0-22) 827-4513/827-3040 (24 hour service). Banks offer a slightly worse rate on travellers cheques than on cash and charge up to two per cent commission; hotels charge even more, and *kantors* do not accept them at all. You will always need proof of identity to change travellers' cheques.

Health

Britain (but not the US) has a reciprocal agreement with Poland which entitles British citizens to free medical and dental care in case of accidents or emergencies, including transport to hospital. The ambulance telephone number is ☎ 999. All other medical and dental care will be charged. It is best to take out travel/health insurance for your stay in Poland as the costs are minimal compared to the potential benefits. The Polish public health service is in a sorry state and is free in theory only. Bribery is institutionalised and hospitals will often refuse to treat patients unless they can at least pay for their own medications. For minor ailments you can consult a doctor at an outpatient clinic (*przychodnia*), but it is usually better to go to a private clinic (*klinika prywatna*) or medical co-operative (addresses in the local press) as you will be seen to much faster for little extra cost. Home visits can be ordered through private clinics and are payable in cash. Hotels often have their own medical services and will arrange visits for you if they do not. Your embassy or consulate should be able to provide you with a list of English-speaking doctors in Poland. It may even have its own clinic.

There are no compulsory inoculations required of people arriving from the EU or US, although some doctors advise getting a hepatitis A vaccination. Polish tapwater is officially drinkable, but it doesn't taste too good. Boil it before use, or, better still, simply stick to mineral water, which is easily obtained in shops, restaurants and hotels.

Pharmacies (*apteki*) are run by qualified staff and have a wide selection of foreign and domestic medications. They are generally open from 08.00 to 20.00, but every city will have at least one which is open through the night (though its location may change). Check the local press or the notices posted oustide pharmacies—the keyword is (*nocny*) *dyżur* (night shift).

 ## Crime and personal security

Street crime in Warsaw and other cities has risen dramatically in recent years, but generally Poland is still a lot safer than Western countries. You should keep your personal belongings with you at all times. Never leave valuables in your car, and if you have a bicycle make sure it has a secure lock. Valuables are best left at the hotel reception (ask for a receipt), or at a left luggage office, where items are insured automatically (the cost of the service is proportionate to their value). Beware of pickpockets on crowded buses and trams and in shops. The Polish police are often castigated for taking far too long to arrive at crime scenes and doing little to help the victims. The language barrier may also be a problem. Minor crimes (eg theft) should be reported to the central police station—you will have more chance of finding an English speaker there than by phoning ☎ 997. There is no compulsion on foreigners to carry passports with them, but it is always wise to carry some form of identity and a contact address in case of accidents. Polish police (blue uniforms) carry guns and can stop and search anyone behaving suspiciously. Bigger cities also have black-uniformed municipal police (*straż miejska*), with far lesser powers.

Getting to Poland

By air

There are numerous regular flights to Poland from most major European cities. Both LOT Polish airlines and British Airways fly daily between London and Warsaw. The journey time is approximately 2 hours 35 minutes. LOT also has direct flights from New York (7 a week) and Chicago (5 a week) to Warsaw. The journey time from New York is 9 hours 40 minutes. International flights also land at the following Polish cities: Kraków, Gdańsk, Katowice, Poznań, Rzeszów, Szczecin and Wrocław. BA has a twice-weekly service from London to Kraków; LOT also has a weekly service to Gdańsk. Recently, British Midland has started running cheap charter flights to Poland during the summer months. It is worth checking other airlines for similar deals.

Information about reservations and tickets is available at LOT offices abroad: London, 313 Regent St, ☎ (020) 7580-5037; New York, 500 Fifth Ave, Suite

408, NY 10110, ☎ (212) 869-1074. The cheapest tickets are Apex, which must be bought well in advance and have various restrictions including fixed journey dates. If you change these dates at a later stage you will lose the Apex discount and the penalties are harsh if you cancel altogether. Regular economy-class tickets are valid for up to one year but can be twice as expensive as Apex. It is worth checking the press for operators offering one- or two-week package deals, as these can often work out cheaper than the price of a regular ticket. 'Bucket shops' are also an option. All ticket prices vary with the season. In general, they are lowest in February/March and October/November. See the Warsaw chapter for information on getting to and from Okęcie airport.

By rail

Warsaw has direct rail connections with many European cities, including:

- Hannover–Dortmund–Cologne
- Leipzig–Frankfurt (Main)
- Bratislava–Budapest
- Minsk–Smolensk–Moscow
- Grodno–St Petersburg

There are also Eurocity trains to Berlin (6 hours), Vienna (8 hours) and Prague (9 hours).

The journey from London Liverpool St to Warsaw takes about 30 hours and includes a long ferry crossing between Harwich and the Hook-of-Holland. Trains leave daily except Sundays. Tickets are valid for two months and allow unlimited stopovers, though they are usually more expensive than Apex air tickets.

An increasingly popular option is to fly to Vienna, Prague, Budapest or Berlin and then continue by train to Poland. This cuts down on journey time and may even be cheaper than travelling direct, as bargain flights to these cities are plentiful. Rail tickets can be bought at *Eurotrain*, 52 Grosvenor Gardens, London SW1, ☎ (020) 7730-3402 and at the International Rail Centre, Victoria Station, London SW1, ☎ 0990-848-848. Inter-Rail passes are valid in Poland.

By coach

This is the cheapest way of getting to Poland, but also the most exhausting. The journey from London to Warsaw can take up to 36 hours depending on the company and route. *Eurolines* (a branch of National Express), 52 Grosvenor Gardens, London SW1, ☎ (020) 7730-8235, has air-conditioned coaches with video and toilets and provides the most comfortable and reliable service from the UK. In high season there are up to three departures each week to Warsaw and other cities.

Alternatively, you could try one of the Polish-run companies, such as *White Eagle Lines*, 200 Earls Court Rd, London SW5, ☎ (020) 7244-0054, which offers a good service at competitive rates, as do the tour operators Tazab, Travelines and Fregata (see above).

By car

Poland has many border crossings with all seven neighbouring countries. All those listed below are open twenty-four hours and can be used by Polish and non-Polish nationals alike. Transit traffic runs through Poland from west to east and north to south. This can cause congestion on the main trunk roads and major delays at the eastern border crossings. Anyone travelling to Russia or the Ukraine by car should check the waiting times at the border before departure. If you are crossing from Germany at Forst–Olszyna, beware that the first stretch of the E-30 on the Polish side is in poor condition. Those entering from Slovakia could try the scenic crossing at Javořina–Łysa Polana in the heart of the Tatra mountains. Another picturesque crossing is at Harrachov (Czech Republic)—Jakuszyce. Petrol is cheaper in Poland than in Germany, so it is best to fill your tank on the Polish side of the border.

From the UK, the quickest route to Poland is via Brussels, Hannover and Berlin, crossing the Polish border at Świecko (for Poznań and Warsaw), Kołbaskowo (for Szczecin), or Olszyna (for Wrocław and Kraków). The distance from the French or Belgian coast to Warsaw is about 1500km.

To drive a foreign-registered car in Poland you must have: a driving licence, car registration documents, a country sticker and Green Card insurance (see also the Driving in Poland section). The latter can be purchased at the Polish Motoring Association (PZM), which has offices at all border crossings. The PZM also sells maps and guides and provides general information on travel in Poland. At all times your car should also carry, by law, a warning triangle for break-downs, a fire extinguisher, and a first aid kit. Until recently, an international driving licence was required to drive a foreign-registered car in Poland, but nowadays licences from EU countries and the US are respected. However, you will need an international licence if you intend to drive abroad in a car registered in Poland.

German border
- Linken–Lubieszyn (for Szczecin)
- Pomellen–Kołbaskowo (for Szczecin)
- Schwedt–Krajnik Dolny
- Hohenwutzen–Osinów Dolny (cars only)
- Kietz–Kostrzyn (for Gorzów)
- Frankfurt am Oder–Słubice (for Poznań)
- Frankfurt am Oder–Świecko (for Poznań)
- Guben–Gubin
- Forst–Olszyna (for Wrocław)
- Bad Muskau–Łęknica
- Görlitz–Zgorzelec (for Wrocław)
- Zittau–Sieniawka
- Zittau–Porajów

Czech border
- Hradek n. Nisou–Porajów
- Habartice–Zawidów (cars only)
- Harrachov–Jakuszyce (for Jelenia Góra)
- Kralovec–Lubawka
- Český Těšín–Cieszyn (for Kraków)
- Dolní Lipka–Boboszów
- Mikulovice–Głuchołazy
- Krnov–Pietrowice
- Bohumín–Chałupki (for Katowice)
- Náchod–Kudowa-Słone

Slovak border
- Trstená–Chyzne (for Kraków)
- Javořina–Łysa Polana
- Mníšek n. Popradom–Piwniczna (for Nowy Sącz)
- Becherov–Konieczna
- Vyš. Komárnik–Barwinek (for Rzeszów)

Ukrainian border
- Šegini Mostiska–Medyka (Lviv/Kiev–Przemyśl route)
- Rawa Rus'ka–Hrebenne
- Jagodin–Dorohusk

Byelorussian border
* Briest–Terespol (Moscow–Warsaw route)
* Bruzgi–Kuźnica Białostocka (Minsk–Białystok route)

Lithuanian border
* Lazdijai–Ogrodniki (Vilnius–Suwałki route)

Russian border
* Bagrationovsk–Bezledy (Kaliningrad Enclave)

By sea
There is a weekly Polish freighter service with passenger accommodation which leaves Tilbury in Essex on Monday, arriving in Gdynia on Friday. The ship also calls at Middlesborough. For more information, contact **Gdynia America Shipping Lines Ltd**, 238 City Rd, London EC1, ☎ (020) 7251–3389, fax (020) 7250–3625.

An alternative is to combine sea and land travel. **Scandinavian Seaways** (Parkeston Quay, Harwich, Essex, ☎ (0225) 241–234), for instance, runs a regular car ferry service from Harwich to Hamburg.

There are also freighter services from the US to Rotterdam and Bremerhaven. For more information, contact Gdynia America Shipping Lines Ltd, 39 Broadway, 14th floor, New York, NY 10006, ☎ (212) 952-1280.

Polferries (Polska Żegluga Bałtycka) has regular car ferry connections with Sweden, Denmark and Finland on the following routes:
* Malmö–Świnoujście (once daily)
* Copenhagen–Świnoujście (five times weekly)
* Rönne (Bornholm)–Świnoujście (once a week, 23 June–4 September)
* Oxelösund–Gdańsk (once weekly)
* Nynäshamn–Gdańsk (twice weekly)

The company has offices in many Polish cities as well as agents in Scandinavia and the UK (Gdynia America Shipping Lines, see above).

Where to stay

Hotel accommodation can be booked direct (see the listings in the city chapters for addresses and telephone numbers) or through British- and US-based agencies before arrival in Poland (see Tour Operators section for details). The busiest period is June to September, and if you visit at this time it is best to book in advance. In cities, rooms can also be scarce during major festivals, trade fairs and conferences—some of these are listed in the relevant sections of this Guide. In general, tourist accommodation in Poland is highly varied in terms of price and quality. For a double room with breakfast in a top-end Warsaw hotel you should expect to pay upwards of £100 ($160) per night. The price for a similar room in a mid-range hotel starts at around £50 ($80). In general, all types of accommodation are cheaper in provincial towns than in the capital.

The Internet has recently become a useful source of up-to-date information on hotel accommodation. A few good addresses are listed below:
* http://www.polhotels.com/
* http://www.hotels.inpoland.com/
* http://www.travel-poland.pl/lodging/index_pl.html

• http:///www.orbis.pl

Information on restaurants can be found at http://www.restauracje.com.

Hotels

Polish hotels follow the international classification system, with categories ranging from one to five stars. Many luxury hotels are run by international chains such as Holiday Inn, Intercontinental, Marriott, Sheraton, Radisson, or Park. The Polish-run Orbis travel agency has a network of high standard hotels across the country. There is also an increasing number of private hotels, some of which are not classified, but of good standard nonetheless. For those travelling by car, country inns (*zajazdy*) and motels (*motele*) may be a good option on account of their convenient out-of-town location within easy reach of major roads; they are also cheaper than city hotels of comparable standard and often provide excellent regional cuisine. Accommodation is sometimes available in castles, palaces and historic country manors, often in pleasant surroundings. Such places are mentioned in the relevant sections of this Guide.

Due to the general shortage of accommodation in Poland, hotels have few single rooms and often charge the same rate for singles as for doubles. In large cities, hotel staff will speak English and/or other foreign languages, but in rural areas the language barrier can be a problem. Check-out time is usually 12.00, but most hotels will allow you to leave your luggage at reception if required. You should always ask if the price of the room includes breakfast. Telephone calls from hotels may be expensive, and it is usually cheaper to use a public card phone. International calls arranged through AT&T, MCI or Sprint are even cheaper. Before you arrive, ask your phone company for up-to-date numbers of their operators in major Polish cities.

Pensions

Pensions or guest houses are a cheap alternative to hotels and are often located in holiday resorts and places of natural beauty. The better ones will offer private bathrooms and half or full board. Some have basic catering facilities. Local travel agents can make reservations, or you can simply look for the signs marked 'pensjonat'.

Private rooms

Private rooms are usually part of the owner's house or flat, but normally you will be given your own key and have full freedom of movement. Local accommodation offices (*biura zakwaterowania*) and some travel agents will arrange accommodation in private rooms, which are especially popular in resort towns and spas. You can also inquire on the spot by looking for the signs marked 'noclegi', 'pokoje', or 'zimmer'.

Hostels

The **Tourist Hotel** (*Dom Turysty* or *Dom Wycieczkowy*), equivalent to hostel accommodation in Western countries, might be a good option for budget travellers. There can be up to six bunks per room, with common toilets and bathrooms, but the better ones offer singles and doubles, too. Geared mainly towards students, tourist hotels are managed by the Polish Tourist Association (PTTK) and are often located along hiking trails and in the countryside. You will also find them in cities. In mountain areas they are known as *schroniska górskie* (mountain shelters), and are obliged to provide at least sleeping room on the floor to all-comers. For more information, contact the PTTK head office, ul. Senatorska 11, Warsaw, ☎ (0-22) 826-2251/55.

Youth Hostels (*schroniska młodzieżowe*) are run by the PTSM, a national organisation affiliated to the International Youth Hostel Federation (IYHF). Holders of IYHF cards are eligible for a 25 per cent discount. Some of the hostels are open all year round, others in summer only. Visitors of all ages are welcome. For more information, contact the head office of the PTSM at ul. Chocimska 28, Warsaw, ☎ (0-22) 498-354.

International Student Hostels offer cheap accommodation in student dormitories when the students are away on their summer holidays. The hostels are located in university towns and cities and are run by the Almatur student organisation. For more information, contact the head office at ul. Kopernika 15, Warsaw, ☎ (0-22) 826-5381.

Campsites

Campsites are plentiful in Poland, especially in the Masurian and Pomeranian lakelands and along the Baltic coast. Most are open in summer only (May to September), though some offer year-round accommodation in wooden chalets. There are three categories of campsite. Holders of FICC-AIT-FIA international camping carnets may get discounts. For more information, including reservations and a list of campsites in Poland, contact the Polish Camping and Caravaning Federation (PFCC), ul. Grochowska 331, Warsaw, ☎ (0-22) 810-6050.

Travelling around Poland

Maps

Maps in English, usually in dual-language versions, are readily available from many bookshops and kiosks. **City maps** are definitely worth buying (ask for *plan miasta*) as they provide additional information not covered in this Guide, for instance on public transport. **Road atlases** contain rudimentary maps of the major cities, but they do not show tourist attractions or places of interest. Hikers exploring mountain regions should always equip themselves with a large-scale topographical map showing hiking trails, shelters etc. A good example is the *Tartzański Park Narodowy* (Tartra National Park) map, which covers the most important part of the Tartra mountain region as well as the town of Zakopane. Likewise, the *Wielkie Pojezierze Mazurskie* (Masurian Lake District) map is very handy for exploring the northeast of the country. **Voivodship (county) maps** may also be convenient if you plan to explore a specific area. Following the administrative reform of 1999, there are 17 voivodships in Poland (as opposed to 49 previously), and new maps have been produced to reflect this change.

By rail

In general, rail travel is the most convenient way of getting around Poland. It is reliable, comfortable and significantly cheaper than in Western countries. The extensive network (24,312km) is run exclusively by Polish State Railways (PKP), with no private operators as yet.

There are four categories of train: *Eurocity/Intercity*, *Expres* (express), *Pospieszny* (fast), and *Osobowy* (local). **Eurocity** services are still in their infancy, with connections from Warsaw to Berlin, Prague and Vienna, but more are planned for the future. Their domestic counterpart, **Intercity** services, are more common, with connections from Warsaw to many cities, including Kraków, Gdańsk, Wrocław, Poznań, Szczecin, Lublin and Katowice. Eurocity/Intercity trains have clean, modern carriages, proper restaurant cars, and six seats per compartment in first and second class. Eurocity/Intercity and express trains carry compulsory seat reservations (denoted by the letter R in a box). **Express** trains travel at the same speed as Intercity services but sometimes stop at more stations, so journey times are slightly longer. There are eight seats per compartment in second class. 'Fast' trains, stopping at larger stations, hardly live up to their name and are often dirty and overcrowded. **Local** trains stop at almost every station and should be avoided except for very short journeys.

On all trains, tickets may be bought from the guard for a small additional charge—you should inform him as soon as you board. They can also be purchased at Orbis offices, sometimes by credit card. First class tickets (*pierwsza klasa*) are 50 per cent more expensive than second class (*druga klasa*); a return ticket (*bilet powrotny*) is usually twice as expensive as a single (*bilet w jedną stronę*). If you want a non-smoking compartment, ask for *dla niepalących*. Many long distance trains have couchette cars (six beds in each compartment) and sleepers (three beds in second class, two in first).

If you plan to do a lot of travelling by rail, you might want to buy a Polrail pass. It gives unlimited travel on Polish railways for 8, 14, 21 or 30-day periods and includes all supplement and reservation charges (not including couchettes or sleepers). Polrail passes must be purchased from an agent—such as Orbis/Polorbis—before arrival in Poland.

Be careful not to confuse departure boards (*odjazdy*, yellow-coloured) with arrivals boards (*przyjazdy*, white-coloured). The boards show the times as well as the platform (*peron*) and track (*tor*) numbers of departing and arriving trains. The types of train are denoted by the following symbols: Eurocity—EC; Intercity—IC; Express—Ex; Fast—Posp., marked in red; Local—Osob., marked in black. If you are travelling to a city, you will usually want to get off at the main station—(*Główny* or *Główna*—though in Warsaw it is, uniquely, *Centralna*). Some regions have narrow-gauge lines with old steam trains—well worth a ride, but nowadays a rarity.

By bus ~ coach

The state bus company (**PKS**) operates **local** (black), **semi-fast** (green) **fast** (red) and **express** (red—Ex) services on regional, national and international routes. In general, buses are useful for getting to out-of-the-way places and when travelling in remote areas. In mountain areas, buses will get you to your destination much faster than trains. There are few services on very long distance routes, eg Kraków–Szczecin, and in these cases it is far better to take the overnight train. Tickets should be bought beforehand at bus terminals or travel offices. You can also buy your ticket from the driver if there are free seats available. On popular and longer routes it is always advisable to book in advance.

An alternative to PKS is the privately-owned **Polski Expres** company, which has newer coaches with air conditioning and friendlier staff. Tickets can be bought at travel offices and at PKS bus terminals in cities serviced by Polski Express lines. Departure boards at PKS terminals indicate the final destinations (*kierunek*) and routes (*przez*) of buses. The place you want to go to will not necessarily be the final destination, so you may have to check the *przez* column also.

By car

While train is the best way of getting from city to city, car travel gives you the freedom to explore regions and visit out-of-the-way places poorly serviced by public transport. The Polish road network is extensive (220,000km) but rather poor by Western standards. There are very few stretches of motorway, though a system of toll motorways linking the major cities is planned to open in 2010. International trunk roads (prefixed by the letter E) are usually well-maintained and relatively fast, but the quality of provincial roads can deteriorate dramatically. In the countryside, asphalt roads are often narrow, potholed and tree-lined, which can make overtaking a problem. In recent years fast foreign cars have appeared on Polish roads without any concomitant increase in road quality. Add to this the bravura of Polish drivers and one of the worst drink-driving records in Europe, and it is clear that special care needs to be taken.

Traffic regulations. Road signs follow the standard continental system. At traffic lights, a green arrow pointing right means proceed, giving priority to vehicles and pedestrians. Cars are supposed to stop at zebra crossings, but often do not, so pedestrians should take special care when crossing roads. Unless signs indicate otherwise, priority is always given to traffic from the right. Special care should be taken at tram stops—you should never drive alongside a stationary tram, as passengers may suddenly jump on or off. In general, priority should always be given to public transport.

On dual carriageways be warned that overtaking on the inside is common, so care should be taken when changing lanes. Seatbelts are compulsory in the front and back seats and children under 12 must sit at the back.

The **speed limit** is 60kph in built-up areas including villages (operative from the white sign with the place name), 90kph on open roads (and when travelling through villages if the place sign is green), and 130kph on highways and motorways (minimum speed is 40kph). Radar speed traps are common.

From 1 November to 1 March dipped headlights must be switched on at all times, regardless of weather conditions. The maximum fine for traffic offences is 500 zlotys and foreigners must pay it on the spot.

The allowable alcohol limit for driving is very low (a small beer) and the penalties are high if you're caught with more. Random breathalyser tests are used. Polish traffic signs are listed and explained in most road atlases.

Accidents/breakdown. All accidents should be immediately reported to the police to determine damage and liability. Make sure you keep the details of all other parties involved. If your car breaks down, contact the Polish Motoring Association (PZM), which has a nationwide emergency breakdown service (☎ 981). Its local centres are usually open from 07.00 to 22.00. The Polmozbyt organisation also has roadside assistance (☎ 954). Failing this, you can contact local garages. Membership in certain Western motoring organisations such as the AA and RAC and certain insurance policies entitle you to discounted or even free PZM services. However, you will need to take out a separate policy to get full cover for driving in Poland. For more details, contact the PZM's head office in Warsaw: ul. Śniadeckich 17A, ☎ (0-22) 825-90-49, or any of the PZM offices at national border crossings.

Fuel. Most filling stations in Poland belong to the state-owned CPN chain, but an increasing number are owned by foreign companies such as Shell and BP. There are fewer stations in Poland than in Western countries. Most are open from 06.00 to 22.00, while 24 hour services are usually only found in larger towns and cities and along international routes. Three types of petrol are available: regular (86 octane, only for very old vehicles), super (94 and 98 octane) and unleaded (95 and 98 octane). Diesel oil is called *olej napędowy* (look for the black ON symbol). Some stations now offer liquid gas.

Car hire. All the major international car-rental agencies have offices in Poland, which are often located in large hotels. You can book a car from abroad but rarely will you be allowed to return it outside of Poland. Rates are generally very high and it is worth checking the local press for cheaper domestic agencies, although bottom-end Polski Fiats should definitely be avoided. Car-rental services are also found at border crossings, airports, and some travel offices such as Orbis. To rent a car you will normally need a passport, credit card and a national driving licence that has been valid for at least a year (international licences are not required). The minimum age for car rental is 21.

Parking. In large cities it is usually best to leave your car at the hotel and travel into the centre by public transport. This is particularly true of Kraków, which has a complex three-zone system of restricted parking. Parking on the pavement is allowed, unless stated otherwise, provided at least 2m of walking room is left for pedestrians. Parking spaces for the disabled are found in most towns and cities. Car theft is common in Poland and it is not advisable to leave your car unattended overnight. Use the hotel's own parking facilities or any guarded car park (*parking strzeżony*). Valuables should never be left in your car at any time. Illegally parked cars will be clamped or towed away.

Cycling
This can be an attractive means of transport in the countryside with its empty roads and predominantly flat terrain. It is possible to rent bicycles at outlets in many towns and cities, but these are not usually suitable for long distance or mountain travel, so it is better to bring your own. Cycling can be hazardous in urban areas due to the lack of segregated bicycle lanes and careless driving. Bicycles may be taken on trains with baggage cars but not on buses. Riding two abreast is illegal.

Hitch-hiking
This is popular in Poland and generally safe. It is illegal to hitch-hike on motorways.

By air
Polish Airlines LOT operates a number of domestic flights connecting Warsaw with other major cities: Gdańsk, Poznań, Wrocław, Kraków, Katowice, Szczecin

and Rzeszów. There are a few direct flights between these cities, but in most cases you will have to catch an onward flight from Warsaw. The airline runs both regular daily services and seasonal ones. Tickets may be bought at LOT and Orbis offices, from travel agents, and directly at airports. You may get discounts on weekend or night travel.

Public transport

Public transport in Poland is cheap and efficient, and consists of trams, buses, commuter trains, and, in some cities, trolleybuses. The only Polish city with a metro line is Warsaw. Regular public transport services run from around 05.00 to 23.00 and can get very crowded at peak hours. Tickets should be purchased in advance from a kiosk or dispensing machine. In some cities they can be bought directly from the driver at a higher price and with no change given. All public transport tickets are flat-rate and interchangeable (except in Gdańsk and Poznań), but cannot be used in other cities. You will need an extra ticket for each large piece of luggage. Tickets should be validated in the punching machines immediately after boarding. 'Plain clothes' inspectors will make fare dodgers pay an on-the-spot fine and will call the police if they cannot pay.

One-day/weekly/monthly passes are available in larger cities. In Warsaw they can be purchased at metro station newsagents and at the Municipal Transport Office (MZK), ul. Senatorska 37, ☎ (0–22) 827–3747.

Night buses (23.00–05.00) cost more (check the information board inside for details), as do 'fast' buses (red numbers or single letters), which stop at fewer places. Commuter trains are particularly useful in cities spread out over a large area, such as Gdańsk-Sopot-Gdynia. Tickets can be bought from dispensing machines or at station ticket offices. Smoking is forbidden on all forms of public transport.

Taxis

Taxis are cheap and plentiful and are a good way of getting around towns and cities. Ranks are found at all airports, most railway stations and large hotels. Taxis can also be hailed in the street. However, it is always best and safest to phone for a 'radio taxi' (in most cities ☎ 919; other numbers are listed in the local press), as these are cheaper than private taxis and the drivers are more likely to be honest. When phoning, give your name, location address, and the number from which you are calling. You should not have to wait more than 10–15 minutes for the taxi to arrive. On Sundays, national holidays, and between 22.00 and 06.00, the standard fare increases by 50 per cent.

When setting off, always make sure the meter is set to the correct rate (night or day) and starting price (check the sticker on the window or dashboard). Meter rates do not apply on out-of-town journeys. This is often the case when travelling to airports: the driver may try to charge you for the return journey, even if you are only going one way. In such instances, it is best to agree on a set price beforehand. By law taxis are not allowed to take more than four passengers and no amount of persuasion will help.

Telephone and postal services

Post offices (*urzędy pocztowe*, or *poczty* for short) are usually open from 08.00 to 18.00 or 20.00 on weekdays and from 08.00 to 14.00 on Saturdays. On Sundays the main section will be closed but you may still be able to make national and international telephone calls. Each major city has at least one 24-hour post office. The best way to make an international call is to buy a magnetic phone card (*karta telefoniczna*; 25, 50 or 100 units) and dial direct from a blue pay phone. You should break the perforated edge of the card before use. To make an international call, dial 0, wait for the tone, then dial 0 again followed by the country code (44 for the UK; 1 for the US), next the area code (dropping the zero, eg 171 or 181 for London), and then finally the subscriber's number. For long-distance calls in Poland, dial 0 followed by the area code (eg 22 for Warsaw) and the subscriber's number. The older pay phones take tokens (*żetony*), also available from post offices: 'A' for local calls (3 minutes), 'C' for national calls. Phone cards and tokens can also be bought at cetain kiosks and hotels. Rates for national (but not international) telephone calls are cheaper after 19.00 and at weekends; they are cheapest between 00.00 and 06.00.

Many new telephone exchanges are being built, with numbers accordingly changing from 6 to 7 digit. There will usually be recorded announcement in Polish and English telling you what digit to put in front of the old number. The numbers in this Guide were correct at the time of writing but some will inevitably change. It is best to check the latest telephone directories, available from post offices. The country code for Poland when dialling from abroad is 48.

Other services provided at main post offices include: parcel delivery, registered mail, courier, telegram, telex, fax, poste restante, and telephone credit card services such as AT&T, MCI and Sprint. You can also order operator-assisted calls to areas which do not have automatic exchanges. Postage stamps, envelopes and postcards are available at all post offices. Out-of-town and international mail should be put into the red post boxes; the green ones are for local mail. A letter takes about one week to reach European countries, two weeks to the US. Polish Telecommunications (*Telekomunikacja Polska*) offers free access to the Internet. Dial 0202122 (in all larger towns and cities you will be charged for a local call) to connect to a public access PPP server (username: ppp, password: ppp). If you have a laptop, you may be able to log on from your hotel room. If not, try an Internet (cyber-) café, found in most major cities.

Useful telephone numbers

Long-distance operator	900	Speaking clock	9226
Telegrams	905	International area codes	9310

Churches and museums

Due to the increasing number of thefts, churches now have more stringent opening times. In cities, historic churches are open all day, but less important ones may be accessible only during mass or at the visiting times indicated outside. It is not considered polite to wander about a church during mass and those who do may get some stern looks or be asked to leave by an irate priest. In the countryside, Sunday is the only sure day for visits, though at other times friendly priests might agree to show you round.

As a rule, **museums** are open six days a week and are closed on Mondays. They open at around 10.00 and close at around 17.00, but times may vary with the season. Last entrance is usually 30 minutes before closing. Tickets are cheap and there is usually one free day. Skansens, or open-air museums, usually close in winter. In cities, exhibits are often marked in English or German, but this is a rarity in the provinces. An irritating practice in many Polish museums is the compulsory use of slippers, worn over the shoe.

Additional information

Emergencies

Ambulance	999	Fire brigade	998	Police	997

Opening hours

Most shops are closed on Saturdays after 13.00 or 14.00 and all day on Sundays. **Food shops** (*spożywcze*) open early, at 06.00 or 07.00, and close at 18.00 or 19.00 on weekdays. Department stores (*domy towarowe*) usually open later, at around 09.00, and close at 20.00.

Large cities have experienced a recent boom in supermarket shopping, with many Western chains opening branches in Poland. Supermarkets are conveniently open all day on Saturdays and until 16.00, but sometimes later, on Sundays. In addition to groceries, they sell household goods, clothes, basic medications, books and newspapers, and often electrical items and car parts. Many supermarkets now accept credit cards but high-street outlets do not. At weekends you can also pick up groceries and miscellaneous items at markets, usually for a lower price than in regular shops. In some supermarkets and, rather irritatingly, in many bookshops, you must collect a basket before entering.

Bakeries (*piekarnie*) and patisseries (*cukiernie*) open early and are a good place to pick up cheap and delicious food for breakfast. Other shops open on weekdays at 10.00 and close at 18.00 or 19.00. **Banks** are usually open from 08.00 to 18.00, weekdays only. Large towns and cities also have 24-hour off-licences, food shops and pharmacies. *Cepelia* shops deal in Polish folk art and are a good place to buy souvenirs. Amber products, (necklaces, rings etc.), also typically Polish, are best bought in reputable jewellery shops (*jubiler*). State-owned *Desa* stores sell antiques, sometimes at bargain prices, but you will need a special licence to export them.

Public holidays

1 January	New Year's Day
Easter Monday	March/April
1 May	Labour Day
3 May	Constitution Day
Corpus Christi	May/June
15 August	Feast of the Assumption
1 November	All Saints' Day
11 November	National Independence Day
25 December	Christmas Day
26 December	St Stephens' Day/Second Day of Christmas

Newspapers

The most popular daily is the left-liberal *Gazeta Wyborcza*, set up in 1989 to help with Solidarity's election campaign and today edited by the ex-dissident, Adam Michnik. Other national dailies include *Rzeczpospolita*, focusing on business and government affairs, and *Życie*, which has broadly Christian-Democratic sympathies. Best-known of the weeklies are *Wprost*, a sort of Polish Newsweek, *Polityka*, a post-communist mouthpiece, and *Tygodnik Powszechny*, a Kraków-based Catholic journal. The best English-language publication is *The Warsaw Voice*, which has national coverage of politics, business, arts and culture, and is available in many cities. Western newspapers are often available in hotel lobbies and foreign-language bookshops.

Public toilets

Public toilets are scarce and rarely clean. It is always better to use the facilities in hotels or restaurants. A charge of 50 groszy is standard. Toilets are sometimes marked with symbols: mens' with a triangle, womens' with a circle.

Tipping

In restaurants a tip of 10 per cent is standard, though you may also simply round up the bill. Cloakrooms are often compulsory in restaurants, theatres and museums. The attendant will expect payment of 50 groszy or more.

Time

Poland lies within the Central European Time Zone, ie. GMT plus one hour in winter and GMT plus two hours in summer (21 March to 21 September).

Electric current

Poland uses standard European two-pin 220V adapters. If you are bringing electrical equipment from the UK, you will need to use a three-to-two-pin adapter (available from electrical shops and airports).

Laundry

Dry cleaners (*pralnie*) offer normal and express cleaning, but laundrettes with self-service washing machines are virtually unknown. As in left luggage offices, you always have to specify the value of the item(s) you leave. Many hotels have their own laundry services.

Sport

For information about sporting activities, contact the relevant organisations listed below.

Angling. Polski Związek Wędkarski (Polish Angling Association), ul. Twarda 42, Warsaw, ☎ (0-22) 620-8966. The association issues licences (compulsory in Poland) and will advise you on boat-hire and the best spots for fishing.

Horse Riding. Poland has a long tradition of Arabian horse breeding and there are numerous stud farms and riding schools around the country, which can be contacted directly. Riding holidays can be booked in the UK or US through Orbis and other tour operators. For more information, contact the national organisation: Polski Związek Jeździecki (Polish Horse-Riding Association), ul. Cegłowska 68/70, Warsaw, ☎ (0-22) 834-7321.

Skiing. There is no national organisation, and it is best to book early through foreign-based tour operators. The most popular resorts include: Zakopane in the Tatra Mountains, Szczyrk in the Beskidy, Karpacz and Szklarska Poręba in the Karkonosze, and Zieleniec in the Bystrzyckie Mountains.

Hunting. Trips can be organised through Orbis or travel agencies co-operating with the following two organisations: *Animex*, ul. Chałubińskiego 8, Warsaw, ☎ (0-22) 302-639, Hunting Bureau, ☎ (0-22) 301-617; or *The Polish Hunting Association*, ul. Nowy Świat 35, Warsaw, ☎ (0-22) 826-2051. Expeditions mostly take place in the north-east of Poland. Hunters are required to pay for game they shoot.

Gliding. It is best to contact air sports centres directly. The best are in Leszno, Jelenia Góra, Bielsko-Biała, Grudziądz, Krosno and Nowy Targ. Equipment, training and accommodation are provided.

Sailing. Yachts should be chartered well in advance through Orbis or other agencies, though it is also possible to hire boats at local resorts. The most popular regions for sailing are the Masurian Lakeland in the north-east, with its numerous lakes and canals, and the less crowded but equally beautiful Pomeranian Lakeland in the north and north-west. Sailing licences are required, and all boats and yachts must be registered. More information is provided by the Polish Sailing Association (Polski Związek Żeglarski), ul. Chocimska 14, Warsaw, ☎ (0-22) 48-04-83.

Kayaking. The best routes are along the Czarna Hańcza and Krutynia rivers, both in the Masurian Lakeland region. The Brda river route flows through the beautiful Bory Tucholskie forest in the west of Poland and is relatively easy. Another popular route is along the Gwda river in the Pomerania region, but in places it involves taking your kayak and equipment across dry land.

Spas. Orbis organises trips to health spas, the best known of which are Nałęczów, Ciechocinek, Krynica, Kudowa-Zdrój, Polanica-Zdrój and Duszniki Zdrój. Health spas specialise in different treatments, so it is best to check beforehand which services and facilities are on offer. For more information, contact the Ministry of Health, ul. Miodowa 15, Warsaw, ☎ (0-22) 826-0894 (Rehabilitation and Spas Department) or ☎ (0-22) 831-3441 (switchboard).

Film, theatre and music

The best way to find out about films, plays and concerts is to look in the local section of *Gazeta Wyborcza*. Publications such as the *Warsaw Voice*, *Warszawa What, Where, When* and *Welcome to Warsaw*, or their equivalents in other Polish cities, also have extensive listings of cultural events.

Mainstream Hollywood films are shown in Polish cinemas soon after their release in Western Europe. Unfortunately, current Polish films are pretty dire, with most trying to imitate American action movies and not really succeeding.

Now and again good films are made by established directors like Andrzej Wajda, but they rarely enjoy commercial success outside of Poland. A notable exception is Krzysztof Kieślowski's widely acclaimed *Three Colours* trilogy of the early 1990s. Foreign films are subtitled in cinemas; on television they are narrated as proper dubbing is considered too expensive.

Contemporary Polish theatre enjoys a far better reputation than cinema. A major problem for visitors is, of course, the language barrier. With the notable exception of the Jewish Theatre in Warsaw, productions in English are a rarity. Avant-garde theatre, though, may be a better bet. The extraordinary *Gardienice* company, for instance, is a kind of medieval theatre troupe which bases its performances on regional music and dance. Likewise, Henryk Tomaszewski's pantomime theatre in Wrocław and Konrad Drzewiecki's dance theatre in Poznań both speak a universal language. At its best, Polish cabaret rivals the best conventional drama can offer, and its reliance on visual gags and music makes it readily accessible to foreigners.

Contemporary Polish music has achieved international renown with the works of Witold Lutosławski, Krzysztof Penderecki, Andrzej Panufnik, Henryk Górecki and others. Performances of classical music are regularly staged in Warsaw and other Polish cities. There are numerous festivals (see the relevant city chapters), which are usually of high standard and always well attended. Concert tickets are still very cheap—you can hear top-class performers for 10–30 PLN—and can be bought direct from city philharmonic halls (*filharmonie*) or at tourist offices. In summer, concerts are often held in churches or in the open air—performances of Chopin in Warsaw's Łazienki park are especially popular. Polish jazz has been held in high regard ever since musicians like Tomasz Stańko and Michał Urbaniak made their names in the West. Jazz enthusiasts visiting in October should not miss the Jamboree in Warsaw, and at other times jazz clubs provide ample opportunity to listen to some good music. Ray Charles, Keith Jarrett and Nina Simone are among the 'big' names who have given concerts in Poland in recent years.

 ## Food and drink

Since 1989, the standards and choice of restaurant food in Poland have significantly improved, and eating out is no longer the exasperating experience it was during Communist times. Cities offer a wide variety of establishments, ranging from the bottom-end *bary mleczne* (self-service 'milk bars', serving mostly dairy-based food), through Western fast-food chains and pizzerias, to exclusive restaurants such as Warsaw's *Bristol* or Kraków's *Wierzynek* (see p. 201). In recent years, there has been an explosion of foreign cuisine, particularly Chinese, Vietnamese and Middle-Eastern, providing an alternative to traditional Polish fare.

Poles are a carnivorous nation. Some say their predilection for meat is a natural outcome of the recent past, when meat was in short supply, and getting it involved a great deal of tedious effort. The old joke: 'what does a Polish cat get for lunch?', answer: 'a mouse coupon' adds a humorous gloss to a situation that was indeed dramatic. In 1980s Poland, queuing was a national pastime and alternatives to meat were not readily available.

It seems, however, that the liking for meat has less to do with Communist shortages than with the mundane fact of Poland's harsh continental climate.

The carnivorous tradition certainly has much earlier roots: *Dinners of the Jagiellonian University's Professors*, published in 1900, describes a typical 16th century professorial meal for five: 'Meat and ragout from a half-dozen capons, to each professor three portions with peeled barley... Boiled chicken ragout seasoned with herbs, one chicken to each... Roast veal and one roast chicken apiece... Pork in apricots'. Today, the average Polish diet is still fatty and extremely meat-based, but times are changing and vegetarian food is no longer dismissed with derision. Vegetarian eateries and restaurants have sprung up in many cities, and elsewhere menus usually offer at least some meat-free dishes.

Polish cuisine is highly eclectic, combining domestic tradition with an assortment of foreign influence. This is hardly surprising: until the Second World War, Poland was home to sizeable German, Jewish, Lithuanian, Ukrainian, and Russian communities, all of which made a strong contribution to national cuisine. Nowadays, though, standard restaurant menus do not differ much. Local specialities may be offered, but regional differences are not particularly strong. You are just as likely to find *kluski śląskie* (Silesian dumplings) or *kołduny* (Lithuanian dumplings) in the north and west of Poland as in the south and east.

Meal times in Poland reflect the working day, which can begin as early as 06.00, ending at 14.00 or 15.00. Breakfast (*śniadanie*) is usually solid, consisting of bread or rolls (*bułki*) served with sausage (*kiełbasa*, infinite in variety), frankfurters (*parówki*), yellow cheese, ham or cottage cheese (*twaróg*). Fried or scrambled eggs are often combined with bacon (*boczek*) or, when in season, with wild mushrooms such as ceps (*borowiki*) or chantarelles (*kurki*). The excellent home-made jam (*konfitura*) is made from a variety of fruits and berries found in Polish woodlands. Hotels will often serve Western breakfasts, including toast, croissants, cereals, etc.

Poles eat their main meal (*obiad*) after work, at around 15.00, though in recent years the concept of 'lunch' has been coming into vogue. A standard *obiad* begins with soup, followed by a main dish and sometimes a dessert. Soups are tasty, nourishing—if a little oily—and usually a safe bet in restaurants. The two classic varieties are: *barszcz* (borscht), made of beetroot stock (fresh or fermented), and *żur*, or *żurek*, a delicious sour soup made from fermented rye flour. Restaurant menus vary with the season, and if you visit in the late spring or summer, you could try, for instance *zupa szczawiowa* (sorrel soup), or *chłodnik*, a speciality from the east, made primarily from young beetroot, cucumber, hard-boiled eggs, buttermilk and sour cream, and served cold. Another good starter is *śledź* (herring) in sour cream or oil, traditionally accompanied by a vodka aperitif.

The most common main dishes are beef, veal, pork and chicken; lamb is virtually unknown, except in the Polish highlands. Meat and poultry are usually fried in batter, less often grilled (*z rusztu*), and served with a side salad (*surówka*) consisting of fresh or marinated vegetables. Of the traditional dishes, best-known are *bigos* (meat stewed in sauerkraut), *kasza gryczana w sosie* (buckwheat in a meaty sauce), *gołąbki* (stuffed cabbage leaves), and the formidable *golonko* (pork knuckle) for those with a mighty appetite. As with fish dishes, *golonko* is usually sold by weight, so the menu will specify the price per gram, not the actual price.

Dumplings (*pierogi*) are a Polish speciality and come in a variety of forms. The most popular savoury fillings are mince, cabbage, and cottage cheese mixed with mashed potatoes, the latter known as *pierogi ruskie*. Some restaurants might also offer a Lithuanian version, called *kołduny* (meat dumplings seasoned with marjoram and served in a clear broth). In season, you will also get a choice of delicious fruit fillings.

For dessert you could try *sernik*, a Polish cheesecake, or *makowiec*, a traditional poppyseed cake. Like pierogi, Polish pancakes (*naleśniki*) come with a choice of fillings, both sweet and savoury, and are often served with a cream, ice-cream or chocolate topping. Cafés (*kawiarnie*), the hub of social life in many towns, are often the best place to eat cakes or desserts. Coffee comes in three forms— *parzona*, boiling water added directly to ground coffee, *z expresu* (expresso), and *rozpuszczalna* (instant). If you want cream, ask for *biała kawa* (white coffee). Tea is taken plain or with lemon, but hardly ever with milk—the latter combination is seen as a quaint British invention.

Supper, or *kolacja*, is a lighter meal, and usually eaten at around 19.00 or 20.00. The format is similar to breakfast, with bread and a selection of meats and cheeses, perhaps followed by cake or a sweet dessert.

Drink

Poles have a reputation as heavy drinkers and many take pride in this fact. Indeed, statistically, the per capita consumption of hard spirits in Poland is one of the highest in Europe.

Vodka, the national drink, comes in many varieties, from the excellent *Chopin* and *Luksusowa*, through the mid-range *Wyborowa* and *Żytnia*, to the insipid *Czysta* and barely drinkable *Stołowa*. Apart from these clear vodkas, there are a number of fine flavoured varieties, including *Cytrynówka* (lemon vodka), *Gold-wasser*, containing flakes of real gold (see p. 320), and *Żubrówka*, seasoned with a blade of sweet-scented grass (hierchloe) found only in the Białowieża Forest (hence its association with bison, or *żubr*; see p. 176). Also worth looking out for are sweet varieties, such as *Wiśniówka* (wild cherry vodka), or *Śliwowica*, an aromatic plum brandy. At a frightening 180° proof, *Spirytus rektyfikowany* is the strongest spirit on the market and one that even many hardened Poles will keep well away from. If you wish to sample this fiery concoction, be warned that it should always be diluted first. Clear vodka is served neat, in tumblers (*kieliszki*), and is best when ice-cold. Shots come in 50 or 100 gramme measures, and are preceded by a simple '*na zdrowie!*' (cheers!) or perhaps a more elaborate toast, as the occasion permits. Flavoured vodkas should be served lightly chilled, sweet ones at room temperature. Diluted hard spirits were until recently considered a heresy, but nowadays, perhaps owing to Western imports, 'mixed drinks' are becoming increasingly popular, and Poles are slowly moving away from hard spirits towards milder brews.

Decent foreign wines are now commonplace on restaurant tables, but anything that advertises itself as Polish wine is best avoided. Polish beer, once considered an 'old man's drink' or 'worker's drink', has experienced a remark-able reversal of fortune; it even made an appearance in politics, with the Polish Beer-Lovers' Party extolling its virtues from the parliamentary tribune. Strong and full-bodied, Polish beers have a distinctive flavour that is not always to the liking of visitors weaned on Western lagers. Famous brands include *Żywiec* and *Okocim* (South), *Leżajsk* (South-East), *Lech* (West), and *Heweliusz* (North). Beer is often consumed in cellar bars (*piwnice*)—the most popular type of drinking estab-lishment—where ventilation can be a major problem, especially for non-smokers.

It is not customary to buy 'rounds' of drinks: you either buy your own, or, if you are invited for a drink, your host will usually pay. Licensing hours are extremely liberal. Pubs will often close when the last guest leaves—03.00 in the morning is not uncommon.

Christmas and Easter

Despite recent improvements in the quality of restaurant food, home-cooking is incomparably better and continues to set the standards of Polish cuisine. To sample Polish food at its best, you would do well to attend a Christmas meal on 24 December (*wigilia*). The culinary customs connected with this event are rooted in a Catholic tradition of abstinence from meat on that day.

The courses, of which there can be up to twelve, vary from region to region and home to home, but the following ingredients are always present: fish (mainly carp), mushrooms, cabbage, and *kutia*, an ancient and popular dish from the east, made from boiled wheat flavoured with poppyseeds, honey, nuts and raisins. Typical dishes might include borscht with dumplings filled with dried wild mushrooms (*uszka*), wild mushroom soup, carp fried in batter, cabbage with mushrooms or peas, marinated herring in apple purée, onion and cream, carp in aspic (often in the Jewish version with vegetables, almonds and raisins), dumplings filled with mushrooms and cabbage, *kluski* with poppyseeds, honey cake, and poppyseed cake.

The *wigilia* meal traditionally begins when the first star appears in the night sky. Close family members will gather around the Christmas table in an atmosphere of goodwill and reconciliation. This is manifested in the tradition of sharing the holy wafer with all present and wishing them well for the coming year. There are also pagan customs associated with the meal: straw is put under the tablecloth, and the holy wafer is shared with animals. Poles are proverbially hospitable ('a guest in the house is God in the house'), and it is customary to leave an empty place at the table for unexpected guests.

During the carnival (*karnawał*), beginning after the New Year, it is customary to eat *chrust*, a biscuit made of dough deep-fried in lard, also known as *faworki*. On Shrove Thursday' (*tłusty czwartek*), marking the end of the *karnawał*, the whole nation traditionally gorges itself on doughnuts. Lent begins the following week, on Ash Wednesday, when the standard dish is herring, served in a number of elaborate forms. Nowadays, the fasting period usually lasts only two days. No meat or alcohol are consumed on Good Friday, while on Saturday food is blessed in preparation for the most important meal of the Easter period: Sunday breakfast. The latter is preceded by a ceremonial sharing of Easter eggs, another pagan custom—the eggs symbolising the beginning of life. A cold buffet is normally served, consisting of sausage, ham, eggs, cold roasts and horseradish.

Restaurant prices

Restaurants listed in this Guide have been divided into three price categories. In 'exclusive restaurants', you should expect to pay from 60–200 PLN for a three course meal, not including drinks; in 'medium price restaurants', anything from

This consolidated opposition against him and he was forced to flee the country in 1079. Stanisław was canonised and the Church successfully promoted his cult as the Patron Saint of Poland. The next outstanding Piast prince was Bolesław's nephew, **Bolesław the Wrymouth** (1102–38). In 1109, he asserted his independence from Imperial authority by defeating Emperor Henry V. In a series of campaigns he conquered and christianised Western Pomerania. At his court the first Latin Polish chronicle was written by a French monk (see p. 80).

To avoid the fratricidal struggles that accompanied the death of every Piast ruler, Bolesław regulated the question of succession by dividing the country between his sons and vesting supreme authority in the eldest member of the dynasty. This system meant that the whole country disintegrated into independent principalities. The fragmentation lasted for about two centuries and brought significant territorial losses.

The weak and divided princes were also unable to defend the country against Tartar invasion. The first, and most devastating, occurred in 1241, when the Tartars reached Silesia. The local prince, Henryk the Pious, was killed at the battle of Legnica, when he tried to stop the invaders (see p. 467).

The most serious threat to the integrity of the Polish lands was posed by the **Teutonic Order of the Hospital of St Mary in Jerusalem**, otherwise known as the Teutonic Knights. The struggle against the Order lasted for over two centuries. The Knights were invited to Poland in 1226 by a Mazovian prince, who enlisted their help to defeat the pagan Prussians. By 1283, the Knights had conquered Prussia. The Order obtained recognition of their conquests from the Emperor and the Pope and quickly renounced any subordination to their Mazovian benefactor. In 1308, they captured Eastern Pomerania and threatened the core Polish lands of Wielkopolska. In the following year the Grand Master moved the Order's headquarters from Venice to Malbork (see p. 333).

Fragmentation of the country was accompanied by rapid economic growth and social change. From a patrimonial state, the private property of the ruling prince, Poland evolved into a society of estates; the Church became a self-ruling corporation and members of the *drużyna* (an armed retinue) turned into a knightly land-owning class.

During the 12C and 13C, Western models of urban autonomy and self-government were imported and assimilated in Poland. This process was helped by the large influx of German burghers, who were particularly numerous in Silesia and Wielkopolska.

Urban life was also enriched by the influx of a large number of Jews fleeing from Germany. The princes of Silesia and Wielkopolska granted them personal inviolability, religious freedom, and the right to engage in commerce. Jewish communities were allowed internal autonomy and their own courts. In the 14C, King Kazimierz the Great made these rights binding on the whole territory of Poland.

In spite of the country's fragmentation, the clergy and the knights retained a sense of belonging to *Regnum Poloniae*. An important role was played by the cult of St Stanisław—like his quartered body, the Polish provinces were to grow back together. Playing on these sentiments, a petty Kuyavian prince, **Władysław the Short**, united the two most important provinces of Wielkopolska and Małopolska and was crowned King of Poland in 1320.

Władysław's son **Kazimierz the Great** managed, by skilful diplomacy, to regain the northwestern Kujawy region from the Teutonic Knights, and persuaded the Mazovian princes to accept his suzerainty. In a series of campaigns against the Tartars and Lithuanians, he incorporated into Poland the westernmost Rus' principalities of Chełm and Galicia with a major trading centre in Lwów (Lviv).

Kazimierz earned the title of 'Great' for his achievements in organising the internal life of the country. Under his auspices, uniform legal codes were drawn up and a supreme court of appeal for urban courts was established. He founded numerous towns, built fortifications and promoted internal settlement. Finally, thanks to his efforts, a university—today the most prestigious in Poland—was established in Kraków in 1364 (see p. 221).

Having failed to produce a male heir, Kazimierz bequeathed his crown to his nephew **Louis d'Anjou**, the King of Hungary. The consent of the Polish nobility was bought with the privilege of Buda (1355), which created the foundation for the exceptionally strong position of the Polish nobility vis-à-vis royal power.

Louis also had to pay the Polish nobility with privileges to ensure the succession for one of his daughters. In 1374, he convened an assembly of estate representatives from Małopolska in Košice (Slovakia). This assembly established a precedent; in future Polish monarchs would have to call on similar assemblies in order to obtain approval from society (above all the nobility) on all major political decisions.

The Jagiellonian Empire (1385–1572)

In 1384, Louis d'Anjou's ten year old daughter **Jadwiga** was crowned king (!) of Poland. The ruling grandees offered her hand to the pagan ruler of Lithuania, **Jagiełło** (Jogaila).

Under the **Union of Krewo**, signed in 1385, in return for Jadwiga's hand and the Polish Crown, Jagiełło and his people were to convert to Christianity and unite the Grand Duchy of Lithuania with the Polish Crown.

The Lithuanians were a Baltic people who, under the leadership of the charismatic clan of Gedymin, created a huge empire stretching from the Baltic to the Black Sea. The empire rested on the coexistence of pagan Lithuanians and Orthodox Rus' (the ancestors of today's Belarusians and Ukrainians).

The union with Lithuania proved invaluable when in 1410 a joint Polish-Lithuanian army defeated the Teutonic Knights at the battle of Grunwald (see p. 417), one of the greatest battles of medieval Europe. But it was only the internal crisis of the Teutonic Order's state that made it possible for Poland to win back Pomerania. In 1453, the Prussian nobility and the rich commercial towns led by Gdańsk rebelled against the Order and appealed for help to the King of Poland, **Kazimierz Jagiellończyk** (1447–1492). Under the Second Peace of Toruń (1466), which ended thirteen years of heavy fighting, the Order ceded Pomerania, with Gdańsk and Elbląg and the diocese of Warmia (Ermeland), to Poland. The Poles also took the Order's capital at Malbork, expelling the Grand Master to Königsberg (which thereafter became the capital of the Order's diminished state). After another series of wars in the first decades of the 16C, the Order finally dissolved. In 1525, the last Grand Master, Albrecht of Brandenburg, adopted Lutheranism, making himself Duke and swearing an oath of allegiance to the Polish King, **Zygmunt the Old** (see p. 197). His domains were turned into a secular principality, thereafter known as Ducal Prussia, held as a fief of the Polish crown.

Jagiełło's sons pursued an ambitious dynastic policy. Kazimierz Jagiellończyk made the House of Jagiełło the dominant dynasty in Central Europe when he secured the Czech (1474) and the Hungarian (1490) thrones for his eldest son Władysław. In 1492, his younger sons **Jan Olbracht** and **Aleksander** became rulers of Poland and Lithuania, respectively.

Heavy defeats suffered by Lithuania at the hands of Muscovy towards the end of the 15C persuaded the Lithuanian grandees to seek a restoration of the Union with Poland. This was achieved in 1501 when the Grand Duke Aleksander accepted the Polish crown after Jan Olbracht had died that year. Under the last Jagiellons—Zygmunt the Old (1506–48) and his son Zygmunt August (1548–72)—Poland enjoyed a period of exceptional prosperity.

Peaceful times, combined with high demand and good prices for Polish grain in the West, triggered an economic boom. In the long term, however, it had deleterious consequences for the Polish economy and society. The nobles expanded their demesnes and converted peasant dues from cash rents into the corvée. To lower the price of manufactured and imported goods, they imposed an extreme version of *laissez faire* trade and customs policy which undercut the economy of Polish towns and the well-being of the burgher estate.

The newly-prosperous middle nobility, educated at Western universities and often sympathetic to Reformation, challenged the oligarchy of spiritual and lay magnates who had been ruling the country under the Jagiellonian kings. In the first half of the 16C, it launched the 'execution' movement—a political movement calling for political and ecclesiastical reform. It built on earlier concessions to the nobility, won from the Jagiellonian kings in the 14C. By the mid-15C, the king could not levy taxes or declare war without the approval of local assemblies of nobility (dietines). Towards the end of the 15C, a country-wide parliamentary representation began to emerge. After 1501, no new laws could be proclaimed without its consent.

The political struggle between the 'execution' movement, magnates and royalty, ended in a compromise. The most important achievement of the movement was the signing in Lublin of the **Polish-Lithuanian Union** in 1569 whereby the last Jagiellonian king, **Zygmunt August**, transferred his hereditary rights to the Lithuanian throne to the Polish Crown. Poland and Lithuania formed a federation, with a common monarch and a common parliament, but with separate armies, treasuries, legal codes and state institutions.

The 'execution' movement failed to reform the Church along Protestant lines. The Jagiellonian kings refused to break with Rome, while simultaneously ignoring its advice to suppress Protestantism with force. Protestantism won numerous adherents among the politically active elite, but most nobles remained with the traditional Church. Around the middle of the 16C, Poland presented the curious picture of a country where predominantly Roman Catholic nobles elected predominantly Protestant deputies to parliament. Religious toleration was officially confirmed by the **Confederation of Warsaw** (1573).

The Commonwealth of Nobility (1572–1772)

After the extinction of the Jagiellonian dynasty in 1572 the checks which had been imposed on the royal prerogative were codified in the so-called **Henrician**

Articles (after the first elected king, Henri de Valois). All nobles were granted the right to participate personally in the election of each new monarch. Before coronation, a prospective king had to swear to uphold the Henrician Articles and the nobility reserved the right to renounce obedience to the king if he broke the oath.

The brittle balance between the Crown, the nobility and magnates broke down within a generation of the first 'free' royal election. The magnates were able to create vast networks of noble clients and use them to subordinate the local dietines and courts. The Most Serene Commonwealth of Poland, as the country was officially called after 1572, gradually evolved into a loose federation of nearly sovereign districts, each dominated by a different magnate family. The final step debilitating parliament was taken in 1652, when the principle of **liberum veto** was put into practice for the first time. This meant that a single noble deputy could veto all parliamentary resolutions. Without a functioning parliament, kings could raise neither taxes nor armies.

For a century the decentralised Commonwealth coped quite well with the absolutist and militaristic states surrounding it. Under **Stefan Bathory**, the Prince of Transylvania, it defeated Ivan the Terrible of Muscovy and extended its rule over Livonia (present-day southern Estonia and Latvia). The election in 1587 of the Swedish prince **Zygmunt Vasa** led to intermittent wars with Sweden in the first half of the 17C, which ended in a draw even though the Swedes were led by a great military leader, Gustavus Adolphus. Similarly inconclusive were a few clashes with the Ottoman Turks.

In 1604, the Commonwealth's magnates sponsored the notorious Muscovite pretender, the 'False Dimitri', who quickly established himself in Moscow. Three years later, Zygmunt Vasa intervened in Muscovy's internal struggles and in 1610 the boyars elected his son Władysław to the Muscovite throne. A Polish-Lithuanian troop entered Moscow together with the pro-Władysław Muscovite forces. Zygmunt, however, demanded the Crown for himself. In response, the boyars elected a new czar, Mikhail Romanov, and besieged the Polish crew in the Kremlin. In the ensuing war the Commonwealth re-conquered most of the territories which Lithuania had lost a century earlier.

In the middle of the 17C a crisis emerged which permanently damaged the well-being of the Commonwealth. It even collapsed for a time under the strain of several simultaneous armed conflicts. The crisis was sparked off by the 1648 uprising of the Ukrainian Cossacks led by Bohdan Khmelnytsky. The Cossacks, a kind of military brotherhood living at the edge of the steppe, claimed noble status by virtue of their martial profession. The attempts of mostly Catholic magnates to enserf them created an explosive situation. It was exacerbated by the religious conflict triggered by the proselytising policy of the Roman Catholic Church. A union with Rome signed in 1596 by a few Orthodox bishops in Brest added fuel to the fire.

In 1648, the Cossacks scored a number of victories against the Polish troops and almost reached the Vistula. Khmelnytsky turned for help to the Russian czar, with whom the Cossacks shared a common religion. In 1654, he signed a union with Russia in Pereiaslav, thus precipitating a war between Russia and the Commonwealth. Russian troops occupied most of Lithuania. In 1655, the Swedish army invaded western Poland. The invasion, which passed into Polish tradition as the '**Deluge**', quickly engulfed the country. Almost the entire nobility swore allegiance to the Swedish king, Charles Gustav.

However, the tide soon turned. The Swedish army treated Poland like a conquered country and the Swedish monarch lost the support of the nobility as quickly as he had won it. A guerrilla movement sprang up, encouraged by Poland's neighbours. **Jan Kazimierz** (1648–1668) returned from exile and rallied the country against the Swedes. Skilfully exploiting their attack on the fortified monastery in Częstochowa, which housed an icon of the Holy Virgin (see p. 267) venerated by the local population, Kazimierz turned the war into a popular crusade in defence of Roman Catholic faith. In a symbolic ceremony he entrusted Poland to the special protection of the Holy Virgin and crowned her Queen of Poland.

The 'Swedish Deluge' revealed the desperate need for internal reform in the Commonwealth. Proposals by the Court in the aftermath of the 'Deluge' to strengthen royal power provoked an armed rebellion. The rebels defeated the royal troops and Jan Kazimierz abdicated. Royal authority had been compromised and the role of the king brought close to nought. Even the brilliant military commander **Jan Sobieski** could not reverse this fact after his election to the Polish throne in 1674.

Sobieski successfully halted a major Turkish offensive in the 1670s, but his efforts at internal reform were thwarted. In 1683, he led the Polish forces to help the Holy League break the Ottoman siege of Vienna and commanded the armies which crushed the Turks in the battle under the city's walls.

In 1697, the first election took place and its result was decided by a foreign army. The noble levy was no match for the professional army brought in by the minority candidate, the elector of Saxony, **August the Strong** of the Wettin dynasty. He was subsequently crowned in Poland as August II (1697–1733). The next election was decided by direct intervention of the Russian army, which supported August's son, who reigned in Poland as August III (1733–1763).

Under the **Saxon kings**, Poland went through one of the gloomiest periods in her history. Poland's neighbours were aware that the anarchic political system was the root of the country's weakness. They agreed to co-operate to preserve the existing 'golden liberties' of the nobility and block any reforms.

The country was ruled in practice by the Russian ambassador in Warsaw. The Diets were dissolved before they could reach any decisions, since foreign powers were always able to find venal deputies prepared to use the *liberum veto*. When bribery was not enough, the Russian ambassador could always resort to the Russian troops garrisoned in the country.

In 1764, the Russian Empress Catherine installed her former lover **Stanisław August Poniatowski** on the throne, the candidate of the powerful Czartoryski clan. By that time the Enlightenment was beginning to have an effect on the Polish elite. A small party formed around the king and the Czartoryskis and began to draw up reform plans. It wanted to abolish the *liberum veto*, strengthen the power of the monarch, curb the anarchy of the magnates and improve the position of the burghers and peasants. Reform projects mobilised the conservative nobility, whose opposition to reform was encouraged and manipulated by Russia. The Russians used the conservatives to thwart the reform plans of the royal camp, but at the same time they prevented them from dethroning the king. In 1768, the opposition launched an armed rebellion, the **Confederacy of Bar**, against both the king and Russian interference. It took the Russian army four years to suppress it. The Confederacy combined elements of a national uprising against foreign rule with fanatical Catholic fundamentalism and a defence of estate privileges.

In 1772, Russia, engaged in a war against Turkey and experiencing difficulties in controlling the Commonwealth, consented to share its spoils with Prussia and Austria. Each of the three Great Powers annexed the neighbouring provinces of the Commonwealth, which lost one third of its territory and population. Russia took the eastern part of Belarus, Prussia seized Pomerania and parts of Wielkopolska, thus cutting Poland off from the Baltic, while Austria incorporated parts of Małopolska and the westernmost Ukraine (Galicia).

Reform and Partition (1773–1815)

The shock of the **Partition** galvanised a reform movement among the Polish nobility. The Diet which approved, under Russian bayonets, the treaties with the Partitioning powers, simultaneously set up a national ministry of education and created a permanent governing body.

The differences that appeared between Russia and Prussia provided the reform camp with an opportunity to realise its plans. In 1788, the Diet demanded the evacuation of Russian garrisons and resolved to increase the army from 18,000 to 100,000. Protected against Russian intervention by an alliance with Prussia, the king and his supporters staged a *coup d'état*, proclaiming on 3 May 1791 a **constitution**—the first written constitution in Europe. It was influenced by the leading political theoreticians of the French Enlightenment as well as by the practice of British parliamentarism. After Jean-Jacques Rousseau, it established the principle of popular sovereignty, and proclaimed that political authority derived from the will of the nation. From Montesquieu it borrowed the idea of the division of power. And, following the British example, it required that every royal decision be countersigned by a responsible minister. The franchise was changed to prevent the great magnates from controlling elections and to turn the middle nobility into the backbone of the political class. Civil and military offices were opened to the bourgeoisie, which was also granted the right to buy landed estates and allowed to have limited representation in the Diet. Protection by public law was extended to the serfs. The architects of the constitution already thought in terms of a modern nation, encompassing members of all social classes and estates, and the constitution included provisions which were intended to make this vision a reality.

In 1792, however, the international environment changed with the outbreak of the First Coalition war against revolutionary France and the end of the Russian–Turkish war. Prussia and Russia closed ranks against the Polish reforms and Catherine the Great prepared to launch an armed intervention. Under the protection of Russian troops, the conservative opposition planned to restore the old political system. It pretended that its manifesto, composed in the Russian capital, had been signed on Polish territory, in the border town of **Targowica**. The name Targowica has since become synonymous in Polish with national betrayal.

The Polish army, caught in the process of expansion, was no match for the Russian veterans. In 1793, Prussia and Russia agreed on the **Second Partition** of the Commonwealth. The May Constitution of 1791 was revoked and its most prominent supporters had to emigrate. What was left of the old Commonwealth was put under Russian protectorate and Russian troops were garrisoned in the land.

In the spring of 1794, an uprising broke out against Russia and Prussia. It was led by **Tadeusz Kościuszko**, a hero of the American War of Independence. Kościuszko tried to involve the peasants in the struggle by granting them personal freedom in the Połaniec Manifesto. The victorious attack of the peasant levy armed with scythes on the Russian cannons in the **battle of Racławice** passed into Polish patriotic mythology. Soon, however, the combined Russian–Prussian force defeated the Polish Army and took Kościuszko prisoner. Warsaw capitulated, terrorised by the carnage of the civilian population committed by the Russian troops after they had stormed the suburb of Praga. In 1795, under the **Third Partition**, Russia, Prussia and Austria divided among themselves the remaining territory of the Commonwealth. Poland disappeared from the map of Europe.

The partitioning of Poland was the most radical international act of the European *ancien régime*. Its perpetrators were able to destroy the Polish state, but not the Polish nation. The 'Polish cause' would become a festering wound in the body politic of both Prussia and Russia for the next hundred years.

Already in 1797, Polish émigrés organised a Polish Legion under French auspices, which fought in Italy against Austria. Another such legion was organised in Germany in 1799. A song written for the Polish Legion in Italy, beginning with the words 'Poland is not yet lost as long as we are still alive', later became the Polish national anthem.

Polish hopes that revolutionary France would help restore an independent Poland were partially realised after Napoleon's victories over Prussia in 1806. Out of the lands of the Second and Third Partition, Napoleon created the **Duchy of Warsaw**, a *de facto* French protectorate, with a constitutional Saxon monarch, but a Polish army, administration and education system. The Duchy introduced reforms, the most important of which were the liberation of the peasants from personal servitude and the introduction of the Napoleonic Civil Code.

The Duchy mobilised almost one hundred thousand men for the 1812 campaign against Russia. After Napoleon's defeat it was occupied by Russian troops. At the **Congress of Vienna** in 1815, the Duchy was divided between Russia and Prussia. The bulk of its territory, including the central Polish lands around Warsaw, was put under Russian authority as the **Kingdom of Poland**. The Kingdom was a constitutional monarchy in personal union with Russia. It had one of the most liberal constitutions in Europe, its own army, and a government separate from that of Russia.

Poland in the 19C: the Struggle for Independence

Growing dissatisfaction with Russian rule led to the emergence of patriotic conspiracies among young officers and students. The outbreak of the July 1830 revolution in France and rumours that the czar intended to send Polish troops to quell the revolution in Belgium provided the spark that set off the **November Uprising**. A small conspiratorial group of military cadets stationed in Warsaw attempted to assassinate the Russian viceroy, the Grand Duke Constantine. The Diet officially dethroned Nicholas I, and the Uprising spread to the eastern territories. By September 1831, however, the Polish forces had been decisively defeated by the larger Russian army.

After the Uprising, the Russians abolished most of the autonomous institutions of the Kingdom and repealed its constitution. Thereafter, the Kingdom was administered by Russian military decree and the Polish army disbanded. In the lands east of the Kingdom the government began to pursue policies of cultural and religious russification, closing the university in Wilno (Vilnius) and all Polish schools, introducing Russian civil law and 'reuniting' the Uniate Church (see p. 253) with the Russian Orthodox Church.

The extensive repression which followed the November Uprising and the heavy-handed rule of the Russian military government ensured that the Kingdom did not participate in the revolutionary events of 1848. In Austrian Galicia, the revolution was pre-empted by a 1846 peasant *jacquerie*, directed against the landed nobility. In Prussia, the Poles took advantage of the upheavals in Berlin to organise a movement for wider autonomy. But with the defeat of revolution in Prussia, the Polish movement was crushed as well.

In January 1863, the leaders of the **January Uprising** set up a clandestine 'National Government' and state structures. Against the odds, the insurgents managed to hold out for a year and a half, but their efforts ultimately ended in failure. The key weakness of the Uprising was that it did not win peasant support despite the radical social policy adopted by the National Government. However, this put pressure on the Russian authorities to grant land ownership to peasants.

In the wake of the Uprising, the Russians followed a policy of total administrative subordination of the Kingdom of Poland ...to Russia—its very name was officially changed to the 'Vistula Provinces'. Russian replaced Polish as the official language of government, right down to the level of village administration. It was also used in schools. In the territories east of the Kingdom the government pursued a policy of 'de-polonisation' in order to reduce and eventually eliminate all signs of Polish cultural influence. Even private tutoring in Polish was a criminal offence.

The defeat of the Uprising led to the rise of an ideology known as 'organic work', which stressed the need for broad-based economic and cultural growth, as opposed to armed struggle for national independence. Conveniently, the last decades of the 19C were marked by intense industrialisation, accompanied by the emergence of a Polish working class. By the beginning of 1880s, the first ephemeral attempts were made by intellectuals to organise a socialist party.

In the 1890s, small groups of activists laid the foundations for two main political camps that dominated the Polish scene until the Second World War. In 1892, a **Polish Socialist Party** (**PPS**) was launched, and in 1893 a group of students set up a **National League**. Both the socialist and the nationalist movement produced charismatic leaders who dominated the arena of Polish politics during the first three decades of the 20C. The socialist leader, **Józef Piłsudski**, was a practical politician with immense personal charisma who embodied and continued the tradition of Romantic insurrectionism. **Roman Dmowski**, the founder and leader of National Democracy, was a brilliant intellectual and the leading theoretician of the movement that was very much his creation.

The two movements took radically different positions on the 1905 Revolution in the Russian Empire. Piłsudski's PPS actively participated in the strikes and demonstrations, hoping to transform them into a national uprising. Its Combat Organisation engaged in terrorist attacks on the Russian security forces and staged 'revolutionary expropriations'; armed attacks on banks and post offices staged to obtain money to support the party. Dmowski was vociferously opposed to Polish participation in the revolution. His strategy was to exact concessions from the Russian government by proving to it that Polish society was loyal to the

Czar and opposed to revolution. The differences led to bloody clashes between the combat organisations of the two parties and mutual assassinations.

While the Poles living under Russian rule repeatedly engaged in armed insurrections, those in Prussia and Austria followed a different method of struggle for national existence. In Prussia, Poles living in the Poznań region initially enjoyed a fair measure of autonomy, but this ended with the defeat of the 1848 liberal revolution, and the creation of a unified German state in 1871. After this they became subject to intense assimilatory pressure from the state. The German Chancellor Otto von Bismarck's anti-Catholic policy of *Kulturkampf* hit particularly hard. Polish language was entirely removed from official use and almost entirely from school education.

In contrast to Prussia, Poles living in the Austro-Hungarian Empire enjoyed far-reaching autonomy and favourable conditions for the development of a national culture. The Habsburgs were forced to liberalise their rule after their defeat by Prussia. The province of Galicia, where Poles predominated, was granted self-rule, with its own diet and provincial government. Polish became an official language there and Poles could pursue careers in the civil service. The two universities in Kraków and Lwów (Lviv), as well as a number of private foundations (the Ossolineum in Lwów being the most famous among them) made the province into a centre of Polish intellectual and cultural life.

The Romantic idealism of those who 'invented' the Polish nation at the beginning of the 19C proved stronger than the material power of the three Empires. Polish communities in Germany, Russia and Austria-Hungary were better organised at the beginning of the 20C, and had a stronger feeling of national identity than a century earlier. The greatest achievement of the Polish elite was the assimilation of the peasantry into the Polish nation. Contrary to Marx's dictum that workers have no fatherland, Polish intellectuals managed to inculcate Polish patriotism among the working class. So the Polish national movement could boast mass popular support in all three Partitions and was in a good position to take advantage of the realignments that were taking place in European politics towards the end of the 19C.

In the 1890s, Russia allied itself with France against the German–Austrian block, thus bringing to an end the solidarity between the three Partitioning Powers. The most far-sighted Polish politicians understood that in the event of war an opportunity might arise to put the 'Polish question' back on the agenda of European politics. Preparing for such an eventuality, Piłsudski organised para-military formations under Austro–Hungarian auspices. They were to serve as the nucleus of a future Polish military force that could be used to restore Polish independence.

The Great War: Independence Restored (1914–1921)

The principle that the Partitioning powers must not exploit the Polish issue died on the battlefields of France. By 1916, the Germans, having suffered huge losses, were desperately looking for manpower. Their attention was drawn to the Kingdom of Poland from which they chased out the Russian armies in 1915. But if Poles were to be persuaded to join the war effort, a political price had to be paid. In 1916, Germany and Austria proclaimed the establishment of the Polish Kingdom under a joint protectorate and created a Polish administration headed by a Regency Council as well as a Polish Armed Force. However, most Poles took a sceptical view of this creation, particularly after Piłsudski, who had fought with his Legion under Austrian command, refused to swear loyalty to the German Emperor. He was interned, as were most of his Legionnaires and soldiers of the Polish Armed Force who followed his example.

In contrast to Piłsudski, Dmowski wanted to tie the Polish cause to that of the Entente powers (Britain, France, Russia). His efforts to win recognition from the Western powers as the representative of Polish interests foundered on their fear of 'interfering in the internal affairs' of their Russian ally. This changed only with the overthrow of the czarist regime in Russia, and the declaration by the new revolutionary government that in principle recognised the right of the Poles to self-determination. Polish units began to form in Russia and the Allies agreed to the organisation of a Polish army in France. In January 1918, President Wilson, thanks in large measure to personal lobbying by the celebrated pianist Ignacy Paderewski, included the restoration of an independent Poland with access to the Baltic sea in his famous '**Fourteen Points**' on war aims. Polish aspirations to independence were gradually winning a cautious recognition in the eyes of the Western powers.

The restoration of Polish independence was made possible by the collapse of the Austro–Hungarian and then the German Army in October and November 1918. On 7 November 1918, representatives of the Socialist and Peasant parties and of the underground Polish Military Organisation organised by Piłsudski, set up a government in Lublin. Piłsudski, released from German prison, negotiated the withdrawal of the German forces from Warsaw on 11 November. On 14 November, both the Regency Council and the Lublin Government passed their authority to Piłsudski, who was declared Chief of State. In January 1919, the first parliament was elected, which proclaimed a provisional constitution.

The frontiers of the new state were carved out between 1918 and 1921 in six simultaneous armed conflicts. The first erupted already in November of 1918 in Lwów (Lviv), where Ukrainians, who formed a majority in Eastern Galicia, proclaimed a West Ukrainian People's Republic. A full scale Polish-Ukrainian war followed, which ended in a Ukrainian defeat and the incorporation of Eastern Galicia into Poland. In December 1918, the Poles in Poznań rose against German rule. Similar uprisings were staged in 1919, 1920 and 1921 by the Polish population of Silesia. Polish forces clashed twice with the Lithuanians over control of the town of Wilno (Vilnius), which was claimed by Lithuanians on historic, and by Poles on ethnic grounds. A minor skirmish took place with Czechoslovak troops, who attacked the predominantly Polish areas around Cieszyn.

The most serious conflict, however, in which the very existence of Polish state-hood was at stake, was fought against Bolshevik Russia. In the spring of 1919, Polish and Bolshevik forces clashed in Belarus, where a political vacuum had been created by the withdrawal of the German troops. In the autumn of 1919, a secret armistice was arranged between the Poles and Bolsheviks. Piłsudski refused to deliver a *coup de grâce* to the Bolshevik forces, which were on the verge of being defeated by the Russian Whites. Though no friend of the Bolsheviks, Piłsudski thought that their victory in the Russian Civil War was less dangerous to Poland than that of the Whites.

The war flared up again in the spring of 1920. With the final defeat of the Whites, Polish and Ukrainian forces launched a pre-emptive strike in May which took them as far as the Ukrainian capital Kiev. The Soviet counter-offensive turned the tide of the war and in August brought the Red Army to the outskirts of Warsaw. However, with a brilliant encircling manoeuvre, Piłsudski surrounded the main Soviet armies east of Warsaw and then rolled them back to the line of the 1919 armistice. In October, Lenin sued for peace. The British Ambassador in Berlin, Lord d'Abernon, compared the significance of the Soviet defeat in the battle of Warsaw to the defeat of the Arab invasion by Charles Martel at Tours: 'The Battle of Tours saved our ancestors from the Yoke of the Koran; it is probable that the Battle of Warsaw saved Central and parts of Western Europe from a more subversive danger—the fanatical tyranny of the Soviet'.

The Second Republic (1921–1939)

The Polish state which arose on the ruins of the three Empires faced an extremely difficult task. It consisted of territories which for a hundred and fifty years had been subject to different political and legal regimes and had been integrated into different economic systems. After seven years of war and ruthless exploitation by occupying armies the country was devastated. Over three quarters of the population was engaged in subsistence agriculture. One third of the population consisted of national minorities (Ukrainians, Jews, Belarusians, Germans). The borders were far from secure. Neither Germany nor Soviet Russia reconciled themselves to their territorial losses.

The political system of the Second Republic was modelled on the French Third Republic. Power rested with the Chamber of Deputies and the position of the executive was extremely weak. With a large number of fractious parties, stable parliamentary majorities and governments were elusive. The political struggle turned violent when a vicious campaign was launched by Dmowski's National Democrats against the first President of Poland, who defeated their candidate thanks to the votes of national minorities. Dmowski's party was frustrated by its inability to control the main levers of power in the new state, even though it was the most popular group among ethnic Poles. The fact that Narutowicz was elected with the votes of national minorities was a convenient pretext to try to change the result. The President was abused by frenzied mobs and finally assassinated. In 1926, Piłsudski, with the support of loyal military units and the left, staged a *coup d'état* against the rightist coalition, which included the National Democrats. He practically ruled the country until his death in 1935, supported by a coterie of veteran Legionnaires and by individuals from a wide variety of political camps, who had become disillusioned with the partisan bickering and instability produced by the parliamentary regime. Judging by the standards of the age, Piłsudski's dictatorship was relatively mild—opposition figures were harassed and even imprisoned without trial, but political parties and trade unions were allowed to function and ran their candidates in elections, the judiciary remained largely free of political pressures, and freedom of the press was maintained.

The Second Republic lasted only 20 years and was brought down by an invasion of its two powerful neighbours—Nazi Germany and Communist Russia. Since the German–Soviet Treaty of Rapallo in 1921, the possibility of such collusion hung like a dark cloud over Polish independence. In the spring of 1939, the Polish government firmly rebuffed German demands for territorial concessions. Polish resolve was strengthened by the British guarantee of Poland's territorial integrity issued in April and the Franco–British–Polish military consultations. In the event of a German attack the French promised to launch a full scale military offensive by the fourteenth day of the war. On 23

August 1939, Germany and the Soviet Union signed the infamous **Ribben-trop–Molotov Pact**. The secret clauses provided for a division of Eastern Europe into Soviet and German spheres of influence. In effect, the Pact meant that Stalin was giving a green light to the German attack on Poland. It was the death warrant of the Second Republic.

The Second World War

On 1 September 1939, Germany invaded Poland from three directions. The *Wehrmacht* enjoyed an overwhelming superiority of three to one in artillery and five to one in tanks and aircraft. The Poles mounted a valiant defence, but were helpless against the German *Blitzkrieg*. On 8 September, German tanks reached Warsaw, which managed to hold out until 27 September.

On 17 September, the Soviet Union, breaking the existing non-aggression treaty with Poland, invaded from the east. The Soviet attack, unanticipated by the Polish high command, thwarted the latter's efforts to organise a new line of defence in the south-eastern corner of the country. On the following day, the Polish government sought refuge in Romania. Individual units continued to fight, trying to break through to the border with Hungary and Romania. The last Polish army, caught in cross fire between the German and the Soviet forces, laid down its arms on 5 October.

On 28 September, Germany and the Soviet Union signed an agreement, dividing the Polish state along the Bug and Narew rivers. The Germans incorporated the western part of their zone directly into the Reich, and from the rest created the General-Gouvernement with its capital in Kraków. German occupation policies in Poland were the harshest in Europe, with the exception of Serbia. In the words of the prominent British historian Norman Davies 'Poland became the killing-ground of Europe, the new Golgotha'. Special SS squads following immediately behind the German troops summarily executed, on the basis of special proscription lists, numerous members of the Polish political, intellectual and social elites. The population was divided into racial categories, with Jews being separated and crowded into ghettos. The aim of German occupation policy was to liquidate the Polish educated class and reduce the Poles to the status of an illiterate labour force. All Polish institutions were closed, including universities and secondary schools. A quarter of a million Poles were expelled from the territories incorporated into the Reich and dumped into the General-Gouvernement. Jewish and Polish industrialists were expropriated and Polish landowners had their estates confiscated. Both the Jewish and Polish population was put beyond the pale of civil law. The only punishment for infringing the occupation rules was death or deportation to a concentration camp. By 1941, street executions, the shooting of hostages, public hangings, mass deportations to labour camps and the razing of whole villages had become a common occurrence.

The worst fate awaited the Jewish population. Hunger and contagious diseases in the extremely cramped ghettos were taking a high toll even before the Nazi leadership decided, at the end of 1941, to exterminate all Jews. The first experiments with the use of carbon monoxide and then Cyklon-B gas were carried out in Chełmno (Kulm). In 1942, a gruesome mass murder operation, unprecedented in history, began in the extermination camps of Oświęcim-Brzezinka (Auschwitz-Birkenau), Treblinka, Sobibór, Bełżec, Majdanek and Płaszów. Almost the entire Jewish population of Poland—over three million people—was wiped out.

The Soviets imposed in their zone their own version of a totalitarian regime. The population was divided into categories, with 'class origin' rather than race as the criterion. Mass arrests and deportations were carried out, which affected primarily the Polish, but also the Jewish, Ukrainian and Belarusian elites. Estimates vary, but from 800,000 to 1.5 million people were deported between September 1939 and June 1941 to labour camps and forced settlement in Siberia, North Russia and Central Asia. Fifteen thousand officers of the Polish army and police officials who surrendered to the Soviets in 1939 were interned and then shot in the spring of 1940 (see below). Thousands of others were liquidated in prisons in Western Belarus and the Ukraine.

The final balance of war losses was staggering. Over six million citizens of the Polish Republic lost their lives, half of them Jews. Only about ten per cent died as a result of military operations, the rest perished in concentration and extermination camps or were killed in mass executions. The casualty rate in Poland was 18 per cent, the highest in Europe. By comparison, the casualty rate in Britain was 0.9 per cent, in Germany 7.4 per cent, 11.1 per cent in Yugoslavia and 11.2 per cent in the Soviet Union.

In spite of the Nazi terror, the Poles managed to organise an effective mass resistance movement and institutions of an underground state. By 1943, partisan units were operating in many areas, especially in the forests of north-eastern Poland, the Świętokrzyskie Mountains and the foothills of the Carpathian range. By 1944, the mainstream military organisation known as the Armia Krajowa (Home Army) could mobilise about 400,000 people. Polish underground intelligence played a major role in helping the Allies to delay the development of the German flying bombs (V1 and V2).

The Resistance movement was loyal to the **Polish government-in-exile**, which was set up in France by all the major Polish political parties in the autumn of 1939, moving to London in 1940. The government, headed by General Władysław Sikorski, was recognised by the Western Allies as well as by most neutral powers including the United States. The Polish Armed Forces organised by the government-in-exile made significant contributions to the Allies' war effort, notably the British victory in the Battle of Britain, and the capture of the fortified abbey of Monte Cassino, which enabled the Allies to advance on Rome.

After the German attack on the Soviet Union Sikorski signed a treaty with Stalin, under which the Soviets repudiated the Ribbentrop-Molotov pact and agreed to liberate all Poles deported to and imprisoned in the Soviet Union. Stalin also consented to the formation of a Polish army on Soviet territory. But the problem of a future border between the two countries was left unsolved and very quickly relations deteriorated. In 1942, matters came to a head when the Soviets cut food supplies to the Polish Army, which was then evacuated to the Middle East.

In April 1943, the Germans announced the discovery of mass graves of Polish officers in **Katyń** near Smoleńsk. The Polish government asked the International Red Cross to investigate, but the Soviets denounced this as collusion with Hitler and broke diplomatic relations. Until the very end of the Soviet Union's existence, its leaders (including Gorbachev) denied responsibility for the deed. It was only in 1991 that President Boris Yeltsin finally released documents proving that the Soviet leadership had ordered the execution.

The Soviets proceeded to set up a Communist-dominated Union of Polish Patriots and organised a Communist-led army composed of Poles still remaining in the Soviet Union and commanded largely by Soviet officers. With the Red Army approaching the pre-war borders of Poland, the Resistance movement loyal to the government-in-exile found itself in a dead-end. The Soviet position was that all territories incorporated into the Soviet Union as a result of the 1939 agreement with Hitler were an inalienable part of the Soviet Union. It regarded the Polish partisan units there as interlopers and Soviet partisans had orders to liquidate them. Polish partisans who helped the Red Army chase the Germans out of Wilno and Lwów were disarmed and sent to Soviet camps. In the summer of 1944, Stalin established a **Polish Committee of National Liberation (PKWN)**, the embryo of Poland's future government. Officials appointed by the Resistance were dismissed and often arrested.

Resistance leaders in Warsaw faced a tragic choice as the Soviet offensive approached the city: they could either keep their forces in hiding, which would lay them open to the charge that they failed to fight the Germans, and allow the Soviets to install the PKWN administration in the capital, or they could try to pre-empt the Red Army by seizing the city from the Germans thus asserting the authority of the government-in-exile in the Polish capital.

The Resistance leaders decided on the second option and launched the **Warsaw Uprising** on 1 August. The partisans managed to liberate several districts of the city, but the Red Army failed to mount a cross-river assault to help them. Stalin even refused to allow British and American planes which dropped supplies for the partisans to land in the Soviet-controlled airfields. After two months of fighting, on 2 October, the Polish forces capitulated. During the fighting almost a quarter of a million civilians were killed. The population was evacuated and demolition teams dynamited what was left of the city.

This was a crippling blow to the underground movement. Its position was further undermined by the results of the **Yalta conference** between Roosevelt, Stalin and Churchill in February 1945. Great Britain and the United States conceded to their Soviet ally that a new Polish government should be formed on the basis of the existing pro-Soviet government in Lublin, with the addition of 'democratic' politicians from the London government and from Poland.

The only major Polish political figure in London prepared to accept the decisions of the Yalta Conference was Stanisław Mikołajczyk, leader of the Polish Peasant Party and Prime Minister of the Polish Government after 1943. Mikołajczyk believed that it was worth trying to reach a compromise with Stalin, and that acceptance of the new Polish-Soviet border would make it possible to preserve national sovereignty. He pinned his hopes on the free elections promised by the Yalta agreements. While Mikołajczyk was negotiating his place in the new Polish government, the Soviets were staging a show trial of sixteen leaders of the Polish anti-Nazi Resistance movement.

Poland under Soviet Domination

When the war in Europe ended in May 1945, Poles were in no mood to celebrate the victory. The toll in human life was staggering—Poland lost about six million of its citizens. Its entire Jewish community of three million was almost totally wiped out. Losses were particularly high among the intellectual and political elites. The country lay in ruins—38 per cent of national wealth was destroyed. Half of Poland's pre-war territory was already annexed by the Soviet Union. The compensation promised at Yalta in the form of German territories east of the

Odra and Nysa rivers—Silesia, Western Pomerania and East Prussia—had still not been confirmed by an international treaty. After Yalta, many Poles could not help feeling that all their suffering had been in vain. After fighting against one totalitarian power threatening Europe—Nazi Germany, they were abandoned by their Western allies to the tender mercies of another—the Soviet Union. It was symbolic that the Polish military units in the West were not even invited to the Victory Parade held in London on 8 June 1946.

At the Potsdam conference in July 1945, the three Great Powers finally approved the new Polish-German border and ordered a population transfer to avoid future complications that might arise from the presence of a large German minority in Poland. Following this decision, about three million Germans were deported to the British occupation zone in Germany. On the basis of the Polish-Soviet agreement, 1.5 million Poles were permitted to leave the former Polish territories in the east and emigrate to Poland, while about 500,000 Ukrainians and Belarusians moved or were deported to the Soviet Union.

While the security forces were hunting down the last resistance units still in hiding, Mikołajczyk's **Polish Peasant Party** was trying to challenge the Communists at the polls. The Communists delayed the elections called for by the Yalta accords until 1947, when they were sure of controlling the electoral process. Mikołajczyk's Peasant Party was subjected to harassment and persecution and the results were rigged on a massive scale. Mikołajczyk, threatened with imminent arrest, had to flee the country.

Having liquidated the legal opposition, the Communists turned against their Socialist allies. In December 1948, the Socialist Party was purged of its right-wing and merged with the Communist PPR to form the **United Polish Workers' Party** (**PZPR**), which was to rule Poland for the next forty-one years. Its new leader was Bolesław Bierut, a staunch Stalinist. The army was fully subordinated to the Soviet high command, with Soviet officers placed in key posts. Konstatin Rokossovsky, a Soviet marshal of Polish extraction, was appointed Minister of Defence.

The Communists launched an offensive against the Roman Catholic Church, culminating in 1954, when the Primate of Poland, Cardinal Stefan Wyszyński, was interned in a remote monastery. In the countryside the party tried to force peasants into collective farms by administrative chicanery. Intellectual life was put into the straightjacket of official Marxist dogma. Censorship intensified, and writers who did not conform to the obligatory doctrine of Socialist Realism were barred from publishing.

After the death of Stalin in 1953, the PZPR slowly began to relax the grip that the secret police had on the country. Bolesław Bierut died of a heart attack in February 1956 after attending Khrushchev's famous speech to the Twentieth Congress of the Communist Party of the Soviet Union denouncing Stalin's crimes. In June 1956, a labour dispute in the city of Poznań erupted into an uprising, and the government had to use armoured units to restore control. Unlike their Hungarian comrades, the party leadership understood that they were sitting on a powder keg and that urgent reforms were needed. The Communist leader Władysław Gomułka (replaced in 1949 by Bierut and imprisoned) and the Primate of Poland Cardinal Wyszyński were released from prison. The former was the only Communist who could count on a measure of popular sympathy as a victim of Stalinist persecution. He accordingly became First

Secretary of the party in October 1956—a move which nearly precipitated a Soviet invasion, because Moscow had not been consulted.

At the outset, Gomułka enjoyed genuine popular support as a politician who had stood up to the Soviets. To a large section of the public he embodied hopes for a democratisation of the political system and an extension of intellectual and cultural freedom. However, this optimism was soon tempered by his restrictive cultural policies and the conservatism of his political regime.

The Prague Spring of 1968 helped trigger the '**March events**' of that year in Poland. After the sudden cancellation (allegedly at the demand of the Soviet embassy) of a performance of a 19C patriotic play at a Warsaw theatre, students marched through the streets and held a protest rally. Student unrest engulfed many Polish campuses. The authorities responded with police violence, arrests, and a massive propaganda effort, in which anti-Semitic rhetoric played a major part.

Gomułka managed to remain in power for two more years. He was brought down by the mass strikes and demonstrations that engulfed coastal towns in December 1970. The workers' were protesting against a sharp rise in the price of basic foodstuffs. Instead of trying to help the economy by allowing some scope for market forces, Gomułka's strategy was to lower workers' living standards. The workers responded by organising strike committees and staging sit-ins; they attacked and burnt down Communist party buildings and police stations. Soon, the shipyards in Gdańsk, Gdynia and Szczecin became the centres of the opposition movement. In response, the government deployed army units and several dozen workers were killed.

To allay the workers' discontent, the party leadership replaced Gomułka with **Edward Gierek**, a district party chairman from Silesia. In a series of meetings with the shipyard workers, Gierek apologised for the bloodshed and promised that the party would never again alienate itself from the working class. In Gdańsk he made the famous plea that later became a subject of popular ridicule and contempt: 'Will you help me?' Lech Wałęsa might well have been among those in the crowd who replied with enthusiasm: 'Yes, we will, comrade general secretary.' He tried to win popular support by promising a fast improvement in living standards, a kind of socialist version of consumerism. To overcome the sluggish economic performance of the 1960s, he resorted to massive borrowing from Western banks and governments. This strategy became feasible with the launching of US–Soviet détente and the normalisation of relations between Poland and West Germany after the treaty of 1970 in which the West German government recognised the post-war border along the Odra and Nysa rivers.

For the first five years Gierek's plan seemed successful: living standards improved fast and Poles enjoyed a minor consumer boom. By 1975, however, it became clear that the funds borrowed from the West had been largely wasted. Polish industry turned out to be unable to earn enough hard currency on Western markets to pay back the loans. There were shortages of even basic foodstuffs and rationing was introduced. Price rises, intended to restore balance on the food market, led to demonstrations and strikes. The most violent protests took place in the industrial town of Radom and in the Ursus tractor plant near Warsaw. Price rises were cancelled, but the protesters were severely punished.

Reacting to the persecution of the former strikers by the authorities, a group of intellectuals led by Jacek Kuroń and Adam Michnik set up the '**Workers' Defence Committee**' (**KOR**). The novelty of KOR's formula was that it acted openly and without breaking any existing laws. Its members were harassed, sacked, repeatedly arrested and threatened with violence, but never imprisoned for long. The Committee published and distributed underground publications, and set up 'initiative groups' to help workers organise independent trade unions. A young shipyard electrician, Lech Wałęsa, joined one such group in Gdańsk. KOR's activities sparked off the development of a broader dissident movement in Poland. It was not a mass phenomenon, but it prepared both the cadres and the ideology, without which the Solidarity revolution of 1980–81 would have been unthinkable.

The election of Kraków's Cardinal, Karol Wojtyła, as pope in 1978, and especially his visit to Poland in 1979, boosted anti-Communist sentiments. The open-air masses, which gathered millions, demonstrated that the power of the Communist party was not unlimited, and that defiance of its authority could not always be repressed.

Solidarity and the Imposition of Martial Law

In 1980, the deteriorating economic situation, shortages of basic foodstuffs, corruption of the party apparatus, and popular contempt for its rule provoked a nationwide wave of strikes. The workers formed regional strike committees, which were joined by many prominent intellectuals and opposition figures. In August, Gdańsk made headline news across the world's media when the huge Lenin shipyard went on strike. Lech Wałęsa, an unknown electrician with hardly any education but amazing political intuition and charisma, famously scrambled over the shipyard gates to assume leadership. The strike committee's demands included not only wage increases and improved work conditions, but also the setting up of free trade unions and the release of all political prisoners. Gierek and the party leadership had learnt their lesson in 1970 and knew better than to send in the soldiers. After tense negotiations lasting several weeks, the party capitulated and signed the historic **Gdańsk agreements**, incorporating the strikers' main demands.

The 'Polish August', as it later came to be known, was an unprecedented and revolutionary event. The strikes precipitated the first open mass revolt against a communist regime, within a couple of months giving birth to a new and powerful political force in the form of the **Independent Solidarity Trade Union**. With a peak membership of almost 10 million people (more than a quarter of the entire population), Solidarity was more than just a trade union: it was a broad social movement grouping all those in Poland who felt that profound economic and social reforms were necessary and that the Communist Party would have to relinquish its monopoly on political power. Only the fear of Soviet invasion forestalled more radical demands.

Between September 1980 and December 1981 a tug of war developed between Solidarity and the party. Twice, in the winter of 1980 and in the summer of 1981, Soviet troops were poised to enter Poland to blackmail Solidarity into submission. As it later turned out, the authorities had only been trying to buy time. On 13 December 1981, General Wojciech Jaruzelski, the newly-appointed Prime Minister and First Secretary of the Communist Party, announced the suspension of civilian government and the declaration of a 'state of war'. The plan, jointly agreed by the Soviet and Polish authorities, was to suppress Solidarity using only the Polish police and army. Many of the union's members were arrested, its offices and bank accounts seized. A curfew was imposed, communications were cut, and military commissars were installed in all enterprises.

The regime destroyed Solidarity as an organisation, but it failed to win popular legitimacy. Poland's foreign debt grew to staggering proportions as the economic situation continued to deteriorate. The workforce was sullen and uncooperative. Solidarity went underground and throughout the 1980s continued its determined opposition to the regime.

The situation in which neither Solidarity could seriously threaten the regime, nor the regime liquidate Solidarity, lasted until the end of the decade. Most of Solidarity's leaders, including Wałęsa, were free, but under constant police surveillance. The failing economy was a major headache for the authorities. In the spring of 1989, faced with the threat of new strikes, the regime decided to enter into negotiations with the opposition. The famous '**Round Table**' talks began between Solidarity and the Communist regime, as a result of which the authorities agreed to legalise Solidarity. In exchange, Solidarity was to legitimise the existing system by participating in parliamentary elections set for June 1989. The terms of the agreement stipulated, however, that the Communists and their allies were to keep a minimum of 65 per cent of the seats. The opposition scored a crushing victory, winning 35 per cent of seats in the Chamber of Deputies (all that were contested) and 99 of the 100 seats in the Senate.

The opposition seemed surprised by the scale of its victory. After some initial hesitation, it agreed to form a cabinet led by Tadeusz Mazowiecki, a Catholic intellectual and an advisor to Solidarity. The government was to share power with a Communist President (Jaruzelski).

Mazowiecki's government, the first non-Communist government in Eastern Europe, launched a programme of radical reform that was to change the face of Poland. Its most important element was the economic 'shock therapy' programme devised and implemented by the finance minister Leszek Balcerowicz. The long process of building a market economy, a democratic political system and a modern pluralist society had begun. After almost fifty years of Communist rule, Poland was to set to rejoin a democratic Europe.

Polish Art and Architecture

By Professor Zdzisław Żygulski

The Piasts (9C–1370)

Early Slavonic architecture

Polish tribes—the **Polanians**, **Vistulanians**, **Mazovians** and **Silesians**—emerged from the proto-Slavonic family after AD 500. Their architecture was almost exclusively wooden, their houses built inside fortified settlements defended by huge wood and earth grille ramparts. They tilled the soil and bred animals, wove linen and wool, used wooden and ceramic vessels, and made bronze jewellery. Thanks to Moravian and Czech influence, the Vistulanians were the most culturally advanced of the tribes.

Under the leadership of the Piast dynasty (see p. 44), the Polanians attempted to unify the tribes in the second half of the 10C. Mieszko I's adoption of Christianity in 966 meant that the **Piast state** became closely interwoven with the hierarchy of the Roman Catholic Church, which was to have a profound impact on the indigenous culture. Latin script appeared, upon which written Polish is based. Places of worship and residence, composed of a palace (*palatium*) and a chapel, were erected in the ducal seats. Examples of these can be found on the peninsula of Ostrów Lednicki, where two baptismal fonts were discovered in 1990, and in Gniezno, Poznań, Giecz, Kraków, Wiślica and Przemyśl. The chapels were usually round, like the rotunda of St Mary on Wawel hill in Kraków. A bishopric and cathedral were founded as early as 968 in Poznań, an archbishopric in Gniezno in 1000, and further bishoprics in Kraków, Wrocław and Kołobrzeg. During the early 11C the first Benedictine monasteries appeared.

Romanesque art and architecture

Romanesque architecture spread throughout the Piast domains during the 11C and 12C. Stone aisled basilicas with twin towers were built, such as St Andrew's in Kraków, or aisleless churches with short chancels and sometimes a tower. Cathedrals acquired crypts. Romanesque churches were marked by the austerity and simplicity of their stone façades. The interiors were plastered and often covered with murals, the floors made of colourful ceramic tiles in relief. The **Gniezno Doors** (1170) bear bronze reliefs depicting scenes from the life and martyrdom of St Adalbert, and are the finest example of Romanesque casting in Poland, influenced by ideas originating from the famous Meuse valley (now in eastern Belgium), which played such a crucial role in the development of Romanesque art (particularly painting). In 1959, two square gypsum slabs were discovered in the crypt of the collegiate church of the Holy Trinity in Wiślica. The fine engraving, filled with black paste, depicts six human figures in prayer, probably Piast Dukes, surrounded by family and court.

The adoption of christianity meant that illuminated manuscripts from various regions, mainly German, Czech and Italian, were brought to Poland. Amongst the oldest examples of Romanesque craftsmanship are the Spear of St Maurice in the cathedral treasury in Kraków, given by Otto III to Bolesław the Brave, a copy of the Holy Roman Spear; the silver Włocławek Chalice, recalling silverwork of the Middle East; and the Kalisz paten (communion plate) from the end of the 12C bearing engraved figures of Mieszko III and the goldsmith Konrad.

In the early 13C, there was a breakthrough in Polish architecture that heralded the approach of the Gothic style. The Cistercians, arriving from their German, French and Danish homelands, with ready-made architectural designs based on pointed arches and rib vaulting, played a major part in this movement. The greatest masterpieces (apart from architecture) dating from this period are: the Płock Chalice, with paten, bearing images of Konrad Mazowiecki and his family; two gold crowns, from which a cross was made in the 15C, now in the cathedral treasury in Kraków; and the coronation sword of Polish kings—the Szczerbiec ('notched sword')—now in the State Art Collections in Wawel (see p. 220).

Early Gothic art and architecture

Gothic art appeared in Poland around 1250 and flourished in the 14C and 15C, surviving well into the 1500s. Brick Gothic architecture is part of the fabric of the ancient cities of Kraków, Wrocław, Toruń and Gdańsk. To some extent, Gothic style was the outcome of the great colonisation that occurred in Poland after the Tartar invasions of the mid-13C, when towns were founded on German law, adopting western models of administration and organising craftsmanship through guilds. Yet despite these foreign influences, Poland was still able to make its own contribution. In **architecture**, the brick Polish Gothic, sometimes called Vistulian, was original not only in its external appearance, but also in building methods. New Gothic buildings appeared, replacing destroyed Romanesque cathedrals, in Wrocław and Kraków, for example. The great surge of building began with the unification of the state and the revival of the kingdom by **Władysław Łokietek** (1320), and lasted throughout the reign of Kazimierz the Great. It was tied to the rapid economic development of the country, the expansion of trade and guilds, particularly in the capital city of Kraków. In the mid-14C, the cathedrals in Gniezno and Poznań were gothicised, and churches in Pomerania, Toruń, Gdańsk, Kamień, Stargard and Szczecin were also erected in this new style.

This was also the golden age of secular architecture. New castles, town halls, burghers' houses, cloth halls, defensive walls and town fortifications were constructed. Wawel castle in Kraków was built in Gothic style; hill-top castles were erected in Będzin, Chęciny, Lwów and Bolków. In addition, there were the Teutonic castles of the monastic-defensive type in Pomerania. These were built on rectangular plans with corner towers and modelled on the Syrian castles of the Crusaders. The Teutonic Knights, brought to Poland in 1226 to convert the pagan Prussians, built 23 such castles before 1300, the finest example being Malbork, the seat of the Grand Master of the Order (see p. 333). Within a short space of time, the Knights acquired sufficient power to threaten the Polish state.

The municipal independence of Polish towns was symbolised by town halls, usually square, with a tall tower occasionally equipped with a clock, as in Kraków, Poznań, Toruń and Gdańsk. In the latter, separate buildings with reception rooms for the meetings of the patriciate, the Artus Court and St George's Court, were added in the 15C. The defence system—walls, ramparts, moats, towers and gate-houses—were a major investment in the towns. In Kraków, the town walls were begun at the end of the 13C and work continued for over 200 years.

In the 13C and 14C, stone **sculpture** was used primarily in architecture, but from the beginning of the 14C, royal tombs were commissioned, such as that of Duke Henry IV Probus in Wrocław, and Władysław Łokietek and Kazimierz the Great in Kraków. Stone and wooden figures of the Madonna and Child, Christ on the Cross, and saints, were produced mainly in Silesia and Małopolska. The finest **gold and silver work** of the period are the silver chalices donated by Kazimierz the Great in Kraków, Stopnica and Kalisz, and the reliquary of St Zygmunt with its 13C gold crown in Płock cathedral.

The Jagiellonians (1385–1572)

Gothic art and architecture

The accession to the throne of the Lithuanian **Duke Władysław Jagiełło** (1386), marked a personal and then political union of the two states which transformed the Polish kingdom into a Central European power. Aided by Lithuania, Poland arrested the expansion of the Teutonic Order, struggled to gain control over the Baltic, and opposed the aggrandisement of Muscovy. Vast eastern territories (including the Ruthenian lands) fell under the influence of Polish and Latin culture. Piast art continued to provide inspiration during the Jagiellonian period, although this was now supplemented by new influences from the Byzantine East. Church and chapel frescoes—examples of Byzantine-Ruthenian art—appeared in Lublin, Sandomierz, Kraków and other towns. New churches, castles, estates and burghers' houses continued to be built in the Gothic style, mainly brick, although some traditional wooden architecture persisted for both secular and religious buildings.

The art of the guilds flourished—particularly **sculpture and painting**—of which Kraków was the leading centre. From the end of the 14C until the mid-15C the 'Beautiful' or 'International' Gothic style prevailed, finding expression in the so-called Beautiful Madonnas—sculptures of the Virgin—which embodied the court ideal of female beauty, both physical and spiritual. The wooden Madonna of Krużlowa (c 1410), in the National Museum in Kraków, is a masterpiece of this genre.

In the mid-15C, a new bourgeois Gothic style—expressionist-realist—emerged in Polish sculpture as well as painting and graphic art. It is often called 'Broken style' from the way folds of fabric were represented and reached its apogee in the work of **Veit Stoss**, who came to Kraków from Nürnberg on a commission to make the gigantic retable of the high altar in the church of St Mary (see p. 199). This monumental work, carved in lime wood, painted and gilded, depicting the Life and Dormition of the Virgin, was begun in 1477 and finished in 1489. Using a broad range of artistic techniques, Stoss achieved an astounding expressiveness in the representation of human figures and super-natural creatures. At the dawn of the Renaissance he left an indelible mark on the imagination of his contemporaries, becoming widely admired and imitated. He also made the crucifix in St Mary's, and the red marble memorial sculpture of Kazimierz the Jagiellon (1492), in Wawel cathedral.

The Gothic **painting** of the guilds, mainly religious, flourished in Kraków, Silesia, Wielkopolska and Pomerania, first in the 'Beautiful', then in the 'Broken' style, under the influence of German, Czech, Italian and Flemish art. Several painted polyptychs, serving as retables but simply called altars, date from the second half of the 15C, the best examples of which are preserved in the National Museums in Kraków, Warsaw, Wrocław, Poznań and Gdańsk.

Gold and silver work thrived. Of the many silver sceptres made for the rectors of the Jagiellonian University, that carved by the Cracovian goldsmith Marcin Marciniec in 1493–95 is particularly fine. Marciniec also made an exquisite reliquary for the head of St Stanisław in the Wawel Cathedral. The *Behem Codex*, the book of privileges of the Cracovian guilds (now in the Jagiellonian Library) dating from the early 16C, is richly illustrated with miniatures.

Renaissance art and architecture

The **Renaissance** in Poland first appeared in **architecture** at the beginning of the 16C. Around 1503, Franciszek Włoch (Italus) from Florence, also known as Francesco Fiorentino, carved the stone framing of the tomb of King Jan Olbracht in Wawel cathedral in this style. He carried out reconstruction work on Wawel Castle between 1507–16, which was finally completed in 1536. This sumptuous residence, with a quadrangular arcaded courtyard, consisted of three habitable wings with reception rooms (piano nobile) on the second floor. King Zygmunt I was a great connoisseur and patron of Renaissance art. He first encountered it whilst staying at the castle in Buda, where, as Crown Prince, he visited his brother Władysław, King of Bohemia and Hungary. His admiration for Italian culture became even greater after his marriage to the Milanese princess, Bona Sforza.

In 1530, Bartolomeo Berrecci, a sculptor and mason from Florence, took over supervision of work on Wawel. He was responsible for the Royal Mausoleum and the Zygmunt Chapel, pure Renaissance with grotesque and mythological decoration, in the Italian style. The mausoleum became the resting place of the last Jagiellons, their tombs carved in red marble by Berrecci himself and other Italian masters. They were assisted by local masons and sculptors, who in architecture often employed transitional Gothic-Renaissance forms, and in tombs—characteristic reclining and sleeping figures, imitating Italian models. Most famous amongst them was Jan Michałowicz, known as the 'Polish Praxiteles'.

Following the King's example, the nobility and magnates funded Renaissance-style domed sepulchral chapels, castles and palaces, country villas, and burghers' houses in the towns. Renaissance motifs were superimposed on older Gothic structures, the Cloth Hall in Kraków, for example, was rebuilt in 1557. The preponderance of horizontal lines was achieved by the addition of parapets—a kind of high ornamental wall atop the roof. From the mid-16C, the Renaissance style made its appearance in the northern and eastern towns of the Kingdom. In Poznań, Italian architects constructed a beautiful town hall, with an arcaded gallery, parapet and mythological interior decoration. In Gdańsk, the imposing Green Gate was erected, and in Lwów an Orthodox church, based on Italian designs, of exceptionally harmonious proportions.

At the very beginning of the 16C, **miniature painting** with Gothic-Renaissance characteristics evolved, especially in Kraków, with works such as the gradual used by King Jan Olbracht, and the pontifical (book of offices) of Bishop Erasmus Ciołek. An outstanding painter of this period was Stanisław Samostrzelnik, a miniaturist and painter of murals, whose work can be seen today at the Cistercian Abbey in Mogiła, near Kraków (see p. 236). Painting was to serve the glory of the rulers and their victories: the *Battle of Orsza* (after 1514), by a painter influenced by Lucas Cranach, probably commissioned by King Zygmunt I (now in the National Museum in Warsaw), is a good example.

The last of the Jagiellons were great patrons and collectors of art. A silver cockerel, stylised as the heraldic eagle, is the work of a Cracovian goldsmith. It was donated by Zygmunt August to the Bractwo Strzeleckie (Rifle Guild), and is preserved in the Historical Museum in Kraków. Brass, bronze and tin casting, tile-making and embroidery, all excelled in Kraków. Zygmunt I was an early collector of artistic and decorative fabrics, mainly Flemish tapestries. A rich collection of them, comprising more than 140 items, bequeathed to the Kingdom by his son Zygmunt August, adorns the rooms of Wawel Castle to the present day. The series of tapestries illustrating the life of Adam and Eve, Cain and Able, Noah, the Tower of Babel and Moses, others depicting animals set against landscapes, or bearing royal coats of arms and monograms, originate from Brussels workshops and were designed by such outstanding artists as Michael van Coxcie. Another curiosity in Wawel Castle are the wooden polychromed sculpted heads on the ceiling of the Audience Hall (see p. 220).

The Commonwealth (1569–1795)

King Zygmunt August died without an heir, so from 1572 Poland's kings were directly elected by the nobility. The main role in this process was played by rich magnates, who had their own private armies but were much influenced by foreign powers. It was thus usually foreign kings who got elected—Henry Valois of France, Stefan Bathory of Hungary, the Swedish Vasas and the Wettin line from Saxony—and only on three occasions 'Piasts'—Michał Korybut Wiśniowiecki, Jan Sobieski and Stanisław August Poniatowski. Over two hundred years, amid wars and unrest, the Polish-Lithuanian Commonwealth lost its position as a major power through political and military disintegration, and finally lost its sovereignty in 1795. The cultural vitality experienced during the Jagiellons and first two Vasas—Zygmunt III and Władysław IV—went into serious decline during the Swedish Deluge (1655–60; see p. 49), which brought destruction to the country, depopulation and a falling off in production by craftsmen. Reconstruction was slow in coming and some sectors of the arts were not revived until the reign of Stanisław August (1764–95). The disastrous political system with its 'golden liberty'—allowing each deputy to veto any parliamentary legislation—blocked all attempts at reform. Paradoxically, the nobility's 'liberty' went hand in hand with political dependence on Poland's aggressive neighbours.

Throughout this period, Polish art and culture retained a characteristic duality. Poland was part of Western culture and with it underwent the change in styles from Mannerism, through Baroque and Rococo to Neo-classicism, prompted by artists arriving from Italy, France, Germany and the Netherlands. Creative work revolved around the patronage of the King and the magnates, and was also centred in the great cities of Warsaw, Kraków, Poznań, Lwów, Toruń and Gdańsk. Simultaneously, a local cultural style known as Sarmatism evolved, pervading not only art, but also literature, rhetoric, music, religious life, military and civil customs, and the nation's outlook in general.

Architecture and sculpture

The Commonwealth period began in the **Mannerist** style. King Stefan Bathory (1576–86), preoccupied with military affairs, had little time to spare for the patronage of art. Yet he should be credited for much Hungarian influence on Sarmatism, particularly in dress and customs. King Zygmunt III (1587–1632) was an eminent patron of the arts, himself an amateur artist, dabbling in painting and gold-smithery, well-versed in architecture and music. The 'silver age of the Vasas' was a variety of Mannerism in its own right, with traces of early Baroque.

The driving force behind many artistic commissions in the **Baroque** style were the Jesuits, spearheading the Counter Reformation and enjoying the support of the king. They settled in many places, including Kraków, Poznań, Lublin, Wilno, and Lwów. The Gesù church in Rome served as the model for SS Peter and Paul's in Kraków, designed by Giovanni Trevano. When in 1595 a fire destroyed part of the Renaissance Wawel Castle, the king immediately commissioned Trevano to rebuild it in the new Baroque style. However, soon the king made the momentous decision to move his residence to Warsaw. Under the supervision of Trevano, the medieval castle of the Mazovian Dukes was expanded by the addition of a two-storey building on a pentagonal plan, with a clock-tower in the front façade. In its Vasa form, the Royal Castle survived until the end of the 18C, witnessing many historic events, including the adoption of the 3 May Constitution in 1791. After the Partitions, it fell into foreign hands and underwent major alterations.

Following the Swedish Deluge, Polish Baroque architecture flourished again during the reign of Jan Sobieski (1674–96). An outstanding architect of this period was a polonised Dutchman, Tylman van Gameren, who designed the Krasiński palace in Warsaw (1680–95) and many churches. The polonised Italian Agostino Locci, designer of the Wilanów palace, was employed by the monarch.

The Saxon kings, August II and III, favoured German architects, but also employed Italians. The capital mushroomed with palaces in the fashionable **Rococo** style. Other edifices included a number of churches, such as the Nuns of the Visitation in Warsaw (Karol Bay), the Piarist in Kraków (Francesco Placidi), the Dominican in Lwów (Jan de Witte), and, in the same city, the orthodox church of St Jur (Bernardyn Meretyn).

King Stanisław August favoured a variety of Baroque Classicism and **Neoclassicism**, his court architect being the Italian, Domenico Merlini. The 'Palace on the Water' in Warsaw's Łazienki Park is a fine example of this style.

Sculpture was closely tied to architecture in the 17C. Sarmatian tombs, featuring a reclining figure, usually in full Renaissance parade armour, adorned

Sarmatian Art

Sarmatism was based on the erroneous belief that Poles were descendants of the ancient Sarmatians, a nomadic people living in the Black Sea Steppe, who supposedly settled along the Vistula having conquered the indigenous tribes, and were the forebears of the Polish and Ruthenian peasantry. As the successors of the bold and warlike Sarmatians, the nobility felt they were entitled to a privileged position and exclusive power in the state. They displayed an inflated belief in their historic mission, xenophobia and megalomania, and cultivated the orientalisation of their habits and aesthetic tastes.

The Sarmatian myth went hand in hand with a cult of ancient Rome, in which the nobles detected the origins of their ideals and beliefs. The Sarmatian nobles easily assimilated Mannerist, Baroque and Neo-classical forms, adapting them to suit their own needs in the chapels, triumphal arches and monumental catafalques—the *castra doloris*—which they commissioned.

The Sarmatian style—a fusion of Catholic high Baroque with Oriental culture—was most prominent in objects of everyday life such as dress, military equipment, riding gear, crockery and cutlery and hunting equipment. It also influenced the interior design of innumerable manor houses and estates. The main elements of Sarmatian interior decoration were adorned with tapestries, drapes, rugs, carpets, often decorated with weapons, hunting trophies, gorgets, icons, ancestral portraits, candleholders and mirrors, pewter, silverware and faience. Polish art was at its most original in these areas. To this day its achievements are inseparable from the notion of national culture, clearly originating in the heritage of the nobility.

with insignia and inscriptions, were still in vogue. In 1644, the Column of Zygmunt III in Warsaw (designed by Constantino Tencalla, Clementi Molli and Daniel Tym) was commissioned by King Władysław, becoming the Polish capital's symbolic landmark. In the 18C, ecstatic-religious sculpture flourished in Lwów, where the workshops of the Fesinger family, Antoni Osiatyński and Jan Jerzy Pinzel were active. The latter was the author of the statue of St George in the façade of the Lwów cathedral of St Jur.

There were two distinct currents in **painting** during this period which some-times mingled: the indigenous Sarmatian, and the western, centred on the court. Sarmatian painting is dominated by a large number of portraits, many of them by itinerant, self-taught artists and commissioned by the nobility and magnates. The faces are rendered with forceful expressiveness, bordering on caricature; the dress and insignia painted in shallow perspective and local colours, usually combined with coats of arms and inscriptions. **Coffin portraits**, a peculiar and unique kind of portraiture painted on polygonal sheets of metal, were suitable for affixing to the side of a coffin. Portraits also appeared on funerary banners used in the 'pompa funebris' ceremony. Innu-merable religious works, figures of saints and secular paintings usually of topical content, commemorating great victories and ceremonial assemblies, were created in a similar style.

Marcin Kober, born in Wrocław (c 1550) was an outstanding court painter, who made portraits of the kings Stefan Bathory and Zygmunt III. His famous full-size likeness of Bathory in Hungarian garb is on display in Wawel Castle. A truly unique work is the so-called *Stockholm Scroll*, a 16 metre long gouache painting on paper, depicting the royal entry of King Zygmunt III into Kraków with his newly-wed Queen Konstancja in 1605, now in the Royal Castle in Warsaw. Tommaso Dolabella from Venice, portraitist and painter of historical scenes, served at the court of the Vasas. Sobieski, in turn, employed the battle-scene painter Marcin Altomonte, author of the enormous canvases—*Battle of Vienna* and *Battle of Parkany*—for the parish church in Żółkiew (now in the castle in Olesko near Lwów).

Sarmatian portraiture and court painting continued to develop under the Saxon kings, while modern national painting blossomed, not without foreign inspiration, under the patronage of King Stanisław August Poniatowski (1764–95), a great lover of art, and a patron and collector. His first court painter, later made responsible for the arts as a whole, was **Marcello Baccia-relli**, born in Rome in 1731 and formerly active in Dresden and Vienna. Under the king's watchful eye, he established the so-called 'Malarnia' (painting-work-shop) at the Royal Castle in Warsaw, as an academy of fine arts, training local artists. He himself painted a large number of portraits of the king and other illustrious personages of the time, as well as allegorical and historical works and a gallery of Polish kings. Another artist in the service of Stanisław August was the Venetian **Bernardo Bellotto**, a master of townscapes, the so-called *vedute*. His outstanding cycle of images of Warsaw, remarkable for the precision of line and flawless perspective, was used during the reconstruction of Warsaw after the Second World War. Amongst the foreign painters active in Poland, particu-larly important was Jean Pierre Norblin de la Gourdaine, summoned from France to the court of Prince Adam Kazimierz Czartoryski. A great draughtsman and faithful chronicler of everyday life, he was active in Warsaw and in the Czartoryski residences in Powązki and Puławy from 1774 until 1804. An entire galaxy of Polish painters matured in the Bacciarelli and Norblin circle, many of whom enjoyed royal pensions which enabled them to travel far afield to broaden their studies.

Polish **decorative art** flourished during this period, in many areas acquiring a highly original character. Gold and silver-smithing were traditionally pursued in Gdańsk and Toruń, but also in Poznań, Kraków and other cities of the Common-wealth. Treasuries and museums were filled with hundreds of religious arte-facts, mainly chalices, monstrances and reliquaries, but also ciboria, platters, basins, cruets, candleholders, tin plates and placards. A specifically Polish curiosity were silver spoons with engraved coats of arms and often satirical inscriptions. During the Sarmatian period, great importance was attached to elegant attire, buttons, insignia, ornate weaponry, especially the sabres of the nobility, saddles, horse trappings and carriages. Traditional robes and fur-lined coats were made of rare, usually imported materials. Unique silk sash-belts, at first bought from Turkey or Persia, became an important locally-produced commodity from the end of the 17C. Workshops called *persjarnie* (Persian shops) were first established in Słuck by Armenians (the Madżarski family), later in Kobyłka and Lipków near Warsaw, in Grodno, Gdańsk and Kraków.

The nobility, although increasingly reluctant to wage war, nourished the traditions of chivalry. Polish Hussar armour was a remarkable combination of Western and Oriental armoury, enriched by the addition of the characteristic 'wings' at the back, rising above the helmet. *Karacena*—Polish scale armour—an outstanding product of Sarmatian culture, harking back to Roman traditions, occupies a unique place in the history of European armoury. After August II Sarmatian interiors also included Meissen porcelain, glass engraved with coats of arms, and, of course, furniture, usually imported from Gdańsk (the famous Gdańsk wardrobes), or the more homely Kolbuszowa furniture (from the Sandomierz province). Some of the decorative fabrics came from abroad—Italy, Flanders, Turkey, Persia—but others were manufactured on a large scale by the magnates (eg the Radziwiłłs, Ogińskis) or in smaller workshops on the nobles' estates. The first Polish porcelain workshop was founded in 1789 by Józef Czartoryski in Korzec.

Partitioned Poland (1795–1918)

The loss of independence in 1795 was a turning point in the history of the Polish nation and was to influence society, culture and the economy profoundly for more than a century. At the beginning of the 19C, Sarmatian culture was already in decline. In the Eastern provinces, most of the vast landed estates of the magnates collapsed, precipitating a mass exodus of impoverished nobility to the towns and cities. Together with the enlightened bourgeoisie, they formed a new creative stratum—the intelligentsia.

The fruitful patronage of King Stanisław August ended with his abdication in 1795, a loss that was only partially offset by powerful aristocratic families like the Czartoryskis, Radziwiłłs and Potockis. Profound changes in the national consciousness were tied to the struggle for independence, which began immedi-ately after the dismemberment of the Polish state in 1795, and was to last until

1918, with more defeats than victories along the way. Participation in the French Revolutionary wars, followed by the Napoleonic campaigns and the creation of the Grand Duchy of Warsaw—ephemeral and dependent on France, transformed later under Russian rule into the Kingdom of Poland—as well as national uprisings and the Great Emigrations, all entangled Poland into the web of European politics. Polish parochialism gave way to universalism. Links between Warsaw and Paris, Warsaw and St Petersburg, Kraków-Lwów-Vienna and Poznań-Berlin were forged gradually by secondary and higher education, trade and travel, financial, administrative and military matters and everyday life.

The closely guarded borders did not stop Poles from cultivating feelings of spiritual and material unity, strengthened by the continuous and rich development of Polish culture in almost all its branches—in literature (Adam Mickiewicz, Juliusz Słowacki, Zygmunt Krasiński, Cyprian Kamil Norwid), music (Frédéric Chopin), theatre (Wojciech Bogusławski) and art, especially painting and the graphic arts. Polish art came under the sway of all the Western currents, from Directory and Empire to Art Nouveau. Yet Polish artists always tried to imbue their works with their own individual style.

Architecture
Neo-classical architecture was in keeping with the attitudes of the late 18C. **Christian Piotr Aigner** was an outstanding representative of this style. He studied classical architecture in Italy and became a member of St Luke's Academy. While in the service of the Czartoryskis, he designed two museum buildings in Puławy (the first in Poland) commissioned by Princess Izabela Czartoryska: the Temple of the Sybil (1801) and the Gothic House (1809). In Warsaw, he built the church of St Alexander on pl. Trzech Krzyży, its form reminiscent of the Roman Pantheon, and the Koniecpolski Palace. Many Neo-classical palaces and churches were erected during this period, both in Warsaw and in the provinces, with Stanisław Zawadzki and Jakub Kubicki the leading architects. The style continued over subsequent decades. In Warsaw, the Italian Antonio Corazzi designed the Grand Theatre and a house for the Warsaw Society of Friends of Learning (today called the Staszic Palace). His younger compatriot, Henryk Marconi, was the architect of the Pac Palace. Józef Bem designed the Neo-classical building of the great Ossolineum library in Lwów. In Kraków, many old houses were given new façades, some of them designed according to the plans of Szczepan Humbert.

In tune with Romantic trends, the **neo-Gothic style** appeared sporadically in architecture from the early 19C. In 1840, the cathedral of St John in Warsaw was remodelled in the Gothic style by Adam Idźkowski, while in Kraków, the Collegium Maius of the Jagiellonian University was given a neo-Gothic shape. At the end of the century, the Collegium Novum was built in the same style. From the mid-19C, Neo-Renaissance predominated, particularly in public buildings, palaces, villas and burghers' houses. Its chief exponent was Teodor Talowski, active in Lwów and Kraków. Grand theatres in Kraków and Lwów were modelled on the Paris Opéra by Jan Zawieyski and Zygmunt Gorgolewski respectively.

Towards the end of the 19C, **Art Nouveau** began to make an appearance in Polish architecture, exemplified by the Fine Arts Society building in Kraków, raised in 1901 to the design of Franciszek Mączyński, who also collaborated with Tadeusz Stryjeński on the Old Theatre. At the same time, Stanisław

Witkiewicz attempted to create a national style in architecture based on traditional highlanders' houses from the Tatra region.

Sculpture

Neo-classical and Romantic styles prevailed in the sculpture (mainly statues) of
the period, influenced to some degree by Thorvaldsen and Canova. The
prevailing atmosphere began to change only towards the end of the century (the
so-called Young Poland period) under the aegis of Impressionism and French
symbolism, whose leading exponent was Auguste Rodin. New forms were especially visible in the works of Xawery Dunikowski (1875–1964), who developed
a personal, highly original style, both synthetic and expressive, apparent in his
series, *Pregnant Women*.

Painting

The 19C was a golden age for Polish painting, much of which was of a standard
comparable to the best of European art. Painters, almost as much as writers, led
the Polish spirit in its struggle for independence.

The works of **Jan Matejko** (1838–1893) are the highest expression of this
phenomenon. At its roots are Stanisław August and the early Polish
National School, initiated by Bacciarelli and Norblin. Matejko, a master of
historical painting, invoking visions of Polish victories and defeats, was
essentially a self-made talent. At the age of 26 he had already produced one
of his best paintings, the *Sermon of Skarga* (1862), soon followed by
Stańczyk (1864) (the Jester) and *Rejtan* (1866). In these patriotic works he
castigated those responsible for the downfall of Poland. In his next phase,
devoted to Polish victories, he created such canvases as *Bathory at Psków*
(1872), *Grunwald* (1879) and the *Prussian Homage* (1882), in which his
dynamic, almost Baroque style crystallised. His paintings are a monumental and striking record of Polish history, still present in the Polish
national consciousness to this day.

The national tradition in Polish painting also produced the spontaneous talent
of Aleksander Orłowski (1777–1832), a master draughtsman and painter of
battle scenes, oriental horsemen and portraits bordering on the caricature.
Michał Płoński (1778–1812), an astute graphic artist, was a keen observer of
everyday life; the Kraków painter Michał Stachowicz (1768–1825) was the
chronicler of the Kościuszko Insurrection (1794). These painters belonged to
the pre-Romantic era, but the prevailing style was Neo-classicism, practised
mostly in the art academies. Antoni Brodowski, the heir to the tradition of
portraiture from the Stanisław August era, was the leading figure in the
Department of Fine Art at Warsaw University. Jan Matejko's teacher, Wojciech
Kornelis Stattler (1800–1875), was a professor at the School of Fine Arts in
Kraków, established in 1818 as a department of Kraków University. His gigantic
biblical canvas *Machabeusze* (Maccabees; 1830–42) was based on the classical
forms of Raphael and the German 'Nazarenes'.

The purely Romantic style was represented by the greatest Polish painter of the first half of the 19C, **Piotr Michałowski** (1800–55), an eminent portraitist enamoured with the Napoleonic period, a painter of horses and battle scenes. January Suchodolski, also a great enthusiast of Napoleon and the military paraphernalia of the Duchy of Warsaw, specialised in the same genre. Henryk Rodakowski (1823–94), educated in Vienna and Paris, acquired fame for his portraits. Another outstanding representative of Sarmatian and battle-scene painting, specialising in water colours, was Juliusz Kossak (1824–99), active in Lwów, the Eastern provinces and Kraków. A great expert on the Cossak, Swedish and Napoleonic wars, and himself an equestrian, he achieved a truly unique style in his paintings of horses. His other works include illustrations to the poems of Mickiewicz and Sienkiewicz's novels. His student, Artur Grottger (1837–67) had a great impact on the Polish consciousness, producing a deeply moving cycle of patriotic paintings connected with the January Uprising of 1863.

The work of Henryk Siemiradzki (1843–1902), a student of the St Petersburg Academy, who later lived in Rome, demonstrated a return to Neo-classicism. He donated his giant *Torches of Nero* to the National Museum in Kraków to mark its inauguration in 1879.

The Munich group

In the third quarter of the 19C, a group of Polish painters was established in Munich under the leadership of Józef Brandt (1841–1915), author of tour-de-force historical genre paintings depicting the Cossak lands, the Swedish Deluge, and the Sobieski era. The most famous among the Munich group were: Alfred Wierusz Kowalski, Józef Chełmoński, and Maksymilian Gierymski. The latter's younger brother, Aleksander, excelled in realist painting with a streak of impressionism. The Sarmatian and battle-scene tradition was continued by the extremely prolific Wojciech Kossak (1857–1942), son of Juliusz. He is best known for his gigantic panoramas, especially the *Panorama of Racławice* (depicting Tadeusz Kościuszko's famous victory), on which he collaborated with Jan Styka and other artists, and which became a national monument (now in Wrocław).

Impressionism was brought to Poland in 1890 by Józef Pankiewicz and Władysław Podkowiński. Leon Wyczółkowski (1853–1936) adopted this new trend, producing many landscapes and genre paintings. Julian Fałat was a master of landscapes, especially winter ones. While Rector of the School of Fine Arts in Kraków he transformed it into the Academy of Fine Arts, the leading art school in the country. In fact, Kraków became the artistic and spiritual capital of Poland and the main centre of the Young Poland Movement, which encompassed all branches of culture and gave unequivocal support to the struggle for independence.

Late 19C landscape painting achieved great subtlety in the works of Jan Stanisławski and his followers. The Hutsul folklore of the Eastern Carpathians became the fascination of the Lwów painters Władysław Jarocki, Kazimierz Sichulski and Fryderyk Pautsch. Artists were also much attracted to the Tatra mountains. One of the painters of Tatra landscapes was Władysław Ślewiński

The Young Poland Movement

Its main representative was **Stanisław Wyspiański** (1869–1907), painter, graphic artist, designer of stained glass, set-designer, poet and playwright, pioneer of new theatrical forms, a reviver of fresco painting and applied art. He is often regarded as the last 'bard' (the first three being Mickiewicz, Słowacki and Krasiński). In his work he combined symbolism, Slavonic folk myths, antiquity and the historico-philosophical heritage of Matejko. Above all, Wyspiański pressed the national cause and the struggle for Poland's independence, especially in the play *The Wedding*, which was not only a drama of words, but also a powerful exercise in visual art. Symbolism dominated the painting of the Young Poland period, often being an expression of obsessions, fears and unfulfilled dreams. A striking example of this was Władysław Podkowiński's painting *Szał uniesień* (The Revelry of Ecstasy) (1894). The artist himself attempted to destroy it, and eventually committed suicide. The works of the excellent Young Poland painter Witold Wojtkiewicz were marked by fairy-tale dreams and neurotic eroticism.

(however, he had stronger ties with Brittany, befriended Gauguin, and maintained active contacts with the Pont-Aven group of artists). The best Polish woman painter of the period was **Olga Boznańska** (1867–1940); her man portraits and still-life paintings are characterised by their soft, almost hazy colours. Paris became a home from home for her. A whole gamut of painters whose debut coincided with Young Poland were active well into the inter-war period. The same goes for the outstanding painter and stained glass designer Józef Mehoffer (1869–1946), the main representative of Polish Art Nouveau.

Symbolism, which dealt with both national concerns and the eternal questions of life, love and death, dominated the works of **Jacek Malczewski** (1854–1929), a student of Matejko, the Paris and Munich academies, and eventually a professor in Kraków. His paintings, teeming with fauns, harpies, chimeras, nymphs and centaurs, death-angels and goddesses of victory, were to enliven the national consciousness for a long time. Simultaneously, in Warsaw circles, neo-Romantic and Art Nouveau trends appeared in the works of Kazimierz Stabrowski and Edward Okuń, social motifs in Stanisław Lentz's work, and peculiar expressionism combined with broad post-Impressionist painting technique in the remarkable portraits of Konrad Krzyżanowski.

Craft and design

Craft work developed and flourished during the period. Handicrafts acquired a more national character over the course of the century, while decorative art was separated from its strictly functional variety. William Morris' ideas influenced Adrian Baraniecki, who, in 1868, founded in Kraków the Municipal Museum of Technology and Industry. In 1901, the Polish Applied Art Society was created in Kraków; its statutory aim was 'to inspire original work in the area of art as applied to industry and construction and to imbue it with the national character'. For many years, decorative art was dominated by the traditional styles, but towards the end of the century, thanks to the efforts of Wyspiański, Mehoffer and others, Art Nouveau, combined with stylised folk motifs, arrived on the scene. In 1913, in the new building of the Museum of Technology and Industry, the so-called Kraków Workshops were inaugurated, introducing new trends: an emphasis on the beauty of form and the functionality of objects.

Polish Art and Architecture from 1918 onwards

Architecture

After the restoration of independence in 1918, historical styles and Art Nouveau were superseded by Constructivism and Functionalism, originating in the Bauhaus, and analogous to Cubism and Futurism in painting and sculpture. Postwar construction work was hampered by a lack of funds and the need to channel part of the effort towards the reconstruction of damaged buildings. The 'Warsaw School' soon appeared, relying on the legacy of Neo-classicism and Art Nouveau, but open to new Constructivist thinking and the use of reinforced concrete. Various public buildings serving the needs of the new state were built in Warsaw: the Ministry of Religious Denominations and Public Enlightenment (Zdzisław Mączyński), the Main Telecommunications Office (Julian Puterman-Sadłowski) and the Grodzki Court (Bohdan Pniewski). Stanisław and Barbara Brukalski designed their now famous own residential house in 1935 in the district of Żoliborz. In Kraków, the monumental, somewhat Palladian Post Office Savings Bank designed by Adolf Szyszko-Bohusz was erected in 1925. Silesia also saw much construction work during this period; most notable was Karol Szayer's Silesian Museum, completed just before 1939. However, the most outstanding achievement—due largely to Eugeniusz Kwiatkowski, the Trade and Industry Minister (1926–30)—was the new port town of Gdynia on the Baltic coast.

The Second World War put an end to the young state and caused unprecedented destruction to its cities, particularly the capital, which was virtually annihilated on Hitler's orders. In 1945, the Nazi occupation troops were driven out by the Red Army and Poland became a Soviet satellite. The nation undertook the gigantic task of reconstruction and town planning assumed paramount importance. Modern Western ideas championed by talented town planners like Maciej Nowicki were relegated to the margins in favour of Socialist Realism, for which the Soviet architect Lev Rudniev's **Palace of Science and Culture** in Warsaw—a gift from Stalin himself—was to be the model. However, the combination in this building of an American skyscraper with adornments, gilding and allegorical sculptures ineptly imitating the decoration of Renaissance palaces led it to be judged an artistic failure. The MDM (Marszałkowska Housing District), designed by Stanisław Jankowski, Jan Knothe and Józef Sigalin, and completed in 1952, was an entire complex of Socialist-Realist architecture which still stands today. A year later, Warsaw regained its Old Town, a masterpiece of restoration, though somewhat marred by the many decorative elements and inscriptions proclaiming the ideological slogans of the time. The reconstruction of the Royal Castle was initially delayed for political reasons, but under popular pressure was finally accomplished with remarkable success during the 1970s. The Polish School of Conservation specialising in the full restoration of almost completely destroyed historic monuments came into being. The methods it developed were also used abroad, particularly in West Germany and the Soviet Union. Work was carried out under the aegis of a powerful state institution, the Conservation of Historic Monuments Workshop (PKZ).

For decades priority was given to pre-fabricated residential housing to meet the population's growing needs. Whole towns, like Nowa Huta near Kraków and Nowe Tychy in Silesia, were built in the Socialist-Realist style. Somewhat more of an achievement in architecture and town planning was the 'Eastern Wall' of ul. Marszałkowska in Warsaw, designed in 1960 by Zbigniew Karpiński and today part of a busy shopping precinct.

Rather unexpectedly, church architecture flourished between 1970 and 1990, as a form of political protest against official atheism. Hundreds of churches were erected, usually in the modern synthetic style, sometimes with traces of Neo-Gothic, or—as in the case of Our Lady Queen of Poland Church in Kraków's Nowa Huta—with an overt symbolic meaning (see p. 235).

Sculpture

Many excellent sculptors who had made their names during the Young Poland period were still active after 1918 and even 1945, most notably **Xawery Dunikowski**. A survivor of Auschwitz, Dunikowski undertook in the post-war period a series of monumental statues, including one on St Anne's Hill in Silesia. The most talented of his many students was **Jerzy Bandura**, who created the unfinished Grunwald monument (1960); another was **Marian Konieczny**, who also attended the Moscow Academy of Fine Arts, returning to champion the Socialist-Realist style. His best work is the *Monument to the Heroes of Warsaw*, also known as the *Warsaw Nike* (1964). Some of the many monuments typical of Eastern Bloc countries after the Second World War, including sculptures of the leaders of the October Revolution, were dismantled following the downfall of the communist regime in 1989.

There were other currents as well, one of them a traditional, slightly modernised Neo-classicism, represented by the Warsaw artists Edward Wittig, Henryk Kuna and August Zamoyski. **Formism**, a home-grown brand of Cubism, appeared in sculpture and even more so in painting. Its main protagonist was **Zbigniew Pronaszko** with his synthetic and geometrically simplified representation of human figures. Formist inspiration, combined with Aztec and supposed 'Proto-Slavonic' elements can be found in the works of Stanisław Szukalski, later active in America. Radically new abstract and expressionist elements were introduced into sculpture by Katarzyna Kobro-Strzemińska (1897–1951), who based her work on the theoretical foundations she and her husband, Władysław Strzemiński, developed in their dissertation *Composition of Space, Calculation of Space-Time Rhythm* (Łódź, 1932). In contemporary sculpture, it was again women who distinguished themselves, amongst them **Magdalena Abakanowicz**, the author of remarkable abstract fabric designs. A singular originality of form, ostensibly primitive and usually carrying some political message, was achieved in wood sculpture by **Władysław Hasior**, who won international recognition in the area of symbolic sculpture by using unconventional media such as flame and sound.

Painting

Painting and graphic art, which had developed so impressively in the 19C, continued a vigorous evolution. Many new artistic groups were formed. As early as 1917, the 'Polish Formist' group was founded in Kraków. Its aim was to break away from both Impressionism and Art Nouveau, and to draw upon Cubism and

Italian Futurism, or even Surrealism. The best known and most influential member was **Stanisław Ignacy Witkiewicz**, better known as Witkacy, a painter, novelist, playwright and art theorist (see p. 86). The Warsaw group 'Rhythm' invoked the traditions of the Young Poland movement, as well as Formism. Its ideologist was **Władysław Skoczylas**, an outstanding practitioner of the woodcut and a great admirer of Highland culture.

During the inter-war period, most Polish painters came under the influence of the French Avant-Garde, associated with the so-called École de Paris, which was central to Post-Impressionism and Cubism. In 1928, the 'Polish Artists in Paris Group' came into being. Its most eminent member was **Tadeusz Makowski** (1882–1932), a painter of lyrical canvases depicting the world as seen through the eyes of a child.

Polish painting owes much to the group known as the '**Paris Committee**' ('Kapiści', the name derived from KP—the Polish abbreviation for 'Paris Committee'), founded at the Kraków Academy of Fine Arts in 1923. The group was initially formed to organise a study trip to Paris for its members. In 1924 the plans were realised and soon a branch of the Kraków Academy had been formed in Paris under Pankiewicz's leadership. Its aesthetic doctrine, known as Colourism, was centred on the belief that the main condition for the creation of a picture was a scheme of artistic colour-qualities. From 1923 to 1931, the 'Kapiści' who included such leading artists as Józef Czapski (1893–1993) and Jan Cybis (1897–1972), produced still life paintings, landscapes, portraits and nudes, marked by a carefully balanced, subtle spectrum of colours. Similar concerns preoccupied the members of another group, 'Prism'. In the wake of Formism followed many kinds of abstract avant-garde art. Władysław Strzemiński from Łódź, a student of Kazimierz Malewicz, studied perception theory and painted in the styles of Cubism, Neo-plasticism, and his own Unism. Avant-garde ideas and radical social beliefs were promoted by the members of the 'Kraków Group', founded in 1931.

The Soviet period

After the Second World War, three conflicting tendencies continued the age-old struggle for dominance in Polish art: the traditional forces, encamped in the academies and represented by senior professors; forces backed by the communist regime attempting to graft Soviet-born **Socialist-Realism** onto Poland; and lastly, the avant-garde, trying to import the latest artistic fashions from Western Europe and America. One of the paradoxes of this struggle was that some of the formerly left-oriented artists (including members of the 'Kraków Group' and several young outstanding artists such as Tadeusz Kantor) opted for the avant-garde.

Yet Socialist-Realism was gaining momentum, its aesthetic justification being Lenin's theory that art reflects reality, and that life in the new order, particularly the glory of socialist work, ought to be the subject matter of art. Portraits and statues sang the praises of revolutionary leaders and the vanguard of the workforce. A showpiece of the style was Aleksander Kobzdej's *Pass the Brick*, depicting a trio of cheerless masons building a house.

However, Socialist-Realism could not last in Polish art. Its rigidly doctrinaire vision of the world was in deep conflict with both the traditions of Polish independence and everyday life. Andrzej Wróblewski's work, *Death by Firing Squad* (1949) and *The Shadow of Hiroshima* (1957) for example, though ostensibly Socialist-Realist, in fact conveyed a shocking, synthetically terse vision of humankind oppressed by war and the post-war tragedy.

In 1955, the National Exhibition of New Visual Art was staged at the Warsaw Arsenal, giving voice to expressionist currents, poetic and metaphoric painting, and protest against the hypocrisy of official art. The political breakthrough in October 1956 also had an impact on artistic life, opening the country to Western currents. In this, independent art galleries had an important role to play: Foksal in Warsaw and Krzysztofory in Kraków. An indefatigable champion of independent art and links with the Western avant-garde was **Tadeusz Kantor** (1915–90), painter, draughtsman, set-designer and founder of the experimental 'Cricot' theatre, who addressed universal and eternal themes such as man's relation to the passage of time and death. Kantor achieved what had hitherto eluded his compatriots: he became an artist of truly international standing.

In the 1960s artists associated with the revived and enlarged 'Kraków Group' produced various kinds of abstract and figurative painting, particularly surrealist and metaphorical. Nikifor and Teofil Ociepka became famous for their 'naive' painting. Jan Lebenstein came closest to the 'painting of matter', and after emigrating to Paris in 1959 gradually moved towards figurative expressionism. Radical realism, drawing upon American hyper-realism, was practised by a group of Warsaw artists. Modern religious painters, whose chief representative was Stanisław Rodziński, had the same aim as the Kraków group 'Wprost': both were anti-communist and actively involved in the Polish independence movement. The hardships of everyday life were captured in the expressive figurative forms of Edward Dwurnik and Jerzy Duda-Gracz. International reputation was gained by the satirical cartoonist Andrzej Czeczot, who eventually established himself in New York. During the 1980s, Expressionist 'savage painting' came to Poland from Germany, finding proponents in the Warsaw 'Gruppa'. Through intentionally sloppy forms and garish colours it evoked fears and obsessions, flaunting an ironic attitude to the problems of the contemporary world.

The father of modern Polish **set design** was Stanisław Wyspiański, who used artistic techniques to give extra depth to the stage, structured it into planes and strata, appreciated the importance of lighting, and stressed the need for harmony between the elements of decoration and costume. Later in the 20C, set design became a specialised branch of study at the Kraków and Warsaw academies.

Polish **graphic art** blossomed after the Second World War, becoming an autonomous discipline with an international standing. This achievement was made possible by the expansion of graphic art departments at the academies in Kraków and Warsaw and colleges in Łódź, Wrocław, Poznań and Gdańsk. Many accomplished painters practised graphic arts. Linoleum-block printing, silk-screen printing, etc., were added to the traditional techniques of woodcutting, copper engraving, etching, aquatint and lithography. Soon after the war, the '9 Graphic Artists' group was formed in Kraków. Its members enjoyed high prestige thanks to their many foreign contacts and the International Graphic Arts Biennale, held in Kraków from 1966 (Triennale, from 1991). After 1945 **poster**

design achieved some international repute. The Warsaw 'Zachęta' gallery became the venue for international poster exhibitions and a permanent Museum of Poster Art was set up in Wilanów (see p. 146).

Craft and design

While decorative art flourished during the Young Poland period, it struck out in new directions after the First World War. In addition to the extant Kraków workshops, the School of Decorative Arts in Poznań was opened in 1919; other schools in Warsaw and Lwów were reformed and modernised. In 1925, Poland took part in the Exhibition of Decorative Arts in Paris, with a display of interior decoration that achieved a singular unity of style through a combination of folk art and austere, geometric forms. The tradition of Polish applied art survived in the work of artists associated with the 'Ład' (Order) cooperative, established in Warsaw in 1926, which opposed philistine bourgeois tradition, historicism and Art Nouveau. Its main contribution was in furniture design, carpets, tapestries, ceramics and metal-work. At the same time, art graduates from the Warsaw Technical University were promoting pure functionalism and extreme simplicity of form.

After the Second World War, the main emphasis was put on craft cooperatives and increased state assistance to rebuild Polish craftsmanship. In 1949, the **Centre for the Production of Folk Art** ('Cepelia') was established, soon to encompass hundreds of workshops, shops and cooperatives, with its own licensing committees and Board of Artistic Standards Control. Export was encouraged. Cepelia dealt mainly in fabrics, especially tapestries, designed and produced by traditional techniques in Zakopane, Nowy Targ, Żywiec, Oliwa, Opole, Poznań and Warsaw. It also specialised in furniture, functional and decorative ceramics, metal-work, various types of folk art, wood sculpture, embroidery, lace and paper art. Cepelia was often criticised for the homogeneity of its mass-production and was opposed by some individual artists and artistic schools; it is these artists who should be credited with the breakthrough in applied art. A new Department of Industrial Forms was opened at the Kraków Academy of Fine Arts. Much work was done in the fields of artistic ceramics, ceramic mosaics and tiling. The main media used in jewellery were silver, amber, coral and semi-precious stones, glazing and copper. The most radical breakthrough, however, was in the field of artistic fabrics. In the 1960s, literally within a single generation, it was elevated to the status of 'pure' art. A group of students from the Warsaw Academy rejected the functional-decorative convention, replacing it with a concept of 'unique fabric' to act solely as a vehicle of artistic expression. These trends came to the fore in 1962 during the first International Biennale of Artistic Fabrics in Lausanne, where three-dimensional fabrics were displayed, breaking the age-old canon of two-dimensionality. In this way fabric acquired the qualities of sculpture. The chief protagonist of this movement was Magdalena Abakanowicz, also known for her sculpture and unconventional architecture.

Polish Literature and Theatre

By Krzysztof Myszkowski

The Middle Ages

Polish literature is more than seven centuries old. It begins with the Latin chronicles, annals and hagiographies, so typical of European literature of the Middle Ages. Of highest historical and artistic value are the chronicles of **Gallus Anonymous** (d. 1118) and **Master Wincenty**, also known as **Kadłubek** (c 1150–1223), as well as the annals of Jan Długosz (1415–80) and the hagiographies of St Adalbert and St Stanisław. There is an intimate relationship between early Polish literature and the Bible. Translations were made of the Psalms, the most noteworthy being the *Florian* and *Puławy* psalm books. The **earliest Polish Bible** (c 1510), prepared for Władysław Jagiełło's wife (hence its name—*Bible of Queen Zofia*) was probably based on a Czech translation (as betrayed by numerous errors and solecisms); the original manuscript was destroyed during the Second World War, but a photocopy made in 1930 survives. **Sermons**, especially the *Świętokrzyskie* and *Gniezno* collections, stand out as beautiful examples of early Polish prose. **Religious songs**, including such gems of medieval lyric poetry as the rhythmically sophisticated Marian prayer-hymn *Bogurodzica* (Mother of God), marked the inception of Polish poetry, while the apocryphal Świętokrzyski lament *Hark, Fair Brethren*, as well as carols and Marian songs of high artistic merit, shaped the main types of Polish verse. Early Polish drama includes countless liturgical plays, which later developed into the Mystery Play genre, their main topics, unsurprisingly, being the birth, death and resurrection of Christ. Of the few lay poems one could mention the *Colloquy between Master Polikarp and Death* invoking the popular motif of the Dance of Death, and Słota's (d. 1419) satirical poems—*On Table Manners* and *On the Indolence of Peasants*.

The Renaissance

The Renaissance chapter of Polish *belles lettres* begins with **Mikołaj Rej** (1505–69), a petty noble from Nagłowice. Born in 1505, he enrolled at the Kraków Academy, but dropped out after only a year. His life is known to us mainly from a somewhat apologetic appendix to one of his works, allegedly written by Trzecieski, but rumoured to have been authored by Rej himself. He accomplished the Herculean task of distilling clear sense and pure voice from the morass of contemporary language, thereby demonstrating that Polish was a fit language to express thoughts and emotions. Rej recorded the everyday speech of the nobility; he wrote in much the same way he spoke, giving his writings a literary gloss. His work is a curious mixture of genres, styles, themes and tensions: from the graceful prose translation of the Psalms and a book of sermons entitled *Postylla to Menagerie*—a lively collection of epigrams, or *Looking Glass*—a meditation in prose and verse, to the ribald and occasionally obscene *Frolics*. Rej is a good example of the tension in mainstream language and literature of the period between the stately cadences of Latin and the unwieldy rhythm and syntax of Polish. Neither Copernicus nor Andrzej Frycz Modrzewski (c 1503–72), whose prose was widely known in Europe, ever wrote a single word in their mother tongue. Other noteworthy poets of the period based their Polish and Latin verse on Classical models. In his *Parliamentary Sermons* and *Hagiographies*, Piotr Skarga (1536–1612) endeavoured to achieve a biblical style in Polish, while Maciej Stryjkowski's (1547–93) *Chronicle*, inlaid with fragments in verse, enjoyed wide popularity among the nobility (it was read by the heroes of *Pan Tadeusz*—see below), and was even translated into Latin for use in Lithuania. The Polish language achieved a higher level of refinement thanks to new translations of the Bible, especially an epoch-making effort by the Jesuit Jakub Wujek (1541–97); some of its linguistic inventions have even become stock phrases in modern Polish, and it continues to inspire translators, Czesław Miłosz (see below) among them. The greatest secular masterpiece of the period was Piotr Kochanowski's (1566–1629) rendering of Tasso's fantastical chivalrous poem, *Gerusalemme Liberata*.

The apogee of Old Polish is the work of **Jan Kochanowski** (1530–84), perhaps the greatest Slav poet prior to the early 19C. Kochanowski cultivated the rhythms of Polish, turning the language into a rich and versatile medium capable of the most subtle meanings and sounds. Himself a bilingual Polish-Latin poet, he drew his inspiration from the greats of Classical literature: 'wdarłem się na skałę pięknej Kallijopy' (I scaled the rock of beautiful Calliope), he wrote in the dedication to his version of the *Psalm Book of David*. His other tour de force, *Laments*, is a poetic cycle on the poet's inner moral and philosophical transformation, an expression of a father's grief at the death of his beloved child. Elaborate vocabulary and a wealth of stylistic devices convey the depths of sorrow in a sublime and masterly fashion. Kochanowski's most popular work was *Facetious Verse*, a delightful collection of some 300 lyrical miniatures, spanning nearly half a century, in which rigour of form and linguistic discipline combine with informality and an almost unlimited variety of content. An altogether different achievement, inspired by Horace, is the collection *Songs*, a fascinating mosaic of religious, philosophical, patriotic, social and erotic pieces. Finally, Polish Humanist drama is at its best in Kochanowski's *The Dismissal of the Grecian Envoys*—a moral-political tragedy of rhetorical exaltation and crystalline simplicity, which became a model for Polish Romantic and Neo-Romantic drama.

The Baroque

At the turn of the 16C metaphysical poetry reigned supreme. Its finest examples, such as the psalm-inspired poetry of **Mikołaj Sęp Szarzyński** (c 1550–81) and **Sebastian Grabowiecki** (1543–1607), rivalled the best English metaphysical poetry of the period. Szarzyński's only volume—*Polish Rhythms or Poems*—which owed much to Kochanowski's *Psalm Book of David*, introduced metaphysical tones that were to become one of the most fruitful currents in Polish verse. A different kind of mystical tension, not so intense as Szarzyński, can be found in Grabowiecki's *Spiritual Rhythms*.

At the opposite end of the spectrum was the 'poetry of worldly delights', best represented by **Jan Andrzej Morsztyn** (1621–93), author of *Holiday or the Dog Star, Lute* and an excellent translation of Corneille's *Le Cid*. **Maciej Kazimierz Sarbiewski** (1595–1640) was the last Polish poet to write Latin verse; it earned him a great European reputation and even a laurel wreath from Pope Urban VIII.

One of the most colourful figures of Polish literature is **Jan Chryzostom Pasek** (c 1636–c 1701), a petty noble, soldier, unscrupulous litigant and indefatigable trouble-maker, five times banished from the Commonwealth before finally being condemned to infamy in the year before his death. His renowned *Memoirs*, written in a peculiar mélange of Polish and Latin, were published in 1836 from a damaged copy of the original manuscript and are a curious essay in Sarmatian prose (see p. 68), a combination of historical fact and psychological insight with preposterous self-glorification. The Romantic poet Mickiewicz was later to see in the *Memoirs* the origin of the historical novel; the Positivist Sienkiewicz likewise admitted his debt to the work.

The Enlightenment

The keystone of Polish language and literature in the 18C is the work of bishop **Ignacy Krasicki** (1735–1801), the 'Prince of Polish poetry', author of celebrated fables and satires, heroic-comic poems—*The Mousiad, Monachomachia or Handbook of the Natural History of Monks* and *Anti-Monachomachia*—as well as the first Polish novels: *The Adventures of Mr Nicholas Wisdom* and *Pan Podstoli*. His epigrammatic fables, in which strikingly simple words and terse form combine to express a profound moral message, are a great artistic achievement, many of the punch-lines subsequently becoming proverbial. Apart from the fables, the most valued and popular of Krasicki's works are his satires, modelled on Horace, but highly original for their intricate and sophisticated form, sparkling with wit, irony, sarcasm, caricature and parody. Krasicki continued the tradition of clear and precise language inherited from Kochanowski.

Other prose writers of the Enlightenment include **Stanisław Staszic** (1755–1826) and **Jan Potocki** (1761–1815). Staszic, an eccentric priest who saw all religion as a tool of oppression, is best known for his rhetorical and didactic *Warnings for Poland and Remarks on the Life of Jan Zamoyski*. His pioneering work in many areas of public life and science earned him a permanent place in the annals of Polish culture. He was the founder of the grand headquarters of the Society of Friends of Learning in Warsaw, since known as the Staszic Palace (see p. 124). His contemporary Potocki, who wrote only in French, authored the *Manuscrit trouvé à Saragosse*, a bizarre philosophical 'tale within a tale', full of fantasy and adventure, befitting his own eventful life. A scientist and traveller, honorary member of the Petersburg Academy of Sciences, he published numerous accounts of his sojourns in exotic climes like the Caucasus, Mongolia or Morocco, and even flew the hot air balloon with its inventor J.P. Blanchard in 1790.

Romanticism

The early 19C was a golden age for Polish literature. Its supreme master was **Adam Mickiewicz** (1798–1855), the foremost of the three Romantic poets, whose *Pan Tadeusz* is a national epic, the very heart of the Polish language. Zygmunt Krasiński (see below) said of Mickiewicz, 'we are all his children'; for him, Mickiewicz was 'the greatest bard not only of the nation but of all the Slavonic tribes', an opinion that later was to gain wide currency. Mickiewicz's debut—*Ballads and Romances* published in Vilnius in 1822—was the embryo of new Polish poetry and heralded a transformation in the national consciousness. Never before or since has there been in Polish literature such refreshingly original talent, drawing upon and creatively developing literary tradition. The first milestone in the poet's artistic life was *Forefathers' Eve*, a play in four parts written in verse, unique in world drama. This visionary work, with a deep moral and metaphysical meaning, is a succession of scenes linked by the spiritual evolution of the main protagonist, the 'Polish hero'. It was followed by the superb and much-translated *Crimean Sonnets*, in which impressionistic glimpses of nature are interspersed with lyrical confession. Mickiewicz grappled with the moral dilemmas of treason in *Konrad Wallenrod*, a novel in verse, whose entire plot revolves around the inner life of the eponymous hero. The messianistic idea of the third part of *Forefathers' Eve*, which hailed Poland as the Christ of Nations, was further developed in the *Books of the Polish Nation and of the Polish Pilgrimage*. The form of the work is modelled on biblical verse, evolving in the second part into a parable. *Pan Tadeusz* (subtitled *The Last Foray in Lithuania*), combines realism and fable in its description of the twilight years of the Polish nobility. It is a truly metaphysical work in which the natural and supernatural orders are merged in a marvellous and baffling way, yet so effortlessly as to seem almost mundane. After *Pan Tadeusz* Mickiewicz wrote little; what he did write—*Statements and Remarks*, a collection of epigrams based as much on German mysticism as the author's inner experience, and the *Lausanne Verses*—is pure metaphysics and music that defies any attempt at translation either into another language or meaningful idiom.

The second of the Romantic bards was **Juliusz Słowacki** (1809–49), the 'King-Spirit of Polish poetry', a great and rare talent, an unrivalled stylist, who possessed perfect pitch in language and a powerful imagination. Deeply immersed in literature, in words, Słowacki was seemingly able to tap all the rhythmical possibilities of the Polish language. Yet his entanglement in nationalism, so ubiquitous in Polish literature of the period, hampered his creative genius. Throughout his entire life he competed with Mickiewicz, although the two were quite dissimilar. His historico-metaphysical *Kordian* was intended as a polemic against the messianic message of *Forefathers' Eve*. His other plays became part of the canon of Polish drama: the fable-like *Balladyna*, two historical tragedies, *Mazeppa* and *Lilla Weneda*, *Fantasy*, a fusion of pathos and comedy, or the dramatic romance *Silver Dream of Salomea*. Słowacki's lyric poetry again and again surprises with its richness, artistic skill, the music of its words and a rare virtuosity. *Beniowski*—a digressive biographical poem—and the *Journey to the Holy Land from Naples* impress with their witty irony. In the late period of his short life he came under the spell of mysticism, which found its artistic expression in *Genesis from the Spirit*, a poem in prose expounding the philosophical credo of the poet, and the unfinished *King-Spirit*, a grand religious and poetic vision, monumental in design.

The third writer in this Polish Romantic group was **Count Zygmunt Krasiński** (1812–59), whose work and personality complemented those of the other two. His main dramatic piece—the *Undivine Comedy*—is about the absence of love. It warns against revolution, which Krasiński saw as a tool used by the Devil to impose a demonic order on earth. The play ends with a vision of Christ (the Galilean), the dispenser of love, the only salvation against the diabolical menace. The *Undivine Comedy* is also an appraisal of all Romantic poetry and the Romantic attitude itself: 'Beauty passes through you, but you are not beauty', he declares at the beginning of the play, underlining the chasm between art and life. Krasiński's works include the historical and philosophical drama *Irydion*, and several volumes of letters, which together form a magnificent and fascinating narrative fresco considered to be the summit of Polish Romantic prose.

Cyprian Kamil Norwid (1821–83) was an altogether unique personality. His poetry—abstruse, thought-provoking, dark and murky—is infused with a mysterious glow, with 'invisible matter' and insight, expressed in a language as hermetic as it is original, resonant with omission and silence. His most important collection of lyric verse—the posthumous *Vade-mecum*—is a pioneering work, heralding a revolution in poetry, though itself untranslatable. A good example of Norwid's more traditional poetic craft is *The Lament of Bem*. A fine introduction, perhaps even the key, to this difficult, hermetic poetry is provided by *Promethidion*, an exposition in verse of the poet's artistic credo, and several pieces of prose, such as *White Blossom, Black Blossom* and *Silence*.

The greatest Polish comedy writer was **Aleksander Fredro** (1793–1876), author of such masterpieces as *Vengeance, Maidens' Vows, or the Magnetism of the Heart, Ladies and Hussars*, and *Life Sentence*. To this day these plays are frequently staged in Polish theatres and always enjoy popularity—a remarkable feat, considering that their subject-matter (the life of the Polish nobility) and the apparently parochial sense of humour could be considered rather exotic by the contemporary theatre-goer. Moreover, Fredro employs rather sophisticated comic effects, particularly in the mysterious prose piece *Mr Jovial*. Also readable are his lively memoirs, *Stuff and Nonsense* and a collection of witty aphorisms, *Scribblings of an Old Codger*.

Positivism

The literature of Positivism was dominated by prose. Its maestro, easily surpassing his peers in popularity, was **Henryk Sienkiewicz** (1846–1916), the first Polish Nobel prize winner for literature (1905) and a writer of international repute. His greatest achievement was the *Trilogy (With Fire and Sword, The Deluge, Fire in the Steppe)*, a splendid tapestry of stylistic imitation and caricature, a grand historical epic which transcends the limits of this genre. Its ostensible purpose was merely to comfort the suffering nation with heroic tales of Poland's resistance to the Swedish invasions of the mid-17C, though in actual fact it was a great show of narrative art and an unexpected eruption of talent in the Polish language, well ahead of its time. Sienkiewicz earned fame for *Quo Vadis*, a world best-seller about the beginnings of Christianity. The absurd attacks mounted on him, which even became a kind of fashion, did much harm to Polish writing.

Another gifted prose writer was **Bolesław Prus** (1847–1912). The main protagonist of his novel *The Doll* embodied both Romantic and Positivist ideals. Its plot, characterisation, structure and, most importantly, the language, were somewhat inferior to the best Sienkiewicz had to offer, but it still deserves a place in the top league of Polish prose. Prus's other notable works include the historical novel *The Pharaoh and the Priest*, a series of robust novellas, and a collection of essays entitled *Chronicles*.

Neo-Romanticism (Fin-de-Siècle)

The fin-de-siècle marks a return to Romantic influences. It produced one of the greatest Polish poets, **Bolesław Leśmian** (1877–1937). An author of exceptional originality, Leśmian spoke a hermetic and lyrically pure language, abounding in neologisms and musical and metaphysical almost in the literal sense. Rhythm was his sole *Weltanschauung*, as he confessed in sketches on poetry. In its last phase, Leśmian's exquisite work was enriched by new themes of nihilism and death, by elegiac and grotesque tones.

Another great poet who made his debut at the turn of the century, but transcended the limits of Neo-Romanticism, was **Leopold Staff** (1878–1957). In later years, including the Second World War, his work became more Classical and moralistic, his last volume of beautiful, terse poetry appearing posthumously in 1958.

The greatest prose writer of the period was **Władysław Stanisław Reymont** (1867–1925), best known for his huge four-volume Realist novel, *The Peasants*, for which he was awarded the Nobel Prize (1924). Narrative overtures to this epic were the novels *The Comedienne* and *The Promised Land*, still in print and widely read.

The showpiece of Polish Neo-Romantic drama is **Stanisław Wyspiański's** (1869–1907) *The Wedding*, often considered the most Polish of all Polish plays, the crowning of the great Romantic theatrical tradition, though of course in an altogether different key. It is a realistic and fantastical account of a wedding feast, which in the course of the night becomes a grand symbol of national tragedy and the impotence of Poland's would-be insurgents. The guests indulge in visions of rebellion, of the country's glorious past and radiant future; yet they flounder in a drunken and gibbering present. The play scintillates with irony, sarcasm and tragi-comedy. Wyspiański, also an outstanding painter, produced an entire series of Polish historical dramas. His great, visual theatre, deeply immersed in tradition, was also highly modern, even avant-garde.

Inter-War Years

The interwar years (1918–39) were a short interlude during which literature could develop in an independent Poland. However, the euphoria of new-found independence gradually subsided, giving way to the pessimism of the 1930s. Writers who had first been published in the closing years of the 19C were still active after the First World War. One striking example is **Stefan Żeromski** (1864–1925), who had begun his career with his remarkable short stories and novels—*Homeless People*, *Ashes* and *The Faithful River*. An outstanding stylist and man of letters, he earned a reputation as the 'conscience of Polish literature'. In 1924, he published *The Coming of Spring*, an uneven novel redeemed by passages of great beauty, trying to come to terms with the post-war reality.

In poetry there were two rival groups: the eclectic and traditionalist 'Skamander', led by **Julian Tuwim** (1894–1953), and the Avant-Garde. An important poet, though outside both these currents, was **Konstanty Ildefons Gałczyński** (1905–53), a strong, even legendary artistic personality, a reveller, scandal-monger and extravagant 'poet of the world', who dismissed all authority bar poetry itself. His literary programme was the grotesque, the attitude of satirical negation and mock catastrophism, whose quintessence is the cycle *Green Geese* begun in 1945. After the war, entangled in the dilemmas of a writer's life under a totalitarian regime, Gałczyński, like many others, was forced to write elegies in praise of Stalin. Today his works enjoy the status of near-classics, still managing to surprise with their vitality and subtle melancholy.

In prose, most enduring are the achievements of Witold Gombrowicz (see below) and **Bruno Schultz** (1892–1942), a Polish writer of Jewish origin. Always an outsider, Schultz spent his entire life amongst Galician Jews in the small remote town of Drohobycz in the far east of Poland. The imaginary town that is the setting for his stories is a mirror image of Drohobycz, while the narrator-protagonist becomes indistinguishable from the author. For Schultz, reality is merely a shadow cast by words: only that which has a name is real; bestowing a name on something promotes it to the realm of the universal. The action has a dreamlike aura, as if events were taking place in a child's reverie. 'Maturing to childhood' is Schultz's ideal. It was on the contradiction of the morass of conflicting, even inimical, but still co-existing systems of values—the idea of God and evil and sin—that Schultz built his expressionistic, highly atmospheric writing, which is permeated with lyricism and rich in biblical-mythological associations and symbols. Schultz counterbalances the Bible with the allure of matter, of woman and of creation, while recognising that the creation myth originates in the Bible. The narrator-protagonist of Schultz's stories effectively transforms reality into myth, endowing it with religious meaning. The perfection with which Schultz does this puts him among the best Polish or indeed even European authors. His work is collected in two volumes: *Cinnamon Shops* and *The Street of Crocodiles*. He was shot dead by the Gestapo during a pogrom of Jews in the Drohobycz ghetto on 'Black Thursday', 19 November 1942.

Stanisław Ignacy Witkiewicz (1885–1939), otherwise known as Witkacy, occupies a unique place in Polish literature. This bizarre figure, branded a lunatic and megalomaniac, always elicited strong if opposing reactions: worshipped by some, dismissed with contempt by others. Only after his death was he given recognition as a first-class dramatist. He was also a painter, prose-writer, and even philosopher, who based his art on his own principles of 'pure form'. His novels, the most important of which were *Farewell to Autumn* and *Insatiability*, were narrative 'cauldrons' into which he threw history, eroticism and metaphysics to eerie and disturbing effect. In his catastrophic and comic plays, of which the most important and commonly staged are *Them, The Cobblers, In a Small Manor House, The Water Hen, Mother, The New Deliverance, The Madman and the Nun*, or *Beelzebub Sonata*, he departed from any verisimilitude, creating a grotesque Theatre of the Absurd that was to become fashionable in Europe after the war. The characters in his plays live 'artificial lives' and experience the 'strangeness of being'. Witkacy foresaw not only the spiritual impoverishment of rich consumer societies, the hopelessness of luxurious yet empty life, but also the totalitarian menace. He committed suicide in September 1939 upon hearing that Soviet army had entered Poland. Though buried at an unknown spot in the remote eastern village of Jeziory, his symbolic grave is in Zakopane, with which, like his father Stanisław, he was intimately connected throughout his life.

The Second World War

The Second World War and the German/Soviet occupation had a great impact on Polish literature. The suffering of the war years and the horror of the concentration camps were the dominant themes of **Tadeusz Borowski's** (1922–51) short stories, published in English as *This Way for the Gas, Ladies and Gentlemen*. What is most shocking in them is the mundane, matter-of-fact tone in which the author describes everyday life in occupied Warsaw and in the camps; he presents a vision of a concentric universe from which there is no escape: Warsaw being the first circle of hell, a cell in Pawiak prison the second, Auschwitz the third, with the outside world extending beyond.

A curiously un-heroic account of perhaps the most heroic event of the war is given by **Miron Białoszewski** (1922–83) in his *A Memoir of the Warsaw Uprising*, a forerunner of his later works, such as *Reality's Denunciations, Noises,*

Blockages, Draughts and *Heart Attack*. These diary-like records of daily events consist of coherent, highly lyrical threads of narrative prose, remarkable for their flexible language and deft imitation of colloquial speech. They extend the author's previous experiments in poetry, and wonderfully broaden the stylistic scope of modern Polish.

Gustaw Herling-Grudziński's (b. 1919) *A World Apart* is an outstanding literary work, a methodical account of life in Soviet labour camps, almost a moral and philosophical treatise, with the spirit of Dostoyevski hovering above its pages. The book was blacklisted in communist countries, and even in France it took years before it could be published, on account of its anti-Soviet content, despite an enthusiastic review from Camus, while in Britain it appeared only after the intervention of Bertrand Russell, who wrote the forward to the 1951 edition. The Polish text was published in London in 1953 and since 1989 has become mandatory reading in Polish schools.

The war experience also found its expression in poetry: the moralistic and Classical poems of Czesław Miłosz (see below), and the simple, restrained and rough-hewn verse of Tadeusz Różewicz (b. 1921), infused with moralistic and melancholy undertones often under-pinned with irony. Różewicz is also a talented playwright, as attested by *The Card Index*, *Marriage Blanc* and *The Trap*.

Post-War Period

After 1949 literature in Poland came under the spell of Socialist Realism. The most important works of this period were by émigré writers associated with the Parisian monthly *Kultura*: Witold Gombrowicz, Czesław Miłosz and Gustaw Herling-Grudziński.

Witold Gombrowicz (1904–69) made his debut in 1933 with a collection of short stories—psychological portraits combined with bizarre fantasy—and soon afterwards published his first novel, the grotesque and comical *Ferdydurke*. At the outbreak of the war, he found himself in Argentina, and what had been intended as a brief journalistic sojourn turned into permanent emigration. Ostracised and ignored by conservative émigrés and reduced to making his living as a petty clerk, Gombrowicz struggled to assert his genius. His vanity was considerable, though a dose of self-irony always filtered through. Passing himself off as a Count and a European writer of great repute did not spare him from scornful rejection by the literary establishment in Buenos Aires. At his table in the café 'Rex', he gathered around him a circle of young admirers and imitators, all of whom were to pass into obscurity. Having finally achieved some recognition, Gombrowicz was able to return to Europe in 1963, first spending a year in west Berlin, and then settling in France. Here, again claiming noble birth, he attacked the entire Parisian literary world, Sartre in particular, for usurping his rightful claim to being the inventor of existentialism. He won several prestigious literary awards, though none could make up for the Nobel Prize, which always eluded him.

In his prose, Gombrowicz struggles with the cultural traditions of his native country and perhaps even more with his own fascinations, or rather obsessions, such as 'form' and 'immaturity'. *Transatlantic, Pornografia* and *Cosmos* are the best-known examples of his prose-writing, bar the three volumes of the *Diary* (1953–66), a peculiar self-portrait of the writer which is an uncanny mixture of disparate elements. He also wrote two valuable plays: *The Marriage*, a parody of

Shakespearean drama, and a historio-philosophical grotesque work entitled *Operetta*. For many, this colourful, eccentric and tragic-comic figure will endure as a source of fascination, as one of those few who shaped European literature of the twentieth century.

Czesław Miłosz (b. 1911) began his career in the inter-war period and made his name as a talented poet. He participated in various underground cultural initiatives during the Nazi occupation. After the war (1946–50) Miłosz worked as a cultural attaché in Washington and Paris, but in 1950 was recalled to Warsaw and had his passport confiscated. Miraculously, he recovered it in January 1951, which allowed him to leave the country for good as a political refugee. It was that year that Miłosz wrote his best-known work, *The Captive Mind*, a Kafkaesque-Orwellian parable sketching the portraits of four imaginary writers, Alfa, Beta, Gamma and Delta, based on real people who in varying degrees collaborated with the new communist regime. Miłosz had already spoken of the schizophrenic personality of those who succumbed to the allure of the 'nameless evil' in his *Moral Tractatus* (1947), which parodied Socialist Realism. In the introductory chapter to *The Captive Mind* entitled 'Murti-Bing', he describes the mechanism of conversion to the New Faith. Karl Jaspers described the book as 'not so much a political as a moral work, inspired by the voice of conscience raised in the defence of fundamental values'. Banned in the People's Republic, it was translated into countless, sometimes exotic languages, and is now mandatory school reading.

In 1960, Miłosz was offered the post of Professor of Slavonic Languages and Literature at Berkeley, where he engaged himself in teaching, translation, and above all writing poetry, for which he received the Nobel Prize in 1980. His translations from the Bible established a modern, hieratic style in Polish. He was also an avid propagator of English and American poetry in Poland, with his Polish versions of Milton, Blake, Yeats, T.S. Eliot and Walt Whitman. In America, he published an anthology—*Post-War Polish Poetry*—bringing such writers as Różewicz, Herbert, Wat and others to public attention. His elegiac-epiphanic volume of poetry entitled *On the Riverbank* appeared in Kraków in 1994.

In Poland, Socialist Realism was abandoned after the 'thaw' of 1956. That year marked several important poetic debuts, Białoszewski and Herbert among them. Born in Lwów, **Zbigniew Herbert** (1924–98) received his schooling at an underground university during the Second World War and fought as a Home Army soldier during the Warsaw Uprising. After the war he worked in odd jobs, but continued to write poems, essays, theatre and radio plays. He is perhaps best known for his much-translated *Mr Cogito* (1974), lofty and ironic, carrying a heroic moral message, and sometimes contrasted with Białoszewski's parodic and grotesque *Kitty Kitty Cabaret*. Herbert is one of the most widely-read Polish poets outside the country. He lectured extensively on Polish and European literature in Europe and America.

Some readers will have heard of only one Polish writer—**Stanisław Lem** (b. 1921), author of popular science fiction novels like *The Cyberiad*, *Solaris* (filmed by Andrei Tarkovski) or *The Star Diaries*. Lem goes beyond the standard fare of commercial science fiction. Under the guise of parody and humour, his novels explore the possibilities and limits of human knowledge, posing profound existential questions. Pastiche, allegory, grotesque and philosophical fable are devices he has turned into a fine art. An equally numerous, though rather different readership is enjoyed by **Ryszard Kapuściński** (b. 1932), an outstanding journalist with literary ambitions and talent. His books give a vivid and suggestive picture of the drama of the contemporary world. He has witnessed at first hand several dozen civil wars and revolutions, probing their mechanisms and causes, and sometimes, as in *Caesar* or *Imperium*, portraying them by means of paradox, irony and self-irony. Very different in character and tone to Kapuściński's reportage are the timeless aphorisms of **Stanisław Lec** (real name Tusch-Letz, 1909–66), collected in a volume entitled *Unkempt Thoughts* and translated into many European languages. They are remarkable for their terseness of form, paradox, allusion and wordplay. An indefatigable enemy of dogmatism, Lec often parodies received wisdom, revealing its unsuspected double meaning.

Gombrowicz and Różewicz aside, the most outstanding achievements of Polish post-war drama are the grotesque-satirical plays of **Sławomir Mrożek** (b. 1930). Mrożek portrays an absurd world, distorted and undermined by stupidity that bears many names. A sophisticated satirist and humorist, he is perhaps at his best as an acute and penetrating observer of the surrealism of daily life in the People's Republic. In his plays, the most famous of which are *Tango*, *The Emigrants*, *Portrait*, and his latest *Love in the Crimea*, events carry an implied message, bringing them closer to the morality genre or philosophical fable and giving them a universal significance. Mrożek's comic effects, ostensibly cabaret-like, have in reality a false bottom, beyond which one catches glimpses of their sometimes terrifying metaphysical and existential depth.

Further reading

History

Acherson, Neal. *The Struggles for Poland* (Pan, London, 1988).

Garton Ash, Timothy. *The Polish Revolution: Solidarity 1980–82* (Jonathan Cape, London, 1983).

Brandys, Kazimierz. *A Warsaw Diary 1977–81* (Chatto, London, 1983).

Ciechanowski, Jan. *The Warsaw Rising.* (Cambridge University Press, Cambridge, 1974)

Davies, Norman. *God's Playground: A History of Poland* (2 vols) (Clarendon Press, Oxford, 1981).

Davies, Norman. *Heart of Europe: A Short History of Poland* (Oxford University Press, Oxford, 1984).

Halecki, Oscar. *A History of Poland* (Routledge, London, 1983).

Michener, James A. *Poland* (Corgi, London, 1983).

Torańska, Teresa. *Them: Stalin's Polish Puppets* (Collins Harvill, London, 1987).

Wat, Aleksander. *My Century. The Odyssey of a Polish Intellectual* (University of California Press, Berkeley, 1988)

Zamoyski, Adam. *The Polish Way: A Thousand-year History of the Poles and their Culture* (John Murray, London, 1987).

Polish Jews

Abramsky, Chimen. Jachimczyk, Maciej, and Polonsky, Antony (eds), *The Jews in Poland* (Blackwell, Oxford, 1986).

Bartoszewski, Władysław. *The Warsaw Ghetto: a Christian's Testimony* (Lamp, London, 1989).

Bauman, Janina. *Winter in the Morning* (Virago, London, 1986).

Fink, Ida. *A Scrap of Time* (Penguin, London, 1989).

Gilbert, Martin. *The Holocaust* (Collins, London, 1986).

Keneally, Thomas. *Schindler's Ark* (Hodder & Stoughton London, 1982).

Levi, Primo. *If This is a Man, The Truce* (Abacus, London, 1987).

Singer, Issac Bashevis. *Collected Stories* (Penguin, London, 1984).

Art and Architecture

Buxton, David. *The Wooden Churches of Eastern Europe* (Cambridge University Press, Cambridge, 1981.

Chrzanowski, Tadeusz. *The Wonders of Poland* (Kluszczyński, Kraków, 1998).

Karpowicz, M. *Baroque in Poland* (Arkady, Warsaw, 1991).

Knox, Brian. *The Architecture of Poland* (Barrie and Jenkins, London, 1971).

Kozakiewicz, Helena and Stefan. *The Renaissance in Poland* (Arkady, Warsaw, 1976).

Lorentz, Stanisław and Rottermund, Andrzej. *Neo-classicism in Poland* (Arkady, Warsaw, 1986).

Olszewski, Andrzej. *An Outline of Polish 20th Century Art and Architecture* (Interpress, Warsaw, 1989).

Świechowski, Zygmunt. *Romanesque Art in Poland* (Arkady, Warsaw, 1983).

Polish Literature
General

Czerniawski, Adam (ed.). *The Burning Forest* (Bloodaxe, UK, 1988).

Kott, Jan (ed.). *Four Decades of Polish Essays* (Northwestern University Press, USA, 1990).

Krzyżanowski, Julian. *A History of Polish Literature* (PWN, Warszawa, 1978).

Miłosz, Czesław. *The History of Polish Literature* (University of California Press, USA, 1983).

Miłosz, Czesław. *Post-War Polish Poetry* (University of California Press, USA, 1983).

Literature in translation
Renaissance

Kochanowski, Jan. *Laments* (Faber and Faber, London, 1995). Translated by Seamus Heaney and Stanisław Barańczak

Baroque

Pasek, Jan Chryzostom. *The Memoirs of Jan Chryzostom Pasek* (The Kościuszko Foundation, Twayne Publishers, USA, 1977).

Enlightenment

Krasicki, Ignacy. *The Adventures of Mr Nicholas Wisdom* (Northwestern University Press, USA, 1992).

Potocki, Jan. *The Saragossa Manuscript: A Collection of Weird Tales* (Orion, USA, 1960).

Romanticism

Fredro, Aleksander. *The Major Comedies of Aleksander Fredro* (Princeton University Press, USA, 1969).

Krasiński, Zygmunt. *The Undivine Comedy* (Greenwood, USA, 1976 [reprint]).

Mickiewicz, Adam. *Pan Tadeusz* (Polish Cultural Foundation , UK, 1990).

Mickiewicz, Adam. *Konrad Wallenrod* and *Grażyna* (University Press of America, UK, 1989).

Positivism

Prus, Bolesław. *The Doll* (Central European University Press, London, New York, Budapest, 1996).

Sienkiewicz, Henryk. *Trilogy* (*With Fire and Sword, The Deluge, Fire in the Steppe*). (Hippocrene, USA, 1992).

Sienkiewicz, Henryk. *Quo Vadis?* (Alan Sutton, UK, 1989).

Fin-de-Siècle

Reymont, Władysław. *The Peasants* (A. A. Knopf, USA, 1942).

Inter-War Years

Gombrowicz, Witold. *Ferdydurke* (Grove, USA, 1968).

Schultz, Bruno. *Cinnamon Shops and Other Stories* (MacGibbon and Kee, UK, 1963).

Schultz, Bruno. *The Street of Crocodiles and Sanatorium Under the Sign of the Hour Glass* (Picador, UK, 1988).

Witkiewicz, Stanisław Ignacy. *The Madman and the Nun and Other Plays* (University of Washington Press, USA, 1969).

Witkiewicz, Stanisław Ignacy. *Insatiability* (Quartet, UK, 1985).

Żeromski, Stefan. *Ashes*. (A. A. Knopf, USA, 1928).

Second World War

Białoszewski, Miron. *A Memoir of the Warsaw Uprising* (Ann Arbor, Ardis, USA, 1977).

Borowski, Tadeusz. *This Way for the Gas, Ladies and Gentlemen* (Penguin, UK, 1976).

Herling-Grudziński, Gustaw. *A World Apart* (Oxford University Press, 1985).

Różewicz, Tadeusz. *Selected Poems* (Penguin, USA, 1976).

Post-War

Andrzejewski, Jerzy. *Ashes and Diamonds* (Penguin, USA, 1980).

Gombrowicz, Witold. *Diary* (vols I and II) (Quartet, 1988).

Gombrowicz, Witold. *Pornografia* (Calder & Boyars, 1966).

Gombrowicz, Witold. *Cosmos* (Grove, USA, 1967).

Herbert, Zbigniew. *Selected Poems* (Oxford University Press, 1977).

Herbert, Zbigniew. *Report from the Besieged City* (Oxford University Press, 1987).

Hłasko, Marek. *The Eighth Day of the Week* (Minerva Press, 1992).

Kapuściński, Ryszard. *Imperium* (Granta, 1994).

Konwicki, Tadeusz. *A Dreambook for Our Time* (Penguin, 1976).

Konwicki, Tadeusz. *A Minor Apocalypse* (Faber & Faber, 1983).

Lec, Stanisław. *Unkempt Thoughts* (St Martin's Press, 1962).

Lem, Stanisław. *Solaris* (Faber & Faber, 1970).

Lem, Stanisław. *The Cyberiad: Fables for the Cybernetic Age* (Secker and Warburg, 1975).

Lem, Stanisław. *The Star Diaries* (Avon, USA, 1977).

Miłosz, Czesław. *The Captive Mind* (Random House, USA, 1981).

Miłosz, Czesław. *Native Realm: A Search for Self-Definition* (Sidgwick and Jackson, 1981).
Miłosz, Czesław. *The Issa Valley* (Sidgwick and Jackson, 1981).
Miłosz, Czesław. *Collected Poems 1931–1987* (Penguin, 1988).
Mrożek, Sławomir. *Tango: A Play in Three Acts* (Grove, USA, 1968).
Mrożek, Sławomir. *Six Plays* (Jonathan Cape, 1968).
Mrożek, Sławomir. *The Emigrants* (Samuel French, 1984).
Szymborska, Wisława. *Sounds, Feelings, Thoughts: Seventy Poems* (Princeton University Press, USA, 1981).
Szymborska, Wisława. *People on a Bridge* (Forest Books, 1990).
Wat, Aleksander. *Lucifer Unemployed* (Northwestern University Press, USA, 1990).

Literature by foreign writers

Grass, Günter. *The Danzig Trilogy* (*The Tin Drum, Cat and Mouse, Dog Years*) (Sidgwick and Jackson, 1959, 1961, 1963).
Hauptmann, Gerhart. *The Weavers* (Methuen, 1980).
Hoffman, Eva. *Lost in Translation: Life in a New Language* (Viking Penguin, 1990).
Kosinski, Jerzy. *The Painted Bird* (Grove, USA, 1995).
Styron, William. *Sophie's Choice* (Random House, 1992).

Mazovia

The historic Mazovia region (Mazowsze) lies in central Poland, bordered by Wielkopolska to the west and Byelorussia to the east. Predominantly low-lying and rural, it forms part of the Central European plain stretching from the Urals to the French Atlantic coast. While considered to be one of the less attractive Polish regions, without the distinct cultural tradition of, say, Silesia or Pomerania, Mazovia does have a number of places of interest. All of these are within easy reach of **Warsaw**, the region's chief city. Going south along the Vistula, you could visit the pilgrimage town of **Góra Kalwaria** or the ruins of the medieval castle at **Czersk**. To the north and west extends the **Kampinos forest**, with a skansen (open-air museum) and war cemeteries, and beyond it **Żelazowa Wola**, the **birthplace of Chopin**. Day trips can also be made to the medieval town of **Pułtusk** (see p. 153), the grand Baroque palace at **Nieborów** and idyllic Romantic park in nearby **Arkadia** (see p. 157). The other major cities of the region are Łódź and Białystok, the latter an ideal base for excursions into the **Białowieża National Park** (see p. 176), home of the last European bison.

Warsaw

Warsaw (population 1,700,000), the Polish capital, straddles the river Vistula in the heart of the Mazovia region. It is, paradoxically, both an ancient and a very young city. In the course of 800 years, from a humble trading settlement there emerged one of the leading royal capitals of 18C Europe, a vibrant centre of cultural life, where the continent's first democratic constitution was proclaimed. Yet, in the 20C, this rich legacy suffered almost complete annihilation at the hands of Nazi Germany. In 1945, 20,000 people emerged from the rubble of a city that six years earlier had held one and a quarter million. From the 1950s onwards, there began a massive influx of people from the countryside, with the result that today's inhabitants are relative newcomers. Families with traditional roots in the city have all but vanished.

In the decade since the fall of Communism, Warsaw has been developing at breakneck speed. It has managed to attract the lion's share of domestic and foreign investment, and the effects are visible in the proliferation of new business and the city's rapidly changing appearance. Huge advertising billboards, fashionable boutiques, postmodernist hotel façades and high-tech shopping malls would have been unthinkable in the 1980s, when Warsaw conformed to the dour, grey 'eastern bloc' stereotype. Today, over 70 per cent of new construction in Poland is concentrated in Warsaw. With the city quickly approaching Western standards in many areas (retailing, real-estate prices, computerisation, to name but a few), the gulf between it and the rest of the country is getting wider. Indeed, the foreign visitor who stays within the confines of the city will get a distorted picture of Poland and Polish life.

Highlights of Warsaw

When you visit Warsaw, most of your time will probably be spent on the river's west (left) bank, where the city centre and main commercial zone are located. The centre is bordered by the districts of Żoliborz (north), Wola (west) and Mokotów (south). To the east, across the river, extends the vast residential suburb of Praga.

All the important sites are situated on the left bank, which is described in nine walks, beginning with the **Old Town** (walk 1). This area, included on UNESCO's World Heritage List, is packed with sites and it is unlikely that you will be able to see everything in a day. The showpiece **Royal Castle** houses some of the best art in Poland, contained in lavishly restored interiors, and should not be missed. Poland's major religious ceremonies take place in the **Cathedral of St John**, while the **Old Town Square** has two museums and many fine tenement houses. Further to the north, beyond the ring of medieval fortifications, lies the **New Town** (walk 2), with many fine churches.

The **Royal Way**, described in three walks begins at pl. Zamkowy in the Old Town and proceeds south along two of Warsaw's most famous streets— **Krakowskie Przedmieście** and **Nowy Świat** (walk 3). Thereafter, it enters the city's government and embassy district around **Ujazdów Avenue** (walk 4), before bringing you to Łazienki (walk 5), a beautiful park with many historic buildings and museums, including the famous **Palace on the Water**. The Royal Way ends at Wilanów (walk 9) in the southern suburbs of Warsaw, where king Jan Sobieski put up the magnificent **Wilanów Palace**, today an impressive museum.

Two of the walks follow a specific theme: walk 7 takes you through the bleak cityscape of the former **Jewish ghetto** and traces the history of the tragic Ghetto Uprising of 1943; walk 8 concentrates on architecture of the Stalinist period, and includes the huge **Palace of Science and Culture**, Stalin's gift to Warsaw, which dominates the city skyline. Central Warsaw is described in walk 6, the highlights of which are the imposing **Krasiński Palace** and **National Theatre**, as well as the **John Paul II Collection**, containing some of the best art in the country.

One of Warsaw's strengths is its great variety of tourist attractions, but it is also unique among Polish cities for having no clearly-defined centre, where entertainment and cultural life are focused. The main attractions are spread out over a large area and often situated on broad, busy roads, which can make sight-seeing on foot a frustrating experience. After 22.00hrs the streets empty quickly, and in terms of night life Warsaw certainly lags behind West European capitals and even some other Polish cities. Public transport is fairly efficient, but often time-consuming, while the much-delayed underground system has only one line and is not particularly useful for getting to the major sites, except Wilanów.

Further afield. Warsaw is not only an ideal base for visiting the Mazovia region, but also places further afield. Fast rail connections to Poland's major cities mean that the latter can be visited on one or two-day trips, though most deserve a longer stay. Direct trains to Kraków do not stop on the way and make the journey in 2 hours 35 minutes. Łódź is the closest major city—just 1 hour by train. There are regular express and inter-city services to Gdańsk (3 hours 30 minutes), Poznań (3 hours), Szczecin (5 hours 30 minutes) and Wrocław (4 hours). If cities are not your top priority, attractive trips can be made to the town of **Kazimierz Dolny** on the Vistula (see p. 291), and to the **Masurian Lake District** (described in the Warmia and Masuria chapter).

■ Practical information

Accommodation

Unless you are prepared to pay top-of-the-range prices, finding suitable accommodation in Warsaw can be a problem. Considering the number of visitors to the city each year, there is a distinct shortage of hotels, particularly in the low- to mid-range bracket. June, July and September are the worst months, and if you are arriving at this time it is wise to book well in advance. Rooms can also be scarce during major festivals, international conferences and national holidays. If you do not have a car, the most convenient hotels are those located on or near ul. Krakowskie Przedmieście and ul. Nowy Świat, as they are within easy reach of most major sites.

If you are mobile, then places out of town, such as the Jabłonna Palace hotel, might be more appealing. Standards vary: the luxury apartments at the Secessionist *Bristol*, for instance, are the plushest in town, but with inflated prices to match. Down the scale, the three-star *Polonia* offers basic, if slightly cramped accommodation at reasonable rates. Going below this standard is risky. Converted former workers' hotels, in particular, are not recommended.

Recommended hotels
★★★★★
Orbis-Victoria Inter-Continental. Ul. Królewska 11, ☎ 657-8011. Excellent facilities. Air conditioning, swimming pool, business services, car park, travel office and wheelchair access. Central location with views over pl. Piłsudskiego and the Saxon Garden. 291 rooms.
Bristol. Ul. Krakowskie Przedmieście 42/44, ☎ 625-2525. Since recent modernisation, the most luxurious hotel in Warsaw. Excellent cuisine. Swimming pool, gym, business services, air conditioning, wheelchair access. 206 rooms, some with attractive views.
Sheraton. Ul. Prusa 2, ☎ 657-6100. Most recent hotel in Warsaw. An American chain, geared towards businesspeople. Air conditioning, business services, gym, car park, wheelchair access. Quiet, central location. 350 rooms.
Mercure-Fryderyk Chopin. Al. Jana Pawła II 22, ☎ 620-0221. Modern and French-owned, with Le Balzac restaurant offering genuine French cuisine. Air conditioning, gym, business services, wheelchair access. 250 rooms.
Sobieski. Pl. Zawiszy 1, ☎ 658-4444. Very clean and modern (1992), with a rooftop garden and a two-storey royal apartment under the glass dome. Air conditioning, business services, gym, swimming pool, wheelchair access. 414 rooms.
Marriott. Al. Jerozolimskie 65/79, ☎ 630-6306, ☎ 630-71-41. Huge, modern tower block situated next to the main railway station. Many boutiques, shops and restaurants on the ground floor, including a LOT ticket office. Popular among visiting businesspeople. Plush conference rooms and luxury apartments. Excellent facilities. Swimming pool, gym, car park, business services, air conditioning, wheelchair access. 521 rooms with panoramic views.

★★★★

Orbis-Holiday Inn. Ul. Złota 48/54, ☎ 620-03-41/620-65-34. Central location. Air conditioning, gym, business services, car park, wheelchair access. 336 rooms, some with good views.

Orbis-Europejski. Ul. Krakowskie Przedmieście 13, ☎ 826-50-51. Travel office. Reasonably priced for its central location. Oldest hotel in Warsaw (mid-19C). 237 rooms.

Orbis-Forum. Ul. Nowogrodzka 24/26 ☎ 621-02-71/823-03-64. Central but noisy location. Largest hotel in Warsaw, with the useful Mazurkas Travel Office ☎ 629-18-78. Air conditioning, business services, swimming pool, gym, car park, wheelchair access. 733 rooms, some with views.

Orbis-Solec. Ul. Zagórna 1, ☎ 625-4400. Situated close to the river. Business services, air conditioning. 137 rooms.

Orbis-Novotel. Ul. 1 Sierpnia 1, ☎ 846-36-86. Out of town, on the way to the airport. Outdoor swimming pool and garden. Business services, wheelchair access, car park. 146 rooms.

★★★

Metropol. Ul. Marszałkowska 99a ☎, 629-4001. Central location, opposite the Forum. Business services. 192 rooms.

Orbis-Grand. Ul. Krucza 28, ☎ 629-40-51. Built in the 1950s, with rooms of modest standard. Quiet, central location. Business services, travel office, swimming pool. 314 rooms.

Polonia. Al. Jerozolimskie 45, ☎ 628-72-41. Central location, reasonably priced. Original turn-of-the-century décor in the restaurant and reception area. 234 rooms.

Warszawa. Pl. Powstańców Warszawy 9, ☎ 826-94-21. Tower block, centrally located. Built in the 1930s for the Prudential Insurance company. 144 rooms, some with panoramic views.

MDM. Pl. Konstytucji 1, ☎ 621-6211. Genuine Socialist Realist building, part of the Marszałkowska Housing District (MDM; see p. 145). Clean and sparsely furnished. Air conditioning, business services, wheelchair access. 111 rooms.

Restaurants
Exclusive
Belvedere, ul. Agrykola 1 (the New Orangery in Łazienki Park). French.
Casa Valdemar, ul. Piękna 7/9. Catalan.
Fukier, Rynek Starego Miasta 27.
Polish, French.
Malinowa, ul. Krakowskie Przedmieście 42/44. Polish, French.
Przedmieście, 42/44. Polish, French.
Polska, ul. Nowy Świat 21. Traditional Polish.

Medium-priced
Tsubame, ul. Foksal 16. Japanese.
Santorini, ul. Egipska 7. Greek.
Chianti, ul. Foksal 17. Italian.
Tokio, ul. Dobra 17, Japanese.
Gessler, Rynek Starego Miasta 21. Polish.
99, ul. Jana Pawła II 23. Italian.
Barbados, ul. Wierzbowa 9. French.
Blue Cactus, ul. Zajączkowska 11. Mexican.
Quchnia Artystyczna, al. Ujazdowskie 6. International, vegetarian.
Montmartre, ul. Nowy Świat 7. French.
Rycerska, ul. Szeroki Dunaj 11. Polish.

Maharaja Indyjska, ul. Marszałkowska 34/50. Indian.
Maharaja Tajska, ul. Szeroki Dunaj 13. Thai.
Nowe Miasto, Rynek Nowego Miasta 13/15. International, vegetarian.
El Popo, ul. Senatorska 27. Mexican.

Bazyliszek, Rynek Starego Miasta 3/9. Polish.
Flik, ul. Puławska 43. Polish, French.
Ugarit, pl. Konstytucji 1. Arabic, Polish.
U Szwejka, pl. Konstytucji 1. International.

Cheap eateries
Pod Samsonem, ul. Freta 3/5.
Fuks, ul. Madalińskigo 38/40. Vegetarian.
Bar Pod Barbakanem, ul. Mostowa 27/29.
Bar Mleczny Familijny, ul. Nowy Świat 39.
Krokiecik, ul. Zgoda 1.

Cafés
Pożegnanie z Afryką, ul. Freta 4/6.
Café Bristol, ul. Krakowskie Przedmieście 42/44.
Café Blikle, ul. Nowy Świat 33.
Literacka, ul. Krakowskie Przedmieście 87/89.
Batida, ul. Nowogrodzka 1/3.

Tourist information
Tourist Information Centre. Pl. Zamkowy 1/13, ☎ 831-0464; open Mon–Fri 09.00–18.00, Sun 11.00–18.00.
Tourist Information (PAPT). Al. Jerozolimskie 54 (Main Railway Station) ☎ 654-2447.
ORBIS. Ul. Świętokrzyska 20, ☎ 826-2011/826-20-16, Krakowskie Przedmieście 13, ☎ 828-1810, ul. Marszałkowska 142, ☎ 827-2786, pl. Mickiewicza 27, ☎ 39-46-44 (train information), ☎ 39-15-66 (flight information), pl. Konstytucji 4, ☎ 628-8222/628-01724, ul. Grójecka 56/58, ☎ 822-7751, 822-4655.

Main railway station (Warszawa Centralna). Al. Jerozolimskie 54 (opposite the Marriot hotel and the Palace of Science and Culture) ☎ 620-0361, domestic; ☎ 620-4512, international. The queues in the ticket hall can be long, so it is best to arrive at least 30 minutes before departure.

Main coach station. Al. Jerozolimskie 144 (next to the Warszawa Zachodnia train station, west of the city centre) ☎ 94-33 (coach information and ticket reservations). Coaches depart from here to many cities in Poland and abroad. An alternative to the state bus company (PKS) is the privately-owned **Polski Express**, which has its own stop at the airport and another at the corner of ul. Złota and al. Jana Pawła II, near the main railway station. For more information, ☎ 620-0326, 620-0330.

Airport. Okęcie (10km from the city centre) ☎ 650-3943 (24 hours), ☎ 650-4220, ☎ 846-1700 (6.00–22.00), ☎ 846-1731 (6.00–22.00), international enquiries, ☎ 650-41 00/846-1803 (after 21.00), domestic enquiries.
   Okęcie has a new passenger terminal, built in 1992, which caters for most of the foreign flights. All the usual airport services are available (duty free shop, travel office, car rental, currency exchange etc.). Bus no. 175 runs from the airport to the main railway station (Warszawa Centralna). You should buy your

ticket before boarding. Alternatively, take the special City Line service, which leaves every 20 minutes. City Line buses stop at all the major hotels in the city centre and have more luggage space. Tickets are bought directly from the driver. Private taxis from the airport are very expensive—much more than travelling by 'radio taxi'. There is also a luxury Fly and Drive with LOT service.

LOT. Al. Jerozolimskie 65/79, ☎ 630-5007/630-5009, reservations, ☎ 952-953 (24 hours), flight information, ☎ 630-5757 (business class information), ☎ 630-5858 (information for Voyager Club members). Ground floor of the Marriot hotel.
British Airways. Al. Krucza 49 ☎ 628-9431.

Taxis. It is always best to phone for a 'radio taxi' as these are cheaper, safer and more reliable than private cabs. The largest radio taxi company in Warsaw is MPT, ☎ 919. Try to avoid, in particular, taking taxis from the ranks at the airport, main railway station and pl. Zamkowy—the fares can be much higher than normal, especially for foreigners.

Metro. Currently, there is only one line, which connects the city centre with the southern suburbs of Mokotów, Ursynów, Natolin and Kabaty. Tickets are the same as those for buses and trams, but have to be punched by the entrance to the platform.

Disabled travellers. The Fundacja TUS (ul. Bohaterów Getta 2, ☎ 831-93-31) runs a special transport service for disabled travellers (only within Warsaw). A trip, regardless of departure place and destination, costs 9 PLN, and can be made beween 08.00 and 22.00. The office takes calls 09.00–15.00.

Post office. Ul. Świętokrzyska 31/33, telex and fax, poste restante, courier services, open 24 hours.
Telephone code: (0-22).

Embassies
Australian. Ul. Estońska 3/5 ☎ 617-6081 to 85.
British. Al. Róż 1 ☎ 628-1001 to 05.
Canadian. Ul. Matejki 1/5 ☎ 629-8051 to 58.
US. Al. Ujazdowskie 29/31 ☎ 628-3041 to 49.

Lost property. The lost property office in Warsaw is at ul. Floriańska 10 (☎ 619-5668). For property lost on public transport, ☎ 663-3297.

Major festivals
January. Warsaw Drama Festival
March. International Biennial of Poster Art
May (third week). International Book Fair
June on Sun. Chopin concerts (by the Chopin monument in the Łazienki Park)
Mid-June–Sept. International

Street Theatre Competition
Mid-June–Aug. Mozart Festival
July–September. Festival of Organ Music, in St John's Cathedral
July–September. Warsaw Summer Jazz Days
September (third week). Warsaw Autumn Festival of Contemporary Music

October. Warsaw Film Festival
October. Jazz Jamboree
October–November. Festival of
Renaissance and Baroque Music

Every five years. Chopin Piano
Competition–next one in the year
2000

English language publications. *Warszawa What, Where, When* and *Welcome to Warsaw* provide comprehensive listings of cultural events in the city. The *Warsaw Voice* and *Warsaw Business Journal* have extensive coverage of politics and the economy.

Cemeteries

A pleasant afternoon may be spent at the Catholic **Powązki Cemetery** (open 07.00–dusk) near the western district of Wola (ul. Powązkowska 14; bus nos 122, 148, tram nos 12, 17, 19, 22,19 and 33 from the city centre). The first plots in this, Poland's oldest historic cemetery, were financed as early as 1790 by the Szymanowski family, and soon a modest church of St Charles Borromeo arose, designed by the royal architect Merlini. Today, the oldest part of Powązki lies in the vicinity of the church and is reached through the St Honorata Gate. Many of the early 19C graves have survived, some plain and unpretentious, others ornate Neo-classical monuments with columns, sculptures and pedestals. Visiting Powązki on All Saints' Day and All Souls' Day (1–2 November) is an unforgettable experience. On these public holidays Poles traditionally turn out *en masse* to pay their respects to the dead. Relatives meticulously tidy the graves of their loved ones, forgotten tombs are suddenly lavished with an abundance of flowers, and crowds wander the 'Lane of Honour' bathed in the light of a million candles.

History

The first traces of human settlement on the terrain of present-day Warsaw date from the 10C. In the 13C, on a steep cliff (35m) rising above the left bank of the Kamionka river, the Mazovian dukes built their fortified wooden stronghold of Jazdów, the very site where, 600 years later, King Stanisław August Poniatowski would lay out his famous Łazienki Park. Jazdów was sacked twice, then replaced, towards the end of the 13C, by a new stronghold located a few kilometres downstream, on the site of today's Royal Castle. At the turn of the 13C, the Old Town (20ha)—as it is called today—was laid out north of the fortress. The urban plan consisted of a rectangular market square and a grid of perpendicular streets. By 1379 it was encircled with new brick walls, supplemented in the following century by an outer ring.

As Warsaw flourished, so it began to expand territorially. To the north arose the New Town, with its own market square, municipal administration (after 1408), and late Gothic church of St Mary (1411). Its inhabitants were mainly craftsmen, who supplied and serviced the nearby rural communities. By contrast, the patriciate of the (original) Old Town monopolised the production of luxury goods and the lucrative grain and timber trade along the Vistula. By the early 17C, the vast quantities of goods shipped along Vistula had made it the most frequented waterway in Europe, surpassing even the Thames.

With the heirless death of the last Mazovian dukes in the 16C, the Duchy was incorporated into the lands of the Polish Crown. On 25 August 1526, **King Zygmunt the Old** arrived from the Polish capital, Kraków, to make a ceremonial entry into his new domain. Warsaw had one major advantage over Kraków in the south: its location at roughly the geographical centre of the Jagiellon realm. Thus, when the union between Poland and Lithuania was formalised at Lublin in 1569, it was Warsaw that was chosen as the venue for the **joint parliament**, or *Sejm*. The first session was held in April 1570. Two years later the city hosted the first royal election (Poland-Lithuania was now an elective monarchy). A fire on Kraków's Wawel Castle in 1596 proved to be the decisive factor prompting King Zygmunt Vasa finally and irrevocably to move the royal court to Warsaw, which thereafter became the official capital.

Warsaw developed rapidly during the 17C. The existing castle was rebuilt as a royal residence, which also housed the joint Polish-Lithuanian parliament. As the Old Town was already densely populated, the magnates, who flocked into the city to be closer to the royal court, put up their residences on the peripheries, beyond the line of walls. These new residences were built in the prevalent Counter-Reformation Baroque style, with its severe and monumental forms, and numerous artists and craftsmen furnished the buildings in a manner befitting the wealth and conceit of their noble patrons. Many churches and monasteries were founded, others rebuilt, with projects often being financed by the rising bourgeois community. Various royal privileges and the right to exact customs duties on the Vistula trade after 1589 had enabled many of Warsaw's merchant families to amass considerable fortunes, and it was they who financed much of the new construction in the Old Town.

The steady rise of Warsaw as a centre of political influence and economic prosperity was violently interrupted by the Swedish Deluge of 1655 (see p. 49). In the space of three years, Charles Gustav's army wrought havoc and destruction on an unparalleled scale: the New Town, along with nearly all the suburban churches and palaces, was burnt to the ground. Elsewhere, Warsaw's buildings were ruthlessly looted, their treasures exported never to return.

The reconstruction of Warsaw did not get fully under way until the accession of **Jan Sobieski** to the throne in 1674. It was Sobieski's court architects who put up the best buildings of the Baroque period. **Tylman van Gameren** (1632–1706), a Pole of Dutch descent, rebuilt much of the city in his distinct, austere Palladian style, and redesigned the chaotic layout of the city suburbs. The prolific work of G. S. Bellotti and A. Locci gave the capital, then still numbering only 20–30 thousand inhabitants, something approaching its present shape. Yet the most enduring achievement of Sobieski's reign was the grand royal palace he began at Wilanów, a few kilometres upstream from the city.

The reign of the last Polish king, **Stanisław August Poniatowski** (1764–95), coincided with Neo-classicism in art and architecture. A vigorous patron of the arts, Poniatowski did much to promote the remarkable cultural revival of the mid–late 18C. He made a lasting contribution to the city's architecture with his splendid royal residence at Łazienki (see p. 129). Concomitantly, the urban layout of southern Warsaw was radically changed when the so-called **Stanislavian Axis**—a broad avenue beginning at the Ujazdów Palace and linking a series of 'radial' squares (Na Rozdrożu, Zbawiciela, Unii Lubelskiej and Politechniki)—was laid out in 1768–73.

Poniatowski managed to attract a formidable team of painters, sculptors and architects to carry out his ambitious plans for the capital. **Giacopo Fontana**, until 1773 the chief royal architect, and his successor **Domenico Merlini** redesigned the Royal Castle; **Marcello Bacciarelli** supplied it with some excellent art. Another Italian, **Bernardo Bellotto**, a nephew and pupil of Canaletto, acquired fame for his *vedute* of Warsaw. These townscapes, of great topographical precision, were used to help with the reconstruction of the city after 1945.

In 1794, Warsaw's population rose against the partitioning powers in support of an insurrection led by Tadeusz Kościuszko (see p. 51). By 1795, however, the insurrection had been crushed, and Prussian troops entered the capital. As part of the Prussian sector, Warsaw was relegated to the status of a provincial town. Brief hope was rekindled in 1806 with the arrival of Napoleon's *grande armée* and the establishment of the autonomous Duchy of Warsaw, but Napoleon's final defeat in 1815 ensured that the peacemakers at Vienna could overlook Polish claims to independence.

Despite the strictures of foreign rule, after 1815 Warsaw developed rapidly, and by 1830 the population had reached 140,000. **Industriali-sation** entailed the construction of residential housing for the flourishing bourgeois community. Instead of palaces and manors, single-family town houses were built in the dominant Neo-classical style, and the urban appearance of Warsaw began to change. Ul. Nowy Świat is perhaps the most striking example of this new trend.

The struggle for independence came to a head in 1830 with the outbreak of the **November Uprising**. Czarist troops laid siege to Warsaw and eventually crushed the rebellion. There followed a period of heavy repression which saw the Russian authorities revoke the autonomy that had been granted to the Congress Kingdom. In the northern suburb of Żoliborz, the occupiers erected the infamous Citadel (1832–36), a gruesome fortress-cum-prison where Polish political prisoners were incarcerated. It was there that the leaders of the 'National Government' were imprisoned and then executed during the 1863 **January Uprising**.

Despite the unfavourable political climate, the city's economy continued to grow. In less than half a century its area grew tenfold and by 1913 its population had reached nearly 700,000. The Russian authorities fled in 1915 and the city was occupied by the Germans for the final three years of the **First World War**. With the restoration of independence in 1918, Warsaw became the capital of the reborn Polish state. Modernisation became top priority, with vast improvements being made in municipal transportation and housing. Old historic buildings were restored, while others were built to accommodate the new parliament, government, civil administration and educational institutions.

The **Second World War** took a terrible toll on the city and its inhabitants. The Germans destroyed 85 per cent of the buildings, and a staggering 800,000 people—over half the 1939 population—perished. Hitler's plan had been to erase Warsaw from the map of Europe to symbolically under-

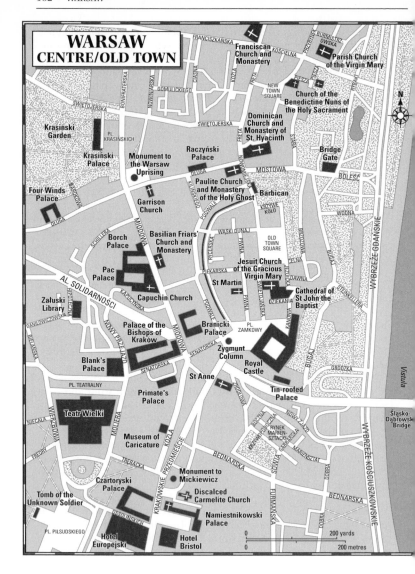

WARSAW CENTRE/OLD TOWN

Franciscan Church and Monastery

Parish Church of the Virgin Mary

Church of the Benedictine Nuns of the Holy Sacrament

NEW TOWN SQUARE

Dominican Church and Monastery of St. Hyacinth

Krasiński Garden

PL KRASIŃSKICH

Raczyński Palace

Bridge Gate

Krasiński Palace

Monument to the Warsaw Uprising

Paulite Church and Monastery of the Holy Ghost

Barbican

Four Winds Palace

Garrison Church

OLD TOWN SQUARE

Borch Palace

Basilian Friars' Church and Monastery

Pac Palace

Jesuit Church of the Gracious Virgin Mary

St Martin

Załuski Library

Capuchin Church

Cathedral of St John the Baptist

Palace of the Bishops of Kraków

Branicki Palace

PL ZAMKOWY

Blank's Palace

Zygmunt Column

St Anne

Royal Castle

Primate's Palace

Tin-roofed Palace

PL. TEATRALNY

Teatr Wielki

Śląsko-Dąbrowski Bridge

Museum of Caricature

Monument to Mickiewicz

Czartoryski Palace

Discalced Carmelite Church

Tomb of the Unknown Soldier

Namiestnikowski Palace

PL. PIŁSUDSKIEGO

Hotel Europejski

Hotel Bristol

Vistula

0   200 yards
0   200 metres

score the annihilation of Polish culture. Yet most of the destruction took place only after the failure of the Warsaw Uprising (August–September 1944), when the Germans set about the systematic demolition of the city, house by house, street by street.

After the war, there were plans to leave the ruined city as a gigantic war memorial, a reminder of Nazi atrocity for generations to come. In the end, reconstruction got under way and continued until the 1960s. Buildings were put together from fragments found in the rubble, the conservators using old maps, photographs and paintings to accomplish their task. The medieval plan of the old town was reconstituted in 1952–55. It was decided to reconstruct the buildings in their earliest retraceable form, usually 17C–18C, with many 19C additions being removed to make way for space and greenery. The conservators' best effort was perhaps ul. Krakowskie Przedmieście, where, even today, the Warsaw of Bellotto seems to echo at every step.

Walk One ~ The Old Town (Stare Miasto)

The Old Town is situated along the high river Vistula escarpment in the northern part of the city centre. It can be reached by **bus** (nos E-1, 116, 122, 144, 174, 175, 179, 195, 495, 503), or by **tram** (nos 4, 13, 26 and 32; get off by the underpass). Alternatively, it is about a 25 minute walk from the city's main railway station (Warszawa Centralna).

Royal Castle

The walk begins at the ****Royal Castle**, which spans the east side of PL. ZAMKOWY. Fully restored since the war, the Castle is Warsaw's most famous monument. The interiors have been opened as a splendid museum of galleries, royal suites, courtiers' chambers and parliamentary rooms from various periods in Poland's history. The exhaustive tour is well marked in English and covers four floors beginning with the cellars below the east wing. The most interesting rooms are on the first floor, so if you are pushed for time, energy or patience it is better to omit what comes first than to miss out later.

History of the Royal Castle

The earliest extant fragments (reconstructed) are found in the base of the Gothic Grodzka Tower (the medieval keep). Major expansion of the Castle did not get under way until 1569, when Warsaw was annexed by the Polish Crown and chosen as the seat of the Parliament, or *Sejm*. Another spate of building commenced after 1600, when the Vasas moved the official royal residence from Kraków to Warsaw. It was then that the Castle received its present shape of a five-winged pentagon around an inner courtyard. Italian architects, notably Giovanni Trevano, gave the building homogeneous architectural form, remodelling its mass and incorporating earlier elements in the predominant Vasa style—a version of early Roman Baroque. During the Vasa period, the Castle became one of the most splendid royal residences on the European mainland, unique in that it housed both monarch and parliament. The interiors, connected by grand staircases, were modelled on the royal apartments in Kraków's Wawel Castle and lavishly decorated with a multitude of paintings, tapestries, exquisite ceilings and portals.

Following a fire in 1767, the south wing was rebuilt in Baroque-Classical style by Stanisław August Poniatowski's chief architect, Giacopo Fontana. His successor, Domenico Merlini, remodelled the state rooms (Royal Residential Suite) on the east side (1774–85) and fitted a small chapel into the south tower. In collaboration with Jan Chrystian Kamsetzer, Merlini also reshaped in Neo-classical style the Grand Suite in the northeast range (1779–85). Taken as a whole, Merlini's is the best extant work in the Castle. His, too, is the long narrow Library, the only wing to survive the Second World War.

The only major addition in the 19C was Jakub Kubicki's Neo-classical terrace on arcades (1818–21) below the east elevation (now being restored to house part of the museum collections). After 1830 the Castle served as the residence of Poland's Czarist governors. With the restoration of independence, it became the official seat of the President of the Republic (1926). During this period some Gothic elements were exposed and the Neo-classical decoration of the façades was removed to restore the 17C appearance of the building.

After the Second World War, during which the Castle was severely bombed and blown up, conservators again opted to restore it to its 17C form, preserving historical layering to show its varied function throughout the ages. Fortunately, many of the furnishings and decoration had been courageously hidden during the war. The reconstruction, financed almost entirely from private donations, did not begin until 1971. By 1974 the clock on the Zygmunt Tower had been restarted, with most of the remaining interiors finally reaching completion in 1984.

■ **Open** 1 Oct–14 Apr, 10.00–16.00, 15 Apr–30 Sept, 10.00–18.00, closed Mon; last admission one hour before closing. Refreshments can be bought at the café and restaurant on the ground floor by the main vestibule. The ticket office is at ul. Świętojańska 2 (☎ 635-3995). Advance group bookings are available for weekdays only. The Castle Shop (open 10.00–19.00, closed Mon) offers a selection of books and souvenirs.

The Castle is best viewed from ul. Krakowskie Przedmieście, or from across the river. Here, the austere yet elegant features of the Vasa style reveal themselves with full clarity: rusticated corners, portals, and regular arrays of windows with stone window frames punctuating the smooth red plaster. Above the three-storey main block rise domed towers and a tiled roof, all in perfect harmony with the distant skyline of the Old Town. Entering through the vaulted hallway below the Clock Tower you emerge into the courtyard, where each wing represents a different period in the Castle's history: the Gothic façade of the former Great Manor (east), the Władysław Tower and early Baroque façades of the Vasas (west and northeast), the 18C elevations to the north and south.

Cellars
The **Great Cellar** contains silver collected for the National Defence Fund in 1936 which had still not been minted by the outbreak of war in 1939. Adjoining it is the 15C **Duke's Cellar** with a single pillar supporting a quadripartite cross vault. The tiny **Gaol** at the end is the lowest part of the tower. Its walls bear inscriptions made by prisoners. From here stairs lead up to the ground floor.

Ground floor (rooms 1–6)
Deputies' Chambers (east and south wings). You emerge from the cellars into the former **Deputies' Anteroom** (1). This room, and the two further north (2–3), originally housed the Mazovian Sejm and the Ducal Court. After the Union of Lublin, until the 1670s, the Parliament of the Polish-Lithuanian Commonwealth held its sessions here. Around 190 deputies sat on the benches placed around the Speaker's chair in the former **Deputies' Chamber** (2). Stretching east from the Deputies' Anteroom is Merlini's **Royal Library** (4), an

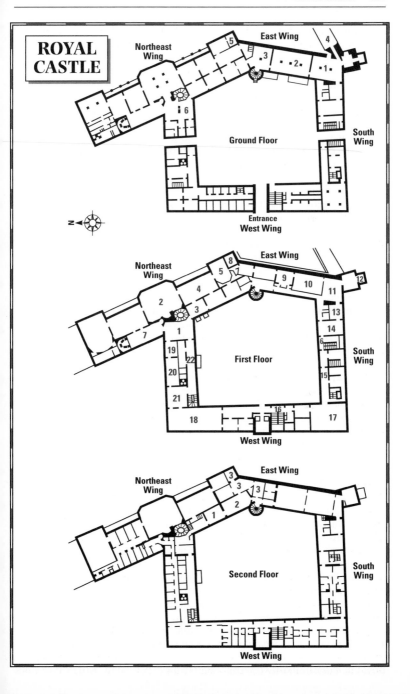

extension built out along the north wing of the Tin-roofed Palace (see p. 108) in 1779–82. The library's rich collections were moved to St Petersburg in 1820, never to return.

Courtiers' Chambers (northeast wing). The northeast wing beyond the **Single Pillar Hall** (3) was originally the ground floor of the New House built for King Zygmunt August. The rooms (16C–17C) served as living quarters for the royal courtiers and king's pages. Of interest is the small **Riverside Closet** (5), the only part of the building to survive the explosion in 1944. The projecting bay still has the drilled holes (visible from the outside) into which the Nazis placed the dynamite. From the **Main Vestibule** (6) ascend the north staircase to the first floor.

First floor (rooms 1–22)

The **Royal Suites**, covering the entire first floor bar the west wing, constitute a compositional whole planned out in the late 18C by Poniatowski and his team of architects, sculptors and historians. By far the most impressive section is the **Grand Suite**. Guests seeking audience with the monarch would ascend the Senators' Stairs and be led through the Antechamber (1) to the Great Assembly Hall (2), the Marble Room (3) and the Knights' Hall (4), before finally reaching the monarch in the Throne Room (5). Beyond these rooms was the Royal Residential Suite, reached via the **Grand Staircase** (6).

Grand Suite (northeast wing). You emerge in the **Oval Gallery** (7) with magnificent Flemish tapestries and portraits of Polish monarchs. The *Great Assembly Hall** (2), also known as the Ballroom, dates from the Saxon period, though its interior was designed later by Merlini and Kamsetzer. Grand and bright, with Corinthian columns and mirrors, the room overlooks the Vistula. Its highlight is Marcello Bacciarelli's huge allegorical ceiling painting (restored) depicting the *Dissolution of Chaos*. Notice, also, André Le Brun's statues of Apollo and Minerva, and his sculpture of *Peace and Justice* (with G. Monaldi). Other bronze busts and statues by Le Brun and Monaldi, notably *Chronos*, *Fame*, and a series of 22 eminent Poles, are found in the fabulous *Knights' Hall** (4). On its walls hang six paintings by Bacciarelli showing famous scenes from Polish history.

Adjoining but not always accessible from the Knights' Hall is the appropriately named *Marble Room** (3), designed by G.B. Ghisleni during the reign of Władysław IV, but later remodelled by Fontana. Here the theme of Polish royal history is continued with portraits of all 22 Polish monarchs, including a large one of Poniatowski, again by Bacciarelli, who collaborated with J.B. Plersch on the painted ceiling.

The *Throne Room** (5), abounding in mirrors and generous gilding, is the most elegant room of the Grand Suite, with small Italian statues of Scipio Africanus Major, Hannibal, Pompey and Julius Caesar, French candelabra, two marble mantelpieces and, of course, a gilded throne, looking curiously forlorn without its base or canopy. The last room in this wing is the **Cabinet of European Monarchs** (8), small, oval, with a beautiful parquet floor. Poniatowski dedicated the room to the monarchs of Europe, whose portraits adorn the walls. The central table, with a painted porcelain top, is from Sèvres.

Royal Residential Suite (east and south wings). Beyond the **King's Bedroom**

(9), with paintings by Bacciarelli above the doors, is the more attractive **Old Audience Chamber** (10), where again Bacciarelli's allegorical work stands out. His ceiling painting (restored) depicts the *Development of Science, Arts, Agriculture and Trade*, while ovals above the doors frame the four royal virtues: Prudence, Fortitude, Faith and Justice. Most interesting is the **Canaletto Room** (11), decked out in a series of *vedute* of Warsaw and its environs painted by Bernardo Bellotto (Canaletto's nephew) between 1767 and 1780. The adjoining **Small Chapel** (12) consists of a nave and a tiny chancel with eight columns crowded together under a rosetted dome. Inside are Poniatowski's regalia. An urn in the sanctuary contains the heart of Tadeusz Kościuszko (see p. 51). The sparsely furnished **First Anteroom** (13) has a Le Brun sculpture—the *Flaying of Marsyas*. Next door, the **Room of the Royal Horse Guards** (14) stands out for its excellent stuccowork on a pure white background.

The Royal Residential Suite ends at the Grand Staircase. From here you may return via the long corridor (with portraits) to the east wing or continue along the **Four Seasons Gallery** (15), named after its four 18C tapestries. The gallery is actually part of the **Suite of Prince Stanisław**, the king's nephew.

Parliamentary Rooms (west wing). The Parliamentary Rooms are usually reached via the **Deputies' Stairs** (16). Originally housed in the Great Manor, the **Deputies' Chamber** (17) moved to its present location in the second half of the 17C. Its walls are decorated with portraits of Polish field commanders. The most impressive room in the west wing is the ***Senators' Chamber** (18), dating from the reign of Augustus III, where joint parliamentary sessions, attended by the king, were held from the early 1740s onwards. It was here that the 3 May Constitution was proclaimed in 1791. During restoration the 18C décor was retained, including opulent stuccowork reconstructed from precise inventories preserved in the Dresden archives, and, at the far end, an authentic throne under a rich scarlet canopy.

Crown Princes' Rooms and Gallery (north wing). These rooms (**19–22**) have been restored to their 17C appearance, when they were inhabited by the sons of the Vasa kings. Here you will find some of Matejko's (see p. 72) great 19C canvases, which capture the high and low points of Polish history. The Gallery has portraits of rulers with whom the Polish-Lithuanian Commonwealth maintained diplomatic relations in the 17C–18C, including Charles II of England and Ferdinando de Medici.

Second floor (rooms 1–3)

The smaller exhibition on the second floor deals with the more recent period of Polish history. Most interesting is the **Room of the Government-in-Exile of the Second Republic of Poland** (1). All the furnishings, including the presidential insignia, were brought to Poland in 1990 from Eaton Place in London, the seat of the government-in-exile. After the first democratic elections, the insignia were officially handed over to Lech Wałęsa, the first non-communist Polish president for nearly half a century. **President Ignacy Mościcki's Study** (2) has been recreated to look as it did when inhabited by Poland's inter-war president (1926–39). Portraits of other famous Polish statesmen, Mościcki's contemporaries, adorn the walls. Finally there is the **Apartment of the writer Stefan Żeromski** (3), where he spent the last years of his life (see p. 85).

Leaving the Castle, walk around to the sloping south side, which runs parallel to a noisy underpass (al. Solidarności). Down the steps is the Baroque **Tin-roofed Palace**, so-called on account of its sheet-metal roof. Poniatowski bought the building in 1777 and incorporated it into the Castle. Merlini remodelled the interiors as courtiers' lodgings, while the upper storeys of the north wing housed the royal library (see p. 104). The low wings to the north and south—the only parts of the building that survived the war—frame a paved courtyard.

Plac Zamkowy (Castle Square)

Return to the gently sloping pl. Zamkowy (Castle Square), on which stands one of Warsaw's most famous historical landmarks—the *Zygmunt Column (1643–44, Constantino Tencalla). Carved in stone, the monument commemorates King Zygmunt Vasa, and was erected by his son, Władysław IV. The marble shaft, topped by a Corinthian capital, rises 22m to a bronze statue of the king, who is shown leaning forward on a cross and wielding a sabre. This bold and unique work—previously only saints could grace the tops of columns—symbolises the glory and elevation of the Vasa dynasty. The original column was destroyed in 1945 by a direct tank hit, though the statue survived. A photograph (on display in the Historical Museum, see p. 112) taken shortly after the German withdrawal shows the fallen king buried in rubble, with only his cross rising defiantly above it.

Cathedral of St John the Baptist

Walking north along UL. ŚWIĘTOJAŃSKA you reach the *Cathedral of St John the Baptist, Warsaw's oldest (late 13C) and most revered church.

> The Gothic edifice was used on several occassions for royal coronations, and, at the turn of the 18C, was promoted to the rank of a cathedral. Only the chancel walls, apse, crypts and Baryczka Chapel survived the Warsaw Uprising (1944), and post-war reconstruction dispensed with Neo-Gothic elements accumulated during the 19C, producing a brick aisled hall in Mazovian Gothic.

At the foot of the bare brick façade is a portal with a copper-plated door bearing scenes from the life of John the Baptist. Going clockwise from the west end of the north aisle, you come first to the modern chapel-mausoleum of Cardinal Stefan Wyszyński (1901–81), 'the Primate of the millennium', so-called because he was Primate on the 1000th anniversary of the baptism of Poland—1966. Next are the Chapel of St John the Baptist, and the Baptistery (often closed), containing a black marble font with a gilded cover (1631). Continue past the former south porch (now a storeroom) to the domed Flagellation (Blessed Sacrament) Chapel, originally 15C, remodelled in early Baroque style during the 17C.

The reconstructed black marble altar contains a striking sculpture in white marble—the *Flagellation of Christ*. Extending the south aisle is the **Baryczka Chapel**, the most interesting in the church, designed in 1708–16 by Kacper Bażnka. It is sealed off from the aisle by a marble portal filled with an 18C grille, both late Baroque. Inside, the altar contains an excellent late Gothic crucifix, of Silesian origin, which miraculously survived the storm of 1602, when the tower and most of the church's interior were destroyed.

The chancel was partially reconstructed after the war and contains a modern high altar (1963) with a copy of the Black Madonna of Częstochowa. Move on to the south aisle, which is extended by the *Mariae Litterarum*, or Literary Fraternity Chapel, a domed Baroque structure of 1690, with rich stuccowork, a large 18C altar behind a grille, and 16C–17C paintings. Further along the aisle stands the monumental black and white marble tomb of Stanisław Małachowski (1736–1809), Marshal of the Four-Year Sejm, which passed the 3 May Constitution. Towards the west entrance is a 16C slab commemorating the last Mazovian dukes. Sculpted in red marble, the tomb is one of the earliest examples of Renaissance art (B. Gianoti, 1524–28) in Mazovia and shows the two armour-clad brothers in a fraternal embrace. Below the church are crypts (entrance from the north aisle) containing the tombs of Polish notables, including recent personages such as the author Henryk Sienkiewicz, of *Quo Vadis* fame, and the engineer Gabriel Narutowicz, assassinated in 1922 two days after taking office as President.

Next to the cathedral stands the unassuming **Jesuit Church of the Gracious Virgin Mary**.

The Jesuits began construction of their Warsaw outpost in 1609–26. The central location—close to both the castle and cathedral—is significant: as the spearhead of the Counter Reformation, the Jesuit Order came to enjoy a pre-eminent position at the court of King Zygmunt Vasa, setting the tone for religious affairs throughout the Vasa period. Their early Baroque church of St Mary suffered major destruction in 1944 and was rebuilt in 1950–73.

The plain interior of the church takes the form of an aisleless box covered by a tunnel vault with net-like stucco decoration typical of Polish vernacular architecture of the 17C. The well-lit chancel, with just a plain slab for an altar, contains a miraculous oval painting of the Gracious Virgin Mary, which, indeed, miraculously escaped wartime destruction. The north aisle has two chapels and a fragment of wall with remnants of the late Baroque tomb of Jan Tarło, the Palatine of Lublin. Figures from the tomb can be seen in the church crypts (entrance in front of the church) along with other architectural fragments discovered in the wartime rubble.

Walking down the narrow UL. DZIEKANIA, next to the cathedral, you will emerge onto **UL. KANONIA**, a charming triangular space, which served as the parish graveyard until 1780. From the 15C, the houses on the square were inhabited by the canons of the cathedral (hence the name). The three-storey, Neo-classical façades, some revealing earlier Gothic fragments, are post-war reconstructions. In the middle of the square stands a bronze bell (1646) designed by Daniel Tym, who also cast the statue on top of the Zygmunt Column (see p. 108). The gateway (south) leading to the castle area dates from the Vasa period. Above it is a covered passageway linking the castle with the cathedral (the next fragment crosses ul. Dziekania), which was built in 1620 after an attempt on the king's life as he was walking to mass.

> The would-be assassin, Michał Piekarski, was hanged from the gallows on a square near the intersection of today's ul. Piekarska and ul. Rycerska. During the 16C–17C, the square came to be known as *piekiełko* (little hell) after the scores of witches, heretics and criminals executed here, but also perhaps because it was the only part of the city where brothels were allowed.

Either walk north along UL. JEZUICKA to the Old Market Square, or return to the west front of the cathedral. From here a passageway leads through to **UL. PIWNA**, the longest street in the Old Town, running parallel to ul. Świętojańska, with small two- and three-bay houses enlivened by rusticated doorways. At No. 9/11 stands the former Augustinian **Church of St Martin**.

> Founded in 1356, the monastery was used as a base by the Augustinian monks on their missions to Christianise the pagan Lithuanian and Ruthenian tribes to the north and east of Warsaw. The church was thoroughly remodelled in 1631–36, and then again in 1744–64, when Karol Bay added the Baroque façade and the Gothic appearance was completely lost.

The only remnant from the Gothic period is the square brick base of the tower (left). A passageway at its foot leads through a vaulted vestibule to a modest arcaded courtyard, with the Baroque monastery buildings clustered around it. Best is the church façade with a huge broken semicircle for a pediment, great half inset columns, and convex side bays heightening the undulating effect.

At the corner of ul. Piwna and **UL. ZAPIECEK** is the **Zapiecek Gallery of Contemporary Art** (open Mon–Fri 10.00–20.00, Sat 11.00–16.00), which has frequent exhibitions by modern Polish artists, but no permanent displays. The gallery is one of Warsaw's best-known art shops, offering an abundant and varied collection of paintings, ceramics, jewellery, sculpture, tapestry, graphics and glass. From here, continue to the Old Town Square (Rynek Starego Miasta).

Old Town Square

Laid out in the Middle Ages, the **Old Town Square** (90m x 73m) was for centuries the focal point of life in the city. Due to frequent fires, Duke Bolesław IV issued a ban on wooden construction, and by the turn of the 15C new brick tenement houses, with pointed-arch portals and decorative arcades or friezes of moulded brick, had begun to appear on the square. In the centre stood a two-storey Gothic Town Hall (1429), finally demolished in 1817. It was surrounded on all sides by wooden market stalls, which Tylman van Gameren redesigned in 1701, to make them more decorative. Another fire in 1607 destroyed most of the existing houses. Those one sees today date primarily from the 17C, when wealthy burghers put up new residences with richly decorated, colourful façades and opulent interiors. With the exodus of Warsaw's élite to the new city suburbs from the late 18C onwards, the square gradually lost its exclusivity and fell into disrepair. Major improvements began in 1911, when the market was removed, the square paved, and the houses renovated. During the First World War the sides acquired their present names—Zakrzewski, Barss, Kołłątaj, Dekert—after famous personages of Enlightenment Warsaw. Later, in 1928, the façades of the buildings were given painted decoration by leading artists of the day, though the Second World War reduced all this fine work to rubble. Reconstruction (1949–53) was carried out with a meticulous, almost fanatical zeal, and today the square rivals ul. Krakowskie Przedmieście as the restorers' showpiece. The buildings were rebuilt to reflect their pre-war state, though the façades have new murals and sgraffito, as well as a number of modern decorative features. The sides of the square are described in ascending order of importance, with only the more significant houses mentioned.

South side (Zakrzewski)

Going from west to east, first is the **Lion House** (No. 13) at the corner of **ul. Świętojańska**, so called after the gilded Rococo lion at the second floor level. Originally 15C, it was remodelled c 1669, and a Renaissance parapet was added. Notice the sgraffito sun-dial on the wall facing ul. Zapiecek (where pigeon fairs were held in the 19C). The appropriately named **Golden House** at No. 7 (15C) has gilded window frames dating from the 17C when it was rebuilt by the owner, Stanisław Baryczka, the town mayor. Look for his crest and initials in the grate within the rusticated stone portal.

East side (Barss)

The 15C **Burbach House** at No. 2 was rebuilt after a fire in 1626, when the present portal and the delightful second floor oriel window (facing ul. Celna) were added. Jesuits from Vilnius made it their seat in 1752, remodelling the façade and the interiors. It currently houses a **gallery** displaying work by young artists (**open** 11.00–18.00, Sun 13.00–18.00, closed Mon).

Take a small detour along **UL. CELNA**, which runs southeast off the square towards the river. In the Middle Ages the street was known as ul. Gnojowa (Dung St), as it led to a rubbish dump beyond the city walls, through the Dung Gate (demolished in 1838). Note the interesting **house** at the corner of ul. Brzozowa. The elevation facing ul. Celna combines fragments of three Gothic buildings merged in the 17C. The carriage gateway is framed by a Gothic pointed arch—probably part of a medieval granary—and has a passageway that was once a street running along the inside of the city walls. Slightly further on a block of exposed brick indicates the position of the former Dung Gate. The elevation facing ul. Brzozowa is pure Baroque, with cornices framing three long niches. **UL. BRZOZOWA** was once lined with granaries owned by rich Warsaw merchants. Examples can be seen at **Nos 12, 22 and 37**, where characteristically large gables testify to the buildings' former function. Return to the terrace by ul. Celna, which offers a panoramic view over the right bank of the Vistula.

The rhythm of narrow houses along the Barss side is broken by the four bays of the 17C **Orlemus House** (No. 18), whose Neo-classical façade sports a triangular pediment—the only building on the square to have one. At ground level there are two portals with rusticated jambs. Together with the adjoining Balcer House (No. 20; see below), the Orlemus accommodates a **Museum of Literature** (**open** Mon, Tues, Fri 10.00–15.00, Wed, Thur 11.00–18.00, Sun 11.00–

17.00) with a display devoted to famous Polish writers, particularly Mickiewicz and the Romantic period. The 15C **Balcer House** is interesting for its 17C stone portal, which was superimposed onto a Gothic arcade (the edges of which are just visible). The owner's crest is on the keystone. In the hallway a Gothic niche with three pointed arcades and fragments of painting have been preserved.

Leading off the northeast corner of the square is the picturesque UL. KAMIENNE SCHODKI—a long flight of stone steps (1780) descending down towards the Vistula.

North side (Dekert)

All the houses along the Dekert side were completely burnt out during the Second World War, but the façades, with their 17C stone portals, window framings and decoration, have survived.

The interiors of the eight tenement houses along the Dekert side were rebuilt to collectively house the **Warsaw Historical Museum** (open Tues, Thur 12.00–19.00, Wed, Fri–Sat 10.00–15.30, Sun 10.30–16.30; entrance at No. 42). The tour is a long one, covering approximately 60 rooms of varying quality, and charting the history of Warsaw from earliest times to the present day. More interesting than the exhibits are the interiors themselves. Some of the rooms have been reconstructed to reflect their 17C appearance and function, including a goldsmith's workshop, a printing shop, and a bourgeois room. The display is partly labelled in English. At the back of No. 42 a small cinema shows a daily film (except Sun) of the devastation of Warsaw during the Second World War and post-war reconstruction (ask at the reception for details and times).

The 15C **Falkiewicz House** at No. 28 was remodelled in early Baroque style in 1643, as shown by the date (hardly visible) inscribed on the parapet wall. Next to it, and on the keystone of the portal, are the initials SF (Stanisław Falkiewicz) and the Falkiewicz family crest. The parapet itself is topped with Vasa-style decoration. Two doors down is the **Baryczka House** (No. 32), one of the best examples of a 17C patrician house in the city. It was remodelled in 1629–33 by the then owner, Wojciech Baryczka, purveyor of oats to the royal stables. Many original (17C) elements have been retained, notably the finialled and bobbled parapet wall (Mannerist), the main portal replete with sculpted pine cones, rosettes and angel heads, and the interiors (part of the museum), with low vaulted rooms sporting decorative stucco ribs and bosses, a double window bisected by a Tuscan column, and a splendid wooden stairway rich in sculptural elements. Like its neighbour, the **Kleinpoldt House** at No. 34 was remodelled in the 17C in early Baroque style, as indicated by the date on the portal (1620). The house is unique for its original wooden beamed ceilings with painted decoration, the only surviving examples in the Old Town (visible in the museum). **No. 36** (15C) is named after the Moor's head (a copy) looking out from a niche in the façade and symbolising the slave trade, the occupation of the building's former owner—Jakub Gianotti—a wealthy merchant and town mayor. The façade, conspicuous for its sgraffito, rises to a rooftop pavilion (17C).

From the northwest corner of the square you may want to take a short detour along UL. WĄSKI DUNAJ. The house at **No. 8**, closing ul. Piwna, has a green façade decorated with rosettes and angels. It is topped by a decorative parapet wall (Mannerist, c 1625) with heads and mythical creatures. Next door stands the 17C **Shoemakers' House** (No. 10), presently owned by the Leather Crafts

Guild and accommodating a small but unique **Museum of Leather Crafts** (**open** Thur–Sat 10.00–15.00). The exhibits (mainly 18C–19C) in the two-room display include the furnishings of a shoemaker's workshop and selected footwear of the Polish nobility. Just around the corner you emerge onto a picturesque mews (UL. SZEROKI DUNAJ), the site of a 17C market selling salted fish and meat (hence the **Butcher's Gate**, c 1632—part of the city walls—at the far end). The 18C house at **No. 5** bears a commemorative plaque to its former owner, the shoemaker Jan Kiliński (see below). You might try the pricey but good *Rycerska* restaurant at No. 11, which offers traditional Polish fare.

West side (Kołłątaj)

St Anne's House, one of the best in the Old Town, was built c 1300 to accommodate the town mayor. Late Gothic remodelling resulted in the addition of decorative niches with pointed arches, today visible from ul. Wąski Dunaj, and a 17C oriel window. The frontage facing the square incorporates a 16C figure of St Anne (with Mary and the Baby Jesus) in a corner niche set into the buttress. The decoration of the façade is mainly late Renaissance (after 1635), with scrolled friezes on the former parapet wall, a gilded doorway (similar to the ones at Nos 32 and 34), gilded window tops, stone detailing, and bands of sgraffito separating the storeys.

From 1810 until 1945, the **Fukier House** at No. 27 was home to a famous tavern and Hungarian wine cellar run by the Fukier family, descended from the famous German banking family of Fugger. The building is originally 16C, though the façade was designed by S.B. Zug in 1782 and reconstructed after the war. Notice the delicate, gilded stucco (medallions, flowers, grapes) and the pediments over the windows. The cellars accommodate the excellent *Fukier* restaurant and wine bar within a stylised interior. The 15C **Wilczek House** at No. 21 is noted for its curious Gothic doorway, with its arch superimposed on an earlier one. Inside is another good restaurant, owned by the Gessler chain.

Leave the Old Town Square from its northwest corner along UL. NOWOMIEJSKA. You will soon arrive at the 16C **Barbican**, adjoined by fragments of the medieval city walls, which mark the limits of the Old Town proper.

> The **city walls** were constructed in stages from the mid-14C onwards. The first (inner) wall enclosed an area of 8.5ha. As weapons technology changed, so a new outer wall, with loopholes and semicircular turrets for firearms, was raised in the mid-15C. Between the walls was a dry moat and beyond the outer wall a moat proper. The last addition to the fortifications was the Barbican (1548), built to defend the adjacent New Town Gate. From the mid-18C, the city walls were gradually dismantled and incorporated into houses, while the towers were converted for use as storehouses or workshops. During wartime destruction fragments of the walls were exposed, and later reconstructed.

Unlike its contemporary in Kraków, the Warsaw Barbican had all but vanished by the 19C. Reconstruction did not take place until after the Second World War. The hollowed out round tower is topped with a parapet and inner and outer walkways. On each side are two three-storey towers supported by the buttresses of the arcaded bridge across the moat. The towers, walkways and many loopholes allowed the Barbican to be defended from all sides, making it a formidable piece of military technology.

To the left and right of the Barbican stretch the city walls. Going east (right) along the former sentry-walk you will come to the **Marshal Tower** (25m), of which only part of the lower storey remains. Perched on the edge of a cliff, the tower originally served as a lookout post, later as a prison (16C–17C). The **Mermaid Statue** (1855) was moved here from the Old Town Square in 1928. A fine view extends out across the Vistula to the district of PRAGA. Looking down and to your left, notice the building at the junction of UL. BOLEŚĆ and UL. RYBAKI (the last one before the boulevard). This is the former **Bridge Gate** (c 1573), so called because the road on which it stands formerly led to the first brick bridge across the Vistula (destroyed by floods in 1603). In the 18C, after the Gunpowder Tower (see below) had fallen into disuse, the Bridge Gate was expanded to contain a powder magazine. It was later converted into a prison (1769), and then rebuilt in Baroque-Classical style by Stanisław Zawadzki in 1778. The building currently houses a theatre and gallery.

Following the moat west of the Barbican you skirt the Old Town back to pl. Zamkowy. First along is the **Gunpowder Tower** with a conical brick dome. Adjoining both the inner and outer walls you will notice traces of numerous other towers. Just beyond the intersection with ul. Wąski Dunaj are the free-standing walls of the Gothic **Knight's Tower**, whose loopholes were bricked up when it was turned into a tenement house during the 17C. The modern house at the corner of ul. Piekarska (No. 20) is home to a small **Museum of Artistic and Precision Handicraft** (open Mon, Wed–Thur 10.00–15.00) with items, the oldest dating from the 16C, produced by various city guilds. The highlights include a collection of clocks and jewelry, as well as some excellent goldwork. Slightly further west (by PL. KILIŃSKIEGO) stands a bronze **Monument to Jan Kiliński** (1760–1819), which shows him defiantly wielding a sabre.

> **Jan Kiliński**, a local cobbler, is remembered for his role during the abortive Kościuszko Uprising (see p. 51). The revolt was directed against Russia and Prussia, who had annexed most of Poland under the Second Partition (1793). On 17 April 1794, Kiliński managed to rouse the inhabitants of the Old Town to storm the residence of the Russian ambassador, Igelström, on ul. Podwale (No. 10). The Russian occupiers were promptly expelled from the city, leaving 4000 dead on the streets. Unveiled in 1936, the monument originally stood on pl. Krasińskich. The Nazis, disturbed by the monument's patriotic connotations, moved it to the cellars of the National Museum in 1942. On the following day, graffiti appeared on the walls of the museum: 'People of Warsaw, I'm in here!—Jan Kiliński'.

Continue along the dry moat back to pl. Zamkowy, passing one of the oldest fragments of the city walls with characteristic Gothic arcades, now filled with hundreds of plaques and crosses. By the square are remnants of a Gothic bridge spanning the moat, discovered during excavation work in 1977.

Walk Two ~ The New Town (Nowe Miasto)

Walking north along UL. NOWOMIEJSKA from the Barbican (see p. 113), you enter Warsaw's **New Town**. In contrast to its richer neighbour—very much the restorer's showpiece with its pastel-coloured buildings and fairy tale Gothic—

the New Town is a more modest affair. In summer, when tourists flock to see the castle and its environs, the churches, squares, and quiet back streets of the New Town come as welcome relief from the noise and crowds.

On the left, at the junction with UL. DŁUGA, stands the unobtrusive **Paulite Church of the Holy Ghost** (No. 23), a twin-towered, early 18C basilica, preceded by steps and a figure of the Madonna (1863). To the south, it adjoins the oldest almshouse and hospital in Warsaw (1388), which the Paulites ran after they arrived from Częstochowa in 1662.

Next door (ul. Długa No. 7) is the more interesting **Raczyński Palace**, a pedimented Neo-classical edifice. Converted from a tenement house in 1701–04, the palace was rebuilt for the Raczyńskis some eighty years later by the renowned Warsaw architect, Jan Chrystian Kamsetzer, to whom the interiors, once unrivalled in beauty and opulence, are also attributed. The building currently houses the Main Historical Records Archive.

Continue north along ul. Nowomiejska, which merges with UL. FRETA. On the right (Nos 8–10) stands the Dominican **Church and Monastery of St Hyacinth** (visiting times: 05.45–08.45, 11.00–13.00, 17.00–19.00), whose bland Baroque façade conceals a medieval chancel with star vaults and ogival windows, but only a slab for an altar. The main building, modelled on St John's in the Old Town (see p. 108), was built in 1614–38, with the late Baroque bell tower being added in 1753. Adjacent to the long, cross-vaulted nave (north) is the small Kotowski Chapel topped by a dome. Designed in 1691–94 by the ubiquitous Tylman van Gameren, the chapel contains the Gameren family crypt.

The Baroque-Classical **Samson House** (1771) at No. 5 was once inhabited by the German Romantic author, composer and artist, E.T.A. Hoffmann (1776–1822). Bas reliefs of *Samson and the Lion* and *Delilah Shearing Samson's Locks* adorn the façade. Inside is the small **Museum of Asia and the Pacific** (**open** Tues–Sun 11.00–17.00) with a gallery of Asian art.

S.B. Zug designed the house at No. 16 (1770–80), the birthplace of Maria Curie-Skłodowska (1867), who discovered the elements radium and polonium,

---

Maria Curie

Maria Curie née Skłodowska, is without doubt the best known woman-scientist in history. As a child she displayed exceptional intellectual aptitude, but being born in Warsaw—at that time a provincial city of the Russian Empire, subjected to harsh repression in the aftermath of the January Uprising—Skłodowska had to go abroad in order to study. In Paris she met several eminent French physicists and chemists, among them Pierre Curie, 8 years her senior, whom she married. Working together in an unheated shed provided by the Institute of Physics and Chemistry in Paris, the Curies processed over a ton of raw material derived from uranium ore, specially imported from a mine in Czechoslovakia, in order to extract from it two hitherto unknown elements: polonium and radium. For their research into radioactivity they received the Nobel Prize in 1903 (with Henri Becquerel). Marie was awarded the prize a second time in 1911, for the isolation of pure radium. She died in 1934 of leukaemia caused by exposure to radioactivity. A year later, her daughter Irène and her husband Frédéric Joliot won the third Nobel Prize in the family for their work in artificial radioactivity.

and was twice awarded a Nobel Prize, one for physics (1903), the other for chemistry (1911). Predictably, the house has been converted into a **Maria Curie Museum** (open Tues–Sat 10.00–16.30, Sun 10.00–14.30). The exhibits are marked in English.

The quiet and irregular NEW TOWN SQUARE (Rynek Nowego Miasta) was laid out in the 14C, but post-war reconstruction saw it return to its late 18C appearance. By 1955, all the houses around it had been rebuilt in mock Neo-classical style, their façades decorated with modern sgraffito and murals. A town hall once stood in the middle, but this was demolished in the early 19C, when many historic buildings all over Poland succumbed to the 'modernising' zeal of city planners. Today, the New Town Square may seem to lack opulence and colour, but it preserves a discreet charm. The vegetarian *Nowe Miasto* restaurant in the centre is an excellent place to sit outside in summer and absorb the atmosphere of the square.

The east side of the square is graced by the finest single building in the New Town: the ***Convent and Church of the Benedictine Nuns of the Holy Sacrament**.

> The Nuns of the Holy Sacrament arrived from France in 1687. Their church of St Kazimierz was begun by Jan Sobieski's wife, Maria Kazimiera, as an offering for her husband's historic victory against the Ottoman Turks at Vienna in 1683. She commissioned Tylman van Gameren, who took five years to complete the work (1688–92), achieving one of the finest examples of Polish Baroque. The exterior was rebuilt in Baroque style after the war; the interiors are modern.

The church takes the form of a central octagon on a Greek cruciform plan with four arms of different sizes. Above rises a grand dome topped by a stone windowed lantern. The west arm projects outwards to a pediment supported on pilasters. Inside, the highlight is the late Baroque funerary chapel of Maria Karolina Sobieska de Bouillon (Sobieski's granddaughter, the last member of the family line), designed by Lorenzo Mattielli in 1746. The sarcophagus bears the Sobieski coat of arms and an armorial cartouche of the Dukes de Bouillon. Do not miss the curious high altar with a glass oval surrounded by white plaster.

From the square follow UL. PIESZA, passing the tiny church of St Benon. Opposite the exit of ul. Piesza is the ***Parish Church of the Virgin Mary**, whose fully preserved medieval bulk is a real surprise—a sudden burst of Mazovian Gothic. Founded as early as 1411 by the Mazovian Duke Janusz, the church is one of Warsaw's oldest. Gothic star vaults, ogival windows and murals were discovered during post-war reconstruction, though most of the original furnishings have been lost. From the terrace behind the church there is a **fine view** onto the Vistula boulevard and the district of Praga across the river.

Continue west along UL. KOŚCIELNA past the Franciscan church and monastery, and turn right into UL. ZAKROCZYMSKA. At No. 6 is the elegant **Sapiecha Palace**, built for Jan Fryderyck Sapiecha, chancellor of the Grand Duchy of Lithuania. The long central block, its pediment adorned with trophies, was designed in 1731–34 by Johann Sigismund Deybel. The building was remodelled after 1817 for use as an army barracks. It currently houses the Cambridge School of English and a school for deaf children.

Approximately 1km further north, beyond Traugutta Park, is a complex of decaying fortifications known as the **Citadel**, a giant fortress built by Czar Nicholas I to punish Warsaw for its part in the November Uprising of 1831. The site is best reached from the Vistula boulevard, where steps lead up the hill to the Gate of Executions, where prisoners were shot or hanged. A path continues to the main prison complex, a singularly grim and forbidding place, with a **Museum of the Independence Movement** inside (open Wed–Sun 09.00–16.00). Wandering through the gloomy labyrinth of corridors, you may visit the cells where the greatest Polish insurgents and revolutionaries of the 19C were incarcerated. The walls carry harrowing photographs and drawings, as well as descriptions of the unspeakable acts of torture that took place within.

Walk Three ~ The Royal Way

To the south of pl. Zamkowy (see p. 108) stretches UL. KRAKOWSKIE PRZEDMIEŚCIE, a long thoroughfare running parallel to the river.

When King Zygmunt Vasa moved the royal court to Warsaw in 1596, magnates and church dignitaries began to line the street with their palaces and mansions, the finest of which had beautiful gardens cascading down the escarpment towards the Vistula. Together with its southerly extension—UL. NOWY ŚWIAT (New World St)—Krakowskie Przedmieście later came to be known as the Royal Way, as it linked the monarch's official and private residences: the castle in the Old Town to the north, and the palaces at Łazienki (see p. 129) and Wilanów (see p. 145) to the south. On coronation days, the royal cortège would pass along the street under triumphal arches to make its ceremonial entry into the city proper.

During the 19C the character of the Royal Way somewhat changed: royal processions gave way to patriotic marches and demonstrations against the Russian occupiers, while further south, the 18C manors and stately homes lining ul. Nowy Świat were replaced with Neo-classical tenement houses inhabited by the rising bourgeois community. Both ul. Krakowskie Przedmieście and Nowy Świat suffered badly during the Second World War. Reconstruction of the latter preserved only the 19C façades, with the interiors being completely refurbished and modernised. The result is that, for all its elegance, ul. Nowy Świat has a slightly counterfeit air. Krakowskie Przedmieście is far better, with more variety and quirks, but here too one has to be content with admiring the exteriors only, as most of the palaces are used by the government and state administration, and are consequently inaccessible.

The walk begins at the misleadingly named **Canaletto Gallery** (after Bernardo Bellotto 'Canaletto', not his more famous uncle), which stands at the corner of pl. Zamkowy and Krakowskie Przedmieście (open 10.00–16.00). A few doors down is the elegant **Prażmowski House** (No. 87) with a Rococo façade executed by Giacopo Fontana in 1745. Reconstructed after the war, it now accommodates the Polish Writers' Union and *Literacka café*. The last building on the right before ul. Miodowa is the **Roessler and Hurtig Building** (No. 79) designed by S.B. Zug in 1785, almost an apartment block, with a long row of Doric columns along the bottom and semicircles above.

You may take a short detour along ul. Miodowa and then left into a quiet lane

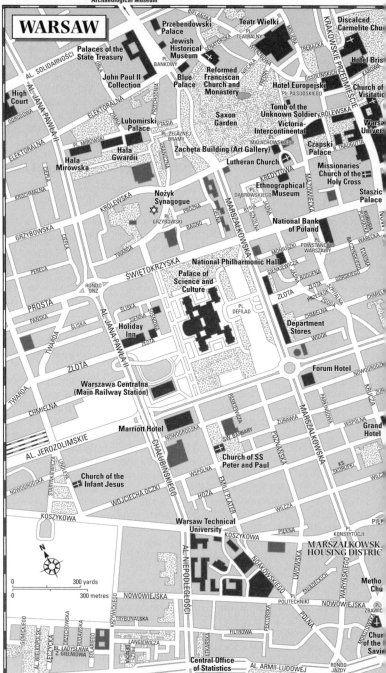

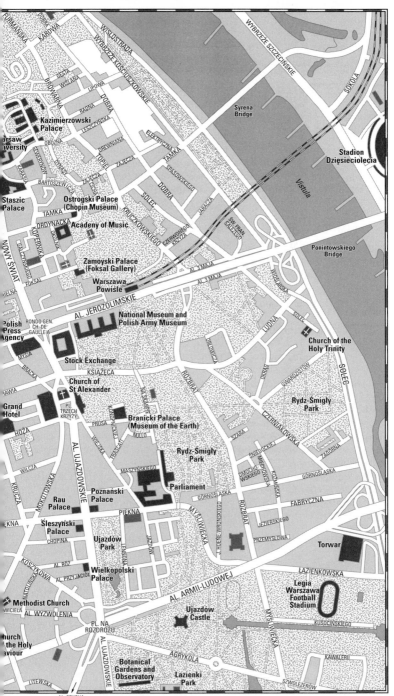

(ul. Kozia) by the Irish pub. At No. 10 on the right is a small **Museum of Cari-cature** (**open** Tues–Fri 11.00–17.00, Sat–Sun 12.00–17.00) exhibiting numerous sketches, cartoons and drawings satirising Poland's political leaders.

St Anne's Church

Returning to ul. Krakowskie Przedmieście you will emerge opposite the striking white plaster façade of **St Anne's Church* (No. 68), one of the city's most picturesque landmarks.

> Three women by the name of Anne (Anna) played an instrumental role in erecting the church that bears their name. The original, late Gothic structure was funded in 1454 by Anna, Duchess of Mazovia. Anna Radziwiłł expanded the body of the church in 1518–33, and in 1578 her Jagiellon namesake funded the detached square belfry to the left of the façade. After the Swedish invasion the body was remodelled with the addition of high Baroque chapels (1660–67). In the late 18C, Piotr Aigner added the Neo-classical façade.

Gothic remnants are still discernible in the north portal, chancel, and monastery (see below). The superbly ornate façade has statues of the four evangelists in niches, attributed to Giacopo Monaldi, four Corinthian columns and two pilasters below a huge pediment, with the initials of Stanisław August Poniatowski inscribed in the tympanum. The belfry, redesigned by Aigner in 1820–21, accommodates a shop and the HQ of the Katyń Committee (see p. 57).

The Baroque **interior** is dominated by illusionist paintings (Rococo, 1753) depicting scenes from the life of St Anne, on the vaults, and scenes from the life of Władysław on the walls of the Gielniów Chapel (see below). The high altar, in the form of an arcade on columns, frames a 17C painting of *St Anne, the Virgin and Jesus*, further into the chancel. Two chapels abut the nave to the north: the Our Lady of Loreto Chapel (H. Marconi, 1837), restored in 1957 by the accomplished post-war architect, Barbara Brukalska, and the square-domed Chapel of the Blessed Władysław of Gielniów (d. 1505), an early Baroque design of 1620. The relics of the Blessed Władysław, a composer credited with introducing folk rhythmns and melodies into Polish medieval song, and later a patron of Warsaw after beatification in 1753, are contained in the Rococo altar.

The long grey building (No. 66) adjoining St Anne's to the south is a wing of the former Bernardine monastery, which Piotr Aigner converted into a Neo-classical guardhouse in 1818. Through the cloister is the monastery's older, Gothic wing (1513–33), but only fragments remain.

Continue along the left side of ul. Krakowskie Przedmieście. Crossing ul. Bednarska you will come to the Neo-classical **Deanery** (No. 56), entered through a huge niche. It was built for the Dean of the Warsaw Chapter in 1780–84. A plaque on the façade commemorates Chopin's mentor, J. Elsner. Level with the Deanery, on the green, stands an august **Monument to Mickie-wicz**, unveiled in 1898 on the centenary of the poet's birth.

Still on the left, at No. 52/54, stands the impressive **Discalced Carmelite Church of the Assumption*, one of the few city buildings to escape wartime destruction. The Baroque interior (1661–1701) is overshadowed by the excellent, finely wrought façade—a rare example of genuine Neo-classicism in Poland—designed by Ephraim Schröger in 1761–83. Figures of St Teresa and St

John stand between the pairs of columns on the upper storey, where a gallery extends left and right towards two sturdy obelisks erected in place of towers. The crowning consists of a green orb (the earth) held in the coils of a serpent with an apple in its mouth (Sin) and surmounted by a chalice containing the Host (Good Triumphant). Inside, most noteworthy are Gameren's high altar (1687), framed in free-standing columns and statues, with a sculptural group representing the Nuptials of the Virgin Mary (late Baroque) and a 15C icon of the Madonna of the Rosary. There are plans to open an archdiocesan museum in the former monastery buildings opposite the church.

The political traditions of the grand (but inaccessible) *__Namiestnikowski Palace__ (No. 46/48, left) date from the early 19C, when Piotr Aigner redesigned the original Baroque building as a sumptuous residence for the Russian governor-general of the Congress Kingdom. Aigner remodelled the front elevation in Neo-classical style, extended the wings up to the road, and refurbished the first and second floor interiors. Before the gate stands a bronze equestrian statue (a copy) of Józef Poniatowski (1763–1813), Commander-in-Chief of the Polish Army during the Duchy of Warsaw, who is shown heroically astride his mare. The Danish sculptor Bertel Thorvaldsen designed the original statue in 1832, modelling it on the figure of Marcus Aurelius on the Roman Capitol. After the Second World War, the palace reassumed a political function as the seat of the Council of Ministers. The Warsaw Pact was signed here in 1955, as were the 'Round Table' agreements between the opposition and the authorities in 1989 (see p. 62). Five years after the fall of Communism the government moved out to make way for President Wałęsa, and the palace is now the official residence of Polish heads of state.

Across ul. Krakowskie Przedmieście, at No. 15, stands the 18C __Czartoryski Palace__, also known as the Potocki Palace with a columned portico designed by Jan Chrystian Kamsetzer in the 1780s. Reconstructed after the war, the building is currently occupied by the Ministry of Art and Culture. Exhibitions of modern art are held in the small __Kordegarda__ (guardhouse) gallery (c 1770, S.B. Zug) by the wrought iron entrance gates (__open__ 10.00–18.00).

Further down ul. Krakowskie Przedmieście are two hotels of historical interest: the *Europejski* (No. 13, right), the oldest modern hotel in Warsaw, designed by Henryk Marconi in 1854–55 (reconstructed after 1945), and the Neo-Renaissance *Bristol* (No. 42/44), across the street, the work of Marconi's son Władysław (1899–1901). The *Bristol* was formerly owned by pianist and inter-war statesman Ignacy Paderewski (1860–1941), though even he could not save the exquisite fin-de-siècle interiors from eradication during the 1930s. Today, after lengthy refurbishment carried out by the Trusthouse Forte chain, the *Bristol* is once again unrivalled as the city's plushest (and most expensive) hotel.

Skirting the green, you will reach the *__Church of the Nuns of the Visitation__ (No. 34, left), arguably the best Baroque church in Warsaw, and one of the few to survive the war undamaged.

> The Visitation Nuns were brought to Poland in 1654 by the wife of King Jan Kazimierz, Maria Gonzaga. The first chapel and convent were razed to the ground during the Swedish Deluge (see p. 49), and it was not until 1727 that work began on a new church, supervised by the architect Karol Bay, who took

six years to complete the small, three-span nave with aisles in the form of arcaded chapels. Ephraim Schröger finished the façade and Rococo interior in 1762. In the 19C, Chopin played the organ here for school services.

The splendid west front has two equal storeys of full round columns and a pilastered summit topped by angels. All the sculptures, notably figures of St Augustine and Francis of Sales on the second level, are by Jan Jerzy Plersch. Above a window are emblems of the royal couple (the sheaf of the Vasas and the eagle of the Gonzagas). There is more Rococo sculpture by Plersch inside, including *God the Father* over the high altar and a pulpit in the shape of a boat (1754–57). The high altar itself is by Schröger and includes a mid-18C painting of the *Visitation of Our Lady*, as well as a 17C French ebony tabernacle.

Past the Visitant church is a group of buildings forming the campus of **Warsaw University**.

Warsaw University

The establishment of Warsaw University in 1818 was made possible thanks to the tireless effort of two leading figures of Enlightenment Warsaw: Stanisław Kostka Potocki and Stanisław Staszic. Closed by the Czar in 1831 in retribution for the November Uprising, the University was reopened in 1869 under the strict control of the Russian authorities. All lectures and seminars were conducted in Russian, which predictably led to a mass student boycott. The Imperial University survived until 1914, and its Polish-speaking counterpart was revived a year later. During the Second World War, all educational activity, with the exception of vocational schooling, was treated as a capital offence. At great risk, some 300 professors continued teaching courses in private apartments (the legendary 'Flying University'), or, secretly, in vocational schools. Heavily bombed and looted, the University buildings were rebuilt after the war.

As in the West, 1968 became a year of protest and upheaval at the universities. The background to the street demonstrations, sit-ins and gatherings was quite different, though. Today most historians agree that the March Events (see p. 60) were deliberately caused by a group within the Communist party that wanted to oust Gomułka, then First Secretary. Police agents had little difficulty in provoking applause at poignant moments during performances of Mickiewicz's *Forefathers' Eve*, bringing out the anti-Russian, pro-independence import of the 19C play. When further performances of the play were banned, people took to the streets, with banners castigating the censor's ruling. The police responded with violence against the demonstrators in Warsaw, Kraków, Gdańsk and other cities. Some university departments were dissolved, thousands of students were expelled, arrested, or drafted into the army; professors were dismissed (including the sociologist Zygmunt Bauman, and the philosopher Leszek Kołakowski). To fill the vacancies, the authorities promoted loyal but under-qualified graduates to the rank of associate-professor, derogatorily known thereafter as 'March professors'. A fierce anti-Semitic campaign was mounted by the Communist party, forcing the few remaining Polish Jews to flee the country (total emigration caused by the 1968 events is estimated at 20,000).

The Neo-classical **Tyszkiewicz Palace** (No. 32) dates from the late 18C, and houses a branch of the University Library, which has an extensive collection of graphic art.

> The core of the collection, comprising drawings by Polish, Italian, Dutch, Flemish and German artists, as well as a vast archive of architectural plans, was purchased from the royal estate of Stanisław August Poniatowski in 1818. Over half the collection was looted or destroyed by the Nazis. The losses included three original drawings by Albrecht Dürer and numerous sketches and ground plans by Tylman van Gameren. Today the collection numbers more than 30,000 items.

Two buildings flank the Neo-Baroque entrance gate (c 1900) to the grounds proper: on the left stands the Neo-Renaissance **Uruski Palace** (1844–47); on the right—the former **Hospital of St Roch** (1707).

Directly in front of you is the main building of the **University Library**. Most of the pre-1939 collection survived the war by being walled up in the cellars, though only 5 per cent of the manuscripts looted by the Nazis have been recovered. The library is flanked by two Neo-classical outbuildings (1815–20); Chopin lived in the one to the south of it from 1817 to 1827. Behind the library stands the more interesting **Kazimierzowski Palace** (No. 26/28), where the University's main administrative offices are located. Its present crisp pilastered shape was planned by the royal architects Pöppelmann and Jauch in 1732.

> During 1765–95, the College of Chivalry, established by Stanisław August Poniatowski was based here. Headed from 1772 by the Englishman John Lind, it was the first entirely secular state-run college, training military and administrative cadres. Among its students was Tadeusz Kościuszko (see p. 51). After a fire in 1814 the palace interiors were remodelled to house the University's central library, and Neo-classical elements were added to the façade, notably Wacław Ritschel's four-columned portico (1824). Since the war, the building has been reconstructed to reflect its appearance of 1830.

Across ul. Krakowskie Przedmieście stands the late Baroque **Czapski Palace** (1752–65) at the far end of an elongated courtyard. The modern interiors are now used by the Academy of Fine Arts. Before the entrance is a bronze copy (1950) of a 15C statue by Verrocchio depicting the Venetian mercenary soldier Colleoni. Of greater interest are the palace's Neo-classical wings (c 1792, Jan Chrystian Kamsetzer). Chopin's family inhabited rooms in the left (south) wing from 1827, just prior to the composer's permanent exile to France. Their stay is commemorated by a plaque on the wall facing the street. You can see the **Salon of Chopin's Parents** (open Mon–Fri 10.00–14.00) with its period furniture and mementoes, on the second floor.

The gate at street level, topped with eagles, is also attributed to Kamsetzer.

Continuing along the right side of ul. Krakowskie Przedmieście you will reach No. 3, the ***Missionaries' Church of the Holy Cross** (1682–96, Giuseppe Simone Bellotti). The twin-tower façade (mid-18C, Giuseppe and Giacopo Fontana) conceals a broad, light nave, flanked by deep chapels between the massive internal buttresses. A shallow cap serves in place of the intended dome above the crossing. Most of the furniture dates from the 18C, though the richly gilded high altar, adorned by a modern *Crucifixion*, is a copy. The original (1700) was destroyed during the war. Go right to the south transept, where there is an altar to St Felicissima (1704, Tylman van Gameren) surrounded by martyrs and blessed virgins. Next to the altar stands a funerary monument (1719–22) in black and white marble to the church's founder, Primate Radziejowski. **Chopin's heart**, which, in accordance with the composer's wishes, was brought to Poland after his death, rests inside an urn by one of the nave pillars (north). During the Warsaw Uprising (see p. 58) a group of civilians barricaded themselves inside the church, managing to withstand a Nazi siege for two weeks. The survivors were rounded up and used as human shields when German tanks advanced on Polish positions along ul. Nowy Świat.

Left along ul. Oboźna is the **Teatr Polski** (1913), with its rounded end bays and large foyer windows. If you wish to spend an evening in the company of Warsaw's Young and Upwardly Mobile, there is no better place than the popular *Harenda* bar across the street.

The south end of ul. Krakowskie Przedmieście is closed by the grandiose, Neo-classical **Staszic Palace** (ul. Nowy Świat No. 72), named after the writer and reformer Stanisław Staszic (1755–1826; see p. 82).

> Designed by Antonio Corazzi (1821–23), the palace was the first building in Poland to be designed specifically for academic purposes, in this case as the headquarters of the Society of Friends of Learning (1808), of which Staszic himself later became president. The Society was dissolved and its property confiscated in 1831 after the failure of the November Uprising. Later in the 19C the palace was remodelled to house a Russian grammar school. The original Neo-classical shape, except for the side projections, was finally restored during the 1920s. Reconstructed in 1947–49, the palace is now occupied by the Polish Academy of Sciences.

Corinthian pilasters and columns rise two storeys to griffins and the inscription 'Societas Scientiarum Varsoviensis', proclaiming the academic traditions of the building. Staszic also funded the **Monument to Copernicus** (1830, B. Thor-valdsen), which stands in front. The Nazis removed the monument during the war, after which it was discovered in the Silesian town of Nysa and returned to Warsaw.

Definitely worth the detour is the **Ostrogski (Gniński) Palace** at ul. Okólnik No. 1. Turn left off Nowy Świat into ul. Ordynacka and walk to the end of the street, passing the Academy of Music on your right. Perched on a large, built-up terrace above the east-west underpass, with a small park to the right, the Ostrogski Palace (1681–85) is one of Gameren's Warsaw masterpieces.

The **interiors**, boasting a variety of architectural styles, house the head-quarters of the Chopin Society and a **Chopin Museum** (open 1 Oct–30 April, Mon–Wed, Fri–Sat 10.00–14.00, Thur 12.00–18.00; 1 May–30 Sept, Mon, Wed, Fri 10.00–17.00, Sat–Sun 10.00–14.00, closed Tues). The tour is not enhanced by a poor-quality tape of polonaises and mazurkas played through loudspeakers. Beginning on the ground floor, the display comprises paintings and drawings on the subject of Chopin, most by modern artists. Upstairs is the highlight of the museum: the last piano to have been played by Chopin (1848). Concerts are occasionally held in the hall on the second floor (ask at reception for details). The Chopin Society also organises the renowned Chopin Piano Competition, held every five years.

Chopin Piano Competition

The competition, inaugurated in 1927 on the initiative of Jerzy Żurawlew, ranks among the most prestigious piano competitions in the world. Such celebrities as Wilhelm Backhaus, Arturo Benedetti-Michelangeli, Artur Rubinstein, Nadia Boulanger, and Martha Argerich have all sat on the jury. The list of prize-winners is no less impressive, and includes Vladimir Ashkenazy, Maurizio Pollini, Martha Argerich, Garrick Ohlsson, Mitsuko Uchida, and Krystian Zimerman. From its inception, the competition has inspired enormous interest and enthusiasm among audiences, who invariably follow the contest with bated breath and have their own favourites, often different from the jury's choice. Those who attended the awards ceremony in 1937 were so disappointed that Japan's Chieko Hara failed to win that they spontaneously had a whip-round and awarded their own prize. Such 'scandals' were to happen again. Years later, for instance, Martha Argerich resigned from the jury after Ivo Pogorelic failed to qualify for the finals.

Return to UL. NOWY ŚWIAT. Next left is the tree-lined ul. Foksal, actually a polonisation of London's 'Vauxhall', after the pleasure gardens that existed here (and in Vauxhall) in the 18C. Closing the street at the far end is the **Zamoyski Palace**, a Neo-Renaissance building designed by Leonard Marconi in 1878–79, now headquarters of the Polish Architects' Association. Exhibitions of contemporary art are held in the **Foksal Gallery** (open Mon–Fri 12.00–16.00), located in the palace's north wing (ground floor). For refreshments, try the *Foksal* café and restaurant to the right of the main entrance gate.

Continue down ul. Nowy Świat to the busy intersection with al. Jerozolimskie (Rondo Charles de Gaulle). Across it are two modern buildings of note: on the right, R. Świerczyński's essay in Functionalism (1931), now housing the Polish Press Agency and offices of the National Bank of Poland; and, on the left, the imposing former headquarters (1948–51) of the Polish United Workers' Party (Communist Party). Following the latter's dissolution in 1990, the building was, ironically, converted into a business centre housing the Stock Exchange, banks and offices.

National Museum

AL. JEROZOLIMSKIE (Jerusalem Avenue) proceeds west towards the central railway station, and east towards the Poniatowski bridge. The name of the street dates from the 18C, when it led to a Jewish colony on the outskirts of the city. Going left towards the bridge, do not miss the ****National Museum** (open Tues–Wed, Fri–Sun 10.00–16.00, Thur 11.00–18.00), whose treasures are contained within a daunting Functionalist edifice of the 1930s (No. 3). Though heavily pillaged during the Second World War, and only partly recovered after it, the collections comprise some of the best domestic and foreign art found in Poland.

Ground floor

The well-labelled display begins on the ground floor with a room of mediocre 19C self-portraits, shortly followed by the excellent **Gallery of Medieval Art** (12C–16C), with a rich and varied assemblage of altarpieces, mostly Gothic. The highlights include a polyptych from Grudziądz in Pomerania (c 1390) showing the *Death and Coronation of the Virgin* in the centrepiece and the *Birth and child-hood of Christ* in the wings, a painted *Pietà* from Tubądzin near Łódź (c 1450, anonymous), and a triptych from Opatówek near Kalisz (c 1460, Jan of Nysa) with a central scene of the *Virgin and Child flanked by SS Matthew and Adalbert*. Particularly good among the religious sculpture are the *Madonna* (c 1390, anonymous) from St Elizabeth's church in Wrocław, a striking example of the 'Beautiful' style (see p. 65), and the *Pietà* (c 1370, anonymous) from the abbey church in Lubiąż, Silesia.

The **Gallery of Ancient Art**, housed in a separate wing, has a valuable collection of items from Greece, the Roman Empire, Etruria and Egypt, as well as numerous finds made by Polish archaeologists in the Near East. The prize exhibits include an Egyptian papyrus (c 1300 BC), measuring 9.5 metres in length and containing verses from the *Book of the Dead*, and a collection of Greek amphorae from Attica, decorated with black and red figures.

The adjoining **Faras Collection**, the largest European display of Nubian culture, presents items discovered on a Polish archaeological expedition to Faras (ancient Pachoras) in the northern Sudan. The fine murals (8C–14C) depicting Old and New Testament scenes combined with images of Nubian dignitaries originate from the cathedral church in Faras. Other exhibits include architec-tural sculpture and painted ceramics (c 100 BC–9C), a group of Ethiopian crosses (14C–20C), and items of Coptic culture, such as fabrics (4C–11C), ceramics and papyrus. Most of these were found during a joint Polish-French archaeological expedition to Edfu in southern Egypt in 1936–38.

First floor

Upstairs, there is a good section on **Oriental Art**, including a valuable collection of Chinese porcelain from the Ming dynasty (1368–1643) and Japanese *ukiyo-e* woodcuts (18C–19C) by such artists as Hokusai, Kunisada and Harunobu. The most precious items in the Islamic art collection are Persian and Turkish fabrics (16C–19C), including some magnificent *kilimy*, or tapestries, originating mostly from the collections of the Potocki and Radziwiłł families. Fine examples of Polish fabrics can be seen in the **Gallery of Polish Decorative Art** on the same floor.

The **Gallery of European Art**, located in the east wing of the museum, concentrates on the 15C–18C, with French and Italian works displayed on the first floor and North European art (Dutch, Flemish and German) on the second. Much of the collection, numbering some 4000 items, was purchased by the Polish nobility on their travels abroad, later finding its way into the hands of the Polish state. Major works include Botticelli's *Madonna and Child*, Giovanni Bellini's *Mourning of Christ*, Tintoretto's *Portrait of a Venetian Admiral*, Cranach the Elder's *Adam and Eve*, Rubens's *Mary and Child*, Salomon van Ruysdael's *Road through Dunes*, and Gustave Courbet's *Landscape near Ornans*. The highlights of the accompanying graphic art section are etchings by Bruegel the Elder (*Hunting for Wild Rabbits*, c 1560), Callot (*The Temptation of St Anthony*, 1635) and Rembrandt (*Three Crosses*, c 1660).

Equally impressive is the **Gallery of Polish Painting**, which excels in its coverage of the 1870–1914 period, particularly the art of Young Poland (see p.

74), with all the leading figures represented. Major works include: H. Rodakowski's *Portrait of Leonia Blühdorn* (1870), J. Matejko's *Battle of Grunwald* (1878), which shows the famous medieval battle (see p. 417) between the joint Polish-Lithuanian armies and the Teutonic Knights (the huge canvas was recently lent to the National Museum in Vilnius), M. Gierymski's *Insurgent Patrol* (1873), a genre scene set during the January Uprising of 1863 (see p. 52), J. Chełmoński's *Storks* (1900), J. Stanisławski's *Musk Thistles in the Sun* (1895), W. Ślewiński's *Orphan from Poronin* (1906), S. Wyspiański's *Rose Bushes in Winter* (1899), O. Boznańska's *Grandma's Name Day* (1889), J. Malczewski's *Self-Portrait in Armour* (1914), F. Ruszczyc's *Earth* (1898), and W. Wojtkiewicz's *Circus* (1907). The earliest work in the collection is the *Battle of Orsza* (c1530, anonymous), an excellent Renaissance military painting which shows the Polish-Lithuanian armies defeating the Muscovites at Orsza on the Dnieper river in 1514. The extensive and rather tedious display of 17C–18C portraiture is enlivened by some fine coffin portraits from the Małopolska and Mazovia regions and M. Bacciarelli's allegorical painting of King Stanisław August Poniatowski holding an hourglass (1793). Not to be missed are the works of Poland's greatest Romantic painter, P. Michałowski, including *Parade in front of Napoleon* (1837) and *Portrait of a Country Boy* (1841). There is also a small graphic art section with some good watercolours, including J. Kossak's *In the Stable* (1866) and L. Wyczółkowski's *Rogalin in Winter* (1925).

Gallery of 20C Polish Art. This last section is housed in five rooms on the first floor. Due to lack of space, only a small portion of the 5,000 items in the collection are displayed, with frequent changes. Major works include: S. I. Witkiewicz's *Fairy Tale* (1933), T. Makowski's *Le Sabotier* (1930), Z. Wasilewski's *Feast* (1933), A. Zamoyski's *Femme Accroupie I* (1927), J. Cybis's *Still Life with Butterfly* (1931), W. Strzemiński's *Sun–Heart of the Day* (1948), A. Wróblewski's *Firing Squad* (1949), T. Brzozowski's *Props Room* (1952), J. Nowosielski's *Cellist* (1959), and T. Kantor's *Parasol and the Invisible* (1973). The museum also has a collection of contemporary graphic art, including works by Kandinsky (*Third Anniversary of the Kandinsky Society*, 1928), Dufy (*Horses in a Yard*, c 1927) and Picasso (*Portrait of a Woman in a Hat*, 1962).

The **Polish Army Museum** (open Wed–Sun 10.00–16.00), further down al. Jerozolimskie, is easily recognisable by its outdoor display of tanks, guns and aeroplanes. The 18 (reconstructed) halls trace the history of Polish warfare from the Piast period until 1945. Numerous weapons and armour (including a 16C Hungarian sabre belonging to Stefan Bathory), as well as uniforms, banners, orders and documents, are supplemented by military art, notably 19C equestrian paintings by Wojciech Kossak.

Walk Four ~ Southern Warsaw

Warsaw's main government district stretches to the south of ul. Nowy Świat, and has something of the affluent flavour of London's Westminster or Kensington. Grand mansions, today housing embassies and ministries, line the edge of the high Vistula riverbank, along which runs UJAZDÓW AVENUE (al. Ujazdowskie), one of the city's finest streets. Towards the river, extensive parkland merges with the Łazienki estate (see below), making this an ideal area for walks.

You should begin on PL. TRZECH KRZYŻY (Three Crosses' Square) at the northern end of al. Ujazdowskie. The square is dominated by the Neo-classical *Church of St Alexander (1818–25, Piotr Aigner), whose design was inspired by the Roman Pantheon. Partly destroyed in 1944, the church has been well restored to its original, central plan, with two large columned porticoes (north and south) preceded by steps. Inside, the dome is panelled with stuccoed flowers. The highlight, on the left, is an anonymous Baroque sculpture of Christ in the sepulchre, brought to Poland from Italy at the end of the 17C.

Facing the south side of the church is a **Statue of St John Nepomuk** (1756), with cross-topped columns either side marking the end of the Ujazdów calvary.

The Ujazdów Calvary

Laid out in 1731 for Augustus II, the Ujazdów calvary comprised some 30 wooden chapels symbolising the Way of the Cross, which lined the avenue (today's al. Ujazdowskie) leading from pl. Trzech Krzyży to the suburb of Ujazdów. While only scattered remnants of the calvary remain (the chapels were dismantled in 1770), al. Ujazdowskie has survived as a grand southerly extension of ul. Nowy Świat. The first villas were built along it in the 1830s, with the tenement houses near pl. Trzech Krzyży and the palaces beyond ul. Piękna appearing from the late 19C onwards.

From the south end of pl. Trzech Krzyży take UL. WIEJSKA to the charming columned rotunda of the *Sejm*, or **Polish Parliament** (Nos 4–8). Begun in 1925 by Kazimierz Skórewicz, the building is one of the better examples of the official 'Piłsudski' style prevalent in Poland after 1918 (the assembly chamber is **open** to the public, Sun–Thur 10.00–14.00, when parliament is not in session).

For a shortcut to Ujazdów Castle (see below), continue south along UL. JAZDÓW and cross the footbridge, passing a chequerboard of small wooden houses built by the Finns as war reparations after 1945. Alternatively, return to al. Ujazdowskie along ul. Matejki, whose exit faces the US Embassy (ul. Matejki 31). Many more fine embassy buildings, mostly late 19C, line al. Ujazdowskie to the south. Running parallel to the avenue between ul. Piękna and pl. Na Rozdrożu is the small **Ujazdów Park**, with an artificial hillock, pond and stream. A large **statue** of the pianist, composer and statesman Ignacy Paderewski (1985) stands by the main entrance. Paths converge at the *Ujazdów Castle**.

The estate is first mentioned in the 13C as a place where the Mazovian dukes kept their menageries. Work on the castle did not begin until 1624, when Zygmunt Vasa commissioned the Italian architect, Giovanni Trevano, to construct a royal suburban residence. Most of the sumptuous furnishings were pillaged by the Swedes, after which the castle passed to the Grand Marshal Lubomirski (1683). The present structure is one of many built on Lubomirski's estate by Tylman van Gameren. August II leased Ujazdów from the Lubomirskis at the beginning of the 18C in order to build a Versailles-style residence, but only the Piaseczyński canal, meant to be the main element of the menagerie garden, was ever completed. Around the turn of the 18C the castle served as a barracks, and later, until the Second World War, as a military hospital. The ruins were rebuilt according to Trevano's original design in the 1970s.

The castle is perched on a high terrace overlooking part of the Piaseczyński canal and a park landscaped in the early 20C. In the distance, to the left, notice the stadium of Legia Warszawa, a football club which inspires almost religious devotion and hostility in equal measure. To the right, beyond ul. Agrykola, stretches the Łazienki park (see below). The castle itself accommodates a **Centre for Modern Art** (open Tues–Sun 11.00–17.00), as well as a theatre, bookshop, library, audio-visual room, exhibition and conference halls. There is also a good restaurant (*Quchnia Artystyczna*) in chic surroundings with seating on the terrace in summer. Concerts are held in the main hall and annexe.

Returning to pl. Na Rozdrożu, you might want to take a short detour to No. 25 al. J. Szucha, which houses the **Museum of Struggle and Martyrdom** (open Wed 09.00–16.00; Thur, Sat 09.00–16.00; Fri 10.00–17.00; Sun 10.00–16.00; entrance from the courtyard of the Ministry of Education). Housed in a former Gestapo headquarters, the small and predictably grim display begins with a quotation from an anonymous prisoner: 'It is easy to talk about Poland, harder to work for her, harder still to die for her, hardest of all to suffer for her'. A line of empty cubicles culminates in the notorious 'streetcar' cells where prisoners would wait to be interrogated. The guardroom and corridor display documents and instruments of torture.

Alternatively, continue south along al. Ujazdowskie to the inviting **University Botanical Gardens**, established in 1818 (open May–Oct). In their southeast corner rises a hillock with the ruins of the **Temple of Providence** (1792, Jakub Kubicki), built to commemorate the first anniversary of the 3 May Constitution. Never completed, the Temple was the scene of patriotic rallies during the Partition era. Next to the Gardens stands a Neo-classical **Observatory** (1824), partly reconstructed after the war.

Walk Five ~ Łazienki

The name 'Łazienki' is invariably associated with one man—Stanisław August Poniatowski—Poland's last monarch, who transformed the game park of the Ujazdów estate into one the finest palatial complexes of late 18C Europe. Landscaped in the 18C English style, and complete with orangeries, Chinese pavilions, temples, fountains, a Roman rotunda and even an amphitheatre, Łazienki Park reflected the tastes of the Enlightenment and dominant vogue for antiquity. The apogee of Poniatowski's achievement was the splendid **Łazienki Palace** or **Palace on the Water**, which the Italian architect Domenico Merlini designed as a royal summer residence. So great was Poniatowski's personal involvement in the project, so vigorous his eye for detail, that he is credited with developing a new mode of expression in architecture, known subsequently to historians as the 'Stanislavian' style.

Over the centuries Łazienki has endured as one of Warsaw's chief attractions. The expansive park is well preserved and closely resembles its 18C appearance. On Sundays in summer open-air classical concerts are held close to the Chopin monument (see p. 136), but should you wish to escape the crowds there is ample space to do so. Numerous palaces, houses and annexes, some with exhibitions, may be visited (separate tickets for each). Fortunately, most of the furnishings were concealed from the Nazis or recovered after the war, so many of the interiors one sees today are original, with the exception of the Palace on the Water.

Łazienki Park was originally situated on land belonging to the Ujazdów estate (see above). Buildings began to appear in 1674, when the Grand Marshal of the Crown, Stanisław Herakliusz Lubomirski, a philosopher, writer and patron of the arts, purchased the estate and built on it a small retreat known as the Hermitage (see p. 135). Additionally, he commissioned Tylman van Gameren to construct a bathhouse (*łazienki* in Polish), enclosed on all sides by water, which would later form the core of the Palace of the Water.

Stanisław August Poniatowski bought the estate in 1776, intending to convert it into a summer residence. A team of top artists and architects were assigned the task under the direct supervision of the monarch. The foremost member, Domenico Merlini, rebuilt the bathhouse, raising it one storey (1775–76) and redesigning the south façade in Baroque-Classical style (1784). Four years later, Merlini gave the palace a purer Neo-classical form, adding a north front of 13 bays—the centre emphasised by columned portico and modest pediment—as well as lateral wings. Meanwhile, J.B. Plersch (1788) and Merlini's successor Jan Chrystian Kamsetzer (1793–95) worked on the interiors, with Marcello Bacciarelli supplying the best painted decoration.

Łazienki was more than just another royal residence: it was also an aesthetic statement that was to have a lasting effect on Polish architecture, inspiring many nobles to build their residences in the much-vaunted 'Stanislavian' style. All the buildings in Łazienki were fitted with the most modern technology then available. The former hunting grounds, redesigned by Agrikola and Schulz as the Łazienki Park in 1774–80, revealed both French and English influence, with the latter gaining the upper hand when Johann Christian Schuch landscaped the area in 1784. The park was never fenced off to restrict public access. On the contrary, visitors were encouraged, and crowds flocked to see the performances staged at the Amphitheatre and Old Orangery. A select few would be invited to attend the monarch's celebrated 'Thursday dinners' held at the Palace on the Water.

Łazienki remained in the possession of Stanisław August's family until appropriation by the Czarist authorities in 1817. Thereafter, the park was extended south, the Botanical Gardens were established to the northwest, and the Belvedere Palace (see p. 136) was separated from the grounds proper. During the Second World War the Nazis planned to blow up the Palace on the Water, but, with the Red Army at their heels, only managed to burn out the interiors.

In the 18C Łazienki was situated on the outskirts of the city, but nowadays it lies at the heart of the government and embassy district. The grounds may be reached from al. Ujazdowskie or ul. Agrykola. If you are following the itinerary suggested here, you should enter through the gate nearest the Botanical Gardens (see above). The opening times of the various buildings differ, and are therefore listed separately.

Water Tower

This circular building (1), with banded masonry and no external windows, was begun in 1777 by Merlini, who drew inspiration from the tomb of Cecilia

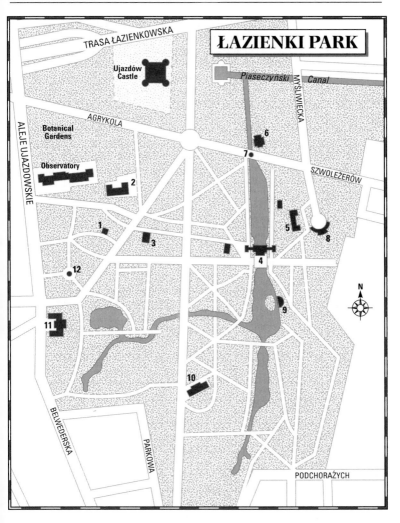

Metella in Rome. Aigner added the small two-columned portico in the 1820s. Inside, tiny rooms look onto a miniature courtyard with a well. Temporary exhibitions are held here in summer (**open** 09.30–16.00).

Old Orangery and Royal Court Theatre

The ***Old Orangery** (2; **open** 09.30–15.00), also by Merlini (1786), is perhaps the most authentic example of the Stanislavian style. The 17-bay south front, divided by pilasters and large arcaded windows, is remarkable for its classical simplicity. Here the monarch kept his beloved orange trees to protect them from the winter cold. The east wing housed the ***Royal Court Theatre** (2), which opened on 6 September 1788. In the words of Renaud, who attended the first performance: 'An effortless combination of Roman and French taste, recalling the glorious times of Louis XVI, endows this theatre with the unmistakable stamp of greatness and opulence'. Renaud was not mistaken, for the theatre won instant popular acclaim. It could seat 200 people, in pews and in nine boxes, with one box directly opposite the stage reserved for the monarch. Excellent acoustics were ensured by the entirely wooden design. In 1791, the theatre was given over to public use, with performances staged by Wojciech Bogusławski, the founding father of Polish theatre.

Spared destruction by the Nazis, the theatre is one of very few in Europe to have retained its original 18C décor. The majestic tondo of Apollo riding a quadriga, with four painted medallions of Sophocles, Shakespeare, Molière and Racine at the corners, is by Jan Jerzy Plersch. His too are the wonderful *trompe l'oeil* effects: 'marble' walls and columns, the Commonwealth crest above the stage, and, best of all, a row of boxes above the cornice from which an 18C audience looks out. Notice, here, the contrasting fashions of Enlightenment Poland: the boorish Sarmatian noble (see p. 68) with his shaven head, long moustache and traditional robe, and the upstart 'progressive' in his dandyish dress coat and designer French wig. The prominent sculptures of women holding candelabra are attributed to Le Brun and Monaldi. Behind the stage, to the left and right, are three tiers of actors' dressing rooms linked by stairs and galleries.

Poniatowski originally intended the south wing to serve as a kind of winter garden, where, besides the orange trees, visitors could admire an array of antique sculptures. With this in mind, a **Sculpture Gallery** filled with plants and exhibits from Stanisław August's collection has been opened here. The sculptures, however, mostly gypsum and marble, are reconstructions. Authentic exhibits can be found in the **Polish Sculpture Gallery** (west wing), where nine small rooms crammed with over 140 items trace the development of Polish sculpture from the 16C to 1939. The Łazienki Museum organises classical concerts and art exhibitions in the Old Orangery. Outside, on a small terrace facing the south wing, are the remains of a formal garden designed by Poniatowski as a kind of open-air museum, a counterpart to the winter garden. Eight stone busts of Roman emperors and two statues of Apollo and Venus, all 18C, have been brought here from the Palace on the Water.

White House

The White House (1774, Merlini; **open** to visitors, 09.30–16.00.) was the first building (3) founded by Poniatowski in the Łazienki Park, serving as a royal residence while the Palace on the Water was under construction. Small, square and regular, with a wooden attic and belvedere, it is predominantly Neo-classical, though certain elements, notably the large ground-floor windows, still echo the late Baroque. Poniatowski's sisters and his mistress, Elżbieta Grabowska, reputedly lived here.

Interior. From the hallway enter the impressive **Dining Room** (left) with striking frescoes (1777, Jan Jerzy Plersch). In a semicircular niche stands an original antique sculpture of Venus. The **Parlour** and adjoining **Bedroom** are decorated in the 'Chinese style' which was fashionable during the Enlightenment. *Trompe l'oeil* decoration by Plersch and Ścisło adorns the **Octagonal Boudoir**, where the intended impression is that of a garden pavilion surrounded by beautiful vistas. Water, the symbol of Venus, is the dominant motif. Go back through the Bedroom and along the corridor, passing a *cabinet d'aisance* with an 18C bidet. The two **Dressing Rooms** contain some fine Polish and French furniture (18C) and Per Krafft's *Portrait of a Boy* (18C).

Palace on the Water

The **palace (4) is fronted by a picturesque south terrace with steps descending to the water. In the middle stands a Baroque fountain flanked by two mythological sculptures (c 1770), and next to it a sundial bearing the date 1788 and the initials of Stanisław August. Notice also the four satyrs—two against the recessed wings of the Palace (1776, Le Brun), and two by the terrace entrance (c 1770, J. B. Plersch).

Ground floor

The principal style of the palace (**open** 09.30–16.00; group tours available) is Neo-classical, though Baroque elements have been preserved from the original bathhouse. Above the entrance a Latin inscription proclaims Lubomirski's motto for the building: 'This house loathes melancholy, loves peace, offers a bath, extols country living, and welcomes the virtuous'.

Enter through the **Vestibule**, where Gameren's legacy survives in the pebble-coated walls—a stylistic device widely used in 17C grottoes and rustic pavilions. Facing you are two Baroque stuccoes: *Mars Resting* and *Poland Flourishing*; the ceiling bears the initials of Stanisław August and Stanisław Lubomirski. The **Bacchus Room** was also part of the original bathhouse, and here again Gameren's Baroque decoration has been preserved. As in Wilanów (see p. 145), the walls are decked out in blue Dutch tiles, some original (the slightly darker ones). An admirable 17C Flemish painting by Jacob Jordaens—*Silenus with Bacchantes*—hangs above the 18C fireplace.

The **Bathroom**, the last Baroque room, constitutes the core of Lubomirski's bathhouse. Scenes in bas-relief from Ovid's *Metamorphoses* decorate the walls, and the motif of water is continued in the Cupids above the doors and the statue of Venus emerging from her bath (c 1780, Francesco Lazzarini). Diana bathing with nymphs appears in relief on the right wall. Next is the ***Ballroom** (1788–93), Kamsetzer's glittering showpiece and one of the best examples of Polish Neo-classicism. Here, Baroque extravagance cedes to balance, simplicity and restraint. Light flooding in through two rows of windows accentuates the whiteness of the stucco and breathes life into the marble sculptures. Two chimney pieces in the form of porticoes grace the ends of the room. Above the south one is a sculpture of Hercules (1793, Giuseppe Angelini), with two of his adversaries—Centaur and the hound Cerberus—below (Le Brun). The whole group symbolises the triumph of Man over hell and the elements. Opposite stands an 18C sculpture of Apollo above figures of Midas and the satyr Marsyas, also by Le Brun, symbolising the triumph of the spirit over folly and pride. To the right of the orchestra pit are bas-reliefs of Hercules and his wife Deianeira, and to the left, of Apollo and Daphne (all by Le Brun). The vertical tempera panels by Plersch on the walls show the four elements, three ages of Man, three fates, three times of day, three (not four) seasons, and finally the signs of the Zodiac (above the doorways).

The **Portrait Gallery**, **Solomon Room** and **Picture Gallery** were built specially to house the royal art collection. In the first are portraits of the friends and relatives of Poniatowski and the entourage of August II. Look out in particular

Palace on the Water

for Bacciarelli's famous portrait of Stanisław August with an hourglass. The second room, in shades of ebony, gold and ivory in imitation of the Temple of Solomon, was until 1944 filled with paintings by Bacciarelli illustrating the life of Solomon, builder of temples, and equated with his own patron, Poniatowski, as architect of Neo-classical Warsaw. Prominent also are Le Brun's marble putti and a complete set of Louis XVI furniture.

Finally, the **Picture Gallery** offers a small taster of Poniatowski's vast collection of European art, once numbering over 2500 works, in which Titian, Van Dyck, Rubens and Bruegel were most favoured. Most of it was looted, including two Rembrandts, with a third—*Polish Rider* (1655)—being controversially sold to the Frick Gallery in New York before the First World War. The paintings have been hung densely, in rows, as was the 18C fashion. Two of the portraits are of Englishmen admired by Poniatowski: *Sir Francis Bacon* and *Sir Charles Williams*, the latter an 18C British ambassador to Russia.

The modest **Antechamber**, remodelled several times, was where guests waited to be received by the monarch. The adjoining **Chapel** was badly disfigured during the Czarist period when a roof was added between the dome and the lower storey.

From the Antechamber enter the **Dining Room**, the earliest purely Neo-classical Palace interior, where Poniatowski would hold his 'Thursday dinners' in the company of artists and scholars. An 18C bust of the monarch shows him as a Roman emperor, with Caracalla, Caesar, Galba and Hadrian completing the set.

The centre of the palace is occupied by the **Rotunda**, the only chamber to survive the Second World War fully intact. Poniatowski refashioned the original Baroque décor of Lubomirski's grotto in hues of white, grey and yellow, which he felt befitted a Polish pantheon. Four statues of the 'greatest' Polish kings stand in niches: Kazimierz the Great (Monaldi), Zygmunt I, Stefan Bathory (both Le Brun), and Jan Sobieski (Pinck). Busts of 'good' Roman emperors are placed above the doors: Titus, Trajan (both Le Brun) and Marcus Aurelius. The Latin inscription around the base of the dome is from the tenth book of Lucan (1C), and reads: 'Set for the world to emulate and profit by'. Recently, paintings by Plersch representing the four times of the day were uncovered on the dome.

First floor

The royal apartments on the first floor were completely destroyed by fire in 1945. Every architectural detail, therefore, is a reconstruction; even the marble for the fireplaces had to be imported from Italy. The rooms have been fitted with 18C period furniture.

First comes the **Vestibule**, its walls decked out in green silk and covered densely in Italian and Dutch paintings. Look for Bacciarelli's *Monk in a Brown Habit*. The east wall carries a portrait of *Catherine the Great*, the Russian Czarina who maintained with Poniatowski one of the great love affairs of the late 18C. More art, mostly by 17C Dutch artists, is found in the **Small Gallery**. The adjoining **Balcony Room** has some fine portraits and Rococo furniture.

Continue to the **Royal Study**, the most formal room on the first floor, whose highlight is a view of Łazienki from 1775 by Bernardo Bellotto (see p. 69). Only Bacciarelli's portraits of the king's parents have survived from the original interiors of the **Royal Bedroom**. A Neo-classical four-poster bed with an eagle crowning the baldachin dominates the room. A portrait of *Anna Szaniawska*, another of Poniatowski's mistresses, shows her against a backdrop of the Łazienki park (1782). The **Royal Dressing Room** is where the monarch kept his most valuable Rembrandts (11 in all), but today the walls are covered with mediocre, mostly 17C Dutch works from the royal collection.

Further on is the **Library**, which once accommodated some 2000 volumes from the king's personal collection. Walk along the long narrow corridor to the **Rooms of Ryx**, formerly the quarters of the king's personal valet, Franciszek Ryx. Of most interest is the **Study**, with paintings by Bacciarelli (*Portrait of Stanisław Sołtyk*), Nicholas Maes (*Portrait of a Woman*), and Antoni Albertrandi (*Self Portrait*).

Grand Annexe

This large but outwardly modest U-shaped building (5) was designed by Merlini in 1788 for the royal staff. During the Congress Kingdom it housed a military college. The bust by the south front is of Piotr Wysocki, leader of the college cadets who fired the first shots of the November Uprising in 1830. The interiors have, since 1988, housed the **Paderewski Museum** (open Tues–Sun 10.00–15.00), with a monographic display of scant interest to all but fans of the composer.

North of the Grand Annexe runs UL. AGRYKOLA, once the main avenue leading to the Palace on the Water, and today lined with 19C gaslights. The avenue marks the perimeter of Łazienki proper. Close by are two monuments of historical interest.

The Hermitage (6) a small, single-storey retreat, topped by a mansard roof, was built by Gameren for his patron Lubomirski in 1683–90. Struck by lightning, it was later reshaped by Merlini in Baroque-Classical style (1775–78) and inhabited by Madame Lhullier, a cabalist and favourite of Poniatowski. The building overlooks the Piaseczyński Canal (ul. Agrykola 9). The best view of the Palace on the Water can be had from the stone bridge linking the Piaseczyński Canal with the north pond. On it stands the **Monument to King Jan Sobieski (7)**, an equestrian monument to the victor of Vienna (1788, Le Brun and Pinck), whom Poniatowski held in great esteem, and who is shown clad in antique armour, trampling Ottoman Turks underfoot.

Myślewicki Palace

The Baroque-Classical *****Myślewicki Palace** (1775–78, Merlini; 8) was the second building in Łazienki to be constructed for Stanisław August, who gave it to his nephew, Prince Józef Poniatowski (look for his initials on the façade). Never modified, the palace survived the war intact, and afterwards was reserved for visiting heads of state, Indira Gandhi among them. Plersch's well-preserved interiors were opened to the public in 1981 (09.30–16.00). The building is often used as a location for period films, and in summer, **chamber concerts** are held here (18.00 and 20.00, Tues, Thur and Sat).

Behind the Myślewicki Palace is a **Museum of Equestrianism** (open Tues–Sun 10.00–16.00) located inside the former Palace stables, with a plethora of stuffed animals, hunting and riding equipment, and a few 19C horse paintings by Wojciech Kossak.

Theatre on the Island

Kamsetzer's delightful open-air *amphitheatre (1791; 9) faces an island with a stage and artificial ruins modelled on the Temple of Jupiter in Baalbeck, Syria. An audience of one thousand watched the opening performance of *Cleopatra*, a historical ballet, on 7 September 1791. During the naval battle scene, 'ships' sailed dramatically towards the stage, an event later depicted in paintings by Norblin. Around the crest of the amphitheatre are eight of the original 16 statues of the 'greatest' poets from Antiquity to the 18C, including, somewhat idiosyncratically, the Poles Naruszewicz and Trembecki. The amphitheatre is still used for concerts on Sunday lunchtimes in summer.

New Orangery

Located in the south part of Łazienki, the New Orangery (10) was built in 1869 to house the Czar's orange trees. In 1876, sculptures and busts representing the four seasons were added to the façade. Today, it is a tropical greenhouse and houses the exclusive *Belvedere* restaurant.

Belvedere Palace

The back of the Belvedere Palace (11; closed to the public) is visible from the park behind a large stone wall. Originally a 17C wooden villa, surrounded by an Italian garden, it came to be known as the Belvedere on account of the fine view (in Italian *bel vedere*). Stanisław August bought the villa in 1767 and made it part of Łazienki. It was used as a guesthouse until Kubicki radically remodelled it as a Neo-classical country manor with columned porticoes for the Czarist governor of Warsaw, the Grand Duke Constantin Pavlovich, in 1818–22. The Belvedere was the official residence of Polish heads of state from the First World War until 1993, when President Wałęsa moved to the Namiestnikowski Palace (see p. 121).

Monument to Chopin

This huge monument (12), a post-war replica, overlooks a pond just beyond the main entrance to the park on al. Ujazdowskie. The original was designed by Wacław Szymanowski in 1908, but its unveiling was delayed due to opposition from the Czarist authorities. The Nazis denounced the monument as an overt symbol of Polish culture, and dismantled it for scrap iron in 1939.

Walk Six ~ Central Warsaw

Begin this walk at the bottom end of **UL. MIODOWA**, near pl. Zamkowy (see p. 108). Walking north you enter the heart of pre-Partition Warsaw, an area where in the 18C Polish magnates put up their mansions and grand palaces, almost all of which were destroyed during the Second World War. Today, the reconstructed buildings accommodate offices, and are mostly inaccessible. Close to the under-pass, on the right, is No. 6: the **Branicki Palace** (1774), built at the height of

Saxon Baroque for Hetman Branicki, a man of unrivalled wealth and influence (see p. 175). The mansion is best seen from UL. PODWALE, where three wings, with a fine central portico and sculptures on the attic (J.C. Redler), frame a quiet inner courtyard. Stay on ul. Podwale to see the striking white façade of the adjoining **Młodziejowski (Morsztyn) Palace** (No. 10), with a tall relief-decorated pediment above four pilasters. The Palace lost its original shape after 19C alterations, but the original form was revived during post-war reconstruction.

Returning to ul. Miodowa, proceed to the Baroque **Capuchin Church** (No. 13), which Sobieski funded in 1683 as a votive offering for the victory over the Turks at Vienna. The plain façade, preceded by an entrance to the crypts (19C), is attributed to Gameren and in time served as a model for many provincial parish churches. Inside, chapels flank a modest, cross-vaulted nave. In the last one on the right (1736) a sarcophagus contains Sobieski's heart and there is also a bust of him sponsored by Czar Nicholas I.

Next up on the left is the unmistakable **Pac Palace** (No. 15), whose concave front building (1824–26, Henryk Marconi), three large niches under medallions and a frieze, faces the street at an angle. Originally raised for the Radziwiłłs, and extended by Gameren (Baroque, 1673), the Palace emerged as the most splendid private residence of the Congress Kingdom after being remodelled by Marconi for General L. Pac in 1824–26. The Czarist authorities punished Pac for his active role in the November Uprising (see p. 51), confiscating the Palace and turning it into a district court (until 1939). Since the war the building has been occupied by the Ministry of Health and Social Welfare. Look for the bas-reliefs (facing ul. Miodowa) of Titus Flavius at the Corinthian Games, laying down the law for Greek cities. Moorish and Gothic elements dominate the interior, whose highlight is the vaulted and galleried hall on the first floor.

The Primate of Poland (currently Cardinal Glemp) resides at the **Borch Palace** (No. 17/19), whose three wings were redesigned in Neo-classical style by Merlini c 1780. The Rococo ironwork gate looks across ul. Miodowa to the **Basilian Friars' Church and Monastery** (No. 16), another work of Merlini's (Baroque-Classical, 1781–84). The house at No. 22/24 was once a liberal boarding school for young noblemen known as the **Collegium Nobilium**. Established in 1740 by the reformer, political writer, and Piarist monk Stanisław Konarski, the school was one of the leading educational institutions of Enlightenment Poland. Confiscated by the army in 1807, the Neo-classical building was subsequently used for administrative purposes. The Piarists' former church and monastery are found at the corner of ul. Długa (No. 13–15).

Ul. Miodowa terminates at two adjoining squares: PL. POWSTANIA WARSZAWSKIEGO and pl. Krasińskich. The first is distinguished by a **Monument to the Warsaw Uprising** (see p. 58), unveiled in 1989, and depicting figures emerging from the wartime rubble: soldiers, a priest, a mother and child.

From the monument there is a fine view onto the imposing ***Krasiński Palace**, or 'Palace of the Kingdom', which dominates PL. KRASIŃSKICH to the north.

Tylman van Gameren began work on the palace in 1677 for the Palatine of Płock and Warsaw Starost, Jan Krasiński, creating in little over five years what is still revered as the most magnificent Baroque residence in the city. The Krasińskis commissioned Andreas Schlüter, better known for his work in Gdańsk, to carve the reliefs for the huge central pediment (front and back). In keeping with the prevalent fashion for antiquity, Schlüter produced two heroic representations—on the front and back elevations—of the Roman tribune of Marcus Valerius Corvinus, a man the Krasińskis claimed as their ancestor.

Stanisław August Poniatowski's court architect Merlini rebuilt the Palace in 1783 when it was already the seat of the Crown Treasury Commission and had been renamed the 'Palace of the Kingdom'. From the early 19C until the Second World War the building housed law courts.

The front elevation is a full nineteen bays long. Look for Schlüter's fine relief scenes in the tympanum showing Corvinus doing battle with the leader of the Gauls. The back elevation overlooks a pleasant park—the Krasiński Garden— originally a Baroque formal garden laid out by Gameren, later redesigned (1766). Since post-war reconstruction the Palace has housed the special archives of the National Library. The collection comprises many rare and valuable documents, including the first printed Polish texts (16C). Entry to the archives is by permission only, but you may visit other parts of the building to admire Merlini's splendid Neo-classical interiors (reconstructed).

Pl. Krasińskich was formerly the Palace courtyard, later becoming a wool market during the Congress Kingdom. Two iron wells (1844, C.P. Aigner) have survived from this period. The Square was one of the last bastions of resistance during the Warsaw Uprising (see p. 58), when all its buildings were devastated, and when 5000 partisans made a final dramatic escape through the sewers to other districts of the city.

Like Miodowa, UL. DŁUGA was formerly lined with the palaces and mansions of Poland's political and ecclesiastical leaders, though wartime destruction has left only a few scattered remnants. A short detour south along ul. Bielańska brings you to the **Przebendowski Palace**, located on a small green in the fork of al. Solidarności (No. 62). J.S. Deybel built it in 1728 for the Lord Treasurer of the Crown, Jan Jerzy Przebendowski. Distinctly late Baroque in style, it consists of a long central block with rounded ends and lower pavilions attached to each corner. During the first half of the 19C the Palace housed a waxworks, later passing to the Radziwiłłs, who owned it until 1944. Throughout the post-war period the building contained a hagiographical Lenin Museum frequented by visiting Soviet heads of state. Lenin was expelled in 1990 to make way for a more politically correct and no less edifying **Museum of the Independence Movement** (open Tues–Fri 10.00–17.00, Sat–Sun 10.00–16.00), covering the period up to and including the First World War. Currently, only two rooms are accessible with a patriotic display of photographs, documents, and memorabilia tracing the history of the struggle for independence. Far better than the exhibits are the oval upper tier and the ground floor 'art house' cinema.

Returning to ul. Długa, you could briefly stop at the **Archaeological Museum** (No. 42; **open** Mon–Fri 09.00–16.00, Sun 10.00–16.00) just before the junction with ul. Gen. Andersa. The Museum is in Władysław IV's 17C Royal Arsenal, erected on a quadrangular plan within a bastion of the former city fortifications. The firearms kept here supplied the rebels during the uprisings of

1794 and 1830, after which the building served as a Czarist prison. The entrance overlooks the Krasiński Garden.

South of UL. GEN. ANDERSA extends PL. BANKOWY, its west side dominated by a fine group of buildings designed by Antonio Corazzi for the State Treasury in 1825. Facing the skyscraper (see p. 141) at No. 5 is the imposing **Building of the Revenue and Treasury Commission**, formerly the Leszczyński-Potocki Palace (17C), with a spacious courtyard and two pavilions on the street. Within are the offices of the city administration, where the great Romantic poet, Juliusz Słowacki (see *p.83*), worked as a clerk in 1830. Corazzi adapted the adjoining **Palace of the Treasury Minister** from an 18C mansion. The building, fronted by arcades and a mass of columns, was used by the revolutionary Jacobin Club as a meeting place during the Kościuszko Uprising (see p. 51).

Corazzi's best composition on the square, built in collaboration with J.J. Gay, is the *****Bank of Poland and Stock Exchange** (1828–30) at No. 1. Surprisingly, the exterior of this central-domed structure has no columns at all—just two storeys of round-headed arches set into banded masonry. Inside, the highlight is the broad domed hall lit by lunettes (the floor of the former stock exchange), with an upper tier supported on columns.

John Paul II Collection

Until recently the building housed a museum of the Polish Revolutionary Movement, but today Poland's Communist heroes have given way to the *****John Paul II Collection** (open Tues–Fri 09.30–16.30; entrance from ul. Elektoralna). This is an impressive, if uneven display of European art of the 14C–20C. The gallery has some 400 works by such illustrious names as Titian, Van Dyck, Goya, Rubens, Rembrandt, Jordaens, Murillo and Velázquez. In the 1980s, all the works were donated to the Polish Church by the Carroll-Porczyńskis, who had emigrated to England during the war. Recently a scandal erupted after a Polish art historian claimed that many paintings in the collection are forgeries.

Most of the works are not divided into schools, but into seven sections, each with a separate, usually religious, theme. Downstairs you will find (1) **Impressionism**; (2) **Portraiture**, with special emphasis on self-portraits, including works by Titian, *Child from the Medici family* (1537), Van Dyck, *Portrait of a Nobleman* (c 1625), Rubens, *Self-portrait*, Rembrandt, *Portrait of a Bearded Man* (1643), Jordaens, *Portrait of an Old Man*, Murillo, *Self-portrait*, Velázquez, *Self-portrait*, Sir Joshua Reynolds, *Portrait of Miss Nelly O'Brien*, Goya, *A Woman Carrying Water*, Renoir, *Portrait of Pierre Renoir, the Artist's Son* (1910) and (3) **Myth and Allegory**.

Upstairs, section (4) is devoted to **The Life of Mary**, including Lucas Cranach the Younger's *Madonna and Child*; section (5) to **The Bible and the Saints**, including Albrecht Dürer's *St Anne* (1523), Tintoretto's *David Learning of the Death of Uriah* (1552), *The Sacrifice of Abraham* (1597) attributed to Caravaggio, Rubens' *The Way of the Cross*, and Guido Reni's *The Judas Kiss* (1637); section (6) to **Still Life and Landscape**, including Constable's *Donkeys in the Stable*, Van Gogh's *A Farm in Hoogeveen* (1883), Sisley's *Riverside Landscape*, and Renoir's *Cauliflower and Pomegranate* (c 1890); and finally section (7) to **Motherhood**. Be sure to visit the upper tier of the hall to sample Gerson's huge canvas, *Baptism of Lithuania*, and the full sweep of Corazzi's achievement.

UL. SENATORSKA leads east off the square. At No. 35/37 is the **Blue Palace**. The inscription on the façade reads 'In the year the kingdom was reborn', a reference to the creation of the Congress Kingdom in 1815. That year F.A. Lessel finished rebuilding the Palace for the Zamoyskis in severe Neo-classical style. Chopin gave one of his first concerts here at the age of six. Before it was destroyed in 1944, the Palace, together with its adjacent pavilion (1868, Neo-Renaissance), housed the famous Zamoyski library with a collection of over 250,000 books and documents, some dating from the 11C.

Further east, ul. Senatorska emerges onto **PL. TEATRALNY**, where one is immediately overwhelmed by the vast, grandiose proportions of the *Teatr Wielki (Nos 21/23/25), which combines the National Theatre, Ballet Theatre and Opera House. Piotr Aigner began the east wing in 1818, and Antonio Corazzi the three-tiered main body and west wing with ballrooms (1826–33), using the Berlin Schauspielhaus as his model. Post-war reconstruction has lent the building a severe, almost dehumanising character befitting the canon of Stalinist architecture. Only the façade overlooking pl. Teatralny is original. In front of the building stand two monuments to the fathers of Polish opera and stage, Stanisław Moniuszko (1819–72) and Wojciech Bogusławski (1757–1829).

A suite of superb reception rooms along the main façade reveals both Corazzi's Neo-classicism and B. Pniewski's post-war remodelling. Here you will find a small but excellent **Theatre Museum** (open Tues, Thur, Fri 11.00–14.00, and daily from 18.00 for audiences only), with the emphasis on Polish theatre in the late 19C and early 20C. The gallery has portraits of famous thespians including Irena Solska (1875–1958) and the peerless Helena Modjewska (Modrzejewska) (1840–1909).

The north façade of the Teatr Wielki faces the **Nike Monument** (1964) commemorating the city's wartime resistance to the Nazis: a sword-waving figure rising from a stone plinth. The south façade overlooks pl. Piłsudskiego (formerly pl. Zwycięstwa), a vast empty space bordered by two hotels—the *Victoria Intercontinental* and the *Europejski* (see p. 121)—with the west part leading onto the **Saxon Garden**.

> The square was once a magnificent 18C garden, landscaped in 1816 by John Savage. In 1925, the ashes of a Polish soldier who fell in Lwów were deposited under the colonnade of the 18C Saxon Palace to form a Tomb of the Unknown Soldier—the only part of the palace not blown up by the Nazis in 1944. A few days after the imposition of Martial Law, in the winter of 1981, a gigantic cross composed of flowers appeared on pl. Zwycięstwa. Each night the police would remove the cross, but each day a fresh one would appear. The floral warfare ceased when the city authorities fenced off the whole area, ostensibly for renovation purposes.
>
> On Sundays a ceremonial changing of guard takes place by the **Tomb of the Unknown Soldier**. The urns at the corners of the tomb contain soil from Second World War battlefields where Poles died (including Tobruk, Lenino, Monte Cassino and Westerplatte).

Beyond the tomb stretches the main avenue of the **Saxon Garden**, with a blackened 19C fountain, Baroque sandstone sculptures, and a sundial. A Neo-classical **Water Tower** (1852–54, Henryk Marconi) overlooks an oval pond from a hillock in the north part of the garden.

Walking south from pl. Piłsudskiego you emerge onto another square, PL. MAŁACHOWSKIEGO. On the right is the eclectic **Zachęta Building** (No. 3), built in 1899 for the Society of Fine Arts (1860–1940). The first President of Poland, Gabriel Narutowicz, was assassinated here in 1922. Today, the Zachęta is home to the excellent **National Gallery of Modern Art (open** 10.00–18.00), which regularly hosts some of the best exhibitions in the country. There is no permanent display.

On the left, at the corner of UL. KREDYTOWA, stands the *****Lutheran Church** (No. 1), an impressive if severe Neo-classical edifice built by S.B. Zug in 1777–79 and funded by contributions from Warsaw's Lutheran community. Visiting times are restricted to weekdays between 09.00 and 15.00. Firebombed in 1939, the church has been reconstructed to its original central plan, with a Doric portico, three matching pedimented wings, and a huge dome (the largest in Warsaw) topped by a tall windowed lantern. Owing to the excellent acoustics the building is often used as a concert venue; Chopin began the trend in 1823.

Close by, on UL. KREDYTOWA (No. 1) is the **Ethnographical Museum (open** Tues, Thur, Fri 09.00–16.00, Wed 11.00–18.00, Sat–Sun 10.00–17.00). The Neo-Renaissance building (1856–58, Henryk Marconi) and the collection—30,000 items in all—were destroyed during the war. The museum's highlight is the rich and diverse display of Polish regional dress.

Walk Seven ~ Jewish Warsaw

West of the Old Town stretch the districts of Mirów and Muranów, today a sullen patchwork of modern housing estates, empty squares and suburban streets. Half a century ago, the area roughly delineated by UL. STAWKI to the north, UL. FRETA to the east, UL. ZŁOTA to the south and UL. OKOPOWA to the west was the scene of one of the darkest episodes of the Second World War, for it was here, on 16 November 1940, that the Nazis established a special district for Warsaw's 300,000 Jews—the infamous **Warsaw ghetto**. The tragic fate of the largest Jewish community in pre-war Europe is still within living memory. In 1939 Jews accounted for a third of the city's population. Yet within six years all but a handful had perished: in the gas chambers of the Treblinka death camp (see p. 170), of starvation and disease, or in the blazing inferno that was the Ghetto Uprising of 1943. Today, few remnants of Warsaw's rich Jewish heritage remain. As the final act in their attempted eradication of Jewish culture, the Nazis burnt the Great Synagogue on ul. Tłomackie to the ground. After the war, a huge skyscraper of tinted glass was controversially erected on the site. This building overlooks pl. Bankowy (see p. 139), where the walk begins.

The **Museum of the Jewish Historical Institute** is in a narrow side street behind the skyscraper (ul. Tłomackie 35; **open** Mon–Fri 09.00–15.00; library and research archive Mon–Fri 08.00–16.00). The display, well-marked in English, concentrates on daily life in occupied Warsaw. Harrowing photographs show the obscene, at times bizarre forms of punishment and humiliation that were used: Jews being made to sift and re-sift dirt, with the caption 'useless work for Jews'; a Polish woman at the moment of her arrest, condemned to death for helping Jews. A few liturgical items have been salvaged from the synagogues, all of which were destroyed. The museum building itself stands on the site of the pre-war Jewish Library.

The Warsaw Ghetto

The racial segregation of Warsaw began on 2 October 1940. Jews all over the city were evicted from their homes and forced to move to the newly-established Jewish district. On 16 November 1940, the district was formally sealed off. It was surrounded by a brick wall, topped with barbed wire, in which there were 15 exits guarded by the German *Schutzpolizei* (Security Police). As of 15 October 1941 the punishment for leaving the ghetto without a permit, or for helping Jews inside the ghetto, was death.

The Warsaw ghetto was the largest in Europe, with a peak population of 450,000 crammed into an area of only 5 sq. km. Disease caused by over-crowding and poor sanitary conditions was widespread. Even before the first transportations to the death camps, as many as 100,000 people had died of starvation. The authorities banned most religious, educational and cultural institutions, forcing all such activity underground. From 1941, some elementary and vocational teaching was allowed. Theatres could stage plays, provided they were not by Jewish playwrights. There was even a Jewish symphony orchestra.

The liquidation of the ghetto began on 22 July 1942, and lasted six weeks. Each day 5000–6000 people would assemble at Umschlagplatz (see below) ready for transportation to the Treblinka death camp. Officially, 35,000 remained in the ghetto after liquidation, and it was they who formed the core element of armed resistance. In late 1942, two fighting organisations were established: the Jewish Combat Organisation (JCO) (500 members), with Marek Edelman and the legendary Mordechaj Anielewicz among its leaders, and the Jewish Army Union (JAU) (250 members). The **Ghetto Uprising** broke out on 18 January 1943, when JCO fighters successfully managed to stop German detachments entering the area. Three months later, heavily outnumbered, the fighting organisations fought the last, decisive battle. In May 1943, the leaders were uncovered at their bunker on ul. Miła (see below) and committed suicide rather than be taken alive. In total, 7000 partisans died in the fighting, another 6000 were burnt to death. With the collapse of the Ghetto Uprising, the Germans levelled most buildings in the ghetto. Any still standing were destroyed during the Warsaw Uprising the following year (see p. 58).

Walk north along ul. Gen. Andersa, turning left into ul. Nowolipki and then right into UL. ZAMENHOFA, where you enter the ghetto area proper. A short detour left along ul. Dzielna will bring you to the **Museum of Pawiak Prison** (No. 24/26) at the junction with al. Jana Pawła II (**open** Wed 09.00–17.00, Thur, Sat 09.00–16.00, Fri, Sun 10.00–16.00, under-14s not allowed). Built in 1829 as a political prison, the Pawiak was later taken over by the Gestapo. Of the 100,000 inmates, a third were executed in and around the ruins of the ghetto, another 60,000 were deported to the death camps. The Nazis blew up the prison in 1944, and it has been partly reconstructed for museum purposes since. A sandstone wall with commemorative tablets surrounds the former courtyard. Enter the gloomy interiors for a macabre display of prison life contained within reconstructed cells.

Ul. Zamenhofa comes out into the vast and empty **PL. BOHATERÓW GETTA**, the first stop on the Jewish Martyrdom Memorial Trail laid out in 1988 to commemorate the 45th anniversary of the Ghetto Uprising. Dominating the east part of the square is the **Monument to the Heroes of the Ghetto**, unveiled in 1948 on the site where the fiercest fighting took place. The stone facing is made of labradorite, which Hitler ordered from Sweden in 1942 for a monument to the anticipated victory of the Reich. At the junction with ul. Miła, stop at the mound surmounted by a stone block. This marks the head-quarters of the Jewish Combat Organisation, whose leaders perished here in 1943.

> Marek Edelman, one of the survivors, recounts the story: 'On 8 May detach-ments of Germans and Ukrainians surrounded the headquarters of the ŻOB (JCO) Command. The fighting lasted two hours, and when the Germans convinced themselves that they would be unable to take the bunker by storm, they tossed in a gas-bomb. Whoever survived the German bullets, whoever was not gassed, committed suicide, for it was quite clear that there was no way out, and nobody even considered being taken alive by the Germans. Jurek Wilner called upon all the partisans to commit suicide together. Lutek Rotblat shot his mother, his sister, then himself. Ruth fired at herself seven times. Thus 80 per cent of the partisans perished, among them the ŻOB (JCO) Commander Mordechaj Anielewicz.'

Continue along ul. Miła and turn right into ul. Karmelicka. A rectangular monument (1988) at the junction with ul. Stawki marks the spot of Umschlag-platz ('Reloading Point'), where the mass deportations of Jews from the ghetto to the Treblinka death camp took place. Continuing west along ul. Stawki and left into ul. Okopowa you should not miss the **Jewish Cemetery** (open 10.00–15.00, Fri–Sat closed), one of the few functioning Jewish burial grounds in Poland, and reputedly the largest in Europe. Most of the gravestones are of the traditional *matzevah* type, with wealthier families occupying the *ohels* (mausolea). Mordechaj Anielewicz is buried here, as are Ludwik Zamenhof (the creator of Esperanto (see p. 175), and many others. Close by is the Roman Catholic cemetery of Powązki (see p. 99).

> Warsaw's Jewish community founded its own burial ground on ul. Okopowa in 1806. Due to overcrowding, by the 1870s only people of note—rabbis, writers, wealthy merchants—were being interred here, the poor being banished to Stanisław August Poniatowski's former royal estate in Targówek. During the Second World War, mass graves were dug at the end of the main avenue to accommodate the dead from the ghetto. Though fighting took place here during the Ghetto Uprising, the stones remained largely untouched, because in Warsaw, unlike in other areas of Poland, the Nazis were not short of construction materials. Restoration work began in 1979.

The **Nożyk Synagogue** (1902) on ul. Twarda, north of central railway station, is the only ghetto synagogue still standing. Used as a stable-cum-warehouse and then gutted by the Nazis, it was reopened in 1983. It is the only synagogue in Warsaw currently running religious services and may be visited on Thursdays (10.00–15.00). On nearby pl. Grzybowski (No. 12–16) is the Jewish Theatre, which regularly stages plays in Yiddish.

Walk Eight ~ Socialist-Realist Warsaw

Palace of Science and Culture

This walk begins at PL. DEFILAD, opposite the main railway station. Here, dominating the city skyline, stands one of Warsaw's most famous landmarks—the monumental ***Palace of Science and Culture**.

Begun in 1952, a year before the death of Stalin, the palace was hailed as a Soviet 'gift' to the Polish people. It remains a classic example of Socialist Realism, the architectural doctrine of the early 1950s, which renounced Western influences in favour of an art that was 'Socialist in content and national in style'. Like its counterparts in Moscow, the palace abounds in grandiose, monumental forms, with numerous bas reliefs and statues of heroic workers proclaiming the triumph of the proletariat. In deference to 'national' concerns, the Soviet element was supposedly tempered with 'Polish' additions such as mock Renaissance attics and statues of Mickiewicz and Copernicus.

Upon completion in 1955, the 'Russian cake'— as it popularly came to be known—easily surpassed all other buildings in the city in terms of height (234m) and volume (817,000 cubic metres). In a possibly apocryphal anecdote, one of the great Polish theatre directors, Konrad Swinarski, once amused himself while waiting for a tram by counting windows of the palace. He noticed a particularly dirty one next to the windows of an office he had often visited, and this led to the discovery of a hitherto unknown room which had been accidentally walled up by the builders of the palace. For most Poles the Palace of Science and Culture was a 'gift' they could have done without; a symbol of Soviet hegemony and of the primacy of ideology over aesthetic concerns, today a lasting reminder of a closed chapter in Poland's past.

The Palace of Science and Culture

The palace interiors still evoke the stifling atmosphere of the 1950s, even if some of the more obsequious inscriptions in honour of Stalin have now been removed. Apart from office space, the palace contains restaurants, foreign language bookshops, four theatres, three cinemas, an art gallery (**open** 11.30–16.00), casino, and even a swimming pool. Enter from the station side—the Palace of Youth—for the **Zoological Museum** (open: Tues–Sat 08.00–16.00, Sun 10.00–15.00). More interesting is the **Museum of Technology** (open 10.00–16.00; entrance facing ul. Marszałkowska). Take the lift to the viewing terrace on the 30th floor for a magnificent panorama of Warsaw, and, on a fine day, the Mazovian plains.

Here, as the old joke goes, you get the best view of the city, as it is the only place where you cannot see the Palace of Science and Culture.

Go south along UL. MARSZAŁKOWSKA, past the huge *Forum Hotel*, to PL. KONSTY- TUCJI, the hub of the **Marszałkowska Housing District**—a grandiose complex of residential housing built in 1949–52 at the height of post-war Stalinism. The best parts are towards pl. Zbawiciela. Notice, for instance, the heroic figures of workers hewn in stone, a short way up on the right. The 1950s Latawiec (kite) housing estate is centred around the plush and verdant al. Wyzwolenia, which branches off to the east. From pl. Zbawiciela return north along ul. Mokotowska and then ul. Krucza, passing 1950s ministry buildings (energy, agriculture) and the *Grand Hotel*. A short detour left along ul. Nowogrodzka takes you to the **Nusantara Gallery and Museum of Asia and the Pacific** (No. 18a; open Mon–Fri 10.00–18.00), with a display of applied art from the Far East.

Cross al. Jerozolimskie and continue down ul. Szpitalna. The eclectic **tene- ment house** at the corner of ul. Górskiego was built in 1893 for the Wedel family, founders of the world-famous chocolate factory. It is now a shop offering a fine selection of Wedel confectionery. Further on you emerge onto PL. POWSTAŃCÓW WARSZAWY (originally pl. Warecki; 1823–26), renamed after the war in honour of the victims of the Warsaw Uprising. On the north side, a monument (1979) in the form of a barricade commemorates the spot where the Uprising is said to have begun (see p. 58). A passageway leads off the square to the **National Philharmonic Hall** (1902) on ul. Jasna (main entrance on ul. Sienkiewicza). Rebuilt in 1955–56, the Philharmonic is the venue for Warsaw's top music events: the annual Warsaw Autumn Festival (Festival of Contempo- rary Music; September), the Jazz Jamboree (October), and the celebrated Inter- national Chopin Piano Competition (every five years). Famous virtuosos to have played here include Horowitz, Menuhin, Paderewski, Rachmaninov, Richter and Rubinstein.

Walk Nine ~ Wilanów

One of Warsaw's chief attractions is the **Royal Palace at Wilanów**, which lies on the southern outskirts of the city (ul. Wiertnicza 1). Wilanów is both the finest Baroque palace in Warsaw and one of Poland's oldest museums (1805), with breathtaking interiors and lavish gardens that have prompted some to call it the Polish Versailles. It is also the last stop on the Royal Way, a route linking three grand royal residences—the Old Town's Gothic Castle, Neo-classical Łazienki, and Baroque Wilanów—each redolent of a different period in Poland's past.

Getting there

For those not travelling by car, Wilanów can be reached by **bus** nos 130, 139, 164, 165, 188, 410, 522, 710, 728 and E-2 from the city centre. Going by **metro** it is best to get off at the Wilanowska stop and then take a bus (or walk) to the site along al. Wilanowska. If you want to visit all the museums and parks, it is best to arrive early, as the full tour can take the best part of a day.

Refreshments. The *Wilanów* restaurant, a former 17C **inn**; the *Kuźnia*, once the **Royal Smithy**, and the *Hetmańska* café, another 17C **inn**.

History of the Palace

Seeking refuge from the crowds and squalor of Warsaw, Jan Sobieski commissioned his chief architect, Agostino Locci, to transform a mansion that stood on the site of today's palace into a royal country residence. By 1682, the main block was complete. The painters Michelangelo Palloni, Jerzy Eleuter Siemiginowski and Claude Callot embellished the interiors, with a team of Italian artists led by Bellotti providing the rich stuccoes. Situated *entre cour et jardin*, the palace, or Villa Nuova, recalled French Baroque residences of the period, though its interior layout relied heavily on a Sarmatian (see p. 68) interpretation of Roman Baroque. When Sobieski died in 1696, he left a small but rich palace, thereafter known as Wilanów (a combination of 'Milanów' and 'Villa Nuova').

Wilanów fell into ruin under Sobieski's heirs until Elżbieta Sieniawska bought it in 1720. She commissioned Giovanni Spazzio to erect the north and south wings (1722–25), with J.B. Plersch producing the stucco scenes from Ovid for the façade. The two subsequent owners—August II and Izabela Czartoryska—did little to improve the palace. It suffered greatly during the 18C at the hands of marauding Polish and Russian armies, but when Stanisław Kostka Potocki inherited the estate in 1799, a brighter future seemed assured. Fabulously wealthy, and an avid collector of art, Potocki fed his obsession with works of art from Poland's golden age by recovering many of the items Wilanów had lost—paintings, antique sculptures, a well-stocked library and numerous Sobieski mementoes. With Chrystian Piotr Aigner's help he erected the 'Chinese' pavilion and 'Roman' bridge, landscaping the gardens in the English style. A gallery, also designed by Aigner, was opened to the public in 1805. Despite some remodelling and restoration, the palace later fell into decline, and during the Second World War, the Nazis stole the best of the art and tore up the park and surrounding buildings. Reconstruction saw the removal of many 19C accretions and the restoration of older features, notably some 18C murals discovered under layers of peeling plaster.

Palace environs

Clustered around the palace, but outside the grounds proper, are buildings formerly used by the staff, servants and administrators of the Wilanów estate. Paths and tree-lined alleyways were added in the mid-19C by August Potocki. He also commissioned the Marconi brothers to rebuild the **Church of St Anne**, the chief attraction of the group. Numerous 19C tablets in memory of the Potockis can be found inside. A curiosity is the nave floor, whose rounded granite plates originally formed a column in Hadrian's Temple of Peace in Rome (donated to Potocki by Pope Pius IX). Facing the church is a 17C **inn**, presently occupied by the *Wilanów* restaurant. Closer to the main gate stands the Potocki **Mausoleum**, designed by Henryk Marconi in sombre Neo-Gothic style (1836). Walk south along the alley to the former **coachhouse** and **riding-school** (1845–55, F.M. Lanci). Inside is the **Museum of Poster Art**, displaying some of the best Polish poster art since the war (**open** Tues–Sun 10.00–16.00).

** *The Royal Palace*

Two statues symbolising War and Peace adorn the Baroque entrance gate through which you enter the palace courtyard. To the left, the palace's north wing culminates in a **pergola** of 1852. To the right stand four buildings: the **Royal Kitchen** and **Guardhouse**, both designed by S.B.Zug in Baroque-Classical style (1775–76), the **Bathhouse of Izabela Lubomirska**, and, obscured from view, the former **stables**.

Across the green rises the palace's central block, adorned with sculptural detail and inscriptions, which express the apotheosis of Sobieski, the self-styled imperial ruler. References to antiquity begin with the boastful line '*Quod vetus urbs coluit nunc Nova Villa tenet*'—'what the ancient city (Rome) revered, the new villa (Wilanów) possesses'. Above a rounded window the rays of a gilded sun—the ancient symbol of imperial rule—surround Sobieski crests supported by putti; and below, a quotation from the Old Testament reads: '*Refulsit sol in clipeis*'—'the sun is reflected in the shields'. Szwaner's bas-reliefs in the balustrade depict the monarch's greatest victories. In the wings (north and south) the main doors are framed by blind arches with carved tympanums above. Those on the south side represent the *Triumph of Jan III*, while those along the north side symbolise the virtues of Sobieski's wife, Maria Kazimiera.

Viewed from the Baroque garden (back), the palace resembles a Polish country manor, but here, too, the façade sparkles with sculptural detail glorifying the royal couple. To the south, look for the exquisite sundial surmounted by Chronos, which tells the time as well as the current astrological sign.

■ The palace interior (**open** 09.30–14.45, Feb–Dec, closed Tues; individual visits on Sat–Sun only) spans the 17C–19C, with the best rooms—the royal apartments of Sobieski and Maria Kazimiera—located on the ground floor of the main block.

First and second floors

Normally in Baroque palaces the *piano nobile* occupied the first floor, so the layout here is further evidence of Wilanów's rustic origins.

The tour, covering some 50 rooms, starts with the **Polish Portrait Gallery** on the first floor, where a unique collection of coffin portraits, 250 in all, is followed by official paintings of magnates and royalty, Sarmatian portraiture (see p. 68), and a section devoted solely to Sobieski and his family. *Trompe l'oeil* frescoes (c 1696) of Greek goddesses adorn the sparsely furnished **Quiet Room**. Equally impressive is the 17C **Faience Room**, whose walls are clad in blue and white tiles, imitations of Delftware. Within the shallow coffered cupola, rich stuccoes and painted decoration provide another royal apotheosis—an eagle carrying the Sobieski crest to the heavens. The adjoining **Three-Windowed Room** has a plafond of Flora and excellent stuccoes and medallions symbolising the four seasons by Schlüter.

Return to the **Middle Room**, where a beamed ceiling and Dutch, English and Polish furniture recreate the atmosphere of a 17C Polish country manor. On the walls hang equestrian portraits of Sobieski's sons, Konstanty and Aleksander. *Trompe l'oeil* frescoes by Giuseppe Rossi (his self-portrait is in the southeast corner) adorn the walls and ceiling of the **Anteroom**. The **Rooms of Agostino Locci**, Wilanów's chief architect, are notable for their 17C beamed ceilings and Rossi's landscape frescoes, all recently uncovered. English furniture (18C) predominates in the **Al Fresco Room**, so-called for its 18C decorations. If open, you should ascend the 18C staircase to the **Banquet Hall** (second floor), decorated with murals by Rossi (1724) and rich ceiling sculptures by Marconi (1873). The **Pastel Study** contains pastel portraits of people connected with Wilanów. Go north for a continuation of the **Polish Portrait Gallery**, with the emphasis on luminaries of the Enlightenment. Many more portraits, chiefly 19C, are found in the north wing, where cast-iron stairs descend to the ground floor.

Ground floor

You emerge in the **Lower Vestibule**, whose highlight is the *grisaille* decoration in the first part, and an oval cupola filled with an 18C depiction of Flora in the second. Going east you enter rooms formerly occupied by the Potocki Art Museum. The **Great Crimson Room**, the largest and grandest interior of the north wing, was converted into a Gallery of Foreign Art in 1805. On the walls hang 17C–18C works, mostly from Potocki's personal collection. Note, especially, the huge canvas entitled *Polish Ambassador Michał Radziwiłł's Entry to Rome* by A. Vivani and P. van Bloemen, and *Cortège of Bacchus* from the Jordaens workshop. Potocki redesigned the adjoining **Crimson Room** for use as a Landscape Gallery, but only mediocre French and Italian genre scenes (17C–18C) have survived. A plafond with a central tondo depicting allegories of repose decorates the **Crimson Study**, which is dominated by J. Brandt's large canvas— *Jan Sobieski and Maria Kazimiera leaving Wilanów*. Situated in the base of the northeast tower, the **Etruscan Room** originally displayed Potocki's collection of antique ceramics, some of which remain.

You reach the main block via the **Northern Gallery**, where a cycle of frescoes by Michelangelo Palloni (1688) recounts the story of Cupid and Psyche. During the 19C, the **Courtyard Room** constituted the first section of Potocki's gallery, hence the Latin inscription embedded into the floor: '*Cunctis patet ingressus*' ('open to all').

The Royal Apartments

The plush royal apartments begin with the **Queen's Antechamber**, which has a fine plafond by Siemiginowski depicting Autumn. More of his frescoes, based on Ovid's *Metamorphoses*, are found in the adjoining **Queen's Study**. The four seasons' cycle (Spring) is continued in the **Queen's Bedchamber**, where walls covered in Genoese velvet surround a French four-poster bed. The centre of the main block is occupied by the impressive **Great Vestibule**, originally 17C, redesigned by S.B. Zug in Neo-classical style, with sculpted personifications of the four winds in the corners of the plafond, and allegories of the four elements in the moulding. Inset Ionic columns flank an arch leading through to the **Dutch Room**, where Sobieski's collection of Dutch art was hung. The present décor dates from 1730–33, with elements glorifying Poland's Saxon kings. To the south of the two central rooms stretch the king's apartments, perfectly symmetrical with those of his spouse. The velvet-lined **King's Antechamber** contains many paintings, notably *Apotheosis of Jan III* by Agostino Scilla and *Portrait of the Sobieski Family* (anonymous) in a rich Baroque frame. A Baroque console-table supports five Delft vases. Siemiginowski painted the allegorical plafond depicting Winter, and his four seasons' cycle (Summer) is completed in the adjacent **King's Bedchamber**. Here rich stucco decoration on the ceiling symbolises repose: cherubs riding dolphins and sea-horses. The canopy over the bed was seized as war booty during the siege of Vienna.

Backtrack a short distance through the King's chambers to the **King's Library**. This is the last 17C room, where two circular paintings representing Theology and Philosophy, and 17 portrait medallions of artists, poets and scholars (including Ovid, Homer, Plato, St Augustine, Ptolemy, Copernicus, Raphael and Horace) look down from a stuccoed ceiling. Situated next to the library is the Neo-Renaissance **Royal Chapel**, erected at Potocki's behest to commemorate the spot where Sobieski is said to have died. Small, domed, and built of white marble, the chapel deliberately imitates the royal mausolea on Kraków's Wawel castle. Fragments of Roman sarcophagi and sculpture collected by the Potockis were placed in the **Lapidarium**, originally part of the **Southern Gallery**. In a niche below the south tower stands a large 17C gypsum statue of Jan Sobieski, on which Le Brun later modelled his statue of the king in Łazienki Park (see p. 135).

By far the most impressive room of the south wing, perhaps even of the palace, is the *****White Hall**, which J.S. Deybel raised c 1730 for the Saxon king, August II. Great fluted pilasters rise two storeys to galleries for the royal music ensemble, while double rows of windows directly face mirrors for extra light and brilliance. On the walls hang royal portraits, the best by Louis de Silvestre of August II and III. The remaining rooms in the south wing comprise the 18C apartment of Izabela Lubomirska, whose portrait, executed by Bacciarelli, hangs in the **Anteroom**. Detached from the south wing is Lubomirska's private **Bathhouse**, built by S.B. Zug at the end of the 18C, and later converted into a residential pavilion. The suite, which culminates in a bathroom decked out in green and white marble, is usually closed to visitors.

Palace Gardens

Be sure not to miss the extensive park (**open** 09.30–dusk, closed Tues), whose three distinct parts—the Baroque Garden, Anglo-Chinese Park and English Park—reflect the changing tastes of Wilanów's successive owners.

The east façade of the palace can be best appreciated from the formal **Baroque Garden**, laid out for Sobieski in 1682, and later redesigned by the Potockis. A sandstone balustrade topped with putti symbolising the four seasons and four stages of love (Fear, Kiss, Indifference, Quarrel) encloses the upper terrace, where geometrically placed parterres are interspersed with fountains, espaliers, and 18C statues of classical deities. Steps lead down over a small grotto to the lower terrace, with more handsome parterres and well-pruned hedges. A long promenade skirts the shore of the lake. Here, on the palace axis, stand two figures of Hercules, affording a fine view of the garden façade.

South of the Baroque garden lies the **Anglo-Chinese Park**, which S.B. Zug laid out in Romantic style for Izabela Lubomirska (c 1784). Two 19C **Monuments** by the oval pond commemorate the Potockis: a marble sarcophagus and a stone obelisk surmounted by an urn. To the southwest rises a low hillock, where a column set on a plinth is topped by a 17C Maltese cross. Closer to the palace, a 19C representation of Victory surveys the surroundings from Sobieski's **Hill of Bacchus**. A small **Rose Garden**, with a central fountain, abuts the palace's south wing, while on the north side is the **Grove of Akademos**, a quiet oval space with a semicircular stone bench among ornamental hedges. Nearby, the former **Orangery**, rebuilt by Aigner in 1811, houses a **Gallery of Decorative Art** (**open** 09.30–15.00, closed Tues).

The picturesque **English Park**, landscaped by Potocki, Aigner and Wojciech Jaszczołd in 1799–1821, stretches north along the lake. By the shore stands Marconi's Romantic **Pump House** of 1852, made to look like a miniature medieval castle. As in Potocki's day, the pump house supplies Wilanów's fountains, canals, and flower beds with water. Eventually, the lower park narrows to a spit separating the lake and pond. Here you can admire Aigner's **Chinese Pavilion**, its eight columns supporting a pagoda-like roof surmounted with a lantern, half moons and a Turkish cap. The restored frescoes date from 1806–09. Cross the **Roman Bridge** to an artificial island with a **Monument to the Battle of Raszyn** (which the Poles fought against the Austrians in 1809) in the form of an antique tomb.

Day trips from Warsaw

❖ Palmiry (Kampinos forest) • Modlin Fortress • Jabłonna Palace •
Lake Zegrzyńskie

This day trip takes you west of Warsaw to the Second World War cemetery at Palmiry, and then on to the fortress at Modlin and palace at Jabłonna. Palmiry can be reached by suburban bus from Warszawa Zachodnia coach station (ten daily), but a car is essential if you plan to visit all the sites in a single day.

Leave Warsaw on road 7 (E77) heading north. After 25km, turn left into the Kampinos forest. The small village of **PALMIRY** (population 300) will be remembered as the final destination of more than 2000 inmates from Pawiak and other Warsaw prisons, who were secretly executed here by the Nazis.

The victims, including many public figures, were buried in anonymous graves that were then sown over with trees to cover up the traces. After the war, exhumations were conducted and a memorial cemetery and mausoleum were set up. The cemetery, surrounded by forest, is a huge rectangular field full of stone crosses and a few Jewish gravestones, the majority of them identical, except for the larger graves of Janusz Kusociński, the legendary long-distance runner, and Maciej Rataj, the leader of the pre-war Polish Peasants' Party. On the wall of the **Mausoleum** (open Tues–Sun 09.00–14.30) is an inscription by an unknown prisoner written in a cell on al. Szucha (see p. 129). There is a small Museum (accompanying tape in English) on the history of Palmiry.

Return to the main road and turn left, following signs to Nowy Dwór Mazowiecki (road 579). The large **fortress** in the suburb of **MODLIN**, (12km) is also worth a visit. Built by Napoleon, it was later captured and extended by the Russians to become one of the last outposts of the November Insurgents in 1830 (see p. 51). Long and fierce resistance was also put up here against Hitler's forces in 1939.

After you cross the second bridge, take a sharp left turn along a cobbled road. You will pass under the red brick **Ostrołęcka Gate**, designed by J.J. Gay in 1856. To see the interior of the fortress, you should ask for a guide at the Officers' Mess (up the hill). Alternatively, continue along the driveway, which ends at a terrace with a fine view onto a derelict Neo-Renaissance brick granary (1844, J.J. Gay) situated at the confluence of the Narew and Vistula rivers (inaccessible, a military area).

The Baroque-Classical **palace** at JABŁONNA is 20km southeast of Modlin. Return to the main road, turn right across the bridge, and join road 630, which passes through hilly, sandy woodland. The yellow entrance gate appears on the right just past a roadsign to Legionowo.

Until the mid-18C, the estate belonged to bishops of Płock, later becoming the property of Prince Józef Poniatowski. The architect of Łazienki (see p. 129), Domenico Merlini, designed a palace here in 1775–79. It was partly restored after the Second World War. To the right of the palace stands an orangery, and, on a hillock close by, a 'Chinese' temple (1783, S.B. Zug) topped by a sculpture of a bat. Behind is an expansive park (**open** 06.00–22.00) with many old trees and a solitary arch with columns, statues of Roman warriors, and the inscription 'to Poniatowski'. Today the palace is used mainly for conferences (☎ 0-22 628-1675), but there is no tourist accommodation as yet. To get there by public transport, take bus no. 723 from the centre of Warsaw (20km).

NIEPORĘT, 13km northeast of Jabłonna (roads 61 and 631), is a resort on shores of the artificial LAKE ZEGRZYŃSKIE (800ha, 2–5.7m deep), formed after the construction of the Narew dam in Dębe (1963). It offers beach facilities and watersports, but is usually overcrowded. Turning left after the village, you could drive to the quieter resort of BIAŁOBRZEGI further along the lake.

❖ Warsaw • Zaborów • Kampinos forest • Żelazowa Wola • Brochów

Leave Warsaw along al. Solidarności. Bear right at the petrol station (unmarked) and continue along road 580. The highlight of this trip is ŻELAZOWA WOLA (60km from Warsaw), the birthplace of Frédéric François Chopin (1810–49). It can be reached by suburban bus from the Warszawa Zachodnia coach station (three daily).

If travelling by car you could visit a couple of places on the way. At ZABORÓW there is a Secessionist **palace**, a former royal hunting lodge, set in a large 19C park. At the back, a terrace affords an idyllic view of the garden with a large pond, two stone lions and a stone bridge. The palace is now a hotel, and you can make reservations by writing to *Hotel Pałac*, 05–083 Zaborów, or by ☎ (0-22) 725-9723.

Within easy reach is the primeval KAMPINOS FOREST, set in a pre-glacial valley, and enclosed by the Bzura and Utrata rivers. It is 336 sq. km in area, with a varied terrain of forest, dunes, meadows, and marshland, in which there are 20 nature reserves, containing elks (Sieraków) and black storks (Krzywa Góra). The area is ideal for walks.

Beyond the village of Kampinos continue along road 580, turn right at the sign to Granica, and drive for 2km. The narrow straight road brings you to the **Kampinos National Park Museum** (**open** Tues–Sun 09.00–16.00), actually a skansen, with thatched cottages from the region, a forester's house, and a small natural history display of plants and animals native to the park.

Żelazowa Wola is about 14km to the west of Kampinos, on the same road. Chopin's family house (19C), set in a large park, has been turned into a museum (**open** Tues–Sun 10.00–17.30, 2 May–30 Sept, and 10.00–16.00 off season). The first room (with the fireplace) contains period furniture from Chopin's day. In the music room (with Directory-style furniture) performances of his music are held on Sundays during the season, with the audience gathered in the park.

A famous portrait of the composer by Scheffer hangs on the wall. In the dining room, images of Warsaw in Chopin's times have been assembled, including engravings by Bernardo Bellotto. The park, laid out by Krzywda-Polkowski in 1932–39, has a pond with stone bridges, artificial hillocks, avenues and other Romantic garden features.

Frédéric Chopin

Like Mozart, Frédéric Chopin died young, and with an even greater, single-minded passion, he devoted his brief life to the art of piano music. He was a great innovator, and although adored by Parisian high society, and financially successful as well, he was misunderstood, and his achievement was fully appreciated only many years after his death.

In the age that idolised virtuoso performers to the same degree as rock stars are idolised today, this magician of the keyboard, whose technique could dazzle as much as Paganini's, refused to give public concerts! He preferred to teach and, best of all, to write music in the secluded Nohant villa of his mistress, George Sand. Luckily, he knew how to deal with his publishers and make them pay well.

His art is startlingly original, and the fads and fashions that preoccupied the artistic salons of 19C Paris had no effect on him. The sources that fired his imagination were remote from his surroundings—by some 1400 kilometres.

He left Poland as a 20 year old student, with the career of a child prodigy behind him. He thought he was going only on a short trip to Germany and Italy, where he wanted to learn more music. News of the outbreak of the November Uprising (1830) caught up with him in Vienna. Lost and hesitant for a while, he eventually set out for Paris, where he spent most of his adult life, and where he died in 1849.

His output is not large, but extremely varied, despite the fact that he wrote almost exclusively for solo piano. All his works are unmistakeable for their tone, colour and unique approach to the instrument, but the range of expression and emotion is vast. Although the forms most suited to his personality were miniatures (as demonstrated by the Preludes, Études and Mazurkas, in which simple Mazovian folk tunes are transformed into unrelentingly perfect art), Chopin also produced larger works, such as sonatas, scherzi and ballads—gripping musical narratives, full of drama and suspense. Shortly before tuberculosis overtook him, he had launched into a serious study of counterpoint.

A short detour (10km) brings you to **BROCHÓW** where Chopin's parents were married, and where the composer was baptised. Leaving Żelazowa Wola, continue along the main road west. Turn right (signposted 'Śladów'), and right again after the level crossing. At Konary, turn left for BROCHÓW. The round brick towers of the fortress-like **church** appear from behind trees. Rebuilt in the late 16C, when tunnel vaults and a Renaissance coffered ceiling were added, the church is a rare example of religious-cum-defensive architecture. The towers have loopholes and the grounds are surrounded by a thick brick wall. The interior, with its white arcades, is airy and quiet. Deserted and tranquil, the setting provides a pleasant contrast to the crowds and souvenir shops of Żelazowa Wola.

❖ Warsaw • Konstancin-Jeziorna • Góra Kalwaria • Czersk

The highlight of this trip is Czersk Castle (39km south of Warsaw), which can be reached by suburban bus from the Warszawa Zachodnia coach station (one daily). If travelling by car, you could also visit the towns of Konstancin-Jeziorna and Góra Kalwaria on the way.

Leave Warsaw south along the Wilanów road (724) for **KONSTANCIN-JEZIORNA**, a spa town with quiet, tree-lined streets, handsome villas from the inter-war period, broad promenades, parks and clean air. The writer Stefan Żeromski lived in 'Świt' villa on ul. Żeromskiego (now a modest museum) in 1920–24. Other villas of interest include: 'Ukrainka' on ul. Batorego; 'Anna' on ul. Żeromskiego; and 'Maja' on ul. Sienkiewicza. Recently, Konstancin has become a fashionable Warsaw suburb, where the rich and famous have their sumptuous and heavily guarded villas, among them the notorious journalist Jerzy Urban, Jaruzelski's spokesman during Martial Law.

The town of **GÓRA KALWARIA** is 18km further south along the 724. As you approach, the towers of the Bernardine church will come into view on a bluff, high above the river. Head for the Market Square. The town, today a popular pilgrimage spot, was founded in 1670 by Bishop Wierzbowski, and planned according to how Jerusalem was imagined at that time. Its main attraction is the **Bernardine Church** and convent, built by Giacopo Fontana in 1755, and furnished in Baroque style. By the side altar on the north side a sarcophagus of black marble with the reliquary of St Valerian. The church grounds are entered through an arch with tiny stone statues of saints on high pedestals (18C): Bernard of Siena, Anthony of Padua, Francis of Assisi, and John Capistrano. Walk through the pleasant convent garden towards the river, down a flight of stone stairs, to the stone chapel of St Anthony, with a handsome interior (**open** Tue only).

The hamlet of **CZERSK**, a 10C–11C stronghold, about 4km south of Góra Kalwaria, is one of the oldest settlements in Mazovia.

> The foundations of the present castle were laid in the 13C, and soon afterwards the settlement became the capital of the Duchy of Czersk, famous for its cloth and beer. It received a charter in 1350, but from the 16C began to decline due to the dominance of Warsaw and the altered course of the Vistula. The castle likewise suffered, especially during the Swedish Deluge (see p. 49), and again when the soldiers of the Margrave Friedrich of Baden took refuge here, starting a fire which led to severe devastation.

Today the **castle** is a ruin, but two round towers and a square gatehouse still stand, visited by countless wrens, which seem to have a special liking for the place. The renovation work has been somewhat overdone—the amount of new brick added gives the castle the appearance of a 19C fort. You may climb to the top of the west tower (30m), formerly an armoury, which offers a fine view onto the Vistula valley.

Pułtusk

As early as the 11C, Pułtusk (population 17,400) was an important stronghold guarding the northeastern borderlands of Mazovia. Given a charter in 1339, it became a residence of the bishops of Płock, but its heyday was in the 15C–16C, when it flourished as a commercial centre and a seat of learning. The Jesuits ran their famous college, employing such illustrious teachers as Piotr Skarga and Jakub Wujek who both contributed to the translation of the Polish Bible (see p. 81). In 1806, Pułtusk witnessed a major battle between Napoleon's *Grande Armée* and Russian troops. As a result, its name was later immortalised on the Arc de Triomphe in Paris.

Today Pułtusk justifiably lays claim to being one of the most attractive Mazovian towns. Situated 60km north of Warsaw, it can be easily visited on a day trip (nine buses daily from the Warszawa Zachodnia coach station). If travelling by car, leave Warsaw along road 61, which follows the right bank of the Vistula. At Jabłonna (see p. 151), stay on this road, passing through the satellite town of Legionowo. The route then crosses Lake Zegrzyński (see p. 151) and continues along the high ridge above the Narew river, with the Biała Forest (Puszcza Biała) to the east.

The town centre is situated on an island formed by an arm of the Narew river. The elongated Market Square is bisected by the Town Hall, its Gothic tower (1405) offering a fine panorama of Pułtusk and the surrounding Mazovian plain. Inside the building is the **Archaeological Museum** (open Tues–Fri 10.00–16.00, Sat–Sun 10.00–14.00), with finds from excavations carried out in Pułtusk in the late seventies, during which two 12C settlements and a 13C–14C stronghold were uncovered. The latter, thanks to the conserving power of the humid soil, includes some 300 pinewood huts in excellent condition.

The Gothic **Collegiate Church*, founded in 1449, was converted into a basilica during the 16C. It miraculously escaped destruction in 1507, when two shells lodged themselves in the vault and failed to explode—the event is mentioned in Henryk Sienkiewicz's *Deluge* (see p. 49). In 1560, Gianbattista of Venice set to work on the interior, and the result was pure Renaissance elegance. The last serious remodelling was attempted in 1833–35; today, the church's Gothic provenance is suggested only by the star vaults in the aisles. Its most striking features, at least inside, are the splendid coffered tunnel vaults, and the tall arcade of square white piers. The family chapel of Bishop Noskowksi (1554) is decorated with Renaissance frescoes and a 16C tombstone.

Adjoining the south end of the square is a small park spread over a hillock, on which stands the **Castle of the Bishops of Płock** (now a hotel and good restaurant serving traditional Polish cuisine), as well as the Renaissance **Chapel of Mary Magdalene** (16C), rebuilt after the Second World War and currently inaccessible. The castle stands on the site of a former 13C stronghold (see above). It was built in Gothic style after 1319, and expanded during the 16C–18C. The late Gothic brick bridge was constructed after 1618.

UL. ŚWIĘTOJAŃSKA leads off the square to the **Church of St Joseph** and former **Franciscan Monastery**. Both escaped major damage, not only during the Second World War—when 80 per cent of Pułtusk was devastated—but also during earlier periods of unrest, which makes them unique monuments in a largely reconstructed town centre.

The church, initially Gothic, was rebuilt in 1649 and in the 19C. Its west façade is unusual, with a richly moulded late Renaissance stone gable adorned with a painting of St Joseph, and a plain sloping roof below. In keeping with the ascetic character of the Franciscan rule, the interior is simple, almost austere. Of the passageways to the monastery and sacristy, only Baroque portals remain. The two-storey rectangular monastery with tunnel vaults on the lower floor is currently a prison.

On UL. PIOTRA SKARGI, off ul. Benedyktyńska, stands the grand **Church of SS Peter and Paul** (18C), a cross-vaulted basilica with pilastered exterior walls. The famous **Jesuit College** is right next to it, while at the back, in an overgrown garden, you will find a crenellated brick **tower** (16C), once part of the city walls.

Walk north along UL. KOŚCIUSZKI and turn right. The **Church of the Holy Cross** (late Gothic, 1531), is scenically located in a cemetery on a hillock, with fine views. It contains Renaissance murals (second quarter of the 16C), and a sculpture of Jesus in a niche in the convex façade, bearing the date 1531.

Nieborów, Arkadia and Łowicz

❖ Warsaw • Nieborów • Arkadia • Łowicz • Łódź

This trip takes you to the sumptuous Baroque palace at Nieborów, one of the finest in Poland, now housing an excellent Museum of Baroque Interiors. It then continues to the Romantic park at nearby Arkadia, followed by the town of Łowicz, rich in local Mazovian folklore. Using public transport, it is best to do the trip in reverse: first to Łowicz by suburban bus from Warszawa Zachodnia (81km, two daily) or by train from Warszawa Centralna (three daily), then by local bus to Nieborów (10km). If travelling by car, leave Warsaw on the E30 heading west. At Kompina, turn left for the village of **NIEBORÓW** (8km) (population 1000).

The Baroque palace was built in 1690–96 by one of the leading architects of the day, Tylman van Gameren, a Pole of Dutch descent. His work in Nieborów was commissioned by Primate Michał Stefan Radziejowski, a vigorous patron of the arts, who had just purchased the estate from the Nieborowskis. Later it passed to the well-known aristocratic families of Ogiński (mid-18C) and Radziwiłł (1771–1945). Prince Michał K. Ogiński, who inherited the estate in the 1760s, is remembered for having constructed a system of canals linking the Black Sea with the Baltic. Under the ownership of Prince Michał Hieronim Radziwiłł and Princess Helena (see below), the palace entered its heyday.

The ***palace**, boasting a pedimented façade and mansard roof, is set in beautiful gardens at the end of a long driveway. Entering the grounds, you will pass the former brewery and a series of outbuildings, all designed in the late 18C by the Warsaw architect, Szymon Bogumił Zug. The **Museum of Baroque Interiors** (**open** Tues–Sun 10.00–16.00), inside the palace, is administered by the National Museum in Warsaw, and in summer attracts large crowds of visitors.

Enter the spacious cross-vaulted vestibule, where the prize exhibit is a marble **head of Niobe** (1C Roman copy of a 6C BC Greek original), which is said to have inspired the 20C poet K.I. Gałczyński (see p. 85) to write a poem of the same name. The bust of a Roman woman, also found in the vestibule, is dated at 235–212 BC.

The staircase to the upper floor (1766–68) is covered with Dutch blue cobalt tiles from the Harlingen factory (c 1700), and adorned by several cupids, two granite sphinxes, Roman urns (1C–3C) and a portrait of King Stanisław Poniatowski.

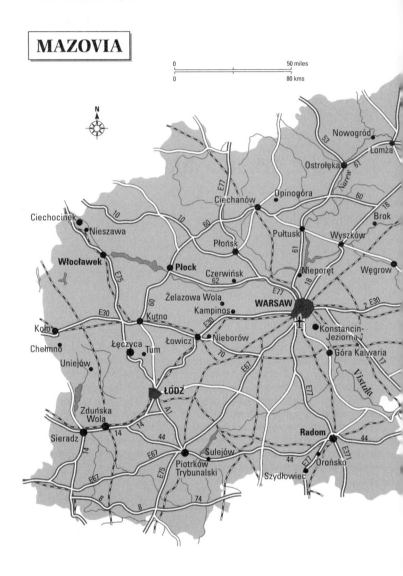

The **White Room** on the first floor, with fine stuccowork, is lit by 18C crystal chandeliers, and equipped with two small corner chapels; notice, also, the tripod with three portraits of childrens' heads (1C). Continue to the **Yellow Study**, carpeted with an Afghan *tebriz* and decorated with early Neo-classical murals. On display is a glass harmonica (1800). Portraits of the Radziwiłł family have been hung on the walls of the bedroom.

Pass through the **Green Study** with a Rococo stove made of green Gdańsk tiles, to the **Library**, where some 11,000 volumes are stacked in 13 mahogany bookcases (early 19C). The mahogany sofa upholstered in red saffian dates from the same period. Among the books are numerous valuable incunabula, including the first printed document in Polish—the *Statute of Jan Łaski* (1506)—an atlas of China published at the beginning of the 18C and two 17C Venetian globes showing the earth and the sky. A small portrait gallery of European monarchs occupies the free space above the bookcases.

The **Red Drawing Room**, which follows the Small Dining Room, is the only room that preserves the original period style from Ogiński's times (mid-18C). It contains a portrait of *Anna Orzelska* by Antoine Pesne, and six unique china vases from the Meissen factory, all made for August II. The tour ends with a bedroom with marble fireplace (1784) and mahogany double bed, a boudoir, and a library study, whose Rococo fireplace has a cast-iron plate decorated with the Ogiński coat of arms.

Almost as impressive as the palace is the 17C–18C *park. Its parterres and regular alleyways following French models are the work of Tylman van Gameren, while the park beyond it was mostly landscaped by Szymon Bogumił Zug. Do not miss the four Turkish stone idols (12C) placed in a small clearing in the centre of the park; of the two columns placed on its main axis, one is early Romanesque, and bears images of demons. Other attractions include an L-shaped pond, and a miniature maze of trimmed hedges. A café and restaurant can be found to the left of the palace; behind it are the historic stables and two orangeries (18C).

Leave Nieborów, turning right (east) for a 4km drive along a lime tree-lined avenue to ARKADIA (population 280), where Szymon Bogumił Zug created a *Romantic park** for Princess Helena Radziwiłł in 1778–1821, complete with an

'Isle of Feelings' on an artificial lake, a 'Grotto of the Sibyl' made of granite blocks (inaccessible), and a 'Roman Arch' of which only the columns remain. An artificial ruin of a classical amphitheatre stands by the lakeshore. The fanciful buildings scattered around the park must have appealed to the Romantic mind. Be sure to visit the **Temple of Diana** by the lake, with a four-columned Ionic portico bearing the inscription 'Dove pace trovai d'ogni mia guerra' ('Here I found peace after each struggle of mine'), and a ceiling painting entitled *Dawn* by Jean Pierre Norblin inside (usually closed to tourists); a mock-Roman aqueduct, closing off the lake with a stream flowing under it; the High Priest's House, constructed of brick, stone and iron-ore masonry; the Margrave's House; and, finally, the Gothic House. The idyllic surroundings could not fail to attract artists and writers: Maria Konopnicka lived in the house with the small porch, visible behind the park fence, in 1893–1903; later, the writer Władysław Reymont sought inspiration in this bizarre skansen.

Łowicz

Łowicz (population 29,500), 5km along the road (70), is a town which cultivates the folk traditions of the Mazovian plain: weaving, embroidery, woodcarving, paper design and colourful costumes. This rich and original culture provided Władysław Reymont with the language, imagery and subject-matter for his Nobel Prize-winning novel, *The Peasants* (see p. 85). During the famous **Corpus Christi procession** (usually in June), and certain other church festivities, the local men and women can be seen wearing traditional dress. The town has two squares: pl. Kilińskiego and the larger PL. KOŚCIUSZKI.

The ***Collegiate Church**, a twin-towered basilica with a richly decorated Baroque interior, stands on this square. For centuries the Gniezno archbishops (Primates of Poland) resided at Łowicz castle (now vanished), and many are buried inside the church.

> The 15C collegiate church was rebuilt in 1625–68 by Tommaso and Andrea Poncino in Renaissance-Baroque style. A fire in 1939 destroyed the towers, roof and organ, but post-war reconstruction restored the church to its original form. The spires by Ephraim Schröger (third quarter of the 18C) crown late Renaissance towers (1624).

Inside, the Rococo high altar (1761, Ephraim Schröger) is adorned with sculptures by Jan Jerzy Plersch. Next to it stand marble statues of Gniezno archbishops. Over the richly carved stalls (1684) hang three large age-blackened paintings of the Flemish school. On the columns are epitaph stones of the bishops and canons of the Łowicz chapter (17C–20C) and, under the choir, a Renaissance double statue (1578).

The church has several elaborate chapels. Most interesting is perhaps the **Chapel of St Victoria** (1580–83), containing a reliquary of the saint brought from Rome in 1652, and the Mannerist tomb of Primate Jakub Uchański, his figure superbly carved by Jan Michałowicz of Urzędów (considered by some to be the greatest Polish sculptor). The chapel itself was rebuilt to Ephraim Schröger's design in the Neo-classical style in 1782–83. The Mannerist Tarnowski (Holy Trinity) Chapel, erected in 1609–11, recalls the famous Zygmunt Chapel on Wawel Hill in Kraków (see p. 216). It contains a white marble *Crucifixion* and the

Tarnowski family tomb, probably carved by the renowned Gdańsk sculptor, Willem van den Blocke (see p. 311). The Chapel of Jesus the Crucified (1759, Ephraim Schröger) has the tomb of Primate Adam Komorowski in black and white marble. In the rectangular Chapel of St Anne (1638), look for Primate Jan Wężyk's coat of arms amid late Renaissance/Mannerist vault decoration. The domed Chapel of the Holy Sacrament (1640–47) has late Baroque frescoes by the Franciscan artist Adam Swach (1718). In addition to the many fine 16C–18C tombstones and memorial tablets other than those already listed, those of Primate J. Przerembski (c 1562, by Girolamo Canavesi, in late Renaissance style), and H. Firlej (1626, Mannerist, probably by Willem van den Blocke), should be visited.

On the **west side** of pl. Kościuszki a group of Baroque houses includes the Curia, Dean's House, six Canons' Houses (Nos 18–20a and No. 21), and the Vicar's Court (No. 29). The **north side** is dominated by a bland Neo-classical **Town Hall** (1825–28). On the **east side**, Tylman van Gameren built the **Missionaries' Seminary** (Baroque, 1689–1701). Reconstructed in 1950–52, it houses a **museum** (open Tues–Sun 10.00–16.00) covering the region's folk art and culture, particularly weaving, embroidery, woodcarving and paper design. Inside the former **chapel**, decorated with frescoes of the life of St Charles by Michelangelo Palloni—court painter to Jan Sobieski III—is a display of Baroque art.

From PL. KILIŃSKIEGO, follow ul. Ciemna, which broadens into UL. SIENKIEWICZA. On the right you will pass the Baroque **Bernardine Nuns' Church and Convent** (c 1650, Tommaso Poncino). Turn right into UL. 1 MAJA, on the corner of which stands the **Church of St Leonard and St Margaret** (1635), a small white building restored after the Second World War. The ruined brick tower on the left (behind a children's playground) used to belong to General Klicki's garden. A road just opposite the tower leads to General's Klicki's **house**, built by Karol Krauze in 1823, using iron-ore masonry and stone fragments (including a coat of arms) from a dismantled palace of the Gniezno archbishops.

> **General Stanisław Klicki** (1775–1847) proved his mettle in several campaigns: the Polish-Russian war of 1792, the Kościuszko Uprising, the Napoleonic wars, the November Uprising. His most glorious deed was to save 4000 Napoleonic soldiers from slaughter by the Cossacks, for which he received a special reward: an exact copy of a set of maps prepared for Napoleon to aid his Asian campaign. Unfortunately, the maps were stolen by Russian soldiers when Klicki left the mansion to fight in the November Uprising (1830). On another occasion he was himself rescued by Duke Beauharnais, Napoleon's stepson; the event has been immortalised on a canvas, which hangs in Kórnik castle near Poznań (see p. 513).

The present owner of the mansion, Mrs Zofia Artymowska, Gen. Klicki's great-granddaughter, is usually willing to show visitors round.

Łódź

Łódź, 135km southwest of Warsaw, was once an obscure village situated close to the larger towns of Pabianice, Zgierz and Konstantynów. It eventually swallowed them up during the Partition Period to become Poland's second largest city, with a population of 870,000. Rapid growth began during the 19C, when Łódź flourished as a centre of the textile industry, earning the nickname of the 'Polish Manchester'. The Nobel Prize-winning author Władysław Reymont (see p. 85) used it as the setting for his *Promised Land*, later filmed by Andrzej Wajda, in which he describes the inhumane ruthlessness of capitalism, the limitless greed of the wealthy, and the helplessness of the poor. Numerous 19C palaces and residences of the industrial magnates, as well as grim, prison-like workers' tenement houses, better described as barracks, have survived to this day as a thought-provoking relic of the past. Though present-day Łódź remains an industrial city, it is more attractive than one might expect, and certainly not lacking in cultural interest. Predictably, it has a well-stocked **Museum of Textiles**, but it also has what is possibly the best **Museum of Modern Art** in the country. Celebrities associated with the city include the poet Julian Tuwim and the pianist Arthur Rubinstein (both were born here in the late 19C), as well as the post-war film-makers Andrzej Wajda, Roman Polański, Jerzy Skolimowski and Krzysztof Kieślowski, who were educated at its famous **Film and Television Academy**.

■ Practical information
Hotels
★★★★
Orbis-Grand. Ul. Piotrkowska 72, ☎ 33-99-20. Ideally located right in the city centre, the Grand is a historic monument in its own right, with preserved fin-de-siècle interiors and a decadent atmosphere to match. Business services. 149 rooms.
Centrum. Ul. Kilińskiego 59-63, ☎ 32-86-40. Air conditioning, car park. 186 rooms.
★★★
Światowid. Al. Kościuszki 68, ☎ 36-30-44. Central location. Car park. 210 rooms.

Tourist information (***PAPT***). Ul. Traugutta 18, ☎ 33-71-69.
ORBIS. Ul. Piotrkowska 68, ☎ 36-65-63, 37-11-01.
Main post office. Ul. Tuwima 38.
Telephone code: (0-42).

History
The hamlet of Łódź was granted to the bishops of Wrocław in 1332, and in 1423 it received a municipal charter from Władysław Jagiełło. Almost four centuries later it passed from the hands of the Kujawy bishops to the state. Due to Łódź's geographical location the liberal reformers R. Rembieliński and S. Staszic (see p. 82) saw in it great potential as a centre of the textile industry. Accordingly, a new cloth-producing settlement was established in 1823 around an octagonal Market Square (now pl. Wolności). The first

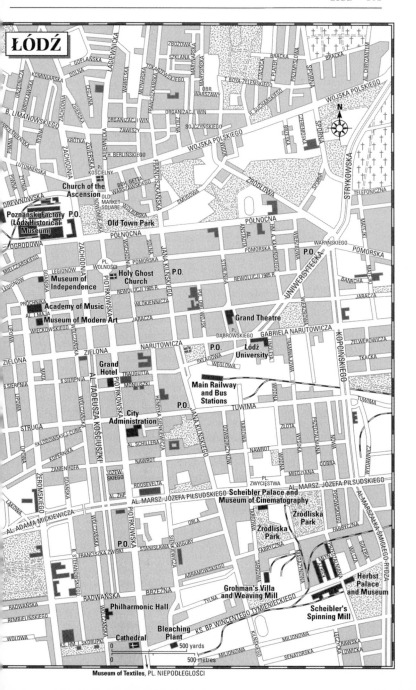

Museum of Textiles, PL. NIEPODLEGŁOŚCI

bleaching plant began operating in 1824, followed, five years later, by the first steam-powered spinning mill, which L. Geyer imported from Great Britain. The abolition of customs barriers between Russia and the Polish Kingdom after 1850 led to a frenzy of money-making led by such entrepreneurial families as the Geyers, Scheiblers, Schweikerts or Poznańskis. Naturally, the accumulated wealth failed to trickle down the social pyramid, causing great resentment among the city's population, which was growing at a breakneck rate (from a few thousand in 1820 to over a quarter of a million by the turn of the century). The six-day **Łódź Rebellion** in 1892 was the first mass strike in Poland. The city became a fertile ground for socialist ideas, championed here by such well-known figures as Julian Marchlewski (who in 1920 set up an abortive Polish Soviet Republic), Józef Piłsudski (regarded by many as Poland's greatest 20C statesman), and Feliks Dzierżyński (the future leader of the fearful Cheka in the Soviet Union). The Second World War brought wide scale destruction and decimated the population. Hardest hit were, of course, the Jews; at one time they constituted a third of the city's population, but almost all perished in the ghetto or in the Chełmno concentration camp 70km to the northwest of the city (see p. 166). During the War the Nazis renamed the city Litzmanstadt.

The imposition of Soviet-style socialism failed to improve the living standards of the city's working class, and in 1979–80, Łódź once again became a hotbed of public protest. A memorable demonstration took place in 1981, when thousands of women employed in the textile factories took to the streets. On a lighter note, in 1987 the Wrocław-based **Orange Alternative** (see p. 424) organised a 'happening' on ul. Piotrkowska, the city's main thoroughfare. Participants wearing T-shirts with the slogan 'Galloping Inflation' ran down the street and were, of course, promptly arrested. In a press release following the event they announced: 'Government economic policy has scored another historic victory: today, the Łódź police force managed to halt galloping inflation.' Indeed, at that time inflation was running into three figures.

Walk One ~ Piotrkowska Street

This walk takes you along ul. Piotrkowska, the city's main axis and shopping district, before heading east to the old industrial area, with its 19C mills, tenements and palaces. A good place to begin is on pl. Niepodległości, at the south end of ul. Piotrkowska. Walking north, notice the statue of Nobel Prize-winner Władysław Reymont (see p. 85) on the right. Further on, at the corner of ul. Przybyszewskiego, stands the Neo-classical **Geyer Villa** (1830). Passing the Reymont Park and a pond on your right, continue to Geyer's *White Factory* at No. 282 (Neo-classical, 1835–39), currently a **Museum of Textiles** (open Tues–Sat 10.00–16.00, Sun 10.00–15.00), with an extensive collection of looms and other machinery, the earliest dating from the 17C.

On the left, at the junction with ul. Ignacego Skorupki, stands a huge yellow brick **cathedral** (Neo-Gothic, 1901–10) designed by the German architect Zelman. The **statue** in front of it represents Father Ignacy Skorupka, an army chaplain who died fighting Soviet troops at the battle of Radzymin in 1920. Opposite the church is the Scheibler Palace, one of two in the city named after the 19C industrialist.

The walk now leaves ul. Piotrkowska and takes you along UL. WINCENTEGO TYMIENIECKIEGO. Here you enter a district of historic **19C factories**. On the right, at the junction with ul. Sienkiewicza, is the **Stary Bielnik** (bleaching plant). Crossing ul. Kilińskiego, you arrive at the Grohman Park (left), where **Grohman's villa** and **weaving mill** are found. Passing a fire station, in front of which stands an original Manchester steam engine, you reach Scheibler's huge redbrick **spinning mill** on the right. Cross the road to see a group of **workers' homes** on UL. KSIĘŻY MŁYN. The entire quarter has preserved its original late 19C plan, linking factories, tenements and palaces. The gloomy redbrick workers' houses, still inhabited, could have been taken straight out of London's East End.

At the next junction turn right into ul. Przędzalniana, which runs south alongside a park. Inside the Herbst Palace, at the edge of the park, is a **museum** (**open** Tue 10.00–17.00, Wed, Fri 12.00–17.00, Thu 12.00–19.00, Sat–Sun 11.00–16.00) which recreates the interiors of 19C industrialists' mansions. Returning north along ul. Przędzalniana you will reach the Źródliska Park with 250-year old oak trees. Walk through it to another fine palace named after Scheibler (pl. Zwycięstwa 1), which contains the **Museum of Cinematography** (**open** Tue–Fri 10.00–15.00, Sat–Sun 11.00–15.00). Turn left to return to ul. Piotrkowska.

Walk Two ~ The city centre

This walk starts from PL. WOLNOŚCI at the north end of ul. Piotrkowska. The noteworthy buildings on the square are the **Archaeological and Ethnographical Museum** at No. 14 (**open** Tues, Thur–Fri 10.00–17.00, Wed 09.00–16.00, Sat–Sun 10.00–15.00); the Neo-classical **Town Hall** (1827); the **Monument to Kościuszko** (M. Lubelski); and the twin-towered **Holy Ghost Church**, whose interior seems almost circular with its two-tiered gallery over the aisles and two domes.

Head north along ul. Nowomiejska, across ul. Północna and the Old Town Park (1953), and pass the neglected area of the Old Market Square. You will finally arrive at the twin-towered **Church of the Ascension** on pl. Kościelny, propped up by massive buttresses, and entered through an imitation-Gothic portal with a rosette. During the Second World War, the Nazis used it as a prison. Inside, the high altar has a Gothic triptych by Antoni Panasiuk, modelled on Veit Stoss's famous altar in St Mary's in Kraków (see p. 199). The wooden reliefs depicting the *Way of the Cross* are a gift of the Brajer family from Radogoszcz, and were made in the Tyrol. In the chapel at the end of the south aisle hangs a painting of *Our Lady of Łódź*, the oldest extant copy of the Black Madonna of Częstochowa (1670–90; see p. 267), according to legend found in a boat on the Łódka river.

Return to ul. Północna, going west along UL. OGRODOWA. Soon the Neo-Gothic façades of the vast **Poznański Factory** will come into view. The complex consists of textile and cotton mills, tenement houses, warehouses, and the Poznański's **Palace** at No. 17, built for the industrialist in the 1880s and currently housing the **Łódź Historical Museum** (**open** Tues, Thur–Sun 10.00–14.00, Wed 14.00–18.00). The highlight of the exhibition is a section devoted to **Artur Rubinstein**, a native of Łódź, who for many will remain the greatest pianist of the 20C.

Continuing along ul. Ogrodowa you will reach an **Orthodox Cemetery**, with many graves bearing inscriptions in Russian. Turn south into ul. Cmentarna

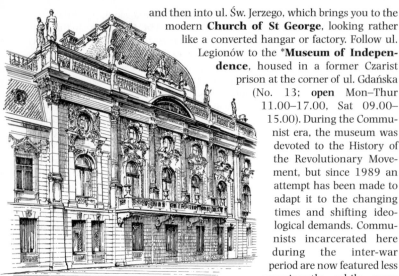

Poznański Palace

and then into ul. Św. Jerzego, which brings you to the modern **Church of St George**, looking rather like a converted hangar or factory. Follow ul. Legionów to the ***Museum of Independence**, housed in a former Czarist prison at the corner of ul. Gdańska (No. 13; **open** Mon–Thur 11.00–17.00, Sat 09.00–15.00). During the Communist era, the museum was devoted to the History of the Revolutionary Movement, but since 1989 an attempt has been made to adapt it to the changing times and shifting ideological demands. Communists incarcerated here during the inter-war period are now featured less prominently, while more emphasis is given to **Józef Piłsudski**, the restorer of Polish independence in 1918 (see p. 54). His cell has not been preserved, but to compensate for this, a room from his Łódź flat has been reconstructed, showing the semi-portable press on which he manually printed the underground paper *Robotnik* (The Worker) until his arrest in February 1900. In the cells on the ground floor are sundry objects illustrating the life of the inmates. The other rooms trace the history of Łódź and Polish participation in the Second World War.

Museum of Modern Art

Continue south along ul. Gdańska, passing another of Poznański's palaces (1904) on the right (currently the Academy of Music). At the corner of ul. Więckowskiego, be sure to visit the splendid ***Museum of Modern Art** at No. 36.

The museum (**open** Tues 10.00–17.00, Wed–Fri 11.00–17.00, Thur 12.00–19.00, Sat–Sun 10.00–16.00), established in 1925, is surprisingly unfrequented. Connoisseurs of 20C avant-garde might spend hours wandering through the rooms, admiring works by Pablo Picasso, Paul Klee, Marc Chagall, Nancy Hold, Christo, Victor Vasarely, Henri Michaux, and Max Ernst; tracing the roots of contemporary art in displays devoted to the 1930s and 1940s, covering S.I. Witkiewicz (Witkacy), W. Strzemiński, the Polish Formists, Unism, Surrealism, Neo-Plasticism, Cinematic Art, Systemic Art, Expressionism, Sign Script, Constructivist Print, the Kraków Group and the Zero Group; or reading about the 'happenings' once staged here (for example, Chris Burden crawling over broken glass, or being bolted to the floor with copper bands near buckets of water attached to live wires from 8–10 pm for three consecutive nights!).

Day trips from Łódź

❖ Łęczyca • Tum • Góra Św. Małgorzaty • Chełmno • Uniejów

The highlights of this trip are the historic town of Łęczyca (38km northwest of Łódź) with its Royal Castle, and the Romanesque church in nearby Tum. Both these places can be reached by bus from Łódź. There are also several trains daily from Łódź to Łęczyca. If travelling by car, you could continue the trip to the remote village of Chełmno, the site of a Nazi Death Camp (34km from Łęczyca).

Łęczyca (population 16,600), one of the earliest Polish settlements, was initially fortified by Kazimierz the Great, who also erected the castle (see below). The town, chartered in 1400, rose to prominence as the seat of the palatinate and the venue of various assemblies and regional councils. It fell into decline during the 17C, and never recovered.

Leave Łódź along ul. Zgierska and then take road 1, signposted 'Gdańsk'. After 38km turn left off the main road when the brick tower of the *Royal Castle comes into view. The castle was built in the 14C as a residence for the Łęczyca starost. Its east wing suffered much damage during the Swedish Deluge (see p. 49), and remnants of the medieval Old House were pulled down by the Prussians at the end of the 18C. What you see today is largely a post-war reconstruction. The interiors house a **Regional Museum** (open Tues 10.00–17.00, Wed–Fri 10.00–16.00, Sat–Sun 09.00–14.00), which begins with an archaeological section in the cellars. The earliest finds date from 150 BC to AD 400 and include weapons from Roman times, Roman, Thracian and Macedonian coins, as well as 12C–13C objects retrieved from the graves of church dignitaries. Also on display is a model of the monastery in Tum (see below). On the ground and first floors the display covers 18C–20C art and furniture from the region, folk culture and household items. The highlight of the museum is the largest collection in Poland of statues and statuettes of the evil spirit Boruta, who crops up in many folk tales, officially repugnant, but such a pathetic loser that one cannot help but like him. Most are carved in lime-wood, some are made of glass.

The Market Square has a Neo-classical **Town Hall** (1788) and a **Monument** to the Poznań corps, defeated here in 1939 by the Wehrmacht. Follow ul. Kościelna to the **parish church** (1425). Its original Gothic character was lost during reconstruction in the 18C–19C, save for the rood arch and crucifix. The rest of the furniture and decoration is unimpressive Baroque. Ul. Waryńskiego will take you from the square to the 17C **Bernardine Church and Priory**, with a small tower above the dome, and a fronton decorated with pilasters. The interior has 18C painted decoration, and ornate side chapels and altars. Outside, a statue of the Virgin commemorates the restoration of the church to Bernardine monks in 1946.

Tum, 3km from Łęczyca, is well worth a visit. Leave Łęczyca on road 703 signposted 'Łowicz/Gdańsk'. After 2km turn right. The village of Tum came into prominence in the 9C, when the Benedictines founded a monastery here. The monastery was pulled down, however, after the monks had abandoned it for Mogilno (see p. 521) in 1140. Soon after their departure, Princess Salomea, the widow of King Bolesław the Wry-mouthed, founded a Romanesque *Collegiate Church* on the site, constructed of huge granite blocks. Its history is marked by distinction (27 Łęczyca synods were held here), interspersed with the usual calamities: it was destroyed by Lithuanians in 1293, burned down by the Teutonic Knights in 1306 and by the Swedes in 1705, finally to be hit by German bombs in 1939. In 1487, the interior was reconstructed in brick Gothic style; in 1569, a Renaissance narthex was added to protect the precious Romanesque portal; and in 1765–85 it acquired a Neo-classical appearance. Apart from the exquisite portal, with a tympanum scene of the Virgin and Child, few other Romanesque elements have survived: a barely-visible mural representing Christ the Pantocreator (12C, discovered in the 1950s), a relief figure of a knight, canons' tombstones, and granite blocks in the apse. Worthy of note are the Renaissance painted decoration and several coffin portraits (see p. 69).

If the dirt road southwest across fields is passable, you could visit the site of a 6C–7C ring settlement, destroyed many times and rebuilt in 1106-07 by King Bolesław the Wry-mouthed. It once guarded the river crossing, and today affords an attractive view over the collegiate church and the surrounding marshes, which must have inspired many of the legends about the evil spirit Boruta (see above).

For a pleasant drive through rural Poland leave Tum and head for the Hill of St Margaret (GÓRA ŚW. MAŁGORZATY), 7km to the east. This leads across plains and fields, along tree-lined roads, past orchards and ramshackle houses. On top of the hill (21m) stands a **church**. Originally built in 1143, it was later Gothicised, but what you see today dates from a much later period, mostly the 19C.

Return to Łęczyca and continue westwards along minor roads to Chełmno. Past Dąbie watch out for a white sign marked 'Obóz straceń'. Set in woodland, **CHEŁMNO** (population 360) was the site of a **Nazi Death Camp**, in which more than 300,000 people perished, mostly Jews. Among the victims were 82 children from Lidice in former Czechoslovakia, whose inhabitants were all executed in retaliation for the assassination of Reinhard Heydrich by the Czech resistance in 1942. There is a slab stating this, and a modernist stone sculpture commemorating the fallen.

Return to Dąbie and continue south to **UNIEJÓW** (population 2600), in medieval times the main residence of the bishops of Gniezno. Today, the main attractions are the Gothic **Church of the Ascension**, with a south chapel devoted to the Blessed Bogumił, Archbishop of Gniezno, and the small Gothic **castle**, situated across the river. Raised in the mid-14C by Archbishop Jarosław Skotnicki, the castle is now a hotel and conference centre, organising balls, weddings and receptions. Parts of it are open to tourists (Sat 14.00–16.00, Sun 14.00–18.00), such as the cellars, several rooms with period furniture, and the chapel. You can climb the tower for a bird's eye view of Uniejów.

To return to Łódź, stay on the 473 heading south. In Balin, turn left onto road 709.

❖ Piotrków Trybulanski • Sulejów • Podklasztorze

This excursion is best done by car. The highlight is the Cistercian monastery in Podklasztorze, set on the banks of Lake Sulejowskie. If travelling from Łódź, you should head south on the E-75 motorway to Piotrków (see below) and then proceed east to Sulejów (road 74).

PIOTRKÓW TRYBUNALSKI (population 80,200), 44km south of Łódź, is the most attractive town of the region. It figures prominently in Polish history as the venue of parliaments and regional assemblies (1354–1567), and as the seat of the Crown Tribunal (1578–1792). The Swedish Deluge brought destruction and decline, though in 1876 the town was raised to the status of a provincial capital. During the Second World War, the Nazis established the first ghetto on Polish territory here.

If you enter Piotrków along ul. Wojska Polskiego, turn right down ul. Rwańska and head for the MAIN SQUARE, which is bordered by 17C–18C houses. You could stop for refreshments at the traditional **Armenian teahouse**, now converted into a café. From the Square, walk down ul. Konarskiego to the junction with UL. PIJARSKA. Squeezed into the narrow side street is the **Jesuit Church** (1695–1727), noted for its *trompe l'oeil* painted decoration by A. Ahorn (1755–69). At the back it abuts the former college building, with a planetarium inside, and, to the right, the monastic building (ring there if the church is locked).

Continue east along ul. Pijarska towards the lofty brick tower of the Gothic **parish church** (14C–15C). The interior, decked out in dark hues, has paintings depicting angels, saints and popes; epitaph stones (16C and later), carved wooden stalls, a black-and-gold high altar, and two Baroque side chapels.

Return to the Main Square and head east along the maple-lined ul. Zamkowa. You will come to a Gothic/Renaissance-style **palace** built for King Zygmunt the Old by Benedykt of Sandomierz, and decorated with stonework by the Italian architect Bartolomeo Berrecci, designer of the famous Zygmunt Chapel in Kraków (see p. 216). Indeed, the stone elements you see here were carved in Kraków and later transported to Piotrków. The palace, like its sister in Lublin, was used by Zygmunt the Old and his successor Zygmunt August as a royal residence during sessions of the Crown Tribunal. The present palace building dates from the turn of the 17C, when it was rebuilt by Starost Michał Werszycki after a fire. During the Partitions, it was turned into a warehouse, and then an Orthodox church. The second floor was dismantled, and what you see today is a 1960s reconstruction of the 17C interior. Originally, the ground floor of the three-storey tower was used by the servants, the first floor housed the royal apartments, and the second floor the reception rooms. In some places the wall is 2.5m thick. A moat and wooden ramparts constituted the palace's defences. A museum inside the palace (**open** Tues 10.00–17.00, Wed–Sat 10.00–16.00, Sun 10.00–16.00) offers a display of 19C Gdańsk furniture, items relating to the pre-history and history of Piotrków, and Renaissance and Baroque furniture.

From Piotrków, head 16km east to the resort of **SULEJÓW** (population 5800) with its artificial lake (2117ha) and recreation facilities scattered over its wooded banks. This was an early medieval trading settlement, which grew around a ford across the Pilica river. At the beginning of the 12C, it was given to the wealthy Cistercian order, and had its charter confirmed in 1308. Decline set in after the Swedish wars of the 17C. The town's Neo-Gothic basilica, built in 1901–08, is set high upon a hill overlooking the Pilica, on the bank of which stands the **Ligęza Chapel** (1644). A Gothic Madonna (1420) hangs just opposite the pulpit, and there are two 16C sculptures.

Cistercian monastery at Podklasztorze

After Sulejów the road forks; take the left branch, signposted 'Kielce', and then immediately left again for **PODKLASZTORZE**, skirting the Pilica river. On the left, the ancient *Cistercian Monastery* will come into view. The whole cluster of buildings is divided into two parts, one of which has been restored to the Cistercians, the other turned into a hotel and **museum**. The latter occupies a small room and has an exhibition devoted to the history of the abbey. A curious item on display is a human skull, probably dating from the 11C, with a piece of bone inserted into it. This may well be the skull mentioned by Gallus the Monk (see p. 80), who tells the story of a knight injured in battle and saved only by speedy trepanation. Other exhibits include early medieval objects of daily use, such as arrowheads and paintings, the most interesting of which is an anonymous oil on wood, depicting the welcome given by the monks to a German bishop from Riga, sent by the king to administer the abbey. The monks are visibly displeased, but have no choice but to bow to the bishop.

The abbey was founded in 1176 by Kazimierz the Just, and a late Romanesque *church (13C) was built soon afterwards. The best surviving element of the church is the main portal of 1230, with a tympanum dating from the end of the 12C. Its sculpted capitals and keystones bear floral and fruit motifs, referring to the Cistercians' traditional occupation—agriculture. The rosette above contains original tracery. Another Romanesque portal is found at the entrance to the north aisle, and shows a Passion scene in relief. The south transept adjoins the sacristy and the 13C chapter house, which borders the east wing of the ruined abbey, with 15C cloisters. Inside the chapter house is a curious piece of Romanesque stonework: a vault boss carved to represent four heads of monks, their beards touching, and a fruit in the middle, perhaps symbolising the fruitful conferences held here.

Warsaw to Białystok

❖ Liw • Węgrów • Treblinka • Brok • Łomża • (detour: Nowogród) • Drozdowo Wizna • Tykocin • Choroszcz • Białystok

The town of **LIW** (72km from Warsaw) is in fact one of oldest settlements in Eastern Mazovia (chartered in 1412). It was also the seat of Mazovian dukes and to them it owes its castle, now a ruin, pleasantly sited among meadows with a stream flowing nearby. From Warsaw cross the Gen. Berling bridge and leave the city along al. Stanów Zjednoczonych, joining road 637. Once in Liw, pass the Neo-Gothic church and turn right onto a narrow road, marked 'Zamek'.

The main surviving building is a late 18C Baroque manor house, which contains a **Weaponry Museum and Portrait Gallery** (open Tues–Sat 10.00–16.00, Sun 11.00–16.00), featuring carpets, furniture, weapons, armoury, and 18C–19C portraiture. The sections of wall in the vicinity are remnants of the castle proper. Two cannon shafts that would not fit into the museum are displayed on the low wall to the right of the main building.

> The **castle** was built on an artificial hillock amid marshes to guard the Polish-Lithuanian border, which at that time followed the course of the Liwiec river. Expanded by Bona Sworza in 1570, it fell into ruin following the Swedish Deluge (see p. 49), and a fire in the 19C. The Nazis planned to dismantle it and use the materials to construct the Treblinka death camp. However, the ancient monument was saved from imminent and irreversible

destruction by a local amateur archaeologist, Otto Warpechowski, who managed to persuade the German governor that it had been built by the Teutonic Knights, and thus proved German presence in the area centuries ago. Initially fooled by this clever stratagem, the Nazis even made a reconstruction effort, but eventually German historians discovered the fraud and Warpechowski had to go into hiding to save his own life; by that time, however, the Nazis had abandoned their plans for the ruin. He later joined the Soviet-backed Second Polish Corps, and died in combat.

In the hall is an oval portrait of Ludwika neé Szuyski Kuczyńska, the 'yellow lady', heroine of a hackneyed legend involving unjust suspicions of adultery, leading to her murder, and repentance and eventual suicide by the jealous and belatedly remorseful husband.

WĘGRÓW (population 11,600), (6km from Liw; turn right onto the main road) chartered in 1441, was a wheat-trading town on the Ukraine-Gdańsk route during the 16C–18C, as well as an important centre of **Polish Calvinism**. In 1570, a seminary, printing house and hospital were founded, followed by textile works in the 17C. The town's growth was checked by the Swedes, and later by the Napoleonic wars. In 1863, the Russian army clashed here with the Polish insurgents.

The **parish church** on the Main Square was originally a late Gothic aisled hall, but only a wooden Gothic crucifix, bells, a few paintings and one epitaph stone were saved from destruction in 1703. It was later rebuilt as a Baroque basilica (1703–06). Only minor damage was done in 1939 and 1944, and the good stuccoes, painted decoration (1707–08, Michelangelo Palloni), and 18C paintings have survived. The weather-vane on the highest tower is a mobile heraldic emblem, the 'Ślepowron' (night heron). Another curiosity, 'the Black Prince's looking glass', is kept in the sacristy. According to tradition, it once belonged to Twardowski.

The Legend of Twardowski

Twardowski, a figure familiar to every Pole, is largely the product of 19C Romantic fancy, but his prototype may well have been a real alchemist-cum-astrologer in the service of King Zygmunt August. Twardowski reputedly signed a pact with the Devil, in return for which he was able to perform such amazing feats as balance an enormous boulder on its tip (the 'Club of Hercules'; see p. 264), create a lake during a single night (Lake Augustowskie), or fashion a whip out of sand. Under the terms of the pact, the Devil could only take Twardowski's soul from Rome. Unable to entice him to Italy, he built an inn in the village of Sucha Beskidska, which he called 'Rome', and thus trapped the unsuspecting magician. The Holy Virgin took pity on Twardowski and saved him from the torments of Hell. He still lives on the moon, and is usually portrayed astride the crescent.

Walk down ul. Kościuszki to the Baroque **Reformed Franciscan Church and Priory**, about 200m down on the left (if locked, enter through the adjoining priory). It was erected by Tylman van Gameren and Ceroni in 1693–1706, and furnished in the early 18C, with fine painted decoration by Palloni. The façade bears statues of kneeling monks at the corners; above the roof rises a black-and-gold lantern. Murals cover the main dome, four chapel domes, and cloisters.

Treblinka

Follow signs to Treblinka (42km) along a narrow road which cuts through pine forest and meadows. In Kosów, follow signs to Łomża (road 63); finally, turn left for *Treblinka. The first Nazi slave labour camp (Treblinka I), in which 7000 died (now commemorated by a monument and cemetery), is adjoined 2km further on by Treblinka II, a death camp built in 1942, where 800,000 Jews and Poles were exterminated. The Nazis built a fake station next to the railway siding, a field hospital, and other buildings to mask the true nature of the destination. The prisoners were gassed in chambers masquerading as showers; their corpses were then burnt on pyres. You can examine photocopies of documents connected with the camp inside the small museum (open 09.00–19.00). Brace yourself for a long walk if you wish to see the whole site. A trail of concrete slabs mark the route of the former railway, ending at the former station where the 'selection procedures' would take place. To the left is the Road of Death, which leads up to a symbolic cemetery with thousands of roughly-hewn stones, most unmarked, set into a concrete base. In the centre is a monument with the inscription 'Never Again' repeated in five languages. The sculpture behind it symbolizes the mass grave of the 800,000 people exterminated here: a bluish-black contorted mass resembling volcanic lava encased in a rectangular shallow ditch. The whole site is surrounded by pillars of rough granite delineating the former perimeter fence. The mausoleum is surrounded by pine forests; three or four weeping willows planted near the monument add a poignant touch. To get to the labour camp (Treblinka 1), follow the cobbled road for 2km. Among those who perished here was Janusz Korczak, a teacher who pioneered many modern ideas of child education, and who chose to die with a group of children from the Warsaw Ghetto rather than abandon them.

Continue north to Małkinia along a bumpy road parallel to the railway lines. Cross the Bug river over a narrow road and rail bridge. In Małkinia, turn left, signposted 'Łomża', and continue straight (road 63). Alternatively, soon after the turn go left again, signposted 'Brok' (16km). The brick Renaissance **parish church** in BROK was erected in 1650 by the accomplished master-mason, Gian-battista of Venice. It contains elegant stucco decoration on the barrel vaults (so-called Pułtusk vaults), and a pretty organ carved in wood at the back.

The next stopping point is ŁOMŻA (59km; population 54,800), an old Mazovian town set on the high bank of the Narew river. Every second year in May it hosts a cultural festival, with performances of early Polish music, poetry reading competitions, and a traditional Polish fair.

The initial 10C–13C settlement in Stara Łomża (Old Łomża) was destroyed during Lithuanian and Jatzvingian (see p. 412) raids, but already by the end of the 14C a new settlement had been founded, which received a charter in 1418 from the Mazovian duke Janusz I. The 17C–18C saw a sharp decline in the town's prosperity, culminating in a revolt against the starost and Łomża's takeover by the mob in 1711. Until the First World War, Łomża remained a provincial capital, defended by a system of forts and redoubts raised in 1889–1902.

The road by which you enter Łomża ascends to a tree-lined square, on the right of which is the large **Church of the Ascension**. Park there and continue on foot, turning right into ul. Dworna to get to the Gothic *****cathedral**. This brick basilica (1504–26), renovated by G. S. Bellotti after a fire in 1621, is one of the most celebrated late Gothic churches in Mazovia. Very spacious and grand, if a little sombre, it has some delightfully intricate vaults: star vaults in the nave and, even more impressive, cellular ones in the aisles. In contrast, the main altar is unusually decorated with five rectangular silver reliefs. The chancel, paved with black and white marble slabs, is dimly lit by three tall stained-glass windows piercing the apse. The best monument is to be found in the south aisle: the magnificently ornamented Renaissance tomb of Mikołaj Troszyński (1611).

Walk further down ul. 22 Lipca and take the next left. You will emerge on the leafy MARKET SQUARE, with a Neo-classical **Town Hall** of 1823. Walk across the Square to ul. Krzywe Koło. On the opposite side of the street, you will see the late Baroque **Capuchin Church** (1781–84, expanded in 1859) and adjoining monastery. Continue down ul. Krzywe Koło to the **Regional Museum** (open Tues–Sun 09.00–16.00), which overlooks a park and amphitheatre. The five permanent exhibitions are devoted to the history of the region, ethnography, local art and handicrafts (including a collection of kerosene lamps), archaeology and numismatics, and a unique collection of amber and amber manufacturing equipment. The amber on display was not fished out of the Baltic sea, as might be expected, but was mined in the Narew valley. The largest piece weighs more than half a kilogram.

Detour to Nowogród

A 16km detour to **NOWOGRÓD** will take you to the heart of the Kurpie region; for a glimpse of the rich local culture, be sure to visit the small but excellent skansen. Leave Łomża heading northwest along ul. 22 Lipca and then ul. Nowogrodzka. The road passes through the Zielona Forest (Puszcza Zielona). Once in Nowogród, follow the signs to 'Muzeum/Skansen'.

> Situated at the confluence of the Pisa and Narew rivers, Nowogród was a trading settlement given a charter by Bolesław IV in 1434 and later fortified. It flourished for some time under the Mazovian dukes, becoming the seat of a castellanship, but began to decline in the 17C, like so many other Polish towns. The two occupations of its inhabitants that brought it most fame were bee-keeping and the manufacture of amber jewellery.

The *****skansen**, one of the oldest in Poland—founded in 1927 by Adam Chętnik—is pleasantly compact (4ha). Its setting on a wooded slope by the Narew and Pisa rivers is truly enchanting, but, as the guide will inform you, a typical Kurpie village, always clustered around the main road, would look rather different. To see the interiors of the 20 or so cottages you should first visit the **manor house** on the hill by the main entrance, and hire a guide (available Mon–Fri 09.00–16.00, Sat–Sun 10.00–17.00). All the farmsteads were moved to the skansen from various villages in the Kurpie region. Other items of interest include smithies, water mills and revolving windmills (to accommodate changing wind direction), two granaries, hollow tree-trunks used for bee-keeping, a thousand-year-old fishing boat with an original fisherman's hut next to it, and a wooden carved monument to Stach Konwa (d. 1733), leader of the Kurpie people. The forester's house contains an exhibition of traditional, lavishly embroidered Kurpie dress. Two granaries are cleverly set on wooden mushroom-shaped stands to exclude mice from the fruits of the summer harvest. In the barn you will see hand-driven ploughs, a hand loom, a treadmill driving various machines, a wooden harrow (the sandy soil predominant in the region harrowed well), and a crane for hauling water, once common in Poland, and still used in a few places. There are plans to open an inn and to make some of the cottages available for tourist accommodation.

Return to Łomża and first take road 64 marked 'Białystok', later (25km) turning right for the village of **DROZDOWO**. The **museum** (open Tues–Sun 09.30–15.30) occupies the former manor house of the Lutosławski family, which had many illustrious members, including Wincenty—a philosopher best known for his dating of Plato's dialogues—and Witold—a celebrated 20C composer. However, with the exception of one room tracing the history of the family and the house (in which the statesman Roman Dmowski died on 2 January 1939), the museum is devoted to the varied **flora and fauna** of the Biebrza and Narew valleys, the largest expanse of marshland in Europe. Hundreds of stuffed animals and dried plants from the Ice Age to present times have been assembled, mostly for the benefit of school parties.

After Drozdowo the road passes through peaceful countryside, skirting the Narew river. At the T-junction turn right. In **WIZNA**, an old Mazovian town chartered in 1435, turn right and head for the square. The **parish church** (1526), in Prussian Gothic style, has large gables on both sides and elaborate net vaults.

TYKOCIN, an old Mazovian town, lies in the marshy valley of the Narew river. Continue along road 64, turning left after Jeżewo (road 671) for an 8km drive to the town.

> Tykocin received a charter in 1425. King Zygmunt August began work on expanding the castle, but eventually, in 1661, donated the town to the Polish general Stefan Czarniecki as reward for his victory over the Swedes. Tykocin's last owners were the Branicki family. During the 18C–19C, the town handled most of the trade in Eastern Mazovia and the area to the south of it. At that time, its population increased rapidly thanks to a massive influx of Jews; a community that was completely wiped out during the Second World War.

The town has preserved its cobbled streets and an historic, 18C urban plan, with the Main Square overlooked by a Baroque **monument of Stefan Czarniecki**. The east side is dominated by the large **parish church** (1742–45). Inside, you will find some good paintings by Szymon Czechowicz, frescoes by Sebastian Eckstein, and busts of various nobles. White curved galleries link the body of the church with two belfries (1742–49). Nearby, just before the bridge, is a late Renaissance **Hospice for Retired Soldiers** (1634–38) with an inner courtyard, which remained functional until the First World War.

Head west from the square along ul. Złota, which becomes ul. Piłsudskiego across the river. On the left is the *****Talmudic House and Synagogue**, with a museum inside (open Tues–Sun 10.00–17.00). The late Renaissance synagogue building (1642) had a tall Baroque roof added in the 18C, as well as a Baroque corner tower and, on the south and west sides, two *babini* (prayer halls for women). Despite fires in the 18C–19C, and damage during the First World War, the synagogue has preserved Renaissance decoration inside and Lublin-style stucco-work adorning the *bema*. Notice the rare nine-part vault structure, cupboards with liturgical vessels, chandeliers, *menorahs* (seven-branched candelabra) and a *chanuk* lamp, used during the Chanukah, or Festival of Lights. In the *babini* is a display showing the history of Tykocin. Next door in the Talmudic house are three permanent displays including a reconstructed apothecary. The stone foundations opposite the synagogue are the remnants of the 18C stalls. Further away are 19C wooden houses, once inhabited by Jews.

Walk south of the square along ul. Bernardyńska to the former **Bernardine Monastery**, founded in 1771 by J. K. Branicki. This horse-shoe shaped building, with a Neo-classical gate-tower (19C), a large courtyard, and a polychromed chapel in the north wing, serves as a home for retired priests.

Cross the bridge north of the square and soon turn left along a dirt road to the ruins of the 15C **royal castle**, where archaeologists unearthed remnants of an early medieval settlement. The castle was extended by King Zygmunt August to become one of the largest fortified structures in the Mazovian lowlands. Its destruction during the 17C Swedish wars was described by Henryk Sienkiewicz in *Deluge*, the second volume of his famous *Trilogy* (see p. 84).

Before reaching Białystok it is worth visiting the Summer Palace at CHOROSZCZ. Drive east from the square and join the main road to Białystok at Złotoria. After 3km, at Żółtki, turn right for 2km south to **CHOROSZCZ** (population 5100). As you enter the town, you will pass on your left the Baroque **Dominican Church and Monastery**, founded in 1756 by J. K. Branicki. Branicki's **Summer Palace** has an adjoining 28ha **park**. There is a **museum** in the palace (open Tues–Sun 10.00–15.00), but it is a little tricky to find: drive along ul. Branickiego opposite the church until you see a birch-wood cross on the left; take the left turn, which takes you up to the hospital; park, and walk through the gate. Alternatively, you could try the dirt road which skirts the hospital to the right.

The museum specialises in 18C interiors from Branicki's time, and has a decent collection of furniture, porcelain, glass and portraiture. The master of the house was a man of enormous wealth (see p. 175), and, as historical records seem to suggest, of comparable vanity. In his will he forbade his wife to remarry on pain of losing the inheritance (she married her lover in secret anyway).

Białystok and the Byelorussian borders

Białystok

Białystok (population 259,600) lies at the heart of the historic **Podlasie** region, marking Poland's border with Byelorussia and the Ukraine. Its name derives from the White river (biały—white, stok—river) which flows into the Supraśl to the north of the city. Because of its border location, Białystok preserves a slightly eastern flavour: there are some fine Orthodox churches, and the eastern dialect, instantly recognizable to Poles from other regions, is widely spoken. Most of the city's sites are conveniently located around ul. Lipowa—the main thoroughfare—delimited by the church of St Roch at its west end, and the church of the

Ascension to the east. The centre itself is fairly nondescript, though happily lacking in industry, and with some charming cobblestone streets spread out over hilly townscape.

Białystok experienced its heyday when it came under the powerful Branicki family in the 18C. Jan Klemens Branicki, the Royal Hetman (Field Commander), transformed the existing castle into a sumptuous residence modelled on Versailles. After the Treaty of Tilsit (1807), the town became part of Russia, and remained so until the restoration of Polish independence in 1918. Before the Second World War, it had one of the largest Jewish populations in Eastern Europe. During the liquidation of the ghetto in August 1943, an armed Jewish uprising broke out under Moszkowicz, predictably ending in defeat. The war years took a terrible toll on the city: over half the population was wiped out, including the entire Jewish community and all traces of Jewish culture; three-quarters of the centre was razed to the ground.

■ Practical information
Hotels
★★★

Cristal. Ul. Lipowa 3, ☎ 42-50-61/3. Central location, helpful staff. Fitness room, car rental. 82 rooms.
Turkus. Al. Jana Pawła II 54, ☎ 51-32-78. Reasonably priced. Car park. 51 rooms.
Leśny. Al. Jana Pawła II 77, ☎ 51-16-41. Situated near woodland. Car park. 53 rooms.

Tourist information (PAPT). Ul. Piękna 3, ☎ 45-46-00.
ORBIS. Rynek Kościuszki 13, ☎ 42-16-27/42-16-28.
Main post office. Ul. Warszawska 10.
Telephone code: (0–85).

The city centre

The modernist Church of St Roch stands on a hillock at the west end of UL. LIPOWA, its asymmetrical, grey mass—a combination of brick and reinforced concrete—visible from a distance. It is possible to climb its tower (81m) for a panoramic view over the city. Walk down ul. Lipowa, passing, on the right, the grand Neo-classical **Orthodox Church of St Nicholas** (1846), and turn left into ul. Zamenhofa. At the end of the street is a plaque on the wall of a modern building (No. 26), commemorating **Ludwik Zamenhof** (1859–1917), the creator of Esperanto. Zamenhof was born in the now vanished house at No. 4.

The area between ul. Zamenhofa and ul. Malmeda (two blocks west) is where the Jewish Uprising took place in 1943. Return to ul. Lipowa. On the opposite side of the street stands the Baroque **Town Hall** (1745–61), situated at the apex of the triangular Rynek Kościuszki (18C), the historic centre of Białystok. The building houses a **museum** (open Tues–Sun 10.00–17.00) with an interesting ground floor display of Polish painting (18C–20C).

Continue east to the the Neo-Gothic **cathedral church** (1905) with imposing towers. To circumvent the Czarist ban on the construction of new Catholic churches, the cathedral was built as an annexe to the adjoining **parish**

Esperanto

Esperanto, originally described in a book called *Lingvo Internacia* (1887), was neither the first nor the last artificial language to be proposed as a medium of international communication; to date, however, it has certainly been the most successful. A century ago it had just one speaker: Doctor Esperanto (the pen-name of Ludwik Lejzer Zamenhof), author of the above-mentioned book. Today, around 2 million people speak the language, and several thousand have learnt it as their native tongue. It has its own literature, theatre, rock music and comic strips.

Zamenhof's aim was to create a language in which people from different national backgrounds could converse on an equal footing. His initiative was inspired by a very real social need: Central Europe at the turn of the century was home to a plethora of linguistic groups, but few people could afford the time and effort needed to learn another natural language. Esperanto, with its simple, regular grammar and flexible, intuitive rules of word formation, was an attempt to solve the problem. Some critics continue to see the language as parochially European, but the evidence suggests otherwise: speakers from the Far East find Esperanto easy to master; indeed, the language is especially popular in China.

Judging by the hostile attitudes towards Esperanto by the most oppressive governments in recent history, Zamenhof was right about its potential to promote freedom and openness. The Czarist authorities banned all publications in Esperanto; Stalin had all its speakers arrested and either shot or sent to labour camps; Hitler denounced it as an instrument of Jewish world domination. The language survived.

church (1617–21). Inside the latter are tombs of the Branickis, including that of Jan Klemens Branicki, the Royal Hetman.

Close by, at the corner of ul. Kilińskiego and ul. Kościelna, stands a former 19C **Masonic Lodge**, now a public library. Walk down ul. Kilińskiego. At No. 7 is the **Polish Army Museum** (open Tues–Sun 09.30–17.00), with sections covering the history of the Polish armed forces, portraiture, battle sculpture, and folk art images of the Polish soldier. Among the highlights are a rare early medieval sword found in Supraśl, and a collection of silver eagles showing the evolution of the Polish national emblem.

Branicki Palace

Continue along ul. Kilińskiego, which brings you to a small square by the gate to the **Branicki Palace*, the city's best monument, and arguably the finest Baroque palatial complex in Poland.

The palace began its life as a Gothic castle (1570), extended in 1602–21, and reconstructed in 1697 by the renowned architect Tylman van Gameren. When the Białystok estate passed to Hetman Jan Klemens Branicki, pretender to the Polish throne, the palace entered its heyday. Branicki's ambition was to build a residence befitting a man of his wealth and influence; a monument that would rival the Versailles palace of his contemporary, Louis XIV. The modest central block was transformed into a Baroque building of grandiose proportions, complete with a theatre, gallery, library and arsenal. The façade overlooked two vast courtyards. At the back, a lavish two-tiered formal garden was laid out, with an orangery, fig-house, and Italian and Chinese pavilions. The end result was truly impressive.

In 1920, during the Polish-Bolshevik war, the Provisional Revolutionary Committee led by Julian Marchlewski and Feliks Dzierżyński was set up in the Branicki palace, with the aim of establishing a Polish Soviet Republic. Its plans folded, however, owing to weak public support and the Bolsheviks' eventual defeat. In 1944, the palace suffered devastation at the hands of the Nazis. It was painstakingly rebuilt after the war, but today the only original interior is a Rococo staircase.

You enter the grounds through a Baroque gate (1758), with a tablet commemorating the Provisional Revolutionary Committee of 1920. Beyond it stretch two large courtyards separated by a wall topped by two statues of Hercules (J. C. Redler). A statue of Atlas stands on the tympanum of the central block. Most of the modern interiors are occupied by the city's medical academy. Feel free to wander through, but there is not much to see.

Opposite the Voivodship Office on ul. Mickiewicza is the **Planty park**, with fountains, ponds, and double rows of trees. In the east part you will find a rosary with Stanisław Horno-Popławski's sculpture *Praczki* (Washerwomen). Beyond the Planty stretches the Zwierzyniec forest (129ha), formerly an 18C game park where Branicki and his entourage would hunt, and today a zoo, military cemetery, and stadium.

The Białowieża National Park

The vast *BIAŁOWIEŻA FOREST* (Puszcza Białowieska) is one of the largest forests on the Central European plain (128,921ha), part of which lies in Poland (58,000ha), and part in Byelorussia. For centuries it was used as a royal hunting ground, first by the Ruthenian and Lithuanian dukes, then by Polish royalty, and finally, after the death of Stanisław August, by the Czars of Russia. Because the forest was protected by royal guards and gamekeepers, a fragment of it— contained within the Białowieża National Park (see below)—has survived in an almost virgin state. This area of primeval forest is unique in Europe, and has accordingly been entered onto UNESCO's World Heritage List.

The forest lies about 100km from Białystok. Using public transport, the only way to get there is by bus. There are two buses daily from Białystok to the village of Białowieża, and many more from Hajnówka. The Hajnówka–Białowieża railway line has unfortunately been closed and is not likely to re-open in the near future. If travelling by car, leave Białystok southeast along ul. Branickiego, following signs to Lublin (road 19) and Białowieża; at the fork, follow the main road left. In Bielsk Podlaski head east along road 689 to Hajnówka.

A narrow strip of uncultivated primeval forest (0.5km on each side) borders the road (689) leading to BIAŁOWIEŻA (population 2500). Before you reach the village, turn left at the sign marked 'Rezerwat Żubrów' (bison reserve). The animals here— all indigenous inhabitants of the Białowieża Forest—are kept in special enclosures. They include wild boar, deer, tarpan ponies and elk, as well as some cross-breeds, such as the *żubron* (cow-bison). The rarest and most famous species, however, is the European bison, the largest European mammal, which has almost vanished from its native continent. There are only 3000 left in the world, 2000 of which are here in Białowieża. The forest was once populated by many of these great animals, but they were wiped out when it was heavily exploited for timber during the First World War. Today, thanks to breeding programmes, some 300 bison have returned to the wild. To see them in their natural habitat, you can take one of the horse-drawn *britzka* rides into the Białowieża National Park (5096ha), which begins about 1km north of the village. Established in 1921, the park is a strict nature reserve, most of which is completely protected.

A small fragment is accessible to tourists, but even here special restrictions apply: no cars are allowed, and entry is with a guide only (ask for information about tour operators at the wooden PTTK hostel in the village). The daily tours, taking from one to four hours, can also be made by bicycle, on foot or horseback, but for the latter permission is required from the Forest Directorate in the museum building (see below). Białowieża has the largest number of European bison in the world, but you will be lucky to see any on your tour. There are many other rare mammals and birds to see, though, including lynxes, beavers, reindeer, wolves, black storks and eagle owls, as well as some ancient trees, mostly oaks, spruce and lime trees.

Further along the road, past the PTTK building, you will arrive at the entrance to the **Palace Park** (botanical gardens). Founded in 1894, the park has 150 varieties of trees and shrubs, including Douglas spruce, and Canadian and Weymouth pines. It originally enclosed a Czarist palace, which was destroyed during the Second World War and never rebuilt. Within the grounds is the **Białowieża Forest Museum** (open Tues–Sun 09.00–15.30), inside an ugly Communist-style building, and offering a disappointing display, consisting of fading diagrams, a few stuffed animals, and such stirring exhibits as jars of bilberry marmalade and pickled mushrooms.

Other parts of the Białowieża Forest can be visited on foot or by car: for instance, you can take the yellow route (first turning right after the PTTK building going towards Hajnówka) to the village of Narewka and then further on to Siemianówka on the shores of an artificial lake. Be warned, however, the roads are pretty rough. Stick to the marked trails, or you might suddenly have to explain your presence to a Byelorussian border guard (not recommended).

Tartar villages on the Byelorussian borders

❖ Sokółka • Bohoniki • Krynki • Kruszyniany

Leave Białystok along ul. Sienkiewicza, heading northeast and following signs to Kuźnica (road 18), the border crossing with Byelorussia. You soon enter the **Knyszyn Forest** (Puszcza Knyszyńska), an undulating terrain (90,000ha) of post-glacial hillocks covered mostly in spruce and pine, and rich in wildlife. As late as the 16C, uninterrupted tracts of primeval forest stretched from here deep into Lithuania. The area has a long history and is dotted with prehistoric burial grounds, early medieval ruins and battlefields from the Swedish invasions (17C), the Napoleonic campaigns, the January Uprising (1863) and the Second World War. There is also much vernacular wooden architecture to be seen, including granaries, watermills, windmills and primitive distilleries.

SOKÓŁKA (42km from Białystok; population 18,700) was originally an estate belonging to the Lithuanian dukes, situated on the old Wilno–Warsaw road. Later, as an autonomous part of the royal demesne (17C–18C), it was settled by the Tartars (see below), whom King Jan Sobieski rewarded with land and titles. The presence of the Tartars in the region is documented in the **museum** (open Wed–Fri 10.00–16.00) on ul. Piłsudskiego, just off the square. On the latter stands a 19C **Orthodox church**.

Turn right onto the 674, marked 'Krynki'. Soon you will see a left turn sign-posted 'Drahle'. Continue straight at the junction and stay on the 'Szlak Tatarski' (**Tartar Route**), which takes you through some of the most beautiful countryside of Eastern Poland: sparsely populated, with undulating meadows interspersed with copses and remote villages.

Bohoniki

Bohoniki (8km) is an ancient Tartar settlement close to the Byelorussian border.

The **Tartars**, a war-like tribe, began arriving from their homelands in the Crimean and Volgan Khanates from as early as the 13C. In 1241, their armies—known as the Golden Horde—swept across Poland, leaving chaos and devastation in their wake (see p. 466). Rather than return east, some settled in the Duchy of Lithuania and, after subsequent invasions, in Poland, too. Polish monarchs valued the Tartars highly for their loyalty to their new homeland, which they defended even against other Muslims. In return, they were granted privileges, such as the right to build mosques or go on pilgrimages to Medina and Mecca. Tartar horsemen fought alongside the Poles at the Battle of Grunwald in 1410 (see p. 417); in 1683, they helped Sobieski save Christendom from the Turks, and were rewarded with land in the Białystok and Lublin provinces; some were even ennobled. Olejewski—a captain in the Tartar cavalry regiment—and his subordinates received the village of Bohoniki for their efforts.

Along with Kruszyniany (see below), Bohoniki is today one of two villages in Poland almost entirely populated by ethnic Tartars. Among its inhabitants are the descendants of Sobieski's soldiers, although, over the centuries, many Tartars moved to other parts of the country, and were replaced by new arrivals from the east. Islamic culture in Bohoniki is still very much in evidence. The main attraction is the wooden 18C **mosque** (*meczet* in Polish). It is usually closed, but the family at No. 24 have the key and will show you round. (The present authors were given a guided tour by Janusz Bohdanowicz, a 12-year-old Tartar boy, who wanted his name in print!) The spartan interior consists of an anteroom (with a rack for shoes), women's prayer hall, and main prayer hall. In keeping with Islamic custom, the latter two are separated by a partitioning wall with a horizontal gap draped with a curtain. Most interesting is the main hall, with a *mihrab* (prayer niche) in the south wall facing Mecca and, to the right of it, a *mimbar*, or pulpit. The walls are decorated with *muhirs* (paintings), with verses from the Koran.

To get to the **Muslim Cemetery** (*mizar*), turn left up a dirt track just after the village. Overgrown with trees and shrubs, the cemetery is scenically set among pastures at the edge of a forest. The graves are placed in a haphazard fashion and bear inscriptions in Arabic and Polish. Typically, the names are of eastern origin, later Polonised, such as Sulkiewicz, Achmatowicz, etc.

Krynki

Return to the main road (674) and continue south (22km) to **KRYNKI**, a border village with a large Byelorussian community and many 19C houses. Preserved is the original 18C town plan, with 12 roads converging like rays on the Main Square, where a trading hall used to stand. The **parish church**, an aisled hall of 1907–13 with three oak altars, is visible as you approach the village. In its grounds stands a Baroque belfry. Turning right at the square you reach a stone **Orthodox Church** and 19C cemetery chapel. The church has a flat, blue ceiling decorated with ribbon-shaped patterns. Two chapels—of the Holy Sepulchre (right) and of St Mary (left)—flank a fine iconostasis with six circular paintings of saints.

From the square, take a minor road to **KRUSZYNIANY**, the second of the Tartar villages, situated at the east edge of the Knyszyn Forest. On the way, you will again travel through landscape of exceptional beauty. Jan Sobieski gave the village to the Tartar captain S. Murzy-Krzeczowski, who saved his life at the Battle of Parkany in 1679. Today, most of Kruszyniany's inhabitants are Byelorussian. Their modern **Orthodox church** is situated about 100m after you turn left towards Łosiniany. Of greater interest is the **mosque**, shrouded by trees, in the centre of the village (turn left off the main road, further up). This wooden twin-towered structure, with a dome and small minaret, dates from the 18C. The interior is similar to the mosque in Bohoniki, with two prayer halls and sparse furniture. If it is shut, ask for the key at the house next door (No. 57). The **Muslim Cemetery** (400m) is set among pines behind a low stone wall. The most recent graves are located at the edge of the wood, with the older ones further in, concealed by tall grass. Most impressive is the tomb of the last imam (Muslim leader) of Kruszyniany. His modern counterpart lives in Warsaw and comes to the village a few times a year to take services.

Warsaw to Płock

Leave Warsaw along the left (south) bank of the Vistula, joining road 7, sign-posted 'Gdańsk'. At Zakroczym, join the Płock road (62), after 24km exiting left for **CZERWIŃSK**, where the towers of the basilican *abbey church, set on the high north bluff of the river, will come into view.

Czerwiński Abbey

The Bishop of Płock, Piotr Dunin, founded the abbey in 1117 for the Canons Regular of the Lateran. The church is today ranked among the best architectural monuments in Poland. Despite Gothic, Renaissance and Baroque alterations, it has preserved its essentially Romanesque core, which pre-dates 1140. The **façade** consists of two Romanesque stone towers flanking a Gothic red brick fronton, decorated with a mosaic depicting the Virgin and Jesus. The porch is entered through an intricately carved Romanesque portal (c 1140) with partly-uncovered Romanesque columns, showing French and Lombardic influence. Inside the porch, as well as in the chancel, original Gothic and Renaissance murals have been preserved on the vaults. More **murals**, the largest piece of Romanesque painted decoration in Poland—can be found in the **Chapel of the Crucifixion** (early 13C). The walls of the church are overhung with paintings. The alternation of piers and columns is a device characteristic of Brabant architecture.

In front of the church, on the right, a gabled brick bell tower (late Gothic, 1497, adapted in 1663) may be climbed with the help of a wooden ladder. Behind it is a terrace commanding a breathtaking view over the Vistula valley. The late **Gothic-Renaissance monastery** (c 1529), rebuilt in early Baroque style before 1633, adjoins the church to the right and behind. Its main interest lies in the late Gothic **murals**, and an ethnographical collection, consisting of objects brought back by the monks from their missions abroad. The statue of Mary and Jesus standing by an old lime tree in front of the church was made in 1916.

Continue into the sleepy village, where the pleasant square is more like a garden overgrown with trees.

Płock

Płock (population 117,600), beautifully sited on the Vistula Bluff, looks surprisingly handsome for a city that is saddled with the largest petrochemical works in the country and the elephantine Pipeline of Friendship, joining the former USSR to the former GDR. It is also one of the oldest Polish towns, evolving from a 9C settlement, and mentioned as early as 1047. From the 11C it was the capital of Mazovia, a bishopric (after 1075), a seat of learning (1180 marks the foundation of the collegiate school by the Church of St Michael), and a centre of political power (it served as a residence for monarchs—Władysław Herman and Bolesław the Wry-mouthed, from 1079 to 1138—and later for the Mazovian dukes).

Płock suffered destruction at the hands of Lithuanians, Prussians, Ruthenes and Teutonic Knights, and yet it flourished from the mid-14C onwards, acquiring fortifications and a castle. After the death of Janusz II, the Duke of Płock, in 1495, the town entered the royal demesne, and continued to expand, particularly during the 16C. This heyday came to an abrupt halt in the 17C; after the Second Partition the town fell under Prussian rule, though it was later incorporated into the Congress Kingdom. During the November Uprising in 1830, the Town Hall hosted the last session of the revolutionary government before it was forced into exile. The insurgents' attempts to take it during the January Uprising (1863) ended in failure.

■ Practical information
Hotel. ★★★ *Orbis-Petropol*. Al. Jachowicza 49, ☎ 262-4451. Central location. Car park. 87 rooms
Tourist information (*PAPT*). Al. Jachowicza 38, ☎ 262-9497.
ORBIS. Al. Jachowicza 47, ☎ 262-2989.
Main post office. Ul. Bielska 14; pl. Narutowicza 5.
Telephone code: (0–24).

The city centre
From PL. NARUTOWICZA walk south along ul. Tumska towards the cathedral, which appears on the left. The castle, cathedral and Benedictine abbey were built

on TUM HILL, also known as Castle Hill, and later Royal Hill. Archaeological excavations by the cathedral uncovered fragments of an ancient settlement with a Romanesque *palatium* and stone rotunda, dated to the 11C–12C.

The Romanesque ***cathedral** (**open** to visitors Mon–Sat 10.00–17.00, Sun 14.00–17.00), built c 1126–41, is a stone basilica, to which two late Gothic brick towers were added in the 15C. They are separated by a fronton pierced with a rose window above a fine Romanesque portal (reconstructed) framing a faithful copy of the famous Płock Door. Commissioned in the 12C, probably in Magdeburg, the splendid bronze door is divided into twelve paneled sections and shows the Apostles (the original is in the Orthodox Church of St Sophia in Novgorod, Russia). The cathedral was first rebuilt in 1531–34 in Renaissance style, and again some 20 years later by Gianbattista of Venice, who lengthened the chancel. In the 20C it was further remodelled, this time to restore its original Romanesque forms. The dark, sombre interior is covered with cross vaults and a large, richly painted dome over the crossing. Embedded in the walls are many Renaissance and Baroque tombstones from the 16C–17C, especially in the south aisle. The Royal Chapel contains 19C **sarcophagi** of Władysław Herman and Bolesław the Wry-mouthed. Other objects of interest include the wooden stalls, the pulpit, some Gothic and Mannerist paintings, and late Gothic sculptures.

Płock's two main museums, the Diocesan Museum and the Mazovian Museum, stand conveniently close to the cathedral. The redbrick ***Diocesan Museum** (**open** Tues–Sat 10.00–15.00, Sun 11.00–16.00) offers a baffling and chaotic display of objects of varying importance, arranged with no apparent order or plan. The ground and upper floors are crowded with exhibits relating to Mazovian folk art, documents and **first editions** of books (such as the early 12C *Płock Bible*, the 14C hymn book of Płock Cathedral, and a 13C Franciscan hymn book), textiles, furniture, ceramics, glass and metal-ware, sgraffito, numismatics, vestments (some lavishly ornamented), religious folk art (several examples of the Pietà, *Christ in Distress* from the Kurpie region, and an early 20C sculpture of St Michael fighting the Devil), numerous paintings of bishops and nobles, weaponry, armour, innumerable crucifixes, monstrances and altars.

Facing the cathedral on the opposite side of ul. Tumska is a cluster of buildings consisting of the castle towers, the Benedictine abbey, and the former church of St Adalbert. Look for a stone tablet set into a small patch of grass between the abbey and the avenue that skirts the edge of the bluff, marking the spot where the early 11C Romanesque rotunda was discovered. From the avenue you get a fine view over the river and the southern suburbs of Płock. The brick Gothic castle erected by Kazimierz the Great was torn down during the second half of the 18C. All that remains of it are the towers, set diagonally opposite each other: the 14C late Gothic **clock tower** (south) with a panelled upper section and corner turrets was converted into the cathedral bell-tower in 1492, and remodelled in the mid-16C by Gianbattista of Venice. The **Noble's Tower** (c 1353) was lowered in 1796. Sandwiched between them is the former ***Benedictine Abbey** and **Church of St Adalbert**, founded before 1172. The early Baroque church (1632) is the work of Giovanni Battista Ghisleni, who incorporated some earlier Gothic remnants. It became a lycée in 1856. The abbey's fine 14C courtyard is visible from inside the Mazovian Museum.

Mazovian Museum

The *Mazovian Museum has the largest collection of Secessionist art in Poland (ul. Tumska 2, ☎ 624-491; open Tues–Sat 09.00–15.00, Sun 10.00–15.00). The museum was established at the beginning of the 19C. It moved to pl. Narutowicza in 1930, and was robbed of its collections during the Second World War. Nationalised in 1949, it moved to its present spot in the early 1960s and began to specialize in Secessionist art, attempting to recreate the atmosphere of the *fin-de-siècle* by showing old objects in their natural setting. There are plans to purchase a Secessionist house and move the collection there, and to set up a research centre entirely devoted to Młoda Polska (Young Poland, the Polish counterpart of Jugendstil). All the rooms are furnished throughout in *fin-de-siècle* style, and decorated with well-arranged porcelain, glass and paintings.

The **first floor** comprises a dining room with Viennese furniture; a drawing room with ornate chandeliers and bronzework; the so-called Belgian drawing room and a bedroom with Mehoffer's *Geniuses* (a sketch of the painted decoration for Wawel cathedral) hanging over the bed. The corridor has a good collection of Polish paintings, Secessionist glass and ceramics, and, perhaps most interesting, Mehoffer's stained-glass designs for Freiburg cathedral.

On the **second floor** is a curious exhibition connected with the January Uprising (1863). There is also a mid-19C drawing room, a section devoted to Freemasonry in Płock, and, in the corridor, a collection of prints and drawings of Płock in times past. You can see the preserved west wing of the monastery (16C) behind the museum.

Return to pl. Narutowicza and follow ul. Teatralna and then UL. PIEKARSKA, which skirts the edge of the bluff. Down below, at the foot of the hill, you will notice an amphitheatre and harbour. Ul. Piekarska ends at a former PTTK hostel, designed by Marek Leykam and held by some in great esteem. Return to UL. MAŁACHOWSKIEGO (off ul. Piekarska), which leads to the Old Town Square. On the way you will pass (right) the former **Collegiate Church of St Michael**, a brick Gothic building with Romanesque cellars, and the **Jesuit College** (1607), converted into schools in 1786 by Stanisław Zawadzki, and rebuilt in Neoclassical style in 1843 by Antonio Corazzi. The Collegiate School of St Michael is the oldest school in Poland, dating from 1180. Continue to the pleasant Old Town Square with an elegant Neo-classical **town hall** (1824–27).

On the same side of the square, but partly obscured from view, stands the **Parish Church of St Bartholomew**, originally Gothic (1356), with two high towers flanking the fronton, two entrances, and Gothic vaults supported on 12 columns. It was expanded into an aisled hall with an ambulatory, and encircled with a ring of late Gothic chapels in 1540. After two major fires, repairs were carried out in 1687. The church retained its original form and size (150m by 19m by 25m), but the Swedish war in 1704–09, subsidence, and remodelling in 1731–75, divested it of architectural merit. Today, the modest interior deserves a visit for the early Baroque **high altar** (c 1632, Giovanni Battista Ghisleni), transferred from the Benedictine church, and the beautiful ebony tabernacle of 1912.

From the parish church, walk along ul. Wieczorka for about 100 m to an old granary (early 19C) containing a **Museum of Folk Art** (open Mon, Wed–Sun 10.00–15.00). The museum, expertly run by its enthusiastic curator, holds temporary exhibitions every three to four months, focusing on aspects of

Mazovian folk art: sculpture, pottery, embroidery, weaving, paper design, costume, hunting, Christmas customs, the cult of St Mary.

Return to pl. Narutowicza and head east along ul. Kościuszki. The north side of pl. Obrońców Warszawy is occupied by the large white building of the **Prussian Kammer** (now offices), erected in Neo-classical style in 1803 by David Gilly, and expanded in the 19C. In the southern part of the square stands a **monument** to the poet Władysław Broniewski. The house where he was born is further along ul. Kościuszki at No. 24. A commemorative plaque on the wall refers to him as 'the great poet-revolutionary, honorary citizen of Płock'.

Władysław Broniewski (1897–1962) was a Polish fellow-traveller harassed for his convictions during the inter-war period, and then imprisoned by the Soviets in Lwów in early 1940. Aleksander Wat recalls how he kept other inmates awake by reciting his poems and singing revolutionary songs at night. Released in 1941, he left the Soviet Union with Gen. Anders's army, returned to Poland after the war, and dutifully served the Communist regime.

Płock to Toruń

❖ Włocławek • Nieszawa • Ciechocinek • Podgórz • Toruń

Włocławek

Leave Płock southwest across the Piłsudski Bridge and join the 62 heading west. Włocławek (50km from Płock; population 119,200) lies on the border of the Kujawy region. Under the Piast dynasty, it was one of the largest Polish towns, chartered before 1255, and then owned until 1793 by the Kujawian bishops. It was a river port, and from 1520 had a customs house, which drew large revenues from the Vistula river trade. The Swedish wars dashed all hopes of prosperity, and it was only during the 19C that the town saw some development (the first paper mill was established in 1799). Today, it is most famous for its hand-painted earthenware.

As you approach the centre, you will see the lofty towers of the Gothic *cathe-dral** on pl. Kopernika, just before the iron bridge (**open** Mon–Sat 12.00–16.00, and Sun 15.00–16.00).

The present brick basilica is a successor to a Romanesque stone cathedral, built after Bolesław the Wry-mouthed established the Włocławek diocese in 1123, and burnt down by the Teutonic knights in 1329. It retains some late Gothic elements characteristic of the Pomeranian region, and others typical of Małopolska.

The chancel and the south sacristy date before 1365, while the nave, aisles and the two towers were raised in 1365–1411. The remaining three sacristies and the Baroque lanterns are later additions. The church was re-Gothicised in 1891–93. It is a huge, overwhelming mass of red brick held up by massive buttresses and dominated by its twin towers, the south one with a clock, the north with a round window.

The spacious interior is rich in works of art. J. Mehoffer designed the stained glass for the apse window. In the centre hangs a Renaissance seven-branched bronze candelabrum, 310 cm high and 378 cm wide (1596), which was stolen from the church of St Peter in Riga in 1940, and somehow found its way to Włocławek. There is also another, smaller Renaissance candelabrum, made in 1563. Notice the mid-17C stalls, and the silver altar of 1744 from the monastery in Ląd (see p. 526). Impressive are the Mannerist square domed chapels, accessible from the aisles. The stone **Chapel of St Mary** has a sundial on the outside, and inside a 19C Renaissance painting of the Virgin. The **Chapel of St Martin**, entered through a wrought-iron gate of 1527, is one of the oldest in the cathedral (1521). The stained glass (1881–83) in the pointed-arch window depicts the legend associated with its patron. The **Chapel of St Joseph** contains the tombstone of Bishop Piotr of Bnin (1493) carved by Veit Stoss. The Renaissance **Chapel of St Kazimierz** (1619) has an 18C Baroque altar, while **St Barbara's Chapel** is noteworthy for its Gothic stained-glass window (14C). Of all the chapels, the largest is the **Chapel of the Assumption** (1541). Inside is a sculpture of *The Last Supper*, a painting of the *Assumption* (before 1475), and a Baroque font (1700). The late Gothic **Chapter House** (c 1560) consists of two vaulted rooms containing 15C–16C epitaph tablets of bishops and canons. An elaborate Renaissance portal leads into the nave.

To the south of the cathedral, in a park, stands a **monument** to Copernicus (he may have briefly studied here). Further south is the brick Gothic **Church of St Vitali** (1330), the oldest in the city. The aisleless interior, accessible only from the adjoining seminary (1843), contains a mid-15C triptych from the collegiate church in Wieluń.

Walk down ul. Tumska along the river to get to the **OLD MARKET SQUARE**, a pleasant area sloping down to the riverside and overlooked by old houses. At its far end rises the brick late Gothic **Parish Church of St John**, erected in 1538. The squat tower was given a Baroque lantern in 1780, when the whole church was renovated. In the exterior wall of the chancel two glazed bricks mark the highest flooding point of the Vistula in 1745 and 1758—the water rose to about one metre above present ground level. The fine, short interior is lavishly ornamented with gilding, modern painted decoration, and a pseudo-coffered vault in the Renaissance **Chapel of the Five Wounds of Christ** (1565). The furniture is mostly Baroque.

On the east side of the square two Gothic-Baroque houses (Nos 14 and 15) accommodate the **Museum of the History of Włocławek** (entrance at ul. Spichlerzna 19; **open** Tues 10.00–18.00, Wed, Fri 10.00–15.00, Thur 10.00–12.00 and 15.00–18.00, Sun 10.00–14.00). The ground floor is devoted to a display of weights and measures, archaeology (a particularly valuable find is an amphora from Kruszynek in Kujawy, dated to 2500–2300 BC), earthenware, porcelain, Polish and Italian numismatics, armour, locks, weaponry, royal seals, and portraits of Polish noblemen. There is also a recreated turn-of-the-century pharmacy and a copy of the famous **Włocławek Chalice** (see p. 63); the original is in the National Museum in Kraków), which probably originated from the old Romanesque cathedral, and was discovered during archaeological excavations that also unearthed skeletons of town officials and more than a hundred old coins. The exhibition on the first floor covers the November and January Uprisings, the Second World War, and a collection of 19C photographs.

Ul. 3 Maja leads south off the square to pl. Wolności. On nearby ul. Słowackie-go (No. 1a) is the **Museum of the Kujawy and Dobrzyń Lands** (same opening times as the museum on the Old Market Square), with a fine collection of earthenware. A plaque outside commemorates Copernicus.

Leave Włocławek heading north on the E75, signposted 'Gdańsk', and turn right to **Nieszawa** (population 1800). This picturesque, sleepy town, spread out over a hill, has a historic urban plan with many 18C–19C houses. It was granted a charter in 1460 by Kazimierz the Jagiellon, and had its heyday in the 16C. As you enter, turn left (north) just before the waterfront and drive to the **Parish Church of St Jadwiga** (1460–80), an example of late Vistulian Gothic. Its five-storey tower (1592–95) has a clock, constructed one year after the tower was complete. Entrance is through an ornamented Gothic portal. The original vaults have been replaced, except in one chapel. The Renaissance high altar was made in Gdańsk in the early 17C, and contains a Dutch painting from the same period. The bishop's throne and stalls also originate from Gdańsk; the latter bear an image of Queen St Jadwiga painted on cloth in 1635 (on the left).

The **house** at the end of ul. Noakowskiego is the birthplace of Stanisław Noakowski (1867–1928), an art historian, painter and university professor. To get to the house where he lived (now a **museum**, **open** Tues, Thur 10.00–18.00, Wed, Fri–Sat 10.00–15.00, Sun 10.00–14.00), return along ul. Noakowskiego to pl. Kazimierza Jagiellończyka; the house is located in the northeast corner. Walking east from there along ul. Mickiewicza you arrive at the ferry **harbour**, with regular crossings to the far bank of the Vistula, where a large expanse of forest begins.

Leave Nieszawa on the minor road to **Ciechocinek** (population 11,200), a large spa and health resort, attracting visitors with its salt springs rich in iodine. Its career began in the 19C with the construction of two salt graduation towers, and a salt-works in nearby Słońsk (although the existence of the springs was known at least since the 12C). Soon the springs came to be exploited for their medicinal properties, too. The town did not receive municipal rights until 1916.

Ciechocinek's greatest tourist attraction are the **Graduation Towers**, espe-cially the original 19C ones. These wooden structures resemble very long free-standing walls, with galleries on top from which you can see the salt crystals being deposited on brushwood constantly washed in brine. Walks along the towers are recommended for various ailments due to the saturation of the surrounding air with ozone and salt particles.

Regain the E75 and continue to Toruń, which you enter via **Podgórz**, until 1938 a separate town. During the Second World War, the Germans set up an internment camp here for British and Soviet POWs.

Turn right towards the centre of Toruń, passing the ruins of **Dybowski Castle**, built during the reign of Władysław Jagiełło for the royal burgraves, and destroyed during the Swedish wars. Notice on the right the picturesque Kępa Bazarowa. It was here that Jagiełło signed the first **Peace of Toruń** in 1411, which ended the war between Poland and the Teutonic Order.

Małopolska

The region of Małopolska (literally 'Lesser Poland') is associated with the beginnings of the Polish state, for centuries being coveted and fiercely defended by
Poland's rulers. To the south it is bordered by the **Carpathian Mountains**,
which also mark the national border with the Czech Republic and Slovakia.
Zakopane, a popular ski-resort and centre of *Górale* ('highland') culture, is situ-
ated at the foot of the highest Carpathian range—**the Tatras**. Further to the
east lies a lower, but no less spectacular range—**the Pieniny**—cut by the
Dunajec river. In the remote southeast corner of the region, the **Bieszczady
Mountains** offer unspoilt landscape and the remnants of local Lemko and
Bojko culture.

Kraków

Kraków (Cracow) (population 755,000), the capital of Małopolska and Poland's
fourth largest city, lies in a broad valley on the banks of the Vistula river. Nearly
all the major sites and attractions, of which there is a vast number, are located
in and around the medieval Old Town. Seen from a distance, Kraków's skyline is
dominated by the twin towers of St Mary's church on the Main Market Square
(*Rynek Główny*). To the south, perched on a hill, is the magnificent Wawel Castle,
overlooking the scenic 'Vistula bend', where the river turns at almost 90
degrees.

Geographical location has played an important role in the history of the
ancient royal capital. For centuries Kraków rivalled the great Central European
cities of Budapest, Prague and Vienna, like them becoming a centre of cultural
development in the region. The affinities have remained strong. Even today,
some Cracovians wistfully refer to themselves as 'Galicians' to distinguish their
cultural legacy from that of Warsaw, and speak with disdain and amusement of
the Polish capital as a 'large, ugly, communised village'; for native Varsovians,
the corresponding stereotype sees Kraków as petty-bourgeois and conservative,
a city more akin to a quaint museum than a modern metropolis.

There is indeed something of a provincial flavour to Kraków. In the Old Town's
quiet, narrow backstreets, almost totally devoid of modern buildings, life generally seems to proceed at a slower pace. Yet there is also much going on, and in
summer the Main Square really comes alive. In recent years a plethora of new
restaurants, cafés and cellar bars has appeared, and today the city enjoys a
nightlife that is the envy of visitors from other parts of Poland. In terms of
cultural life Kraków is admittedly losing ground to Warsaw, but it does regularly
play host to a variety of events, the **Festival of Jewish Culture** (June), the
International Graphic Art Triennale (September), and **Music in Old
Kraków** (August) among them. In 1992 it was chosen as the venue for the
European City of Culture, and it is in the running to host the event again in the
year 2000. The historic centre is itself a treasure-trove of architectural monuments, given recognition in 1978 when Kraków was included on **UNESCO's**

World Heritage List. Nowa Huta aside, all the sites are within easy walking distance. May or September are the best months to visit: the weather is mild and sunny, and there is lots to do and see.

The Old Town and its environs are described in five **walks**, each beginning on or very close to the **Main Market Square**, itself described in walk 1. The next walk begins by the city walls north of the square and proceeds southwards to the Wawel castle. A full day could be spent visiting the **Castle and Cathedral**, which are covered in Walk 3. The university district, southwest of the square, is described in walk 4. Finally, in walk 5, you follow the medieval city walls around the northern part of the Old Town.

A further four walks begin outside the perimeter of the Old Town. Walk 6 describes the former **Jewish district of Kazimierz**, south of the Main Market Square, and the story of Kraków's Jews is continued in walk 7, which takes you across the river to Podgórze, where the Nazis set up a ghetto during the Second World War. The final two walks (8 and 9) go slightly further afield, exploring Kraków's communist legacy in the suburb of Nowa Huta, and providing a panoramic view of the entire city from the Kościuszko Mound.

A number of interesting day trips can be made from Kraków. Heading upstream along the Vistula river, you could visit the secluded **medieval monasteries of Bielany and Tyniec**. Some 50km further west, towards Upper Silesia, is the town of Oświęcim, where the Nazis established their infamous **concentration camp of Auschwitz-Birkenau**. A mere 12km south-east of Kraków lies Wieliczka, where you should not miss the historic **11C salt mine**.

To the northwest of Kraków extend the grottoes and cliff-top castles of the 'Jura' limestone valley, reaching beyond the pilgrimage town of Częstochowa, and thereafter merging with the great Mazovian plain. Going northeast into Małopolska you reach **Kielce**, an ideal base for excursions into the ancient **Świętokrzyskie (Holy Cross) Mountains**, with hill-top abbeys, easy walking trails and beautiful views. The sub-region of Lubelszczyzna near the Ukrainian border has many worthwhile towns, such as Kazimierz Dolny, Zamość, Sandomierz and Przemyśl. They are best reached from the regional capital, Lublin, but could also be visited on a long weekend trip from Kraków.

■ Practical information
Hotels
★★★★

Orbis-Cracovia. Al. Marsz. F. Focha 1, ☎ 422-8666. Noisy, fairly central. Orbis travel office, car rental, car park, business services, wheelchair access. 314 rooms, some overlooking the Błonia park.

Orbis-Forum. Ul. M. Konopnickiej 28, ☎ 261-9212. Situated on the right bank of the Vistula, overlooking Wawel Castle. Business centre, travel services, air conditioning, wheelchair access, car park, swimming pool. 276 rooms.

Orbis-Francuski. Ul. Pijarska 13, ☎ 422-5122. Historic building in a quiet, Old Town location. Business services, car rental, excellent cuisine. 42 rooms.

Orbis-Continental. Ul. Armii Krajowej 11, ☎ 637-5044/423-8622. Situated in an out-of-town residential district, close to the E-40 motorway. Largest hotel in Kraków. Travel office, swimming pool, car park, business services, air conditioning, wheelchair access. 304 rooms, some with a view onto the Kościuszko Mound.

Orbis-Wanda. Ul. Armii Krajowej 15, ☎ 637-1677. Next to the Orbis-Continental. Car park, swimming pool, garden, wheelchair access. 80 rooms.
Elektor. Ul. Szpitalna 28, ☎ 423-2317. Modern hotel inside a 19C town-house. Central location (5 minutes walk from the main railway station). Guarded car park nearby. Business services. 15 rooms, some overlooking the Słowacki Theatre.
Grand. Ul. Sławkowska 5/7, ☎ 421-7255, A few metres from the Market Square. Plush restaurant and turn-of-the-century decor. Wheelchair access. 56 rooms.

★★★
Pod Kopcem. Al. Waszyngtona 1, ☎ 427-0355. By the Kościuszko Mound, with a view over the city. Car rental, wheelchair access. 22 rooms.
Pod Różą. Ul. Floriańska 14, ☎ 422-1244. Historic building (see p. 205), with two good restaurants. Situated on the Old Town's busiest street. 54 rooms.
Royal. Ul. Św. Gertrudy 26, ☎ 421-3500. Art Nouveau building situated opposite Wawel Castle. 97 rooms. Backs on to the less expensive Garnizonowy Hotel.
Polski. Ul. Pijarska 17 ☎ 422-1144. Central location, opposite the medieval city walls. 54 rooms.
Ariel. Ul. Szeroka 17 (and 6), ☎ 421-3870. Situated in the heart of Kazimierz. Good restaurant serving Jewish cuisine.
Pollera. Ul. Szpitalna 30, ☎ 422-1044. Central location (5 minutes walk from the main railway station). Excellent value. Guarded car park nearby. Good restaurant. 42 rooms, some overlooking the Słowacki Theatre.
Saski. Ul. Sławkowska 3, ☎ 421-4222. Art Nouveau building, a few metres from the Market Square. Good value. 62 rooms.
Europejski. Ul. Lubicz 5, ☎ 423-2510. The best of the hotels close to the main railway station. Recently refurbished, but often full. 56 rooms.

Recommended restaurants

Exclusive
Wierzynek, Rynek Główny 15. Polish and international.
Tetmajerowska, Rynek Główny 34. Polish and international.

Villa Decius, ul. 28 Lipca 17a. Polish.
Cyrano de Bergerac, ul. Sławkowska. French.

Medium-priced
Amarone, ul. Floriańska 14. Italian.
Hotel Francuski, ul. Pijarska 13. French.
Hotel Elektor, Szpitalna 28. Polish.
Da Pietro, Rynek Główny 17. Italian.
Adong, ul. Brodzińskiego 3. Chinese.
Chlopskie Jadlo, ul. Św Agnieszki 1. Polish.
Wentzl, Rynek Główny 19. Central European.

CK, ul. Bracka 4. Polish.
Gulliver, ul. Bracka 6. Polish and French.
Lemon, ul. Floriańska 53. Balkan.
Paese, ul. Poselska 24. Corsican.
Ariel, ul. Szeroka 17. Jewish.
Cechowa, ul. Jagiellońska 11. Polish.
El Paso, ul. Św. Krzyża 13. Mexican.

Cheap eateries

Piccolo, ul. Jagiellońska 2.
Chimera, ul. Św. Anny 3. Upstairs restaurant of the same name.
Vega, ul. Św. Gertrudy 7. Vegetarian.

Jadłodajnia u Pani Stasi, ul. Mikołajska 16.
Jadłodajnia Kuchcik, ul. Jagiellońska 12.

Cafés

Ariel, ul. Szeroka 17.
Jama Michalika, ul. Floriańska 45.
Larousse, ul. Św. Tomasza 22.
Pożegnanie z Afryką, ul. Św. Tomasza 21.
Redolfi, Rynek Główny 38.

Maska, ul. Jagiellońska 1.
Manggha, ul. Starowiślna 10.
Noworolski, Rynek Główny 1/3 (Cloth Hall).
U Literatów, ul. Kanonicza 7.
Krzysztofory, ul. Szczepańska 2.

Tourist Information (PAPT). Ul. Pawia 8, ☎ 422-0471/422-6091; open Mon–Fri 08.00–18.00. In the same building is the Waweltur office (☎ 422-19-21), which can arrange accommodation in private lodgings.

Cultural Information Centre. Ul. Św. Jana 2, ☎ 421-7787; open 10.00–19.00. The office has listings of cultural events in the city and provides information on how to get tickets.

ORBIS. Rynek Główny 41, ☎ 422-4035 (with an American Express desk) and al. Marsz. F. Focha 1 (Orbis-Cracovia hotel) ☎ 421-9880.

Main railway station (Kraków Główny). Pl. Kolejowy ☎ 9313 domestic; 422-4182, international. The station has been recently refurbished and has all the usual facilities, including money exchange, left luggage, and a good self-service restaurant. There is a post office on the square opposite the station, as well as numerous stalls selling food and miscellaneous goods. Walk through the underpass to get to the Main Market Square (10 minutes). Kraków has direct, daily rail connections with Berlin, Vienna, Prague, Budapest, Kiev and Odessa.

Main coach station. Pl. Kolejowy (next to the main railway station) ☎ 9316. Coaches leave from here to many domestic and foreign destinations. There are also private mini-bus services to nearby towns.

Airport. Balice (15km from the city centre) ☎ 411-67-00. Though recently modernised, Balice does not have all the services found at Okęcie airport in Warsaw. Notably, there is no duty free shop for departing passengers, although on the first floor you can buy gifts and souvenirs, including Polish vodka. Public transport bus No. 208 runs from the airport to the main railway station; No. 152 to the Cracovia Hotel. A 'radio taxi' into the centre of Kraków should cost around PLN 30 (GBP 5; USD 8). Taking a private taxi from the rank may cost significantly more, though you could try to negotiate a set price with the driver.

LOT. Ul. Basztowa 15, ☎ 422-4215; open Mon–Fri 08.00–19.00, Sat 08.00–15.00; ☎ 952 or 953 for 24-hour reservations and enquiries.
British Airways. Ul. Św. Tomasza 25, ☎ 422-8621.

Disabled travellers. The information centre for the disabled takes calls on Mon and Wed 15.00–17.00, ☎ 422-2811.

Main post office. Ul. Westerplatte 20 (entrance from ul. Wielopole; **open** Mon–Fri 08.00–20.00, Sat 08.00–14.00, Sun 09.00–11.00), telex, fax, poste restante, and 24-hour telephone service.

Telephone code: (0-12).

Taxis. There are numerous 'radio taxi' companies in Kraków. Popular numbers include: ☎ 9666; 919; 9625; 9628; 9667. The private cabs at the rank by the main railway station may charge twice as much as a radio taxi. Radio taxis are not allowed to queue at this rank, but they can pick up and drop passengers there and now have their own rank in the car park above the platforms.

Driving. Unless you know your way around, driving in the centre of Kraków can be a frustrating experience. There are many one-way streets, frequent delays, and three traffic zones (A, B and C). Zone A (basically the Main Market Square) is for pedestrians only. To drive in zone B (most of the Old Town) you need a special permit, which is only available to local residents. You may drive freely through zone C, but in order to park you have to buy a special pay-and-display ticket (*karta postojowa*), available from kiosks. These restrictions apply Mon–Sat 09.00–18.00. Do not park in zones A or B at any time—your car will be clamped or towed away. The two car parks closest to the Main Market Square are on pl. Szczepański and pl. Św. Ducha. However, it is nearly always best to leave your car where you are staying and travel into the centre by public transport, or simply walk.

US Consulate. Ul. Stolarska 9, ☎ 422-1400, fax 421-8292.

Lost property. The district office (Urząd Rejonowy) has a section dealing with lost property: al. Słowackiego 20, ☎ 616-9289. For property lost on public transport, contact the municipal transport authority (MPK) at ul. Sławka 10, ☎ 655-4300 (open 0630–16.00).

Major festivals. International Advertising Festival (**February**); Organ Festival (**April**); Juvenalia Student Festival (**May**); International Short Film Festival (**June**); Festival of Jewish Culture (June); Wianki (Midsummer's Eve on the Vistula river); Tyniec Organ Recitals (**July–August**); International Festival of Street Theatre (July); Music in Old Kraków (August); International Graphic Art Triennale (**September**; next one in 2000); Zaduszki (All Souls') Jazz Festival (**November**).

History

The earliest written record of Kraków appears in the travelogue of Ibrahim ibn Yaqub, a Jewish merchant from Moorish Spain, who visited the region in 960–65. Yaqub writes of the lands of the Czech Duke Bolesław and the city of 'Karako', an important trading centre on the Vistula river three weeks' journey from Prague.

The **Piast dynasty** did not assert itself in Kraków until the late 10C, after the first Piast duke—Mieszko I (d. 992)—had converted to Christianity. Kazimierz the Restorer (1038–58) made it his capital city in 1038, and from then until the 17C Kraków became the home of Poland's rulers. The city benefited from its location on important trade routes, particularly the old 'amber trail', and close to rich salt deposits in Wieliczka. In the late 11C, a Benedictine abbey was founded at Tyniec, a few miles up the Vistula. Through their contacts with Western Europe, the monks provided much of the cultural impetus that served the regeneration of the Polish state under Bolesław the Bold (1058–79).

Brick building came with the arrival of monastic orders from Western Europe in the early 13C. Kraków experienced rapid growth: trade and crafts flourished, and the city gained its first taste of municipal government. These halcyon days were rudely interrupted in 1241 by the **invasion of the Tartars**, a warrior race from eastern Asia. Like other Polish cities, Kraków was sacked by the invading army; most of its inhabitants killed, their severed heads being ceremoniously stuck on wooden pikes, as was the Tartar custom. Yet though it caused much havoc and destruction, the Tartar invasion did foster at least one positive development: in 1257 Bolesław the Chaste (1243–79) endowed Kraków with a new and lasting municipal charter, which saw the city shift north of the old settlement. The new town consisted of a grand market square (the largest in Central Europe) at the centre of a regular grid of streets.

Kraków entered its golden age during the reign of **Kazimierz the Great** (1333–70), who established the Jagiellonian University, and founded the new town of Kazimierz, named after himself, just south of the castle. The flourishing of architecture was mirrored and in part financed by the growth of commerce. As the Polish state expanded eastwards, merchants benefited from the new trade routes with Lwów and the Black Sea coast. Traditional links with the Hanseatic League and cities like Nürnberg were maintained, while the city's rising significance was confirmed in 1364, when it was chosen for a conference of European monarchs. Following the **union of Poland and Lithuania** at Krewo in 1385 (see p. 46), Kraków— formerly lying close to the geographical heartland of Poland—suddenly found itself in the outlying provinces of a vast new state.

Under **Zygmunt the Old** (1506–48), an archetypal Renaissance monarch, Italian influence reached its apogee in Kraków. Royal patronage of Italian artists began with the reconstruction of the old Gothic castle on Wawel hill as a palatial residence. In the later, Mannerist phase of the Renaissance, the architect **Santi Gucci** stands out.

After the union with Lithuania, political power gradually shifted away from Kraków. Already by the mid-16C most sessions of the joint *Seym*, or Parliament, were being held at Piotrków Trybunalski. The final blow to the royal city came in 1569 when the *Seym* was moved to Warsaw. The last king to reside in the city was Zygmunt III (1587–1632) of the Swedish Vasa line, but a fire on Wawel in 1595 forced him to move to Warsaw, which from 1609 became the official royal seat, although coronations still took place in Kraków.

Kraków's declining importance had an inevitable impact on social and urban development. Few new buildings and not a single church went up in the 16C. Economic prosperity was undermined by Gdańsk's monopoly over the grain trade and the Ottoman and Tartar occupation of the Black Sea coast (the lucrative eastern trade route). The population rose to 20,000, in part due to the influx of Jews and Italians, but this figure fell drastically after the wars and plagues of the following century. The university was affected, too: student numbers fell, and prestige suffered to the extent that a rival school was set up by the Jesuits in 1579.

During the '**Swedish Deluge**' (see p. 49), the army of Charles X laid siege to Kraków in 1655, razing the district of Stradom. The city again suffered destruction at the hands of foreign armies in the first half of 18C. Augustus III of Saxony (1733–63) was the last king to be crowned in Kraków, the ceremony set to the music of J. S. Bach, his court composer. The reign of Stanisław August Poniatowski (1764–95) saw the centre of cultural and political life shift decidedly and irrevocably to Warsaw. After the **First Partition of Poland** (1791), the Vistula river marked the border between Kraków and the Austrian Empire. A new Austrian town (today's district of Podgórze) soon emerged, taking over much of the city's south-eastern trade and accelerating her economic decline.

Under **Austrian rule** after 1795, Kraków was initially made the capital of the northern province of Western Galicia, but when the latter was merged with its eastern namesake, the city lost its autonomous status and the provincial capital moved to Lwów (Lviv). A vigorous campaign of Germanisation was begun.

The Poles saw in Napoleon a potential liberator from imperial rule, but the defeat of his *grande armée* in 1812 led to the **Russian occupation** of Kraków in the following year. At the **Congress of Vienna** in 1815, the peacemakers endowed the city with the status of a **mini-republic**, under the direct supervision of its three powerful neighbours, Austria, Russia and Prussia.

For a state under foreign rule, the **Republic of Kraków** (1815–46) was blessed with a relatively liberal constitution. The Austrians turned a blind eye to the ceremonial funerals of Polish national heroes—Józef Poniatowski (1817) and Tadeusz Kościuszko (1818)—who were both laid to rest on Wawel. (Kościuszko even had a mound raised in his honour in 1820–23.) The modest economic revival that had begun under Austrian rule continued into the Republic. In the early years of the century, the obsolete town fortifications were torn down and replaced by the *Planty* green belt encircling the Old Town.

The Kraków Republic was eventually dissolved and annexed to Austria in November 1846, following a **peasant revolt** (see p. 52). The next 20 years were the most repressive period of Austrian rule in the city. Economic decline was exacerbated by two natural disasters: famine and a typhoid epidemic in 1847, followed by a massive fire in 1850 which destroyed half the Old Town.

Kraków's fortunes were to turn again in 1867, when the constitution of the new Austro-Hungarian Empire gave Galicia wide-ranging autonomy. In the freer atmosphere of the mid to late 19C, the city experienced an unprecedented upsurge in artistic and intellectual activity. Literature and art came to be dominated by the Modernist 'Young Poland' movement, with Kraków becoming its Bohemian centre. A parallel process was taking place in architecture. New public buildings went up, soon to be dominated by Art Nouveau. The physical appearance of urban Kraków changed rapidly after the election of Józef Dietl as mayor in 1861. The city spread outwards from the historic centre, with its old approach roads being adapted into a radial system of new streets.

The late 19C witnessed a proliferation of socialist ideas in Kraków and Galicia. For Lenin, who lived on ul. Królowej Jadwigi 41 between 1912 and 1914, the city was a safe haven from the Czarist authorities. The **First World War** years were relatively kind to Kraków: no fighting took place within its borders, and once the Austro-Hungarian Empire had finally disintegrated, it was the first Polish city to be freed.

Between the wars Kraków once again fell into relative obscurity, though it managed to retain its status as the leading centre of the arts and sciences. In 1939, it surrendered to the invading German army without a fight, and consequently avoided the mass bombing and destruction that befell Warsaw. In October, it was designated as the seat of the *General Gouvernement*. Racial segregation of the city began almost immediately. The best districts in the west were reserved for Germans. Poles were expelled to the poorer, Jewish districts of Kazimierz and Stradom, the Jewish community to labour camps in Germany or, after 1941, to the new ghetto in Podgórze across the river. Before the **Second World War**, a fifth of Kraków's 250,000 inhabitants were Jews, but as few as 1000 managed to survive it. Mass exterminations began in 1942 with the first transports to concentration camps at the nearby Płaszów, and at Auschwitz-Birkenau, 50km east of Kraków. Priceless works of art, such as Veit Stoss's altarpiece in St Mary's, were looted by the Nazis; the rooms of Wawel castle were converted into the offices of the Governor, Hans Frank. In spite of hardships and extreme risk, cultural life in the city refused to die: the university carried on underground teaching; school lessons were organised; Tadeusz Kantor began his famous Independent Theatre. At the end of the war, again, Kraków escaped destruction, though it needed a small miracle: Marshal Koniev's Red Army division arrived on 18 January 1945, just in time to stop the Germans detonating the vast amounts of explosive that had been placed all around the city.

For Kraków, the **Communist period** spelled disaster. With the erection of the huge Lenin steelworks in the 1950s, pollution levels soared. Buildings in the historic city centre began to turn a blackish-grey and fall into disrepair. Lack of funds meant little was done in the way of renovation, though the city's entry onto UNESCO's World Heritage List in 1978 did help to reverse the trend somewhat. Few good buildings went up. Worst of all were the drab, dehumanising housing estates that mar the city's skyline even today.

Walk One ~ The Historic Old Town

The Main Market Square

Much of your time in Kraków will probably be spent in and around the **Main Market Square**, located at the centre of the city's historic Old Town. The square, or *Rynek* (from the German, 'Ring') is the largest medieval market square in central Europe (200m by 200m). In the Middle Ages, it was the commercial and administrative centre of the city, the venue for ceremonies and parades, public meetings and executions. Later, it was where the magnates put up their grand palaces to be closer to the royal court on Wawel. Today, in summer, children feed the swarms of pigeons, the flower-sellers open their stalls, and the cafés move their chairs and tables outdoors, providing an excellent vantage point from which to admire the ancient buildings—the Cloth Hall, Town Hall Tower, church of St Mary—or just watch the crowds.

The history of the Market Square begins in 1257, when Bolesław the Chaste endowed Kraków with a charter based on Magdeburg law. A new market square was laid out at the centre of a regular grid of streets. The plan was symmetrical, though in some places concessions had to be made to accommodate extant buildings, such as the churches of St Mary and St Adalbert. Likewise, the existing street plan had to be taken into account: ul. Grodzka, for example, the old thoroughfare running south towards the castle, broke the rule that streets should enter the square at right angles. With urban expansion limited by the town walls, the Rynek was soon crammed with a plethora of stalls and municipal buildings: a Gothic town hall; Renaissance granary; large weighing house; foundry; pillory; and cloth hall. Over the centuries, the Gothic appearance of the Market Square gradually changed: the narrow medieval buildings around the periphery were demolished or combined to form new houses and palaces. Bare Gothic brick gave way to plaster; storeys and decorative parapets were added, and buttresses were often used to bolster the frailer buildings. A major transformation took place during Austrian rule in the 19C, when the stalls and the old buildings, except the Cloth Hall and the Town Hall tower, were demolished to make way for a broad open space lined with trees. The façades on the palaces one sees today generally date from this period. Most are Neo-classical, often concealing older elements: beam-framed ceilings, numerous portals (15C–18C), painted and stucco-work decoration (16C–19C).

From the 14C onwards, royal coronations and burials were preceded by grand parades along the Royal Way (see p. 203), from the Floriańska Gate to Wawel Castle. Some medieval ceremonies have survived to the present day. In June, the spectacular **Corpus Christi procession**, attended by vast crowds, begins at Wawel Cathedral and ends with an army of monks and nuns kneeling in prayer on the Market Square. In the following week, you might catch a glimpse of Lajkonik, a horseman dressed in a costume designed by the early 20C painter and playwright, Stanisław Wyspiański, and meant to represent a Tartar chieftain. The **Lajkonik parade** sets out from the Premonstratensian Convent in Salwator (see p. 237) and proceeds to the Market Square. In December, the Rynek is the venue for a competition of *szopki*, or Christmas cribs, which are put on display around the statue of Adam Mickiewicz (see p. 197).

St Florian

N

KARMELICKA

Carmelite Church

GARBARSKA
P.O.

RAJSKA

Building of the Fine Arts Society

KRUPNICZA

STUDENCKA

GARNCARSKA

LORETAŃSKA

JABŁONOWSKICH

Collegium Novum

PIŁSUDSKIEGO

SMOLEŃSK

FELICIANEK

RETORYKA

ZWIERZYNIECKA

STRASZEWSKIEGO

WIERZYŃSKIECKA

POWIŚLE

KONOPNICKIEJ

Dębnicki
Bridge

Vistula

BASZTOWA

Academy of Fine Arts
Reformed
Franciscans'
Church and
Monastery

DUNAJEWSKIEGO

PL
SZCZEPAŃSKI

Old Theatre

SW. REFORMACKA

St Mark

Czartoryski Mus.

Jama Michalika Café

Matejko Museum

St John

PL
TOMASZA

Szolajski House (Mus.)

Historical Mus.
of Kraków

Town
Hall Tower

Collegium Maius

Rams'
Palace

Archbishop's
Palace

Mon. to Adam
Mickiewicz

Cloth
Hall

St Adalbert

FRANCISZKAŃSKA

Franciscan
Church

Archaeological Museum

Collegium Iuridicum

Wyspiański Museum

Archdiocesan Museum

Dean's House

House of Jan Długosz

PODZAMCZE

Wawel

BERNARDYŃSKA

Bernardine
Church and Monastery

Grunwald
Monument

Piarist
Church

Joiners'
Tower

Carpenters'
Tower

Barbican

Main Bus
Station

PL
KOLEJOWY

PAWIA

i

P.O.
Main Railway
Station

LUBICZ

St Florian
Gate

Trimming-
makers' Tower

BASZTOWA

Słowacki Theatre

Holy Cross Church

ZAMENHOFFA

House under
the Cross

SW. KRZYŻA

RADZIWIŁŁOWSKA

St Mary

St Barbara

Dominican
Convent

St Nicholas

KOPERNIKA

ZYBLIKIEWICZA

Dominican
Church

PL
WSZYSTKICH
ŚWIĘTYCH

DOMINIKAŃSKA

Main
Post Office

WIELOPOLE

POSELSKA

SENACKA

SS Peter
and Paul

SW. GERTRUDY

SAREGO

GRODZKA

St Andrew

St Martin

SW. SEBASTIANA

St Giles

Arsenal

STRADOM

Missionary
Fathers

BLICH

DIETLA

STAROWIŚLNA

KRAKÓW
OLD TOWN

0   500 yds
0   500 metres

JAGIELLOŃSKA

SW. ANNY

PL
SŁAWKOWSKA

FLORIAŃSKA

SW. JANA

SZEWSKA

PODWALE

BRACKA

GOŁĘBIA

SIENNA

STOLARSKA

MIKOŁAJSKA

WESTERPLATTE

LIBROWSZCZYZNA

SZPITALNA

KANONICZA

Town Hall (Ethnographical Museum)

The Cloth Hall

In the middle of the Rynek is one of Kraków's best-known and best-loved architectural monuments, the **Cloth Hall**, or *Sukiennice*. Rectangular in shape, and measuring almost 100m in length, the Cloth Hall was the medieval city's main centre of trading, surrounded on all sides by a labyrinth of market stalls. Nowadays, the building's mercantile traditions are sustained by a covered market offering a variety of souvenirs, folk art, handicraft and leather goods; everything from carved chess sets and amber brooches to Stalin dolls with miniature Yeltsins inside. You may want to visit the *Noworolski* café under the east arcade, notably the Red Room with its Art Nouveau ornamentation. The upper floors of the Cloth Hall house a Gallery of Polish Painting (see below).

The earliest fragments of the Cloth Hall date from the 13C, when Bolesław the Chaste promised to provide stalls for the cloth traders under the terms of the city's charter. In 1555 the Gothic edifice was gutted by a huge fire, and its rebuilding was entrusted to the best architect of Polish Renaissance,

Santi Gucci. His grand opus was the Cloth Hall, which he gave new Mannerist form in 1556–60, crowning it with a decorative parapet wall. The 'Polish Parapet', as it later came to be known, took the form of a lively cresting in place of the traditional battlements, with a sunken roof as additional protection against fire. Gucci's version, consisting of a blind-arcade frieze with volute crowning, is the earliest example of its kind. His too are the grotesque masks on the parapet, their faces contorted with pain or convulsed in satanic laughter. Inside, the Cloth Hall was given a massive vault with lunettes, while the Paduan architect, **Giovanni il Mosca**, added columned loggias reached by stairs to the external lower sections (north and south ends). Due to increased traffic, a passageway through the centre of the hall was built at the beginning of the 17C.

Originally the Cloth hall was hemmed in on all sides by stalls, demolished in the 19C to make way for the massive central projections you see today. **Tomasz Pryliński**, the architect in charge of the reconstruction project, skilfully masked the bare hall façades with Neo-Gothic granite arcades (1875–79), allowing entry to the stores within. The capitals on some of the columns were adorned with sculptures designed by Jan Matejko, who also made new stalls in carved wood. In 1883, a National Museum was opened exhibiting works donated by local artists, a trend established by Henryk Siemiradzki, who presented his huge *Torches of Nero* for public display in 1879.

Entrance to the ***Cloth Hall Gallery** (open Tues–Wed, Fri–Sun 10.00–16.00, Thur 10.00–18.00), is from the east arcade. Most of the canvases on display are by 19C Polish artists. The most popular exhibits are the huge 'patriotic' paintings by Jan Matejko—*The Prussian Homage*, *Kościuszko at Racławice* and *Wernyhora* (see below and p. 72).

The imposing ***Town Hall Tower** (70m, 50cm off vertical) in the southwest part of the Rynek is all that now remains of Kraków's 14C Town Hall, demolished in 1817 after falling into a state of disrepair. The tower is mainly brick, resting on stone blocks, and with Gothic stone fluting. On the north side, fronted by two stone lions and stairs, is the entrance. The upper sections of the building suffered extensive damage during a fire in 1680. During reconstruction a new crowning was added: a mediocre Baroque double-lantern, all of copper. Another fire in the 18C destroyed the Nürnberg clock and oriel windows. The latter were rebuilt in the 1960s, but the end result outraged many conservators as unauthentic.

The Town Hall Tower is now a branch of the **Historical Museum of Kraków** (open Mon–Fri 10.00–16.00, Sat–Sun 10.00–17.00, summer only). More interesting than the display (history of the city authorities) is the interior itself, which has some fine Gothic masonry. Inscribed on the stone facing in the former ground floor Treasury are a dozen or so stonemason's marks dating from 1444 when the tower was reconstructed. Upstairs you will find the chambers of the City Council, and on the third floor a series of rooms, former prison cells, offering a fine view over the city. The cellars, reached by a separate entrance, house the Maszkaron Theatre.

Close to the Town Hall Tower are two slabs set into the stone paving. Both commemorate famous historical events that took place on the square: the Prussian Homage, and Kościuszko's Oath.

The '**Prussian Homage**', immortalised on canvas in the 19C by Jan Matejko (see p. 72), refers to an event that took place here in 1525. On 10 April, the Grand Master of the Teutonic Order (see p. 333) swore a historic oath of allegiance to the Polish king, Zygmunt the Old. Through his act of feudal tribute, the Order formally recognised Polish dominance in the Baltic region. By the late 18C, however, the balance of power had diametrically changed. The partitioning powers, among them Prussia, were seeking to wipe Poland off the map of Europe. In 1794 a national insurrection broke out under Tadeusz Kościuszko's leadership. On 24 March, crowds gathered on the Market Square and watched as Kościuszko took a public oath to defend the integrity and independence of the Polish state. Yet his efforts came to nothing: under the Third Partition (1795) Poland was formally abolished, and Kraków found itself in the northern reaches of the Austrian Empire. With the restoration of independence in 1918, Austrian eagles and other reminders of imperial rule were symbolically smashed to the ground at precisely the spot where Kościuszko had made his famous call to arms two centuries earlier.

Southwest of the Cloth Hall stands **St Adalbert's church**, a modest, domed building on a square plan. It is in fact one of the oldest surviving examples of Romanesque architecture in the city, pre-dating the Market Square.

A pagan temple on yew-wood foundations already existed at this spot in the 10C. In the 11C a stone church appeared with a rectangular tower on its west side, eventually giving way to a Romanesque church of cobbled stone. As successive layers of stone were added to the market square, so the church began to sink—almost 3m over the centuries. In 1611, the somewhat spartan nave was improved with the addition of an elliptical dome and lantern.

St Adalbert's has been restored right down to its foundations. Small Romanesque windows with slanting jambs are preserved in the lower sections. Adjacent to the north is a sacristy (1711), and to the south, a chapel (1778). Underneath the church are cellars housing a small but worthwhile **museum** (**open** June–August, Mon–Sat 10.00–15.00), with a display devoted to the history of the Market Square.

Walking north to St Mary's church you will pass the **Monument to Adam Mickiewicz**, the greatest Polish poet of the Romantic period. Teodor Rygier designed the piece in bronze in 1898. It stands on a solid granite plinth decorated with allegorical figures symbolising Patriotism, Learning, Poetry and Valour. Destroyed by the Nazis in 1940, the monument was rebuilt and placed in its present spot in 1955—the hundredth anniversary of the poet's death. It serves as a convenient meeting point (popularly known as '*pod Adasiem*'—'by Adam') and favoured venue for the occasional Anarchist rally.

The Church of St Mary

When viewed from afar, the city's skyline is dominated by the ****Church of St Mary**, revered by many as Poland's finest architectural monument, surpassing even the Cathedral on Wawel. St Mary's is the quintessential Cracovian church; it is also one of the city's oldest, pre-dating the Rynek around it by almost half a century.

Discoveries of Romanesque foundations suggest that a stone basilica existed at this spot as early as 1221, replaced in the 1290s by a low brick hall. A chancel, sponsored by Mikołaj Wierzynek (see p. 201), followed in 1355–65, and finally a Gothic brick basilica with transept was raised in 1392–97 under the supervision of the Prague builder, Mikuláš Werner. As its contemporary—Wawel Cathedral—was the royal and episcopal church of Kraków, St Mary's became the town church, financed not by royalty, nobility, or clergy, but by wealthy burgher families whose memorial slabs still adorn the walls and chapels.

The lowest sections of the giant twin towers of St Mary's are remnants of the 13C Gothic hall church. The shorter south tower, late 14C, was set aside for the belfry and has five bells, the largest—the 'Half-Zygmunt', in reference to the greater bell on Wawel—cast in 1438. It is topped with a Renaissance spire. The taller north tower reached its present height of over 80m in 1478, when Mathias Heringk gave it a steep Gothic spire adorned with a wreath of eight turrets and smaller spires lower down. A gilded crown was later mounted on the spire. In the Middle Ages the tower served as the city watchtower, when the trumpeter at the top would give the signal to open or close the city gates.

Local legend has it that during the Tartar invasion in 1241 the dutiful watchman sounded his bugle to warn the city's inhabitants of impending attack. Before he could finish his call, his neck was pierced by a Tartar arrow. Today, to commemorate the event, the bugle call on the hour ends abruptly, mid-way through the melody.

The somewhat severe **façade** of St Mary's is enlivened by stone detailing and a decorative pattern of different coloured brick. Tall thin panels and Gothic windows rise up the towers, between which nestles a huge pointed arch window with fine 15C tracery, its lower section concealed by the west **Porch**. On its outer doors are the sculpted heads of church dignitaries and apostles. Enter the church through the porch. Two chapels adjoin the **Vestibule**: to the right, the **Chapel of the Virgin of Częstochowa**, its altar containing a copy of the famed Black Madonna (see p. 267), and usually crowded with believers kneeling before the Holy Sacrament; to the left, the more sombre **Chapel of St Anthony**, originally used for prisoners awaiting execution. The altar here dates from the 18C.

The **nave**, 28m high and four bays long, is separated from the aisles by huge piers. The Gothic cross vault is divided by a net of stone ribs, its clarity contrasting with the Baroque opulence of the altars below. In the distance you will see a giant crucifix of c 1520 high above on the rood beam; beyond it, in the chancel, Veit Stoss's celebrated high altar. The 19C murals covering the walls are by Jan Matejko, who included, amongst the plant motifs, guild emblems and royal crests. Either side of the entrance to the nave are aldermen's and town councillors' benches, covered by canopies from the 16C, and further on, adjacent to the middle pillars, early Baroque benches. 18C black marble altars, by Bażanka and Placidi, adorn the pillars separating the nave from the aisles; many contain valuable paintings by such masters as the Venetian Giovanni Battista Pittoni, whose best piece—the *Annunciation*—is on an altar to the left of the rood.

Between the buttresses in the north and south aisles are six chapels (1435–46) with late Gothic vaults, closed off from the nave by Baroque gates and marble portals. Begin at the west end of the north aisle (clockwise). Before the aisle chapels, first there is the small **Lady of Loreto Chapel**, containing one of the best tombs: a great bronze slab of 1538 to Seweryn and Zofia Boner from Vischer's Nürnberg workshop. Murals by Józef Mehoffer decorate the **Chapel of John the Baptist**. In the adjoining **Chapel of St Lawrence**, Jan Bukowski's 19C murals are partly obscured by photographs of abortions and starving children. Last in the north aisle is the **Chapel of the Transfiguration**, again with murals by Bukowski. Moving across to the south aisle, you will pass, to the right of the chancel arch, a Renaissance tabernacle of marble and alabaster with three small medallion heads above two pensive angels. It was here that Tadeusz Kościuszko reaffirmed the oath of insurrection on 25 March 1794. Standing in a Baroque altar next to the tabernacle is Veit Stoss's huge sandstone *crucifix, an outstanding example of 15C stone sculpture. The south aisle chapels begin with the **Chapel of St John Nepomuk**, which has early 20C murals by Włodzimierz Tetmajer. Next is the **Chapel of St Valentine**, with a 15C tomb in the form of reclining figure, and finally the **Chapel of St Lazarus**, founded slightly later (1494).

The **chancel** (open 12.00–18.00; 14.00–18.00 Sun) is as long and tall as the nave, but, unlike it, has a truly Gothic slimness of proportion. In 1442, the stonemason Czipser put up the present vault of four-pointed stars. Then, in the late 19C, Jan Matejko covered the vault and walls with murals depicting angels playing musical instruments and holding banners with verses of the Litany of Loreto. The upper sections of the walls sport a painted frieze with royal and ecclesiastical coats of arms, emblems of the various city guilds, and other heraldic motifs. Notice, to the right and left as you enter the chancel, the raised Mannerist tombstones of the celebrated Montelupi and Cellari families, depicted as a group of bronze effigies. These, like the Renaissance bronze tablet to Piotr Salomon (d. 1506) at the east end of the chancel, originate from Vischer's Nürnberg workshop and are among the best sculptural monuments in the church. Running down the sides of the chancel are early Baroque stalls, 1632, with reliefs by Fabian Möller, a magnificent example of local woodcarving from the first half of the 17C.

Dominating the east wall of the chancel is Veit Stoss's **High Altar**, a massive 15C polyptych (13m by 11m) carved in limewood with folding wings.

Stoss began the piece in 1477 and continued for 12 years. He achieved a work of true genius, a superb example of European late Gothic, today coveted as Poland's greatest cultural treasure. During the Second World War the altar was removed to Germany by the Nazis, and eventually retrieved from the cellars of Nürnberg castle. After extensive conservation, it was restored to its original place in the church in 1957.

The proportions of the altar are huge: even 'closed' it commands the whole church, its lavish gilding in striking contrast to the chancel's sombre surroundings. The main scene in the *Corpus* represents the **Dormition of the Virgin**. Huge (up to 2.7m high), three-dimensional figures of the apostles support the fainting Mary. The figures, in their dramatic poses, reveal the artist's astonishing eye for detail: not a single muscle contour, expression or facial blemish seem to have escaped Stoss's attention. Above the apostles, still in the main *Corpus*, is a scene of the *Assumption* carved with equal meticulousness and sensitivity. On the hinged wings of the *Corpus* are six scenes in flat relief: (left, top to bottom) *Annunciation, Nativity, Adoration of the Magi*; (right, top to bottom) *Resurrection, Ascension, Descent of the Holy Ghost*. The scene in the altar crowning depicts the *Coronation of the Virgin*, flanked by the patrons of Poland—SS Stanisław and Adalbert; below the main *Corpus* is a predella panel with the genealogical tree of Jesus and Mary. When closed, the wings of the altar reveal a further twelve scenes in low-relief from the life of the Holy Family. The mood of the entire work is enhanced by the opalescent light filtering in through the medieval stained glass windows in the apse behind.

Completed in 1370–1400, and attributed to the mysterious Michael, 'vitraetor de Cracovia' (glass-maker of Kraków), the windows behind the altar are stylistically linked to the French early Gothic school of stained glass. Each window consists of three columns, containing on average 40 scenes from the book of Genesis and the life of Jesus and Mary.

The door in the north wall of the chancel leads to the **sacristy**, its ceiling decorated with 18C murals depicting the triumph of the Christian faith. Behind it, in a 16C Mannerist annex, is the **Treasury** (c 1600). The Baroque interior holds a rich collection of liturgical vessels (14C–18C), including late Gothic chalices and embroidered chasubles.

Leave St Mary's from the south side of the chancel. Notice the strong buttresses finished with pinnacles above the chapels, nave and aisles. Rich thematic sculptures (c 1390) decorate the supports of the moulding encircling the chancel and the keystones of the window frames. By the south entrance are two sets of stocks.

St Mary's Square, comprising the area between St Mary's church and the church of St Barbara to the south-east, was the parish graveyard until demolition in 1804. In the middle stands a 'pigeon fountain' with a bronze figure of a schoolboy—a copy of one of the figures from Stoss's altar—which was donated to the city by local sculptors in 1958. The house at No. 8, nearest the Main Square, has a late Gothic bas-relief—*Christ in the Garden of Olives*—at the first floor level, a copy of a work from Veit Stoss's workshop (the original is in the National Museum).

The Gothic **Church of St Barbara** began its existence as a mortuary in 1338. It was later remodelled by the Jesuits, who built their college (today facing the Small Market Square) adjacent to its chancel. Of the original Gothic elements, only two were left intact: the west gable and the small Chapel of Gethsemane to the left of the main entrance (St Mary's Square). The chapel, containing stone figures of Jesus and three apostles, 1488–1516, from Veit Stoss's workshop, is one of the best of its kind in the city. Along the north exterior wall are two more chapels: of the Virgin (1608, rebuilt 1731), domed, with a bricked-up Renaissance portal, and a late Renaissance one of Jesus (1605–08) with rich stone ornamentation. The interior of St Barbara's underwent significant alterations during the Baroque period. By far the finest work is a late Gothic Pietà (c 1410), which rests in a niche in the north aisle.

Houses on the Main Market Square

Between St Mary's Square and ul. Grodzka (east side)

The huge, three-storeyed **Grey House** at No. 6 (corner of ul. Sienna) dates from the 16C. Its name derives from Sara (in Polish *Szara*, Grey)—a mistress of King Kazimierz the Jagiellon—who lived in the former Gothic house at this spot. Later, the Grey House became the town residence of the powerful Zborowski family, after whom it is sometimes still called. In 1794, it served as the headquarters of Kościuszko's High Command, briefly accommodating the revolutionary Provisional Government of the Republic of Kraków half a century later. Murals by Józef Mehoffer adorn the Gothic vaults in the ground floor shop.

The **Italian House** at No. 7 was from the 16C the residence of the wealthy Italian family of Montelupi. The first Polish postal service was established here in 1558, when a stagecoach set off bound for Venice. The event is commemorated by the plaque beside the Mannerist portal. The mock stagecoach by the house (summer only) is actually a post office selling stamps and postcards.

The 15C **Lizard House** further on at No. 8, is named after a late Gothic bas-relief of two entwined lizards above the entrance (original in the National Museum). Inside, there is well-preserved 'Piast' vaulting on the ground floor. The building is currently host to a loud student disco and occasional jazz concerts (entrance from No. 9; the passageway is a convenient short-cut through to the Small Market Square).

Between ul. Grodzka and ul. Wiślna (south side)

The **Morsztynowski House** at No. 16 and part of the adjoining Hetman House were combined to form one building after restoration work in 1975–79. It is home to the renowned **Wierzynek Restaurant**, whose culinary traditions stretch back to the 14C.

> In 1364, Kraków was chosen as the venue for a Congress of Monarchs. Among the guests of Kazimierz the Great were such illustrious figures as Emperor Charles IV and Louis, King of Hungary. Once the official ceremonies had finished, the guests were treated to a lavish banquet hosted by Mikołaj Wierzynek, a wealthy patrician and city councillor. A restaurant was opened in Wierzynek's house after the Second World War. Since then it has acquired the—some say—undeserved title of Poland's most exclusive restaurant, frequently visited by politicians, diplomats and foreign dignitaries.

The first floor rooms have beam-framed ceilings. In one there is a huge 19C canvas depicting the historic feast of 1364.

The 14C **Hetman House** at No. 17 was in the 16C the residence of the king's field commanders (hetmans), hence the stone heraldic emblems above the entrance and high up on the façade. One of the ground floor rooms, presently occupied by the *Hetmańska* bookshop, has well-preserved Gothic ribbed vaulting (c 1390), recalling the east parts of the Cathedral, with carved stone bosses, two of which depict Kazimierz the Great and Queen Jadwiga. Another bookshop upstairs (entrance from the passage) has a miniature Gothic stone arch and, embedded in the wall, a stove decked out in Baroque tiles that were found during restoration work in the 1980s. The cellars of Hetman House are occupied by the *Da Pietro* Italian restaurant.

Over the centuries, the 16C **Zbaraski Palace** at No. 20 (corner of ul. Bracka) was successively owned by many of Poland's great noble families. The Flemish architect van Pecne remodelled the three wings in the early 17C, adding a tiny, late Renaissance arcaded courtyard with loggias (occasionally the venue of plays and concerts). The building acquired its present Neo-classical appearance after major renovation and alteration work in 1777–83.

Between ul. Św. Anny and ul. Szczepańska (west side)

The Potocki Palace at No. 27, better known as the *Rams' Palace (Pałac Pod Baranami), was created in the 17C when Justus Decius, secretary to King Zygmunt the Old, purchased two Gothic buildings at this spot and transformed them into his town residence. After numerous alterations—a new façade was added in the 18C—the palace was given its present architectural form in 1874. The ground floor rooms off the inner courtyard have 15C Gothic ribbed vaulting, while upstairs the interiors are mainly Neo-classical. The name 'Rams' Palace' probably derives from the fact that there was originally an inn here, with rams for sale in its courtyard. Three stone ram heads can be seen on the façade just below the balcony. The Potockis owned the palace from 1822 until expulsion by the Nazi authorities, recovering it again after reprivatisation in 1990.

After 1945 the Rams' Palace began a new life as a Cultural Centre, comprising reading rooms, music studios, a library and cinema. In 1956, in the cellars off the courtyard, a group of actors, artists and musicians established what came to be known as the **Piwnica Pod Baranami Cabaret**. During the 40 years of its existence, it acquired a legendary status, and its performances, combining music, poetry and witty sketches enjoyed huge popularity. The cabaret closed in 1996 following the death its host and founder, Piotr Skrzynecki, but there are now plans to revive it, perhaps in a different form. You can visit the rooms where the cabaret was held (turn right at the bottom of the stairs). The wall decoration, designed by the performers and associates of the cabaret, still manages to capture the special mood of the place.

The **Spiski Palace** at No. 34 was bought in 1592–98 by the wealthy magnate Stanisław Lubomirski, the starost of Spisz (hence the name), who turned it into a palatial residence. Later architectural accretions somewhat ruined the original Baroque façade. The first floor of the building is now occupied by the *Tetma-jerowska Restaurant*, which tries to outdo the nearby Wierzynek (see above) in prestige and especially prices. Its Tetmajer Room, which the artist decorated in 1891, has a frieze depicting Twardowski's grotto and three banquets: the patri-cians', nobles', and court.

The **Wodzicki Palace** (called 'Krzysztofory') at No. 35, an amalgamation of three Gothic burghers' houses, is named after a figure of St Christopher (1380), which adorned the façade until the 18C (presently in the National Museum). The palace accommodates the **Historical Museum of Kraków** (open Thur 11.00–18.00, Wed and Fri–Sun 09.00–15.00). The two best rooms, with stuc-coes by Baldassare Fontana, are on the first floor overlooking the Rynek. Upstairs on the second floor is an exhibition of clocks. The vestibule entered from ul. Szczepańska 2 gives access to a courtyard with a columned loggia. Just before it on the right is a door leading down to the *Krzysztofory* café and modern art gallery in the cellars. Tadeusz Kantor's avant-garde Cricot 2 Theatre (see

p. 208) put on a number of performances here in the 1960s and 70s. His work has recently been performed at the Edinburgh Festival.

Between ul. Sławkowska and ul. Floriańska (north side)

Opposite the Wodzicki Palace stands the 14C **Pear House** (ul. Szczepańska 1). Two first floor rooms house the Journalists' Club bar and restaurant; a third, usually closed, has fine stucco decoration by Baldassare Fontana (c 1700) concealing Gothic rib vaults and the remnants of Renaissance murals. The walls are decked out in 17C Dutch tiles.

> According to the medieval historian Jan Długosz, the Pear House was where Prince Wilhelm—a suitor to the Polish Princess Jadwiga—lived during his secret visit to Kraków in 1386. Apparently, the two lovers would meet at night in the Franciscan cloister (see p. 207), as Wilhelm was banned from entering the castle. Their plans were wrecked, however, when Jadwiga, much against her will, finally married the Lithuanian Duke Jagiełło, thus beginning the Polish Jagiellon dynasty.

The **Eagle House** at No. 45 was where one of the first city apothecaries was established in 1625. High up on the Gothic red brick façade is an ornamental stone eagle. Renaissance coffered ceilings have been preserved on the first floor and part of the ground floor.

Small Market Square (Mały Rynek)

The covered passageway next to St Barbara's church will bring you onto the Small Market Square. Some of the houses around it date back as early as the 14C. Those on the east side used to be fronted with *przedproża*, or raised platforms covering partly sunken cellars, of the kind found on ul. Mariacka in Gdańsk (see p. 318); today, only a section of stone terrace remains.

Return to the Main Market Square along ul. Sienna. At No. 5 (corner of ul. Stolarska) stands the **Salomon House** with a Rococo portal. Rebuilt in 1590–95 from a Gothic burgher's lodge, the building accommodates the oldest charitable institution in Kraków—the Fraternity of Mercy—established in 1584 by Piotr Skarga, as well as a library (ground floor) and the Catholic Intelligentsia Club (first floor). The house has one of the best-preserved 18C interiors in the city.

Walk Two ~ The Royal Way

The **St Florian Gate** marks the beginning of the 'Royal Way'—a route south through the city to Wawel Hill traditionally taken by Polish monarchs on coronation day. At royal funerals, the cortège would assemble in the district of Kleparz to the north and proceed along the same route to bury the deceased in the Cathedral. It was also through the St Florian Gate that the invading Tartars in 1241 and Swedes in 1655 made their victorious entry into the Royal City.

The St Florian Gate and the Furriers' Tower above it were constructed in 1300–07 as part of the city's fortifications. In the 15C a brick upper storey with machicolations and a steep roof were added, the Gothic crowning being replaced with a Baroque one in 1656. At night, or in times of danger, the gatekeeper would lower the heavy portcullis, remnants of which are visible at the corners of the gate. Notice the 18C bas-relief of St Florian above the south entrance, and on the opposite (north) side a stone coat of arms bearing the Piast eagle, designed by Jan Matejko. The classical altar, with a painting of the Virgin, was placed inside the gate in 1835.

To the west and east of the gate are fragments of the city's medieval fortifications, consisting of a section of wall with three towers linked by a guards' gallery: the **Carpenters' Tower**, integrated into the corpus of the two-storey former Renaissance Arsenal (which now houses part of the Czartoryski Museum; see p. 226); the **Joiners' Tower**; and the semi-circular **Trimming-makers' Tower**, east of the gate, decked out in zigzags of glazed brick. By the gate is a street gallery where works by local artists and students are put on display in spring to late autumn.

Beyond the St Florian Gate lie the *Planty*, a ring of parks created in the 1810s to replace the former city walls and moat. Facing you is the Gothic ****Barbican**.

> Built in 1498–99, when Kraków was subject to Ottoman raids, this turreted and machicolated circle of reddish brick arose as a remarkable piece of military technology modelled on Arab fortifications from the times of the Crusades. Its purpose was to defend the St Florian Gate, to which it was connected by a covered passageway allowing supplies and ammunition to be swiftly replenished at all times. With an upper gallery, machicolation, and 130 loopholes on four levels, it was virtually impregnable to enemy attack until siege techniques changed. Today the Barbican endures as a unique example of medieval defensive architecture. In the summer months, plays and concerts are occasionally staged inside.

Beyond the Barbican is PL. MATEJKI (Matejko Square); in the middle stands the **Grunwald Monument** commemorating the victory of the Polish-Lithuanian armies against the Teutonic Knights in 1410 (see p. 417). Funded by the pianist, composer and inter-war statesman Ignacy Paderewski, the monument was erected in 1910 to mark the quincentenary of the battle. During the Second World War the Nazis destroyed it for its 'anti-German' connotations. It was eventually reconstructed in 1975 combined with the Tomb of the Unknown Soldier.

Ul. Floriańska

Return to UL. FLORIAŃSKA, one of the Old Town's showpiece streets. Over the centuries it was bought up by Kraków's wealthiest burgher families. Most of the houses, originally Gothic, were extensively rebuilt in the 19C and 20C, though a number of fine portals and façades have survived. With the massive towers of St Mary's church looming in the distance, the street today preserves a unique and captivating charm.

The first building of note is the renowned *Jama Michalika* café (No. 45, left). In the early years of the 20C, it was a mecca for the Cracovian *Bohème*, especially members of the modernist 'Young Poland' movement. Artists, poets and literati would meet here to enjoy provincialism being ridiculed by the satirical *Green Balloon* literary cabaret (1905–12). In a separate show, Karol Frycz's puppets would lampoon ivory-towered professors, Austrian bureaucrats and petit-bourgeois mores in a sort of fin-de-siècle *Spitting Image*. Frycz, a talented set designer, also did the lavish Art Nouveau interior (1910), much of which has been preserved. Nowadays, Jama Michalika tends to attract an elderly, tea-drinking Sunday clientele, though efforts have been made to reinvigorate the traditions of the puppet theatre, with a popular show being staged on Monday, Friday and Saturday nights.

Two doors down (**No. 41**) is the house where Jan Matejko (1838–93; see p. 72), the greatest exponent of Polish historical painting, lived and worked. Twenty years before his death, Matejko himself remodelled the façade of this 16C house in Neo-Baroque and built a new studio on the third floor. Inside the house is a small **Matejko Museum** (open Tues–Thur, Sat–Sun 10.00–15.30, Fri 10.00–18.00) with original 19C interiors and memorabilia.

With over 150,000 exhibits, the **Museum of Pharmacy** at No. 25 is the largest of its kind in Europe (open Wed–Sat 11.00–14.00, Tues 15.00–19.00; entry for group tours only; ☎ 421–92–79). The display traces the history of Polish pharmacy from medieval times until the present day. The highlight is a reconstruction of an old dispensary in the basement.

The *Rose Hotel* (*Pod Różą*) at No. 14 was originally known as the Hôtel de Russie in begrudging honour of Czar Alexander I, who stopped here in 1805. The building dates from the 16C, though only a fine Renaissance portal (c 1550) has survived the numerous later alterations. The Latin inscription reads: 'May this house stand until the ant drinks the waters of the oceans and the tortoise travels the earth'.

Crossing ul. Św. Tomasza, notice the building at No. 13, one of the best on the street. It is known as the **Kmita Palace**, 16C, after a former owner—the magnate and Palatine of Kraków, Piotr Kmita. The façade has Renaissance window frames and is topped by a Neo-classical attic with scenes in relief. Inside you will find the DESA antique shop, a gallery of modern art in the basement, and an excellent gallery of interiors on the first floor, where there are also some fine Renaissance fragments, including a Renaissance column of 1508, frescoes, and wooden beamed ceilings.

At the corner of the Market Square stands the **Ethiopian House** (No. 1)— alarmingly translated by some local guidebooks as 'The House Under the Negroes'—so-called on account of the 16C sculpture, facing the square, of two Ethiopians holding a basket of fruit. The house once belonged to an apothecary known as *Sub Aethiopibus*.

The Royal Way continues along **UL. GRODZKA**, one of Kraków's oldest streets, which exits from the southeast corner of the Market Square. After the great fire of 1850, the section up to pl. Dominikański was broadened to give it a more august appearance, and today ul. Grodzka remains the city's chief showpiece street, with many pastel-coloured buildings, exquisite portals, and grand churches.

The Dominican Church

At the first crossroads is the ***Dominican Church** (Basilica of the Holy Trinity), which stands to the left on a small square, PL. DOMINIKAŃSKI, once the heart of the medieval city.

> The Dominicans were brought to Kraków from Bologna in 1222 by Bishop Iwo Odrowąż, who endowed them with the parish church of the Holy Trinity at this spot. After the Tartar invasion (see p. 191), a new Gothic church went up on the south side of the existing cloister, preserving only

the refectory from its Romanesque predecessor. The church attained its present form in the late 14C and 15C. Much of its lavish interior was lost during the great fire of Kraków in 1850.

Viewed from outside, the church is immediately striking for its east and west gables, adorned with spikes and panels. The slender Gothic body is flanked by sumptuous chapels from later periods, clearly visible on both sides. Around the external chancel wall runs a moulded brick frieze marking the height of the original 13C church. Enter through the Neo-Gothic vestibule, beyond which is a splendid medieval doorway abounding in carved stone leaves. The interior, cold and empty, had to be thoroughly rebuilt after 1850, which resulted in much arid detail, particularly in the Neo-Gothic altars.

By far the greatest attraction are the **chapels**, beginning with the **Zbaraski Chapel** at the west end of the north aisle. Designed by Constantino Tencalla in 1629–33 on a rectangular plan with an elliptical dome, it was modelled on the Zygmunt Chapel in the Wawel Cathedral. Inside are the tombs of the last Zbaraskis, the brothers Jerzy and Krzysztof. The oldest, and perhaps best, chapel—of St Hyacinth—is reached via the white marble staircase further along the north aisle. Originally built in 1581, it contains stuccoes (c 1700) by Baldassare Fontana, particularly impressive around the inside of the dome, and the Baroque sarcophagus of St Hyacinth, the first abbot of the monastery. The painted decoration is by the Venetian Tommaso Dolabella (c 1570–1650).

In the **chancel**, at the east end of the north wall, you should not miss Veit Stoss's exquisite bronze tablet (c 1500) to **Filippo Buonaccorsi** ('Callimachus'; d. 1496), a great Humanist scholar and the Florentine mentor to King Jan Olbracht's (1492–1501) children.

Crossing to the south aisle, you will notice the entrance to the **Our Lady of the Rosary Chapel** (1685–88), which backs on to ul. Poselska. Almost a church in itself, it was built as a votive for Sobieski's victory at Vienna (see p. 49). The highlight is a miraculous image of the Virgin, which was copied from the Basilica of Santa Maria Maggiore in Rome.

Close by is the **Myszkowski Chapel**, a somewhat pompous Renaissance mausoleum (1603–16) attributed to the Santi Gucci (see p. 195) workshop. Again modelled on the Zygmunt Chapel, it has an eight-sided coffered dome, around the inside of which is a gallery of busts representing members of the Myszkowski family. The external walls, of rusticated sandstone, bear a cartouche with the founding tablet. Another Renaissance mausoleum—the Lubomirski Chapel—has painted decoration from the same period and stands at the west end of the south aisle.

Adjoining the church to the north are impressive Gothic **cloisters** (enter from the north aisle or from ul. Stolarska 12) with a refectory (after 1225), chapter house (c 1250), remnants of medieval frescoes, and many paintings. Embedded into the walls are over 150 tombs and memorial tablets.

PL. WSZYSTKICH ŚWIĘTYCH (All Saints Square), to the west of the Dominican church, is dominated by the 16C Wielkopolski Palace, currently home to the city authorities. In front of it stands a statue of Józef Dietl (1938), a former Mayor of Kraków (1866–74).

The Franciscan Church

The chancel of the *Franciscan Church backs onto the square to the right of the Wielkopolski Palace. You may sometimes enter through the monastery cloisters. Otherwise, walk around to the west entrance.

The Friars of St Francis arrived in Kraków from Prague in 1237. The construction of their church (1252–69) was the initiative of Bolesław the Chaste (d. 1279), who, along with his sister, the Blessed Salomea, was laid to rest in one of the chapels. The cruciform plan of the first Gothic brick church was somewhat altered in 1401–36, when the nave and chancel were lengthened, and when the huge Corpus Christi Chapel in the form of an aisle was added. Major changes carried out in 1850–1912 gave the interior its present Neo-Gothic appearance. The monastery (south), with its two cloister gardens, was begun in the 14C, but like the church suffered extensive damage during the fire in 1850 and had to be reconstructed (1900–12).

All that remains of the original Gothic church is the north transept. The best view of it is from ul. Bracka, where you can admire the large ogival windows and the triangular gable with an arcaded moulded-brick frieze. By far the greatest attraction of the Neo-Gothic interior are the **murals and stained glass** executed by Stanisław Wyspiański at the turn of the last century. The best murals—a composition of floral and heraldic motifs, geometric patterns and religious scenes—are found in the chancel and transepts. Equally good is the stained glass rising up above the musicians' choir (west), a *tour de force* of modern religious art. The scene, with its blue, green, yellow and red hues, depicts God the Father in the Act of Creation. There is more stained glass in the chancel, with a scene of St Francis, the church's patron, and the Blessed Salomea, whose tomb lies in a chapel adjoining the north transept. The spacious Corpus Christi Chapel (north side of the nave) dates from the 17C and was once used as a place of worship by Kraków's large Italian community. The stations of the Way of the Cross were painted by Józef Mehoffer, an accomplished artist of the Young Poland period.

Enter the cloisters either from the south transept or from the Our Lady of Sorrows Chapel (south side of the nave), where there is a Baroque altar containing a celebrated 16C painting of the Virgin. Like the chancel, the cloisters have mostly kept their 15C Gothic vaults. Along the walls you will see fine **murals** from the same period, though now in desperate need of conservation. Better still is the Gallery of Cracovian Bishops, a series of some 30 portraits begun in 1520. The finest piece, perhaps, is a portrait of Bishop Piotr Tomicki painted by the best Polish artist of the 16C, Stanisław Samostrzelnik, a Cistercian monk from the monastery at Mogiła (see p. 236).

Leave by the west exit. Facing the green at the back is the vast 16C **Archbishop's Palace** (ul. Franciszkańska 3), a three-winged building with an irregular courtyard, whose present form dates mainly from 1642–47, when it was thoroughly rebuilt in Baroque style. Like so many other buildings, the palace suffered badly during the great fire of 1850, when most of its treasures were lost. The palace is famous for being the former residence (1964–78) of **Cardinal Karol Wojtyła**, later Pope John Paul II, whose monument stands in the courtyard.

Return to ul. Grodzka. The corner house (**No. 26**) was built in 1909 on the site of an older building from which only a figure of the Virgin (set below the first floor oriel) has survived. The attic was modelled on that of the Cloth Hall. Further down is the 14C **Lion House** (No. 32), so called on account of its Gothic emblem—a gilded bas-relief of a lion. Many buildings on the Royal Way possess such emblems, which were formerly used as a system of numbering—**No. 38**, for instance, has two from the 17C: an elephant and a rhinoceros. Turn right at the first intersection, UL. POSELSKA, which in the Middle Ages delineated the limit of Kraków proper. A few yards down the street a cobbled alleyway (ul. Senacka) leads off to the left. The complex of buildings you see here is dominated by the severe-looking building at **No. 3**, a prison in the 19C, and today housing the **Archaeological Museum** (open Mon 09.00–14.00, Tues, Thur and Sat 14.00–18.00, Fri 10.00–14.00, Sun 11.00–14.00). The display is divided into four sections: Mediterranean culture in antiquity; the ancient and medieval history of Małopolska; Nowa Huta in prehistoric times; and the history of the former prison. The prize exhibit is a stone statue of the pagan Slav deity, Światowid, believed to date from the 10C. The attractive museum garden (further west along ul. Poselska) offers a fine view onto Wawel and is occasionally the venue for classical concerts.

Ul. Kanonicza

The Royal Way continues south along ul. Kanonicza (first right), one of the most beautiful streets in Kraków, evoking the atmosphere of the medieval city. Mentioned in municipal documents as early as 1401, 'Canonicorum'—today's ul. Kanonicza—is named after the Canons of the Cathedral Chapter House, who from the 14C put up their houses here. Most of the buildings date from the 14C–16C. The façades, attics and portals reveal a diversity of styles—Gothic, Renaissance, Baroque—and conceal quiet courtyards reached by carriage gateways.

No. 2 is conspicuous for its crenellated attic, which originally served both a defensive and decorative function. **No. 3** has early Renaissance stone window frames, sgraffito decoration, and a fine Rococo portal. The **Chapter House** at No. 5 was built in the 15C by Jan Długosz, who gave it over for use as a student hostel. Some fragments from this period have survived. The building is currently occupied by Tadeusz Kantor's Cricot 2 Theatre.

The Cricot Theatre

Considered to be Poland's leading avant-garde theatre, Cricot began in the 1930s. Its surrealistic presentations became famous for their acid humour and merciless attacks on Cracovian philistinism. Forced underground during the war years, it re-emerged in 1956 as Cricot 2. The *spiritus movens* of this new and unusual initiative was Tadeusz Kantor (1915–90). The theatre put on a number of memorable performances, including plays by Witkacy (see p. 86) and Kantor's groundbreaking *Dead Class*.

The **Three Crowns House** at No. 7, rebuilt in 1504 and in 1756–78, has a Renaissance façade and some fine late Gothic detailing in the vestibule. The ground floor accomodates the *U Literatów* café. In summer you can sit out in the pleasant garden-cum-courtyard at the back. **No. 9**, originally 14C, was once the home of Hugo Kołłątaj (1750–1812), a noted Enlightenment author and thinker, and rector of the Jagiellonian University. Preserved on the first floor are some fine 18C murals depicting seascapes. Following renovation in 1979–83, a branch of the National Museum was opened here, the **Wyspiański Museum** (**open** Wed, Fri–Sun 10.00–15.00, Thur 12.00–17.00), tracing the life and work of Stanisław Wyspiański as painter, set-designer and dramatist (see p. 74).

To the left ul. Kanonicza borders PL. ŚW. MARII MAGDALENY (St Mary Magdalene Square), a delightful corner of medieval Kraków, offering an excellent view onto the grand façade of the SS Peter and Paul church, just the other side of ul. Grodzka. There are four buildings of interest here. Going clockwise, first is the recently renovated **Collegium Iuridicum** (ul. Grodzka 53), which was purchased by the University in 1403 and turned into a college of law; hence the name. It was remodelled in Baroque style in 1709, when arcades were added to the charming inner courtyard. Some Gothic elements have remained, though, notably the brick gable adjacent to ul. Kanonicza, as well as parts of the window frames, portals and vaulting.

Church of SS Peter and Paul

Dominating the square is the ****Church of SS Peter and Paul**, the earliest and best example of Baroque architecture in the city.

> The Jesuits arrived in Kraków in 1582 and set up their headquarters at ul. Grodzka 52 (currently housing University departments). Work began on their church in 1596, and was completed by Giovanni Trevano in 1619. The overall design was modelled on the first Jesuit Baroque church in Rome—the Gesù: a Latin cross plan with two series of chapels in place of the aisles, but no galleries, and with a large dome above the crossing. Work on the interior continued until 1633, with Giovanni Battista Falconi executing the exquisite stuccoes in the apse, side chapels and dome.

Most interesting is the two-storey façade, consisting of three pedimented bays on top of five, and achieving a remarkable slenderness of proportion. Between the sculptures of saints are the coats of arms of Poland and of the Vasa line, as well as the Jesuit emblem. Due to the narrowness of ul. Grodzka in the 17C, the façade had to be set back from the street, thus forming a small court in front of the church. In 1715–22 Kacper Bażanka turned the space into a monumental enclosure preceded by rhomboidal stone plinths—a clever *trompe l'oeil* effect which disguises the fact that the church is not perpendicular to the street. The apostles on top of the plinths were originally designed by the unfortunately named Jesuit sculptor Daniel Hell in 1721–25, but owing to their poor condition, had to be replaced after the Second World War. Bażanka also designed the gate to the neighbouring church and convent of St Andrew, as well as the High Altar (1726–35) and two of the tombs.

The **interior** is characterised by sharp architectural detail (not a single fresco) and an austerity reminiscent of the Vasa style. Spartan chapels linked by a passageway run down the nave. In the chancel, before the High Altar, is a **crypt** (**open** 10.00–17.00) containing the surprisingly modest tomb of the preacher Piotr Skarga (d. 1612), whose writings promulgated the idea of unity between the Eastern and Western churches. This theme finds expression in Bażanka's High Altar, in the scenes in stucco relief on the apse ceiling, and indeed in the very dedication of the church: Peter, the first Pope, and Paul, the Apostle of the East. On the left of the chancel is the funerary monument to Andrzej Trzebicki (d. 1679), with a bust of the Bishop surrounded by cherubs and saints.

The stone towers to the south belong to the ***Church of St Andrew**, one of the few examples of completely preserved Romanesque architecture in Poland.

Built in 1079–98 to celebrate the birth of King Władysław Herman's son, St Andrew's was located at the centre of the medieval settlement of Okół. It was designed as a stone basilica with a transept, galleries and two slender towers. Initially, the church served a defensive as well as a religious purpose, as evidenced by the loopholes in the lower part of the façade. After transfer to the austere order of Poor Clares in c 1318, the church acquired a brick Gothic oratory (now the sacristy) and later, in the 17C, the towers were topped with copper lanterns. The convent was begun shortly after the arrival of the nuns, c 1325, though today it bears the legacy of Neo-Romanesque remodelling carried out in 1843.

The most interesting aspect of the exterior are the pairs of deep Romanesque windows in the towers and the arcaded frieze around the apse and chancel. The small interior, completely rebuilt in 1701, immediately surprises with its Baroque elegance and gilding. Especially good is the stucco decoration by Baldassare Fontana and the frescoes illustrating the life of the Blessed Salomea. Notice the Rococo pulpit in the shape of a gilded limewood boat with huge mast, meant to represent the boat of St Peter. The convent contains some unique 14C Nativity figures and a portable Byzantine mosaic of the Virgin with Child from the turn of the 13C.

The house opposite Collegium Iuridicum, **No. 2**, originally dates from 1520. The portal supported by atlantes was added during remodelling in 1776. After recent renovation the ground floor was bought up by the Pizza Hut chain, which has thankfully managed to keep its neon signs discreet and disturb neither the aesthetic appearance of the building nor the square on which it stands.

Continue south along ul. Kanonicza. In 1979, conservators discovered a treasure-trove of iron hatchets (a pre-monetary form of payment), weighing a staggering four tonnes, buried underneath the house at **No. 13**. Next door, the portal of the **Szreniawa House** (No. 15) displays a variety of different styles. The original Gothic was supplanted in the 16C by a Renaissance frieze bearing plant motifs; in the 18C, above the frieze was placed a Rococo armorial cartouche, itself topped by a crown and then by a hat of the type formerly worn by higher members of the clergy.

The **House of Bishop Erazm Ciołek** (No. 17) dates from the 16C when its eponymous founder integrated two Gothic buildings, one of which was a brick bastion, into his lavish town residence. The Renaissance portal has an armorial cartouche of the Jagiellon line consisting of a stone eagle and crown intertwined with the letter 'S', which refers to King Zygmunt (Sigismund) the Old. To the right of the portal is a Gothic window set askew to the façade in order to catch more daylight.

The 14C house at **No. 18** was remodelled in 1560–63 by Jan Michałowicz of Urzędów (the 'Polish Praxiteles'), who also designed the excellent Renaissance portal and the arcades around the inner courtyard supported on slender Tuscan columns.

The Neo-classical façade of the **Chapter House** at No. 19 disguises the 16C origins of the building. Suffragan Bishop Karol Wojtyła, later Pope John Paul II, lived here in 1951–63, and later in the Dean's House next door. Inside is a small **Archdiocesan Museum** (open 10.00–15.00; closed Sun–Mon). The display, well-marked in English, comprises altarpieces (mainly 15C–16C), triptychs (15C–17C), liturgical vestments, paintings, including an excellent religious cycle by Hans Suess of Kulmbach (1514), and two items from St Mary's church: a Gothic sculpture of the Adoration of the Magi, and a predella illustrating the Entombment of St John the Evangelist (1516). Finally, don't miss the room where John Paul II once lived, complete with typewriter, skis and chamber pot.

The 14C *Dean's House** at No. 21 is one of the best preserved buildings on the street. It was rebuilt in 1582–88 by the celebrated architect Santi Gucci (see p. 195). The façade has a sgraffito decoration and sumptuous portal modelled on a Roman triumphal arch. Beyond it is a delightful arcaded courtyard containing a Baroque statue of St Stanisław.

No. 25, at the foot of Wawel, is the **House of Jan Długosz** (15C) where the historian lived from 1450 until his death in 1480. On the façade facing the castle is a 17C painting on wood of the *Virgin and Child*. Further along the wall is the foundation plate of the no-longer extant Psalterists' House on Wawel Hill (1480), which shows Długosz kneeling before the Virgin.

Here the Royal Way ends. Turning left into ul. Podzamcze, you might wish to visit the tiny 14C **Church of St Giles** at the intersection with ul. Grodzka. On Sundays at 10.30 a Catholic mass is held here in English. Opposite the church, at ul. Grodzka 64, stands Władysław IV's **Arsenal** of 1643, currently the University's department of geography.

Walk Three ~ Wawel

You can approach **Wawel Castle** (pronounced *Vah-vel*) from several directions. From the Old Town, via ul. Kanonicza or the *Planty*, you will arrive at the foot of the hill (228m) along its north side, on the busy ul. Podzamcze. The brick fortifications, more massive further to the left, opposite ul. Grodzka, are reduced on this side to a round bastion and a wall running along the stone-lined path. These dark-red brick additions are the most recent in Wawel's history: in the mid-19C, after removing the last vestiges of medieval defences, the Austrians endeavoured to turn Wawel into a citadel.

Wawel Castle

Higher up, partly hidden by trees, looms the solid mass of buildings from other, more distant epochs in the castle's long history. Most conspicuous are the two towers with copper crownings: the thicker and lower one, with spires, four corner turrets, a crown and a weather-cock in the form of a galloping horseman, is the **Zygmunt Tower**, named after its founder King Zygmunt Vasa. He commissioned Giovanni Trevano to reconstruct it after a fire in 1595, which destroyed its 14C predecessor. The tower houses the most famous **bell** in Poland—the 'Zygmunt', in memory of King Zygmunt the Old. It is 2.5m in diameter, weighs almost eleven tonnes and is covered with reliefs depicting SS Stanisław and Zygmunt, the Polish eagle, and the Lithuanian coat of arms ('*Pogoń*'). The bell's resounding D-sharp can only be heard a few times a year, on major church and state holidays. The **Clock Tower** to the right of the Zygmunt, is a 15C structure resting on Romanesque foundations. Its graceful two-tiered Baroque crowning, designed by Kacper Bażanka in 1715, is moderately gilded and has four figures of saints in the corners. To the left of the two towers extends a vast expanse of wall belonging to the chapter house, the library and the castle, framed by squat towers with chunky copper domes to the left and right.

Walk up along the stone-paved path towards the brick **Coats of Arms (Herbowa) Gate**, erected in 1921 and decorated with the emblems of Poland, Lithuania and Ruthenia. At night it is barred with a wooden portcullis. Left of the gate, atop the polygonal bastion of Władysław IV (c 1581), stands a stately, equestrian **statue of Kościuszko**, designed by Leonard Marconi in 1921, and destroyed by the Nazis. The present one is a gift from the city of Dresden, and is modelled on the original. Turn to the arched **Vasa Gateway**. To the right of it is the gabled 14C **Rorantist House**, connected to the **Seminary** further west (right). The two buildings house the **Cathedral Museum** (entrance from the other side; see below).

Lower Castle

Passing through the Vasa Gateway you come out on the Lower Castle grounds. To your left is the Cathedral; to the right, the Cathedral Museum clad in luscious vine and, a little further on, the **Curates' House**, where you can purchase a ticket to the Royal Crypt and the Zygmunt Tower, both entered from the Cathedral. The house is used by the Cathedral clergy as living quarters.

Cathedral

The ****Cathedral** (**open** daily 09.00–17.30, summer; 09.00–15.00, winter; **open** from 12.15 Sun) is a motley of styles, building materials and forms. The cream-coloured west façade is hemmed in between two brick towers, partly concealed in their lower sections by two Gothic burial chapels. Three narrow windows in the gable, a 14C figure of St Stanisław, a Piast eagle and a huge rosette window modelled on French cathedrals make for all the decoration. Pass through the ornate Baroque entrance and walk up a flight of steps under a wooden coffered roof with rosettes (1643–4). A black-marble portal frames a door of 1636 with characteristic inlaid iron decoration: a crowned capital 'K', the cypher of King Kazimierz the Great, repeated over and over again. By the door, bones of antediluvian animals are suspended on chains—a practice common in the Middle Ages—and below, in two small niches, are Gothic stone sculptures representing the dragon-slaying Archangel Michael and St Margaret.

The **interior**, sparsely lit by the rosette and the dim clerestory windows, seems short, as the chancel is concealed behind the large shrine of St Stanisław (see below) at the intersection of the nave and transept. Three bays of cross vaults rest on corbels supporting four sculptures of the Fathers of the Christian Church: SS Jerome, Ambrose, Gregory (all three late Gothic) and Augustine (1900). The walls are hung with somewhat faded Brussels tapestries (mid-17C), partly concealing the aisle arches.

The central place in the Cathedral is occupied by the **shrine of St Stanisław** (1), the most revered martyr of the Polish Catholic Church (see p. 233). His tomb has rested at this spot since the 13C, a fact which determined the unusual proportions of the church, with the chancel longer than the nave. The dome, supported on four pillars, was designed by Giovanni Trevano in 1626–29. Below it is a silver coffin (1669–71), resting on the shoulders of angels, and bearing fine reliefs depicting scenes from the life of the saint.

On both sides of the nave, in the aisle arches, stand **royal tombs**: of Władysław of Varna (2) (a modern imitation of Gothic sarcophagi), and of Władysław Jagiełło (3) (early 15C), under a stone baldachin designed by Berrecci and resting on slender marble columns. Jagiełło's tomb, made of red Hungarian marble, is one of the best sculptures of the Polish Renaissance. It consists of the *tumba* and the supine figure of the king, dressed in a belted coat, holding a sceptre and an orb, with his feet resting against a scaled and winged reptile.

Pass around the shrine and enter the **chancel**, the site of many royal coronations. The Baroque high altar (4) (c 1650) contains a large, mid-17C *Crucifixion*. In front stands the tomb of Cardinal Fryderyk Jagiełło (d. 1503), the brother of King Zygmunt the Old. The Baroque stalls on both sides of the chancel were heavily restored at the beginning of the 20C. Notice also the Gothic vault bosses with figural ornamentation, and the Flemish tapestries.

Go back to the north-west corner of the church and begin the tour of the aisles and ambulatory. Of the 18 chapels in the Cathedral, almost all are often closed and you can only peep through the grills; a pity, as the chapels contain some of the finest works of art to be found in Wawel, or indeed Poland. If you visit in May or June, beware you may be swamped by hordes of noisy school children.

At the west end of the north aisle is the 15C Chapel of the Holy Trinity (5). The Gothic vaults were reconstructed in the early 20C and covered with murals. Below stands the tomb of Anna Wąsowicz. The way to the Royal Crypts, protruding into the aisle and partly concealing its vaults, leads through the **Czartoryski Chapel** (6). The chapel also contains a late Gothic triptych, with a central *Crucifixion* (c 1501), probably by Stanisław Stoss (son of Veit).

Descending the stairs, you enter the ***Crypt of St Leonard**, covered with low vaults supported on eight pillars, and ending in a round apse with three narrow windows that used to supply light, as the crypt was originally above ground.

> The Crypt of St Leonard is the most important remnant of the grand Romanesque Cathedral of St Wacław, begun in 1038 and completed over a hundred years later. The present, Gothic cathedral was begun by Bishop Nanker in 1320. While the west part of the old church was still being used, the Chapel of St Margaret (the present sacristy) and a new, square chancel appeared. In 1330–64, the new nave eventually swallowed up the rest of

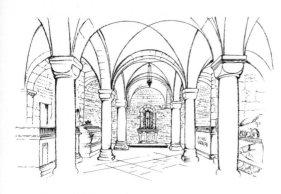

Crypt of St Leonard

the Romanesque church, incorporating its towers and the crypt of St Leonard. Chapels were added over the centuries, and the cathedral itself was repeatedly rebuilt and renovated; it has, however, been essentially preserved in the original Gothic form.

Today, the crypt of St Leonard contains an altar by Eugène Viollet-le-Duc (1873) and several sar-cophagi of Polish monarchs and national heroes. The oldest tomb is that of King Zygmunt the Old; the most ornate are the Vasa coffins, wrought by silversmiths from Gdańsk and Toruń; the most recent ones include the sarcophagi of Tadeusz Kościuszko, 1832, and Władysław Sikorski, 1981, (Poland's war-time general whose ashes were brought from England in 1994). Narrow passages take you to the other crypts which together hold the remains of most of Poland's royalty, with the Jagiellonian, Vasa and Saxon dynasties all represented. You leave the church through the south-west gate; walk back through the main entrance and continue the tour from the entrance to the crypt.

From the short transept you can enter the vestibule of the **Chapter Library** (7), with a Rococo flight of stairs (here also is the exit from the Zygmunt Tower—see below). The library has one of the most valuable Polish collections of codices, incunabula and prints. Adjacent to it and entered through an identical portal with an ornate gate, is the domed **Chapel of Bishop Maciejowski** (8). High up in its west wall is a columned tomb of the bishop, with his figure, carved in Mosca's (Padovano's) workshop. From the ambulatory you enter the under-ground **Crypt of the Bards** (9) containing the tombs of Adam Mickiewicz (1798–1855) and Juliusz Słowacki (1809–49), the greatest Polish poets of the Romantic period. The construction of the crypt was occasioned in 1890 by the return of Adam Mickiewicz's body to Poland from Paris, where he had lived in exile. By the entrance is the **Lipski Chapel** (10), with the tomb of Bishop Andrzej Lipski (d. 1631), by Sebastiano Sala, against the west wall. There are two more chapels before the sacristy: of the Skotnicki family (11), and of Bishop Zebrzydowski (d. 1620) (12). The latter is distinguished by the splendid tomb of the bishop, designed by Jan Michałowicz of Urzędów, who also considerably remodelled the chapel. The **sacristy** (13), originally a Gothic chapel from which the construction of the Cathedral began, was enlarged and acquired its present function in the 15C. The keystones of the vaults are decorated with Gothic reliefs, the oldest in Kraków.

Through the sacristy you can enter the 14C **Zygmunt Tower**, with one of the largest bells in Europe, the 'Zygmunt' (see above), and four smaller ones. From the top there is a good view over Kraków towards the Market Square: to the right

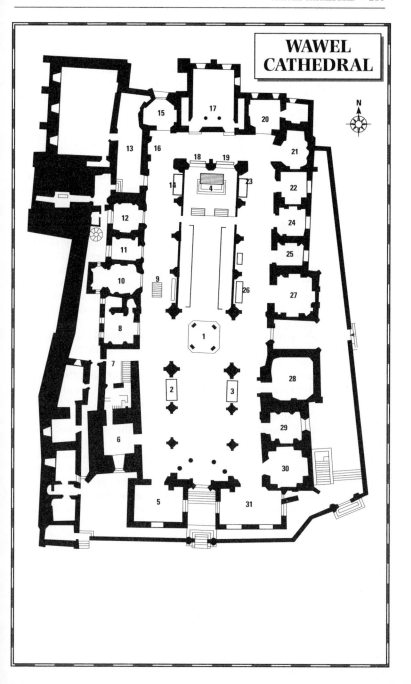

WAWEL CATHEDRAL

you see the twin towers of St Andrew's (see p. 210) and the huge dome of the SS Peter and Paul church; slightly further away is St Mary's.

You leave the tower via the library vestibule. Opposite the entrance to the sacristy stands the sandstone **tomb of Władysław the Short** (14) (d. 1333), the first Polish monarch to be laid to rest in the Cathedral. At the north-east end of the ambulatory, behind a Renaissance bronze grille, is the **Chapel of Bishop Gamrat** (15). Inside is the bishop's tomb (1545–47), designed by Giovanni Mosca (Padovano). By the chapel, on the north wall of the ambulatory, hangs the Gothic **Crucifix of St Jadwiga** (16)—a sheet of beaten silver silhouetting the soft outlines of the 'Beautiful Style' (*Weicher Stil*).

The easternmost end of the Cathedral is occupied by the **Chapel of Our Lady** (17), which Santi Gucci converted into the funerary chapel of King Stefan Bathory in 1594–95; the same artist designed Bathory's tomb. The chapel is covered with tripartite 'Piast' vaults and late 16C painting. In the window jambs are the remnants of even older, Gothic murals. Opposite, on the west wall of the ambulatory, are Francesco Placidi's two 18C black marble memorials to Michał Korybut Wiśniowiecki (18) and Jan Sobieski (19). In the latter, two Turks with hands bound in chains are a reference to the battle that saved Vienna from the Ottoman siege in 1683. At the southeast end of the ambulatory is the **Chapel of Bishop Tomicki** (20), a reduced version of the Zygmunt Chapel, designed by Bartolomeo Berrecci in 1530. The latter also carved the bishop's tomb, which stands by the north wall.

The south aisle begins with the **Chapel of Bishop Załuski** (21), remodelled in Rococo style by Placidi in 1758–66. A black niche in its south wall holds a white-marble figure of Bishop Grot, showing him as a rather corpulent man poised flamboyantly on his right foot. Next is the **Chapel of Jan Olbracht** (22) (d. 1501), with the king's tomb standing against the west wall. The marble relief representing the monarch's figure, probably made by Veit Stoss's son, Stanisław, is still Gothic. The arcaded sandstone niche, however, with decoration meticulously carved by Francesco Fiorentino in 1505, is the earliest Renaissance monument in Poland.

Opposite the Olbracht Chapel is the second oldest **royal tomb** in the Cathedral (23). It was commissioned in the 1370s by Louis of Hungary for his uncle, Kazimierz the Great. The king's figure, carved in Hungarian red marble, rests under a sandstone baldachin. Next is the 14C **Chapel of Bishop Zadzik** (24), converted into a funerary chapel in the 16C, probably by Sebastiano Sala, who also designed the bishop's tomb. The **Chapel of Bishop Jan Konarski** (25) contains a marble tomb of the bishop (d. 1525), which probably originated in Berrecci's workshop. Opposite the chapel is a glass case containing Queen Jadwiga's wooden sceptre and orb. Her sarcophagus (26), further west, with a white marble figure, was made in 1902. Opposite is the Cathedral's most famous chapel—the ****Zygmunt Chapel** (27).

Rightly known as the 'the pearl of the Renaissance north of the Alps', the Zygmunt Chapel has no equal outside Italy. Its pure Renaissance form is entirely the work of **Bartolomeo Berrecci**, whom Zygmunt the Old brought to Kraków in 1516 to work on the new royal castle (see p. 66). After the death of his first wife, Zygmunt decided to build a burial chapel for himself and his former spouse. Little did he know that it would become the mausoleum of the last Jagiellons.

Seen from the outside, the chapel immediately attracts attention with its **gilded dome**, cast in copper. The dome is surmounted with a tall lantern, topped by a spire with a gilded putto carrying a crown and cross. The **interior** is striking for the richness of its sculptural and stucco decoration. The architectonic composition of each wall is based on the form of a triumphal arch, popular during the Renaissance. Each of the deep, broad recesses is flanked by smaller niches containing sculptures of SS Peter, Paul, Wacław (Wenceslaus), Florian, John the Baptist and, the best of all, Zygmunt, the king's patron. The **marble effigy** of the king, Berrecci's true masterpiece, rests in the upper part of the west wall. The figure reclines in an uneasy pose, propped on its elbow, with a bent knee, as if about to wake up and rise.

The original *tumba* was replaced in 1574–75 with the present, smaller version, to make room for another monarch, Zygmunt August, whose similar figure rests in the lower part of the niche. It was sponsored by the king's sister, Anna the Jagiellon, and made by Santi Gucci, who simultaneously worked on his patron's tomb (c 1583), which was placed by the south wall a few years before her death. In the east niche is the altarpiece ordered by Zygmunt the Old in Nürnberg, and designed by Hans Dürer (Albrecht's brother). The six tondi in red marble with representations of the four evangelists, David and King Solomon, are the work of Berrecci. His too is the stucco decoration, no less remarkable than the sculptures, with miniature scenes among a profusion of floral arabesques. The chapel is closed off with an elaborate bronze grille (1530–32) from the renowned Vischer workshop.

The funerary **Chapel of the Vasas** (28) was completed in 1676 after the death of the last Vasa king, Jan Kazimierz. The splendid bronze door, cast in 1673 in Gdańsk, is so thickly ornamented that you cannot see through to the chapel. The Baroque interior, decked out in black marble, exudes a severe Counter-Reformation spirit, characteristic of the Vasas, whose memorial slabs are contained within. Seen from the outside, the chapel is a mirror-image of the Zygmunt Chapel, save for the golden dome of the latter: the Vasa Chapel is more modestly clad in copper.

Behind a Baroque portal by Placidi is the cross-vaulted **Szafraniec Chapel** (29), forming the ground floor of the Silver Bell Tower (one of the few remnants of the former Romanesque cathedral). Rebuilt several times, it has nevertheless retained its Gothic style.

The domed **Potocki Chapel** (30) was refashioned by Jan Michałowicz of Urzędów as a funerary chapel for Bishop Padniewski. His alabaster tomb bears an inscription by the poet Jan Kochanowski (see p. 81). The chapel became a mausoleum of the Potocki family in 1832–40, when it acquired its present Neoclassical form. Inside is a 19C statue of *Christ Giving a Blessing* by Berthel Thorvaldsen, and a 17C *Crucifixion* by the great Italian painter Giovanni Francesco Barbieri (Guercino).

At the west end of the south aisle is the **Chapel of the Holy Cross** (31), built in the 15C as a royal mausoleum. The founder, Kazimierz the Jagiellon, is buried in the Gothic tomb standing in the southwest corner, which Veit Stoss carved in spotted Salzburg marble in 1492. Stoss and Jorg Huber of Passau made the rich baldachin resting on columns with biblical scenes carved on the capitals. A larger tomb, standing by the west wall, was made by Piotr Aigner in 1789 to designs by Domenico Merlini. This Baroque classical composition is a reminder of the banishment of Bishop Kajetan Sołtyk for his defence of Poland against Russian interference: an eagle is struggling to get out of a coffin, which a malicious figure is trying to shut. The chapel also has stained glass by Józef Mehoffer and some rare 15C Byzantine-style murals executed by artists from Pskov. The bosses of the vault are decorated with the crests of Lithuania, Poland and Hungary.

Cathedral Museum

The Cathedral Treasury, whose beginnings reach back to the 11C, occupies a late Gothic building reached via the sacristy. The collection is not open to the public, although a few items are occasionally displayed in the Cathedral Museum (**open** 10.00–16.00, closed Mon). The highlight, though usually not displayed, is the spear of St Maurice, which Emperor Otto III presented to Bolesław the Brave in 1000 at the Congress of Gniezno.

The Castle

Leaving the museum, proceed to the **Renaissance castle** (**open** Tues–Sun 10.00–15.00). You will pass, on the right, the sloping expanse of the former Lower Castle, today a tidy, English-style lawn interspersed with the occasional flower bed and white stones marking the foundations of the medieval churches of St Michael and St George. Walk between the former Royal Kitchen building on the right (fronted by a display of cannons) and the Cathedral. **Tickets** to the royal chambers, treasury, armoury and oriental exhibition can be bought inside the long, vaulted passageway of the Renaissance gatehouse. You emerge onto the much-admired courtyard of the castle proper: an irregular pentagon, with three-tiered arcades all around, except for the west wing, most of which is taken up by the Royal Kitchen.

> The first castle on this part of Wawel hill was destroyed during a major fire in 1499. At the beginning of the 16C, King Zygmunt the Old commissioned the Italian, **Francesco Fiorentino**, to construct a new residence befitting the power and influence of the Jagiellon dynasty. After 1530, his work was continued by **Bartolomeo Berrecci**, another Florentine. In 1595, two towers were added—the Zygmunt in the north-east corner, and the Sobieski, adjacent to the Cathedral Treasury. **Tommaso Dolabella** worked on the interiors, decorating them in Baroque style. Swedish troops ravaged the castle twice, most destructively in 1702, when they began a fire that raged for a whole week. The castle suffered during the Partitions, notably at the hands of the Austrian army, who used it as a barracks. It was only after 1905 that serious restoration work began, lasting until the 1960s.

The **courtyard** is the best example of Italian Renaissance architecture in the castle. The arcades, directly borrowed from 15C Florentine architecture, are perfect semi-circles resting on slender columns, of equal length at the ground and first floor level, but twice as long at the upper level; they look so fragile, as if they were about to snap. The upper-storey columns are decorated with stone rings, which serve to visually shorten the shafts. Frescoed friezes depicting busts of Roman Emperors have been preserved just below the eaves in the south and east part of the arcades. The west wing has windows with intricate surrounds in pure Quattrocento style. Above the oriel are the crests of Poland, Lithuania and the Habsburg family. Cross the courtyard diagonally to enter the Royal Chambers. The main part of the exhibition normally open to tourists is on the second floor, the *piano nobile*.

Unless you get special permission from the museum administration to visit rooms that are usually closed to tourists, the Royal Chambers could be a disappointment, apart from the truly magnificent **tapestries**. The collection, one of the largest of its kind in the world, was bequeathed to the Polish nation by the last of the Jagiellons, Zygmunt August, who commissioned them for the interiors of his Wawel residence. The tapestries were painstakingly woven in the mid-16C by several outstanding masters from Brussels to the drawings and designs of Michiel van Coxcie of Mechelen (1499–92), nick-named the 'Flemish Raphael'. More than 350 pieces were made of which 136 have survived. It took a whole year for one craftsman to weave a single square metre of fabric.

The collection comprises three basic groups: figurative tapestries depicting Biblical scenes (Garden of Eden, Story of Noah, Tower of Babel); the so-called verdures—narrow and long, intended for the spaces between the windows, above the portals, and in the corners of the rooms, bearing images of plants, animals and usually hilly landscapes; and finally, the grotesque tapestries, smaller in size, with the cypher of Zygmunt August amid satyrs and other mythical creatures. The verdures abound in contrasts of light and shades of colour; a commonly-used device is the representation of either bright or dark leaves against a contrasting background, creating a strangely scintillating effect. The huge Biblical scenes are rather tawny and subdued, almost faded, but stop for a minute or two in front of, say, *Noah's Offering*, and the fabric reveals its hidden riches. Bizarre creatures suddenly begin to assert their presence, assuming an astonishing depth of perspective. In some miraculous way, the texture of the fabric is for a brief moment transformed into that of smooth human skin, the fur of a dog, the lustre of water, the bark of a tree, or the thick, sticky warmth of fresh blood.

After the Third Partition of Poland in 1795 the tapestries were removed to Russia, where they remained until after the October Revolution. The Treaty of Riga (1921), ending Poland's victorious war against the Bolsheviks, ensured the tapestries' return a few years later. When Hans Frank arrived at Wawel to set up his residence as the head of the *General Gouvernement*, he discovered that the tapestries had vanished. In 1940, the collection surfaced, intact, in Canada, and stayed there until 1961, when the Communist Polish government eventually managed to convince the Canadians of its credentials and reclaim the treasure.

Royal Chambers

You begin the tour of the Royal Chambers with the Servants' Quarters on the ground floor. The main items of interest here are the original Gothic and Renaissance stone portals and wooden beam ceilings. From a room with a Renaissance fireplace you ascend a flight of stairs, first to the mid-floor landing and then, via the monumental Envoys' Staircase, to the **first floor**. Here you can see a 17C Brussels tapestry depicting a battle scene, after Rubens's painting, *The Death of Decius Mus*. On the opposite wall hangs a large canvas showing a royal election.

Second floor

The state apartments in the north and east wings consist of spacious, sparsely furnished rooms hung with Zygmunt August's splendid tapestries and decorated with richly gilded coffered or painted ceilings. Some of the rooms get their names from the subject-matter of the broad friezes painted below the ceilings.

Thus you have the Tournament Hall, the Military Review Room, the Zodiac Room, or the Planets Room. Some rooms are closed to the public; the best accessible ones are the **Audience Hall** and the Senators' Hall. The former, where the monarch would receive foreign ambassadors and preside over Coronation Parliaments, has a coffered ceiling remarkably decorated with carved wooden heads (1531–35). Of the original 194 heads only 30 have survived, but even that is enough to demonstrate the artists' sweep of inventiveness and imagination. Some are solemn, lost in a quiet reverie, others seem bewildered, irritated, malicious or frightened. There is a philosopher, a warrior, a coquettish maid, a drunk, a lunatic. This panorama of human types is a fitting supplement to the frieze under the ceiling, painted in 1532 by Hans Dürer, and showing the cycle of human life from the cradle to the grave.

The **Senators' Hall**, the largest in the castle, originally hosted the Senate assemblies, lavish balls, theatrical performances, and other court festivities. It contains some of the largest tapestries from the royal collection.

Emerging on the second-floor landing of the Senators' Staircase, proceed to the exhibition of **oriental art** housed in the west wing, the oldest in the castle (1504–07). Some of the items on display were purchased, initially by Polish monarchs and eventually by museum curators, but most were taken as war booty, particularly by Jan Sobieski, the celebrated vanquisher of the Ottoman Turks at Vienna in 1683. The most captivating, and indeed most valuable, objects are the Turkish and Persian tents, which constitute one of the best collections of this kind in Europe. Of particular interest is a 16C Persian carpet depicting the Garden of Eden. It is known as the Paris-Kraków carpet, as only one half of it is displayed in Wawel, the other being found in the Musée des Arts Decoratifs.

Royal Treasury and Armoury

The Royal Treasury (mid-15C), housed on the ground floor of the Łokietek Tower, was where the crown jewels were once kept. In 1795, the Prussians plundered and melted down the most valuable items. Nowadays, four rooms in the Łokietek, Danish, Zygmunt Vasa towers, and the north wing of the castle mainly contain items recovered from the Soviet Union after the Second World War. The highlights are the 13C coronation sword 'Szczerbiec', insignia bestowed on Sobieski by the Pope and Louis XIV, and an 11C golden chalice discovered in an abbot's tomb in Tyniec (see p. 239). The Armoury has unique 17C–18C Polish Hussar armour, 15C Nürnberg tournament armour and Italian Renaissance parade shields.

'Lost Wawel'

Leave the Renaissance castle and return to the sloping yard of the Lower Castle. The cellars of the former Royal Kitchen contain an archaeological exhibition—*Lost Wawel*. There, right under your feet, protected by shatter-proof glass, you can see the only remaining vestiges of the earliest stone church in Kraków, the pre-Romanesque **Rotunda of St Mary**, which predates even the establishment of the bishopric. St Mary's was fairly typical of the many round stone temples (10C) built by Slav tribes in Central Europe. It had a sparsely-lit round body surrounded by four semi-circular apses, one of which housed the altar. Gutted by fire in 12C, the rotunda was merged with the castle later built by Kazimierz the Great. Further north there is an open grave with bones, and fragments of medieval fortifications. The second part of the exhibition (west) has glass cases containing various objects found in the former royal coach house and kitchens. The first exhibit on the left is a small stone sculpture of an animal that may well be a 10C pagan relic, related to similar sculptures found on Ślęża hill in Silesia (see p. 447). In the rooms on the ground floor you can see tiles from various stoves in the royal apartments and a lapidary with a fine selection of stonework chiselled by Bartolomeo Berrecci and other Italian masters.

You may leave Wawel by a different route: walk down the sloping grounds of the Lower Castle, passing the Thief's Tower. Behind it, to the right, is the entrance to *Smocza Jama*, or **Dragon's Cave**, which according to legend was once inhabited by a ferocious maiden-eating dragon. Today, the dragon has been replaced with a copper effigy that occasionally breathes fire. If you decide to go down the cave, turn left when you exit, and walk back around the hill.

Walking down the cobbled road skirting the hill on its south side you pass, on your left, the former hospital building and the Sandomierz and Senators' Towers, relics of the medieval fortifications; to the right are the rooftops of ul. Bernardyńska, just a few metres away. Eventually you will reach the intersection of ul. Grodzka (leading back to the Market Square), ul. Stradom (going south towards the Jewish district of Kazimierz) and ul. Podzamcze, which skirts the hill and continues towards the river. There is a good view from this side onto the Austrian brick fortifications, with a round bastion, and the castle towers, including a peculiar-looking one known as the 14C **Hen's Foot** (you can see why).

Across the river, visible from the castle, is the new building of the **Manggha Centre of Japanese Art and Technology** (ul. Konopnickiej 26), which houses a unique collection of Japanese art (**open** Tues–Sun 10.00–18.00 ☎ 267–2703). Concerts and other cultural events are often held in the spacious rooms. The building was designed by the outstanding Japanese architect Arata Isozaki.

Walk Four ~ The University Quarter

The historic university area is centred on three streets—Św. Anny, Jagiellońska and Gołębia—reached from the south-west corner of the Main Market Square.

Collegium Maius

A short way up ul. Św. Anny (entrance facing ul. Jagiellońska) is one of Kraków's most renowned and architecturally complex buildings: ****Collegium Maius**, the earliest extant college of the Jagiellonian University.

As early as 1364, Kazimierz the Great founded the Kraków Academy, an educational institution pre-dated in Central Europe only by the Charles University in Prague. Progress was temporarily halted by the death of Kazimierz in 1370, but a revival soon followed, thanks largely to Queen Jadwiga, who endowed the Academy with most of her considerable fortune. In 1400, Jadwiga's husband, Władysław Jagiełło, purchased a house at the corner of ul. Św. Anny and ul. Jagiellońska. A few months later the theological faculty set up its headquarters in the house, which took the name of Collegium Maius. During the 15C the Kraków Academy flourished, with enrolment rising to a peak of 500 students, of whom nearly half were foreigners. In time, teaching came to focus on the sciences, particularly astrology and astronomy. The Academy's most famous student, **Nicolaus Copernicus**, studied and resided at Collegium Maius in 1491–95.

Though considerable damage was caused to the building through fires in 1462 and 1492, the latter in fact proved to be a blessing in disguise: during reconstruction carried out by the king's brother, Cardinal Fryderyk, the original corner house was integrated with buildings further down the street. This unified architectural whole was given a magnificent inner courtyard encircled by a late Gothic cloister, rather like the loggias of Italian universities. The 16C saw the construction of a new library wing (1518–40), as well as many other colleges around the University quarter. Collegium Maius remained the University's chief building until the 19C. Under Austrian rule, it fell into decline. Much of the original late Gothic architecture and detailing was lost during restoration work carried out in 1840–60, after which the building housed the Jagiellonian library (until 1939). Fortunately, many of the Neo-Gothic accretions were removed when the building once again underwent major restoration after the Second World War. Today's Collegium Maius is thus a mixture of authentic and 'new' Gothic elements, and its appearance is far removed from the original.

Viewed from ul. Jagiellońska, the **façade** presents an unornamented mass of brick and stone, with three panelled gables topped by pinnacles and a delightful bay window at first floor level. The fragment of stone wall at the corner marks the extent of the original house from which Collegium Maius evolved.

Enter through the late Gothic portal. Beyond the vaulted vestibule you emerge onto the cool and peaceful courtyard. Around the rectangular space run pointed arcades, supported on round stone columns, with simple diamond vaults made up of faceted cells between the rib-lines. Above is a stone balustrade, which used to carry long wooden posts supporting the great projecting eaves of the roof. Walking around the gallery, notice the fine bas-relief of the *Adoration of the Magi*.

The rooms off the courtyard accommodate the **Jagiellonian University Museum** (open Mon–Fri 11.00–14.30, Sat 11.00–13.30; guided tour in English), entered through the late Gothic *Porta Aurea*, or Golden Door. The largely ceremonial rooms on the first floor begin with the star-vaulted *Libraria*, the former library, currently used as an assembly hall by the University Senate. There are copies of astronomical instruments used by Copernicus here. Next is the Gothic *Stuba Communis*, or common room, which also served as a refectory. Standing by the bay window is a 14C statuette of Kazimierz the Great. An ornately carved wooden staircase leads up to the living quarters on the second floor. Notice also the wooden beamed ceiling, original pewter plates, and the 17C tiled stove bearing heraldic motifs.

The tiny **University Treasury** is housed in the two small rooms further on. Inside are various items of memorabilia, sceptres endowed by Queen Jadwiga (c 1400), Cardinal Oleśnicki (1454) and Cardinal Fryderyk (1495)—still wielded by the University Rector during official ceremonies—as well as the famous Jagiellonian Globe (1510), the first one to show America (though Australia is still missing), with a built-in calendar and clock. Next are the theology faculty's reading rooms, with Empire style and Biedermeier furnishings. The small **Copernicus Room** has a register of 1491 (copy) where the young Nicolaus is entered as a student having paid his college fees. There is also a later edition of his greatest work *De revolutionibus* (the first edition is in the college library). The oddest exhibit, perhaps, is a photograph of the moon with the inscription 'To the Copernicus Museum in Kraków on the 500th birthday of a Giant', signed 'Neil Armstrong, Apollo II'.

The last and largest room, facing ul. Św. Anny, is the 15C **Auditorium**, formerly the University's main assembly hall. Below the Renaissance coffered ceiling (16C) are professors' stalls, a rector's throne, and a richly carved wooden doorway of 1593 in a stone frame. In keeping with ancient tradition, at the beginning of each academic year a procession of gowned professors begins at the auditorium and proceeds to Collegium Novum (see below). The ground floor *lektoria* (usually closed to tourists) contain a unique display of scientific instruments donated to the Academy by the astronomer Marcin Bylica in 1492. The highlight is an 11C Arabian astrolabe. Copernicus attended lectures in the *Galen Lektorium* and, according to legend, Faust and Twardowski studied black magic in the Alchemist's Chamber. The museum collections also contain many paintings and medieval sculpture.

Leave Collegium Maius and continue south to the first intersection—UL. GOŁĘBIA. Turn right (west) towards the main University complex, which borders the *Planty*. The group of buildings here is dominated by **Collegium Novum**, an imposing Neo-Gothic structure designed in 1883–87. On the façade are the crests of the University and its greatest benefactors. The building houses the Rectorate and main administrative offices and lecture rooms. Ascend the great staircase to the diamond vaulted auditorium, where there are portraits of Jadwiga and Jagiełło, famous University Rectors, and best of all, Matejko's *Portrait of Copernicus*. Classical concerts are occasionally held in the tomato-coloured auditorium. By the entrance to the hall is a plaque commemorating the 184 professors who were deported to Sachsenhausen in 1939.

Return north along the *Planty* to ul. Św. Anny, passing, on your right, a statue of Copernicus (1900) brought here from the courtyard of Collegium Maius in 1953. Soon the ****Collegiate Church of St Anne** will come into view.

The history of St Anne's is closely tied to the University. Władysław Jagiełło funded the construction of a Gothic church here in 1407, which a decade later came under the patronage of the Kraków Academy. In 1689, the professors commissioned **Tylman van Gameren**, an architect widely admired for his work in Warsaw, to construct a new church modelled on San Andrea della Valle in Rome. Gameren continued work until 1703, producing perhaps the greatest example of Polish classicised Baroque, an achievement all the more remarkable in the light of Poland's political and economic decline. As the façade had to be set perpendicular to the street, and could only be viewed from the side, Gameren profiled it in depth, with projecting columns, niches and recesses emphasised by an interplay of light and shade; his clever use of perspective and proportion, moreover, had the visual effect of shortening the nave and enlarging the dome. Gameren's achievement was further enhanced by **Baldassare Fontana**, who did the figural and ornamental sculpture, stuccoes, and main portal.

The **interior** of St Anne's (visiting times 09.00–12.00 and 16.00–19.00) was designed on the plan of a Latin cross, with three pairs of chapels along the broad nave and a dome above the transepts. The impression of space and light is enhanced by the pastel-coloured illusionist frescoes. Fontana's stuccowork immediately stands out for its intricacy and richness, particularly the medallion and fruit stuccoes on the nave piers, and his dynamic sculptures of saints and angels, recalling Bernini, around the altar. His best effort, however, is the **mausoleum** of the church's patron, St John of Cantinus, a 15C theologian and cult figure, which stands at the end of the south transept. The sarcophagus is supported by figures representing the four faculties of the University: Theology, Law, Medicine and Philosophy. On top of the tall spiral columns surrounding the tomb are four of the Saint's namesakes: John the Baptist, John of Damascus, John the Apostle and John Chrysostom. In the north transept, opposite, there is another fine altar by Fontana with a Pietà in stucco relief. Next to it is a Neo-classical monument to Copernicus (1822).

Facing St Anne's No. 12 is the **Nowodworski Collegium**, formerly housing a mint, and later one of Poland's oldest secondary schools (opened 1558). Beyond the portal is a much altered courtyard of 1640 with Baroque arcades. The young Jan Sobieski, then a student, attended the inaugural opening of the Nowodworski Collegium in 1643, and later, as king, became one of its most generous benefactors.

Walking east along ul. Św. Anny will bring you back to the Main Market Square. Alternatively, a short walk from Collegium Novum down ul. Piłsudskiego brings you to a huge park known as the **Błonia** (48ha). From the 15C it served as the city common, and even today, farmers from the outlying villages retain the ancient right to graze their cattle here (and sometimes do). Due to its sheer size, the Błonia is often a venue for large-scale ceremonies: in 1979 a staggering two million turned out to see John Paul II on his first visit to Poland.

At the edge of the park, by the busy thoroughfare (al. Mickiewicza) is the new building of the **National Museum** (open Tues, Thur–Sun 10.00–15.00, Wed 10.00–18.00). The display concentrates on painting and sculpture from the Young Poland period, with a particularly rich collection of works by Wyspiański, followed by 20C art and sculpture, including some fine abstract pieces, and finally post-war Polish art. The building itself is part of the new university district, constructed in the 1930s when functionalism was the prevailing architectural style. Further north along ul. Mickiewicza are two more examples from this period: the **Jagiellonian Library** and the **Academy of Mining and Metallurgy**, the latter with two large statues of 'heroic' workers flanking the entrance.

Walk Five ~ Around the Planty Park

Begin at PL. SZCZEPAŃSKI, west of the Main Market Square. The buildings you see are largely Secessionist, though the square itself dates from 1801. Most impressive is the **Building of the Fine Arts Society** (1901) bordering the *Planty* (west). On the façade are niches containing busts of famous artists, notably Jan Matejko (pl. Szczepański side) and Stanisław Wyspiański (*Planty* side). Running round the building, below the mansard roof, is a decorative frieze by another turn-of-the-century artist, Jacek Malczewski. Exhibitions of graphic art, sculpture and painting—often the best in Kraków—are held inside (**open** Tues–Sun

11.00–18.00). The neighbouring **Arts Pavilion** (BWA) at pl. Szczepański 3, facing the *Planty*, is where the International Graphic Art Triennale is held in September. At other times, the pavilion hosts exhibitions of modern art.

Dominating the south side of the square at No. 1 is the **Old Theatre** (Teatr Stary), the oldest in Poland and still operational. Converted in 1798 from former stables, it received its fine Art Nouveau façade, with a broad stuccoed frieze under the eaves, in the following century. The designers—Tadeusz Stryjeński and Franciszek Mączyński—also remodelled the interiors in the same style. In the basement (entrance from ul. Jagiellońska 1) is the up-market *Maska* café, and upstairs, a small **Theatre Museum** (open Tue–Sat 11.00–13.00, and an hour before performances).

At the end of the 19C the Szołayski family donated their house at No. 9 (east) to a branch of the *National Museum (open Tues 10.00–18.00, Wed–Sun 10.00–16.00). The display, with French and Polish labels, consists of a broad and impressive selection of Polish sculpture and painting, with particular emphasis on medieval art from the Małopolska region. The mainly 15C first floor exhibits include the exquisite *Madonna of Krużlowa* (c 1400), an almost life-size sculpture of *Jesus Riding a Donkey* (c 1470) from the church in Szydłowiec, two reclining figures of knights (c 1480), attributed to Veit Stoss, as well as some fine epitaphs, notably of the *Wierzbięta of Branice* (c 1425). Upstairs the story is taken up to the 18C, with Hans Dürer's miniature *St Hieronymous* (c 1526), Sarmatian portraits, votive paintings, and, the highlight, a huge polyptych—*St John the Almsgiver* (c 1504)—from the Augustinian monastery. As you leave the museum, don't miss, in the vestibule, Stoss's *Christ in the Garden of Olives*, a sculpted group brought here from St Mary's church.

Walk along UL. REFORMACKA from the north-west corner of pl. Szczepański. On the left you will pass the 17C **Reformed Franciscans' Church and Monastery**. The buildings themselves are of little interest, but you might take a look at the crypts below the monastery, where there are over 1000 tombs dating from 1667 onwards. Due to the special atmospheric conditions, the mummified corpses are almost perfectly preserved. The monks will gladly show you round, though visits are deliberately short to protect the relics from further decomposition.

Turn right along ŚW. MARKA, where there is a 13C **church** of the same name (junction with ul. Sławkowska). Originally a Gothic aisled hall, the interior of St Mark's was completely rebuilt in 1624–47 with the addition of the nave arcades and early Baroque decoration. Adjoining the chancel—the oldest part of the church—is a square bell tower set askew to the street. Inside, notice the Mannerist **high altar** (c 1618), built at roughly the same time as the monastery. Facing ul. Sławkowska, between the chancel buttresses, is a Gothic sculpture of Jesus flanked by the Virgin and St John the Evangelist (c 1500).

The bustling UL. SŁAWKOWSKA was once part of the ancient trade route to Silesia. No. 17, opposite St Mark's, is the Neo-Renaissance **Academy of Sciences** (1857–64), accommodating an extensive library and a small book-shop selling academic texts.

Continue east along ul. Św. Marka. At the next junction (right) is the **Palace of the Cistercian Abbots of Jędrzejów** (ul. Św. Jana 20), an amalgamation (1735–44) of three Gothic burghers' houses, which accounts for its sizeable proportions. Francesco Placidi added the Rococo façade. The stone portal, with caryatids supporting the moulding, is also Rococo (c 1744). In the basement is a gallery (**open** Mon–Fri 11.00–18.00 Sat 11.00–14.00) run by the well-known Cracovian sculptor, Dominik Rostworowski.

Lovers of satirical humour may enjoy the gallery (**open** Mon–Fri 10.00–17.00 Sat 11.00–15.00) of the Cracovian cartoonist Andrzej Mleczko, situated further down the street at **No. 14**.

Looking left, you will see the picturesque outline of the Piarist church, which closes the north end of UL. ŚW. JANA. Walk towards it passing, at No. 15 (right), the 17C **Lubomirski Palace**, named after its 19C owner, who remodelled the façade in an eclectic spirit. Preserved are an 18C portal and 17C stuccoes inside the vaulted vestibule. The building across the street (No. 30) is known as the **Peacock House** after the 17C bas-relief on the façade. The corner house next door is occupied by the French Hotel, predictably noted for its excellent cuisine.

The Piarists settled in Kraków in 1654, organising theological schools and teaching. Their Baroque **Church of the Transfiguration** (ul. Pijarska 2–4), with adjoining monastery (1714–27), was designed by Kacper Bażanka. The tall white façade (1761) was completed by **Francesco Placidi**, the last and best Baroque architect in Kraków (active 1742–82), who based it on the Gesù in Rome. Below the front stairs an entrance leads down to the church crypts, where exhibitions of religious sculpture are occasionally held. Above, on the stone balustrade, stands a marble bust of the Piarist monk, Stanisław Konarski, school-reformer and co-author of the 3 May Constitution (1791), whose heart is embedded in the south aisle wall (1882). Inside the church, notice the illusionist vault frescoes executed by the Moravian, Franciszek Eckstein, in 1759, which recall the decoration of the church of St Ignatius in Rome.

The Czartoryski Museum

The former monastery, to the east of the church, is linked to the Czartoryski Palace via a delightful covered passageway across ul. Pijarska. Together, these buildings constitute the *Czartoryski Museum** (ul. Św. Jana 19).

> The Czartoryski Museum, the oldest in Poland, began as the private initiative of Princess Izabela Czartoryska (1746–1835), who amassed at her home in Puławy (see p. 289) a large collection of Polish art and memorabilia. Fearing reprisals after the failed November Uprising in 1831, Czartoryska managed to smuggle the collection to Paris, where it remained at the family's residence—the Hôtel Lambert on the Ile-Saint-Louis—for the next half century. Thanks to the efforts of her grandson, Władysław Czartoryski, the collection was enriched with the addition of ancient, medieval and early Renaissance art, Italian majolica, Meissen porcelain, and other works. In 1876 Władysław moved the collection to Kraków. He purchased the Piarists' monastery, the City Arsenal, and three other buildings on ul. Pijarska, which the French architect, Maurice Ouradou, converted into a unified museum complex (1879–84). During the Second World War, the Nazis looted the most valuable items. The greatest loss was Raphael's *Portrait of a Young Man*, which was never recovered.

Today, the Czartoryski Collection is a branch of the National Museum (**open** Wed–Thur, Sat–Sun 10.00–15.30, Fri 10.00–18.00). It occupies three buildings—the Palace, Arsenal, and Small Monastery (Klasztorek)—and exudes the atmosphere of a 19C museum, which has preserved even the original French-Polish labels and oak showcases. The permanent display is accommodated on the upper floors of the palace.

First floor

This floor is devoted to the history of Poland from the 14C–18C. Here you will find memorabilia of the Polish Jagiellons and Vasas, portraits, including a group of ten miniatures of Zygmunt the Old's family from the workshop of Lucas Cranach the Younger, Persian and Turkish art, such as an Ottoman tent captured at Vienna in 1683, Polish scale armour, or *Karacena*, sabres belonging to Kościuszko, ceremonial shields, including Sobieski's, horse trappings and coffin portraits (c 1700). In addition there is a display of European decorative art—medieval French enamels, ivory, silverware, pottery, porcelain, a 16C Persian carpet, and an early 16C Brussels tapestry, *The Shower of Gold.*

Second floor

This floor accommodates a gallery of European sculpture and painting (13C–19C). Pride of place goes to **Leonardo da Vinci**'s *Lady with an Ermine* (c 1485), painted shortly after he had arrived at the court of Lodovico Moro. Other highlights include Rembrandt's *Landscape with the Good Samaritan* (1638), Alessandro Magnasco's *Temptation of Monks* and *Washerwomen*, and Vincenzo Catena's sculpture, *Madonna and Child with Saints* (1508).

Continue east along ul. Pijarska, skirting the medieval town walls and St Florian Gate (see p. 203). You will emerge onto a broad square—PL. ŚW. DUCHA—dominated by the eclectic **Słowacki Theatre**. Named after the great Romantic poet, Juliusz Słowacki, the theatre was built in 1891–93. The architect in charge, Jan Zawieyski, modelled it on the Paris Opéra, introducing a few local motifs like the parapet around the dome, whose grotesque masks echo the Cloth Hall. Impressive, if overdone, is the rich west façade decorated with groups of allegorical figures: on the right, Music, Opera and Operetta; on the left, Poetry, Drama and Comedy. At the very top stand the figures of Tadeusz and Zosia, the main protagonists of Adam Mickiewicz's epic poem, *Pan Tadeusz* (see p. 82). The highlight of the interior is the exquisite **stage curtain** painted by Henryk Siemiradzki and adorned with allegorical figures representing the arts. Before the First World War, the Słowacki rose to prominence as the leading Polish theatre, staging uncensored plays and developing a national repertoire. In front of the building is a monument to the grandfather of Polish comedy, Aleksander Fredro (see p. 84).

On the east side of pl. Św. Ducha stands the irregular brick shape of the Gothic **Holy Cross Church**, its west tower and steep pointed roof forming a charming silhouette. Most impressive is the late Gothic palm vault, whose sixteen ribs spread out from a single central pillar. Notice also the 15C–16C murals and paintings, restored and complemented by Stanisław Wyspiański in the early 20C. The furniture is all Mannerist and Baroque except for a Gothic bronze font of 1420.

You can return to Main Market Square along ul. Szpitalna (Hospital Street), which runs south off pl. Św. Ducha. You will pass, at the corner of ul. Św. Marka, the 15C **House under the Cross** (No. 21)—the only surviving building of a former medieval hospital—which later acquired its mansard roof. Inside is a small **Museum** (**open** Wed 11.00–17.00, Thur–Sun 09.00–15.00) devoted to the history of theatre in Kraków.

Walk 6 ~ The Synagogues and Churches of Kazimierz

Walking due south from the foot of Wawel Castle towards the Piłsudski bridge you enter the former Jewish town (now district) of Kazimierz. Even after its formal incorporation into the city in 1791, Kazimierz retained its distinctive character. It was separated from Kraków by an arm of the Vistula, its culture providing a sharp contrast to the splendour and pageantry of its royal neighbour. The war years changed Kazimierz beyond recognition—its Jewish population was entirely wiped out—and today, the district is a shadow of its former self. When the ambitious renovation programme properly gets under way, Kazimierz may yet rival the Market Square as the city's main tourist attraction. Signs of new cultural vitality are already in evidence. In June, for example, Kazimierz plays host to an International Festival of Jewish Culture. Concerts of Jewish music are organised in the Old Synagogue, and a new Jewish Cultural Centre has been opened on ul. Meiselsa.

Established in 1335, the town of Kazimierz was named after its founder, King Kazimierz the Great (1310–70). A spacious market square (now pl. Wolnica), almost as large as Kraków's, was laid out at the centre. The square was bisected by the main thoroughfare—ul. Krakowska—and in its northeast corner the parish church of Corpus Christi was built, followed in the 15C by a town hall. Encircling the town were huge stone walls—2850m long, 1.8m thick and 4m–5m tall—interspersed with four gates and two defensive towers. A separate wall later divided Kazimierz into its Christian and Jewish parts. The town remained an island until 1878–80, when the arm of the Vistula separating it from Kraków was drained to form today's ul. Dietla. An old viaduct can still be seen at the east end of the street.

The history of Jewish Kazimierz begins in the late 15C. Following a ruling by the royal court, Kraków's Jewish population was resettled in the east part of the new town, around ul. Szeroka and pl. Nowy. Synagogues, publishing houses and a cemetery appeared. The Jewish community, headed by the Kahal, or council of elders, rapidly came to be associated with scholarship and academic excellence. It established first-rate centres of learning, notably a Talmudic school of European repute. For centuries Kazimierz retained its position as the most important cultural centre of the largest Jewish community in Poland. In 1939 there were over 45,000 people in the district who spoke Hebrew or Yiddish as their native language.

Originally a muddy path leading across marshland to the Old Vistula bridge, ul. Stradom benefited from its location on the main trade route to the south of Poland, gradually acquiring inns, bath-houses, a stagecoach house and a customs house. The street is now the main thoroughfare linking the city centre with Kazimierz and can boast two buildings of major historical interest.

Nestling at the junction with UL. BERNARDYŃSKA, below the imposing Wawel Castle, is the **Bernardine Church and Monastery** (pl. Bernardyński 2).

KRAKÓW
KAZIMIERZ & PODGÓRZE

1 High Synagogue
2 Old Synagogue (Museum)
3 Popper Synagogue
4 Remuh Synagogue
5 Progressive (Reformed) Synagogue
6 Ajzyk (Isaac) Synagogue

The once-wooden Bernardine church was rebuilt in stone in 1455. Five years earlier royal emissaries had brought from the Silesian town of Wrocław the renowned Italian preacher, John Capistrano. A hundred or so of Capistrano's devotees established in 1453 the Order of the Observers of the Rule of St Francis, popularly known as the Bernardines. Their church was destroyed during the Swedish siege of Wawel in 1655 and later rebuilt in Baroque style (1670–80).

The ivy-clad façade, with its two modest octagonal towers and niches filled with saints, bears a clear resemblance to the SS Peter and Paul church on ul. Grodzka (see p. 209). The interior, furnished in stages during the 17C–18C, includes a sculpture of the *Virgin and Child with St Anne*, ascribed to Veit Stoss (1447–1533), and a 17C painting of the *Dance of Death*, in which representatives of all four estates (clergy, nobility, bourgeoisie, peasantry) take part. Both are found in the Chapel of St Anne at the east end of the north aisle. In the sacristy is the reliquary of the Blessed Szymon of Lipnica, whose marble tomb sporting a reclining figure stands in a south aisle chapel parallel to the chancel. The aisles contain huge Passion paintings by the Bernardine monk Franciszek Lekszycki (d. 1668), based on sketches of works by Rubens and Van Dyck. The church dome was set below the roof, apparently to widen the firing range from the battlements of Wawel.

Further down ul. Stradom, walking away from the castle, you will come to the Church of the *Missionary Fathers* (No. 4), considered to be one of the finest examples of late Baroque architecture in the city. Brought to Poland in 1651, the Missionary Fathers found their way to Kraków a year later. A small monastery soon appeared, bordered by a beautiful formal garden, which has survived to the present day (often inaccessible). The church, completed in 1719–32, was designed by **Kacper Bażanka**, whose Roman education no doubt inspired him to base the façade (unfinished) on Bernini's Sant' Andrea al Quirinale. Above the entrance is a protruding semi-circular portico resting on columns, itself encased in a monumental aedicule composed of colossal order pilasters and crowned by a triangular pediment. The interior is modelled on the Chapel of the Magi in Borromini's Collegio di Propaganda Fide in Rome. Tadeusz Konicz, who, like Bażanka, drew his inspiration from Roman art, executed the painting at the high altar, as well as others around the church.

Crossing ul. Dietla you will come on to **UL. KRAKOWSKA**, which splits Kazimierz into its distinct Christian and Jewish halves. The street ends at the Piłsudski bridge, beyond which you will notice the distant outline of the Kraków TV tower. About half way down on the left is pl. Wolnica, dominated by the 16C Renaissance **Town Hall**, with an octagonal tower and crenellated attic. The building was extensively altered in the 19C and turned into a Jewish school. Since 1947 it has housed the **Ethnographical Museum** (open Mon 10.00–18.00, Wed–Fri 10.00–15.00, Sat–Sun 10.00–14.00) containing a rich collection of folk art, particularly from the south of Poland. The museum has an **exhibition centre** further down ul. Krakowska at No. 46 (same opening hours).

The last building of note on ul. Krakowska, further down on the left (No. 48), is the Church of the **Holy Trinity**. Constructed in 1752–58, this is Francesco Placidi's Cracovian showpiece, surpassing even his Piarist church on ul. Św. Jana. Most impressive is the façade, replete with recesses and projections, echoing Borromini's tower on the convent of the Filippini in Rome. The modest interior has a fine vault mural (c 1750) depicting the ransoming of prisoners captured by the Turks.

Return to PL. WOLNICA. Beyond the north-east corner of the square rises the imposing *Corpus Christi Church, set amongst greenery behind a high stone wall. It was the first church in Kraków to achieve truly late Gothic proportions, with the nave more than twice as high as it is broad, and external buttresses of the long aisleless chancel and apse further emphasising the height. The oldest parts visible today are the late Gothic nave vault and pretty pinnacled west gable (c 1500). The northeast tower, dating from 1566–82, is topped with a Baroque crowning. Skirting the wall anti-clockwise you will pass under a huge arcade on which rests a covered passageway linking the church with the adjoining monastery. Further on, near the main entrance, is the only remnant of the former graveyard—the Chapel of Gethsemane, enclosed by an iron grating, containing a number of late Gothic and Renaissance wooden sculptures.

The magnificently gilded **interior** of the church juxtaposes severe Gothic architecture with exceptionally rich wood carving. Of particular interest are the lavishly decorated stalls of 1624–32 and the **pulpit** shaped in the form of a boat with a mast and oars, supported by two mermaids. The huge high altar, completed in 1634, contains two paintings—*Nativity* and *Descent from the Cross*—attributed to Tommaso Dolabella. Of the many paintings, mainly 17C, in the chancel and aisles, those near the Renaissance memorial slab of Bartolomeo Berrecci (c 1480–1537) in the Chapel of St Anne, deserve particular attention. To the right is the Mannerist tomb of the Blessed Stanisław Kazimierczyk (c 1632), a famed miracle-worker.

Continuing east along ul. Św. Wawrzyńca you enter the more run-down, Jewish part of Kazimierz. On the left, as you walk up ul. Wąska is a school (**No. 5–7**), formerly the headquarters of the Gestapo in Kraków, which bears a plaque to the scores of victims who were tortured here during the war. The street ends at the dilapidated 16C **High Synagogue** (ul. Józefa 38), disused since 1939. To the right, an alleyway, actually an extension of ul. Józefa, leads through to most famous street of Jewish Kazimierz—UL. SZEROKA. The well-preserved *Old Synagogue** at the south end (No. 24) houses a **museum** (open Wed–Thur, Sat–Sun 09.00–15.00, Fri 11.00–18.00) devoted to the history and culture of Kraków's Jews. Matteo Gucci thoroughly redesigned the building in Renaissance style in c 1557–70. The almost empty Hall of Prayer has rib vaults arising from two pillars, in clear imitation of the Staronová Synagogue in Prague. In the middle stands a small podium encircled by an exquisite *bema*, or wrought-iron grating in the shape of a cage. On the east wall, facing Jerusalem, is a 17C Ark of the Covenant bearing the scrolls of the Torah. The two remaining rooms on the ground floor are devoted to an exhibition of Jewish decorative arts. On the upper floor numerous photographs, posters and documents offer a grim reminder of the extermination of Polish Jews during the Nazi occupation, when the building was desecrated and many of its works of art looted. The original chandeliers, for example, were used to decorate the wartime residence of Hans Frank.

At ul. Szeroka 16, concealed behind trees and an iron gate, stands the early 17C **Popper Synagogue**, today housing an art studio and gallery. Two nearby café-cum-restaurants—both, confusingly, called *Ariel*—offer Jewish cuisine in pleasant surroundings and put on evenings of Jewish, Gypsy and Ukrainian music. The larger and better establishment (No. 17; left) has a few guest rooms here and at ul. Szeroka 6 (☎ 421-3870).

Of more interest than the Popper is the small *Remuh Synagogue** on the opposite side of Szeroka (No. 40), which continues to perform a religious function (services on Friday afternoon and Saturday morning). The curator is usually willing to show visitors around and will provide skullcaps for men wishing to enter the synagogue or adjoining cemetery. Constructed in 1553 when Israel Isserles, a trusted banker to King Zygmunt August, converted one of his properties into a house of prayer, the Remuh nevertheless came to be associated with his son, the famous scholar and philosopher Rabbi Moses Isserles (1525–72), who is buried here. The inscription on the rabbi's tomb reads 'From Moses [the prophet] to Moses [Isserles], there was no greater Moses.' Strangely enough it was the only tomb to survive the Holocaust—the remaining 47 were destroyed. After the war the shattered gravestones were cobbled together to form a Wailing Wall. In the 1950s conservationists unearthed another 700 that had apparently been concealed from the Swedish army during the invasion of Poland in the 17C.

Ul. Szeroka ends at the **Jordan House** (No. 2), built in the 16C, but probably a remnant of Kazimierz the Great's efforts to set up a university in the district. There is a small Jewish bookshop and café inside. Leaving ul. Szeroka you may want to take a small detour to a more recent but no less fascinating **Jewish Cemetery**, actually outside Kazimierz proper. Go right along ul. Miodowa, across ul. Starowiślna and walk under the rail bridge. This peaceful and secluded spot with its beautiful gravestones and tree-lined alleys makes for a delightful afternoon walk. If the gates are locked, enter the building at No. 55: the back entrance leads conveniently onto the cemetery. Returning along ul. Miodowa you will come to the **Progressive (Reformed) Synagogue** (No. 24), so-called because services were given here in Polish and German as well as in Hebrew. Built in 1862, it is the venue of organ concerts and religious ceremonies attended by Jews from all over the world.

In the maze of streets directly south are two more synagogues. Turn left into ul. Estery and left again at the first junction (ul. Warszauera). The derelict **Kupa Synagogue** of 1590 (No. 8) is so named because it was financed with Kahal funds (*kupa*—purse). Here too is a stretch of medieval town wall (another fragment runs along ul. Paulińska). Straight down ul. Kupa, at the intersection with ul. Izaaka, is the **Ajzyk (Isaac) Synagogue** (No. 16), an early Baroque building of 1640. Thanks largely to the efforts of its curator, Dominik Dybek, the synagogue has been thoroughly renovated, including Giovanni Battista Falconi's original stucco decoration. The former gallery for women, located on the first floor, is separated from the main room by an ornamental wooden wall with five arcades. Most interesting is the continuous film show, based on German archive footage, which traces the life of Kraków's Jews before the Second World War.

Ul. Izaaka opens out onto pl. Nowy, a square devoid of historic buildings but at weekends occupied by a fruit and vegetable market around the circular abattoir in the middle. Ul. Meiselsa leads off the square to the newly-built **Jewish Cultural Centre** (No. 17), housing a gallery, cinema and café.

Across ul. Krakowska begins the Christian half of Kazimierz. The area enclosed by ul. Paulińska, ul. Augustiańska and ul. Skałeczna, in many ways one of the most attractive parts of the city, is home to the lush, but inaccessible gardens of the Augustinian monastery, bordered by a high limestone wall. The ***Church of St Catherine** (ul. Augustiańska 9) is the purest example of Cracovian Gothic. It was a gift from Kazimierz the Great to the Augustinian Order, brought from Prague in 1343. First to go up was the chancel, completed in 1378, followed by the main body (1426). The oldest extant vaults, designed by Master Hanusz (1503–05), are in the chancel. Outside, its buttresses are topped with intricate stone pinnacles. Close by stands a rustic belfry with a wooden roof (15C). The towerless west façade faces the monastery gardens, so you enter the church from the north aisle or through the cross-vaulted cloisters.

The plan of the tall and empty **interior** is very similar to that of the Corpus Christi church (see p. 230). The rectangular chapel in the south-west corner, its magnificent vault resting on a single pillar, is known as the Hungarian Chapel after its founder, the Palatine Ścibor, a condottiere in the Hungarian army. Built in 1402–14, it is still used by the Augustinian nuns and is connected to their convent by an arch which crosses ul. Skałeczna. Especially fine is the church's south porch, with its rich portal, pinnacles, and sumptuous stone detailing (1430). Notice also the large Mannerist high altar of 1636 with a painting of the mystical wedding of St Catherine (1674). In the south aisle stands the fine tomb of the magnate Spytek Jordan (1600), crowded with figures.

The adjoining monastery (south) has beautiful cloisters (1378) with elaborate piers and medieval frescoes. At their east end is the Gothic Chapel of St Thomas, currently the sacristy. The vault, again resting on a single pillar, has the name of Kazymirus (Kazimierz the Great) emblazoned on the bosses. Here, too, you will find the impressive Chapel of St Dorothy (the former chapter house), its vault carried on two slender pillars.

Ul. Skałeczna terminates at an elaborate wrought-iron gate. Walking down, parallel to the garden wall, you will notice in the distance the silhouette of the Church of St Michael the Archangel and St Stanisław, commonly known as the 'Skałka' Church after the hillock of Jurrassic limestone (skałka) on which it rests.

'Skałka' Church

The original Romanesque rotunda was replaced with a twin-towered Gothic church in the 13C. Some 500 years later, the Pauline monks, influenced by the cult of St Stanisław (see below), built an adjoining monastery and in 1733 commissioned Georg Müntzer to redesign the *church in Baroque style. The final version was completed by Antoni Solari in 1740–42.

Enter the church via a sumptuous stone staircase (1749). The **interior** has some fine 18C stucco decoration and sculpture. To the right of the nave is a bust of Pope John Paul II, commemorating the Holy Father's audience here in 1979. Situated below the entrance stairs is the **Crypt of Honour**, a national pantheon built in 1880 to commemorate the 400th anniversary of the death of Jan Długosz (1415–80), whose ashes were the first to be moved to the crypt. Other famous names at rest here include the painter and playwright Stanisław Wyspiański, the novelist Józef Ignacy Kraszewski, the composer Karol Szymanowski, and the painters Henryk Siemiradzki and Jacek Malczewski.

> The history of the church is interwoven with the legendary struggle between secular and ecclesiastical power, represented respectively by King Bolesław the Bold (c 1040–81) and the cult figure of Stanisław Szczepanowski, Bishop of Kraków (c 1030–79). In 1079 the bishop was accused of treason and executed—according to legend, in the 'Skałca' church, later to become the centre of his cult. He was recognised as a saint and canonised by Pope Innocent IV at Assisi in 1253 and his remains are now kept in Wawel Cathedral. Each year on 8 May, a reliquary containing the bishop's remains is ceremoniously brought from the cathedral to the 'Skałca' church. The bishop's decapitated corpse is said to have been cast into a pool outside. A more recent pool was constructed in 1688–1731, and is known as the Stoup of Poland. A statue of St Stanisław stands on a plinth in the middle surrounded by water. Silver eagles on obelisks—guardians of the bishop's remains—adorn the four corners.

You can leave the site via a passageway on the north side of the monastery, which brings you onto the banks of the Vistula. Crossing over the Grunwaldzki bridge, you may want to get a bird's eye view of the area. For this purpose **Hotel Forum**, a monstrous vestige of 1960s planning, is excellently suited; the appropriately named *Panorama* café at the top offers a splendid view over Wawel Castle, Kazimierz and its environs.

Walk Seven ~ Podgórze

Facing Kazimierz on the south bank of the Vistula is the district of **Podgórze**. It lies at the foot of a wooded hill known as Krzemionki, occupied in its north part by the Kraków TV station and surrounding park, and in its south part, beyond al. Powstańców Śląskich, by a large cemetery, allotments, and the mysterious

Krakus Mound (16m). The origins of the mound have been traced to the 8C and it is said to contain the grave of Krak, the legendary founder of the city that bears his name. During the 19C Podgórze developed as an Austrian town (Josephstadt), primarily noted for its industry, but always in the shadow of its richer neighbour, Kraków, to which it was joined in 1915. This partly explains the absence of historic buildings, though the Austrians did leave a number of 19C houses on ul. Limanowskiego and the large Neo-Gothic **Church of St Joseph** (1909) on the main square—RYNEK PODGÓRSKI. By far the most interesting aspect of Podgórze, however, is its association with the tragic fate of Kraków's Jews during the Second World War. Their story is told in Thomas Keneally's novel *Schindler's Ark*, filmed by Steven Spielberg in the original Kraków setting. Some of the city tourist agencies still run a 'Schindler's List' tour, which takes you round some of the original sites, as well as those recreated for the purposes of the film. Schindler's factory was located on ul. Lipowa near Kraków Zabłocie station.

> The war years were a catastrophic turning point in the history of Kraków's Jews. In 1941, the Nazis set up a new 'Jewish District' in Podgórze, into which Jews from Kazimierz and other areas of Kraków were moved. The ghetto was delineated by today's Rynek Podgórski, pl. Bohaterów Getta, and the intersection of ul. Limanowskiego and ul. Wielicka. Enclosed by a ring of walls and barbed wire, nearly 17,000 were crammed into the ramshackle buildings. In 1942, the Jews were systematically moved out to a new concentration camp erected in nearby Płaszów, after which the ghetto was destroyed (13 March 1943). Between 1942 and liberation in 1945, Płaszów housed approximately 150,000 inmates; most perished. The Camp Kommandant, Amon Leopold Göth, was found guilty of crimes against humanity and executed in Kraków in 1946.

Today, there are few visible remnants of Jewish Podgórze. During the war, pl. Zgody (pl. Bohaterów Getta) was the most gruesome and feared area of the ghetto. It was here that Jews were selected for execution or transportation to the concentration camps. Today, the square is dominated by the ugly mass of tinted glass that is the BPH Bank building. The house at **No. 6**, now a mini-market, bears a plaque commemorating the Jewish Resistance Organisation, which had its headquarters here in 1942–43. **No. 18** was formerly a pharmacy, whose Polish owner, Tadeusz Pankiewicz, received permission from the Nazi authorities to do business here. It was chiefly through Pankiewicz and his staff that food, medicine, false documents, and other kinds of aid were brought in from the outside. In 1983 the house was converted into a museum (**open** Mon–Fri 10.00–16.00, Sat 10.00–14.00, Sun closed) documenting life in the ghetto.

Walk Eight ~ The Solidarity stronghold of Nowa Huta

A few kilometres east of the city centre lies **Nowa Huta**, the largest district in Kraków, with a population of 220,000. The main attraction is the massive Sendzimir (formerly Lenin) Steelworks, a fully-preserved Stalinist monolith of the type that is thankfully fast disappearing in Eastern Europe. Of interest, too, is the urban layout of the district, formerly a town in its own right (until 1951) and the first to be built in post-war Poland. Unless you only want to visit some of the sites, Nowa Huta is best visited by car. The main square—pl. Centralny—can be reached by tram nos 4, 15, 22 or 44, or by express bus 'B' from the city centre.

The post-war Communist elite saw in Kraków a hotbed of bourgeois values and reaction. Consequently, it was felt that the ancient royal capital had to be symbolically punished. To this end, in 1949, the authorities decided to build a huge iron and steel works, serviced by a model 'workers' town', on the periphery of the city. The construction of the Lenin Steelworks began in 1951. At its completion four years later it was the largest steelworks in Poland. By 1976, its 37,000 staff were producing on average 6.5 million tons of iron and steel per year. Yet the Communists' plans for bourgeois Kraków backfired somewhat when, in the 1980s, Nowa Huta became a stronghold of the Solidarity movement.

The 'model' housing estates—grey, uniform, run down—still carry names redolent of the past, in some cases sounding almost as if they were borrowed from Orwell's *1984*: the Estate of Youth, the Estate of Peace, the Estate of Enlightenment. Pollution is a major problem. The black smoke billowing from the chimneys of the steelworks has for decades done untold damage to Kraków's architectural heritage; more importantly, the incidence of pollution-related diseases has soared. Some of the tourist agencies in Kraków even run an 'ecological disaster tour' to the site. Yet there exists no more poignant reminder of the scale of the problem than the steelworkers' cemetery in the shadow of the rolling mill: looking at the dates on the graves one sees that very few of the workers buried there made it to old age. The environmental situation has improved slightly in recent years with the most polluting sections of Nowa Huta being closed down, but this, in turn, has caused new social problems in the form of poverty and unemployment. Frustrated also by the lack of civic amenities, many young people have turned to violence and petty crime. Unless you know your way around, Nowa Huta is not the place to be after dark.

Begin at PL. CENTRALNY, from which the main thoroughfares of the district fan out in all directions.

Going north along al. Róż you pass the spot where until 1990 there stood a giant statue of Lenin. Many demonstrations against the Communist regime took place here. In the late 1970s, a small explosive charge ripped off Lenin's heel. The statue was speedily repaired, which gave rise to the joke: 'Lenin tried to take a Great Leap Forward, but they welded him back into place.'

Turning left off al. Róż into ul. Żeromskiego you will come to the **People's Theatre** (Os. Teatralne 34). The first play performed here in 1955 was Wojciech Bogusławski's *Cracovians and Highlanders*, set in the nearby village (now suburb) of Mogiła. Under its recently appointed director, Jacek Fedorowicz, the theatre has put on a series of highly acclaimed performances involving a local neighbourhood cast.

The construction of new churches in Nowa Huta was forbidden for many years as the Communist authorities sought to prove that the proletariat had no need for religion. Needless to say, the ban led to numerous riots and demonstrations, with especially fierce street battles taking place in November 1982. In the spate of building that followed the lifting of the ban, the **Our Lady Queen of Poland Church**, further north along ul. Obrońców Krzyża in the district of BIEŃCZYCE, stands out for its interesting design. The exterior is peculiarly shaped like an ark and encrusted with thousands of pebbles. The interior, set on several levels, looks more like an arts centre than a place of worship. The highlight is a grand modern sculpture of *Christ Crucified*, his limbs spread out like the wings of an eagle.

The long avenue (al. Solidarności) leading northeast from pl. Centralny, formerly Lenin Avenue, takes you right up to the gates of the **Sendzimir (formerly Lenin) Steelworks**. The vast complex is truly astonishing, its seemingly endless rows of antiquated furnaces and ovens resembling a Dickensian film set. Visits can be made by special arrangement (PTTK, Os. Stalowe 16/2 ☎ 643–7905). Right next to the mill (near the junction of ul. Ujastek and al. Jana Pawła II), amid tramlines and shrubbery, is a more ancient site—the **Wanda Mound**, one of four in the city, whose origins are enshrined in popular myth.

The Myth of Wanda

Following the death of her father, Krakus (the legendary founder of Kraków), Princess Wanda was subjected to incessant courtship by the German Prince Rytygier (Rytogar). Repelled by this Teutonic upstart but fearful of forfeiting her lands (Rytygier threatened to invade if she did not marry), Wanda threw herself into the Vistula to avoid an even more terrible fate. She was buried close to the spot where she drowned. Local people covered her tomb with a mound of earth, known till this day as the Wanda Mound. In deference to tradition, each year on the Feast of Wanda young Cracovian males are entitled to hurl into the Vistula all unsuspecting women so-named.

On top of the mound (14m), until 1970 enclosed by Austrian fortifications, is a small marble monument, designed by Jan Matejko (1890). The emblem of Princess Wanda is inscribed on the marble block in bas-relief.

Returning back along al. Jana Pawła II, turn left into ul. Klasztorna. The **Cistercian Abbey** at Mogiła will come into view on the left.

Bishop Iwo Odrowąż founded the abbey in 1225 for the Cistercians, who settled in the village of Mogiła. Their church of St Wenceslaus, an early Gothic basilica on a Latin cross plan, went up in c 1266, remaining largely unchanged until the late 18C, when it was rebuilt in Baroque style and received a new façade. A 13C miniature arcaded frieze and three pointed arch windows have been preserved at the east end (visible from the garden).

The Baroque west front of the church masks some fine 13C stone detailing within, notably sculpted early Gothic bosses in the aisle vaults. The chancel, unusually flanked on one side by a pair of chapels, features a late Gothic polyptych of 1514 serving as the high altar. The highlight are the Renaissance frescoes in the transept and chancel, executed in the early 16C by Stanisław Samostrzelnik, a monk at the abbey and also a talented artist, who did a number of Royal prayer books and miniatures. A 13C portal (often closed) in the south aisle leads through to the cross-vaulted 14C cloisters, where Gothic and Renaissance monks' tombstones are embedded into the walls. Here, as in the library (c 1533), are more frescoes by Samostrzelnik, notably his monumental *Crucifixion* of 1538, now looking very time-worn. The library itself (ask the porter for permission to enter) contains over 15,000 documents amassed by the Cistercians over the centuries. In the oldest, east wing there is an early Gothic chapter house (late 13C). From the cloisters you may enter the pleasant monastery garden.

Opposite the abbey, hidden among trees, is the small Parish **Church of St Bartholomew** (1347), an early example of Polish wooden architecture, rebuilt many times. Of note inside is a Gothic portal, carved in wood and dated 1466, as well as Rococo murals. Above the entrance gate rises a domed belfry of 1752.

Walk Nine ~ Salwator and the Kościuszko Mound

Salwator, in the west part of Kraków, can be conveniently reached by tram (nos 1, 2, 6) from pl. Wszystkich Świętych in the city centre. You should get off at the terminus. To the left, in a picturesque setting at the fork of the Vistula and Rudawa rivers, stands the Premonstratensian Convent (ul. Kościuszki 88), one of the oldest in Kraków, founded in 1162. From here, the ancient district of ZWIERZYNIEC stretches northwest along ul. Królowej Jadwigi and west up towards the Kościuszko Mound. The area was owned by the convent as early as the 12C, the surrounding woodlands later being used as royal hunting grounds. Today, Salwator rivals Wola Justowska as Kraków's richest and most exclusive suburb: quiet, leafy, yet only ten minutes' ride from the city centre. Walk up the hill or east along the river, passing some fine Secessionist villas. On Easter Monday the popular Emaus fair takes place near the convent, and in June the Lajkonik procession begins here (see p. 194).

The **Church of St Augustine**, adjoining the convent, dates from the first half of the 13C. Thorough rebuilding carried out in 1596–1626 preserved only a late Romanesque portal (north entrance) and a section of wall from the former church. The interior of the chancel was redone in Baroque classical style in 1777. The fortress-like convent has spacious grounds enclosed by a late Renaissance decorative parapet wall with towers and loopholes.

Walk up the hill along ul. Bł. Bronisławy, a beautiful cobbled avenue lined with trees and villas. On the left you will pass the deserted wooden **Chapel of St Margaret**, a small domed octagon of 1690 associated with pagan worship, which stands in an overgrown garden.

Further up on the right is the **Church of Our Saviour**, set in its own grounds behind a wall. According to legend it was consecrated in the 9C by St Adalbert before his last mission to convert the heathen Prussians to Christianity. Inside are a *Crucifixion* (1605), which shows Christ giving his golden shoe to a minstrel, and two Renaissance pulpits, the one by the entrance in the shape of a chalice. Of greater interest is the underground archaeological site, open to the public, where excavations were carried out in 1962. Amongst the finds were a stone mensa and fragments of early Gothic murals.

Ul. Bł. Bronisławy eventually merges with al. Waszyngtona, a long avenue leading up Bł. Bronisława Hill (333m) to the **Kościuszko Mound** (34m). Raised in 1820–23, the mound contains earth from many of the battle sites where Kościuszko fought (see p. 51), some as far afield as America. In 1856 the Austrians encircled the mound with brick fortifications, which in 1977 were converted into a hotel and restaurant. Close by is the Neo-Gothic **Chapel of the Blessed Bronisława** (1861), housing a small display of Kościuszko memorabilia. Wind your way up to the top of the mound where there is an open vista of Kraków, its Old Town sadly dwarfed by chimneys of the huge Łęg powerplant and Sendzimir steelworks in the distance, closed in on all sides by grey housing estates. The inscription on the granite boulder reads: 'To Kościuszko'.

Day trips from Kraków

❖ The Wolski Forest, Monasteries of Bielany and Tyniec, Auschwitz and Wieliczka

In the west of Kraków lies the **Wolski Forest** (412ha), an area of hilly wood-land and nature reserves. If you are not travelling by car, take bus no. 134 from the Cracovia Hotel and get off at the Zoo (last stop). The various sites within the forest are linked by a web of well-marked trails and are all within easy walking distance.

The Camaldolite Monastery ~ Bielany

The suburb of Bielany is situated in the south-west part of the forest. Here, on a verdant hillside overlooking the Vistula, is the *Camaldolite Monastery*, its twin towers visible on the horizon as one approaches Kraków from the west. Bielany derives its name from the white habits worn by the Camaldolite monks ('*biel*' means the colour white).

> The austere Camaldolite Order was brought to Bielany from Italy in 1603 by the Grand Marshal of the Crown, Mikołaj Wolski. A suitably beautiful site was chosen for the church—a remote wooded hill, later known as 'Silver Mountain' after an exquisite set of silver cutlery which Wolski presented to the former owner of the land. Wolski himself supplied the Roman designs for the church. First to be constructed, though, were the monks' dwellings (1605–09) in a large rectangular garden divided into plots. The nave, chancel and twin-tower stone façade followed in 1609–30.

Due to the strict monastic rule, the church is only open to tourists on Sunday mornings and women are forbidden to enter the monastery (except during Easter and on a few other days of the year). You approach the site along a narrow path flanked by walls, with the church's broad monumental façade of white stone and black marble coming into full view beyond the gatehouse. The grounds are designed according to an early Baroque axial scheme: monastic buildings symmetrically flanking the inner yard and rows of monks' dwellings at the back.

The church is one of the finest examples of early Baroque in Poland, its interior bearing striking similarities to Italian architecture of the period. The plain, tunnel vaulted nave is flanked by richly decorated chapels, with rich stuccowork (1622–42) and paintings by Tommaso Dolabella. Mummified corpses of monks are preserved in the church crypts. Wolski is buried in a tomb by the main entrance; his portrait, showing him dressed in foreign clothing, hangs in the monastery.

The green and affluent suburb of **Wola Justowska** borders the Wolski Forest to the north-east. It is named after Justus Decius (1485–1545), the Royal secre-tary to King Zygmunt the Old, who in the 1530s commissioned Bartolomeo Berrecci to build the **Decius Villa** (Willa Decjusza), which stands in the park just off ul. Królowej Jadwigi. The present appearance of the building is the result of remodelling carried out in the 17C and 19C. Especially fine are the three tiers of arcaded galleries on the east façade. The recently renovated interior now houses conference rooms and the exclusive *Villa Decius* restaurant. Close by (ul.

Panieńskich Skał, left off ul. Kasztanowa) is a small **skansen** consisting of a reconstructed 17C wooden church, a wooden inn with arcades, currently the priest's house, and a wooden granary of 1764 with characteristically large eaves, all brought here from villages in the Małopolska region. From the skansen a path leads up Sowiniec Hill (358m) to a mound raised in honour of Józef Piłsudski (1934–37). Also in the vicinity is a limestone ravine—Panieńskie Skały—with a nature reserve.

A small **castle**, built during the inter-war period, overlooks the Vistula from a hill in the suburb of **Przegorzały** (southeast). The adjoining two-storey building was erected by the Nazis in 1941, who used stone from the destroyed Carmelite church in Nowy Wiśnicz. The complex has been recently converted into a luxury hostel for foreign students. From the *U Ziyada* restaurant balcony there is an excellent view over the river and the monasteries at Bielany and Tyniec.

The Benedictine Abbey ~ Tyniec

The *****abbey** is scenically perched on a limestone rock—the southernmost elevation of the Jura uplands—on the south bank of the Vistula river. To get there you have to return to the city centre and cross the river by the Dębnicki Bridge. Then proceed along ul. Tyniecka, or better still, take the boat from the riverside near Wawel Castle. The round trip (May–September only) takes four hours with a 30 minute stop in Tyniec to see the abbey. Unfortunately, there are plans to close the service, so it is best to check at one of the tourist agencies before you depart.

> Recent archaeological discoveries suggest that the first church, a Romanesque stone basilica, was built as early as c 1060–70. It is likely that the abbey, which dates from the same period, initially served a defensive purpose. In the 15C, a new, towerless Gothic church was constructed. A few fragments from it have survived—foundations, buttresses, two windows in the chancel, stairs and a founding tablet—but what you see today is largely Baroque (1618–22). The abbey was later surrounded with fortifications, but this offered little protection against the heavy attacks launched by the Confederates of Bar in 1772–73. It suffered even greater damage during a fire in 1831, after which only the church was rebuilt. The Benedictines returned to Poland during the inter-war period to begin reconstructing their abbey. Work is still in progress.

The abbey is reached along a winding road punctuated by two medieval gates. In the middle of the courtyard stands a well covered with a rustic timber cone (1620). The church, a modest, twin-towered structure, which lost its most valuable furnishings

Benedictine Abbey, Tyniec

MAŁOPOLSKA

0   50 miles

0   80 kms

in the 19C, adjoins the partly ruined monastic buildings. Of note are the black marble high altar, designed by Francesco Placidi in the mid-18C, and the original Rococo pulpit in the shape of a boat. In the abbey buildings you might want to take a look at the medieval chapter house and cloisters, where there are fragments of Gothic murals. On the south side of the hill, behind a stone wall with two towers, stretches the 18C abbey garden.

Auschwitz

Regular train and bus services connect Kraków with the industrial town of Oświęcim (population 43,400), 50km to the west. It was here in 1940 that the Nazis built their largest and most notorious extermination camp— **Auschwitz-Birkenau**—where an estimated four million people perished during the Second World War. In 1947 the grounds of the former camp, the largest cemetery in the history of mankind, were declared a memorial to the martyrdom of nations. The Polish Government turned the site into a museum, meticulously reconstructing all the evidence the Nazis had tried to destroy.

The first camp was erected in June 1940 as an internment centre for 10,000 Polish political prisoners, chiefly members of the intelligentsia and the resistance movement. The local population was removed to make way for a 'death zone' around the camp, whose purpose was to maintain the camp's secrecy and render escape impossible. In March 1941 Auschwitz was extended to accommodate 30,000 inmates. Once inside, each prisoner was assigned a tattooed number, a striped uniform, and a wooden bunk. No one was expected to live longer than three months. In October 1941, further extensions were made to accommodate prisoners from other countries subjugated by the Reich. Soon, the camp became an enormous death factory consisting of three parts: Auschwitz I (the original camp), Auschwitz II—Birkenau (constructed in 1941 in the nearby village of Brzezinka), and Auschwitz III—Monowitz (set up in 1942 near a factory in Dwory). Birkenau, the largest camp, had a capacity of 100,000 inmates. A special railway was built, with the tracks extending right up to the crematoria. Prisoners would be loaded off the cattle wagons onto a long concrete platform where the 'selection procedure' would take place. Those fit to work would be marched off to the barracks; the old, infirm, the young, and mothers with children would be stripped and led directly to the gas chambers, their corpses then burnt in open pits or incinerated in the crematoria. The gas chambers consumed their first victims on 4 May 1942 and it was then that the mass extermination of Jews began. At its peak, the Nazi war machine was able to slaughter 60,000 people during a single night, with a train arriving approximately every hour. Those who avoided the gas chambers were condemned to slave labour for the Reich. Life in the camp was almost unimaginable: daily beatings, torture, executions, disease, mass starvation, cannibalism. Inmates were subjected to sterilisation and medical 'experiments'. When the Soviet Army liberated the camp on 27 January 1945, they discovered 7500 living people, including 90 pairs of identical twins whom the Nazis had used in the name of 'scientific research'.

The **Museum** (open 08.00–15.00, and sometimes later depending on the time of year) takes a 'no holds barred' approach and the experience can be distressing. Every gruesome detail of life in the camp is documented. You enter through the original iron gateway with its slogan 'Arbeit Macht Frei' (work makes you free). The prisoners barracks contain exhibitions devoted to daily life in the camp, living and sanitary conditions, as well as the fate of various nation-

The concentration camp, Auschwitz

alities. Blocks 4 and 5 present the story and evidence of mass extermination: a room of women's hair, piles of broken toys, collections of gold teeth, suitcases and artificial limbs, all revealing the insane bureaucracy of murder. Executions were carried out in the Block of Death. The bunkers underground, where prisoners were starved and tortured during interrogation, contain the notorious 'standing cells'. Beside the Block of Death is the Wall of Death, where the condemned were shot. Two of the grimmest places are the Crematorium I, and Assembly Square with its mass gallows. The cinema shows a film of the Soviet army liberating the camp in 1945.

A special bus service is provided for those wishing to visit the camp at **Birkenau** (3km). Here one gets an idea of the sheer scale of the Nazis' plans. The camp was actually subdivided into smaller sections housing men, women, Jews, Gypsies, etc. More than 300 prisoners' barracks were erected on the vast site, of which only 67 have survived intact. The rest were demolished or burnt by the fleeing Nazis, though the chimneys and the outlines of the foundations are still visible. The railway enters through the main gate, flanked by watchtowers, and proceeds towards the ruins of gas chambers and crematoria at the far end of the camp. About halfway along is the unloading ramp where the 'selection procedure' would take place. A Monument to the Victims of Fascism

(1967) stands at the end of the track. Further to the right are two more cremato-ria, pits and pyres where corpses would be burned, and a pond into which the ashes would be dumped.

The Salt Mine at Wieliczka

Wieliczka (population 18,500), 12km to the southwest of Kraków, is best reached by bus or minibus from Kraków's main station. The town is a major tourist destination on account of its ancient Salt Mine. Opened as a museum in 1950, the mine predates the Polish state itself. Approximately 200km of tunnels and corridors stretch out in a vast web underneath the town. Such was the level of exploitation, that in the 19C cave-ins and flooding were common. A massive recent flood (1992) endangered the very existence of the historic site, and it was only thanks to special EU funds (Wieliczka was placed on the UNESCO World Heritage List in 1978) that enough water was pumped out in time to prevent total collapse.

> The huge salt deposits were formed 18–20 million years ago during the Miocene era, and were already being mined long before Wieliczka received its town charter in 1290. As early as the 11C the settlement here was known as *Magnum Sal*, or Great Salt. Kazimierz the Great encircled the town with walls, eleven towers and two gates. In this way he hoped to protect the precious deposits, which provided a staggering one-third of the revenue flowing into the royal coffers. It would be no exaggeration to say that the Wieliczka mine financed most of the architectural construction in Kraków and southern Poland during the Middle Ages. In 1826, a spa was set up in the town when it was discovered that the salt waters had rich medicinal qualities. More recently, a small spa hospital treating asthma and other respiratory diseases was opened in the mine, at a depth of 211m.

The length of the tours varies, but a standard one covers only 3.5km of tunnels, and takes up to two or three hours. You are advised to bring suitable clothing, as the temperature below ground is around 14°C. The exhibition area (**open** 08.00–18.00) is contained on levels I, II and III (64m–135m), reached by a long staircase. The remaining four levels, descending to a depth of 300m are closed to the public. The highlights, as you wander the long galleries, are the chambers containing underground chapels. Everything is sculpted in salt—the altars, candlesticks, columns and pulpits, even the figures of saints. The best chapels are St Anthony's, sculpted by the miner Antoni Kuczkiewicz, and the Holy Cross, both 17C. Truly breathtaking is the 19C Chapel of the Blessed Kinga. There is also a display of old mining equipment and ancient excavation techniques. The largest chamber has excellent acoustics and is occasionally the venue for opera and concerts. A genuine mine lift takes you back up the main Danilewicz shaft, sunk in 1638.

South of Kraków ~ Zakopane

Zakopane (population 28,500), Poland's best known resort, lying at the foot of the **Tatra mountains**, is a popular destination for day-trippers escaping the noise and fumes of Kraków (108km), but it really merits more time, particularly if you enjoy hiking in the mountains. There are good tourist facilities, though in the winter and summer accommodation may be scarce, so it is best to book in advance. The fastest road from Kraków is the 7 to Nowy Targ (a dual-carriageway up to Myślenice), followed by road 95 heading south. The train is exasperatingly slow, and it takes longer to get from Kraków to Zakopane than to Warsaw.

Zakopane occupies a unique place in Polish culture. Beginning in the mid-19C, its reputation as a fashionable retreat grew rapidly. City dwellers would come to enjoy the fresh mountain air, live in a *pension* run by a highlander family, or perhaps take an afternoon stroll along UL. KRUPÓWKI, the town's main street. Kraków's and Warsaw's *bohème* paid frequent visits, some even settling permanently, and the town's popularity, or, some would say, snob appeal, continues to this day. The **folklore** of the Tatras, and Zakopane itself, became inextricably woven in the fabric of Polish culture; it found its way into, or at least influenced the works of composers Mieczysław Karłowicz (who died here in an avalanche), Karol Szymanowski, Wojciech Kilar, Henryk Górecki and artists Leon Wyczółkowski, and Władysław Skoczylas. Cultural influence has worked in both directions: Stanisław Witkiewicz (father of Stanisław Ignacy, see p. 86), using elements of the native highlander style, created a unique, highly artistic and successful '**Zakopane style**' in architecture, which to this day gives the place its special flavour. The best examples are the **Pod Jedlami house** (ul. Na Antałówkę), which Witkiewicz designed in 1895–6, and a **chapel** in Jaszczurówka. The mountain people speak a distinct dialect, dress in an easily recognisable way, and set themselves apart from the rest of the country, taking special pride in their independence and in their familiarity with the mountains, which inspire such awe among the *cepry* ('lowland folk', in highlanders' disparaging dialect). Usually in the last week of August, Zakopane plays host to the International Festival of Mountain Folklore, which features dance, music and exhibitions.

Pod Jedlami house

■ Practical information

Accommodation can be arranged through TPT 'Tatry' (corner of al. 3 Maja and ul. Kościuszki, ☎ 201 4000). There are scores of good, reasonably priced pensions, as well as rooms in private houses (look for the signs '*noclegi*' or '*pokoje*' meaning rooms and accommodation). The more adventurous could try one of the several mountain shelters, such as *Murowaniec* in Hala Gąsienicowa (☎ 126-33), or the shelter in Morskie Oko (☎ 776-09), but during high season you are likely to be offered floor space only.

Hotels
★★★★

Orbis-Kasprowy. Polana Szymoszkowa, ☎ 201-4011. The best hotel in Zakopane, situated on the slope of Gubałówka hill. Car park, swimming pool, fitness centre, wheelchair access, tennis court, private garden, business services. 286 rooms, some with spectacular views over the Tatra mountains.
★★★

Orbis-Giewont. Ul. Kościuszki 1, ☎ 201-2011. Located in the town centre. Car park. 43 rooms.

Gazda. Ul. Zaruskiego 2, ☎ 201-5011. Central location. Car park, swimming pool, tennis court. 55 rooms.

Biały Potok. Ul. Droga do Białego 7, ☎ 201-4380/201-4903. Car park, tennis court, swimming pool. 32 rooms.

Tourist information. Ul. Kościuszki 7 (PAPT), ☎ 201-2211, or ul. Krupówki 12 (PTTK), ☎ 201-5848.

ORBIS. Ul. Krupówki 22, ☎ 201-2238/201-5051.

Main post office. Corner of ul. Krupówki and ul. Zaruskiego.

Telephone code: (0–18).

History
Until the second half of the 19C, Zakopane was an impoverished, remote village at the foot of the inaccessible Tatras. However, by the mid-19C, visitors had begun to arrive from Kraków, Warsaw and other Polish cities, lured by the magic of the mountains, their natural beauty, and the exotic folk culture of the *górale* (highlanders). In the 1870s, Tytus Chałubiński, a Warsaw physician, mounted a vigorous campaign to bolster its popularity further. Some years later, Count Władysław Zamoyski, owner of Kórnik Castle near Poznań (see p. 515), purchased large tracts of land in the vicinity of Zakopane (such as the area around the lake of Morskie Oko), and later bequeathed the land—as well as his entire fortune—to the Polish nation, thus laying the foundations for the **Tatra National Park**. In 1929 and 1939, Zakopane hosted the World Skiing Championships; the cable car to the summit of Kasprowy Wierch became operational in 1936. In little over a century, the resort has been visited by practically all the luminaries of Polish art, science, religion and politics, from Maria Curie-Skłodowska, Henryk Sienkiewicz, and Pope John Paul II (once an ardent skier and mountaineer), to ex-President Lech Wałęsa.

The Town and the Mountains

Life in Zakopane centres around UL. KRUPÓWKI. The funicular at its north end will take you to the summit of Gubałówka in 5 minutes (1 hour 30 minutes walking distance, blue trail), where you can enjoy an excellent panorama of the Tatras. Also close to the north end of ul. Krupówki, across a creek, is the **Tatra Mountain Museum** (open Wed–Sun 09.00–16.00), which occupies an early 20C house designed by Stanisław Witkiewicz in the 'Zakopane style'. Close by, on UL. KASPRUSIE, stands the *Villa Atma*, where the composer **Karol Szymanowski** lived in 1930–5.

Further south, ul. Kasprusie becomes ul. Strążyska, bringing you to the bottom of the scenic **STRĄŻYSKA VALLEY** (see below).

Perpendicular to ul. Kasprusie, at its north end, runs UL. KOŚCIELISKA, where some 19C peasant houses still survive, as well as the *Villa Koliba*, designed by Witkiewicz. Inside is a **Museum of the Zakopane Style** (open Wed–Sun 09.00–16.00). The street leads west to Kościeliska Valley (see below). Further to the east, running roughly parallel to ul. Krupówki, is ul. Jagiellońska, at the north end of which is the bus station. Also on this, at No. 18b, is the Gallery of the renowned and controversial artist Władysław Hasior (open Wed–Sat 11.00–18.00, Sun 09.00–15.00).

Surrounding walks and cycle routes

To protect the natural environment of the Tatras, trails have been carefully prepared and marked (look for coloured strips painted on rocks, trees or other objects). By straying from the trail, you risk paying a heavy fine. There is a small charge for entering the Tatra National Park; **car parks** by the entrances may cost as much as 1 PLN per hour.

Bicycles can be used in the Tatra National Park only on specially designated routes:
* Siwa Polana to the mountain shelter in the Chochołowska Valley
* Kuźnice to the mountain shelter in Kalatówki
* Brzeziny to the Murowaniece mountain shelter
* Siwa Polana to Bystre

Walks

* **Strążyska Valley**. This is about half an hour from the centre of Zakopane. Walk up ul. Kościeliska and then follow the red trail. It offers excellent views of the mountains, particularly the Giewont range. The red trail continues to the summit of **Mt Giewont** (1894m, 4hrs), on which a 15m iron cross was erected in 1901 (beware of storms!). The trail is closed in winter. Another possible route to Mt Giewont is from Kuźnice to Kalatówki, then across Hala Kondratowa and the Kondracka Pass—blue trail, 3hrs 30mins.

* **White Creek Valley**. Also half an hour from the town centre. Take ul. Kasprusie from the west end of ul. Krupówki and turn into ul. Do Białego; then follow the yellow trail. The yellow and black trails lead to the *Kalatówki* mountain shelter (2hrs).

• **Kościeliska Valley**. This is perhaps the most popular walk, usually accessible in winter, too. Take a bus from the centre of Zakopane to Kiry. The narrow, dark valley is the starting point for many attractive trails into the Western Tatras. You can visit several caves (well-marked and safe, provided you have a torch; black trail, 40mins to the **Frosty Cave**), wander along the 'streets' cut by water in the limestone rocks of the narrow **Kraków Ravine** (so-named by highlanders who thought it resembled Kraków's Old Town), walk to the Ornak mountain shelter (1hr 30mins), or climb **Mt Ciemniak** (2096m).

• **Chochołowska Valley**, further west from Kiry (black trail from the Kościeliska Valley, 2hrs, or by bus from Kiry to Hucisko). This is the longest valley in the Tatras, with a convenient mountain shelter (1hr) which can serve as a base for excursions into the Western Tatras. The most attractive trails lead to **Mt Ornak** (yellow and green; 3hrs), **Mt Trzydniowiański Wierch** (red; 2hrs 30mins) and **Mt Grześ** (yellow, blue and green; 4hrs).

The road continues north for about 25km to the unmissable **Chochołów*, a 16C village where fine 18C–19C wooden houses, typical of highlander architecture, have been preserved. The house at No. 75 contains a **Museum** (**open** Wed–Sun 10.00–14.00; closed in November and December) featuring a mid-19C rural interior.

• **Kuźnice** can be reached from the town centre on foot or by bus (4km from ul. Krupówki). From there you can take the cable car (or walk) to **Mt Kasprowy Wierch** (1985m). During summer and winter, tickets are hard to come by, so either arrive very early in the morning at the Kuźnice station or make a reservation two days in advance at the Orbis office on ul. Krupówki. Several attractive trails lead down, the most frequented being the one to Hala Gąsienicowa and the *Murowaniec* mountain shelter, which is a good base for several excellent trails into the High Tatras (closed in winter). The most scenic routes lead to **Mt Granaty** (2239m; blue and yellow trail; 3hrs) and to the **Zawrat Mountain Pass** (2159m; blue trail; 2hrs 45mins).

• The classic Zakopane excursion is to **Morskie Oko* (Eye of the Sea). During summer, the trail can be crowded, but the stunning views amply justify the effort of getting there. Either take a bus or drive to the car park in Palenica Białczańska. From there you can take a horse-drawn *doroshka* in summer or a sledge in winter to Morskie Oko. The glacial lake, 862m long, 566m wide, and 1393m above sea level, is known for its striking greenish-blue colour, especially when viewed from the steep trail leading up to another lake—**Czarny Staw** (Black Tarn, 1580m above sea level)—at the foot of Mt Rysy. The mountain shelter by the north shore of Morskie Oko is a convenient base for excursions to **Mt Rysy** (2499m; red trail; 4hrs), the **Mięguszowiecka mountain pass** (red and green trail; 3hrs), and the **Szpiglasowa mountain pass** (yellow trail; 2hrs 30mins).

Kraków to Nowy Sącz

❖ Kraków • Łopuszna • Harklowa • Dębno • Czorsztyn • Niedzica • Stary Sącz
• Nowy Sącz

This trip explores the Carpathian highlands south of Kraków, except for the Tatras, which are covered in the Zakopane chapter. The highlights are some outstanding wooden churches, the castles in Niedzica and Czorsztyn, and the scenic Pieniny Mountains.

Leave Kraków by ul. Zakopiańska going south. Up to Myślenice, the road is a dual-carriageway. **Nowy Targ** (population 31,800) 79km from Kraków, is a dreary town whose appearance belies the rare prosperity of its inhabitants. Polish highlanders have maintained strong ties with their relatives abroad, particularly in the USA, where large, close-knit emigré communities are common. In villages around the Nowy Targ region, the evident diffusion of American money into provincial lifestyles is somehow incongruous, even comical in its effect: tatty traditional cottages, for instance, with satellite dishes on the roofs and BMWs in the driveways.

Leaving Nowy Targ, follow signs to Nowy Sącz (road 969). In **ŁOPUSZNA** (8km) take the first left to the Baroque **manor house** of the Tetmajer family (**open** Wed–Sun 10.00–16.00). Further on, across a wooden bridge, is a 16C wooden **parish church**, with a frescoed ceiling and a late Gothic triptych in the high altar. Another wooden **parish church**, late Gothic with 19C accretions, has survived in nearby **HARKLOWA** (4km). Most of the furnishings and decoration are Baroque, except for remnants of Gothic polychromy (c 1500) under the bell tower.

By far the best example of **wooden religious architecture** of the Podhale region (in the foothills of the Tatras) can be found in **DĘBNO** (1km). The fascinating *parish church contains well-preserved Gothic painted decoration (c 1500) with an astounding variety of motifs (animals, knights, floral patterns, St George slaying the dragon, etc.), supplemented by sculptures and elaborate carved furnishings, including a high altar with an early 16C triptych featuring a scene depicting a *Sacra Conversazione*. Outside, note the steep shingled roof. Continue east along road 969 to the village of Czorsztyn (15km).

Czorsztyn

Close to the village, up on a hill, is a weird spiky steel construction created by Władysław Hasior to commemorate the 'Protectors of the People's Government' (in other words, members of the Communist Fifth Column killed during the brief struggle against Soviet occupation after the Second World War). The **monument** is supposed to whine and jingle, but only does so in a gale. The view from the top is well worth the climb.

Czorsztyn was gradually flooded in the mid-1990s when the dam across the Dunajec river reached completion, leading to much protest from environmental groups. Once all the inhabitants had been evicted, Czorsztyn continued for a while as a bizarre ghost town of empty streets and deserted houses. Nowadays, all that you are likely to see are the ruins of a forlorn 14C **Castle** (**open** daily 10.00–17.00) erected by Kazimierz the Great on the hill. Some fear that it too may not last long, as the limestone on which it stands is gradually eroding.

Visible across the flooded Dunajec valley is its better-preserved twin in **Niedzica** (5km), built in 1330 for the Hungarian Berzevicy family (the Spisz region, east of Nowy Targ, was part of Hungary until 1918). It consists of two parts: the Gothic upper castle, and the Renaissance lower castle added in 1601 by the Horvaths and equipped with round corner towers. The **Castle Museum** (open Tues–Sun 09.00–17.00) contains few exhibits, but the rooms themselves are worth seeing. Apart from folk art and kitchenware (moved here from the village of Frydman), there is a furnished room of Ilona Salamon, the last owner of the castle (d. 1943), a torture room, a well 60m deep, and two terraces offering a good view of the Pieniny mountains and the Dunajec gorge. The lower castle, with its arcaded courtyard, is now a hotel used by the Art Historians' Society.

Niedzica and nearby Krościenko and Szczawnica are the best bases for excursions into the scenic PIENINY MOUNTAINS, well-marked and accessible limestone peaks (*Trzy Korony*, 982m, is the highest). Partly wooded, and dropping steeply to the Dunajec valley below, in places the sheer rock faces of the gorge are 300m high. The spectacular twists and turns of the river can be navigated on a raft steered by local highlanders. An International Canoeing Rally is held every June. In SZCZAWNICA follow the signs to 'Wąwóz Homole', a picturesque ravine cut by the Kamionka creek. Return to the main road (969) and continue to Stary Sącz (58km).

Stary Sącz

Stary Sącz (population 9000), arguably the prettiest town of the region, is small, neat and unspoilt. The town, granted a charter in 1273, was dominated for centuries by the Convent of St Clare, founded in 1280 by the Blessed Kinga (daughter of Bela IV of Hungary). The convent's Church of the Holy Trinity was erected in 1332, and the buildings were surrounded with medieval walls, of which only one tower has survived. The church towers, the sgraffito covering the walls, the annexe above the sacristy with a pretty frieze, as well as the Renaissance **convent building** (1601–05) are all attributed to Jan de Simonii, while Baldassare Fontana is credited with the high altar of 1699. Notice, also, 16C painted decoration on the vaults and two paintings by the high altar. Of impressive proportions (7.6m high) is the wooden carved pulpit (1671) in the form of a Jesse tree. Another curiosity is the palm vault supported on a single pillar in the 14C sacristy beneath the nuns' oratory.

The pride of Stary Sącz is its cobbled ***Market Square** with low 18C houses. Inside one (No. 6) is the **Regional Museum** (open Tues–Sun 10.00–13.00), offering a section on the history of the town, crafts and folklore, 17C–18C paintings, 16C–17C religious books, and various items connected with the famous soprano Ada Sari (1886–1968). South of the square is the 14C **Church of St Elizabeth**, whose Gothic chancel ends in a polygonal apse, and contains a Baroque high altar with wooden sculptures of SS Peter and Paul. The solid west tower was built in 1686.

Continue to Nowy Sącz (8km).

Nowy Sącz

■ **Practical information**

Hotel. ★★★*Panorama*. Ul. Romanowskiego 4a, ☎ 443-7145/443-7100. Central location, car park. 27 rooms.

Tourist information (PAPT). Ul. P. Skargi 2, ☎ 443-5597.
Post office. Ul. Dunajewskiego 10.
Telephone code: (0–18).

Town centre

The centre of the MARKET SQUARE in Nowy Sącz (population 75,000) is occupied by an eclectic **town hall** of 1895–7. East of the square is the twin-towered **parish church**. Built in 1446 and remodelled at the turn of the 18C, it was restored to its Gothic form in the 1970s. The heavily gilded high altar and the four side altars date from the Renaissance, the former containing a valuable 15C Italian painting. On the north pillar below the organ loft, protected by glass, is a fragment of Gothic painted decoration discovered in 1976. A Renaissance font (1557) stands on the left of the nave.

South of the church, behind a wall, is the Canons' House (ul. Lwowska 3), currently a **Regional Museum** (open Tues–Thur 10.00–15.00, Fri 10.00–17.00, Sat–Sun 09.00–14.30). The 15C building has a fine late Gothic portal of 1505, as well as fragments of 16C murals in the first-floor Concert Room. On the same floor is a large collection of works by Nikifor (d. 1968) a celebrated amateur painter from Krynica 45km further south. The museum has some 200 of his watercolours from the inter-war period. Other collections include 18C–20C folk art, Orthodox church art, and 14C craft work, mostly religious in character.

UL. JAGIELLOŃSKA, which exits from the southeast corner of the Market Square, is the main shopping area of Nowy Sącz. At the corner with UL. LWOWSKA is an art gallery with a bookshop and pleasant café inside. North of the square, on ul. Piotra Skargi, stands the **Premonstratensian Nuns' Convent**, founded in the 15C. Walk to the end of the street to see the **Old Synagogue** (1700–46), a low square building now housing a gallery (same **opening** hours as the Regional Museum), which often puts on temporary exhibitions. Across the car park are the ruins of a castle erected by King Jan Kazimierz in the 14C. Only the Smith Tower has been partly reconstructed. Walking back towards the Market Square you will pass two 14C churches: the Franciscan, and the more interesting St Mary's (currently Protestant), with a large dome. At the corner of ul. Jagiellońska and ul. Franciszkańska is the 17C **Lubomirski House**, much damaged when the explosives stored by the Germans in the castle cellars blew up. About 4km out of town (southeast), on ul. Długoszewskiego, is a **skansen** (open Tues–Sun 10.00–17.00), offering examples of regional architecture.

Nowy Sącz to Sanok

❖ Nowy Sącz • Krynica • Szymbark • Biecz • Krosno • Sanok

This trip makes a short detour south to the pretty spa of Krynica, and then continues east to Sanok, passing through the charming medieval town of Biecz with its excellent musuem.

From Nowy Sącz take road 99 due south (35km) to **KRYNICA** (population 12,700), a fashionable **spa** situated in a picturesque valley surrounded by hills. One of these—Góra Parkowa—can be reached by a funicular from the spa park.

The latter has facilities offering mineral cures and mud baths. There is plenty of good accommodation (such as the *Jagiellonka* on ul. Piłsudskiego 24, ☎ 471–5486), but during high season rooms may be in short supply so book well in advance. In September, an **International Competition of Opera Singers** and the **Jan Kiepura Festival** take place here. The architecture is mostly 19C, with many Secessionist villas including the famous 'Patria', which belonged to the singer Jan Kiepura (1902–66).

Leave Krynica on road 99, turning right along road 977 to Grybów. Continue 51km to **SZYMBARK** (road 98), where you may visit a **skansen** (open Tues–Sun 09.00–16.00; during off season months closed on weekends). The exhibits, which include two wooden mills, have been brought here from neighbouring villages, and date mostly from the second half of the 19C.

Biecz

Continue 20km along road 98 to Biecz (population 4900), an ancient town mentioned as early as the 11C, though archaeological excavations prove that a fortified settlement existed on the castle hill already in the 9C. The castle was erected in the 12C, and served as a royal residence of Polish kings from Władysław Łokietek to Władysław Jagiełło. It flourished until the late 17C, after which famine (the most tragic in 1721, which left only 30 survivors), fire and war contributed to its sharp decline. Its historical monuments, however, have

Biecz

been well-preserved, including the medieval urban plan, and the Gothic **Parish Church of Corpus Christi** on PL. KROMERA. This bulky aisled hall of brick and stone stands behind a wall decorated with 13 statues of saints. The wall, as well as the square bell tower (15C), was part of the town's defensive system. The main entrance used to lead through the elaborate Gothic south portal. Inside, notice the ornate late Gothic stalls on the right (south), and more modest Renaissance ones on the left (north), with carved heads representing the burghers of Biecz. Most of the church's furniture and decoration is Renaissance, such as the pews, epitaph slabs, marble and alabaster tombstones guarding the entrance to the chancel, stalls in the apse, and the high altar (end of 16C), with an Italian painting forming the centrepiece of the large, three-tiered structure. The Gothic rood beam supports a passion group (1639).

Across the street, at ul. Kromera 5, is the excellent *****Regional Museum** (open Tues–Sat 09.00–17.00, Sun 09.00–14.00; Nov–April, Tues–Sat 09.00–15.00). It occupies the Renaissance Kromer House (1519), and the Barian Rokicki House (1523) with a round tower. Its varied and well-arranged collections comprise a section devoted to Bishop Kromer (1512–89), an eminent historian, writer and diplomat; a pharmacy section (a meticulously reconstructed 19C pharmacy, with various implements, bottles, mortars, scales, cases and an original 16C prescription); musical instruments (including some curious examples of folk instruments); handicrafts (including famous Russian samovars made in Tuła); contemporary Polish painting; numismatics and archaeology. An interesting item is a bronze bell of 1382 (one of the oldest in Europe), which broke in 1950, as well as fragments of 15C water pipes.

To the east is the Market Square with a **town hall**, whose octagonal tower (40m) is visible from afar. Its original Gothic character was mostly obliterated in the 16C, when the tower collapsed, and the whole structure was remodelled. The remnants of sgraffito decoration preserved in the upper parts date from that period. Convicts sentenced to death would be held in a prison cell down in the cellars.

Krosno

In Krosno (46km) (population 48,300) stop at ul. Piłsudskiego 16 to visit the **Regional Museum** in the former Bishop's Palace (**open** May–Oct, Tues–Sun 10.00–16.00; November–April Sat–Sun 10.00–14.00), which has a display entitled 'Krosno in Old Photographs', a collection of kerosene lamps, an archaeology and history section in the cellars, and some 19C–20C Polish art. Opposite, at No. 17, is a commendable **Museum of Handicraft and Trade** (**open** Tues–Wed, Fri 08.00–15.00, Thur 09.00–16.00, Sat–Sun 10.00–15.00). A complete hairdresser's shop from the turn of the century, bells from the Felczyński foundry, pots from the workshop of Adam Habrat, a smithy in which six generations of the Bochenek family had worked, various documents illustrating the history of the guilds from the 16C onwards—all this is assembled in the former tower-clock factory of Michał Mięsowicz, whose clock is still ticking in the Town Hall, Vienna. Walk further up the street to the 15C **parish church**, which burnt down during the great fire of Krosno in 1638, and was rebuilt soon afterwards. Its southeast domed **chapel** of SS Peter and Paul was founded by Wojciech Robert Portius, a rich Scottish merchant who lived in Krosno in the 17C. The church has a fine collection of paintings, including a late Gothic *Coronation of the Virgin* (c 1480), and twenty-three 17C Baroque canvases in the 'Sarmatian' style (see p. 68) from the Dolabella workshop.

Northeast of the Market Square, which is surrounded with 16C–18C arcaded houses, stands the **Franciscan Church**. Its exquisite early Baroque **Oświęcim Chapel** (1647) was decorated with excellent stuccoes by Giovanni Battista Falconi. The nave has several good Renaissance and Baroque tomb slabs, including Gian-Maria Padovano's marble slab for Jan Kamieniecki.

Continue along road 38 to Sanok.

Sanok

■ Practical information

Hotel. ★★ *Turysta*. Ul. Jagiellońska 13, ☎ 463-0922. Car park. 31 rooms.
Tourist information (PTTK). Ul. 3 Maja 2, ☎ 321-71.
Post office. Ul. Kościuszki 26.
Telephone code: (0–13)

Town centre

Sanok (population 40,000) is not only a good base to explore the unspoilt, scarcely populated **Bieszczady mountains**, but itself has several attractions.

North of the MARKET SQUARE is an excellent **museum** (ul. Zamkowa 2, **open** Tues–Sun 09.00–15.00 mid-April to mid-October), which features two unique permanent exhibitions: the Beksiński gallery; and the largest collection of icons in Poland. The museum is housed in a group of buildings incorporating remnants of a castle raised by Kazimierz the Great in the mid-14C. The most valued part of the collection consists of icons of the Kiev school, dating from the 15C–19C, most painted on wood. The oldest one, depicting the *Dormition of the Virgin*, comes from the village of Żukotyń. All the icons exhibit painstaking attention to detail and adhere to strict rules of composition. They depict the Virgin in a style peculiar to this traditional art-form, marked by the elongation of the whole figure, hands and features of the Madonna. All the inscriptions are in Old Church Slavonic. The museum's other collection of icons comprises many fine examples of Uniate art.

> The Uniates, also known as the Greek Catholics, were formerly Orthodox believers until a schism in 1596, when they converted to Catholicism. They recognise the authority of the Roman Pope, but have preserved the Orthodox rite.

In addition to religious art, the museum has a large collection of highly original works by the celebrated contemporary painter Zdzisław Beksiński, a native of Sanok.

From the museum, follow the white signs marked 'skansen', crossing the San river, to one of the largest (38ha) and best **open-air museums** in Poland. Unfortunately, a fire in 1994, which broke out during the night and spread with astonishing speed (dramatic photographs can be seen and bought in the ticket office), destroyed many of the valuable exhibits; reconstruction work is still under way. The exhibition is divided into sections according to ethnic group, with most emphasis on the Lemko and Bojko (see p. 254), native inhabitants of the Bieszczady region. It features peasant cottages, farm buildings, churches, windmills, inns, water and timber mills, wayside shrines, a fire-brigade HQ, beehives, a smithy, and even a village jail.

Sanok to Przemyśl

Through the Bieszczady Mountains

❖ Sanok • Lesko • Czarna Górna • Bircza • Posada Robotycka • Przemyśl

The *BIESZCZADY are low, mostly bare-topped mountains forming part of the long Carpathian ridge, with the highest peaks already on the other side of the Polish-Ukrainian border. The Bieszczady region is the wildest and least popu-lated part of Poland. Its main attraction lies not so much in architecture as in its pure, natural beauty. There is no difficult or risky mountain-climbing along the scenic trails, but the long distances involved (up to 20 hours on foot) can really put your endurance to the test. One of the most popular and beautiful trails begins in the village of Kalnica (or Wetlina) about 70km from Sanok, with an ascent to **Mt Smerek** (1222m). Thereafter you follow the Wetlińska plateau, with magnificent views, descending to Brzegi Górne, or continuing along the Caryńska plateau (part of the Bieszczady National Park) to Ustrzyki Górne. The high peaks of **Halicz** (1333m) and **Tarnica** (1346m) lie to the southeast of Ustrzyki Górne, and can be covered on a long day-trip from Ustrzyki Górne. From the rocky summits, Ukrainian villages are visible in the distance.

> The region has a grim chapter of recent history behind it, and this provides explanation of its depopulation, and the dereliction of its many churches, houses, even entire villages. The subject is still very touchy in Poland, and even after the abolition of Communist censorship it is hard to find an objective account in Polish sources. The Oxford historian Norman Davies writes in his *God's Playground*: 'Formed in 1943, [the Ukrainian Insurrectionist Army, or UPA] fought with equal ferocity against Hitler and Stalin. In Volhynia [...] it came into conflict with both Polish and Soviet partisans. Its vicious reprisals against uncooperative Polish villagers at this time were subsequently to deprive it of sympathy in Poland'. After the UPA had managed to kill General Karol Świerczewski, a final and ruthless campaign was launched by the Polish Communist government in 1947, when entire Lemko and Bojko villages, deemed sympathetic to the UPA, were razed to the ground, and the villagers were either resettled in western Poland, or expelled to the Soviet Union. 'Operation Vistula', as it came to be known, was jointly carried out by the Polish, Soviet and Czechoslovak armies. To this day the operation remains controversial, inspiring nationalist resentment on both sides of the border.

Road 891 going southeast from Sanok will take you to **Lesko** (13km). The Renaissance **synagogue** is currently an art gallery (**open** during the season, Tues–Sat 10.00–16.00). Driving down past the synagogue you will arrive at a large **Jewish Cemetery** on a hill (right), with tombstones, most in poor condition, scattered among oaks, maples and birches. From Lesko, take the scenic road (894), which skirts the artificial Solińskie lake. In the village of **Czarna Górna** (54km), the 19C wooden **Orthodox church** comes into view on a hill overgrown with trees. Orthodox churches can also be found in the neighbouring villages of **Rabe** and **Równia** further north (the latter one is especially pretty).

Continue via Ustrzyki Dolne (roads 896, 891, 890) to the junction with road 98 heading north to Przemyśl. In **Bircza** (65km from Czarna Górna), instead of continuing along the main road, you could take a detour and visit the place where Lech Wałęsa was put under luxury house arrest in 1981, and where he used to hunt with the then Minister of the Interior, Czesław Kiszczak. Turn right towards Posada Robotycka. When the winding and deserted road forks, bear right and you will come to the former government resort of Arłamowo, Today the luxury house in which Wałęsa was interned is a large hotel. Return to the fork and continue to **Posada Robotycka** (14km). Up on a hillock on the left, stands a whitewashed stone **Orthodox church** surrounded by a wall. The gabled building houses a branch of the **Przemyśl Regional Museum**.

Continue north to Przemyśl (26km).

Przemyśl

Przemyśl is a hilly town on the San river in the remote east of Poland. It is also one of the country's oldest cities, mentioned in the 10C by the Kiev historian Nestor and by an Arabic traveller and geographer Ibrahim ibn Yaqub.

■ Practical information

Hotels

★★★ *Marko*. Ul. Lurowska 36A, ☎ 678-9272. 15 rooms, car park.

★★ *Pod Białym Orłem*. Ul. Sanocka 13, ☎ 678-6107. Central location, car park. 14 rooms.

Tourist information (PAPT). Ul. Ratuszowa 8 or ul. Władycze 3, ☎ 78-73-09.

ORBIS. Pl. Legionów 1, ☎ 78-33-66.

Main post office. Ul. 3 Maja 29.

Telephone code: (0–16).

History

Archaeological excavations in Przemyśl have uncovered traces of human settlement reaching back as far as 30,000 BC, and later finds suggesting the presence of Celts, Romans, Alanians, and Polanians. In the 10C, the town lay on the busy trade route connecting the Baltic with the Black Sea and the Adriatic. After centuries of turmoil, the town was finally incorporated into Poland by Kazimierz the Great in 1340. At that time it was a melting pot of many religions and ethnic groups: Poles, Jews, Tartars, Ruthenians. Its prosperity came to an end with the Swedish Deluge (see p. 49), and the process of decline culminated in the Partitions, which left Przemyśl in Austrian hands. During the inter-war period, the city suffered much poverty and unemployment, leading to numerous anti-government demonstrations and much-publicised trials against Communist leaders.

Old Town

The Market Square in Przemyśl (population 66,000), overgrown with trees and paved with rough stone, has lost most of its original buildings. Best preserved is the south (upper) side, reconstructed in the 1950s. The house at No. 18, with a double fluted pilaster in lieu of a buttress, was built in the early 16C. The fountain in the west part of the square, decorated with bears, modelled on the Przemyśl coat of arms, dates from 1964.

At the end of UL. FRANCISZKAŃSKA (southeast corner of the square) is the **Franciscan Church and Monastery**. The original Gothic church built by the Franciscans was replaced with a Baroque one in 1754–78. In front of it stand three Rococo sandstone sculptures. The ornamental door leads through to the recently renovated, heavily painted interior. The columned high altar has a painting of the *Virgin* in the centre and sculptures (1761–64) by Maciej Polejowski, who also made the matching side altars and pulpit (1778).

Walk up UL. ASNYKA by the side of the Franciscan buildings to the former **Jesuit Church**, currently an Orthodox cathedral. A twin-towered late Baroque façade with a curly gable was added in the 18C, but the church was closed and converted into a military warehouse by the Austrians in 1820. The basilican interior has aisles much lower than the cross-vaulted nave, which is surrounded by a gallery and a prominent cornice above pilasters surmounted with ornate capitals. To the left of the church stands the **Diocesan Museum** (second-floor, **open** Tues–Sun 10.00–15.00), with a Romanesque cross, Gothic sculptures, vestments and tapestries, including one depicting *The Four Evangelists* (1730) from the chancel of the cathedral.

The Cathedral

The *****cathedral** stands further up ul. Katedralna. Originally Gothic, its present Baroque form is largely due to reconstruction work carried out in the 18C by Bishop Aleksander Fredro. Enter through a large pedimented porch, bearing the date 1913. Huge pillars support the cross vaults of the nave, covered with 20C painted decoration.

Beyond the rood arch with a Gothic crucifix is the net-vaulted chancel, lit by stained-glass windows made to the design of Józef Mehoffer. The tapestries hanging on the walls are copies (the originals of 1645 are currently in the Diocesan Museum). A stone Gothic portal in the north wall leads to a twin-room sacristy with original Gothic vaults. Next to the sacristy is the entrance to the octagonal **Drohojewski Chapel** (Renaissance, 1578), with Baroque *trompe l'oeil murals* (18C) and a black marble Renaissance portal.

Walk to the west end of the church to see the only surviving **Gothic mural**, framed in a 20C altar, which is situated behind a marble font (1692) under the choir. Here, by the entrance, you will also find the memorial slab (1545) of an anonymous priest's mother, which survived the collapse of the vault in 1733. At the west end of the south aisle is the 17C tomb of Jan and Anna Fredro. In the same aisle stands a mid-16C red marble statue of Bishop Jan Dziaduski (d. 1559).

The late Baroque oval **Chapel of the Fredro family**, its dome decorated with murals by Stanisław Stroiński, is entered through a Baroque portal bearing the Fredro coat of arms. The black marble altar you see here contains a Gothic *Crucifixion* and, below, an alabaster Renaissance *Pietà*. Epitaph slabs (18C) are embedded in the walls. The free-standing bell-tower belongs to the cathedral (1764).

Walking up UL. ZAMKOWA you will arrive at the Gothic **Castle Gate**, the only remnant of the 14C castle erected by Kazimierz the Great. Archaeological excavations have uncovered remnants of an early medieval settlement on the castle hill, with a rotunda and palatium from the 10C–11C. These were replaced in the 12C–13C by new buildings whose shape can only be surmised from the existing recovered remnants. The stone castle raised by Kazimierz the Great, although remodelled several times, managed to survive until the early 19C, when it fell into ruin under the Austrian rule. Only the gate and two towers were saved from destruction. Other parts have been reconstructed, including the foundations of the pre-Romanesque rotunda and the palatium. Today, the former castle courtyard is often used as a venue for theatrical performances. It also offers a breathtaking view over the San valley.

Return to the former Jesuit church. The **Regional Museum** (open Tues–Fri 10.00–18.00, Sat–Sun 10.00–14.00) is in the adjacent Jesuit College at No. 3 pl. Czackiego. In addition to the usual archaeology and folk art sections (mostly wooden sculptures and paintings), it has a collection of 17C–19C icons, one of the largest in the country, and Orthodox vestments. The room on the first floor has a stuccoed ceiling and a decorative cornice.

Up on the hill, south of the Jesuit church, stands the **Discalced Carmelite's**

Church, with a three-tiered curly gable surmounted by pinnacles. Since the church has no tower, its three bells hang beneath an arch to the right. The most striking piece of furniture inside is a late Baroque **pulpit** in the form of a boat, complete with sail and ropes. An 18C marble portal leads to the sacristy (the high altar is modern).

The church, built by the Carmelite monks in the early 17C, was turned over by the Austrian authorities to the Uniates after 1784—a fact never acknowledged by the Pope. A huge Byzantine dome, built in 1866, completely altered its form, and was followed by other changes required by the Orthodox rite. After the Uniates (see p. 254) were resettled in the Ukraine in 1946, the church was confiscated by the state, only to be returned to the Roman Catholic Church in 1966. Pope John Paul II decided to give it back to the Uniate community in 1991, but this met with fierce resistance from local Catholics. Despite pressure and a rather bad press—the whole affair hit the headlines of the national papers—the Catholics prevailed. Several years later, emotions are still running high.

Still higher up the hill, you could visit the **Discalced Carmelite Nuns' Church and Monastery**—a brick Neo-Gothic hall with a tower and murals painted in 1903.

Return to ul. Franciszkańska and head towards the large intersection of ul. Mickiewicza, ul. Słowackiego and ul. Jagiellońska, passing the Clock Tower (1775–7) on **PL. NIEPODLEGŁOŚCI**. Across the intersection is the **Reformed Franciscans' Church and Monastery**, which has sunk 3m below ground level. It was built after 1641, and remodelled many times most thoroughly in 1870–7. Andrzej M. Fredro, the brother of the great playwright (see p. 84), is buried in the crypt.

Walk along ul. Jagiellońska and across the bridge. To your left is a monument to the 'Orlęta Przemyskie' (The Przemyśl Eaglets—young soldiers who fought against Ukrainians in 1918) and to your right, Fesinger's stone statue of St John Nepomuk. Close by is the **Benedictine Convent and Church**, founded in 1616. The present church, dating from 1768–77, is partly surrounded by defensive walls with loopholes and the remnants of two towers. The interior is noteworthy for Stroiński's painted decoration (before 1784), and the Baroque furniture, including a late Baroque pulpit.

Day trips from Przemyśl

The fort in Siedliska

Przemyśl is surrounded by enormous 19C forts which rank it as the third largest fortress in Europe (after Antwerp and Verdun). The inner defensive ring was built in 1853–55, the outer in 1878–1914. Most of the forts were blown up by the Austrians before their surrender to the Russian army in 1915. The best-preserved fragments are in **SIEDLISKA**, 14km from Przemyśl town centre. To get there, follow signs to Medyka (a border crossing to the Ukraine). About 6km before it, turn right signposted 'Siedliska'. Beyond the village the road ascends, degenerating into a dirt track. Bear left at the fork and drive to the gate, some 50m further on. From here a black trail leads into the fort erected in 1886–90 by Salis Saglio. Be sure to bring a torch.

Krasiczyn Castle

The excursion to *KRASICZYN (10km) will take you to one of the most scenic castles in Poland, a beautifully preserved monument of Renaissance and Baroque architecture set in an 11ha park, handsomely designed and rich in old and varied trees. The **castle** was built by the powerful magnates Stanisław (father) and Marcin (son) Krasicki in 1592–1608, although it incorporated many elements of an earlier stronghold. The Italian architect Galeazzo Appiano endowed the residence with an unmistakable Renaissance air, most prominent in the exquisite, fairy-tale parapets. The rectangular inner courtyard is bordered on two sides by residential buildings, and on the others by walls, with a tall clock tower over the gate in the middle of the west wall. In the corners stand bulky round towers, which, apart from the parapets, are the castle's most characteristic feature. Originally defensive bastions, they were raised and crowned with parapets, the southwest one with a dome. The latter accommodates a **chapel** with excellent stuccoes and murals. All the towers were given symbolic names that already foreshadowed the Sarmatian (see p. 68) fashions of the Polish Baroque: the Divine Tower, the Royal Tower (with six miniature turrets), the Papal Tower, and the Tower of the Gentry (both with parapets). No expense was spared on the vast sgraffito covering the walls, which already exhibits traces of Baroque. The carved stone, originating mostly from excellent Lvov workshops, and decorating the portals, arcades and parapets, is pure Renaissance and Mannerism.

Although the castle was ill-served by reconstruction work carried out during the inter-war period, and was not much improved by being turned over to the Forestry School after the war, it has recovered some of its splendour since renovation sponsored by the FSO car factory in Warsaw. Work is still under way and, in an effort to raise funds, a hotel has been opened in the residential section (☎ (0–16) 671-8321/671-8316).

Przemyśl to Rzeszów

❖ Przemyśl • Jarosław • Leżajsk • Łańcut • Rzeszów

Jarosław

From Przemyśl take road 4 leading north for 32km to **JAROSŁAW** (population 40,800), a delightful quiet town, surprisingly picturesque and unspoilt by tourism, though not lacking in cultural interest. The **annual music festival** held in August combines concerts of old music with workshops, meetings and other artistic events.

Medieval chronicles mentioned Jarosław as early as 1152. Thanks to its location on the San river and the important east-west trade route, it quickly prospered, establishing itself as a wealthy merchant town. In the 16C–17C, its fairs, the longest of which lasted throughout August, attracted traders from all over Europe and the Middle East. This accounts for the peculiar design of the burgher houses which had roofed yards modelled on Byzantine architecture, and labyrinthine two or even three-level cellars used as warehouses and—during the Tartar invasions—as shelters. You can still see both the roofed yard and 200m of underground corridors in the **Rydzik House** at No. 14 on the east side of the Market Square. The soft loess soil made it easy to dig the corridors, but also nearly caused the entire old town to collapse—mining experts from Silesia and Kraków managed to save it in the nick of time.

The centre of the MARKET SQUARE is occupied by a rectangular **Town Hall** with stucco coats of arms adorning the corner towers. But the most amazing edifice stands to the south, its arcades protruding from the row of houses in which it stands. The 16C **Orsetti House* is a veritable castle in miniature, topped by an ornate Mannerist parapet decorated

Orsetti House

with niches, blind arcades and a row of characteristic spoked circles. Inside is a **Regional Museum** (open Wed–Sat 10.00–18.00, Sun 10.00–14.00).

East of the Market Square, at the end of ul. Sobieskiego, is a domed **Uniate Church** with octagonal towers, while to the west, on pl. Piotra Skargi, stands the **Jesuit Church**, built in 1582–94 in late Renaissance style by the Dutchman Joseph Britius, and consecrated by Piotr Skarga himself (see p. 81). A fire of 1862 destroyed all the Baroque furniture, damaging a 16C Gothic figure of the Virgin (now in the chancel) and a 17C crucifix (in the south aisle). Stone sculptures (18C) of the Fathers of the Church and saints adorn the south wall outside.

Continue west to the fortified **Benedictine Convent** on the Hill of St Nicholas, founded in 1609 by Anna Ostrogska. The **church**, much damaged in 1914, is rather bare. In the convent building there is one curious room, completely blackened: the Nazis intended to blow up the whole site, but managed only to start a fire, which charred the walls.

On ul. Jana Pawła II stands the **Reformed Franciscans' Church** sponsored by a wealthy burgher and constructed after 1707 to the designs of Giuseppe Simone Bellotti and Martyn of Kęty. Further west along the same street, visible from afar (left) is the Baroque **Dominican Church** built by Jakub Solari in 1698–1708. In the 18C, a rich, late Baroque east façade was added, twin-towered, with a convex gable and a balustraded parapet. The interior is dominated by late Baroque pilasters with huge capitals and a prominent cornice. In the chancel, as tall as the nave, the vaults are densely covered with *trompe l'oeil* murals painted in 1723–31. Walk west of the church, down a flight of steps, to the **Miraculous Spring Chapel** (1752), with a well inside. According to legend, in 1381 shepherds found here a figure of the Madonna (now on the high altar of the church), and soon a spring appeared on the site. Science has determined that the water contains no health-giving agents, but some believe it can cure all kinds of diseases. Taps have been installed, so try for yourself.

Leave Jarosław following signs to Rzeszów. In Przeworsk turn north along road 835 to Leżajsk (43km), or, if pressed for time, continue straight along road 4 to Łańcut, the highlight of the route.

LEŻAJSK (population 13,100) is most widely known for its beer, but its name is also familiar to lovers of organ music. Though it suffered badly in the past from Tartars, Swedes and troops fighting during the First World War, its famous Bernardine monastery has managed to survive in good shape within a ring of defensive walls. The road leading to the monastery from the town centre is marked 'Nisko', and the grounds are entered through an early Baroque gate. The **Basilica and Monastery** were built in the first half of the 17C. Most of the furnishings and interior decoration are the work of the monks themselves, such as the splendid carved and inlaid oak stalls (1648), the beautifully carved and gilded pulpit, or the imposing early Baroque high altar (1637), with Franciszek Lekszycki's painting in the centre. The huge, lavishly ornamented organ, made in 1678–82 and said to be the best in Poland, fills the west end of the nave and spills over to the aisles and nearby pillars. The church's two chapels, placed symmetrically at the east ends of the aisles, have vaults with stuccoes attributed to Giovanni Battista Falconi. In the southeast corner of the church is the entrance to the four-winged monastery, which houses a small **museum**, normally shown only to groups of tourists by request.

Łańcut

Continue to Łańcut (29km) along road 877.

History

Two powerful magnate families—the **Lubomirskis** and the **Potockis**—made Łańcut what it is today. Yet it could already boast a string of famous (and infamous) owners by the time Stanisław Lubomirski acquired it in 1629. In the 14C–15C, it was the seat of another influential clan—the **Pileckis**, distant relatives of the Jagiellon dynasty. Subsequently, the small town and castle passed into the hands of Stanisław Stadnicki, a violent, unscrupulous man, whose constant litigations, robberies, and assaults against his neighbours earned him the nickname of 'the Łańcut Devil'.

Stanisław Lubomirski, who purchased Łańcut in 1629, was of an entirely different character. His passion was architecture, and he possessed the requisite funds to nurture it. The architect **Maciej Trapola** and stuccoist **Giovanni Battista Falconi** were among the eminent artists he employed. By 1750 the castle had become a splendid fortified residence worthy of its owners. However, its real heyday would come later, when Elżbieta Lubomirska (née Czartoryska), by that time a widow, settled here having been driven out of Paris by the French Revolution. Along with her came many prominent exiles, such as the Count of Provence (the future Louis XVIII), the Prince de Bourbon, Madame de Staël, and Louis de Sabran, as well as several outstanding artists, among them Chrystian Piotr Aigner, Jan Chrystian Kamsetzer and Szymon Bogumił Zug, who remodelled the castle in the new, Neo-classical and Romantic style.

Elżbieta Lubomirska bequeathed the castle to the two sons of her daughter and Jan Potocki, a magnate as well as a scientist, traveller and writer, the author of the novel *Manuscrit trouvé à Saragosse* (see p. 82). Potocki's grandson Alfred, a politically influential figure, played host in Łańcut to Emperor Franz Joseph II. Alfred's son Roman used his fabulous fortune (he owned some 50,000ha of land, factories mines and palaces) to improve the residence, giving it all the latest trappings of civilisation that he and his wife Elżbieta (née Radziwiłł) had encountered on their travels around Europe. When the Red Army was approaching Łańcut in 1944, their son Alfred fled to Vienna, taking a trainload of treasures with him: some 600 crates filled with paintings, sculptures, porcelain, furniture, tapestries, gold-work and jewellery. Upon arrival at the castle, General Kurochkin was dismayed to discover that all the most precious objects had disappeared, while on the door he read a notice in Russian, cleverly hung there by Potocki's plenipotentiary, proclaiming the castle to be the 'Museum of the Polish Nation'. This may well have saved Łańcut from the fate of many aristocratic residences plundered by the Soviets, and marked the beginning of today's museum.

The ****Palace** (open Tues–Sat 09.00–14.30, Sun 09.00–16.00; during off-season months Tues–Sun 09.00–14.30; closed in December and January) is square in form, with an inner courtyard and four towers at the corners, two of which have Baroque crownings, probably by Tylman van Gameren. The main entrance is through a 17C portal in the west façade bearing the Lubomirski coat of arms. During the 18C–19C, two annexes on the south and north sides were built to house the library, the dining room, kitchens and servants' quarters (currently an exclusive hotel), as was another tower, the 'Hen's Foot'. Projecting westward from the northwest corner is a large Neo-classical orangery by Aigner.

Passing through a vaulted vestibule—lined with oak blocks to muffle the sound of horses' hoofs—and ascending the stairs, you enter the *Piano Nobile*. The first room on the left, one of the oldest, is covered with a polychromed beamed ceiling. It also contains a curious early 18C wardrobe in the shape of a pear. The walls of the corridors are cluttered with medallions, paintings, reliefs and sculptures, the rooms crowded with furniture. The opulence is almost cloying, and one can only wonder how the interiors must have looked before Potocki removed the most precious items to Vienna. Admittedly, much of what you see today has been brought to Łańcut during the post-war period, and bears no relation to the original collection. The dome of the Zodiac Room in the northwest tower was adorned by Falconi with stuccoes of fruit amid geometric forms. But the most exquisite room of all is the **Ballroom**, designed by Aigner, and decorated with stuccoes by Fryderyk Baumann. Concerts are often held in this two-storey hall, permeated with warm golden hues and brilliant whites reflected in the mirrors. Aigner and Baumann also collaborated on the Grand Dining Hall in the south annexe, but it was already badly damaged in the 19C. The crockery and cutlery on display are also a poor substitute for what disappeared in 1944: a one-hundred-piece set given to King Jan Sobieski by the Chinese Emperor, a golden Turkish coffee-set that once belonged to Kara Mustaffa, Meissen porcelain and cut glass from Vienna and France.

Be sure to visit the **exhibition of icons**, a rich collection ranging from the 15C to the 20C. The most precious items are a 16C *St Nicholas* from Łodyny, and a 15C icon from Owczary. The present **park** was shaped at the turn of the century when Roman Potocki commissioned the Viennese landscape gardener Franz Maxwald. It is generously sprinkled with sculptures, statues, decorative hedges and geometric flower beds. On the site of the former Arsenal, in the northwest part of the Park, Aigner built a colonnade that once half encircled a statue of Diana (now indoors). He also erected the **Romantic Castle** in the northeast corner, which Baumann graced with stuccoes. On the opposite side of the castle, across ul. 1 Maja, are the vast stables with a display of innumerable carriages. Potocki's Rolls-Royces, reportedly 'ordered three at a time' are no longer there.

From Łańcut it is a mere 17km drive to Rzeszów.

Rzeszów

■ Practical information

Hotel. ★★★ *Rzeszów*. Al. Cieplińskiego 2, ☎ 374-41. Car park, travel services. 291 rooms.

Tourist information (*PAPT*). Ul. Asnyka 6, ☎ 52-46-12.

ORBIS. Rynek 7, ☎ 371-29/343-66.

Main post office. Ul. Moniuszki 1.

Telephone code: (0–17).

History
In the 19C, Rzeszów (population 152,000) was a small, provincial town in Galicia, the poorest of all the regions of Austrian Poland. Indeed, it was never very prosperous, despite lying on the medieval trade route connecting Kraków to Ruthenia. Originally owned by the Ligęzas, later by the Lubomirskis, Rzeszów was dealt a severe blow by the Swedish Deluge of the mid-17C, from which it never really recovered. Today it is a large regional capital, but its parochial atmosphere has remained.

Old Town

On the main MARKET SQUARE is a **museum** (open Tues–Thur, Sun 09.00–14.00, Fri 09.00–17.00). This is the ethnographical branch of the Regional Museum, offering a large collection of folk costume and wooden religious sculpture. Close by stand a **Monument to Tadeusz Kościuszko** and a Neo-Gothic **town hall**, with the date 1847 inscribed on its gabled façade. The first town hall on this site was built before 1591 by the owner of Rzeszów, Mikołaj Spytko Ligęza, but major remodelling followed in the 19C, when the building received angle towers, a second storey, pointed-arch windows, a clock and stuccoes.

Walk west along ul. Kościuszki to the nearby PL. FARNY. The oldest part of the **parish church**—the star-vaulted chancel framed by buttresses and lit by pointed-arch windows—dates back to the first half of the 15C. The nave, aisles and belltower are later additions, heavily remodelled in 1754 in Baroque style. Most of the furnishings are Baroque and Rococo. In the chancel, note the Renaissance epitaphs of the Rzeszowski family from the turn of the 16C.

Return to the square and continue east, turning left into UL. BÓŻNICZA. At No. 4 is the late Renaissance **Old Synagogue** with an angular tower, now the Centre for Jewish History. Further down ul. Bóżnicza is the **New Synagogue**, built in the 17C–18C by Giovanni Battista Bellotti, and presently used as a gallery.

The ugly superstructure housing studios was added during post-war reconstruction, when the former steep roof was dismantled.

Follow ul. Słowackiego from the southwest corner of the Square to ul. Dekerta. On the left is a former summer residence of the Lubomirskis, a graceful house with a porch on the west side, gables and niches to the south and north, and a decorative portal in the east façade, now a Teacher Training College. It was built in the early 18C, probably by Tylman van Gameren, and expanded in 1750 in the Regency style. Further south is the **castle**, now law courts—a huge quadrangle surrounded by a wall. Only fragments of stone fortifications and the early Baroque gate tower (1620) have survived from the original castle built by Mikołaj Spytko Ligęza, expanded by the Lubomirskis, and pulled down in the early 20C.

At ul. 3 Maja No. 19 is the **Piarist Church and Monastery**. When the monks arrived in 1654, they decorated the refectory, cloisters and guest room with murals. After the dissolution of the Order in 1772, the Austrian authorities confiscated the building, converting it into offices and then a school. Since the war it has housed a **Regional Museum** (open Tues, Fri 10.00–17.00, Wed–Thur 10.00–15.00, Sun 09.00–14.00). The cloisters, guest room and refectory contain mostly paintings furniture and porcelain. Among the best exhibits are some good Polish 19C–20C paintings. The **Piarist Church** was rebuilt by Tylman van Gameren, who added two towers and the Chapel of St Joseph. Falconi executed the stuccoes, particularly fine on the vaults of the chancel, while Baldassare Fontana designed the high altar. The church is adjoined to the north by the former Piarist College (currently a secondary school), founded in 1658 and rebuilt by Tylman van Gameren in 1703–4.

Continue the walk along ul. 3 Maja, turning into ul. Sokoła for the **Bernardine Church**, founded by Mikołaj Spytko Ligęza as a family mausoleum and preserved almost intact in its original late Renaissance form. The alabaster **tomb statues** of the Ligęzas, probably by Sebastiano Sala, and the Renaissance high **altar** are the main attractions of the chancel. The south transept contains a late Gothic figure of the Madonna (15C–16C), believed to be capable of working miracles (examples of the miracles are shown on two large panel paintings).

Kraków to Częstochowa through the Jura

❖ Modlnica • Ojców • Pieskowa Skała • Ogrodzieniec • Kroczyce •
Mirów • Bobolice • Janów • Olsztyn • Częstochowa

To the north of Kraków stretches a picturesque limestone terrain known as the **Jura uplands**, studded with medieval castle ruins, caves and fancifully shaped rocks.

Leave Kraków along ul. Armii Krajowej. Turn right with the road, and at the roundabout keep straight ahead, following signs to Wrocław, then Olkusz (road 4). The first stop is in MODLNICA (8km). Its fine late Gothic wooden **parish church** (1553) has Renaissance murals, the late Renaissance Kucharski Chapel, and contemporary murals by Włodzimierz Tetmajer. Nearby is a Baroque-Classical **manor house** (1783–95) in an Italian formal garden and landscaped park (18C–19C), which contains the remains of a castle: 15C cellars, a yard, and a Renaissance loggia.

Turn left in BIAŁY KOŚCIÓŁ (5km), following a sign to 'Jaskinia Wierzchowska'. After 3.5km, the last stretch of which has to be walked, you will come to the **Wierzchowska Cave**, where 900m of tunnels and 11 caves can be visited in summer (**open** 09 Apr–30 Nov, 09.00–16.00, guides available).

The main attractions of the route are **Ojców National Park** and **Pieskowa Skała**. Despite what the map might suggest, do not turn right in Murownia, as the road is open only to buses further on. Instead, continue along road 4 to Jerzmanowice, turning right at the poorly-visible signpost to **OJCÓW** (500m after Jerzmanowice). The winding, hilly road will take you to Sąspów and into the Ojców National Park (16km). From Złota Góra, where you can see the **Chapel on the Water** (1901), either walk for about 2km, or hire a horse-driven *doroshka* to the **Kraków Gate** and the **Łokietek Cave**. The Prądnik valley offers an excellent example of the region's karst landscape, with rocks, caves and an exceptionally rich variety of flora.

Pieskowa Skała Castle

Turn left in Złota Góra and left again in Ojców, signposted 'Olkusz' (road 733) for Pieskowa Skała (6km). Soon, on the right, a tall limestone rock, aptly named 'The Club of Hercules' will come into view. Further on, up on the hill, is the Gothic and Renaissance *****Royal Castle**. The courtyard is **open** daily 07.00–20.00; the museum inside is **open** Tues–Sat 10.00–15.30, Sun 10.00–17.30 (to 15.30 off season). On display is a motley of objects from various epochs and European countries that Wawel could not accommodate (the museum is a branch of the Wawel collections—see p.211). More interesting than the exhibitions is the castle itself. Originally built by Kazimierz the Great in the 14C, it was expanded and remodelled several times afterwards, particularly in the 16C, when it received Mannerist arcades typical of the Italian style so dominant at that time in Kraków. Notice the Renaissance sgraffito and mascarons. A curiosity, especially popular with children (the castle seems to be a favourite destination for school excursions), is the well in the courtyard, drilled into solid rock and reaching the level of the Prądnik river, which flows by the foot of the hill. Inside the Castle is a café and restaurant.

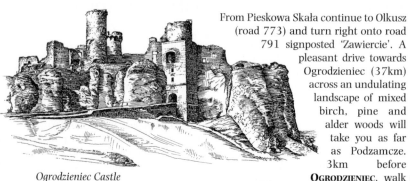

From Pieskowa Skała continue to Olkusz (road 773) and turn right onto road 791 signposted 'Zawiercie'. A pleasant drive towards Ogrodzieniec (37km) across an undulating landscape of mixed birch, pine and alder woods will take you as far as Podzamcze. 3km before OGRODZIENIEC, walk

Ogrodzieniec Castle

up Janowski Hill (504m) to the 13C *castle. Once a magnificent Renaissance residence, it fell into ruin after suffering damage during the Swedish Deluge (see p.49). Incorporated into the existing limestone rocks, it has a regular, three-winged form with a gate, towers, and the remnants of arcaded galleries around spacious forecourts. Reinforced concrete staircases allow you to climb the tallest tower for a glimpse of the Jura and a whiff of smoke from the Silesian mills and mines in the distance.

From Ogrodzieniec, join road 791, signposted 'Zawiercie', turning right onto the 78. In Kroczyce (16km) turn left, signposted 'Żarki' (road 792). Hotel *Ostaniec* and Mt. Zborów (462m) will appear on the right after about 2.5km. The **Kroczyce Rocks** and the **Zborów Mountain Nature Reserve** form one of the most beautiful parts of the Jura, abundant in rocks of fantastic shapes and scenic views. The hotel is a good base for walking excursions.

Continue straight along the tree-lined road to Kotowice. Turn right at the junction and drive for 3km to the **castle** ruins in MIRÓW. Built in the mid-15C, the castle began to decline after the Swedes destroyed it in 1657. From the hill, another castle is visible in the distance, less than 2km away. To get there, take the dirt road to **BOBOLICE**. The ruins here are smaller and more remote, the setting idyllic. Continue along the asphalt road to Niegowa, Żarki (road 789) and Janów (road 793), passing through the Wiercica valley—a 153ha landscape reserve with forests, caves, springs, wild flowers, and the remnants of a prehistoric settlement. Continue Road 76 brings you to the vast ruins of the Gothic **Royal Castle** in OLSZTYN. This irregular stone structure was erected in the mid-14C by Kazimierz the Great, who allegedly ordered the Palatine of Poznań, Maćko Borkowic, to be starved to death in its tower.

Continue to Częstochowa along road 76 (10km).

Częstochowa

Częstochowa (population 250,000) lies at the northern extreme of the Jura uplands, which reach south as far as Kraków. Itself rather bland, with the feel of a provincial town aspiring to be something it is not, its **Paulite Monastery** on Jasna Góra is one of Europe's great Catholic pilgrimage spots, and certainly the greatest in Poland. For Częstochowa is the home of the famous *Black Madonna* (see below). The work was described by the medieval historian Jan Długosz as: '.... a picture of Mary .... which has been executed with a strange and extraordinary skill, with a serene expression on her face from whatever direction you look at it'. Throngs of pilgrims can be a mixed blessing, and if you plan to visit Jasna Góra for its architectural, as opposed to religious, interest, try to avoid arriving on a weekend, as the shrine may turn out to be inaccessible due to crowds of worshippers. Especially during the season, the Paulite Order competes with the municipal authorities in broadcasting music, singing and preaching over loud-speakers strategically placed along the main boulevard (al. Najświętszej Marii Panny).

■ **Practical information**
Hotels
★★★ *Patria*. Ul. Ks. J. Popiełuszki 2, ☎ 24-70-01. The best hotel in town. Car park. 102 rooms.

★★ *Vegas*. Ul. Św. Rocha 224, ☎ 620-530/620-515. Car park. 33 rooms.

Tourist information (PAPT). Al. Najświętszej Marii Panny 65, ☎ 24-13-60.
ORBIS. Al. Najświętszej Marii Panny 40/42, ☎ 24-11-83/24-20-56.
Post office. Ul. Orzechowskiego 7.
Telephone code: (0–34).

History
The **Paulite Order**, founded in Hungary by Canon Eusebius of Gran (Esztergom), was given the rule of St Augustine in 1308, but preserved its orginal eremitic character. The Order is characterised by seclusion, asceticism, and severe discipline with periods of hard labour, meditation and prayer. Władysław, Duke of Opole and Palatine of Ruthenia, brought the Paulites to Jasna Góra during the reign of Louis of Anjou. The founding document, affixed with a seal representing a horse and dated 9 August 1382, is still preserved in the monastery archives.

Jasna Góra Monastery
The first church on Jasna Góra was made of wood. It was replaced in the 15C with a late Gothic hall, which in turn gave way to the present **Basilica of the Holy Cross** in 1690, after a major fire. From that period dates its rich Baroque decoration, notably the stuccoes and medallions painted by Karl Dankwart of Nysa. At that time, too, the slender west tower was raised to its present height. The only chapel spared by the flames is the beautifully vaulted, black marble **Sepulchral Chapel of the Denhoff family** (1645–71), modelled on Wawel's Zygmunt Chapel in Kraków, but decorated in Baroque style.

*The Chapel of Our Lady** (**open** daily 06.00–12.00, 16.40–17.30, 19.00–19.30), originally the size of its present chancel, was erected in the mid-15C. Two aisles and an elaborate brass rood screen extended the shrine in 1641–44. The interior was embellished with late Renaissance decorations, replaced in 1689 with Baroque stucco patterns, which spill beyond the chancel, covering the Gothic ribs and original frescoes. The retable is made of ebony and ornamented with silver.

Early in the 20C, the courtyard and cloisters in front of the chapel were converted into a narthex. The altar at the end of the south aisle contains a late Gothic wooden crucifix (early 16C), inspired by the work of Veit Stoss.

The 17C ebony-inlaid high altar (possibly designed by Giovanni Battista Ghisleni) contains the most valued object of all, the *Black Madonna*, which has become not only a Catholic idol, but also a symbol of national resistance and independence, popularly called the 'Queen of Poland'.

From the Chapel of Our Lady proceed to the **treasury** (**open** daily 09.00–12.00, 15.00–17.00) along the walkway above the arcaded southeast cloister built in 1920 in a blend of Rococo and Art Nouveau styles. The treasury contains a stunning display of amber, ivory, gold, coral and turquoise jewellery, tapestries, monstrances and chalices, ornamental clocks, pocket watches, porcelain figures of the Apostles, silverware, silver platters, reliquaries, embroidery, candleholders and liturgical vestments. The most valued items are a Baroque, jewel-encrusted monstrance made by the Warsaw goldsmith Wacław Grottkau in

The Black Madonna

It is impossible to date the *Black Madonna* precisely, as it was painted virtually anew in 1434. Judging by the iconography, however (assuming the restorers were faithful to the original), it is a Byzantine icon modelled on one which, from the 5C, was worshipped in a church in Constantinople's *ton hedgeon* quarter. This type of Madonna, with the infant Christ on her left arm, the latter holding, in older images, a scroll or a book, was known as *Hodgetria*. The Constantinople original was destroyed by the Turks in 1453, but many versions and copies have been preserved, of which the most famous are the *Salus Populi Romani* from the Capella Paolina in the Roman basilica of Santa Maria Maggiore, and this *Black Madonna*. The picture was probably brought to Jasna Góra on 31 August 1384 by Władysław, Duke of Opole.

In 1430, a gang of robbers, allegedly connected with the Hussite movement, raided the Paulite monastery on Easter Day. They stripped the *Black Madonna* of its precious jewel-encrusted robe, slashed the image with a sword and broke the wooden panel. The panel—believed to have been made from cyprus planks from the table of the Holy Family in Nazareth—was mended several years later, and covered with a piece of canvas, on which the Madonna and Child was copied from the damaged original, but now in a style characteristic of early 15C European art. As both monks and pilgrims had become accustomed to the slashes on the Madonna's face, these were also reproduced. The painting acquired a kind of symbolic meaning, expressing the union of Eastern and Western traditions, so characteristic of Poland. The picture was restored several times thereafter.

From the 17C, it became customary to cover it with gaudy robes woven of silver, gold and precious stones. Also, since c 1431, the aureoles around the heads of the Madonna and Child have been covered with diadems of repoussé gilded silver, and since the late 15C, engraved silver plates depicting scenes from the life of Jesus and Mary and a figure of St Barbara have served as a backdrop for the picture. Recently, however, the icon has usually been displayed without its robes, of which the most precious are the Ruby Robe and the Diamond Robe. The latter, with its cloisonné ornaments, studded with diamonds, emeralds, pearls and rubies is a veritable history of European jewellery from the High Renaissance to Art Nouveau.

1672, a late Gothic crucifix from Nürnberg (1510), a silver votive plaque with an engraved knight (before 1650), and a Mannerist ebony-and-silver altarpiece from Dresden (c 1600).

In c 1620, the monastery buildings were encircled with Dutch fortifications, enabling the monks to withstand the Swedish siege of 1655, described by Henryk Sienkiewicz with gripping narrative flair in the second volume of his *Trilogy* (see p. 84). General Burchard Müller commanded the Swedish mercenary forces, while the Prior, Augustyn Kordecki, led the defence. More fortifications were added after the Swedish Deluge (see p. 49), including the **Lubomirski Gate** (1767) in front of which is a stone mosaic representing the coat of arms of the Paulite Order. Fortifications were pulled down by order of Czar Aleksander I, who also dissolved all the branches of the Paulite Order except the one at Jasna Góra.

The 17C early Baroque **monastic building**, remodelled in the 18C, is a fine example of a Polish residence on a par with the palaces in Ujazdów (Warsaw), Kielce and Nieborów. In its south wing is the spacious, tunnel-vaulted **Knights' Hall** (1647), with a display of late 17C historical paintings. A well-marked display of armour and weaponry can be seen in the 17C **Arsenal** (open daily 09.00–12.00, 15.00–17.00). The **Library**, usually inaccessible to tourists, is decorated with a plafond representing the Fathers of the Church and an allegorical image of Divine Wisdom. The **Refectory** (mid-17C) contains murals by Karl Dankwart.

The city centre

The town of Częstochowa is centred on the 1.5km long AL. NAJŚWIĘTSZEJ MARII PANNY, a tree-lined boulevard built in 1818, connecting Jasna Góra at its west end with pl. Daszyńskiego in the east. From Jasna Góra, walk east down al. Najświętszej Marii Panny, passing a monument to H. Sienkiewicz, to the Neo-Byzantine **Church of St James** (1870), initially Orthodox, built on the ruins of a former Roman Catholic church. Opposite, on pl. Biegańskiego, in the former town hall building of 1828, is a small **Regional Museum** (open Wed–Sun 11.00–18.00). Continuing downhill, across the railway lines, you will come to pl. Daszyńskiego on which stands the Baroque **Church of St Zygmunt** (1625–43) with a pseudo-Baroque tower and façade (1783). Going 200m south along UL. KRAKOWSKA you will reach one the largest churches in Poland, the **Cathedral Church of the Holy Family** (1901), 100m long, with aisles 10m wide. Behind pl. Daszyńskiego to the north are the remains of the Old Town, largely destroyed by the Nazis in 1943. The city, darkened by the noxious fumes of the Częstochowa Steel Mill, seems in parts like an industrial wasteland, a good example being ul. Orzechowskiego, where the main post office stands alone on a stretch of barren land strewn with rubbish.

Kraków to Kielce via Jędrzejów

❖ Jędrzejów • Mnichów • Tokarnia • Chęciny • Jaskinia Raj • Kielce

The Clock Museum at Jędrzejów

Leave Kraków on the busy road 7. **JĘDRZEJÓW** (80km) (population 17,500) is chiefly known for its **Clock Museum** (open Tues–Sun 08.00–16.00; guided tours only, on the hour), located on the main square (PL. KOŚCIUSZKI 7–8). The museum has over 500 exhibits spanning the 16C–20C: clocks, old astronomical instruments, and the third largest collection of sundials in the world after Oxford and Chicago. The museum was the brainchild of Feliks Przypkowski (1872–1951), an expert on astronomy and gnomonics, who opened his vast collection for public display in 1909. Among the prize exhibits are two special devices designed for two Polish monarchs: Stanisław Leszczyński's sundial with a gun that fires at noon, and Jan Kazimierz's pendulum clock made in Paris in 1645. There are also clocks and sundials designed by the Przypkowskis themselves. The exhibition rooms contain period furniture and memorabilia. A pavilion at the back has temporary displays and a sgraffito sundial, designed by Tadeusz Przypkowski (1905–77), on its outer wall.

Leaving the square, follow ul. 11 Listopada northwest for 2km to the *Cistercian Abbey, set in a Renaissance garden divided into plots.

> The first Cistercians arrived from Morimond in Burgundy in 1140. Their abbey, consecrated in 1210, was accordingly called 'Mały Morymond' (little Morimond). Like its sister churches in Koprzywnica (see p. 276), Wąchock (see p. 287) and Sulejów (see p. 167), all founded in 1176–86, the abbey still conforms to its original late Romanesque plan: a nave of four bays, transepts with pairs of chapels, and a short chancel. Partially rebuilt in the 15C, it was then expanded in late Baroque style (1728–54), receiving a curious new east façade, an apse, and a fine exterior for the north transept flanked by two symmetrical domed chapels. The adjoining monastery burnt down in 1800 along with its valuable library, and then fell into complete ruin after the dissolution of the Order in 1817. The Reformed Franciscans inhabited the abbey thereafter, but they too were expelled in 1870 for aiding the Polish Insurrection of 1863. The building was dismantled in 1913, leaving only the sacristy, blank arcades and the corbels of the cloister vaults still visible on the external south wall of the church.

The barrel-vaulted nave is overlaid with fading Baroque painted decoration of 1739, depicting the life of Wincenty Kadłubek, a medieval chronicler who spent the last years of his life (1218–23) in the abbey writing the fourth volume of his *magnum opus* (see p. 80). The chapel flanking the north transept to the east is dedicated to him and contains a reliquary at the altar surrounded by figures of angels. The furnishings are late Baroque: altars and sculptures from c 1730, stalls with painted vistas of other Cistercian abbeys (1731), and a fine 54-voice organ (1745). A Gothic tomb slab of 1319, with an engraved figure of a knight, can be viewed in the south chapel. Close to the church stands an 18C Baroque belfry.

On the right of the main road at MNICHÓW (8km) is a wooden **parish church** (Baroque, c 1770), with a transept, dome and free-standing wooden bell tower (Baroque, 1768). TOKARNIA, 9km further on, has a **skansen** (**open** Apr–Oct, Mon–Sun 10.00–17.00, Nov–Mar, Mon–Sun 10.00–14.30), one of the largest in Poland (65ha). The mainly 19C exhibits include 12 traditional farmsteads, a barn, well, chicken-house, windmill, pharmacy, and a manor house with period furniture.

Chęciny

Situated at the foot of a wooded hill, Chęciny (7km; population 4200) is an attractive town with quaint cobbled streets and a preserved medieval urban plan. Scattered around it are 15 houses dating from the 16C–19C. Chęciny was once an important centre of lead and copper ore mining, and there are still a few functioning quarries in the vicinity.

Steps lead up the hill from the Market Square to the **parish church**, an aisled hall in the late Gothic tradition (c 1600), with a Mannerist sepulchral chapel (1614) abutting the south aisle. Follow the yellow trail up the hill for the quickest way to the ruins of **Chęciny Castle**.

Built in c 1300, initially as an episcopal seat, the castle was located roughly at the geographical centre of the Piast realm. In the 14C, it was considered an impregnable fortress, and accordingly the place where the crown jewels were kept. Władysław Łokietek assembled the Polish nobility here in 1331 before the march on Płowce to do battle with the Teutonic Knights. Indeed, after the victory at Grunwald (see p. 417), the captured Knights were imprisoned in the castle. Repeatedly rebuilt until destroyed by the Swedes in the mid-17C, it fell into ruin after 1795.

You enter the lower castle through the 15C gate-tower. The crumbling walls follow the steep ridge to the upper castle with its two round towers, one of which guarded the bridge over the moat; the other was a refuge of last resort during times of siege (the only entrance was a second-floor window). From the ruins there is a breathtaking view over the Świętokrzyskie mountains.

Jaskinia Raj ~ *Paradise Cave*

From Chęciny join the dual-carriageway (762) towards Kielce and watch out for signs marked 'Jaskinia Raj' (6km). Just before crossing the Bobrzyczka river, turn left off the main road for about 1km to the car park. Discovered accidentally in 1964 by a local farmer, the cave is actually a series of limestone corridors, 240m in length, of which 150m are accessible to visitors. Fantastic geological forms, **stalagmites and stalactites**, are the chief attraction of the tour, which lasts about forty minutes. Flint implements discovered inside the cave suggest that it was inhabited by Neanderthal Man, some 50,000 years ago.

The cave is **open** Apr–Nov 09.00–17.00, but due to its huge popularity, visitors often have to wait hours to enter (guided group tours only). To avoid this, you can reserve tickets: ☎ (0-41) 66-74-18. Some of the finds from the cave are on display in the exhibition room.

Stay on the dual carriageway for Kielce, 17km further on.

Kielce

Situated in a valley, Kielce (population 208,100) is an ideal base for trips into the **Świętokrzyski (Holy Cross) National Park**, with its hill-top monasteries, pagan sanctuaries, and ancient smelting furnaces. The city itself is dreary and uninspiring, and were it not for the **Bishops' Palace**, could be safely avoided. Regional rivalries with Kraków to the south, and especially Radom to the north remain strong. For many inhabitants of larger, and perhaps more illustrious Polish cities, Kielce is the classic provincial backwater. Certainly, in the 1930s, the painter and writer Stanisław Ignacy Witkiewicz (see p. 86) spared none of his acerbic wit in tarnishing Kielce's reputation. In a letter to his friend, the celebrated British anthropologist of Polish extraction Bronisław Malinowski, Witkiewicz described the city as 'a symbol of revulsion, the zenith of provincial ugliness'.

■ Practical information
Hotels
★★★ *Bristol*. Ul. H. Sienkiewicza 21, ☎ 368-2460/368-2466. Central location. Car park. 28 rooms
★★ *Stella*. Ul. Krakowska 374, Kielce-Słowik, ☎ 346-5164. Just off the

Kraków-Kielce road. Car park. 27 rooms. **Convenient walking trail to the Paradise Cave**.

Tourist information (*PTTK*). Ul. Zamkowa 3, ☎ 344-5914.
ORBIS. Ul. Sienkiewicza 26, ☎ 368-0562.
Main post office. Pl. Niepodległości.
Telephone code: (0–41).

History

Already by the early 12C, Kielce was the property of the bishops of Kraków, the administrative capital of their vast domain, of which the sumptuous Bishops' Palace would become a lasting reminder. In the 16C, large deposits of copper, lead and iron ore were discovered in the vicinity, and the city soon became a key centre of the Polish armaments industry. In the early 19C, the reformer Stanisław Staszic (see p. 82) established an Academy of Mining here, the first such institution in the country. The ruins of industrial workshops, ironworks and armaments factories from the early 19C, a fine example of building from the Staszic period, can be visited in Samsonów, 12km north of Kielce.

In the political history of Poland, Kielce did not play any role that would be worth mentioning, except for one shameful event that took place on 4 July 1946: in an anti-Semitic frenzy, a mob murdered 40 Jews, making Kielce the site of the last pogrom in Europe.

The Market Square (PL. PARTYZANTÓW) in Kielce is a modest affair, with a few 18C houses (Nos 12 and 18) and a **Regional Museum** at Nos 3–5 (**open** Tues, Thur–Sun 09.00–16.00), focusing on natural history and folk art. From the square, head south along UL. MAŁA until you reach a courtyard enclosed by the **Cathedral** and the ****Bishops' Palace**.

The palace, founded by the Bishop of Kraków, Jakub Zadzik, was probably designed by the Italian, **Giovanni Trevano**. The main block was completed in 1641, a year before Zadzik's death. The palace was built on two storeys: the ground floor was used by the courtiers and servants and as storage space; the upper floor housed the bishop's apartments, a dining hall, chapel, and rooms for the lay lords and higher clergy. In 1720–46, **Kacper Bażanka** erected the Baroque one-storey gallery wings, thus enclosing the courtyard from three sides.

Unlike so many stately residences in Poland, the palace escaped destruction by the Swedes, and was hardly altered, despite being used by the Russian (19C) and then Polish provincial administrations (until 1971). Because it has survived virtually intact since the 17C, it is rightly seen as one of the most authentic and valuable pieces of architecture from the Vasa period. The central block, though, is still semi-Mannerist in effect: the front (east) towers are half-detached, connected to the main block by screen walls; the central part has an entrance 'loggia' of three arches. Likewise, inside, different architectural styles coexist. The interiors are lavishly decorated with sgraffito friezes, stuccowork, marble and stone portals, beamed ceilings, and rich painting. In the senatorial chambers, the ceilings have excellent plafonds from the workshop of Tommaso

Dolabella (c 1641), depicting scenes inspired by Bishop Zadzik's political concerns: *The Trial of the Aryans in 1638* (whom he detested for refusing to acknowledge the Holy Trinity), *The Reception of Swedish Envoys by King Władysław IV at Kwidzyn in 1635*, and *The Fire in the Troicka Suburb in Moscow in 1611*.

Inside the palace is a **museum** (**open** Wed–Sun 09.00–16.00), with four permanent exhibitions. The tour begins on the **upper floor** with historic interiors of the 17C–18C. The exhibits include furniture, tapestries, carpets and silk hangings, Delft faience, Meissen porcelain, silver- and gold-work, as well as portraiture, including two impressive friezes of Cracovian bishops (17C–19C) in the dining hall.

   Ground floor. This houses the **Gallery of Polish Painting**, with about 140 works spanning the 17–20C. These include Sarmatian portraits, landscape painting—mainly 19C Romantic realism, but also some modernist landscapes—portraiture from the Young Poland period, and French-inspired art from the 1920s and 30s, notably a few works by Olga Bozańska. There is also a section devoted to European and oriental armoury and weaponry (16C–19C), and four rooms known as the Sanctuary of Marshal Józef Piłsudski (see p. 52).

Facing the Bishops' Palace is the **cathedral**, an aisled basilica adapted in 1632–35 from a Romanesque temple of 1171. Despite numerous later alterations, the early Baroque appearance has been preserved. Inside, the cross-vaulted nave is covered with dark painted decoration (1898), executed by students of Jan Matejko. The furnishings are Baroque (1726–65). A fine Renaissance red marble effigy of Elżbieta Zebrzydowska (1553, Gian-Maria Padovano) stands at the east end of the south aisle. In the north aisle, the Jesus Chapel (east) has a 16C crucifix set against a background of Jerusalem. Close by is a Gothic triptych (1500), with St Mary in the centrepiece and the patrons of Poland, SS Adalbert and Stanisław, in the wings.

To the south and west of the Bishops' Palace extends the city park with a Romantic **palace** of 1846–58 (ul. Zamkowa 5), formerly owned by the patron of arts T. Zieliński, with two pavilions and a tower, as well as **monuments** to the Enlightenment reformer Stanisław Staszic and the writer Stefan Żeromski (see p. 82).

Oblęgorek

This is a short excursion from Kielce which can be easily done in a couple of hours. Drive northwest from Kielce along road 74, turning left onto the 748, and right along a minor road to **OBLĘGOREK** (13km). Set in a picturesque landscaped park (2ha) is an eclectic **manor house** (1880) given to the Positivist writer and Nobel prize-winner Henryk Sienkiewicz (see p. 84) in 1900 as a reward for 25 years of literary work. It is now the **Henryk Sienkiewicz Museum** (open Wed–Sun 09.00–16.00). The writer lived here from 1902 to 1914, during which time he won the Nobel Prize for Literature. The interiors contain period furniture, memorabilia, and a biographical exhibition.

Kielce to Sandomierz

❖ Św. Katarzyna • Bodzentyn • Nowa Słupia • Św. Krzyż • Opatów • Ujazd
(detour: Szydłów) • Koprzywnica • Sandomierz

The **Świętokrzyskie (Holy Cross) Mountains**, forming part of the Małopolska uplands, are among the oldest mountain chains in Europe, once high and mighty, but now eroded (Mt. Łysica, the highest peak, is only 612m). **ŁYSOGÓRY**, 22km from Kielce, is their most beautiful part, with Mt. Łysica and the Bernardine convent in Św. Katarzyna at its west end, and Łysa Góra (Bare Mountain) with its Benedictine abbey of the Holy Cross in the east. There is a well-marked and easy hiking trail between these two peaks (15km) through the Świętokrzyskie National Park (6037ha), encompassing the remnants of a virgin silver fir forest, with beautiful views and scenery. A peculiarity of the main peaks is the treeless plains of quartzite sandstone blocks caused by rock erosion during the Ice Age. The discovery of Roman coins and pagan sanctuaries on three of the peaks suggests early settlement in the area. Indeed, from the 1C–11C, it was one of the largest centres of iron smelting in Europe; in 1955–61, many ore mines and smelting furnaces ('*dymarki*') were unearthed. Demonstrations of ancient iron smelting techniques can be seen at the festival in Nowa Słupia each September.

Apart from the Holy Cross Mountains, which are best seen on foot, the highlights of this trip are Krzyżtopór Castle and the medieval town of Szydłów. Leave Kielce on road 74, turning left at Górno onto the 752 (unmarked) for **ŚWIĘTA KATARZYNA** (27km). Parking is available at the PTTK hostel (left). Across the road, a short distance into the woods, stands the small **Bernardine Convent** (1471) with a tiny cloister (1633) around a courtyard. The cloister is the oldest part of the group; both the convent and the adjoining church were thoroughly rebuilt after a fire in 1847. Close to the convent, at the edge of the forest, are two **chapels** (18C and 19C). The writer Stefan Żeromski (see p. 85) left his signature on the south wall of the wooden chapel after an excursion to Łysica in 1882. Follow the red trail up the hill to the **Spring and Chapel of St Francis**. God-fearing locals claim the waters are a cure for conjunctivitis (St Francis is the patron saint of sight). The red trail continues to the treeless summit of **ŁYSICA** (1 hr 15 min)—according to local legend the site of a witches' coven—with beautiful views.

BODZENTYN, 6km along the 752, is a pleasant village with narrow winding streets on a steep ridge among hills. Park on the lower Market Square and walk along **UL. LANGIEWICZA** to the 15C Gothic **Parish Church**. In the vestibule, the foundation tablet (1452) shows a scene in relief of Cardinal Oleśnicki offering a model of the church to the Virgin. The immense **high altar** was executed in Kraków in 1545 by Italian sculptors working on the Zygmunt Chapel (see p. 216), and brought to Bodzentyn in 1728. When viewed from beneath the choir, the central Crucifixion scene is almost three-dimensional in effect (particularly the horse and the hands of Jesus). This is why—according to one, possibly spurious account—the altar was removed from Wawel Cathedral: the parishioners there found the protruding horse's rump too off-putting during mass. Visible from the church, further west, are the ruins of a 14C **castle**, later rebuilt as a Renaissance residence.

Twelve kilometres from Bodzentyn, heading southeast along the 751 is the town of **NOWA SŁUPIA**. Turn right at the market square and drive past the **parish church** (1678) to the car park at the end of ul. Świętokrzyska. Backtrack for about 100m to get to the **Museum of Ancient Metallurgy** (open Tues–Sun 09.00–16.00), with an exposition of primitive smelting techniques, and finds of old metalware and tools from the surrounding area. The September festival takes place close by.

Benedictine Abbey of Św. Krzyż

From the museum car park, the 'King's Way' (blue trail) leads up the hill for 2km to the **Benedictine Abbey of Św. Krzyż.

> By the 9C, the summit of Łysa Góra (595m) was already the centre for a pagan cult, as shown by the 5m high stone rampart which encircles the hill. The 15C historian Jan Długosz suggests that the abbey was founded in 1006, though the *Wielkopolska Chronicle* gives the more likely date of 1103. Certainly, by the Middle Ages the abbey was a vibrant centre of religious and cultural life. It guarded the relics of the Tree of the Holy Cross, and one of the earliest Polish texts—*The Świętokrzyskie Sermons*—was discovered in its library (see p. 80).
>
> Dissolved in 1818, the abbey served as a Czarist prison after 1884, and later, during the Second World War, as an extermination camp for Soviet prisoners-of-war.

The **church** façade is late Baroque (1781–89) on Romanesque and Gothic foundations. The interior is substantially Neo-classical (c 1800): a long white nave lined with large 18C canvasses by Franciszek Smuglewicz, and a high altar consisting of a pediment and two Corinthian columns framing a painting of the *Holy Trinity*. From the north aisle you may enter the **sacristy**, with 18C wainscoting on the walls, and murals with symbolic scenes from the *Life of St Benedict* on the barrel vault. Through the marble portal, enter the early **Baroque Chapel** of the Oleśnickis (1614–20), with 17C murals on the cupola and 18C scenes on the walls telling the story of the *Tree of the Holy Cross*. The famous relics are contained within a modern tabernacle which stands at the altar. To the right of it is the red marble tomb of the Oleśnickis. In the crypt below the chapel are open coffins containing the mummified remains of J. Wiśniowiecki, an insurgent of 1863, and a monk, the last of which carries the morbid inscription: 'What you are I once was; what I am you for sure will become!' The sacristy and chapel are **open** 09.00–12.00 and 13.00–17.00.

The **monastery**, abutting the church from the north, has two Baroque wings (c 1643) and Gothic cloisters (entrance by the east front of the church) enclosing a cloister garth. From here you may enter the **Missionary Museum** (**open** Mon–Sat 9.00–17.00, Sun 12.00–17.00), with a four-room display of exotic ethnographical collections brought back by the monks from their various missions around the world.

Inside the monastery's Baroque wing is the **Natural History Museum of the Świętokrzyski National Park** (open Tues–Sun 10.00–16.00), covering the geology, archaeology, flora and fauna of the park. The entrance faces the TV mast.

Opatów

You could return to Nowa Słupia and pick up road 751 to Ostrowiec Świętokrzyski (28km), a town lacking in tourist attractions, but a convenient stopping place with its good Hotel Łysica on al. 3 Maja 13, ☎ 653-181/87. Alternatively, head south on road 756 and then east on the 74 to Opatów (17km).

The castle-like **Collegiate Church of St Martin** was built before 1150, and has retained much of its Romanesque character despite major alterations in the 15C and 18C. The Romanesque elements include an arcaded frieze on the chancel wall, west and north portals, and double windows in the segmented south tower. The nave, separated from the aisles by tall slender arcades, has a late Gothic vault with an odd rib design. All the other vaults are 18C, as is the painted decoration which covers them. In the chancel, scenes depict the battles of Psie Pole (1109) and Grunwald (1410). The highlight is the **north transept**, which contains fine **Renaissance tombs** of the Szydłowiecki family, notably a large bronze effigy (1536, Giovanni Cini) of Krzysztof Szydłowiecki, the Royal Chancellor, who purchased Opatów in 1514 and presided over its best years. It is decorated with a relief known as the *Opatów Lament*—41 figures around a large table mourning the Chancellor's death. Around it are brass and red marble figures of his three children: Anna, Ludwik and Zygmunt. On the wall above, a scene depicts the *Siege of Vienna* (1683).

Krzyżtopór Castle ~ Ujazd

To reach the castle, join road 757 to Iwaniska, turning left onto the 758 for **Ujazd** (16km). Once you enter the village, follow signs marked 'Krzyżtopór'. The ruins will come into view on the left.

There are surely few castles in Poland as immense or ambitious as that begun in 1627 by the Palatine Krzysztof Ossoliński in the unassuming hamlet of Ujazd. The vast *Krzyżtopór Castle took nearly two decades to complete, but its glory was disastrously short lived. Within 11 years, Charles Gustav's marauding Swedish army had razed it to the ground and—despite a brief revival—by 1770 it had fallen into terminal decline. Today, a restoration programme is under way to save the ruins from further disintegration, but given the vast sums of money involved, full reconstruction is unlikely in the foreseeable future.

Ossoliński commissioned the Italian architect, Lorenzo Senes, to execute his grand project. The front entrance consisted of a gate tower backing onto a forecourt flanked by low wings. A narrow passageway led through the main block, four storeys high, to a small inner courtyard surrounded by a horseshoe of vaulted galleries. Behind it, a long dining hall—its glass ceiling serving as the bottom of a huge aquarium—extended out towards a tall octagonal tower overlooking a marshy lake at the back. The entire complex was encircled by a pentagonal bastion fortress, 60m across, of which the gate tower was the only point of entry. The cellars were used as stables for 370 thoroughbred stallions. In places, stone detailing has been preserved on the ruined buildings: circles and quatrefoils in low relief, pilasters and panels, a battle-axe and cross over the entrance gate, and inscriptions in old Polish, including one indicating the date of completion—1644.

From Ujazd, you could make a detour of about 78km southwest (roads 757 and 765) to Szydłów, one of the most beautiful medieval towns in central Poland, situated on a hill and enclosed by long sections of 14C stone fortifications. As you enter, stop at the convenient car park facing the arched east gate. Just beyond the gate stands the **parish church**. Its Gothic bell-tower is actually part of the medieval **town walls**, 1.8m thick, with battlements and shooting galleries. The church's modest double-naved interior has a palm vault carried on two pillars, and a short chancel with a 16C triptych for an altar. Walk straight on to the peaceful Market Square. North along ul. Targowa is a late Gothic stone **synagogue**, with Mannerist decoration inside, and an annexe with a wooden roof and balcony to the left. To the west of the Market Square, you enter a large courtyard enclosed by a battlemented wall. The buildings you see here constitute the remnants of a Gothic **castle** built by Kazimierz the Great in the second half of the 14C. To the left stands the main building—the Knights' Hall—which was already in ruins by 1789. To the right is the 'Little Treasury', converted from the castle tower in 1528, now a **Regional Museum** (open Tues, Thur–Sat 09.00–15.00, Sun 10.00–14.00). The stone gatehouse through which you enter the courtyard was last remodelled in 1723. All the buildings have been restored since the war.

The road which exits south off the Market Square leads to the 14C **Kraków Gate**, a Gothic structure with 16C accretions, notably the attic and foregate, the latter giving it the appearance of a giant chair.

To continue the trip, head southeast on road 758 (or roads 765 and 777 from Szydłów) to **KOPRZYWNICA**. Some 700m west of the Market Square stands a **Cistercian Abbey** founded in 1185 by Kazimierz the Just. The church, a stone basilica with a transept, was begun as early as 1207. In c 1507, brick gables were added, and in c 1697, a sacristy and library (currently the chapel) extended the south transept. The Romanesque four-bay corpus, long and light, is deceptively masked by a late Baroque plastered front (1770–90) with a tower on the roof. Late Renaissance murals are barely visible on the walls of the nave and transept, but a clearer scene of the *The Last Judgement* (c 1400) adorns the south wall of the chancel. The oldest mural (mid-13C), by the westernmost pier in the south aisle, shows Mary as the Mother of Mercy, and the death of a monk observed by the Devil and an angel. Of the furnishings, most impressive is the early Baroque high altar, which has a large painting of the *Ascension* by Bartholomäus Strobel (1645), the court artist of the Vasas, and Gothic murals either side. Abutting the north transept is the only surviving wing of the **monastery** (east). Make straight for the late Romanesque chapter house, a rectangular hall with beautiful Gothic ribbed vaults carried on two short columns

Join road 777 northeast to Sandomierz.

Sandomierz

■ **Practical information**

Hotel. ★★ *Zajazd Pod Ciżemką.* Rynek 27, ☎ 32-36-68. Quiet central location overlooking the Main Square.

Tourist information (**PTTK**). Rynek 25, ☎ 32-23-05/32-37-21.

ORBIS. Rynek 24, ☎ 32-30-40.

Main Post office. Ul. Bulińskiego/Mariacka.

Telephone code: (0–15).

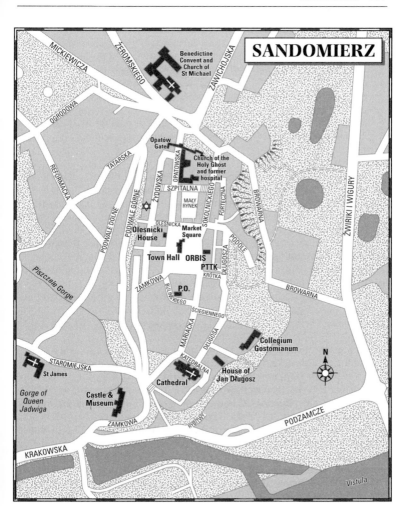

History

Sandomierz, one of the oldest towns in Małopolska, is named after Sudomir, a tribal chieftain who probably built a stronghold here as early as the 8C. During the reign of Kazimierz the Great, Sandomierz acquired the urban plan that survives to this day, a castle, a Gothic cathedral and fortifications. The prosperity of the 15C–16C was underpinned by new commercial links with the eastern provinces and the lucrative river trade in timber and grain. A port was constructed on the Vistula, encompassing numerous riverside granaries. Merchants dug warehouses and cellars into the soft loess soil beneath the town.

Gradual decline set in with the Swedish Deluge (see p. 49) of the mid-17C. Annexed to Austria under the Third Partition (1795), Sandomierz was later incorporated into the Grand Duchy of Warsaw. Many of the buildings fell in 1857 when the tunnels and warehouses underneath the town began to cave in. By the 1960s the rate of subsidence had become so critical that the old town was in danger of sliding down the hill altogether. A major engineering project was launched, with conservators bolstering the Vistula scarp with steel and concrete, and securing the underground tunnels, a fragment of which was later opened to the public (see below).

Sandomierz Old Town

All the principal attractions of Sandomierz are located within, or just outside the perimeter of the Old Town, which overlooks the Vistula from a hill. It is best to enter through the medieval **Opatów Gate** (north)—the only survivor of four gates—built in c 1350, with a later Renaissance superstructure. Climb to the top (**open** 10.00–17.30) for a fine view over the city, the river and the Pieprzowe (Pepper) Hills in the distance. The Opatów Gate faces the former **Benedictine Convent** (ul. Żeromskiego), a Catholic Seminary since 1903. The convent buildings (founded 1613) are of scant interest, but the adjoining Baroque **Church of St Michael** (1686–92), with its skyline of three volute gables surmounted by figures, is well worth a visit. The entrance is preceded by a courtyard with an unusual outdoor pulpit (c 1770). Another pulpit (1694–95) with sculptural decoration can be seen inside. Of the foreign art, a 17C Italian *Visitation* stands out.

Walking south, you can skirt a preserved fragment of the medieval fortifications along ul. Żydowska. The brick walls, originally 8m tall and 2m thick, with turrets every 30–50m, were badly damaged in the mid-17C by the Swedes, and later dismantled. Further along the street is a Baroque **synagogue** (1758), reconstructed after the war to house regional archives. Turning left into ul. Oleśnickich, you could stop at the 18C Oleśnicki House (Rynek No. 10), where begins the disappointing **Underground Tourist Route** (10.00–17.00), opened in 1977 after lengthy conservation work. The tunnels and cellars, some dating from as far back as the 14C, have been combined to form a continuous 400m stretch, which emerges at the town hall on the Market Square. An enthusiastic Polish guide will navigate you through this gloomy labyrinth, but most of it consists of empty rooms and scattered archaeological finds.

Of far greater interest is the handsome medieval **Town Hall**, the oldest building on the MARKET SQUARE. The two-storey main building (after 1550) incorporates earlier Gothic elements and is topped with an arcaded Renaissance parapet. To the west it adjoins a slender octagonal clock tower (17C) on a square base. During the great fire of 1757 the town hall suffered major damage, and was not renovated until 1873. The three ground floor rooms accommodate a small **museum** (**open** Tues–Fri 09.00–16.00, Sat 09.00–15.00, Sun 10.00–14.00). Originally, the sloping Market Square (100m by 120m) could boast a continuous line of arcades, but today only the Oleśnicki House (see above) and *Ciżemka Hotel* (No. 27) evoke its former appearance.

The Cathedral

Walk south off the Market Square along UL. MARIACKA to the **cathedral*,
passing a series of 18C–19C ecclesiastical buildings, some in ruin. Kazimierz the
Great founded a collegiate church here in 1360, apparently as penance for the
murder of the Cracovian curate, Marcin Baryrzko. The Gothic aisled hall was
expanded during the Baroque period (1663–74), and in the 19C, when an
incongruous Neo-Gothic turret was erected above the nave. However, the interior is still impressive: four pairs of solid stone piers support ribbed cross vaults
in the nave and aisles, with modern, dark blue painted decoration filling the
gaps. Wainscoting on the aisle walls (north and south) frames a cycle of twelve
large paintings—*Martyrologium Romanum* (1708–37)—depicting scenes of
torture including the slaughter of the Dominicans at the hands of the Tartars.
The same artist, Karol de Prevot, painted the four works on the west wall below
the organ (1694–98), with equally gruesome scenes from the history of
Sandomierz. The last of these includes the legend of the knight Bobola, who was
suddenly swept across the Vistula by a strong (divine?) gust of wind, only to land
safely on the other side. The north aisle ends at a cross-vaulted sacristy, with a
room above it containing valuable books, manuscripts and incunabula, some as
early as the 12C (inaccessible).

Do not miss the **Ruthenian-Byzantine frescoes** decorating the walls of the
long, three-bay chancel. Painted in the 1420s, the frescoes depict the lives of
Jesus and Mary, and are one of only four examples of such art in Poland (see also
Kraków, Wiślica and Lublin). They are chiefly attributed to Hayl, an Orthodox
priest of unknown nationality, who settled in Przemyśl in 1426. Late Renaissance
stalls (1640) line both sides of the chancel, which has a late Baroque high altar
of black marble and fine bronze candelabra of 1558. In the nave, the piers are
embellished with richly sculpted Rococo altars and 17C paintings of the apostles.

Facing the cathedral is the narrow exit of UL. DŁUGOSZA. Up the street and to your
right is the charming **House of Jan Długosz**, like a brick box (1476) with stone
window frames and a view over the Vistula valley. As well as being a famous
medieval historian, Długosz was a canon in Sandomierz, and he funded this
house for the mansionaries (priests who sang in the church choir). Remodelled
in the 17C, and again in the 1930s, the building is presently used as the
Diocesan Museum (open Tues–Sat 09.00–12.00, Sun 11.00–13.00). Close
by, on the edge of the scarp, is the **Collegium Gostomianum**, a former Jesuit
college (1605–15), affiliated to the church of St Peter (no-longer extant), one of
the oldest seats of learning in Poland. East of the cathedral, at UL. KATEDRALNA
No. 5, you could visit the small **Museum of Literature** (open Wed–Fri
09.00–16.00, Sat 09.00–15.00, Sun 10.00–14.00). Most of the items were
donated by the family of Jarosław Iwaszkiewicz, a writer who had a special fondness for the Sandomierz region.

Continue downhill from the cathedral (ul. Mariacka) to the barrack-like
castle, which overlooks the river.

> The earliest surviving fragment of the castle—the south tower with its
> diamond-patterned brickwork—dates from the 15C. In 1680–86, the west
> wing—the only one to survive the Swedish Deluge—was remodelled to
> serve as the main block, complete with a *piano nobile*. The castle remained in

this state until 1825, when the Czarist authorities found better use for it as a prison. The rooms were swiftly converted into cells, and an unsightly Romantic-style façade overlooking the courtyard was added. The prison was finally closed in 1959.

Today, the castle is home to a modest **Regional Museum** (open Tues–Fri 09.00–16.00, Sat 09.00–15.00, Sun 10.00–14.00), with sections devoted to European silverware and kitchen utensils (17C–20C), numismatics (10C–20C), ethnography and portraiture. Note the '**Sandomierz Crown**' (copy), made of copper and studded with jewels; the original was apparently worn by Kazimierz the Great·

St James' Church

Going west from the castle along the cobbled lane (ul. Staromiejska) you will arrive at the former Dominican Priory and adjoining ***Church of St James**, one of the finest monuments in the city. The Dominicans were brought from Kraków by Bishop Iwo Odrowąż in 1226. Work on their church and priory—two of the earliest brick buildings in Poland—began soon afterwards lasting until the early 14C.

The church is an aisled basilica with a long square-ended chancel. Though the interior was substantially remodelled in the 17C, much of the earlier detailing was restored during conservation work in 1907–09. The Romanesque and early Gothic elements are best viewed from the outside, where glazed and moulded brick is used in the frieze, window surrounds, and elaborate two-part north portal (13C). Baroque vaults with stucco decoration (1624–31) have been preserved only in the chancel. Closing the north aisle is the late Renaissance **Martyrs' Chapel**, the best of the three chapels. Square and domed, it has lively stucco decoration (c 1640) and **frescoes** attributed to Karol de Prevot, whose finest work is found in the cathedral (see above). In the north wall is the tomb of Princess Adelaide (Baroque, 1676), the ostensible founder of the priory (d. 1291). In complete contrast is the modernist **Rosary Chapel** at the end of the south aisle; the 20C decor here is the work of the Cracovian, Karol Frycz (see p. 204).

Within Sandomierz there are a number of loess gorges, the best of which—the **Gorge of Queen Jadwiga**—begins a short distance from the church. Taking this route, you descend through a 'tunnel' of trees and shrubbery for about 500m to ul. Krakowska, where you should turn left to return to the castle. Alternatively, go back to the church of St James and join the **Piszczele Gorge** opposite the portal. Turning right after the bridge, and up the stone stairs, you will emerge through a narrow gap in the wall onto pl. Poniatowskiego. The gap even has a name—Eye of the Needle; it was built to enable easy access between the two Dominican priories: the second, of which only a single wing remains (1645), stands on pl. Poniatowskiego. From here it is a short distance back to the Market Square.

Leszczyński Castle ~ Baranów Sandomierski

A pleasant trip can be made to the ****Leszczyński Castle** in Baranów Sandomierski, some 31km up the Vistula. Set in extensive grounds, the castle has endured as one of the finest and most representative examples of the Polish Renaissance. The quickest way there is via Tarnobrzeg (roads 723, 84 and 985). Once in Baranów, follow the signs marked 'Zamek'.

According to the chronicler Jan Długosz, a manor house belonging to the Baranowski family existed here as early as the 15C, but work on the present castle did not commence until Rafał Leszczyński purchased the estate in 1569. His son, Jędrzej Leszczyński, is said to have commissioned **Santi Gucci** (see p. 195), the best architect of the Polish Renaissance, to complete the project. Gucci accomplished his task in 1606, the year of Jędrzej's death, after which the residence passed to another Rafał, an enlightened member of the Leszczyński clan, who amassed a vast collection of books and manuscripts, and commissioned Giovanni Battista Falconi to provide stuccoes for the northeast tower. Overall, the Leszczyńskis managed to hold on to the estate for about a century. During this period they turned the local parish church into a Calvinist congregation hall, and financed a printing press in the village, promoting Protestant literature.

In 1695, the estate passed to another magnate family—the Lubomirskis—who promptly engaged **Tylman van Gameren**, the leading architect of Polish Baroque, to redesign the first-floor interiors and build a richly ornamented gallery for the west wing. Later illustrious owners included the Sanguszkos, Potockis, and, finally, the Krasickis, whose entire collection of art, furniture, books and manuscripts—as well as numerous mementos of the poet-bishop Ignacy Krasicki—were lost in a fire in 1894. During turn-of-the-century restoration work, one of the ground floor chambers was converted into a chapel, with two leading Polish Impressionists of the day—Jacek Malczewski and Józef Mehoffer—providing the altar triptych and the stained-glass windows. The castle became a museum in 1968.

The castle is built on a rectangular plan, with four round angle towers topped by small green domes, and a square tower in the middle of the front elevation (south). Remarkably, the latter is only decorative: no rooms at all, just an entrance gate below, and a rich parapet above. The residential wings (east, west, and north), together with the decorative wall, frame an arcaded courtyard with the loggias stretching round only three sides (east, west, and south), apparently for reasons of economy. The two elegant storeys of Ionic arcades have mascarons on the ground floor plinths (to ward off evil!), a first-floor balustrade, and roses in the spandrels. Underneath, the ground floor arcades are plain and cross-vaulted, but on the first floor they are decorated with painted crests of successive owners of the estate.

The **museum** is surprisingly modest (**open** Tues–Sun 09.00–14.30). Only three rooms with period furnishing are open to the public (east wing, ground floor). In the former chapel, a documentary film can be seen about the castle and its history; and down in the basement there is a small display devoted to the sulphur industry—huge deposits of sulphur were discovered in the vicinity of Baranów during the 1950s, and even today the castle is formally managed by the local sulphur-processing plant.

Kraków to Tarnów

❖ Nowy Wiśnicz • Dębno • Tarnów

This trip takes you east of Kraków to the castles in Nowy Wiśnicz and Dębno. If using public transport, the best way to reach Nowy Wiśnicz is by bus, changing at Bochnia. All buses from Kraków to Tarnów stop at Dębno. There are also many daily train services from Kraków to Tarnów, all of which stop at Bochnia.

Leave Kraków on road 4 (E40) heading east. Twenty-six kilometres after Wieliczka turn right for **NOWY WIŚNICZ**, a small, attractive town, famous for its imposing *castle.

Nowy Wiśnicz Castle

In terms of sheer size, Wiśnicz Castle rivals Krzyżtopór (see p. 275), but unlike the latter, has seen large-scale restoration work and now parts of it are open to the public (Mon–Fri 09.00–14.00, Sat 11.00–15.00, Sun 12.00–18.00; compulsory guided tour).

> Though a castle probably existed here as early as the 13C, it was not until the estate passed into the hands of the powerful Kmita family that Wiśnicz rose to prominence. Piotr Kmita (d. 1553) fortified it with cannon and three stone corner towers, decorating the interiors with paintings and murals. Soon Wiśnicz became a flourishing centre of Renaissance culture. A frequent guest was Queen Bona Sworza, the wife of Zygmunt the Old, after whom one of the towers (northwest) is named. The estate changed hands in 1593, when Sebastian Lubomirski (d. 1649) purchased it for the sum of 85,000 Polish zlotys. In 1615–21, his son Stanisław—the most celebrated member of the clan, a man of fantastic wealth—employed Matteo Trapola to reshape the central block as a rectangle with three tiers of arcaded galleries around a small courtyard. The fake 'windows' on the north wall were one of the first examples of *trompe l'oeil* painting in Poland. Giovanni Battista Falconi supplied the stuccoes for the new domed chapel. Outside, Trapola fortified the hill with a modern bastioned pentagonal wall, broken only by a sumptuous stone gate with scrolls and banded masonry. During its heyday, the castle was inhabited by some 1000 people. Lubomirski also financed the construction of a fortified monastery for the Discalced Carmelites (see below) next to the castle, as well as a town hall and parish church in the village, both still there. Despite severe pillaging by the Swedes, who took away 150 wagons of goods (see p. 49), and a fire in 1831 which made it uninhabitable, the castle has remained virtually unchanged in form since Lubomirski's day.

The guide will take you through the cellars and selected rooms in the residential wing. The rooms are mostly empty, though some sandstone (ground and first floor) and marble (second floor) portals have survived. Traces of Falconi's murals and stuccoes are discernible on the walls and ceilings, particularly well-preserved in the Chapel and the Tower of Bona. The single-storey Kmita House (16C)—the former kitchens—abuts the castle to the south. To the east, the adjoining domed chapel has five Baroque sarcophagi of the Lubomirski family in its crypt. They were transferred here in 1951 after the Carmelites' church was bombed by the Nazis.

Fragments of the church (the walls and portal) may be viewed from the court-yard of the former **Discalced Carmelites' Monastery** (1622–34), which, since the expulsion of the Carmelites in 1780, has been used as a high security prison, complete with Baroque entrance gate, bastion fortifications, and monastic cells! To get there, turn left up the hill from the castle. Ask at the porter's lodge for permission to enter the courtyard. You might also visit the small wooden house between the castle and prison. Built in the 19C, it was much frequented by the painter Jan Matejko (see p. 72), and now houses a biographical **museum** dedicated to him (**open** Wed–Sun 10.00–14.00).

The Castle at Dębno

Return to road 4 and continue eastwards to DĘBNO (28km). Turn off the main road for the *castle (**open** Tues, Thur 10.00–17.00, Wed, Fri 09.00–15.00, Sat 09.00–13.00, Sun 10.00–16.00) of the Castellan Jakub Dębiński (c 1470). Located in a picturesque setting among lime trees, it is the best-preserved example of **late Gothic defensive architecture** in southern Poland. The castle is composed of four single-storey buildings around a rectangular court-yard, with impressive oriel windows framed in rich Gothic stonework. The red brick walls contrast nicely with the stone foundations. Two turrets, round and stone at the base, brick and octagonal above, flank the west wing. A number of other Gothic elements have been preserved, such as portals and loopholes, as well as Renaissance sgraffito around some of the window frames.

The courtyard, with a gallery at the first-floor level, and a covered well in the middle, is reached through the north entrance. A guided tour of the well-restored interiors reveals the successive phases in the castle's history. You can visit the Gothic chapel with a painted dome, the Renaissance Knights' Hall, Baroque and Rococo rooms, as well as a concert hall, with an organ of 1686 and a 19C piano, where concerts are occasionally given.

Dębno Castle

Continue for 24km along road 4 to **TARNÓW** (population 118,500). Most of the town's sights lie within the pedestrian zone delimited by the ring road (ul. Wałowa), which follows the line of the medieval fortifications, only fragments of which remain. Begin your exploration of the town at the Market Square, laid out in 1330. In the centre stands the ***Town Hall**, the best-preserved building in the Old Town. The Gothic stone base was built first, followed in the 16C by the brick upper storey and the machicolated round superstructure of the tower. The archi-tect of this fine Polish Renaissance building was probably **Gian-Maria Padovano**, the court architect of the last Jagiellons, who was commissioned by the hereditary owner of the town, **Jan Tarnowski**, the Grand Hetman.

The Town Hall currently houses a **Regional Museum** (open Tues–Fri 09.00–15.00, Sat–Sun 10.00–14.00), with a collection of ceramics and glass (16C–18C), a gallery of Polish portraiture (17C–18C), and a small display dedicated to the hero of the national independence movement, Józef Bem (1794–1850), a native of Tarnów. The museum is continued in two Renaissance arcaded houses (16C) on the north side of the square (Nos 20–21), with a display devoted to the archaeology and history of the Tarnów region.

The Cathedral

Northwest of the Market Square stands the cathedral, an early 15C structure, expanded and modified in 1889–97. Enter through the Neo-Gothic arched portal below the square brick west tower (72m). The vestibule has an original Gothic portal leading through to the main part of the church, whose basilican appearance dates from 1816. Of greatest interest are the **tombs**, beginning, in the north aisle, with two reclining sandstone figures (Tarnowskis) under a Gothic ribbed star vault of 1514, and a late Renaissance tomb of sandstone and red marble in the east bay. Gian-Maria Padovano's monument to Barbara Tarnowska (d. 1521), the first wife of the Grand Hetman Jan Tarnowski, rests high up on the wall of south aisle. At its east end stands a large white marble tomb to the Sanguszkos. Padovano's best effort is the huge monument to General Jan Tarnowski (d. 1561), and his son Jan Krzysztof (d. 1567), on the left of the chancel. A relief in the tympanum shows Tarnowski's triumphant entry into Kraków in 1531. Below it are battle scenes in relief and female figures in niches symbolising Tarnowski's self-proclaimed virtues of justice and circumspection. Opposite the monument stands the Mannerist tomb (1612–20) of the Ostrogskis—Janusz (d. 1620) and his wife Zuzanna (d. 1596). Made chiefly of black and red marble, with allegorical sculpture, it is attributed to Johann Pfister and possibly Willem van den Blocke. Notice also, at the west end of the nave, the finely carved 15C **canons' stalls**.

In the northwest corner of the cathedral square stands a group of early 16C canons' houses (No. 5), the best of which is the central **Mikołajowski House** (1524). Since 1947, the interiors have collectively housed the **Diocesan Museum** (open Tues–Sat 10.00–15.00, Sun 09.00–14.00). The display includes Gothic religious art from the Małopolska region, a collection of liturgical vessels and vestments, and folk painting on glass from southern Poland.

Walking east from PL. KATEDRALNY to PL. RYBNY, you enter Tarnów's **Jewish district**, where 18,000 people lived before the war. Today, all that remains of the 17C synagogue destroyed by the Nazis is the *bema*—four brick columns supporting a cupola—on the east side of the square. Nearby, ul. Żydowska is lined with 18C–19C Jewish tenement houses, their fronts characteristically plain with narrow entrances.

Kraków to Kielce via Wiślica

❖ Niepołomice • Wiślica • Busko Zdrój • Pińczów • Kielce

This long trip takes you northeast to Kielce (see p. 270). The highlight is the historic town of Wiślica, with its famous collegiate church. If you are not travelling by car, you could visit Wiślica on a day trip by bus from Kraków.

Leave Kraków heading east through Nowa Huta and join road 777. At Cło, turn south along the 772; just after crossing the river, turn right for NIEPOŁOMICE. The **castle** was raised by Kazimierz the Great in 1340–50 as a base for his hunting forays into the nearby game park (Puszcza Niepołomicka). Zygmunt August later converted it into a Renaissance palace (1550–71) with a large courtyard, to which arcades were added in the 17C. Visible from the outside are the fine Renaissance portal and the remains of the moat and earth ramparts. The nearby **parish church** is roughly contemporaneous with the castle. It has two chapels of note: the Renaissance Branicki chapel (1596) in the south aisle, square and domed, with kneeling marble figures of Grzegorz and Katarzyna Branicki sculpted by Santi Gucci; and the Baroque Lubomirski chapel of 1640 in the north aisle.

Wiślica

Heading northeast to Wiślica (72km), return to road 777 and turn right; 54km later pick up road 973 marked 'Busko', turning left after 4km for WIŚLICA (road 771).

> This famous settlement is perched on a gypsum hillock commanding the flat Nida valley. Until recently, historians believed it to be of 10C origin, possibly the capital of the Wiślanie, a proto-Slavonic tribe. In the 1960s, however, a 9C circular trough—most probably a baptismal font—was discovered in the ruins of a 12C Romanesque church beneath the chancel of the present collegiate church (see below), suggesting that in fact Christianity had arrived in Poland earlier than was previously thought (Mieszko, the first Piast ruler, was baptised in 966). On the crypt pavement of the 12C church, archaeologists also found three figural scenes engraved on a red gypsum slab (a replica can be seen in the town museum), as well as fragments of yet another Romanesque church—a two-towered basilica dating from the mid-13C—underneath the nave. Until 1915, parts of these two towers buttressed the west front of the present church, and even today many 13C sculptural elements, such as the stone ribs of the vault, can be found within it.
>
> In 1326, Wiślica received a town charter. Two decades later the Wiślica statutes were drawn up—the first codification of customary law in Poland. Decline set in after the Swedish invasions of the mid-17C (see p. 49), with the remains of the town walls and castle being dismantled after 1766.

The *collegiate church** stands by the southeast corner of the Market Square. Built in 1350–80 by Kazimierz the Great, this stone church has a plain west gable, an adjoining square bell tower (1460–70), tall buttresses, and three Gothic portals: above the blocked north doorway is a 14C stone crest; above the south portal, a tablet (1464) shows the kneeling Kazimierz offering a miniature of the collegiate church to Jesus and Mary. The remarkable **double-nave hall** is covered, rather like a monastic refectory, with ribbed palm vaults resting on three pillars. The apsed, three-bay chancel, tall and narrow, carries Gothic ribbed cross vaults (1370–80) with sculpted bosses. Fading Ruthenian-Byzantine murals (1398–1400) are discernible on the walls of the chancel. At the high altar there is an early Gothic stone sculpture of the Virgin (1260–1280). Remnants of the first Romanesque church, as well as the celebrated font, can be viewed in an ugly pavilion east of the chancel (ul. Batalionów Chłopskich). Next to the church stands a curate's house (1460), one of the few remaining secular Gothic buildings in Poland. It is also known as the **House of Długosz**, after its founder, the medieval chronicler and custodian of Wiślica, Jan Długosz (see p. 80), who tutored the royal children here. On the Market Square is the **museum** (open Wed–Mon 09.00–16.00), which has in its tatty basement more archaeological finds, including bas-reliefs and three column bases from the first Romanesque church.

From Wiślica, join road 776 north to **Busko Zdrój** (population 16,800), a modest spa town which rose to prominence when mineral springs were discovered here in 1776. From the Market Square, walk south for about 1km through the park to the Neo-classical **Bath-house** (1836–38). Beyond the columned portico is a large pump room where you may sample the waters. There is also a concert hall lined with columns and busts.

Pińczów

Heading west along road 767 (15km) you will arrive at Pińczów (population 10,900), situated on the left bank of the Nida river.

> During its 16C heyday, Pińczów was one of the leading centres of the Polish Reformation. Cultural achievement flourished under the patronage of the Myszkowski family, and by the end of the 16C, the town's stonemasons were producing high-quality 'prefabricated' portals, chapels and tombstones, using local limestone. The workshops were supervised by Santi Gucci and other Italian artists. Though Pińczów's large Jewish population was completely wiped out by the Nazis, a few scattered landmarks are still in evidence.

Driving into town, you can safely ignore the 17C Reformed Franciscan church (left) and head straight for the nearby **synagogue** on ul. Klasztorna (No. 8). This square building, in late Renaissance style, was destroyed during the Second World War, though some painting, stuccoes and stone decoration have survived. Note, also, the altar on Pentateuch scrolls.

The Market Square is dominated by the **parish church**, an early Baroque basilica built in 1642, with preserved Gothic fragments, notably the pointed-arch portal through which you enter. A covered passageway links the church to the former Paulite monastery building, with its Gothic portal and sgraffito frieze. The interiors accommodate a **Regional Museum** (open Wed–Sun 10.00–17.00).

From the church, follow the Kielce road (766) up the hill. On the left, there once stood a huge castle raised by the Myszkowskis (1424–54), but only a 16C Renaissance tower (probably by Santi Gucci) remains. The tower is set into the wall encircling the grounds of the **Wielkopolski Palace** (c 1780) further up the hill. For a fine view over Pińczów, continue to the summit (right). You will have to walk the final stretch to reach the **Chapel of St Anne** (c 1600, Santi Gucci), a plain Mannerist cube sprouting a modest dome, with a fine vista over the Nida valley.

The 766 eventually joins road 73 to Kielce (40km).

Kielce to Warsaw

❖ Wąchock • Szydłowiec • Orońsko • **Warsaw**

Wąchock

This trip takes you north from the Małopolska region into Mazovia. The highlights are the abbey at Wąchock and the Centre for Polish Sculpture at Orońsko. The itinerary can be easily covered in a day, but if you are pushed for time, it is best to omit Szydłowiec.

From Kielce city centre pick up road 73 and then road 7 heading north. Just before entering Skarżysko-Kamienna, turn right along the 746 for Wąchock (52km).

> Archaeological finds testify that flint tools were already being produced in the area around Wąchock during the early Stone Age. The mining tradition was continued by the Cistercian monks, who founded an abbey here in 1179. Using the swiftly flowing waters of the Kamienna river, they established primitive smelting furnaces, smithies, and later, in the 16C, proper ovens. Wąchock lost its town status in 1869 as punishment for helping the insurrectionists of 1863, after which it fell into decline.

The *church, one of the most valuable examples of Romanesque architecture in Poland, was built in the first half of the 13C. It takes the form of a towerless basilica on the plan of a Latin cross. The exterior walls are patterned with grey and brown sandstone blocks, with later Gothic gables, and a rose window at the east end. The **interior**, slightly disappointing, is entered through a 19C vestibule, which has partially covered the richly-carved Romanesque portal. The five-bay nave, only as high as it is broad, carries a Gothic cross vault. Unfortunately, its 19C murals obscure earlier and far better painted decoration. Romanesque windows have been preserved high up (the church also served a defensive purpose) in the walls of the transepts, south aisle, and chancel. The master builder of the church is known only as Simon; his signature—the oldest inscribed monogram in Poland—is found on one of the buttresses. Most of the church's furnishings are Baroque or Rococo.

The much larger **abbey**, consisting of a tower (1643) and two quadrangles, was rebuilt in the 16C–17C and 19C. Romanesque fragments in the walls and buttressing are visible on the exterior of the south and east wings, which overlook a lush garden, containing a statue of St Bernard among chickens and partridges. You can enter the impressive 16C cloisters through a door in the north aisle of the church. It is best to ask one of the monks to show you round, as most of the rooms are usually closed. Of greatest interest is the **chapter house** in the east wing—a small square room whose cross ribbed vault is carried on six carved corbels and four columns, with carved leaf capitals and faces at the bottom, but without a single boss. Nearby are other rooms with similar Romanesque detailing. The door in the centre of the west wing leads, via the abbey vestibule, to the **Cistercian Museum** (open Mon–Sat 09.00–12.00, Sun 14.00–17.00), with a large collection of 19C memorabilia.

Szydłowiec

Return to Skarżysko-Kamienna and continue north along road 7 to SZYDŁOWIEC (32km) (population 11,000), a small town on the Korzeniówka river. For centuries, local white sandstone was mined here for use on the façades of many buildings and monuments in the Polish capital. The Market Square has two monuments of note: a late Renaissance **Town Hall** (1602–26), and, to the south, a **parish church**.

The church is a fully-preserved late Gothic structure founded by the Szydłowieckis in 1493–1509. The nave has retained its 16C flat wooden ceiling and even the original roof trusses. Sculptures (1531) adorn the wooden high altar (1618–27). A Renaissance tombstone of the Grand Treasurer Mikołaj Szydłowiecki (d. 1532), to the left of the altar, depicts him as a sleeping knight in armour; to the right stands the white marble sarcophagus of his wife (1795). A Gothic polyptych of 1505 is on the left of the chancel. Note, also, the Renaissance coffered ceiling below the organ loft, 18 coffers in all, each one different.

UL. KĄPIELOWA leads northwest off the Market Square to the late Gothic **castle** (1510–26) of the Szydłowieckis, in a picturesque setting by a lake. A screen wall (south) was added to the existing three wings in 1620–30, when the castle was rebuilt in Renaissance style. The small, well-preserved rooms house a **Museum of Folk Musical Instruments** (open 09.00–15.00, Sat 10.00–17.00). As you leave town on the Radom road, you could visit the large overgrown **Jewish Cemetery** on UL. KILIŃSKIEGO, situated opposite an ugly housing estate. Turn right by the Biesiada restaurant. There are about 1300 graves here, most of them 19C–20C.

Headstones in the Jewish Cemetery

Continue north along road 7 to **OROŃSKO** (13km). Turn left off the main road, following signs to 'Centrum Rzeźby'. Located within the grounds of a 19C estate is the **Centre for Polish Sculpture**, with numerous 17C–18C sculptures dotted around an attractive landscaped park (c 1840). A small Neo-classical chapel of 1841, with two Latin inscriptions, stands to the left of the main entrance. All the Romantic buildings on the estate are attributed to **Francesco Maria Lanci**: the grandest, the manor house, has a display of mid-19C interiors (**open** Tues, Wed, Fri 10.00–15.00, Thur, Sat–Sun 10.00–16.00). In a separate building, further on, is an exhibition hall with more sculptures of varying quality. Temporary exhibitions are put on in the Orangery.

Stay on road 7 for Warsaw (103km).

Warsaw to Lublin

❖ Puławy • (detour: Janowiec) • Kazimierz Dolny • Nałęczów (detour: Wojciechów) • Lublin

This trip takes you southeast of Warsaw into the Lublin region. The Czartoryski Palace in Puławy and Janowiec Castle are both well worth a visit, but the undoubted highlight is Kazimierz Dolny, one of the most beautiful towns in Poland, and an excellent place to break your journey. To get there by public transport, take the train to Puławy (Warsaw–Lublin main line), and then a local bus. If you decide to make Kazimierz Dolny your base, Puławy, Janowiec and the spa town of Nałęczów can all be easily visited on day trips.

The quickest way from Warsaw to Puławy (127km) is along road 17, eventually turning left onto the 823; alternatively, take the more scenic, parallel Vistula road (801).

Puławy ~ The Czartoryski Palace

Puławy (population 51,200) is a dreary, polluted town, but one that should not be missed on account of the **Czartoryski palace** with its surrounding landscaped park, one of the best in Poland. You can visit the pillared entrance hall and the 'Gothic' room on the first floor, but the palace is presently occupied by the Agricultural Institute, and most of it is inaccessible. Drive through the town centre and park on UL. CZARTORYSKA by the main entrance to the grounds.

The history of the estate begins in 1676–9 when Tylman van Gameren raised a Baroque palace for Lubomirski, the Palatine of Kraków. It then passed to the Czartoryskis, who made it their official family seat in 1731. The marriage of Adam Kazimierz Czartoryski to Izabela Flemming heralded a golden age for Puławy, which became a sort of second court for magnates, artists and scholars, even rivalling Warsaw as the chief centre of cultural life in Poland. In c 1800, the couple commissioned Piotr Aigner, one of the leading Polish Neo-classicists, to redesign the palace and its surroundings. Perhaps inspired by S. B. Zug's Arkadia (see p. 140), Izabela summoned a team of international experts—including John Savage, the designer of Warsaw's Saxon garden (see p. 140)—to landscape the park as a fashionable Romantic garden (1788–1810), with 260 varieties of trees, and scores of Romantic pavilions. Two of the latter—the Gothic house and the Temple of the Sibyl—were purpose-built as the first Polish museum, where the Czartoryskis' vast collections of art and memorabilia were put on display. After the Russians confiscated the estate in 1831, the collections were moved to Paris, and later to Kraków, where today they can be seen in the Czartoryski Museum (see p. 226).

Temple of the Sybil

A map and a potted history of the Czartoryski estate can be found by the entrance. Follow the main alley to the **palace**, situated on what was once a high river bluff. The terrace overlooks water meadows and a pond, with the Vistula occasionally visible in the distance. The exterior is largely the work of Aigner, except for the south façade above the terrace, which was reshaped in 1722–36. Walking west along the terrace you arrive at the charming **Temple of the Sibyl** (1798–1801). An inscription on the portal reads: 'the future's past', Czartoryska's motto for the museum. Close by is the freshly restored **Gothic House** (1800–09). Returning to the palace you could descend the 'English stairs' to Aigner's tiny **Chinese Pavilion** below the terrace. His **parish church** (1800–03) stands on a hillock to the northeast. A **Regional Museum** (open 09.00–15.00) on ul. Czartoryskich (No. 6a) exhibits items from the Czartoryski collection in Kraków.

Leaving Puławy on the Kazimierz Dolny road (824), you will pass the **Marynki Palace** (1790–1804) in the south part of the park. The nine-bay block, with a shallow portico, presents a version of Neo-classicism known as the 'Stanislavian' style (see p. 129).

Detour to Janowiec Castle

Before heading south, you could visit the castle in JANOWIEC (28km), on the opposite bank of the Vistula (turn left after the bridge). The *castle has been a ruin since the 19C, but work is under way to prevent further decay. Built for the important Firlej family in the early 16C, it was expanded by Santi Gucci, and later, during the Baroque period (c1675), by Tylman van Gameren. A modest **museum** (open Wed–Sun 10.00–15.00) may be visited in the nearby 18C manor house, overlooking fields and woodland. The adjoining mini-skansen has stables, granaries, and a 19C boat carved out of a huge tree trunk. On a fine day, walk to the scarp for a breathtaking view onto Kazimierz Dolny and the Vistula valley.

South of Puławy you enter the picturesque **Kazimierz National Park**, where a patchwork of fields is cut across by deep loess ravines and lush woodland. Road 824 follows the river to **BOCHOTNICA**, a hamlet immortalised by the 19C writer Bolesław Prus in his heart-rending novella *Antek*. The ruins of a **castle** on Esterka hill are visible from the road. According to legend, Kazimierz the Great built the castle for his Jewish mistress, Esterka. From the top, there is a spectacular view along the lower part of the Bystra valley. Bochotnica can also be reached along a red hiking trail from Kazimierz Dolny (5km).

Kazimierz Dolny

It is easy to see why many regard Kazimierz Dolny (26km) (population 4000) to be one of Poland's most attractive towns. Its potential as an ideal retreat for writers and artists was recognised in the 1920s, and the tradition has been maintained to the present day, with students arriving from all over Poland to paint the autumnal colours or to find inspiration in the unique atmosphere of the place. Much of this has to do with its tranquil setting: a lush valley on the right bank of the Vistula, surrounded by fields and woods, and thankfully distant from industry and pollution. In June, the town plays host to a **festival of folk music**, with weekend trippers arriving en masse in summer to crowd the numerous bars and cafés.

Kazimierz dates from the 12C, when Kazimierz the Just gave the settlement of Wietrzna Góra (Windy Mountain) to the Premonstratensian nuns of Zwierzyniec near Kraków (see p. 237). They in turn renamed it 'Kazimierz' to honour the gift. Later, in the 14C, Kazimierz the Great endowed the settlement with a municipal charter and numerous royal privileges. Beginning in the 16C, merchant families like the Firlejs, Przybyłas, Górkas and Celejs amassed huge fortunes from the waterway trade along the Vistula, grain being the most lucrative commodity. Traces of this prosperity are still very much alive in the town's architecture, prompting local tourist brochures to dub Kazimierz the 'pearl of the Polish Renaissance'.

Buttressed and gabled **granaries** scatter the riverside as you enter the town along the Puławy road. The earliest of these (1591), remarkable for being entirely of wood, houses a **Natural History Museum** (open Wed–Mon 10.00–15.00); another (17C) accommodates a youth hostel; a third dates from as late as 1792. But the real showpieces are the **merchants' houses** on the MAIN SQUARE, notably those of the Przybyła brothers, Nicholas and Christopher (east). Built in 1615, these two houses are an apotheosis of the **Lublin Renaissance style**. As in Zamość (see p. 299), they are built on arcades, pushing them closer towards the centre of the square. The exquisite façades, replete with floral ornamentation, religious symbols and philosophical dictums, are a true delight. On the left, the *House of Mikołaj Przybyła** has a relief of St Nicholas in a panel on the first storey, with Evangelists above, and two-and-a-half aedicules on the skyline. No less impressive is the adjoining *House of Krzysztof Przybyła**, where pilaster figures of Judith and Salome—both holding severed heads—flank a larger-than-life St Christopher in low relief.

At the corner of UL. KLASZTORNA (south) stands the somewhat later **Gdańsk House**, whose gabled late Baroque

Main Square, Kazimierz Dolny

façade bears the date 1795. Across the street at No. 19, don't miss the **Museum of Goldsmithery** (open Tues–Sun 10.00–16.00), with a rich display of Jewish, Polish and European silverware from the 17C–19C. Continue down ul. Klasztorna and turn right (west) into UL. SENATORSKA. No. 3 is the partly reconstructed **Górski House** (1607), with a late Renaissance façade. Still more remarkable is the *****Celej House** at No. 11. Here, the astonishingly ornate attic (c 1635)—almost as tall as the ground and first floors put together—includes a row of niches rising to statues in frames, and a multitude of griffins, basilisks and dragons. Inside is the **Regional Museum** (open Tues–Sun 10.00–15.00).

Returning to ul. Klasztorna, walk up the hill, via roofed stairs, to the **Reformed Franciscan Monastery**, founded by the Firlejs in 1626. The monastic building (1639–88) was used as a Gestapo headquarters. Adjoining it is a modest Baroque church, where organ concerts are held in summer. More granaries can be found to the southwest on ul. Krakowska, including a late Renaissance one of 1636, now a PTTK hostel.

Before the Second World War, Kazimierz Dolny had a large Jewish population, mostly housed in a district situated to the east of the Market Square. As in so many Polish towns, nowadays there is only scant evidence of this rich heritage: a short way up ul. Lubelska stands a reconstructed **synagogue** of 1677 (now a cinema); close by is a wooden building once occupied by the Jewish butchers' stalls. For a longer walk, continue along ul. Lubelska and ul. Czerniawy to the **Jewish Memorial** (1984) and cemetery (1792). On the way you pass the **Hospital Church of St Anne** (c 1649–70). Next to it, set below street level, is the **hospital** building (1635), currently a community centre.

St Anne's is a miniature copy of the far more impressive **parish church**, which dominates the north end of the Market Square. Here, slender proportions attest to a Gothic provenance, though the church was extensively remodelled in 1586–89, and again in 1610–3 by Jacopo Balin, who added the handsome gables, west belfry, and panelled plaster vaults with geometric patterns typical of

the Lublin Renaissance. The interior (**open** only during mass) has three memorial chapels, the best of which is the Górski chapel (south) of 1625. Notice also the **organ** (1620), chandelier, and carved chancel stalls, all Mannerist.

Continue up the hill to the ruins of a royal *****castle** built by Kazimierz the Great. The Renaissance lower part (mid-16C) was destroyed during the Swedish Deluge of the mid-17C (see p. 49), while all that remains of the Gothic upper castle (14C) is a solid round watch-tower, some 200m further on. For a fine view over Kazimierz Dolny walk to the nearby **Hill of Three Crosses**. The crosses here (copies) commemorate the victims of a cholera epidemic that ravaged the town in the early 18C.

Fragment of the façade of Krzysztof Przybyla House

Return to Bochotnica and join road 830 (east) to **NAŁĘCZÓW** (20km) (population 4800), a picturesque spa town situated on the banks of the Bystra river.

The first owner of the estate was Stanisław Małachowski, who built a Baroque-Classical palace here in 1771–73. His successor, Antoni, later expanded the bath house when the local spring waters were discovered to have medicinal qualities. Thereafter, Nałęczów became a fashionable resort, a favourite haunt of writers and artists. Today, it is a haven for elderly people, who arrive to enjoy the famous micro-climate, or convalesce in one of the many sanatoria.

The **palace**, situated in the main park, contains a **museum** (open Tues–Sun 10.00–15.00) dedicated to Bolesław Prus and other late 19C writers. To the west, bordering the pond, is a **well-house** (open 09.00–18.00), where you can sample the spring waters.

The town's main street is lined with trees and old wooden villas. The best of these is 'Octavia', once belonging to the wife of the writer Stefan Żeromski (see p. 85). Close by, a narrow paved road (ul. Żeromskiego) ascends the hill to a high-lander-style cottage, now a **museum**, where Żeromski lived and worked.

Continuing along the Lublin road (830), a short detour (12km) south brings you to **Wojciechów** (827). Visible from the road is a solitary **tower**, the only remnant of a former Renaissance castle (1520–40), with a small display of smith's work inside. More examples of artistic ironwork may be seen at an old **smithy**, 250m from the tower.

Lublin

Lublin (population 380,000) lies at the heart of a predominantly upland region known as **Lubelszczyzna**, stretching east towards the Bug river (Poland's natural border with the Ukraine), south towards the San, and west towards the Vistula. It is the largest and most important city of southeast Poland. After the Second World War, it grew rapidly, with vast housing estates appearing, inevitably, around the periphery. Though the tiny Old Town escaped the total physical devastation that befell Warsaw, reconstruction was slow and often shoddy. Consequently, for all its discreet charm, today's Old Town looks like a large building site, still very run down, and almost entirely devoid of shops. To the west is the city centre, with second-rate 19C–20C architecture the rule, and little in the way of tourist attractions. Lublin has two universities, including the renowned **Catholic University** (**KUL**)—the only one of its kind in Eastern Europe—which preserved a modicum of independence from the state even under Communist rule.

The fastest way of getting from Warsaw to Lublin is by train. There are several express trains daily, with the trip taking about two and a half hours.

■ **Practical information**
Hotels
★★★★
Orbis-Unia. Al. Racławickie 12, ☎ 533-2061. Close to the Catholic University of Lublin (KUL). Good facilities, helpful staff. Business Centre, car park and rental, travel office. 110 rooms.
Victoria. Ul. Narutowicza 58/60, ☎ 532-7011. Central location. Car park. 170 rooms.
Tourist information (*PAPT*). Ul. Krakowskie Przedmieście 78, ☎ 532-4412, 532-5339.

ORBIS. Ul. Narutowicza 31/33, ☎ 532–2256/59.
Main post office. Ul. Krakowskie Przedmieśie 50.
Telephone code: (0–81).

History

The first traces of human settlement in Lublin date from the 7C. Favourably located on a spur above the Bystrzyca river, the early medieval town flourished as an important commercial centre on the east-west and north-south trade routes. Successive raids by the Ruthenians, Lithuanians and Tartars prompted Kazimierz the Great to build a walled city after 1317, a royal castle, and a monastery for the Dominicans. The 14C–16C mark the golden period in Lublin's history. Grander than the merely ducal Warsaw, it enjoyed many royal privileges, which ensured steady growth. Prosperity was mirrored in the political sphere: in 1569 the **Union of Lublin** formalised the personal union between the Polish and Lithuanian crowns. In architecture, a provincial Renaissance style (known as the '**Lublin Renaissance**'), distinctive and pretty, came to the fore, its finest examples being the Dominican church and the castle Chapel of the Holy Trinity with its **Ruthenian-Byzantine frescoes**. This style still dominates much of the city, its medieval elements having all but vanished.

From the 17C onwards, wars and plague brought the city to virtual ruin. A minor revival came with the industrial boom of the late 19C, and the population rose to 60,000 by 1900. Lublin once again entered the political arena in 1918 when the Provisional Government of the Republic of Poland was established here as the first step on the road to Polish independence.

During the Second World War the Nazis set up a death camp in the suburb of Majdanek, where almost all of Lublin's 40,000 Jews—a third of the city's pre-war population—perished A dubious moment of glory followed liberation on 24 July 1944, when Lublin became the Polish capital for 164 days. It was then that the Moscow-backed '**Lublin Committee**' took power, brushing aside the claims of the Polish Government-in-exile in London, and thereby sealing Poland's fate as a vassal of the Soviet Union for many decades to come. Ironically, in July 1980, factory workers in Lublin initiated the first wave of strikes leading to the historic Gdańsk agreements and the birth of **Solidarity** (p.61).

The Old Town

It is best to enter the Old Town from PL. ŁOKIETKA, which closes the end of ul. Krakowskie Przedmieście. Here stands the medieval **Kraków Gate**, begun in the 14C when the city was encircled with brick fortifications, of which only fragments remain. Inside is the **Historical Museum of Lublin** (open Tues–Sat 09.00–16.00, Sun 09.00–17.00). Climb the spiral staircase to the top room for a panorama of the city supplemented by some old photographs

Walk through the Kraków Gate and continue along UL. BRAMOWA to the *Market Square, whose centre is occupied by the *Old Town Hall. A fire destroyed the original Gothic building in 1575. Three years later its Renaissance successor was designated as the seat of the Crown Tribunal, the highest court of appeal in Małopolska for the Polish and Lithuanian gentry. The celebrated Warsaw architect, Domenico Merlini, gave the building its present Baroque-Classical shape

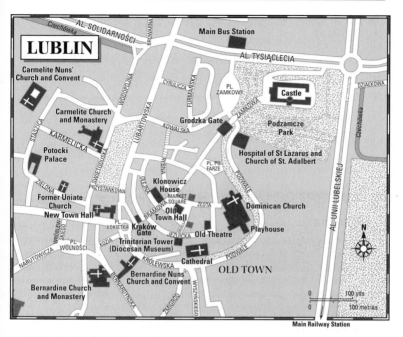

in 1781–87, but due to lack of funds the end result was rather mediocre. The last sitting of the Tribunal was in 1794. Thereafter, the Russians used the building as a regional court, as evidenced by the restored cyrillic inscription on the façade. A small but worthwhile **Tribunal Museum** (open Wed–Sat 09.00–16.00; Sun 09.00–17.00) has been opened inside the maze of Gothic cellars.

The square itself, small and irregular, is surrounded by burghers' houses built in the 15C–16C, though few of the Gothic and Renaissance elements survived the 19C alterations, when new storeys and Neo-classical façades were added. During reconstruction in 1954 a few pseudo-Renaissance parapets were introduced in a vain attempt to re-create the 17C appearance of the square. Beginning with the west side, at No. 2 stands the **Klonowicz House**, named after the 17C poet and city councillor, Sebastian Klonowicz. Moving to the north side, the Neo-classical **Lubomelski House** (No. 8) has a fragment of a Renaissance stone portal bearing the date 1540. Renaissance frescoes (1540) extolling Epicurean life adorn the three-tiered cellars below the building. Most impressive on the east side is No. 12, the Renaissance **Konopnica House** (1597), with preserved Mannerist window frames decorated with masks, rosettes and dragon heads. The south side of the square is unremarkable except for a preserved 17C portal at **No. 18**, and lots of modern sgraffito.

Walking south along UL. GRUELLA you will arrive at the imposing façade of the *Cathedral*, formerly a Jesuit church (1586–96), which Antonio Corazzi redesigned in 1821. The interiors, perhaps the best in Lublin, are noted for their colourful *trompe l'oeil* frescoes (Joseph Mayer, 1756–57). To the right of the chancel is the entrance to the bishop's **Sacristy** (1684), with a small display of religious art. The room is also known as the **Acoustic Chapel**, as two people standing in opposite corners and facing the wall can hear each other whisper. The frescoes here, depicting the Triumph of Truth over Heresy, were reproduced after the war. Mayer's original can be viewed in the adjoining **Treasury** (1697), which suffered much less war damage. Here, there is a curious 'double vault', with Mayer's Old Testament scene—*Heliodorus Expelled from the Temple*—visible through the oval gap. Both the sacristy and treasury are open 10.00–14.00 and 15.00–19.00. The square in front of the cathedral was formerly occupied by the Jesuit College. Most of its buildings were dismantled in 1815, though two wings adjoining the cathedral to the north have survived (now state archives). In between them rises the **Trinitarian Tower**, reshaped in 1819 in ugly Neo-Gothic style, with a **Diocesan Museum of Religious Art** (open Tues–Sun 10.00–17.00) inside. Climb to the top for a fine view over the city.

Walk west along ul. Jezuicka, which skirts the back of the college. The façade of the *Dominican Church comes into view as you turn into the narrow ul. Dominikańska.

> The Dominicans settled in Lublin as early as 1260. Kazimierz the Great founded their first Gothic brick church in 1342, but this fell during a fire of 1575. Reconstruction saw the addition of a Renaissance interior and gable. During the mid-17C the towers were built and the chancel lengthened by means of the sumptuous Tyszkiewicz Chapel. Another fire in 1719 destroyed the furnishings, which were replaced in Rococo style.

The Dominican church rivals the cathedral as the city's finest monument of religious architecture. The interior is only accessible during mass (06.30, 08.00, 09.00, 18.00), but it is well worth a visit.

Tucked away in a side street, the west gable (Lublin Renaissance), consisting of a broad mass of stone with curly edges and segmented by pilasters, hardly gets the exposure it deserves. Most impressive are the chapels, beginning with the **Szaniawski Chapel** (1660) at the west end of the south aisle, where the fire of Lublin in 1719 is depicted in a large anonymous painting. Walk the length of the south aisle to the showpiece **Firlej Chapel** (1615–30), whose tall fluted pilasters rise to a dome and lantern. The exquisite decoration of the underside of the dome and the walls is attributed to the 17C mason and stuccoist Jan Wolff. Behind the high altar is the domed **Tyszkiewicz Chapel** (1645), with Baroque stuccoes and figural sculpture (1645–58, Giovanni Battista Falconi), and a scene of the *Last Judgement*. The Dominican monastery (mid-17C) adjoins the church to the south. Part of it is used by a popular playhouse (reached through an arch off ul. Dominikańska), with a small terrace overlooking the city suburbs.

Continue along ul. Archidiakońska, an extension of ul. Dominikańska, to a square-cum-terrace (pl. Po Farze), with the Lublin Castle looming in the distance (northeast). Turn right towards the castle. The **Grodzka Gate** marks the boundary of the Old Town, though its medieval appearance was lost after remodelling by Merlini in 1785. Beyond the gate, a viaduct, formerly a wooden bridge, connects the Old Town with the castle. Looking down and to your right, notice the freshly renovated **Hospital of St Lazarus and Church of St Adalbert** (1611), now an orphanage.

Despite its medieval origins, Lublin *Castle is almost a blot on the townscape. Founded by Kazimierz the Great, and later expanded during the Renaissance period, it fell into irrevocable decline after the wars and plagues of the 17C. By order of the Czar, the ruined buildings were rebuilt as a prison in 1823–26, the façades in forbidding Neo-Gothic style. Only the tower and castle chapel survived these alterations. The prison, where 80,000 were incarcerated during the Nazi occupation, remained operational until 1954. Today, the most interesting parts of the castle are the tower and chapel. The former, built on 13C stone foundations, was used to impound wayward nobles.

Behind the tower stands the ***Chapel of the Holy Trinity**, founded in c 1385 by Władysław Jagiełło. Remarkably, a single pillar supports the vaults covering the two-tiered Gothic interior. Exquisite **Ruthenian-Byzantine frescoes**, painted in 1418 by Orthodox priests in the service of King Władysław Jagiełło, cover the walls of the chancel, with 'Balkan' versions in the nave. The frescoes, which depict both religious and secular scenes, including an equestrian portrait of Jagiełło, are a European rarity. Since the war they have been undergoing painstaking restoration work, which is now more or less complete. The rest of the castle is a **museum** (open Wed–Sun 09.00–16.00) with exhibitions covering numismatics, prehistory, weaponry (14C–20C), decorative art (14C–19C), and an uncommonly good display of folk art (mainly 19C–20C). A small section devoted to Italian and Dutch Painting (17C–18C) is overshadowed by Polish Art (17C–20C), whose highlights are two Matejko canvases—*The Union of Lublin* and *The Admission of the Jews into Poland*—and some first-rate Polish Impressionism.

Majdanek

Southeast of the city centre lies Majdanek, the second largest Nazi death camp in Europe after Auschwitz-Birkenau, where over 360,000 people perished between 1941 and 1944. The ***museum** is open May–Sep 08.00–18.00, Oct–Apr 08.00–15.00 (children under 14 not allowed). If you are not arriving by car, trolley bus Nos 153 or 156 from the cathedral will drop you by the entrance. Since the war, Majdanek has been preserved as a memorial to the victims of genocide.

Unlike Bełżec and Sobibór, or other camps in the region, Majdanek was never liquidated; even as late as 1944, with the Red Army approaching from the east, the Nazis were planning to expand its capacity from 40,000 to 250,000 inmates. Initially, the camp was used as an internment centre for Soviet prisoners-of-war, but by 1942 most of the inmates were Polish civilians. The mass extermination of Jews began in 1943 with the intensification of Hitler's 'final solution'. Thousands from the Warsaw ghetto, but also from places as far away as Greece and Albania, were transported to the camp in cattle wagons; as survivors would later recount, it was the 'lucky' few who died on the journey. The largest mass execution took place on 3 November 1943, when 18,400 were shot in a single night. Majdanek was liberated by the Red Army on 22 July 1944.

Guidebooks to the camp and background material may be purchased at the pavilion on the left, which also shows a documentary film. The tour takes about two hours and begins with the vast **Monument to Struggle and Martyrdom**, opposite the main road. Thereafter you enter the site proper, with its fully preserved barracks (eleven of them open to the public), gas chambers, guard towers and barbed wire. The crematorium, where up to one thousand bodies were incinerated daily, and the ditches where mass executions would take place are situated at the end of the main alley. Here, too, is a giant urn-shaped **mausoleum**, containing the ashes of the victims. An inscription reads: 'Let our fate be a warning to you all'.

Northwest of the city centre is a well maintained **skansen** (Muzeum Wsi Lubelskiej; **open** Apr–Oct, Tues–Sun 10.00–17.00) on al. Warszawska, which offers a glimpse into the **traditional wooden architecture** of the region. The buildings exemplify different styles of rural architecture ranging from peasant cottages, barns and granaries, to a working windmill and a manor house with adjoining farm.

Chełm and the Borders

❖ Chełm • Włodawa • Sobibór

Leave Lublin going southeast (road 17) turning left at Piaski (road 82). In contrast to the lush parklands of the Vistula valley, the scenery here is wilder, less spoilt. Crossing the Wieprz river, flatness gives way to an undulating terrain of limestone hillocks.

The town of **CHEŁM** (70km, population 63,000) is spread out over a chalk and limestone hill, with the towers of its cathedral visible far off in the distance. The chalk has been mined for centuries, and you can visit a labyrinth of *****tunnels** underneath the town, which in the past were also used as escape routes and storage areas. The entrance is at ul. Lubelska 20, close to pl. Konstytucji, a convenient place to park. A short distance down the hill stands the *****Parish Church**, built to the design of Paolo Antonio Fontana for the Piarist Order in 1753–63. The standard late Baroque façade, with twin towers and a gable, conceals a far more impressive interior, whose plan recalls Fontana's churches in Lubartów and Włodawa (see below). Rich painted decoration by Joseph Mayer (1758) covers the long, elliptical nave.

Walk back to pl. Konstytucji and ascend the hill, whose summit is dominated by the former *****Uniate Cathedral** (1735–56), now the Church of St Mary. The late Baroque façade strikes a familiar note—the architect was once again Fontana—though the Doric portico and free-standing bell tower are the result of 19C remodelling. Next to the church are the buildings of the former Basilian Friars' Monastery (17C) and Palace of the Bishops of Chełm (18C). The site is surrounded by a pleasant park with a view over Chełm, somewhat obscured by trees.

Forty-seven kilometres north of Chełm, on road 83, is the border town of **WŁODAWA** (population 14,400), interesting for its assimilation of three religious cultures: in the vicinity of the spacious Market Square stand a Roman Catholic parish church (Paolo Antonio Fontana, 1741–80), a Russian Orthodox church, with its characteristic onion domes, and the best preserved synagogue (1774) in the Lublin region.

Inside the synagogue is the **Museum of the Łęczna-Włodawa Lake District**. This swampy, forested terrain stretches west of Włodawa, and is attractive for its nature reserves, numerous lakes, and many rare species of flora and fauna. Twelve kilometres southeast of Włodawa is the village of **SOBIBÓR**, the site of a former Nazi death camp (liquidated in 1943). In woodland, close to the railway station, is a monument to the 250,000 Jews who perished in the camp.

The Palace and Museum at Kozłówka

Leave Lublin on road 19 going north. In Lubartów turn west along a minor road to **KOZŁÓWKA**, one of the most sumptuous palatial complexes in Poland, albeit frequently omitted from tourist itineraries. Paolo Antonio Fontana built the initial late Baroque palace for the Palatine of Chełm, Michał Bieliński, in 1735–42, but today the estate is associated with the famous Zamoyski family, who owned it during its heyday (1799–1944). The Francophile and art connoisseur Konstanty Zamoyski remodelled the palace in 1879–1907 to house his vast collection of paintings, which covered almost every available centimetre of wall space (and still do). For a period after the war Kozłówka was used as a museum storehouse, apparently because the communist authorities found Zamoyski's collection too eccentric for public show—even worthless. Happily, the **museum* was reopened in 1977 and today offers 15 rooms of lavish Empire-style furnishings.

Individuals may visit at weekends, otherwise you have to follow the group tour (**open** Tues–Fri 10.00–16.00, Sat–Sun 10.00–17.00).

Be sure not to miss the **chapel** (separate entrance), and the magnificent **French park** at the back, with its fountain, well-pruned hedges and ancient lime-trees. For an amusing, though entirely different experience, visit the unique **Exhibition of Socialist-Realist Art* in one of the forecourt annexes. Here, ironic homage is paid the great heroes of yesteryear: there are busts of Lenin, Dzierżyński and Mao, eulogies to Stalin, paintings of brawny proletarians gazing towards a brighter future, and scores of other gems. The tour is set to some wonderfully tongue-in-cheek background music. Some of the scenes from Andrzej Wajda's *Man of Marble* (1977)—a wry look at the Stalinist years in Poland—were filmed inside the storage rooms. A huge statue of the Soviet-backed communist leader Bolesław Bierut stands behind the theatre building opposite the annexe.

Zamość

Zamość, a work of art in its own right, was designed from scratch. A formidable pair of individuals undertook the task. The first was the magnate **Jan Zamoyski**, who sought to establish a grandiose family seat and the capital of a veritable state-within-a-state, the *Ordynacja Zamoyskich*, which encompassed six cities and nearly 150 villages (and managed to survive until 1944). The other was the Italian architect **Bernardo Morando** of Padua (or perhaps Venice), who laboured to realise Zamoyski's dream. He laid out the entire plan of the compact town—a mere 600m by 400m—taking his inspiration from Pietro Cataneo, and possibly Duke Vespasiano Gonzaga, the builder of Sabbioneta in northern Italy, like Zamość a town designed from scratch to the delight of the Renaissance scientific mind.

■ Practical information
Hotels
★★★ *Jubilat*. Al. Prymasa Wyszyńskiego 52, ☎ 638-6401/05. The highest standard in town. Car park. 55 rooms.
★★ *Renesans*. Ul. Grecka 6, ☎ 639-2001/03. Central location. Car park. 28 rooms.

Tourist information (*PAPT*). Town Hall, Rynek Wielki 13, ☎ 39-22-92.
Post office. Ul. Kościuszki 9.
Telephone code: (0–84).

History
The contract to build Zamość was signed on 1 July 1578. Soon, settlers began to flock to the new city—Poles, Jews, Armenians, Greeks, Germans, Italians, Hungarians and Scots. The town was given a charter, later confirmed by King Stefan Bathory, whom Zamoyski served as Grand Chancellor of the Crown. Construction proceeded quite swiftly: **Zamoyski's palace** was finished in 1586, the wooden **Church of the Holy Cross** in 1584, by which time many houses had arisen (in 1591, of the 250 available lots, only 26 were still vacant), and a significant part of the fortifications had been completed, including the **Lublin Gate**. It was through this gate that in 1588 the Austrian Archduke Maximilian was ignominiously led as Zamoyski's prisoner taken at the battle of Byczyna. To commemorate the event, Zamoyski ordered the gate to be walled up, so that no one after the Archduke would have the privilege to pass through it (travellers from Lublin were thus forced to pay a tribute to the Chancellor's victory by taking an inconvenient detour via the Szczebrzeska Gate).

Morando died in 1600, five years before his patron. He left behind a legacy that has survived to the present day, albeit in a tarnished form. Greatest harm was done in the 19C, when the town was converted into a fortress guarding the border between Austria and the Kingdom of Poland, to which it belonged. Two houses in the Main Square were pulled down, others lost their Renaissance attics in favour of additional storeys, many historic buildings in the town, including several churches, were adapted for military use and rebuilt in the grim 'garrison-cum-prison' style. Restoration began in the inter-war period, but was completed only in the 1970s, and the result was much criticised. Indeed, the façades are already flaky and in need of renovation.

Old Town
The greatest attraction of Zamość is without doubt the *MAIN SQUARE (Rynek Wielki), with its characteristic Italian-style loggias and the 16C **Town Hall**, oddly not in the centre, but almost in line with the houses on the north side, only the guardhouse and huge staircase protruding.

The first town hall was erected by Morando in 1591–1600, and comprehensively rebuilt in 1639–51, when it acquired its tall attic, pilasters and niches. Some Baroque elements were introduced in 1767–70. The building served a municipal purpose and was the seat of the Zamoyski Tribunal, the organ of justice for the whole *Ordynacja*. In the 18C, it became a prison and lost its Mannerist arcades, attic and ornaments. Thanks to renovation in 1937–38, however, it regained its original splendour.

The exceptionally harmonious visual impact of the square was achieved by strict planning and compulsory adherence to Morando's ideas (at least throughout the 17C), exemplified for the benefit of future builders by two houses designed by the master himself: the **Tellani House** (1591–99) and Morando's own house at **No. 25** (1599–1604), both on the south side. Low and squat, they stand in sharp contrast to the slender, tall shapes employed in the burgher architecture of northern Poland, under the inspiration of Dutch models (as in Gdańsk). The Italian *loggia* was combined in Zamość with the uniquely Polish parapet, usually so high as to completely conceal the roof, and intricately ornamented.

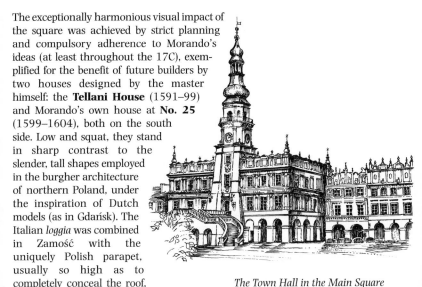

The Town Hall in the Main Square

Another mandatory element was the broad moulded frieze just above the arcades. Below them you can find some remarkable portals, real masterpieces of early Baroque ornamentation.

A somewhat different, rather oriental atmosphere predominates on the north side of the square, which from early on in the history of Zamość was the Armenian sector. The houses here were built in the 17C, and their decoration reflects the cultural influence of their original owners—wealthy Armenian settlers, engaging in trade with Turkey and Persia, who were attracted to Zamość by special privileges granted to them in 1585. The four best preserved houses (**Nos 24**, **26**, **28** and **30**) are now occupied by the **Regional Museum** (open Tues–Sun 10.00–16.00). Some interiors have beamed ceilings, characteristic painted friezes, and stucco decoration on the window jambs. The exhibits range from archaeological finds, through items illustrating the history of the town and the Zamoyski family (with some good portraits), religious art, to folk dress, art and artefacts. Don't miss the unique Armenian 'black kitchen' on the second floor of the house at No. 26.

Also on the north side of the square, one **house** is conspicuous for its style and proportions: it was built in the 17C by Jan Michał Link, whose military calling is clearly shown by the motifs of the frieze over the arcades. The busts in niches above the first-floor windows represent Minerva and Hercules.

A short detour from the Main Square brings you to the former **synagogue** on UL. ZAMENHOFA. In addition to Armenians and Greeks, Zamoyski invited Jewish settlers to his town and allowed them to build a wooden synagogue.

It was replaced with a brick one in 1610–20, initially only for men, later supplemented by a separate room for women (reconstructed after the war). Rich murals and stuccoes have survived inside.

The houses on the east side, like those on the north, originally belonged to Armenians, but then passed to professors of the Zamoyski Academy. Today they are distinguished primarily by the elegant stucco decoration of the arcades, also found in some of the vaulted halls. The art gallery on the first floor of **No. 14**, entered through a Renaissance portal from Morando's workshop, is usually worth a visit.

The Collegiate Church

Leave the square west along UL. STASZICA and walk to the ***Collegiate Church**, designed and built by Bernardo Morando.

> Most of the church was in place by the end of the 16C, and survived with little change until the 19C; the interior, though, is still relatively intact. Jan Zamoyski, the first *Ordynat* needed a church that would bear witness to the prestige of his family and serve as a burial place for many generations of *Ordynaci*, who would also be sworn in before its main altar. Over the centuries, it accumulated numerous mementoes of the great Zamoyskis, and it was precisely these that the Czar's brother, Prince Konstanty, set out to eradicate when he ordered the rebuilding of the church in 1824–26.

The lofty nave leads to a much lower and darker chancel, lit solely by twin windows partly obscured by the heavy, Baroque high altar. In contrast, note the restrained Mannerist stonework of the vaults, cornice and frieze. The splendid **silver tabernacle** is a masterpiece of Rococo art from Wrocław (1744–8).

Adjoining the chancel is the **Zamoyski Chapel**—the best in the church—decorated with excellent stuccoes by Giovanni Battista Falconi. Ask to be let in to see the funerary crypt of the Zamoyski family, located under the chapel (entrance from the south aisle).

At the west end of the nave is the **choir**, designed by Morando himself. In the second chapel from the west end of the north aisle hangs a captivating *Annunciation*, a copy of the famous painting from the Santissima Annunziata church in Florence.

North of the church is a free-standing bell-tower of 1760–75, rebuilt in 1830–1. Nearby, on the south side, stands the **Prelate's House** (*Infułatka*), built by Morando and remodelled in Baroque style in 1620. The **museum** inside (**open** Tues–Sun 10.00–16.00) contains items from the church treasury, including a remarkable Baroque font (1630), liturgical books, gold and silverware.

Leave the Collegiate Church and cross ul. Szczebrzeska to come to the former Arsenal, built in the 16C to store Zamoyski's war trophies. Today it is a **military museum** (open Tues–Sun 08.00–15.00).

UL. AKADEMICKA, which extends ul. Szczebrzeska to the north, used to be the main horizontal axis of the town, dividing Zamoyski's residence in the west from the burghers' district in the east, and connecting the Collegiate Church with the Academy. Walking north along it you will pass a late Baroque **seminary** (right) and the former **Zamoyski Palace** (left) at the far end of a large yard overgrown with trees. The palace was designed by Morando, but subsequently altered beyond recognition, particularly in the 19C, when it was turned into military barracks. It is currently used by law courts and other offices.

The quadrangular, whitewashed building of the **Zamoyski Academy** is a little further on.

Jan Zamoyski was a highly educated man—he studied at the universities of Kraków and Padua—with a discerning taste in art and a strong sense of civic responsibility. Naturally, his *Ordynacja* could not do without an academy, which was officially opened in 1595 in a house designed by Morando. From its inception, the Academy maintained close ties with the Collegiate Church, and was intended as a centre for the Counter Reformation. After the death of its generous and enlightened founder, it quickly fell into decline.

Today's building dates from a later period (1639–48) and was sponsored by Zamoyski's successor, the second *Ordynat*.

Next to the Academy is a park, with a **monument** to children from the Zamość region murdered by the Nazis. Nearby, partly below ground level, stands the **Old Lublin Gate** (see p. 300), currently occupied by a drama school. It belongs to the oldest part of the town's fortifications, begun by Morando, and completed in the 17C by Andrea dell'Aqua.

Continuing north along ul. Akademicka, turn right for the 17C **Reformed Franciscans' Church** opposite the New Lublin Gate. Further along are two brick-and-stone cavaliers, designed by General Mallet-Malletsky, the same man whom Prince Konstanty entrusted in the early 19C to transform the refined Mannerism of Morando's Zamość into a sombre 'garrison-cum-prison' style shorn of superfluous ornamentation. The grim cavaliers of dark brick, with stone arches and grass overgrowing the rooftops, are a good example. One of them—a former prison cell—is occupied by a market, now crowded mostly with Russian and Ukrainian traders. The Polish patriot Walerian Łukasiński was held here after 1822 for his anti-Czarist activities. Close by is the **Old Lwów Gate**, designed by Morando, and walled up in the 19C, when its functions were supplanted by the New Lwów Gate across the street.

War Cemetery

On ul. Męczenników, which joins ul. Szczebrzeska near the Arsenal (see above), you can visit **The War Cemetery** and **Martyrology Mausoleum**. The latter is housed in a rotunda built by General Mallet-Malletsky (**open** Apr–Oct, Tues–Sun 10.00–17.00), later used by the Nazis as a prison and execution site. This brick structure takes the form of a ring divided radially into cells connected by passageways. In the cells, graves, crosses and altars have been placed to commemorate those who perished here at the hands of the Nazis.

Pomerania

The region is known as Pomerania (Pomorze), its eastern part occupied by the **Vistula fens** (Żuławy Wiślane). On the Vistula bay (Zalew Wiślany), at the northeastern edge of the fens, lies the sleepy town of **Frombork**, where the astronomer Nicholas Copernicus lived and worked. Across the bay in **Sztutowo** (Stutthof) the Nazis built a notorious concentration camp, today a harrowing museum. Venturing southwest of Gdańsk you enter **Kashubia** (Kaszuby), with its local folklore, customs and dialect.

Western Pomerania is centred on the port-city of Szczecin, close to the German boder. Within easy reach of it are the preserved medieval towns of **Stargard** and **Kamień**. An attractive option is to follow the long '**Amber coast**', with its numerous resorts, spas and sandy beaches; the coastal scenery is most dramatic in the **Słowiński National Park**, a protected habitat with remarkable shifting dunes. Inland you enter a terrain of pine forests and lakes, one of the most unspoilt areas of the country.

The southeastern part of Pomerania is most interesting as far as art and architecture are concerned. Travelling upstream along the broad, slow-moving Vistula, you can visit numerous **castles built by the Teutonic Knights**, such as at **Gniew** and **Kwidzyn**, often scenically set in the river valley. The Knights had their capital in **Malbork**, 58km southeast of Gdańsk, where today there stands a vast Gothic castle. The Vistula has no shortage of fascinating towns, either: **Grudziądz**, with its riverside granaries, or **Chełmno**, with its preserved medieval plan, are well worth visiting, but **Toruń** has no equal and should not be missed. Founded by the Teutonic Knights, today it is a beautiful university town brimming with attractions, such as the medieval Town Hall, and three magnificent churches of St Mary, St James and SS John the Baptist and Evangelist.

Gdańsk

Gdańsk should be a natural base for anyone wishing to explore northern Poland. The city of Gdańsk (population 460,000) lies in the eastern part of Poland's Baltic coast, near the point where the Vistula river enters the sea. It overlooks the Gulf of Gdańsk (Zatoka Gdańska) and is shielded from the harsh sea winds by the **Hel peninsula**, a 34km strip of land to the north. Even in one week's stay you will probably not see all that the city and its environs have to offer. If the beach is not top priority, then spring or autumn is the best time to visit. The tourist infrastructure is fairly well developed, so unless you come at the very peak of the season, accommodation—whether a luxury hotel or private rooms—should be easy to find.

For those not arriving by car, Gdańsk can be reached easily by Express or Intercity train from Warsaw (3 hours 30 min.) and from most of the major cities. There is an airport in the suburb of Rębiechowo and LOT runs direct flights at least once a week even in low season. For the more adventurous, there are weekly ferry services from Finland and Sweden, and, less frequently, freighter ships with passenger accommodation from Britain.

Gdańsk is actually one element of the so-called **Tri-city** (Trójmiasto), a sprawling conurbation that encompasses the nearby resort of **Sopot** and the port-town of **Gdynia**. Both are worth a visit and can be easily reached by local commuter train.

Gdańsk contains some of the best architectural relics of Poland, in some respects rivalling even the ancient Royal capital of Kraków. Though as much as 90 per cent of this rich heritage was destroyed during the war, the historic centre has been completely rebuilt and is a sheer delight, attracting thousands of tourists each year. Many buildings were recently renovated to coincide with the city's millennium celebrations in 1997.

For centuries Gdańsk was a cosmopolitan city, and today this is reflected in the diversity of its architectural styles. **Flemish Mannerism** is especially in evidence, with rows of gabled and richly ornamented merchants' houses forming the city's characteristic skyline. Industry has also played an important role; the **vast shipyards** and port have been Gdańsk's hallmark since the Middle Ages, providing much of the city's income and prestige, and, more recently, giving rise to the **Solidarity movement**.

The city's major sights and attractions are concentrated in the Main Town (*Główne Miasto*), which is described in Walks 1 and 2. **WALK 1** proceeds along ul. Długa and ul. Długi Targ (The Royal Way). On these showpiece streets stand the imposing **Main Town Hall** and **Artus Court**, both containing excellent museums. **WALK 2** explores the area to the north of ul. Długi Targ, notably ul. Mariacka, Gdańsk's most famous street, dominated by the vast mass of **St Mary's church**. You then return to the riverside to see another famous landmark, **a giant medieval crane** ('*Żuraw*'). The crane houses the **Polish Maritime Museum**, which is continued in three old granaries situated on an island across the Motława river. **WALK 3** visits the **Castle Suburb** (*Zamczysko*) and **Old Town** (*Stare Miasto*). The highlights here are the **Polish Post Office**, scene of a heroic defence by postal workers during the Second World War, and the **Gdańsk shipyard**, the birthplace of Solidarity. On **WALK 4** in the Old Suburb (*Stare Przedmieście*) you should not miss the **Franciscan Church of the Holy Trinity**, and the **National Museum**, located inside the former monastery. **WALK 5** describes the suburb of **Oliwa**, with its famous cathedral and park. **WALK 6**—the bleak **Westerplatte peninsula**, where the Second World War began. The final two, somewhat shorter, walks (7 and 8) cover the remainder of the Tri-city—**Sopot** and **Gdynia**, further along the coast.

■ Practical information

Hotels
★★★★

Hanza. Ul. Tokarska 6, ☎ 35-34-27. The newest luxury hotel in Gdańsk, situated on the Motława river. Wheelchair access, car park, business services. 60 rooms.

Orbis-Hevelius. Ul. Heweliusza 22, ☎ 301-5631. Recently refurbished 1970s tower block in the centre of the Old Town. Orbis Travel office, car rental, car park, wheelchair access, Business Centre. 281 rooms, some with magnificent views over the Baltic coast.

Orbis-Novotel. Ul. Pszenna 1, ☎ 301-5611/18. Situated on Granary Island, close to the Old Town. Business services, wheelchair access. 152 rooms, some with views.

Orbis-Marina. Ul. Jelitkowska 20, ☎ 553-2079. Seaside location in the suburb of Jelitkowo. Car rental, car park, wheelchair access, swimming pool, Business Centre. 163 rooms overlooking the Baltic coast.

Orbis-Posejdon. Ul. Kapliczna 30, ☎ 553-1803. In the suburb of Jelitkowo, close to the beach. Car park, business services, swimming pool. 147 rooms.

★★★

Dom Aktora. Ul. Straganiarska 55/56, ☎ 301-5901. Small hotel-cum-pension located in the heart of the Main Town.

Jantar. Ul. Długi Targ 19, ☎ 301-9532/☎ 301-2716. Excellent central location. 46 rooms, some overlooking Długi Targ.

Mac-Tur. Ul. Beethovena 8, ☎ 302-4170. Small hotel situated close to the beach. Tourist information office, car park. 12 rooms.

Hotels in Sopot
★★★★

Orbis-Grand. Ul. Powstańców Warszawy 12/14, ☎ 551-0041. Art Nouveau building, beautifully situated on the seafront. Car rental, car park, wheelchair access, business services. 112 rooms, either overlooking the park or the sea. Overpriced.

Zhong Hua. Al. Wojska Polskiego 1, ☎ 550-2020. Wooden building under Chinese ownership, situated on the seafront. Clean and modern. Air conditioning, wheelchair access. 46 rooms.

★★★

Pensjonat Maryla. Al. Sępia 22, ☎ 551-0034. Recently refurbished villa, situated close to the seafront. Car park. 16 rooms as well as summer cabins.

Hotels in Gdynia
★★★★

Orbis-Gdynia. Ul. Armii Krajowej 22, ☎ 620-6661. Large hotel situated in the city centre. Orbis travel office, car park, car rental, wheelchair access, swimming pool, business services. 279 rooms, overlooking the sea.

★★

Dworek Paraszyno (near Strzebielino). 84–214 Bożepole Wielkie ☎ 76-25-15. A delightful 18C country mansion set in hilly woodland (14km from Wejherowo, west of Gdynia).

Restaurants in Gdańsk
Exclusive restaurants
Pod Łososiem, ul. Szeroka 52/54. Polish, European.

Tawerna, ul. Powroźnicza 19/20. French. Specialises in seafood.

Major, ul. Długa 18. European.

Medium-price restaurants
Kubicki, ul. Wartka 5. Polish.

Tan-Viet, ul. Podmłyńska 1/5. Vietnamese.

Milano, ul. Chlebnicka 49/51. Italian.

Retman, ul. Stągiewna 1. Polish.

U Szkota, ul. Chlebnicka 9/12. Polish, Scottish.

Halong, ul. Szeroka 37/39. Vietnamese and Chinese.

Cheap eateries

Jadłodajnia u Plastyków, ul. Chleb-
nicka 13/16. Polish.
Bar Pod Złotym Kurem, ul. Długa 4.
Polish.

Dom Aktora, ul. Straganiarska
55/56. Polish.
Napoli, ul. Długa 62/63. Pizzeria.
Kirkor, ul. Słowackiego 48. Polish.

Cafés

Palowa, ul. Długi Targ 47. Inside the
Town Hall.
Cocktail Bar Capri, ul. Długa 59/61.
Pożegnanie z Afryką, ul. Kołodziejska 4.

Café Korzenna, ul. Korzenna 33/35.
Inside the Old Town Hall.
Pellowski, ul. Podwale Staromiejskie
82.

Restaurants in Sopot
Exclusive restaurants

Villa Hestia, ul. Władysława IV 3/5.
Polish, European. Inside the *Villa
Hestia* hotel.
Balzac, ul. 3 Maja 7. French.
Zhong-Hua, al. Wojska Polskiego 1.
Chinese.

Medium-price restaurants

Irena, ul. Chopina 36. Polish.

Cheap eateries

Bar Przystań, al. Wojska Polskiego 11.
Polish.

Restaurants in Gdynia
Exclusive restaurants

La Gondola, ul. Portowa 8. Italian.

Medium-price restaurants

Jack-fish, ul. Jana z Kolna 55. International. Specialises in seafood.
Polonia, ul. Świętojańska 92/94. Polish.

Cheap eateries

Cyganeria, ul. 3 Maja 27. Polish.
Liliput, ul. Świętojańska 75. International.

Tourist Information Office (**PAPT**). ul. Heweliusza 27, ☎ 301-4355/301-
6637.
PTTK. ul. Bogusławskiego 1 (Highland Gate), ☎ 301-6096/301-1761
ORBIS. ul. Heweliusza 22, ☎ 301-12384. Inside the Orbis-Hevelius hotel (with
an American Express desk).

Main railway station. (Gdańsk Główny) ul. Podwale Grodzkie 1, ☎ 308–5260,
domestic; 301–1112, international. There is a tourist information desk inside the
main hall. To get to the historic centre, cross the busy thoroughfare and head
southeast (10 minutes).
    From Gdańsk Główny there are regular commuter services (yellow-blue SKM
trains) to Oliwa, Sopot and Gdynia (40 minutes), and, going in the opposite direction, to Brzeźno (a beach resort) and Nowy Port (for car ferries to Scandanavia).
Tickets (only usable on these trains) should be validated in the yellow machines
before boarding. You can also travel to Sopot and Gdynia by long-distance train
(local, fast, or express), but this does not cut down on the journey time.

Main coach station. ul. 3 Maja 12 (behind the main train station) ☎ 302-
1532, domestic. There is a tourist information desk inside the ticket hall.

Coaches for many domestic and foreign destinations leave from here.

Airport. Rębiechowo (14km west of the city centre), ul. Słowackiego 200, ☎ 341-5251. Public transport **bus B** runs from the airport to the main railway station. Taking a private taxi from the airport rank is expensive—it is much cheaper to phone for a 'radio taxi', which should cost around GBP 5 (USD 8) into the centre of Gdańsk.

LOT. ul. Wały Jagiellońskie 2/4, ☎ 952/953, 301-11-61.

British Airways. At the time of writing there is no British Airways office in Gdańsk, but the INT Express company is an authorised BA agent and runs a 24 hour information service. ul. Grunwaldzka 87/91, ☎ 346-0317/341-6220/341-9872.

Ferries. The ferry terminal is at ul. Przemysłowa 1 (Nowy Port) ☎ 343-1887. There are weekly crossings from Gdańsk to Oxelösund (Sweden) and twice weekly crossings to Helsinki. For more information, contact any Orbis travel office or Polska Żegluga Bałtycka (Polferries) in Gdynia, ul. Portowa 3, ☎ 620-8761/661-3534.

Public transport. Gdańsk is serviced by trams, Sopot and Gdynia by trolley-buses. Thus, you can only travel between the three cities by train. In Gdynia and Sopot, flat-rate tickets are used on buses and trolleybuses. In Gdańsk, the price of a ticket depends on the length of the journey. Bus and tram tickets are available for 10, 30 and 60 minute periods, and must be validated in the machine immediately after boarding. All tickets, including 24-hour ones, can be bought at kiosks.

Disabled travellers. Transport can be arranged through Zakłady Komunikacji Miejskiej, ☎ 341-7637 (Mon–Fri 6.00–15.00), or ☎ 341-9593 (Mon–Fri 6.00–21.30, Sat–Sun 7.00–21.00). A trip costs 0.55 PLN per 1km within the city, and 1 PLN per 1km outside the city.

Main post offices. ul. Długa 23 (Gdańsk); ul. Kościuszki 2 (Sopot); 10 Lutego 10 (Gdynia). The main post office in Gdańsk is **open** Mon–Fri 08.00–20.00, Sat 08.00–13.00; outside these times you may still be able to make telephone calls or send faxes at the telecommunications section (same building).
Telephone code: (0–58).

Taxis. There are numerous 'radio taxi' companies in the Tri-city. Telephone numbers are advertised on the taxis themselves and listed in the local press. By phoning for a radio taxi you can expect to reduce the standard fare by around one third.

Driving. A car is useful in Gdańsk for getting to Oliwa, Sopot Gdynia, and the Hel peninsula; the city centre, though, is best visited on foot. As a rule, only taxis and local residents may drive in the Main Town, while some parts of it (e.g., ul. Długi Targ) are wholly pedestrian zones. Driving is less restricted in the Old Town, but here, too, all the sights are within easy walking distance. Parking meters have been installed on many roads in the city centre, though it is much safer to leave your car at a guarded car park—the difference in cost is minimal. Parking meters take tokens, which are available from kiosks.

Major festivals. International Guitar Festival (**April**); International Festival of Organ, Choral and Chamber Music (**June–August**); International Festival of Organ Music in Oliwa (**July**); Dominican Fair (**August**); Shakespeare Festival (August); Pomeranian Folk Festival (August); International Song Festival in Sopot (August); Polish Film Festival (**October**).

History

We first hear of the city of Gdańsk (Gyddanyzc) in Slavnikovic's biography of bishop Adalbert from Prague *Vita Sancti Adalberti*, written in Rome c 1000. Adalbert was later to become a Polish saint (see p. 44). The text speaks of a city inhabited by many people (approximately 1200), under the rule of the Polish king, **Bolesław the Brave** (Chrobry). Other sources, primarily archaeological, confirm that as early as 997, a fortified settlement existed at the mouth of the Motława river (the present-day suburb of Zamczysko), the point where the old 'amber trail' from the south reached the Baltic.

Until the 14C Gdańsk was ruled by the **East Pomeranian Dukes**, relatives of the Polish Piast dynasty. The town flourished, largely on account of its ideal location as a trading centre. Soon a new port arose on the Motława and in c 1238 Duke Świętopełk (1217–66) granted a charter to the two main centres in the city: roughly the area of today's Old and Main Towns.

Feudal divisions and the extinction of the Pomeranian dynasty in the 12C ushered in a period of instability that was to culminate in the seizure of Gdańsk by the **Teutonic Knights** (see p. 334) in 1308. The Knights destroyed much of the city, including the Duke's Castle, which they replaced with one of their own. In the 1350s they laid out the Main Town on a regular plan, the only part of Gdańsk to have one, and in 1393 the city also embraced the Old Suburb to the south. It was during this period that Gdańsk joined the **Hanseatic League**—a medieval association of free towns in the Baltic region—to which the city owed much of its prosperity during the coming centuries.

In 1454, the Gdańsk burghers revolted against the increasingly oppressive rule of the Teutonic Knights, razing their castle to the ground. Pressure from the Prussian Union on Polish King Kazimierz the Jagiellon to annex the lands seized by the Knights led to the **Thirteen Years War** (1454–66), with the Poles emerging victorious and regaining the city at the Peace of Toruń in 1466. In reality, however, Gdańsk was a free city, and Polish monarchs never exercised more than nominal suzerainty over it.

The Seventeenth–Nineteenth Century

In the 16C and 17C Gdańsk became the pre-eminent city of the **Polish Commonwealth**, with a near monopoly on the lucrative Baltic trade in grain, timber and fish. These halcyon days were reflected in architecture: austere Gothic buildings were given new life; new ones went up infused with Italian and, later, as the Hansa went into decline, Dutch and Flemish influence. Besides Poles and Germans, there was a host of other European nationalities, including the Scots, who even had their own district (Stare and Nowe Szkoty—Old and New Scots). Gdańsk gained a reputation for tolerance, enshrined in King Stephan Bathory's decree of 1584, which provided refuge to the many thousands of Protestants fleeing the religious wars in Western Europe. The city was home to such famous personages as the astronomer Johannes Hevelius (1611–87), the physicist Daniel Gabriel Fahrenheit (1686–1736), the Baroque sculptor Andreas Schlüter (1664–1714), the engraver Johannes Daniel Falk (1768–1826), and Joanna Schopenhauer (1770–1838), mother of the philosopher (also born in Gdańsk in 1788).

Though besieged from 1626 to 1629, Gdańsk was lucky to escape much of the havoc and destruction wreaked by the **Swedish Deluge** in the mid-17C (see p. 49). The Swedes were finally driven out at the Peace of Oliwa in 1660, but the city suffered again, this time badly, during a concerted **Russian attack** in 1734. In the 18C Gdańsk went into decline, a process mirrored by the political weakening of the Polish state. Fires and plagues played their part (an especially pernicious one killed over 20,000 in 1709), and by 1800 the city's population had fallen to half its peak. The **Second Partition of Poland** of 1793 meant that Gdańsk was swallowed up by the powerful Prussian state, and despite the liberation of the city by Napoleon's armies in 1807, Prussian dominance was restored at the **Congress of Vienna** (1815).

The Twentieth Century

Under the **Treaty of Versailles**, which ended the First World War, neither Gdańsk nor the mouth of the Vistula were restored to the new Polish state; instead, Poland was accorded a stretch of barren coastal land to the west of the city (Hitler's infamous '**Polish corridor**'). The peacemakers declared Gdańsk (Danzig) a Free City (as Napoleon had done a century before) under the auspices of the League of Nations, and it retained this status until the Nazis entered in 1939. With no port of its own, Poland had a new one built at Gdynia (now part of the Tri-city), which soon became the largest in the Baltic.

From 1930 onwards the presence of the Third Reich began to make itself felt in the city; on 1 September 1939 German divisions attacked the Polish Post Office in the city centre and a Polish munitions depot on the peninsula of Westerplatte, thus beginning the **Second World War**; the defence was as heroic as the eventual destruction in 1945 was absolute. The war years took a terrible toll on the city—90 per cent of it was destroyed, leaving tens of thousands dead. Most of the destruction came in the final battle between the retreating Germans (forbidden by Hitler to surrender) and the Red Army under Marshall Rokossowski. On 28 March 1945, the Polish flag was raised over the ruins of Artus Court in the Main Town.

After the war, painstaking reconstruction work to salvage old Gdańsk from the ruins began. In most cases the original brick was used, but generally only the façades, not the interiors, have maintained their former appearance. The Main Town you see today has been made to look like the Gdańsk of 1450–1650, with many of the later changes now lost.

Walk One ~ The Royal Way

The walk begins at the *Highland Gate at the west end of UL. DŁUGA. Brick and originally plain, the gate was built in 1574–75 as part of the city's modern fortifications; their architect was Johann Kramer of Dresden. Earth ramparts on both sides reached to the level of the frieze, which, along with the rest of the relief decoration, was made in 1588 by Willem van den Blocke.

> Willem van den Blocke (?–1628), a Dutch sculptor trained in Antwerp and Königsberg, came to Gdańsk in 1584 to work on the Highland Gate. He soon became known in other parts of Poland and commissions were plentiful: he did the tomb of Jan III Vasa (now in Uppsala, Sweden), numerous other tombs and memorial tablets. His two sons were also accomplished artists: the architect and sculptor Abraham, and painter Izaak; most of their works were done in and for Gdańsk. All three died in the same year—1628.

Floral motifs carved in sandstone slabs provide the setting for the sculptures, pilasters, inscriptions and three cartouches in the east façade: of Eastern Prussia on the left, supported by two unicorns, of the Kingdom of Poland in the centre, flanked by two angels, and of Gdańsk, guarded by lions. Four more lions are portrayed above the frieze. Next to the gate, looking towards the Main Town, is the medieval **Torture Chamber** and **Prison Tower**, now a branch of the Museum of the History of Gdańsk (**open** Mon–Fri 08.00–17.00). The two parts—the Tower and the Chamber—are linked to 15C Gothic walls, forming the so-called 'neck'. The Torture Chamber has four pretty Renaissance gables (1593) decorated with sculptures, facing both the outside and inside of the small courtyard in between the walls of the 'neck'.

Slightly further west stands the ***Golden Gate**, designed by Abraham van den Blocke in 1612–14, with a balustrade surmounted by eight allegorical sculptures (four on each side) representing peace, freedom, wealth, fame, prudence, piety, justice and concord. To the left is the **Court of the Fraternity of St George** (a kind of exclusive archery club). It is a splendid example of lay Gothic architecture in the Flemish style, once so popular in Gdańsk, with its angle towers, crenellated parapet, and curious turret topped by a copper-green St George fighting the dragon (a copy; the original is in Artus Court; p. 314).

Ul. Długa

Pass through the Golden Gate onto ul. Długa (Long Street), which curves down towards the river. The street was laid out in the 13C, but most of the wealthy burghers' houses that you see are later additions, commissioned by rich merchants during the Hanseatic era. In 1945 ul. Długa was turned into smouldering rubble; nearly everything you see today is the result of reconstruction and renovation work, sometimes not of the highest quality, and in constant need of maintenance.

The dark red house at **No. 12**, with a carved door and pilastered portal, was built in 1776 for the Flemish town councillor Uphagen, after whom it is also called. The owner established it as a museum of 18C Gdańsk interiors, but most of its Rococo furniture and decoration was destroyed in 1945. Today, the house accommodates a branch of the **Museum of the History of Gdańsk** (open Tues–Fri 10.00–16.00, Sun 11.00–16.00). The elegant **Ferber house** (No. 28; right) was built in 1560 in Italian Renaissance style. It is also known as 'Adam and Eve' after the relief decorating the door which shows the unfortunate pair. **No. 29**, with medallions of Roman emperors on the façade (reconstruction), was built c 1620, allegedly by Abraham van den Blocke (see previous page), who also did **No. 30** (a barber's shop), with sculptures above the portal and an ornamental door. Both are fine examples of Mannerism. No. 35, known as the **Lion House** (after two lions sitting on the capitals of the portal), is the work of Johann Kramer of Dresden (1569); the sculptures decorating the façade are by F. Vroom of Haarlem. **No. 45**, on the corner of ul. Długa and ul. Ławnicza was built around 1560 for the wealthy Konert family. Its rich, almost palatial façade is decorated with fluted pilasters running from top to bottom.

The Main Town Hall

Gdańsk has two town halls. The **Main Town Hall** on UL. DŁUGI TARG (No. 47) was restored after severe destruction in 1945. It is now occupied by the ***Museum of the History of Gdańsk** (open Tues–Fri 10.00–16.00, Sun 11.00–16.00).

> The Town Hall received its present form in the 16C, when the original Gothic architecture was remodelled in Renaissance style by several outstanding artists, such as Hans Vredeman de Vries, Izaak van den Blocke (see previous page), Willem van den Meer the Younger, Simon Herle and Antoni Möller, working under the supervision of Anthonis van Opbergen. It was then that the interiors received their sumptuous decoration. However, the hall itself, damaged and rebuilt many times over the centuries, dates back to 1379–82; the murals in the 'Mały Krzysztof' chamber are the only remnants preserved from those times. The building served as a royal residence: Kazimierz the Jagiellon, Aleksander, and Zygmunt the Old all stayed here. It was surmounted by a gilded statue of King Zygmunt August (1561), placed on top of the tower, and a 14-bell carillon, which melted during the fire of 1945.

The building attracts attention with its 81m tall tower (the highest in Gdańsk), corner turrets and a sandstone parapet of 1562 in the east façade. Enter through a late Baroque portal, with the Gdańsk coat of arms supported by two lions looking towards the Golden Gate. The low-vaulted staircase behind the massive door is a surprise. It leads to the ground floor hall, where there is a wooden winding staircase and a Baroque portal (c 1680) richly carved in oak. The eagle above bears Jan Sobieski's coat of arms (Janina). Sobieski's victory at Vienna, when Christendom was saved from the Ottoman Turks, is depicted in the large, modern ceiling painting. The east wall has a stone portal of 1570.

Walk left through the Baroque portal to the **Red Hall**, formerly the Great Council Chamber. The **portal** on this side is Simon Herle's true masterpiece of 1596, its decoration corresponding to the inlaid wooden frieze running around the room. Above it are seven allegorical paintings by Hans Vredeman de Vries (1595). The ceiling is covered with paintings, including 25 by Izaak van den Blocke, 1608–09, with a centrepiece of *The Apotheosis of Gdańsk*, all framed by Simon Herle. They form a rich and varied mosaic of scenes of Gdańsk. The Renaissance **fireplace**, carved by Willem van der Meer, is equally impressive.

An inlaid portal by Simon Herle leads to the **Winter Room**. Most of its original furniture has been destroyed; the 17C fireplace, shattered by a bomb in 1945, was painstakingly reassembled by conservators. Only one of the bosses is original (with the coat of arms of Royal Prussia). The next room—the **Small**

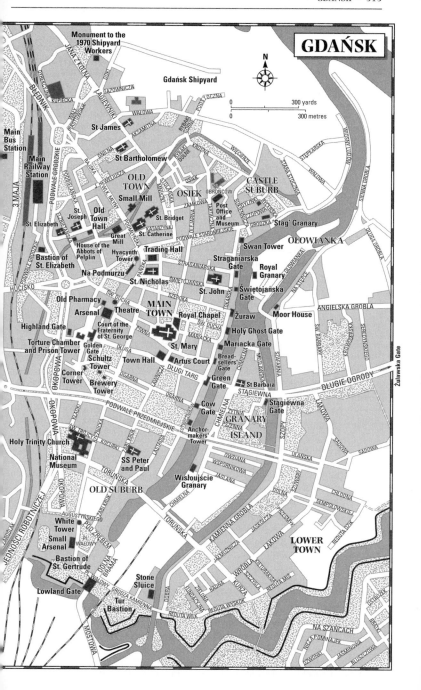

GDAŃSK

N

0   300 yards

0   300 metres

Monument to the 1970 Shipyard Workers

Gdańsk Shipyard

Main Bus Station

Main Railway Station

St James

St Bartholomew

OLD TOWN

OSIEK

CASTLE SUBURB

Small Mill

Post Office and Museum

'Stag' Granary

St. Joseph

Old Town Hall

St. Bridget

St. Elizabeth

Great Mill

St. Catherine

Swan Tower

OŁOWIANKA

House of the Abbots of Pelplin

Hyacinth Tower

Trading Hall

Straganiarska Gate

Royal Granary

Bastion of St. Elizabeth

Na Podmurzu

St. Nicholas

St. John

Świętojańska Gate

HUCISKO

St John

Old Pharmacy

Theatre

MAIN TOWN

Royal Chapel

Żuraw

Moor House

ANGIELSKA GROBLA

Arsenal

Court of the Fraternity of St. George

Holy Ghost Gate

Highland Gate

St. Mary

Mariacka Gate

Torture Chamber and Prison Tower

Golden Gate

Schultz Tower

Town Hall

Artus Court

Bread-sellers' Gate

Corner Tower

Brewery Tower

Green Gate

St Barbara

DŁUGIE OGRODY

Żuławska Gate

Cow Gate

Stągiewna Gate

GRANARY ISLAND

Anchor-makers' Tower

Holy Trinity Church

National Museum

SS Peter and Paul

Wisłoujście Granary

OLD SUBURB

LOWER TOWN

White Tower

Small Arsenal

Bastion of St. Gertrude

Lowland Gate

Stone Sluice

Tur Bastion

NA SZAŃCACH

Court Room—has original vaults, a Renaissance fireplace with a statue of King David (1730) from St Bridget's Church, and a display of photographs of honorary citizens of Gdańsk, including German President Paul Hindenburg and the neo-Kantian philosopher Heinrich Rickert. From the **Zodiac Room** ascend the stairs to the upper floor, which houses a display of artistic crafts, mostly 16C–18C Gdańsk productions. Two rooms are devoted to the cultural heritage of the city; the main exhibit is a statue of Schopenhauer. From there continue through to the '**Kamlarnia**'—the chamber of the city treasury. Its most precious item is Antoni Möller's arc-shaped painting *Penny Rent* (1601), with the Gdańsk Main Town forming the backdrop. The **Small Treasury** contains a display of coins, while the large Maritime Room is used for temporary exhibitions. To get a good view of Gdańsk you can climb the tower. Refreshments are served in the popular *Palowa* café, downstairs in the cellars.

Ul. Długi Targ is a short and broad street that extends ul. Długa and forms the last section of the Royal Way. It begins at the Town Hall and terminates at the Green Gate, behind which is the Motława river. Ul. Długi Targ is the main tourist attraction with souvenir shops, a hotel and street art. The raised terraces (*przedproża*) give the street the unique flavour of Gdańsk's Main Town (see below).

Walking down towards the river you pass on your right several magnificent residences, many times honoured by royal visits. The stone slab embedded into the terrace of the house at **No. 2** is original and dates back to 1577; the other Mannerist elements of the façade had to be reconstructed. Likewise, the Neoclassical **No. 1** and the Baroque **No. 3–4** are reconstructions. **No. 19** is now the Hotel Jantar. The house at **No. 20** was built in 1680 by Andreas Schlüter. Its Baroque façade has some original sculptural decoration.

The *****Green Gate** (probably named after the bridge behind it), though intended as a royal residence, never fulfilled this role. It was built in 1564–68 by Johann Kramer from Dresden and Regnier from Amsterdam; it was also from Amsterdam that the special small bricks used in its construction were imported. The gate, or rather palace, has rich stonework, with sculptures, door and window surrounds, and a fine heraldic frieze.

Turning back towards the Town Hall, don't miss the humorous grotesque masks on the house at **No. 25** (corner of ul. Długi Targ and ul. Pończoszników), depicting several architects and renovators who restored ul. Długi Targ after the war. The greatest expression of Gdańsk Mannerism is the *****Golden** (or **Steffens**) **House** (No. 41); the stone façade has four storeys of pilasters and herms, with biblical and antique scenes in entablature panels, surmounted by statues of Cleopatra, Oedipus, Achilles and Antigone on the balustrade, and a statue of the goddess Fortune on the roof, all carved in 1616–18 by Johann Voigt from Rostock (workshop of Abraham van den Blocke). The **Nowy Dom Ławy** (No. 43) has an original 15C Gothic façade, a Mannerist portal (1617) and Baroque gable (1712). The ground floor hall, called 'Sień Gdańska', (Gdańsk Hall) is traditionally used for art exhibitions. The **Stary Dom Ławy** (No. 45) at the corner of ul. Kramarska (west of Artus Court) has a few original elements, such as pilasters and sculptures in the gable; the sculptures on the terrace, depicting Minerva, Cronus and Apollo, were carved c 1750 by Johann Heinrich Meissner, who also did the Rococo porches of the neighbouring Artus Court.

*****Artus Court** was erected in 1478–81, and served the city's merchant corporations and guilds. The Renaissance façade, designed by Abraham van den Blocke (see p. 311) and constructed in 1617, is dominated by three large pointed-arch windows, above which is a gable with allegorical sculptures depicting Justice and Might. Other sculptures found in the façade include Scipio, Themistocles, Marcus Furius Camillus and Judas Maccabaeus. The stone portal has reliefs of King Zygmunt Vasa and Władysław IV.

The **interiors** were opened in 1997 after lengthy refurbishment to mark the beginning of the Gdańsk millennium celebrations. The huge hall, covered with elaborate Gothic vaults supported on four slender pillars, is now a **museum** (**open** Tues–Fri 10.00–16.00, Sun 11.00–16.00). Its highlight is a magnificent 16C **Renaissance stove**, decorated with tiles portraying European rulers, coats of arms, and personifications of the virtues and planets. Note, also, the beautiful late Gothic sculpture of St George killing the dragon, c 1485, by Hans Brandt. Some of the treasures that accumulated in the hall over the ages are now in the National Museum (see p. 326).

In front of Artus Court stands the **Fountain of Neptune**, cast by Peter Husum in 1613 and renovated several times afterwards. The overall design and some of the stone decoration is by Abraham van den Blocke.

The houses in **ul. Ogarna**, running parallel to ul. Długi Targ, are the oldest in Gdańsk except for the Royal Way. They suffered badly in 1945 and their reconstruction was not always faithful to the original form. Apparently the name '*Ogarna*' (hound) originated in the late 14C: it was along this street that a pack of vicious dogs was led each evening to Granary Island, to guard the treasures amassed by the Gdańsk merchants. **No. 27** houses the British Council library. **Daniel Fahrenheit**, the inventor of the temperature scale that bears his name, was born in 1686 in the former house at **No. 94**—to commemorate this event, a plaque in the form of a thermometer hangs on the wall.

Walk Two ~ Town Centre

Begin the walk at the **Bread-sellers Gate** on the waterfront north of ul. Długi Targ. This is one of seven Gothic watergates-turned-storehouses lining the promenade along the river Motława. They constitute the most imposing remnant of the **medieval walls** and belong to Gdańsk's most characteristic sights, recalling the urban plan of her sister cities—Toruń, Elbląg, and Lübeck—with parallel main streets running from west to east, down to the riverside. Dating from 1454 (rebuilt in 1961), the Bread-sellers' Gate bears the Gdańsk coat of arms without the crown, bestowed upon the city only later by King Kazimierz the Jagiellon. Continue through the arch and up **ul. Chlebnicka**, where, looking back, you will get the best view of the gate's broad asymmetrical mass and panelling.

Local ferry trips. Next to the Bread-sellers' Gate is a ferry harbour with local tours (☎ 301-4916):

Westerplatte	(15 Mar–15 Nov)	10.00 and 14.00
Sopot	(15 May–30 Sep)	08.00 and 13.00
Gdynia	(15 May–30 Sep)	13.00
Hel	(15 May–30 Sep)	08.00

The **English House** at UL. CHLEBNICKA No. 16 (also called the Angel House—in Polish the two words sound alike) was once the city's tallest. Built in a Mannerist spirit by Johann Kramer in 1569, the broad mass of the façade abounds in pilasters, adorned with sculpture and plasterwork, and is topped by a large gable. Next door is a reconstructed early Baroque house of 1644 (**No. 15**), twin-gabled, with an admirable stone carved portal leading through to the *Jadłodajnia u Plastyków* (cheap nutritious fare). The square-gabled **Schlieff House** (No. 14), c 1520, has a reconstructed Gothic façade, complete with imitation tracery.

Continue along ul. Chlebnicka, which merges with UL. PIWNA; right at the end, facing the Arsenal (see below), is a group of reconstructed houses (Nos 1–3), 17C–19C; the best is **Schlüter the Elder's House** at No. 1 with an Mannerist façade of 1640, adorned with wrought-iron signs.

At the end of ul. Piwna is the *****Arsenal**, a masterpiece of Flemish Mannerism. The design is by van Opbergen, the sculptures by two other Flemish masters—Abraham van den Blocke (see p. 311) and Willem van den Meer. Although the building itself was greatly damaged in 1945, the decoration is mostly original. Between the two doorways on the east façade is a well covered with a canopy resting on four pillars—it was used to bring cannon balls up from the cellars by a special lift. Crowning the gables on the west side are stone balls with radiating metal spikes, supposed to represent exploding cannon balls and attesting to the original purpose of the building (now a shopping centre and art school). A covered passage connects the Arsenal to the medieval **Straw Tower**; the passage was originally used to carry gunpowder stored beneath the tower.

The north side of Targ Węglowy is dominated by the **Theatre** (Teatr Wybrzeże); behind it on ul. Teatralna is the **Old Pharmacy**, built in 1636 by Anthonis van Opbergen. The name is rather misleading, as it was used to manu-facture munitions and cannon balls. In the tympanum, stone lions support the Gdańsk coat of arms. The Baroque façade has kept its original decoration of stone cannon balls of many sizes. Continue through the passage (ul. Teatralna) and walk west along ul. Św. Ducha towards St Mary's Church.

St Mary's Church

The construction of the Gothic *****Church of St Mary** began in 1343 and took 159 years to complete. It is one of the largest brick churches in the world and certainly the largest of its kind in Poland: 105m long and 5000 sq.m in area. The interior is truly vast—25,000 people can be accommodated with ease—and one is immediately struck by the emptiness of the place; the interior walls, sheer and whitewashed, serve to accentuate the enormous breadth and depth. Outside, St Mary's could almost pass for a Teutonic castle, its massive brick walls rising skyward, the buttresses entirely hidden from view and in fact forming 29 chapels.

> Originally built as a basilica, St Mary's was subsequently remodelled as an aisled hall with transepts, completed in 1447 along with the aisled chancel. The nave and aisles followed in 1484–98, while the impressive vaults—star, net and cellular—were constructed by Henryk Hetzel in 1498–1502. In 1945 the church suffered severe damage: nearly half of the vaults collapsed, the roofs burned down, the bells melted. Fortunately, many of the works of art that could be moved were taken away, and some are still

waiting to be restored to their original places. Reconstruction began soon after the war and is still under way.

■ St Mary's is **open** to visitors Mon–Sat 08.00–17.30 and Sun 13.00–17.30. **Tower open** Mon–Sat 09.00–17.00, Sun 13.00–17.00; summer only.

The main entrance is through a portal in the west façade, which is dominated by the massive tower (70m). In the **nave** you first reach an octagonal grille surrounding the font and supported on a relief-decorated stone base (1554). Behind you is an 17C early Baroque organ loft moved from the derelict St John's Church, while further east hangs a splendid brass chandelier of 1490 in the form of a basket; the wooden sculpture of the Madonna it once contained is lost. The pulpit (1617) also comes from the Church of St John.

North Aisle. Situated at the west end, the Chapel of St Rajnold contains a copy of Hans Memling's *Last Judgement* (see p. 326) and a Gothic *Pietà*, c 1410. Close by is the entrance to the **tower** which you can climb for a **magnificent view** of the city. Inside the Chapel of St Magdalene, first in the north aisle, is the memorial tablet of Michał Loytz (1561) and a 17C painting, *The Finding of Moses by the Pharaoh's Daughter*. The next chapel has a 15C Gothic altar and five alabaster reliefs (c 1420). St Anne's Chapel follows with a 'Beautiful Madonna' (c 1420).

North Transept. On the west wall are two recently restored Gothic murals, a landscape (c 1400) above and a townscape (c 1500) below. An exquisite 17C grille surrounds perhaps the best **tomb** in the church: that of **Szymon and Judyta Bahr** (1620, Abraham van den Blocke). Nearby is an astronomical clock—a reconstruction of the original work by Hans Düringer, dating from 1464–70—which shows the time, date and moon phase. Further on, by a pillar facing the Gothic portal to the sacristy, hangs an intricate wooden tabernacle of 1482. The adjacent pillar to the west has an allegorical panel painting by Antoni Möller (1607).

Moving to the **chancel**, the rood beam supports a Passion group, 1517, of monumental proportions (the figure of Christ is 4.35m tall). The **high altar** is a late Gothic polyptych depicting the *Coronation of the Virgin* and originates from the workshop of Master Michael of Augsburg (1536). Its back has a stone relief (1536), depicting the *Garden of Olives*. In the east wall of the chancel, on the right, is the entrance to the **Chapel of St Jadwiga**, closed off with a Gothic wrought-iron grille. Inside is the altar of St Jadwiga, c 1435, and, set in the floor in front of it, two tomb slabs. The most precious in the church, these belong to Konrad Letzkau and Arnold Hecht, two prominent Gdańsk burghers, who were murdered by the Teutonic Order in 1410.

The corner Chapel of Balthazar, by the **south transept**, contains the sumptuous tomb of the Ferber family. On the wall to the right of this chapel hangs the fine memorial tablet of Edward Blemke, 1591, by Willem van den Blocke, which depicts the *Last Judgement*.

The former Chapel of the Brotherhood of Mary, at the east end of the **south aisle**, is now dedicated to the 2779 priests murdered by the Nazis during the Second World War. Further west, in the vestibule, is a Gothic sculpture of St Anne, and the memorial tablet of Jan Brandes (1586).

On the square in front of the church (clock side) is the half-timbered **Ferber House** (1518; ul. Plebania No. 5–7), once used by the clergy of St Mary's and now containing a religious bookshop.

The **Royal Chapel**, at the corner of ul. Św Ducha and ul. Plebania, is the only Baroque church in Gdańsk. A renowned team consisting of architect Tylman van Gameren, sculptor Andreas Schlüter, and chief mason Bartholomäus Ranisch began work on the chapel in 1678. The fine sandstone sculptural decoration on the façade is by Schlüter, while Gameren devised the central plan with the dome carried on an octagonal drum. The gabled wings rise above low doorways to look almost like narrow houses, while the central section is topped by a balustrade with open lanterns flanking the main dome. Above the main doorway is a decorative cartouche bearing the emblems of Poland and Lithuania; inside, the chapel is contained within a first floor chamber (often closed) with a fresco running around the inside of the dome.

Ul. Mariacka

Skirting the Royal Chapel you enter *UL. MARIACKA near the east end of St Mary's Church. The street, once popularly known as the Polish Montmartre, was traditionally home to artists and writers, though nowadays they have made way for boutiques selling amber to tourists. With the castle-like St Mary's looming at one end, and the Mariacka Gate at the other, the street has an atmospheric, almost picture-postcard feel to it; the tranquillity is only disturbed during the first two weeks of August, when the street is taken over by the Dominican Fair, a tradition dating back to 1260. The amber boutiques are set below ground level between raised terraces with low carved stone parapets. The terraces, or *przedproża*, quite unique in Poland, front the reconstructed Gothic and Mannerist buildings down both sides of the street. An especially fine example is the terrace of the house at **No. 1**, ornamented with a pair of unique late Gothic slabs. **No. 6**, from 1600, has Tuscan pillars framing the porch. Best of all is perhaps **No. 26**, adjoining the gate. Built in 1598 (and reconstructed) it was once the main office of the Natural Science Society. The central block is topped by a gable and adjoins a slender seven-storey tower with turret; from the riverside you can catch a glimpse of the charming five-storey oriel. The asymmetrical mass of the impressive **Mariacka Gate** (late 15C) is set between corner towers. Together with No. 26 it houses the **Archaeological Museum** (open Tues, Thur–Fri 09.00–16.00; Wed 10.00–17.00, Sat–Sun 10.00–16.00), with a standard display tracing the history and prehistory of the Slavonic and Germanic tribes in East Pomerania.

The Żuraw and Polish Maritime Museum

Going north along the riverside, you pass the most modern of the water gates, the **Holy Ghost Gate**, originally 15C Gothic but completely remodelled since the war. Beyond it is one of Gdańsk's greatest treasures: the *Żuraw, a massive medieval crane, all of wood, set between two brick towers, the only one of its kind on the European mainland.

> The oldest document mentioning a wooden crane in the port of Gdańsk dates from 1367. After repeated fires, the Żuraw was rebuilt in 1442. It consisted of two solid towers with 4m thick walls supporting a giant projecting hoist, over 30m tall. The mechanism was powered by means of two giant wheels used as a kind of medieval treadmill. The wheels could each lift 2 tonnes in weight and were used to load and unload heavy cargo,

or to step the masts of the city's ships. With the advance of technology and the construction of the New Port in the 19C, the importance of the Żuraw declined; the towers were given over to housing and commerce, while the crane fell into disuse. All that was left of it in 1945 were two empty shells: everything else had been burnt to cinders. Reconstruction work con-tinued until 1962, when the building was reopened as a branch of the Polish Maritime Museum.

The **Polish Maritime Museum** consists of four parts: the main building (and ticket office) at ul. Szeroka 67; the adjoining Żuraw (the medieval crane); three granaries—Virgin (c 1600), Copper (17C–19C), and Oliwa (15C)—across the river on **Ołowianka** island (ferry tickets in the main building); and the ship-turned-museum Sołdek. All four sections are **open** Tues–Sun 10.00–16.00; for guides, ☎ 301-6938 or ☎ 301-8611/12.

The first and least interesting part (main building) has an exhibition devoted to prehistoric and traditional boats from Poland and around the world; the second (inside the Żuraw), with the emphasis on 20C maritime history, is only margin-ally better, though it is perhaps redeemed by the glimpses you catch of the inside of the crane as you pass between the towers. Well worth the ferry trip, however, are the granaries, where the display meticulously traces Polish maritime history from earliest times to the present day. The nine spacious rooms are well laid out and have detailed descrip-tions in English; the exhibits include a 9C

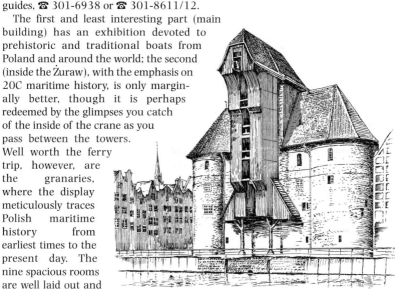

The Żuraw or medieval crane

dugout, 17C Swedish and Russian bronze cannon, navigational instruments, marine art including 18C cityscapes of Elbląg, Riga and Königsberg, and many artefacts from ships that sank in the Gulf of Gdańsk between the 15C and 19C.

Also accessible from the island is the ship *Sołdek*, moored at a reconstructed wooden wharf. This was the first steamship to be built in Poland after the Second World War in the Gdańsk shipyard. The eponymous Sołdek, a workaholic loftsman who helped construct the ship that bears his name, seems to have been something of a communist hero; there are numerous photographs of him joyfully receiving state honours from Edward Gierek, First Secretary of the Polish United Workers' Party in the 1970s. Ironically, another room on the ship chronicles the events of August 1980, when, in the same shipyard, Solidarity was born.

Returning to the Żuraw, you may want to take a quick look at ul. Szeroka; of the many reconstructed houses, most interesting is **No. 52** where the famous Goldwasser, or **Golden Vodka**, was produced from the early 18C onwards. It is now the exclusive *Pod Łososiem* restaurant.

> For those with a taste for **vodka**, this local speciality is well worth a try: it actually contains real flakes of gold and when shaken creates the effect of a snowstorm in miniature. The tradition was apparently begun in the 16C by Flemish merchant Vormöllen, who secured a licence from the city authorities to produce 'beverages for entertainment'. Eager to flaunt their wealth, Gdańsk burghers would impress their guests with this expensive drink, thus contributing to the success of the business, which by the early 1700s had acquired the extant house at ul. Szeroka 52. For centuries, the recipe for Goldwasser remained a closely guarded trade secret, but today it is produced by state distilleries in Stargard and Poznań.

Continue along the waterfront and turn left into ul. Świętojańska. The large derelict **Church of St John** was built from 1371 to c 1415 and altered in the 1460s. During the Second World War the interior was completely burnt out; the only salvaged item was a **Renaissance high altar**, the largest in Poland, made in 1611 by Abraham van den Blocke (see p. 311). In 1986 subsidence caused one of the nave pillars to move, bringing down part of the vault. Today, St John's is a lamentable sight: the green and yellow glazed brick on the tower and transept gables has all but peeled off, and the church itself is inaccessible for safety reasons; though renovation work is under way, it will be some time before its former splendour is revived.

Further up ul. Świętojańska is the more impressive Dominican **Church of St Nicholas**.

> The Dominicans arrived in Gdańsk in 1227 and in the following decade began a church to be used as a base for missions to convert the heathen Prussians. Major expansion work took place in 1340–80, giving St Nicholas's its present form, and preserving only the sacristy and Chapel of St Joseph (east end of the south aisle). The Dominican Order was dissolved in 1835, and their monastic building (adjoining the church to the north) was dismantled by the Prussian authorities; at the turn of the century a trading hall (Hala Targowa) was erected in its place and is still in use today.

St Nicholas's is a brick aisled hall with modest exterior decoration—only an octagonal turret, c 1350, at the east end, and a battlemented sacristy. However, it is the only church in Gdańsk not to have been burnt out during the war, and the surprising richness of the interior testifies to this. Immediately striking is the Dutch Renaissance **high altar** of 1687, which almost touches the vault, with an anonymous central painting of St Nicholas (1643). The altar's stone retable of 1671 (by the south aisle pillar) contains two paintings of *St Rose of Lima* by Andreas Stech. From the same period is the Chapel of St Hyacinth, closed off at the east end of the north aisle. More furniture was added in the 18C: the superb **Baroque organ** (1755), font (1732; by the entrance), pulpit (1715), upper stalls and remaining altars. Two earlier pieces include a late Gothic crucifix of 1520 by Master Alexander, standing on the rood, and, in the north aisle, a 15C 'votive painting' of the Virgin from the Nürnberg school.

Walk Three ~ Castle Suburb and Old Town

The walk begins at the north end of the waterfront, close to where the Motława joins the Radunia canal. Facing the river is a short fragment of brick wall, evidence of the Teutonic Knights' castle that once guarded the approaches to the city.

This area, appropriately known as 'Zamczysko' (castle) was inhabited as early as 997. A document of 1148 mentions that the castle was in the hands of the rulers of Pomerelia, which stood on what is now the forlorn patch of wasteland facing ul. Rycerska (cranes and a bus station in the background). The castle's first owner was the Pomeranian Duke Świętopełk, who brought the Dominicans to the extant Chapel of St Nicholas (see previous page) and probably endowed Gdańsk with a town charter in 1238. The castle remained in the Świętopełk family until it was seized by the Teutonic Order in 1308. The Knights completed their own castle on the same spot in c 1340, but only managed to hang on to it until 1454, when they were unceremoniously ousted during a revolt by the town's citizenry. The castle was razed to the ground, never to be rebuilt.

Turn left into ul. Rycerska and then back west along ul. Grodzka passing the half-timbered **'Stag' Granary** of 1771 at No. 16. Further on ul. Grodzka merges with UL. PODWALE STAROMIEJSKIE—the main thoroughfare separating the Main Town (south) from the Old Town (northwest) and the suburbs of Osiek and Zamczysko (north). On the left, by Targ Rybny (Fish Market) is the odd shape of the **Swan Tower**, once part of the castle's fortifications, but destroyed along with the latter in 1454; it was later rebuilt, raised one storey in the 16C, and integrated in the defensive system of the Main Town, meticulously restored fragments of which can be seen running parallel to ul. Podwale Staromiejskie. The dour and rather uninspiring **Monument to the Fallen in Defence of the Polishness of Gdańsk** signals a right turn into ul. Tartaczna, bringing you up to pl. Obrońców Poczty Polskiej.

The Gdansk **Post Office** building on the square is remembered as the site of a heroic defence by postal workers during the September campaign of 1939.

Built in the mid-19C for use as a hospital, the building became the headquarters of the Polish Post Office in the Free City of Gdańsk during the interwar period. As a building of strategic importance, it was one of the first targets of Nazi attack on 1 September 1939. As few as 50 ragged post-office workers armed with rifles and makeshift bombs withstood the concerted onslaught of SA, Heimwehr, Wehrmacht and armoured SS divisions for a full 14 hours before finally capitulating when the attackers, enraged by the stubborn resistance, set fire to the building; needless to say, the survivors were executed after a mock trial on 5 October 1939. The memory of this legendary defence is very much alive. Günter Grass wrote about it in his best-selling novel *The Tin Drum*. And in 1998, the Polish postal workers were officially rehabilitated by the German government.

The names of the postal workers who died in the combat are engraved on two memorial tablets either side of the main entrance. Inside is a **museum** (open Mon, Wed–Fri 10.00–16.00; Sat–Sun 10.30–14.00), which traces the history of the Polish postal service from the 15C to the present day, with maps, photographs, memorabilia, and an old-fashioned switchboard. In front of the building is a commemorative stone and a heroic brick and metal monument depicting Victory with a fallen postal worker at her feet.

The Gdańsk Shipyard
Head west until you reach the green enclosed by ul. Stolarska and ul. Mniszki; then north along ul. Mniszki and ul. Łagiewniki, passing two churches of no historic or architectural interest, to reach **PL. SOLIDARNOŚCI** and the entrance to the world-famous **Gdańsk Shipyard**, where the Solidarity movement was born.

The Gdańsk (formerly Lenin) shipyard occupies a special place in the history of Poland and communism. It was here that the tragic events of December 1970 took place (see p. 60), when the police and army killed scores of shipyard workers during a wave of strikes and protest. It was not until 1980, on the tenth anniversary of the massacre, that a monument to the victims—hurriedly erected for fear that the authorities might revoke permission to build it—was uncovered by the shipyard gates. In August of that year, following more unrest, striking shipyard workers led by Lech Wałęsa signed the historic **Gdańsk agreements** with the communist authorities, which gave rise to the **Independent Solidarity Trade Union** (see p. 61). Arguably, this was the most important political episode in the history of post-war Europe—the chain reaction set off by events in Gdańsk was to culminate in the East European revolutions a decade later. In 1989, when Polish communism, to cite Trotsky's apt phrase, was 'consigned to the slagheap of history', it was the leaders of Solidarity who formed the core of Poland's first democratically-elected post-war government.

In an ironic twist of fate, the last General Secretary of the communist party, Mieczysław Rakowski, attempted to do away with the troublesome shipyard once and for all by closing it down in the late 1980s, giving as his reason that it was antiquated, inefficient, and could not compete in a free market economy. His efforts came to nothing and the mammoth enterprise was left in the hands of successive Solidarity governments, who tried and failed to privatise it. In 1997 the yard almost collapsed through bankruptcy. True to their capitalist credentials, Poland's new rulers were grudgingly forced to admit that perhaps Rakowski had been right after all.

The **Monument to the 1970 Shipyard Workers** stands in the middle of the square: three large stone crosses bearing anchors with flower crosses below. The plaque reads: 'divine providence could do no better, for in such a place silence becomes a scream' and recalls Pope John Paul II's visit and prayer here in 1987. The full text of the historic Gdańsk Agreements is carved in stone on the wall at the far end of the square.

Group tours of the shipyard are available—for information ask at the reception office by the gates (ul. Doki; ☎ 309-1111); alternatively, the docklands can be visited by boat (the Westerplatte cruise leaving from the Bread-sellers' Gate; p. 315).

Return south to the canal and continue down ul. Mniszki. To the right you will see two churches in close proximity. First is **St Bridget's**, named after the saint whose relics were briefly exposed in a former chapel here on their way from Rome to Sweden in 1374. The new church was built in 1396–1402 and expanded into a late Gothic aisled hall with side chapels in 1514. The interior is spartan—a mass of freshly restored bare brick, with the original chapels along the aisles now no more than niches. The chancel of 1602 has had its cellular vaults restored since partial destruction in 1945, and there are matching ones at the east end. In between, a ribbed vault covers the nave and aisles. There is no furniture to speak of bar a haphazard collection of Solidarity memorabilia: St Bridget's is considered to be the Solidarity church.

Three gables adorn the 16C east front of the **Parish Church of St Catherine**, the central one particularly fine with its three turrets and blank ogival shapes. The church was founded as early as c 1180 and probably acquired its solid stone or brick form under the Pomeranian Duke Świętopełk, in the first half of the 13C. The single narrow chancel went up a century later (1326); a fresco of St Christopher—still visible in the nave—also dates from this period (1320).

In 1575, the west tower, with its long blank panelling, received the first carillon—all of 14 bells—brought to Gdańsk from the Netherlands. The carillon was replaced in 1738 by a grander one, again Flemish, this time with 35 bells. Both it and Jakub van den Blocke's Baroque lantern (today an ugly replica) were destroyed when lightning struck the church in 1905; painstakingly reconstructed, the carillon survived until the Nazis whisked it away; it hangs to this day on the tower of the Church of Our Lady in Lübeck. The vaults too—tunnel in the nave and chancel, star and cellular in the aisles, from after 1500—had to be rebuilt after the war. Most of the original 17C furniture not pillaged by the Nazis was lost when the church burned down in 1945. The best of what remains is perhaps Antoni Möller's *Crucifixion* of 1610, set against a background of Gdańsk with a view over Żuławy and the mouth of the Vistula. There is also a recently restored memorial (1780) to the astronomer Johannes Hevelius (1611–87), who is buried inside the church (see next page).

Facing St Catherine's on the Radunia canal is one of Gdańsk's finest secular buildings—the ***Great Mill**, easily recognisable by its tall steep roof. Decked out in harsh brick and dotted with projecting skylights, the outside effect of the mill somewhat belies its modern interior, which is now a high-tech shopping centre. Further down the canal across the road is an earlier version—the appropriately named **Small Mill** (c 1400), since 1967 the HQ of the Polish Angling Society. Built in the mid-14C, the Great Mill was the largest of its kind in medieval Europe. It had 18 massive waterwheels capable of grinding a staggering 200 tonnes of grain per day. The Second World War left it an empty shell, but work in 1962 managed to restore at least the exterior to its former appearance.

The Old Town Hall

Continuing west across the canal you reach the *Old Town Hall, one of the few buildings in the Old Town to survive the war relatively intact. This elegant example of Dutch Mannerism was built by **Anthonis van Opbergen** in 1587–95, as the inscription on the façade confirms. Willem van den Blocke (see p. 311) was responsible for most of the stone sculpture and ornamentation. The roof has two slender, octagonal corner turrets, with a triple lantern in between, and lots of odd flags and miniature gables. Below, the carved stone portal bears the Polish eagle flanked by angels.

The interior is impressive—much sculpture, painting and original Gdańsk furniture; best of all is an original Renaissance arcaded wall (from the house at ul. Długa 45) with a frieze of reliefs depicting Mercury, Juno and Neptune. There is also a fine 17C ceiling (from the house at ul. Długa 39) with allegorical paintings. The central one, probably by the Pomeranian artist Hermann Hahn is entitled *The Lord's Blessing*. Among the figures shown in the painting is King Zygmunt Vasa, Hahn's patron. The building is now a Cultural Centre, so feel free to walk around inside, but avoid Saturdays if possible, when the place is usually teeming with wedding guests.

> The illustrious figures to have passed through the chambers of the Old Town Hall include the astronomer Johannes Hevelius, one-time member of the Town Council, which had its headquarters here. Though he lived in the 17C, Hevelius was a typical Renaissance man, an expert in many trades whose thirst for knowledge seemed to known no bounds. Initially, Hevelius gained a reputation as a brewer after acquiring two city breweries in the dowry of his first wife Catherine—he stored his beer in the Town Hall cellars (now an Irish Pub). It appears that Catherine chiefly ran the business, allowing her husband to pursue the more abstract pleasures of astronomy and mathematics. After her death in 1662, Hevelius married the 16-year old Elżbieta Koopmann, with whom he had four children. Under her husband's tutelage, she quickly became the first woman astronomer in history and, after his death, the publisher of his works.

Continue west along the path by the canal, turning right into ul. Elżbietańska. At the corner (No. 3) is the charming **House of the Abbots of Pelplin**, built in 1612 in Mannerist style by Abraham van den Blocke, but until recently of disputed authorship. In terms of detailing, this is perhaps the best of the brick and stone Dutch houses in Gdańsk, and partial restoration work carried out in 1912 apparently did much to preserve the original look of the building.

Ul. Elżbietańska runs north between two churches. On the right is **St Joseph's**, an unfinished late 15C work, formerly of the Carmelite Order. The **interior** is very plain: sparse, mainly modern furnishing and a flat beamed roof above the nave, unredeemed by a longer four-bay chancel with a star vault of 1482. If the main entrance is shut, make your way through the monastic building, which adjoins to the north. Originally brick Gothic, the monastery was expanded in Baroque style by Bartholomäus Ranisch in 1690–95. The cannon ball in the vestibule commemorates the Russian siege of the city in 1734.

The history of St Joseph's begins in 1467 when the Carmelites were brought to Gdańsk to guarantee the safety of pilgrims—under attack from the Hussites—coming to pay homage to a miraculous painting of the Virgin. The building's original plans were wrecked, however, through lack of funds; work had to stop in 1496 and the church remains unfinished to this day.

On the left of ul. Elżbietańska, its west front facing the busy thoroughfare of ul. Wały Jagiellońskie, is the brick **Hospital Church of St Elizabeth**. Enter at the west end through a deep open porch topped by a turret. The **interior**, conforming to the original late 14C design, though reconstructed in 1846, has an aisleless nave covered by low star vaults. The murals and stained glass are the post-war work of Zofia Baudoin de Courtenay. Adjoining to the north is the hospital building, formerly an almshouse for lepers. It was redone in Baroque style in 1752–3 and has a portal from the same period.

Walk Four ~ Old Suburb and Granary Island

This walk takes you south and southeast of the Main Town to the Old Suburb, where you can visit the excellent **National Museum**, and **Granary Island**, where wealthy merchants built their closely-guarded granaries.

From the **Highland Gate** (see p. 311) head south along ul. Okopowa, turning left into ul. Św. Trójcy, on which stands the Franciscan complex.

> The Franciscans arrived in Gdańsk in the early 15C. When their second church, dedicated to the Holy Trinity, was nearly complete, the wall of the north aisle, five pillars and part of the vaults collapsed; after this setback, the church was not completed until 1514. In the meantime, the Chapel of St Anne, adjoining it to the west, was erected in 1484, and given to Polish-speaking Protestants. When in 1523 one of the Franciscan monks converted to Lutheranism, the gradual but unrelenting decline of the Order began, ending 30 years later when the last monk handed over the church to the municipal authorities. Since then until the Second World War (except for a short episode during the Napoleonic wars, when it was converted into a military hospital) it belonged to the Protestant community, reverting in 1947 to the Franciscan Order.

The Franciscan **Holy Trinity Church** can be entered either by the north aisle, or through the Chapel of St Anne, which is accessible from an inner courtyard behind a pretty 17C half-timbered house with a wooden gallery on ul. Św. Trójcy (pass through the gate). The broad west façade of the Holy Trinity church has three large pointed-arch windows, a frieze of moulded brick above, and three gables, rich in arcades and pinnacles. Similar late Gothic gables and glazed relief adorn the west façade of St Anne's Chapel. The chapel's net-vaulted interior has a Baroque high altar and an organ of 1650.

A portal to the left of the high altar leads through to the Holy Trinity Church. This aisled hall, the second largest church in Gdańsk, suffered badly in 1945, but has been largely restored since then. Some precious items have survived, such as the two **late Gothic altarpieces** (1515), originating from Augsburg, and the late **Gothic pulpit** (1541) with the four Evangelists sitting in niches decorated with tracery, arches and pinnacles. In the north aisle stands a memorial to Giovanni Bernardo Bonifacio d'Orii (1597; Abraham van den Blocke). The late Gothic stalls (1511) have been moved from the chancel to beneath the organ-loft.

National Museum

South of the church is the former monastery, which now houses the *****National**

Museum (open Tues–Fri 10.00–16.00, Sat–Sun 10.00–17.00; entrance from ul. Toruńska).

Ground floor
The vaulted halls on the ground floor, themselves well worth a visit, contain religious sculpture from Pomerania (largely 15C), gold- and silverware, Renaissance wrought-iron grilles from local workshops, bells, coffers, liturgical vestments, and plenty of Dutch and Gdańsk furniture. Perhaps the best item on display in this section of the museum is the original figure of St George (by Hans Brandt, c 1485) from the building of the Fraternity of St George (see p. 311).

First floor
This floor is devoted to painting, and has a valuable collection of 16C–17C Flemish art, including several paintings by Pieter Bruegel the Younger, as well as 16C–18C works produced in Gdańsk and a 19C–20C Polish collection which includes works by Malczewski, Axentowicz, Weiss, Boznańska, Fałat, Wyczółkowski and Michałowski. The most precious work owned by the museum is Hans Memling's famous and much travelled triptych—the *Last Judgement*.

It is not certain how the *Last Judgement* ended up in Gdańsk. According to one account, it was part of the loot seized in 1473 by Paweł Beneke, the captain of a Gdańsk ship, after he had successfully stormed the English galleon *St Thomas*, on its way from Sluys to London during a period of hostilities between England and the Hanseatic League. As the owners of Beneke's ship were members of the Fraternity of St George, the canvas was placed in the Chapel of St George in St Mary's Church. Other historians believe the painting may well have been commissioned by the Fraternity.

In 1807 it was looted by the Napoleonic armies and put on display in the Louvre, before returning to Gdańsk via Berlin eight years later. Snatched by the Nazis, it was discovered by the Soviets in a mine in Halle, and spent some of the post-war period on display in the Hermitage in Leningrad. The 'thaw' of 1956 saw its return to Poland, though it still awaits restitution to its original place in St Mary's.

The west façade of the nearby **Church of SS Peter and Paul**, a huge mass of brick, has a characteristic squat west tower with two stepped gables. Notice a pretty relief depicting two angels clutching a coat of arms on a fragment of wall to the left of the west façade. At the time of writing the church is still under renovation and only the north aisle, with its deep-cut vaults, is open to visitors. The church, built in 1393, was sponsored by shipbuilders, and hence was dedicated to St Peter the Apostle—himself a fisherman. It acquired its present form in the late 15C after a major fire in 1424 (incidentally on St Peter's day). The interior was stripped of most of its valuable works of art after the church had been taken over by Protestants in 1557, and finally succumbed to fire in 1945.

Going back along ul. Św. Trójcy you pass the rectangular east wall of the Holy Trinity Church, with its gigantic window and gable of three turrets, the central one onion-domed. Turn left into UL. RZEŹNICKA, at the end of which is the **White Tower**, once part of the now vanished New Gate (1461), and presently occupied by a mountaineering club. Walk left (east) to the corner of ul. Augustyńskiego and ul. Żabi Kruk to see the surviving fragment of the medieval **Loft Tower**, which collapsed in 1982. Close by is a large half-timbered house (c 1800), better seen from ul. Pod Zrębem. The street forms one side of a tree-lined square (PL. WAŁOWY), whose west side is occupied by the **Small Arsenal**—a large, double-naved building erected in 1645, as attested by the date on the relief cartouche in the centre of the façade. It is the only extant decorative element of the once ornate front.

Walk past the Arsenal to the nearby **Bastion of St Gertrude**, constructed in the late 16C by Anthonis van Opbergen as part of a system of new Italian type fortifications. Continue east to the granite **Lowland Gate**, built in the mid-17C and now used by an art school. Crossing the train tracks on ul. Grodza Kamienna brings you to the **Tur Bastion**. From the top there is a good view onto the **Stone Sluice** (1619–24). The small towers (quizzically called 'maidens') on the stone walls directing the Motława into the sluice barred access to potential intruders. By closing the sluice during sieges large areas of land were flooded, making attack from this side almost impossible.

Granary Island

Continue past the sluice along a narrow dirt road, then turn into ul. Zielona and cross the bridge to enter the Granary Island. A 200m walk along ul. Toruńska will bring you to ul. Chmielna.

> From the 14C onwards, this area gradually provided visible evidence of the city's great wealth, becoming its 'treasure island'. During its 17C heyday, it had some 340 granaries, with a total capacity of 250,000 tonnes of grain. Other commodities were also stockpiled here, and guards, as well as vicious dogs warded off looters. As recounted by J. I. Kraszewski, the dogs were exterminated after they had killed and eaten several Napoleonic soldiers. Fire ravaged the island on many occasions, especially during wartime.

As you walk along UL. CHMIELNA, the first granary you pass (left) is an almost total ruin. Next is the four-gabled **Wisłoujście Granary**, bearing the date 1744.

Turn right into ul. Stągiewna and walk to the **Stągiewna Gate**, set on the Nowa Motława river, and consisting of two towers connected by a suspended passage. The larger tower was built in 1515, the smaller one in 1456; both were used as artillery outposts.

Cross the bridge and turn left into ul. Szafarnia. At its end is Krzysztof Strzycki's **Moor House** (1727–28). The house burnt down in 1945, but the portal with a Moor's head has survived. From here you may cross the bridge onto Ołowianka island (see p. 319).

Walk Five ~ Oliwa Cathedral and Park

For many centuries, the district of Oliwa was the seat of the wealthy Cistercian Order, and the highlight of this walk is their excellent cathedral with its famous organ.

Though some distance from Gdańsk city centre, Oliwa can be easily reached by the convenient local commuter train (every half hour from Gdańsk Główny). From Oliwa station (Gdańsk Oliwa) head straight for the **Cathedral, crossing a park with numerous ponds.

The Cistercian Order in Oliwa

The Cistercians from Kołbacz, near Szczecin, came to Oliwa in 1186. As in so many other places, the Order, which specialised in agriculture, soon amassed huge wealth. It owned over 40 villages, forests, lakes, mills, smithies, a brewery, and even houses in Gdańsk. The wealth attracted looters: pagan Prussians and the pious Teutonic Knights alike. To protect themselves against attack, the monks built fortifications during the 13C, the remnants of which can still be seen. The church, originally a Romanesque and early Gothic basilica dating from the early 13C, received its present form when it was rebuilt in Gothic style after a fire in 1350.

From the 15C–18C, many industrial buildings were constructed on grounds leased from the Cistercians, and the vicinity of the monastery even became a fashionable luxury district, where the villas of the Gdańsk patriciate were built from the mid-16C onwards. Finally, in the mid-19C, the Prussian authorities ordered most of the monastery buildings to be pulled down; a few, like the Abbot's Palace, survived.

The Cathedral

The Cathedral's 14C west **façade**, remodelled in 1771 in Rococo style, is strikingly narrow, squeezed in between two slender octagonal towers (46m) topped with copper-green spires. From the Baroque portal (1688) a flight of stairs takes you down to the **interior**—the church floor is more than 1m below ground level. The space inside is exceptionally long and narrow, encompassing both nave and chancel, which ends in a swirling mass of stucco clouds symbolising the heavens, and lit by a round stained-glass window. The lower part of the Baroque **high altar** consists of an imposing black marble colonnade, framing a central painting of the *Adoration of Mary* by Andreas Stech (1693). The entire design was clearly influenced by Bernini's art. On the walls of the chancel hang portraits of Pomeranian dukes (north) and Polish kings (south), painted by Hermann Hahn in 1613. The only dark accents in the whitewashed, vaulted nave (1582) are corbels and brick pointed arches separating it from the aisles. A splendid black and gold **Rococo pulpit** with scenes from the life of St Bernard (a copy; the original was looted by the Swedes) matches the pretty carved pews and the magnificent **Mannerist stalls** (1604) in the chancel.

North Aisle. At the west end is the church's best monument—the **tomb of the Kos family**. Two of the three kneeling figures and the child were carved by Willem van den Blocke (see p. 311) in 1620, and are considered by some to be his supreme achievement. The statues, and the black marble background with a crucifix and a monk against which they appear, were two separate memorial sculptures until 1831. Further east is the Baptismal Chapel (1745), its altar adorned with sculptures, reliefs and twisted columns. The ornate altar (1606), found in the north transept, with sculptures, columns, putti and floral decoration, once served as the cathedral's high altar. The **Abbot's Chapel**, entered from the southern part of the vaulted ambulatory, and closed off with a decorative grille, contains a Passion group and a crypt underneath. By the entrance to the south transept is a black marble tomb of the Pomeranian dukes (1615) and a small organ, connected to a somewhat later and larger **organ** at the west end of the cathedral. The latter, with a splendid Rococo loft, is attributed to Rudolf Dalitz and the Cistercian monk Jan Wulff of Orneta. Together, the instruments have 7876 pipes and 110 voices, and are famous for their excellent sound. A short demonstration, featuring such favourites as Bach's Toccata in D Minor, takes place at 12.00 on weekdays and at 15.00 on Sun.

In July and August (vacation break at the seminary) you can enter the **cloisters** (**open** Mon–Fri 10.30–17.00; Sun 15.00–17.00; entrance in the south aisle). They contain several fine portals in various styles—Gothic, Baroque and Renaissance; the two Baroque marble ones, leading to the church, were made in 1660. On the walls hang 18 paintings depicting biblical scenes (1749), and in the south wing a 16C mural by Wolfgang Sporer has survived. Close by is the entrance to the **refectory** (now the Diocesan Museum), with late Gothic-Mannerist vaults (1593–94) supported on three sandstone pillars. The museum's collection includes the original table on which the Peace of Oliwa between Poland and Sweden was signed in 1660; the actual signing took place in the **Peace Hall** (entrance from the west wing of the cloisters).

Leave the church via the north side exit and turn right. Through an arched gate you enter the **park**, east of the Cathedral, laid out in the 18C, in part formal, with parterres, espaliers and canals, in part landscaped. At the edge of the formal park is the **New Abbot's Palace**, late Baroque, 1754–56 (south wing), and the **Old Abbot's Palace**, late Gothic, with vaulted cellars (east wing). Both were burnt down in 1945 by the Germans, and restored in the early 1960s. The New Palace contains a **Museum of Modern Art**, with a permanent exhibition of contemporary Polish art and caricature (**open** Tues, Thur–Sat 10.00–16.00, Wed, Sun 10.00–17.00). In front of the Rococo south façade, amid geometrical hedges, is a fountain with a sculpture of a boy, and further south two busts of early Pomeranian dukes, Świętopełk II and Mściwój II. Walk north to the **Abbot's Granary** (Baroque, 1723), with 18C stables behind the canal. The granary houses an **Ethnographical Museum** (**open** Tues, Sat 10.00–17.00, Wed–Fri, Sun 10.00–16.00), with fishing tackle on the ground floor, and agricultural tools from the Pomeranian region, 18C–19C Kaszubian dowry coffers and furniture on the upper floors.

Return to the west façade of the church and walk south along ul. Cystersów, which runs along the former 13C embankment, part of the water installation that powered the monastery mill. At its end is the 14C **Gatehouse**, with sundials, blank arches decorating its stepped gable, and tiny buttresses. In 1709 the building was dubbed the 'House of Plague' to mark the deaths of nine monks who had tended to the sick during the plague. Beyond the gate, across Stary Rynek Oliwski, you will see a large 19C half-timbered house, called the **Polish House** since it served as a Polish cultural centre in the 1930s when German nationalism was asserting itself with ever-greater confidence.

A 2km walk or drive southwest along ul. Kwietna will take you past several 19C workers' houses (**Nos 32–28**) to the squat, tar-smelling, wooden **Water Smithy**, at the junction with ul. Bytowska. Constructed in the 16C, it was owned by the monastery and leased to Gdańsk entrepreneurs. Currently it is a branch of the **Warsaw Museum of Technology** (**open** May–Oct 10.00–17.00). This relic of industry—still operational—is located amidst the beautiful beech forests of the **Gdańsk Landscape Park**.

Walk Six ~ Westerplatte

The excursion takes you to the historic site where the Second World War began. Certainly the most attractive way of getting there is by pleasure-boat from the quay by the Bread-sellers' Gate (see p. 315). The peninsula is situated about 8km north of the city centre.

The **Second World War** began at **Westerplatte** on 1 September 1939, when the German battleship *Schleswig-Holstein* opened fire on the fort defended by Major H. Sucharski's small garrison. Isolated and hugely outnumbered, some 200 soldiers managed to withstand attacks from sea, air and land for seven days, although they were supposed to hold out for only 12 hours. The Poles capitulated having lost only 15 men, with losses on the German side numbering 300. The story of this heroic defence has since passed into history and legend.

The peninsula, before 1845 an island, had already been an important military outpost: French troops landed here in 1734 to rescue King Stanisław Leszczyński, father-in-law of Louis XV, who was besieged in Gdańsk by the Russians (the attempted rescue, however, was a failure: the king was finally forced to escape in secret, dressed as a peasant).

During the inter-war period, the island was turned into a munitions depot.

The main attraction is the imposing **Monument to the Defenders of the Coast**, erected in 1966 on top of an artificial hill. The sombre granite blocks, weighing 1150 tonnes, are decorated with sculptures, reliefs and the inscribed names of battlefields where Polish troops fought during the Second World War.

In the vicinity of the monument are the ruins of the barracks and two guard-houses, one with a small **museum** (officially **open** 09.00–16.00, but frequently closed). By the water's edge, a tank marks the grave of the Polish soldiers killed during the defence of Westerplatte, and of Major Sucharski, who died in 1946 in Naples; his ashes were brought to Poland in 1971.

Walk Seven ~ Sopot

Sopot is not the place to come for art or architecture, though some might find inspiration in the Secessionist villas and palaces in the back-streets off the main pedestrian precinct of UL. MONTE CASSINO. Sopot is primarily a resort town, albeit a grand and stately one. It can be easily reached by car or, better still, by local commuter train.

A document of 1283 mentions the granting of the village of 'Sopoth' to the Cistercians at Oliwa; from the 16C onwards Sopot became a popular **seaside resort**, but it was not until the arrival of French doctor Jean-Georges Haffner in 1823 that proper sea bathing and spa buildings emerged, as well as a horse-drawn bus service from Gdańsk. The resort developed rapidly in the late 19C; many grand villas in the fashionable **Secessionist style** sprang up, housing a wealthy clientele. Sopot received a town charter in 1901, and the northern and southern baths (on the beach either side of the pier) catering to growing numbers of holidaymakers soon followed. The Grand Hotel appeared in 1927, the famous pier a year later. After the war, Sopot emerged as the largest and most popular resort on the Polish coast, and has remained so to the present day.

UL. MONTE CASSINO, with its bustling bars and cafés, begins close to the main station, from where you can take a leisurely amble down to the **Pier**, the longest in Poland (512m); to the right, bordering the Southern Park, is a bathing establishment (salt and mud baths) of 1903, and close by, a viewing tower. North of the pier you should not miss the **Grand Hotel** (1927) which, for all its charm and idyllic location, is somewhat overpriced and has a reputation for arrogant staff; if you intend to stay during the song festival (see below) be sure to book in advance as accommodation can be scarce. North of the Grand Hotel, the beach, or the park it borders, make for a pleasant stroll; if you arrive in summer you may prefer the beach—even at peak temperatures, the Baltic is always a cool, refreshing swim, though pollution scares are common.

Away from the waterfront is the **Opera in the Woods** (1909; ul. Moniuszki 12) where, in the second half of August each year, the **International Song Festival** is staged (☎ 551-1812 for details); at its worst the festival is on a par with the Eurovision Song Contest, though standards seem to have improved in recent years. To get to the Opera, walk along ul. 1 Maja from the station and then right into ul. Moniuszki (No. 12). There are special services back to Gdańsk after performances. Marked trails lead up into the hills behind the Opera; on Shooting Hill (Wzniesienie Strzeleckie) there is an excellent viewpoint, on Olympic Hill (Wzgórze Olimpijskie) a **Soviet War Cemetery and Monument**; there is also a ski-lift and ski trails for those unable to make it south to the Tatra mountains in winter. When all else fails, there is always the **Racecourse**. Saturday is usually race day; get off at Sopot Wyścigi station, one stop before Sopot.

Walk Eight ~ Gdynia

Today, Gdynia is a thriving commercial centre, one of Poland's most affluent cities. Most of the architecture, and indeed the modern urban plan, date from the inter-war period. Nearly everything there is to see is situated on and around the waterfront; from the main station (*Gdynia Główna*) walk down UL. STAROWIEJSKA, the oldest part of the city, where the fishing settlement used to be. At No. 30 is a small **Museum of the History of Gdynia** (open Tues–Sun 11.00–16.00). More interesting than the display is the house itself, dating from the turn of the last century, when Gdynia was still a village. Set charmingly askew to the road, it is a typical example of urban architecture of the period, its front steps partially covered when the road was raised.

> The earliest document mentioning the village of Gdina (Gdynia) dates from 1253. For nearly four centuries (1380–1772) Gdynia belonged to the Carthusian Abbey in Kartuzy (see p. 341), its population never rising above 100. After the First World War, the new Polish state no longer controlled the port in Gdańsk, so the construction of a new port began in 1922 at Gdynia. The first ship—the *SS Kentucky*—docked on 13 August 1923. As the port grew in size, by 1934 becoming the largest in the Baltic, so the new town of Gdynia arose, reaching 120,000 inhabitants by 1939.
>
> The war years brought terrible devastation to the port and town; 12,000 locals were executed in the Piaśnica woods near Wejherowo (see p. 343). Reconstruction proceeded apace, and the first ship was able to dock as early as July 1945; the post-war years also saw the rapid expansion of the shipyard, which by the 1970s was producing ships of vast tonnage, and much glory to the communist authorities.

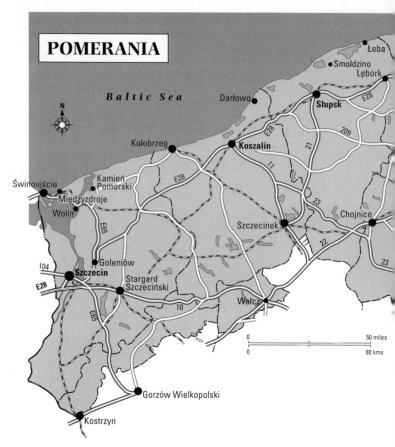

Head for the southern pier via KOŚCIUSZKI SQUARE, to the right of which rises a hill—Kamienna Góra (52m)—with a viewing tower on top; at the foot of the hill is the **Naval War Museum** (accessible from Bulwar Nadmorski), which exhibits rusty anti-aircraft guns, bombs and planes, mostly from the Second World War (open 10.00–16.00).

Return to Kościuszki Square and continue onto the pier; on the north side (left) are two museum-ships (**open** 10.00–16.00). The first is *Błyskawica* (Lightning), a destroyer built in 1937 in an English shipyard; active during the Second World War, it was turned into a museum in 1976 with a display on Poland's role as a seafaring nation. Further along is the *Dar Pomorza* (Gift of Pomerania), a three-masted frigate built in Hamburg in 1909; it was given to the French navy after the First World War as reparation before being bought by the Higher Maritime School in Gdynia in 1929. Moored in Stockholm during the war, it managed to escape damage, making its last voyage in 1981 to Finland; it was opened as a museum in 1983. Nearby is a ferry harbour offering trips around the sprawling port area, out to Jastarnia and the Hel peninsula (see p. 347), or

back to Gdańsk. Overlooking the yacht marina by the south side of the pier are the Higher Maritime School and Fisheries Institute, housing the **Oceanographic Museum and Marine Aquarium** (open Tues–Sun 10.00– 17.00). At the end of the pier is a rather forlorn sculpture of Joseph Conrad gazing out across the sea to Finland.

Malbork

The town of Malbork (58km) is easily accessible from Gdańsk either as a day trip, or if you wish to stay there (perhaps to enjoy the evening *Son et Lumière* show), you will find comfortable accommodation at the Hotel Zamek (ul. Starościska 14; ☎ (0-55) 272-3367), situated next to the castle. Malbork is on the main Gdańsk–Warsaw line, and there are daily express trains from both these cities. If travelling by car, leave Gdańsk on the E75; after Tczew, turn left (road 50).

Castle of the Teutonic Knights

Rising majestically above the banks of the Nogat, the **castle is rightly regarded as the finest example of secular medieval architecture on the European mainland. This vast fortress, so evocatively described by Sienkiewicz in *The Teutonic Knights* (see p. 84) overwhelms the visitor with its sheer size: 4.5 million bricks were used in the construction of the original early 14C convent, and the complex, encircled by towers and multiple walls in places 4.5m thick, has since grown to cover an area of 21 hectares. There are three main sections, all open to the public: **Upper Castle**, **Middle Castle**, and **Lower** (Outer) **Castle**. The first two house the main exhibition rooms and can only be visited with a guide (though it is possible to break away from the group once inside). Tours in English are frequent and begin from the ticket office (see below); however, unless you can afford a private guide, you may have to wait a while for a large enough group to gather. The Lower Castle (or castle grounds) is more accessible and can be visited even on Mondays and public holidays when the exhibitions are closed. In summer, a good way to avoid the crowds and heat is to attend the *Son et Lumière* show, which takes place every day after dusk. The exhibitions themselves vary greatly in quality: the museum presently contains a collection of coins, ceramics, art and fragments of architectural decoration from the entire Teutonic realm, but

Castle of the Teutonic Knights

the modern amber display reeks of the tourist industry and has no connection at all with the castle's heritage. Simply walking through the rooms and chapels, palaces and refectories, courtyards and towers—all painstakingly restored—is where the true delights of Malbork are to be found.

■ **Opening times**

Ticket office:	08.30–17.00 (summer, 1 May–9 Sep)
	09.00–14.30 (winter)
Exhibitions:	08.30–16.30 (summer)
	09.00–15.00 (winter)
Castle grounds:	08.30–18.00 (summer)
	09.00–15.00 (winter)

Lower (Outer) Castle

You will probably approach the castle along its east side, passing on your left the 15C enceinte guarding the Upper and Middle castle; the complex is actually situated on a peninsula between the river and millstream, cut by a railway viaduct; to your right, a range of medieval walls (1300–50) with defensive towers and buildings

The Teutonic Knights

The history of the castle at Malbork is inextricably linked to that of the Teutonic Order of the Hospital of St Mary in Jerusalem, otherwise known as the Teutonic Knights. The Knights were a medieval religious order given to military chivalry and devotion to the Virgin Mary. They were established by a papal bull at Acre in Palestine in 1191. Like their precursors the Templars, the Knights observed a strict monastic regime: chastity, poverty and silence were the guiding principles, and the penalties were harsh for anyone who failed to comply. Daily life consisted of prayer, long punishing marches, and frequent combat—the only moment when the knight-brothers were allowed to speak to one another.

In 1226 the Order was invited by Duke Konrad of Mazovia to settle at Chełmno (see p. 370), a base from which it could wage war against the heathen Prussians. The Knights proceeded to establish an independent theocratic state on Prussian soil, which they had wholly conquered by 1283.

Existing castles were occupied and in 1274 work began on a new one at Marienburg ('The Fortress of Mary', Malbork in Polish). In 1291 the Saracens sacked Acre, forcing the Knights to move their headquarters to Venice. But they were soon ousted again when a papal judgement over their role in the Prussian lands went against them. Marienburg now became the obvious choice of refuge, and with the arrival of the Grand Master from Venice in 1309, it quickly became the capital of the Order's state.

The Teutonic Order ruled from Marienburg for a century and a half, a period in which the self-assurance and aggrandisement of the Knights was translated into the rapid development of their castle. The oldest part—the Upper Castle—was already complete by 1309, serving both a residential and official function. During the 14C work began on the Middle Castle, whose chief purpose was to underline the power and grandeur of the new state and its rulers. Yet the commanding nature of the building was not limited to outer show: spacious, opulent interiors, as well as the façades, provided a backdrop to ceremonies, treaty signings, feasts, and receptions of foreign guests. Outside, beyond the main core of upper and middle castle, stretched numerous farm buildings all servicing the castle's growing needs; further still was the small town of Malbork, built solely as an adjunct to its imposing neighbour. The castle also had a strategic and defensive role to play: standing on the east bank of the Nogat, it guarded a vital crossing—the only bridge across the river at the south end of the Nogat delta.

The Order's dominance in the region came under increasing threat in the 15C. The most serious defeat was suffered at Grunwald in 1410 (see p. 417). Recovery was only temporary, and during the Thirteen Years War the Grand Master was forced to flee his castle, which irrevocably passed to Polish rule at the **Second Peace of Toruń** in 1466. The Order went into rapid decline, leaving only its fortified convents and castles as evidence of a tyrannical and bellicose past. Under its new masters—the Poles—Marienburg seemed to mirror the fate of the Order. Though some modernisation work was undertaken to make it a habitable summer residence for Polish royalty, the decay was terminal, and by the 19C the castle had fallen into a state of abject ruin. Under Prussian rule after 1772, the castle was dismantled for its bricks. Luckily, under the influence of Romanticism, some rebuilding and renovation work supervised by K. F. Schinkel got under way in 1817, mostly of the Middle Castle.

Gradually, over the course of the 19C, Marienburg came to be seen as a symbol of Prussian imperialism; indeed, when Kaiser Wilhelm II paid a personal visit, he invoked the spirit of the Teutonic Knights 'to join the fight against Polish impudence and Sarmatian effrontery'. The most significant conservation work was carried out in 1882–1921 by Konrad Steinbrecht (later succeeded by Bernard Schmidt), who set up archaeological excavations, renovated the castle in Gothic style, and saved it from almost certain extinction. The fortunes of Malbork were to turn again during the Second World War. First it was used as a POW camp for 30,000 prisoners, and then suffered major damage during fierce fighting in 1945, when the east side was destroyed by heavy shell fire.

runs parallel to the road; you will come out onto a large forecourt, built after the Grand Master had moved to the castle in 1309. Across from the ticket office is the **Chapel of St Lawrence** (1358), its gabled west façade decorated with pinnacles and irregular blank arches, and adjoining it to the north, old farm buildings, which have been converted into the Hotel Zamek. Extending northwards from the castle forecourt are a number of other buildings, walls, towers and bastions; the best is perhaps the twin-towered **Bridge Gate**. It is a pleasant walk around these, particularly if you are waiting for entry into the main complex, which is reached by a covered wooden bridge leading to the north gate of the Middle Castle.

Middle Castle

In the late 13C the Middle Castle served as a forecourt; its three wings enclose a large irregular courtyard, open towards the older Upper Castle, which rises to the south, and separated from it by a wall and moat. The most interesting part is the west wing with the Great Refectory and Grand Master's Palace; constructed after 1309, both were used for receptions and official ceremonies—their form in deliberate contrast to the self-contained symmetry and austerity of the Upper castle.

The **Great Refectory** (1), also known as the Knights' Hall is the grandest room; built in 1330–40, the bright interior is lit by two pointed arch windows; the ceiling is a complex structure of stars and ribs vaulting arising from three slender octagonal pillars with sculpted bases and capitals—one depicting a group of dancing figures. The consoles have sculpted heads, plant motifs and tracery. Best of all is a stone boss in the vault depicting a scene of the Flight into Egypt. South of the Great Refectory is the Grand Master's private **Chapel of St Catherine** (2), its three-sided apse projecting onto the courtyard.

The Grand Master's Palace

The southern part of the west wing is dominated by the Grand Master's Palace. Begun c 1330–40, it was remodelled in 1382–99 as one of the grandest Gothic residences in Europe, perhaps rivalled only by the Palace of the Popes at Avignon. The work proceeded in two stages under the supervision of the chief mason, Nikolaus Fellenstein. First a four-storey block with towers was raised on the moat side with reception rooms at the top, next the east front looking onto the courtyard. The best view is actually from the moat, where the buttresses are charmingly interrupted at the third storey (Summer Refectory) by pairs of slender columns supporting the machicolation and battlements above.

Inside the palace, you first pass through the Grand Master's private lodgings (3, 4, 5), which end with the suspiciously named 'bedroom of the Grand Master's companion' (6).

First floor

Continue upstairs to the reception rooms. First are two vestibules (7, 8), shortly followed by the **Summer Refectory** (9), with double rows of windows and a complicated radial vault arising from a solitary granite pillar; food and provisions used to be hauled up via a lift from the kitchen in the cellars below. Adjoining to the east is the slightly smaller but no less impressive **Winter Refectory** (10) with a similar vault; here you can see clearly the holes in the floor through which hot air would rise from the ovens below. On the wall are remnants of frescoes depicting previous Grand Masters; these, like other frescoes

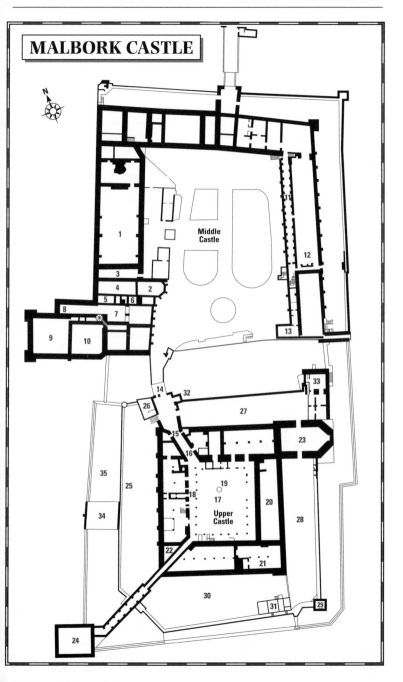

MALBORK CASTLE

Middle Castle

Upper Castle

around the palace, were painted in 1399–1404 by Master Peter. Here you leave the palace.

The mid-14C east wing was almost completely reconstructed in 1898–1908. Behind the cloister (11) running parallel to the courtyard were guest rooms for secular knights (12), separated by a passageway leading to a now vanished latrine tower; the rooms house the main castle **Museum**. The ground floor contains an exhibition on historic monuments from around Europe (Malbork among them) which have been given special EU funding under its heritage programme. Upstairs in the lofts, formerly used for grain storage, is an extensive **display of amber**, both in its raw form and in ornamentation—reliquaries, candlesticks, figurines of angels, Baroque caskets, ornate chess sets, miniature altars and ships, all dating from 17C–20C. Next is a collection of porcelain (mainly 18C–19C), and downstairs a display of 16C and 17C armour and weaponry. You exit from the museum through the former **Chapel of St Bartholomew** (13), cross-vaulted, with a fine glazed brick portal and stone tracery; it is now an amber shop offering souvenirs and jewellery.

In the southwest-corner of the courtyard is the entrance to the Upper Castle, decorated with 19C sculptures of Grand Masters.

Upper Castle

This is the oldest part of the complex, built as a huge convent-cum-fortress, with four wings enclosing a quadrangular courtyard. To the left and right, as you cross the **drawbridge** (14), notice the extensive fortifications: two walls, inner and outer, with dry moats in between, and the moat proper beyond the outer wall. You enter the Upper Castle through a huge pointed niche, its edges framed by slender columns; the back wall of the niche is obliquely set so that the low gateway (15) in it conforms to the diagonal passage to the courtyard. The tunnel (16) brings you into the cloistered courtyard (17, 18) with two storeys of arcades renewed in 1888–91 and a castle well (19) under a wooden hut.

Most of the rooms on the ground floor were used as servants' quarters and store-rooms (20, 21). In the south wing they contain a display devoted to the history of Malbork. The adjoining **torture chamber** (22), in use only during the Teutonic period, has been reconstructed in Kwidzyn castle (see p. 389). More interesting is the oldest **north wing** (1274), which pre-dates the arrival of the first Grand Master: at its west end is the two-tiered castle church: St Mary's (23) above (entrance from the first floor), and St Anne's Chapel below (entrance from the dry moat), where the tombs of the Grand Masters were housed. The adjoining store-rooms were originally used by the monks as dormitories, but were never heated and had no beds; they now contain a permanent exhibition of stained glass. To the left of the storerooms is a dark cell set aside for more privileged prisoners.

First floor

The most impressive rooms of the Upper castle are located on the first floor. The **chapter house** (first room left of the stairs) has an interlocking system of star vaults radiating from three slender octagonal stone pillars, 1320–30, one of the earliest examples of this type of vault. The 14C **frescoes** depicting a galaxy of Grand Masters were restored in the late 19C. On the cloister side is a fine offset portal with plant decoration on the capitals. From the Chapter House you can (at additional cost) ascend the huge tower.

Next to the chapter house is the castle **Church of St Mary** (23) with its famous portal—the **Golden Gate**—(northeast corner of the cloister). Built at the end of the 13C, the gate is framed in a shallow vaulted porch cut in the thickness of the wall. Plant and animal decoration adorns the archivolt and capitals, with figures of the *Wise and Foolish Virgins* on the colonettes and *Christ* in the keystone.

The church is entered through the small vaulted room to the right of the Golden Gate; a winding staircase leads upwards via the bell tower to the second-floor storage rooms (now temporary exhibitions), and downwards to the church. St Mary's was probably built in 1311–44, in the last stages of High Gothic style. While the church is undergoing major and long-term renovation work, many of the most precious items, such as stone figures of Christ, apostles and saints (c 1340) have been moved and are on display in the castle museum (first floor dormitories) or the lapidary in the moat (the latter also includes a beautiful stone figure of *Christ Kneeling in the Garden of Olives*, c 1390).

Along the west wing stretch the rooms of the former **treasury**, which included the living quarters of the treasurer and the housekeeper monk. Inside is a display of coins and various items in silver, brass and copper. In the south-west corner a covered passage runs out on four arches to a squat **Latrine Tower** (24), otherwise known as the *Dansker*, built in 1276–80 along with the outer wall fortifications. The exhibition in the long tunnel-vaulted **dormitories** in the south and east wings is devoted to medieval art and books.

You may tour the inner castle wall (25) via stairs by the Gatekeeper's House (26). Going clockwise along the north terrace (27), you will first come to the sepulchral **Chapel of St Anne** (23), containing the tombs of Grand Masters. The chapel is a bit later than St Mary's dating from 1331–44, when the castle church was extended with the addition of a projecting choir, under which the chapel stands.

Inside, the reconstructed star vaults are embellished with sculpted bosses and consoles (masks, busts and atlantes). Set in the floor are three finely detailed memorial stones to Grand Masters of the Order. The most precious items, however, are the two portals (c 1340) set into the thickness of the wall and forming shallow vestibules; both are sumptuously carved in stone, five columns each side, with leaf and animal decoration filling the voussoirs and capitals. The tympanums are impressive: in the north portal (terrace side), the scene depicts the *Coronation of the Virgin* and the *Wise and Foolish Virgins*, with, on the side walls, the *Adoration of the Magi* and the *Dormition of the Virgin*; in the south portal two rows of figures tell the *Legend of the True Cross*, while on the side walls there are scenes of the *Ascension* and the *Last Judgement*.

Continue along the east terrace (28), which once contained a cemetery and sewer installations. During the Polish period there used to be a gate by the **Dietriech Tower** (29; southeast corner) linking the castle and town via bridge over the south moat. Turn right into the south terrace, actually the Grand Master's garden (30), with the **Gardener's House** (31) on the left. Continue under the covered passageway linking the castle with the *Dansker* (24).

You may also visit the outer castle wall (25). Begin at the Watchtower (32), which has a steep spiral staircase (behind a door) leading 12m down to the dry moat, where prisoners were allowed to exercise. Going clockwise you will pass: the Cleric's Tower (33), late 19C, and adjoining Bell Keeper's house; the Dietriech Tower (29); the *Dansker* (24), Mill (34) and moat (35). From the outer wall and beyond you can admire the exterior of the Upper Castle: walls with patterns of dark glazed bricks, great blank niches towards the river, and, on the skyline, a mass of square turrets with elaborate gables.

Kashubia

❖ Żukowo • Kartuzy • Szymbark • Kościerzyna • Wdzydze Kiszewskie • Będomin • Gdańsk

Leave Gdańsk on road 219, signposted 'Kartuzy', heading west. Kashubia (Kaszuby to the Poles), is an undulating terrain of pine forests and crystal-clear lakes. It is a region of **great natural beauty**, remote and tranquil, and, unlike the Masurian lakeland to the east, relatively unsullied by tourism and industry. For a swift and concise introduction into **Kashubian culture** (see below), visit the skansen at Wdzydze Kiszewskie, or the Kashubian Museums in Kartuzy and Wejherowo (see p. 343). Alternatively, you can wander through the sleepy hamlets and towns, where you will find in the unique architecture and folk art evidence of a local culture that is very much alive.

> ### The Kashubians
> The Kashubians—an ancient ethnic group related to the Pomeranian Slavs—have inhabited western Pomerania for centuries. During the Partition era, the Prussian authorities launched a determined campaign to 'Germanise' Kashubian culture and subsume it within the imperial German state; but resistance was stubborn, and the natives of the region managed to preserve much of their indigenous heritage. Prussian rule did, however, have a lasting effect on the Kashubian language—a dialect of Polish— which acquired many German words and expressions. Indeed, nowadays, Poles from outside the region can often experience problems understanding it. After the Second World War, the Kashubians were omitted from the mass deportation programmes that befell many of Poland's other national minorities. Perhaps it was felt that this small and rather beleaguered ethnic group, with no particular grudge against the Poles, presented little threat to the incumbent communist regime.

Żukowo (21km) is a large Kashubian village on the Radunia river, known locally for its folk embroidery. The road leads past St John's church on the hilltop; turn left signposted 'Kościerzyna', then immediately left again to the **Premonstratensian Nuns' Abbey**.

The abbey in Żukowo was founded as early as 1212 when the Pomeranian Duke Mszczuj invited the Norbertine nuns from Strzelno (see p. 519) to settle here, but its buildings were dismantled after the Prussian authorities dissolved the convent in 1834; all that remains today is a fragment of wall and a vaulted Gothic hall. The former nuns' church (13C) avoided the fate of the convent and became the Parish Church of the Ascension after the nuns had been expelled.

If the doors of the church are locked, ask to be let in at the vicarage next door; the priest also has the keys to the museum.

Inside, the 17C vaults cover a mass of rich furnishing in a variety of styles (14C–18C). Most impressive is the 17C **gallery** for the nuns' choir at the west end of the nave, fenced off by an iron grille which is exquisitely ornamented with gilt leaves and fronted with panels bearing portraits of luminaries associated with the convent. The Renaissance **high altar**, flanked by two smaller ones, is from 1620, its sides draped with tapestries made by the Norbertine nuns. Also of note is the valuable Antwerp **triptych** (early 16C) in a chapel by the north wall.

The **parish museum** in the adjoining building (former stables and coach house) features modern embroidery (some of it for sale) modelled on patterns used by the Norbertine nuns, and a collection of liturgical items from the church and convent.

Kartuzy, 12km further along road 219, is set in a picturesque location among forests in the heart of the Kashubian lake district. Though considered the 'capital' of Kashubia and a centre of regional culture, the town is relatively new, and did not receive a charter until 1923. It survived over the centuries as a small settlement, mainly inhabited by the monks of the Carthusian Monastery, who settled in the region in the 1380s—hence the name 'Kartuzy' (Carthusians).

After crossing the railway lines turn left into ul. Kościerska. A short way up on the left, next to a large car park, is the **Kashubian Museum** at No. 1 (**open** Tues–Sat 08.00–15.00; in summer, also Sun, 10.00–14.00), with a somewhat disappointing display. The ground floor rooms try to capture the essence of daily life in the 19C. Upstairs, there is a collection of toys (some with intricate moving parts) and delightful Christmas masks depicting various animals, as well as traditional musical instruments, art, handicrafts and clothing. In the reconstructed 19C Kashubian bedroom, note the ingenious bed for children that could be extended as they grew.

Carthusian Monastery

From the museum drive along ul. Gdańska, turning right onto road 219, signposted 'Słupsk', 'Lębork'; to the left is Lake Karczemne; to the right, beyond the town park, the towers of the ***Carthusian Church and Monastery** on the shores of lake Klasztorne.

The Carthusian monks were brought to Pomerania from Prague in 1381. The Order observed the rule of St Benedict—very harsh even by medieval standards—which featured asceticism, silence and vegetarian cuisine. A normal day was divided into three equal shifts of prayer, work and rest. There were exceptions to the rule of silence: the monks could greet each other with a festive 'memento mori' ('remember you are mortal'), and speaking was allowed during Sunday lunch, when the monks would gorge themselves on fish and beer. Despite the severe regime, the monks had a knack of persuading wealthy people to part with their riches. Even their rivals, Teutonic Knights, endowed them with various gifts and much land. By 1474 the monks had acquired numerous villages and a staggering 6700 hectares of land stretching to the Żuławy fens. In 1383, the Gdańsk merchant Johannes Thiergart paid for the construction of their Gothic church, completed in 1403. It was surrounded on three sides by 18 hermitages; only one is preserved (14C), and serves as the verger's living quarters (near to the sacristy). A well, refectory (now a museum), part of the cloister, and three of the original farm buildings have also survived, but the other buildings were dismantled after the Order's dissolution in 1823.

The most immediately striking thing about the **church** is the roof. It was remodelled in 1731–33 to resemble a coffin lid so that the monks would be constantly reminded of the transience of the earthly life. Enter through the sacristy (south). The vaults in the nave rest on corbels ornamented with sculptures of mythical creatures and geometric designs; on both sides are exquisite **Baroque stalls** (1641 and 1677), decorated with reliefs of scenes from the lives of saints. Flanking the Renaissance **high altar** (1639) are **leather wall hangings** made in Flanders (1685), gilded and silvered, with delicate ornamentation of floral and animal motifs. Of the four side altars in the nave, the best was carved in black marble and alabaster by Kasper Gockhaller in 1680. It is adorned with sculptures and three paintings, including a central one of the *Last Supper*. In the south wall is the entrance to the **Golden Chapel**, part of the former cloister, containing a famous wooden Gothic **triptych** (1444), only the middle part of which remains (the other two wings were sold by Prussians to the British Museum). The musicians' choir has a balustrade and a clock (1640) with a pendulum in the form of the Angel of Death holding a scythe, moving to and fro right above the entrance to the church. On the exterior wall of the chancel you can catch a glimpse of the sundial, and above it a skull with the Carthusian motto: 'memento mori'.

Next to the church (north side) is the former Gothic **refectory**, accommodating a small **museum of Kashubian folk art and craft** (open Tues–Fri 10.00–16.00; Sat 10.00–15.00; Sun 11.00–14.00). A path leads from the church to a pleasant beech grove on the shores of the lake, with a view of the church from its south side.

Leave Kartuzy south along road 224, passing through the most beautiful part of the Radunia gorge; turn in Egiertowo for Kościerzyna (road 220). On the way (17km) is **SZYMBARK**, described in some zealous tourist brochures as the 'Kashubian Zakopane'; there are indeed ski-jumps and winter sports facilities. The nearby hill—Wieżyca (328m)—is the highest point in Pomerania.

KOŚCIERZYNA (population 21,400) is the largest town of the Kashubian region, (35km) set among morainic elevations, lakes and forests. It was once a stronghold of the Pomeranian Dukes, but their castle has long since gone. The town itself is of little interest; if you want to explore Kashubian culture you should head 15km south to the lakeside resort of **WDZYDZE KISZEWSKIE**, where there is a large **Kashubian Ethnographical Park** (open Tues–Sun 10.00–15.00) consisting of some 20 buildings, most of them traditional cottages from the region. Do not miss the revolving mill and the wooden church of 1700. **LAKE WDZYDZE** (1420ha) is set in forested, sandy surroundings constituting the **Wdzydze Landscaped Park**, with camping, motel and beach facilities, and a riverside hostel (west part of the village); beware that in summer the place can get very crowded.

From Kościerzyna head east along road 221 to Gdańsk (46km). You may want to take a 1km detour north to **BĘDOMIN**, the birthplace of General Józef Wybicki, author of the Polish national anthem. A museum—the appropriately named **Museum of the National Anthem**—has been opened here in his honour (**open** 10.00–16.00).

The Kashubian Coast

❖ Wejherowo • Krokowa • Żarnowiec • Łeba • Słowiński National Park • Lębork • Gdańsk

To the northwest of Gdańsk stretches an area known as the Kaszubian Coast, a post-glacial landscape terrain of great natural beauty. The chief attraction is the Słowiński National Park with its remarkable 'shifting dunes'. There are also several historic sights well worth visiting, particularly the Cistercian Abbey in Żarnowiec

Leave Gdańsk by the E75 to Gdynia, then join the E28 for Wejherowo (45km). **WEJHEROWO** (population 46,500) is a Kashubian town set in the valley of the Reda river, at the foot of forested uplands. It owes its name and existence to Jakub Wejher (1609–57), the Palatine of Malbork, who gave it a charter in 1650 and proceeded to build a priory, church and calvary (see below). Much of the original 17C town plan, with its large market square, has been preserved. For an insight into Kashubian culture, try the **Museum of Kashubian-Pomeranian Literature and Music** at ul. Klasztorna 1 (**open** Mon–Fri 08.00–15.00).

The Main Square has a number of 19C and 20C houses—notably the Town Hall of 1908—and a statue of Wejher (1991) with the inscription 'founder of the town and the calvary'. Ul. Waryńskiego leads off the square to the **Reformed Franciscans' Church** (1650–51). The shallow chancel contains the best piece—a Baroque **high altar** with an inlaid altar-rail and retable, and behind it a fresco of 1658. The ubiquitous Jakub Wejher is buried in the crypts beneath the church, along with most of his family.

Just south of the town is Wejher's lasting legacy—a **Calvary** of 26 chapels (1649–55) spread out over a beech-clad hill on a plan based on the **Way of the Cross** in Jerusalem. The best ones include: Jesus meets Mary; Pilate's Palace; Church of the Three Crosses; and Jesus's Grave. On religious holidays, pilgrims from all over Poland come here to walk the 5936 steps.

From Wejherowo drive north (22km) through woodland along a winding road (217) marked 'Krokowa' (off the E28). The village of **KROKOWA** was for centuries in the possession of the wealthy Krokowski family, who arrived from Franconia in 1232. The oldest parts of their three-winged **palace** date from the 14C, when it served as a defensive castle. Encircled by earth fortifications in 1602—the ditches and ramparts are still visible—it underwent further adaptation in 1784 and in the 19C. Today, it houses a conference centre and lavish hotel (☎ 0-58-673-7706). An added attraction is the surrounding park. In Krokowa turn left onto road 213 marked 'Słupsk' and head for Żarnowiec.

The Cistercian Abbey ~ Żarnowiec

The village of ŻARNOWIEC achieved notoriety as the site of a nuclear power plant (never completed and eventually abandoned due to pressure from environmental groups) on the shores of nearby Lake Żarnowiec. Nowadays, though, most visitors come to admire the *Cistercian Nuns' Abbey*.

The Cistercian nuns settled in Żarnowiec in the mid-13C and began construction of a brick Gothic church soon afterwards. A fire in 1389 destroyed much of the structure, but rebuilding saw the addition of a square west tower, a sacristy and a vestibule (south). The main body of the church received a steep roof, gabled at both ends. Work did not achieve full completion until the early 15C. In 1589 the convent passed to the Benedictine nuns from Chełmno.

If the main entrance to the church is locked, walk around to the back and enter through the convent cloisters; ring the bell and ask to be let in.

Interior. You emerge into a long, narrow eight-bay hall covered by a complicated star vault supported on carved 14C corbels. Between the third and fourth bays on either side of the nave are two relief figures—the Madonna (north) and St Catherine (south). The sumptuous Baroque **high altar** (c 1700) bears a central painting of the *Assumption* (anonymous) ornamented with silver robes. Flanking it are two richly carved smaller altars from the same period. From the nave proceed northwest to the convent cloisters. The Treasury has a large collection of 17C–19C embroidered church vestments, 15C–16C sculptures, including a *Pietà* (c 1430), and many valuable liturgical items.

Continue for about 50km to ŁEBA, a pleasant if frequently overcrowded seaside resort at the mouth of the Łeba river. It is set between two large shallow lakes—Lake Sarbsko (east) and the more interesting Lake Łebsko (west). The latter once formed a bay, but over the centuries, through a combination of wind and sand, it was gradually cut off from the sea by a long spit (17km by 1.2km) serving as a sort of natural dyke.

Such was the effect of the shifting dunes (see below) that in 1558–70 the original medieval fishing settlement, under constant threat of being buried in sand, had to be moved 1km southeast to its present location. Even here, however, flooding was a constant problem, and in the 19C the riverbanks had to be walled up to protect the town from total destruction. Today, in the forest, west of the river, you can still see the decaying remains of Old Łeba—a fragment of wall, once part of a Gothic church, and the site of the former market square.

Łeba itself has little in the way of sights. A few 19C gabled houses overlook the main thoroughfare, ul. Kościuszki (16C). Just off it, on ul. Powstańców Warszawy, is a small box church of 1683, very modern in appearance. Heading seawards you cross the Chełst canal, linking the river Łeba with Lake Sarbsko. Along the canal is a busy fishing port with its stalls and seafood bars. Here, too, is the departure point for boat trips along the river. Further along ul. Kościuszki you reach a strip of sandy pine forest, so characteristic of the Baltic coast, separating the town from the beach and pier beyond.

By far the greatest attraction of Łeba is the 'shifting dunes' in the *Słowiński National Park* to the west of town. To get there turn off ul. Kościuszki into ul. 11 Listopada (second left before the canal) and bear right (northwest) to the suburb of Rąbek. The road ends at a large car park on the shores of Łebsko. The lake itself, 300m above sea level, is surrounded by reeds and peat bogs, and is a paradise for some rare species of water fowl. To get to the dune area (6km further along the coast) you can walk, hire a bike, or jump on one of the special buses. On the way you might notice some concrete slabs strewn about the woods: these are the remains of materials used by the Germans to build V1 rockets during the war. The highest point in the dune area—Łącka Hill (42m)—is an almost sheer wall of sand, well worth the exhausting climb, with a fine view from the top over the desert-like coastal landscape. On occasion you can even see the tops of trees, long since covered by the dunes, sticking up through the sand.

Return south to Wicko and follow signs to Lębork, road 214 (38km).

Lębork is a quiet, unassuming town set in the Łeba valley at the foot of forested uplands. On the main square stands the late Gothic **Church of St James**. Its square west tower is characteristic of Pomeranian Gothic—tall blank panels in the form of arches rising to a roof adorned with stepped gables. The four-bay nave leads to an aisleless chancel where, embedded in the wall, are two sandstone Renaissance memorial slabs. There is also a fine 18C tabernacle adorned with alabaster reliefs.

Opposite St James's on the other side of the square is ul. Młynarska with a **Regional Museum** in the first building on the left (**open** Tues–Sat 10.00–15.00; Sun 09.00–14.00). Further along is an old half-timbered salt granary facing the **Miller's House** (1806), and next to that, the **Castle Mill**, adapted and extended in the 19C along with the Teutonic Knights' Castle, immediately across the canal (ul. Przyzamcze). All that remains from the castle's Gothic period are fragments of wall, the east gable, and the cell vaults underneath the east wing. The building now houses a district court.

From Lębork pick up the E28 (east) for Wejherowo and Gdańsk.

The Gulf of Gdańsk and the Hel Peninsula

❖ Puck • Władysławowo • Rozewie • Jastrzębia Góra • Karwia • Jastarnia • Hel

For the seaside town of **Puck** (52km) leave Gdańsk by the E75 to Gdynia, then join the E28; at Reda turn north on road 27. It lies on the west bank of the Gulf of Puck, a few kilometres south of the Hel peninsula. It has traditionally maintained strong connections with the sea, both as a fishing village, and later, in 1567, as a naval port. For a period during the 16C Puck owed almost its entire wealth to piracy. The seafaring tradition was revived in 1920 when the Polish army under the command of General J. Haller re-established Poland's access to the Baltic, with Puck becoming a temporary naval base shortly afterwards. In the old port area of Korabne (corner of ul. Ceynowy and ul. Marynarska) there is a monument commemorating the 800th anniversary of the town.

Much of the 14C urban plan, centred around the large market square, has been preserved. The houses, however, have not; most of those on the square are 19C with the exception of No. 6 (c 1725). The **Museum of the Puck Lands** is on the north side at No. 28 (**open** Mon, Wed–Fri 09.00–12.00 and 14.00–17.00; Sat–Sun 09.00–13.00). The permanent displays focus mainly on the history of the town; there is also an exhibition of photographs from the turn of the century. Another branch of the museum (same times as above) occupies a half-timbered former almshouse (c 1720) on ul. Wałowa (south from the main square along ul. Gdańska), opposite the now vanished Gdańsk Gate. The interior takes the form of a recreated traditional Kashubian cottage.

The best and oldest monument in Puck is the Gothic **Church of SS Peter and Paul**, just north of the square. The oldest parts, probably dating from 1283, are the lower sections of the squat west tower, which rise up to an arcaded frieze visible on the north and west sides; the roof, closed off at the east end by an intricately ornamented gable, was added in 1466–96. Inside, the original late Gothic star vaults have only survived in the chancel and in the Judycki and Wejher Chapels. The latter (south side of the tower) contains a Mannerist wooden altar with a *Crucifixion* by the Pomeranian artist Hermann Hahn (1574–1628). In the former (south aisle) there is an entrance to the crypts where members of the Judycki family are buried. A 15C baptismal chapel on the north side of the tower contains a richly carved font (1697).

The large resort of **WŁADYSŁAWOWO** (8km) lies at the west end of the **Hel peninsula**. A port was built here in 1935–38, rather unfortunately on the seaward side; this disturbed the natural bolstering effect of the tidewaters on the sandy spit, which has consequently become much more susceptible to storms. An especially violent one in 1983 completely submerged the road and railway, cutting Hel off from the mainland.

From Władysławowo you can drive along the spit, or alternatively go further west along the coast to the Rozewie lighthouse and the seaside resorts of Jastrzębia Góra and Karwia. For the latter, turn left at the first big intersection in the town along al. Niepodległości and then al. Żeromskiego, passing a modern, reinforced concrete church (1957–61).

The cape at **ROZEWIE** (7km) is the most northerly point in Poland (54° 50') with steep cliffs barring the access of vessels. Turn right off the main road for the **Żeromski Lighthouse** (see p. 85), a place the writer Stefan Żeromski often visited. The hexagonal lighthouse (1821) is 21.3m high, and the beam, powered by 13 Argand lamps burning rapeseed oil, is set at 70.3m above sea level; it can be seen 43km away at sea. Inside is a sparse and tedious **Lighthouse Museum** (**open** 09.30–13.00 and 15.00–19.00) with an array of plastic model lighthouses and charts explaining the principles of optics and maritime navigation amid strategically placed quotations from Joseph Conrad. Wind your way up to the top for a view that apparently impressed Żeromski, but which is now obscured by trees. Far better is the steep descent to the sea through lush woodland.

JASTRZĘBIA GÓRA (2km) developed swiftly after the First World War and is considered one of the best Polish resorts. **KARWIA**, slightly further on, has a broad beach looking onto the open sea. 3km southeast Karwia is the village of Karwieńskie Błoto, established in 1599 by Jakub Wejher, who settled Dutch families on the surrounding marshes.

The Hel Peninsula

JASTARNIA (20km) was once an island and now has a fine beach bordering the open sea; there are boat trips to Gdynia and cruises around the gulf. The local population has traditionally engaged in fishing, and some old fishermen's houses can be seen southeast of the **Church** (1932, turn left off the main road). The tunnel-vaulted, sea-green interior is replete with maritime and fishing motifs: the pulpit is carved in the form of a fishing boat—murals in Kashubian colours (white, green, blue), and there is a chandelier in the shape of an anchor.

HEL (14km) is larger than the other resorts along the spit, but like them attracts much tourist traffic, particularly day trippers arriving by boat from Gdańsk. The town and port both face the gulf and are thus shielded from the strong Baltic winds. The town rose to prominence in 1939 as the last Polish base to capitulate during the September campaign after a heroic defence.

The main street, lined with many gabled fishermen's houses (19C), runs parallel to the sea, right up to the port area. Next to the port is a former 15C Gothic church, converted in 1971 into a good **Fisheries Museum** (ul. Wiejska; **open** 09.00–20.00) with a wooden viewing tower of 1959. The ground floor has a display of fishing nets and equipment from prehistoric times to the Second World War, including three complete fishing boats. Upstairs is a display of Polish maritime art, mainly 20C, and numerous model ships.

Close to the intersection with ul. Dworcowa are two **Monuments**: one is dedicated to the Defenders of Hel, and commemorates the sailors who held out against all the odds until 2 October 1939. The other is in memory of Stefan Żeromski (see p. 85), and is placed at the spot where the writer spent the summers of 1922–24.

Stutthof and the Vistula Spit

❖ Stegna • Sztutowo • Kąty Rybackie • Krynica Morska • Nowa Karczma

The main site on this trip is the former Nazi concentration camp at Sztutowo (Stutthof), situated at the edge of the Vistula fens (see p. 390). The first stop is the village and resort of STEGNA (33km from Gdańsk), which lies on the south side of a forested embankment of seaside dunes. Leave Gdańsk on the E77, turning left at Przejazdowo, and continue through Sobieszewo to the car ferry at the mouth of the Vistula (15-minute crossing; 05.00–23.00). The beach is a few kilometres north of the village—a pleasant drive through tall pines; a narrow gauge railway links Stegna with Sztutowo and Nowy Dwór.

Left of the main road is a half-timbered, Baroque **Parish Church** of 1683. The impressive pulpit, altar (both 1687) and an elaborately carved font (1666) are survivors from the original wooden church, but the greatest attractions are undoubtedly the excellent 17C Dutch watercolour paintings on linen (450 sq. m) covering the ceiling.

Stutthof Concentration Camp

Just before SZTUTOWO (6km) there are signs pointing left to 'Muzeum', in fact, the *Stutthof Concentration Camp (**open** May–Sep 09.00–18.00; Oct–Apr

09.00–15.00). There is a large car park by the site; Sztutowo-Muzeum station (narrow gauge) is also close by.

> Stutthof was the first Nazi concentration camp established on Polish terri-tory and the last to be liberated. As early as September 1939, units of the 'Selbstschutz', a locally recruited organisation closely linked with Himmler's SS, began mass arrests and executions. The first prisoners arrived in Stutthof on 2 September. Under forced labour, they immediately began construction of the very camp in which many of their friends and compatriots would later perish. Escape was virtually impossible; even if a prisoner could somehow evade the guard dogs and watchtowers, the camp was almost entirely surrounded by water—the sea to the north, the Vistula river to the west, and the inhospitable Vistula fens to the south and east. Mass extermination of the Jewish population commenced in 1942. A crematorium was built, a year later a gas chamber, ten Jewish blocks, and a 'special' division. The camp claimed the lives of more than 85,000 people. As many as 15,000 died during mass evacuations of prisoners in January 1945, when, in a desperate, last-ditch attempt, the Nazis tried to hide the evidence of genocide from the approaching Soviet army.

The grim legacy of Stutthof is plain for all to see. Four of the barracks, the gas chamber, crematorium, and villa of the camp commander have been preserved. The remaining buildings, barbed wire and watchtowers are reconstructions (more are planned). Inside the barracks is a harrowing documentary record of camp life and the German occupation of Pomerania. There is also a small cinema with regular showings of a film on the history of the camp.

Beyond Sztutowo lies the resort of **KĄTY RYBACKIE** with a beach on the seaward side. This is where you enter the Vistula spit, a picturesque strip of land (500m–2.5km wide) separating the Baltic from the Vistula bay. The bay (5m deep) is a giant, shallow lake, with an abundance of fish due to the low salt content of its waters. In winter, international ice-boat competitions are held here.

If you continue east towards the Russian border you will pass through a terrain of forested dunes, at times rising to a height of 43m. **KRYNICA MORSKA** (15km) is a somewhat larger resort, again facing the bay, with a beach on the north side.

The village developed into a popular resort during the 19C, becoming a frequent haunt of, among others, Kaiser Wilhelm II's family. The earlier history of Krynica Morska is more sinister: in the 14C, it was a place where the Teutonic Knights deposited their mentally ill, leaving them to their own fate.

Ferry services
Direct ferry services to Elbląg, Frombork and Tolkmicko leave from the wooden pier:

Krynica Morska–Frombork:	09.30, 13.00, 16.20
Frombork–Krynica Morska:	11.15, 14.40, 18.00
Krynica Morska–Elbląg:	17.30 (Fri–Sun)
Elbląg–Krynica Morska:	07.30 (Sat–Mon)

On a fine day you can see the towers of Frombork Cathedral (see p. 394) across the bay. If you have time to spare, continue 11km further east along the spit through pine woods to **NOWA KARCZMA**—the last village before the Russian border.

Szczecin

Szczecin (population 420,000), the capital of Western Pomerania, spans a shallow valley in the delta of the Odra (Oder) river. Wooded uplands to the north (Puszcza Wkrzańska), forested areas to the east (Puszcza Goleniowska), and hills to the south (Puszcza Bukowa) shield the city from cold winds, softening the harshness of its maritime climate. Although it does not lie directly on the Baltic coast, it has for centuries been associated with the sea. The huge Szczecin shipyards have only one rival in Poland—Gdańsk. Both were leading centres of opposition during the events of 1970 (when 16 dockers from the Szczecin shipyard were killed), and later, in the 1980s, bastions of the nascent Solidarity movement. The port area of Międzyzdroje is situated between the two rivers, and can be visited by boat (from the Passenger Quay near the Maritime Museum). Świnoujście (see p. 359), 65km to the north, is the closest Baltic port, with regular ferry services to Copenhagen, Ystad and Travemunde.

Szczecin's strong German legacy sets it apart from many Polish cities. Purchased by Prussia in 1720, it practically remained in German hands until the end of the Second World War. With landlocked Berlin a mere 130km away, Szczecin evolved into an important Baltic port. In the late 19C, the French architect Baron Haussmann attempted to redesign the city using as his model the Paris of Louis Napoleon, with its broad avenues and radial squares. The spirit of this urban plan is still very much alive, but unlike Paris, Szczecin has suffered from chronic under-investment. During the Communist period in particular, the authorities, fearful of German revanchism, were disinclined to pour money into a city they thought they would eventually lose anyway. Such fears may in retrospect seem groundless, but it must be said that Poland's border with Germany was not formally ratified until 1990. Today, even if the crude nationalism of 'Szczecin forever Polish!' or other such graffiti is galling, it is nonetheless the fruit of human tragedy still within living memory.

■ Practical information
Hotels
★★★★★

Radisson. Pl. Rodła 10, ☎ 359-5595. Ideal central location; excellent service and facilities, including Business Centre, car park, gym, sauna and swimming pool, shuttle service to and from Berlin. 369 rooms.
★★★★

Orbis-Neptun. Ul. Matejki 18, ☎ 488-3883. Central location. 283 rooms. Car park, car rental, business services.

Orbis-Arkona. Ul. Panieńska 10, ☎ 488-0261. Located close to the castle. Business services, car park. 62 rooms.

Orbis-Reda. Ul. Cukrowa 2, ☎ 482-2461. Situated 5km from the city centre, near the Polish/German border. Wheelchair access, car park, business services. 150 rooms.

Tourist information (***PAPT***). Ul. Wyszyńskiego 26, ☎ 340-440.
ORBIS. Pl. Zwycięstwa 1, ☎ 433-5248.
Airport. Goleniów (45km northeast of Szczecin).
LOT. Al. Wyzwolenia 17, ☎ 339-926/335-058 (reservations and bus to the airport).
Ferries. Polska Żegluga Bałtycka, ul. Wyszyńskiego 28, ☎ 488-0945, 488-0238 (tickets for ferries to Scandinavia, leaving from Świnoujście).
Main post office. Ul. Bogurodzicy 1.
Telephone code: (0–91).

History

Originally an ancient Lusatian settlement clustered around today's Castle Hill, Szczecin was captured in 976 by the Polish Duke Mieszko I. In 1121, Bishop Otto of Bamberg (St Otto) set out on a mission to Christianise the heathen Pomeranians, during which all Szczecin's pagan temples and statues were destroyed, and two new churches—SS Peter and Paul's and St Adalbert's—were built. Polish claims on the region were enhanced in 1140 when Pope Innocent II issued a bull creating the West Pomeranian bishopric. Adalbert, a Polish missionary, became its first bishop. By 1212, the ducal seat had been transferred from Kamień (see p. 360) to Szczecin. Duke Barnim I granted Szczecin a municipal charter in 1243, and the griffin was adopted as the town's heraldic symbol. Such was the prosperity afforded by membership of the Hanseatic League (a member since 1275) that in 1346 Barnim the Great began work on a new castle; but within four years the city had been devastated by the Black Death.

In 1478, the Cracovian-born Bogusław the Great managed to unite the whole of West Pomerania. His marriage to Anna the Jagiellon brought West Pomerania under the aegis of the powerful Jagiellon dynasty, but even this was not enough to forestall the rising dominance of Brandenburg, to which the Duke was forced to swear allegiance in 1521. Despite attempts to stay neutral during the Thirty Years' War, West Pomerania suffered devastation and occupation by the Swedes. With the death of Bogusław XIV, the last West Pomeranian Duke, Sweden seized formal control over the domains under the Treaty of Westphalia (1648), managing to hold onto them for nearly 90 years.

Szczecin's rulers changed once again in 1720, when Queen Ulrica Eleanor sold the city to the Prussians, who Germanised its name to Stettin. In 1729, the future Czarina of Russia, Catherine the Great, was born in a house on ul. Farna. During the Napoleonic wars, Szczecin was briefly occupied by the French (1806–13). Thereafter, it experienced rapid growth, with the population reaching 237,000 in 1911. Carpet bombing raids by the allies in 1944 destroyed 60 per cent of the city. It was liberated by the Soviet army on 30 April 1945, and formally handed over to the Polish authorities a month later.

The city centre

A good starting point for exploring the city is the busy PL. ZWYCIĘSTWA. At its west end stands the **Garrison Church** (1906–09) with a tall tower (65m) and sparse furnishings. To the right (north) is the hardly more inspiring **Church of the Holy Heart of Jesus** (1913–19) with a square stone tower and ugly modern painted decoration. However, a surprise awaits you at the opposite end of the square: the Baroque **Port Gate** (Berliner Tor), the first of the Westphalian architect Gerhard Cornelius Wallrawe's two showpiece city gates, built in 1725–40 and richly decorated with stone sculpture, trophies and reliefs by Wilhelm Meyer and Bartholome Damart (Frederick Wilhelm's court sculptor). A Latin inscription below the gable commemorates the purchase of Pomerania by Frederick Wilhelm of Prussia from the Swedes. The gate closes ul. Wyszyńskiego, which leads east towards the river through the paradoxically modern 'Old Town'.

St James' Cathedral

Half-way down on the left, the huge west tower of the Gothic Cathedral of St James (14C–15C) will come into view.

> The cathedral began its existence as a small Romanesque chapel, much expanded in the 14C and the 15C, and turned into a Gothic hall. In 1504, the whole west front was consolidated into a single huge tower, rising, together with the spire, to a massive 90m. Following a fire in 1677, stone-masons rebuilt the vaults (1693), tower (1694) and Gothic furnishings, but the latter were replaced with Baroque ones in 1720. The church was completely destroyed during the war, and rebuilt only in the 1970s.

Visible from the outside are portals decorated with glazed brick, a huge bell (1681, 5.7 tonnes) mounted onto a wooden contraption by the east end, and a 15C medieval brick annexe to the south. The interior is a brick aisled hall with an ambulatory. Between the interior buttresses are scores of side chapels, dedicated for the most part to the victims of the Second World War. In the Chapel of the Blessed Sacrament, fine 14C sculptures have been preserved. The Chapel of Our Lady of Częstochowa, entered from the N aisle, has cross vaults resting on two round pillars. A 15C *Beautiful Madonna* occupies the centre of the high altar. The modest **Diocesan Museum** (open Tues–Wed, Fri–Sat 10.00–15.00, Thur 12.00–17.00) with a display on the history of the West Pomeranian Church is reached from the north aisle.

Continue along ul. Wyszyńskiego to the **Long Bridge**—the longest drawbridge in Poland—which crosses the river to the port area. Originally 13C, it was destroyed several times and last rebuilt in 1957. Just before it, to the south (ul. Pod Bramą) stands the Gothic **Church of St John**, contemporaneous with the cathedral, but of smaller proportions, with a lantern instead of a tower. St John's is Szczecin's oldest surviving church, built in the 14C by the Franciscans. The west façade is decorated with nine pinnacles, while a low frieze of vine leaves (before 1300) encircles the chancel. Ceramic figural corbels adorn the star vaults inside.

Town Hall and Museum

Returning to ul. Wyszyńskiego, head north along ul. Mściwoja to what remains of the Old Town Square (Stary Rynek), now devoid of historic buildings except for the Gothic **Town Hall**, reshaped in the 15C as a small brick block gabled at both ends—the star-vaulted cellars also date from this period. Note the elaborate ceramic decoration on the north gable. Twice rebuilt in Baroque style during the 17C, it was restored after the Second World War to house the **Szczecin Historical Museum** (open Tues, Thur 10.00–17.00, Wed, Fri 09.00–15.30, Sat–Sun 10.00–16.00). The highlights of this commendable display (with German but no English labelling) are a relief of 1657—*Jesus in the Garden of Olives*—from the church of St John (see above), a triptych in a small vaulted room, and some interesting photographs of old Szczecin.

Ascend the slope (ul. Kurkowa) to the sumptuous late Gothic **Loitz House** (c 1547)—a post-war reconstruction. This extraordinary four-storey building, with a richly decorated white exterior and tower——its windows charmingly askew—was formerly owned by a wealthy family of bankers, whose clients included the Polish monarchy. The two buildings close by are 15C brick **Granaries**, rebuilt in the 17C and after the war. The Loitz House backs onto ul. Grodzka, which leads to the *Castle of the Pomeranian Dukes**.

The Castle of the Dukes of Pomerania

The castle was founded by Duke Barnim III in 1346. However, the oldest surviving part—the **south wing**—dates from 1503–08, and was built by Duke Bogusław X to store the immense dowry of his wife, Anna the Jagiellon. This is where you enter through a Neo-classical gate (1735). The present castle—heavily reconstructed after almost total destruction by allied bombing raids in 1944—consists of five wings, enclosing two courtyards (open all day) on the plan of a large irregular polygon. Just before you enter, look to your left for the **Prison Tower** (1639) with Gothic ornamentation. Once inside the main courtyard, notice the characteristic late Gothic tracery in the gabled attic (reconstructed) of the south wing. There is also a **Clock Tower** here, with a fancy three-part clock. The plain **east wing**, running parallel to the river, was rebuilt by Barnim XI, the son of Bogusław X, in 1538–69. Note the foundation tablet, dated 1538, between the first floor windows, which shows the armorial cartouche of the Pomeranian lands guarded by burly savages. A display of sarcophagi is set to re-open in the crypts.

North wing. This Renaissance wing was built in 1577 during a general overhaul of the castle. There is a commemorative plaque of Barnim III beneath the portico, bearing in relief an armour-clad knight, the Pomeranian cartouche, and a fading German text glorifying the deeds of its founder. Both the Stone Hall and Chapel of St Otto built by Barnim III in 1346 were demolished. The place where the chapel used to stand is marked by a mosaic of tiles in the Great Courtyard and the adjoining Mint Courtyard (see below). The West Wing (Middle Wing) was also completed in 1577.

A passage leads through to the smaller Mint Courtyard. **The Museum (Mint) Wing** was built in 1616–19 by the Dukes of Szczecin, Filip II and Franciszek I to serve as a 'house of art and science', as indicated by the Latin inscription on the foundation tablet set into the wall. It was later converted by Frederick the Great into a mint. A covered passageway connects it to the **Bell Tower** (northwest), which you can climb for a panoramic view over the city and its environs. Embedded into the wall of the tower is a copy of a sandstone sculpture of St Otto (the original is in the National Museum, see below).

The castle regularly stages a variety of cultural events, including concerts, plays, opera, film shows and art exhibitions. Concerts are held either in the courtyard (Sundays in summer), or in the Bogusław Hall. Full details may be obtained from the box office in the North Wing, where there is also a **museum** (**open** 10.00–16.00) charting the history of the castle.

From the castle's east terrace, descend to the Gothic **Maiden's Tower** on ul. Panieńska, a remnant of the medieval fortifications. Head west along ul. Trasa Zamkowa towards the SS Peter and Paul church (see below). Alternatively, proceed north under the busy bridge and up the slope to UL. WAŁY CHROBREGO (Chrobry Embankments), which runs parallel to the river. The street begins with two early 20C buildings of the **Maritime Academy**. Continue north, passing on your right a pavilion with steps leading down to the Passenger Quay. Commanding the wide prospect of the river and harbour is the huge Neo-Renaissance **Maritime Museum** building, a branch of the National Museum (**open** Tues, Thur 10.00–17.00, Wed, Fri 09.00–15.30, Sat–Sun 10.00–16.00), featuring an archaeological section (the most valued exhibits being an early medieval dugout boat from Jawor, and 1C–3C amber and silver jewellery); the maritime history of the Baltic (13C–20C) section; a display devoted to African culture; and—in the north wing—a rich collection of small-scale models of ships and nautical instruments. Behind the museum building there is a small skansen of boats and fishing vessels. Further north along ul. Wały Chrobrego, passing another pavilion, you reach the imposing brick mass of the Neo-Renaissance Voivodship Office (1911).

Return to ul. Małopolska and go west for about 300m to the **Church of SS Peter and Paul**. Founded in 1124 by Bishop Otto of Bamberg, the brick Gothic building you see today dates mainly from 1470–80, though it was extended during the 16C, and the aisles removed in 1677. The highlight of the interior is the inner buttresses, decorated with glazed brick and ceramic mascarons representing 15C Szczecin burghers. On the wooden ceiling a plafond of 1703 depicts the *Holy Trinity*.

Continue west along the main boulevard (ul. Trasa Zamkowa), which marks the border of the Old and New Towns. The mast of a steamship (1929) occupies the middle of PL. HOŁDU PRUSKIEGO, which is named after the Baroque **Prussian Homage Gate** to your right. Also known as the Nakło Gate, it was built in 1726–28 by Wallrawe, and consists of two triumphal arches connected by a tunnel (now a café). The cream-coloured sandstone arches are decorated with sculptures, trophies and reliefs. Lining the south side of the square (Nos 11–16) are the so-called **Professors' Houses** (15C), built initially as homes for the teachers at the nearby Convent of St Mary. The façades were rebuilt in Neo-classical style in 1831–34.

National Museum

Slightly further west is pl. Żołnierza Polskiego, with modern buildings on its north side and historic ones to the south. At the corner of UL. STAROMŁYŃSKA (No. 27) is the **National Museum** (open Tues, Thur 10.00–17.00, Wed, Fri 09.00–15.30, Sat–Sun 10.00–16.00), housed in a pedimented Baroque-classical building built by Wallrawe in 1725–27 for the Pomeranian Estates' Diet, the regional parliament, and reconstructed after the war.

Enter from ul. Staromłyńska through a portal with a crest in the lintel. The ground-floor display covers medieval religious art (mainly wooden sculptures from Pomeranian churches), craftwork, porcelain and glass. Ascend to the first floor for Polish painting and sculpture, including 19C–20C works by Chełmoński, Siemiradzki, J. Kossak, Malczewski, Wyczółkowski, Mehoffer, Pronaszko, Dunikowski, Gierymski and Pankiewicz. A separate section is devoted to the patronage of art, featuring 'Sarmatian' (see p. 68) portraits of the Pomeranian dukes and their genealogical tree (1598), tapestries, costume, and jewels. More of the Museum's collections may be viewed in the 19C **Palace of the Thirteen Muses** across the street (No. 1), with a gallery of modern Polish painting, but no permanent exhibitions.

Continuing down ul. Staromłyńska, note the Baroque-Classical **Velthusen Palace**, currently a music school, at the corner of ul. Łaziebna. Across ul. Łaziebna at No. 2 stands the very ornate **Globe Palace** (originally Baroque, 1723–26, rebuilt 1890), named after the copper globe which tops the balustraded attic (now a medical school). Opposite, on pl. Orła Białego, is a Baroque **Fountain** (1729–32) surmounted by a white eagle with outspread wings and water spurting from its beak. To the southeast rises the Cathedral of St James (see p. 351), where our city tour ends.

Day trips from Szczecin

❖ Kołbacz • (detour Glinna) • Stargard Szczeciński

Around 40km to the east of Szczecin lies the medieval town of Stargard Szczeciński, the highlight of this trip. On the way you can visit Kołbacz (27km), where the Cistercians founded an abbey in 1173, and Glinna (9km from Kołbacz), with its secluded Dendrological Garden. From the centre of Szczecin head east on the 116 for 15km, joining road 3 (south) signposted 'Zielona Góra'. Turn left onto road 143 signposted Kobylanka for KOŁBACZ.

The late Romanesque **Church** (right) is sadly dilapidated. It was built in 1210–30, but only the small round-headed windows have survived from this period. By 1307, the nave had been lengthened and an asymmetrical west front with a blind rose window in the gable had been added. The Gothic chancel, with much larger windows and a five-sided apse followed in 1347. The church has been used as a granary and warehouse since a fire in 1662. Only the north transept, with its stepped gable, is still used as a place of worship. In the early 18C, the chapels were pulled down and the pointed-arch arcades of the aisles were walled in (you can see where).

A few of the 13C priory buildings have been preserved: the **Konwers House** (a house for labourer-monks), which adjoins to the southwest—an original bread oven, in the modern building above it, the charming Gothic **Abbot's House** (now a library) and a grand Gothic barn with blind arcaded walls (across the road to the north). Also visible from the Church, further along the road, is a 16C **prison tower**.

For a short detour (17km there and back) return to road 3 and continue south. In Stare Czarnowo turn right, signposted 'Gryfino' (road 120) for 4km. Just after this you enter **GLINNA**. Turn right at the easily missed sign marked 'Ogród dendrologiczny' and continue for 2km. At the T-junction turn left and park by the entrance to the **Dendrological Garden** (admission free; open all day) with approximately 100 species of rare trees. The shores of **LAKE GLINNO** are 1km further north.

To continue the route, return to Kołbacz and then take road 10, going east and passing **LAKE MIEDWIE**, a popular destination among watersports' enthusiasts.

Stargard Szczeciński

About 20km from Kołbacz is the town of Stargard Szczeciński. The town's chief attraction is its medieval urban plan and a ring of defensive walls encircling the oval Old Town. Four of the nine Gothic towers and three of the four gates still exist. All these monuments were faithfully restored after the war (during which 70 per cent of the historic city centre was destroyed), unlike those in Szczecin.

> The town experienced its best times during the 14C, when it joined the Hanseatic League. However, a fierce conflict with Szczecin over the rights to grain trade along the Odra in mid-15C, as well as fires, sieges, and looting during the Thirty Years' War led to its physical and economic ruin. Ceded to Brandenburg under the Peace of Westphalia (1648), it remained in German hands until 1945.

Just off the OLD TOWN SQUARE is the imposing ***Parish Church of St Mary**. Originally a simple Gothic hall founded in 1292, St Mary's was transformed into a late Gothic basilica at the turn of the 15C by Heinrich Brunsberg. Two towers were begun, but the south one never reached completion. Star vaults were added in 1637–61, when the church underwent general renovation.

The asymmetrical west **façade** is richly decorated with glazed and moulded brick, ornate pinnacles, and intricate tracery. Equally striking are the ceramic faces of humans and mythological creatures adorning the north Chapel of St Mary, and the sandstone reliefs depicting biblical scenes found in the portal on the north side of the larger tower. Ceramic tracery embellishes the main west portal, while the south portal has, in addition to similar decoration, a pretty zigzag pattern of moulded brick.

The most remarkable features of the spacious **interior** are a triforium below the clerestory, unique in the Pomeranian region, and 'Piast' vaults in the ambulatory. 15C frescoes have been preserved in one of the small chapels reached from the ambulatory. Of the furniture, only the 17C Baroque pulpit is worthy of mention.

Three buildings (14C–19C) to the southeast of the church are of interest. The oldest and largest is the Gothic **Parish School** on the corner, with the 16C **Priest's House** next door. On the square (No. 1) is the **Town Hall** (c 1569), unmistakable for its gable composed of quarter-circles with attached blank tracery, creating a complex structure of interconnecting shapes. The building was reconstructed in late Renaissance style in 1638, and restored after the war. Note the windows with rare curtain arches.

To the right of the Town Hall are a couple of Baroque buildings: an arcaded house, and an 18C guardhouse with a curly gable. The latter accommodates a small **museum** (open Tues–Sun 10.00– 15.30). A fine late Gothic **house** (15C)

stands on the opposite side of ul. Kazimierza Wielkiego (No. 13). Now a music school, it has a five-sectioned 16C gable with miniature blank arches, and a moulded portal decorated with glazed brick.

Heading south and then left into ul. Basztowa you reach the **arsenal** (16C, rebuilt in the 1970s), a grim building with glazed brick friezes separating the storeys.

You can begin a tour of the town walls from ul. Strażnicza. The small cylindrical **Prisoners' Tower** (13m high) borders the canal and the Jagielloński Park. As with the other three surviving towers, the entrance is 5–7m above ground, at the level of the wooden walkway which used to circle the walls. Next along is the **Ice Tower** (31m), adjoining a bastion with loopholes and a gabled annexe. Inside the latter is a branch of the **museum** (open Tues–Sun 10.00–15.30).

Town hall, Stargard Szczeciński

Continuing along UL. WAŁOWA you

reach the impressive **Pyrzyce Gate**, the oldest of the three gates, whose 15C brick superstructure rests on an earlier stone base (13C). Close by, at the corner of ul. Mieszka I (No. 43), is the Gothic **Klatzan House**, a fine example of the 16C secular architecture found in Hanseatic towns. The next fragment of wall ends at the **Red Sea Tower** (34m), decorated with rhombic patterns of glazed brick.

Continue along ul. Wałowa to the **Church of St John the Baptist**. The slender Neo-Gothic tower, the largest in Western Pomerania, rises a staggering 99m.

St John's began its existence as a 12C granite chapel by the Hospitallers' monastery. In 1408, work commenced on a brick aisled hall with a tower modelled on St Mary's. The original chapel, fragments of which remain, was later dismantled to make way for a new chancel with an ambulatory. During the late 17C the church was rebuilt after a fire. The tower fell in 1699, and its Neo-Gothic replica did not appear until 1892.

The Baroque **interior** consists of a short nave of three star-vaulted bays and a five-sided chancel apse enclosed by an ambulatory; star vaults also cover the ambulatory chapels. On the walls, 48 ceramic mascarons serve as corbels.

Continue to skirt the town wall, which is interrupted by a playground, but reappears on ul. Klasztorna. At the next junction (ul. Portowa) is the picturesque 15C **Mill Gate** (Port Gate), with two crenellated octagonal turrets and an arch spanning a hideously dirty stream. The modern mill is further north, in the vicinity of the Chrobry Park. Opposite the gate is a large 16C **salt granary**, marking the spot of Stargard's former river port. Cross the stream and continue along the former rampart, currently a promenade, to the **Biało-główka Tower** (30m) at its end. Turning the corner, notice the **Rampart Gate**, which closes the end of ul. Bolesława Chrobrego. Constructed in the 15C, it received its handsome Renaissance stone gables a century later.

Szczecin to Świnoujście via Międzyzdroje

❖ Goleniów • Wolin • Międzyzdroje • Karsibór • Świnoujście

The main attractions of this trip are the mysterious Wolin island, with remnants of an ancient pagan harbour, and the charming resort town of Międzyzdroje on the Baltic coast. The final stop is the ferry port of Świnoujście on the German border.

From Szczecin head east on the 116, joining the motorway (road 3) heading north for Goleniów (17km). Come off the road at the exit marked 'Gole-niów/Gdańsk'.

GOLENIÓW originally had four medieval gates; only one is preserved—the **Wolin Gate** (north)—which you pass on your way to the main square. This impressive 14C structure (26m) has a panelled and gabled front with a passageway below. Now a small cultural centre, it adjoins a fragment of medieval wall with a turret. On the square stands the late Gothic **Parish**

Church of St Catherine, a 15C brick aisled hall erected on the ruins of a 13C Romanesque chapel built by the Knights Hospitallers of St John. Its present appearance owes much to the remodelling carried out in 1865–67, when many Neo-Gothic elements were introduced. Reconstructed after the war, it has a moulded and glazed west portal, four glazed friezes separating the sections of the west tower, and gables of all sizes and shapes to the south, east and north. Two Gothic towers (14C–15C) lie further south towards the river: the round **Prison Tower** and the octagonal **Mint Tower**, both adjoining scraps of medieval wall.

Island of Wolin

Continue north through forests to the island of Wolin (42km), which separates the Bay of Szczecin from the Gulf of Pomerania. The town of **WOLIN** is one of the oldest Slav settlements, mentioned by chroniclers as early as the 10C. It is also the alleged site of *Vineta*, a sort of Slavic *Atlantis*, drowned by the gods for its licentiousness. The rise and fall of this mythical city inspired Feliks Nowowiejski (see p. 408) to write his opera *The Legend of the Baltic*.

The early Wolinians were chiefly fishermen and farmers, by the 9C trading with places as far away as Constantinople, and later turning to piracy. After its capture by the Polish Duke Mieszko, Wolin became the first sea port of the Piast dynasty—with a quay nearly 300m long, defended by a ring of ramparts. In pursuit of his mission to Christianise Pomerania, Bishop Otto of Bamberg ordered the destruction of the pagan idols worshipped in Wolin (the most prominent of which were *Triglav*—literally, 'three-headed'—and *Svantevit*), and in 1140 a bishopric was created by papal decree. However, frequent Danish raids and competition from other Pomeranian towns led to Wolin's decline. A revival began in the 13C, when it received a municipal charter and fortifications, but this, too, proved brief. Today, the only remnant surviving from this twilight period is the ruined church of St Nicholas on the Main Square.

The best place to learn about the ancient history of Wolin is the **Regional Museum** (open Mon–Fri 09.00–16.00, Sat 09.00–14.00) on the Main Square. The small two-room display covers the early Middle Ages, the most interesting period, with well-marked exhibits and a tape commentary in English. The tower of **St Nicholas' Church** (13C–19C) offers a bird's-eye view of the island. Just to the north of it, a low wall marks the spot where the medieval town hall once stood. To the west is a wooden statue with sculpted faces—an enlarged copy of a remarkable 9C statuette of *Svantevit* discovered under the square in 1973. Fragments of Mieszko's ramparts, which existed from the 9C until the demolition of the town walls in 1680, can be seen on ul. Polna (left of the museum), with another fragment, adjoined by a late 18C manor house, nearby on ul. Krzywa. By the riverside, a row of poles stuck into the ground marks the location of the 9C quay.

Hangman Hill, 2km south of town, the site of an ancient lighthouse, offers beautiful views over the Bay of Szczecin. Here too, are 9C–11C barrow mounds, the graves of tribal elders of Wolin. Returning to town you pass an amphitheatre with a statue of *Triglav*, which was built to commemorate the 1000th anniversary of Wolin's fusion with Poland.

After Dargobądź, you enter the scenic **Wolin National Park**, which occupies the central part of the island. If you are leaving Poland by ferry, proceed directly to Świnoujście. If not, turn right off road 3 to the far more enticing resort of **MIĘDZYZDROJE** (13km). Though it offers little in the way of cultural attractions, Międzyzdroje's strength is the natural beauty of its surroundings. Excellent accommodation is provided at the *Amber Baltic Hotel* on ul. Bohaterów Warszawy 26A (☎ (0–91) 328–0800, 328–1000), idyllically situated right on the seashore.

Unlike so many Polish coastal towns, Międzyzdroje seems to have preserved some of the discreet atmosphere of a 19C resort. The seafront has a long promenade and an amphitheatre. From the pier, you can view the cliffs or take a pleasure boat excursion. South of the modest Main Square, at ul. Niepodległości 3, is a **natural history museum** with aviaries and a display of stuffed animals that live, or lived, in the Wolin National Park. A number of excellent hiking trails leading into the park begin in Międzyzdroje, taking you to some crystal-clear lakes, and a section of dramatic coastline with cliffs dropping 100m in places to the sea. Most of the park is thickly forested, and rich in flora and fauna. A small bison reserve (**open** 10.00–16.00, summer only) lies 2km east of town.

Back on road 3, just before Świnoujście, turn south along a minor road towards Karsibór. This brings you to the car ferry that takes you across the River Świna to Świnoujście proper, situated on the island of Uznam (the municipal car ferry on the town's east bank is for locals only). The shuttle service leaves every half hour and takes about ten minutes. Before crossing, you could drive south for 12km to the isle of **KARSIBÓR**. The sprawling village of the same name is an ancient Slav settlement, today offering beach huts, a few 18C houses, and a modest 15C Gothic church. The road stops at the marsh, beyond which lies an archipelago of 40 islands with an abundance of water fowl. Once across the river, drive north to Świnoujście.

Świnoujście

■ Practical information

Hotel. ★★ *Polaris*. Ul. Słowackiego 33, ☎ 321-5412. Car park, swimming pool. 34 rooms.
Tourist information. Ul. Paderewskiego 24, ☎ 326-6113.
ORBIS. Ul. Bolesława Chrobrego 9, ☎ 336-6167.
Main post office. Pl. Wolności.
Telephone code: (0–91)

Ferries to Scandinavia. Ferry terminal, ul. Dworcowa 1, ☎ 321-6140; Polferries, ul. Armii Krajowej 14a, ☎ 322-4396.
German Border Crossing. Pedestrians only. Take bus 'A' from pl. Kościelny in the town centre.

By the standards of border towns, Świnoujście (population 44,100) is quite pleasant, though few come here for the sights. On the waterfront (Wybrzeże Władysława IV) is the **Sea Fisheries Museum** (open Tues–Fri 09.00–15.00, Sat–Sun 11.00–15.00) housed inside the former 19C town hall. Close by, on pl. Słowiański, is a weird concrete **Sailors' Monument**. On a fine day, you can walk north from the city centre through parks to the seashore, where there are spa facilities and a broad beach.

Świnoujście to Kołobrzeg ~ the Amber Coast

❖ Kamień Pomorski • Trzęsacz • Rewal • Niechorze • Kołobrzeg

Kamień Pomorski, 55km east of Świnoujście, is probably the most attractive town in Western Pomerania, its Gothic cathedral alone amply justifying a visit. Further east along the coast, widely known since prehistoric times for its amber, is the village of Trzęsacz with an extraordinary church ruin.

Take road 3 to Międzyzdroje and follow the scenic coastal road (102) east through the Wolin National park (see previous page), and along the narrow spit. After crossing the bridge in Dziwnów, you leave Wolin island; stay on the 102 heading 53km south for the spa town of KAMIEŃ POMORSKI.

Kamień Pomorski

The town is distinguished for its historic medieval plan (reconstructed), and has one of the finest cathedrals in the country. It also hosts an annual **International Festival of Organ and Chamber Music** (July and August).

> Kamień was a 9C Wolinian harbour settlement (see p. 358). It rose to prominence in the late 12C, when it became the seat of the Pomeranian bishopric (1176). From the 19C onwards, it quickly gained a reputation as a fashionable resort and health spa. The historic town centre was rebuilt almost from scratch after the Second World War.

The Cathedral

East of the MAIN SQUARE stands the superb ****cathedral**, founded before 1176. It started as a late Romanesque granite church, but only in the north transept does the stone rise high enough to form a round-headed portal (13C); the rest of the church, completed before 1464, is brick Gothic. Most impressive is the **exterior**, especially the south side, where the concept of the gable is exploited to its limits. Clinging to the south wall, to the right of the portal, is a small hexagonal tower and a tiny pointed-arch entrance.

The **interior**—a nave of three broad bays and a single-bay chancel—is sparsely furnished. A late Gothic triptych serves as the high altar, with traces of 13C murals behind it. At the nave's west end is a splendid **organ**, renowned for its beautiful sound. From the north transept, with a font surrounded by a 17C grille, stairs lead to the first-floor **Treasury** (guided tours at 09.00, 10.00, 11.00, 15.00 and 16.00, weekdays only), begun in the early 14C, above the east wing of the cloister. The walls of its cross-vaulted interior are covered with preserved Gothic murals (c 1350). Originally used as canons' rooms, it was later expanded to perform the function of a library and archive. On display are codices and manuscripts (13C–18C), incunabula (15C), prints (16C–18C), liturgical items and sculptures (14C–17C), as well as written records of what the Nazis looted. A door in the north aisle leads to the medieval cloister garth around a 12C granite font, with old tombstones embedded into the walls.

Opposite the cathedral, on pl. Katedralny, stands the former **Bishop's Palace**, currently a library, with a Renaissance gable on the north side and a 16C oriel to the west. Either head directly west along ul. Hanki Sawickiej, passing a **Renaissance House** (No. 1) with reliefs depicting birds, or walk northwest towards the lake, passing remnants of the 14C **town walls**, and then follow the waterfront to the OLD TOWN SQUARE. On it stands the late Gothic **Town Hall** (15C–16C), rebuilt after the war, with a café inside. East of the square, along ul. Basztowa, stands the 14C **Wolin Gate**, the only survivor of five, with a round crenellated superstructure on a square turreted base. South of the square, ul. Jagiełły rises up the hill to the Gothic Church of St Nicholas with a pentagonal tower and a small **museum** inside (**open** Tues–Sat 10.00–15.00).

From Kamień Pomorski, return to Dziwnówek and continue east (22km) along the 103 to **TRZĘSACZ**, noted for its remarkable Gothic *church (15C), of which only a single wall remains, perched precariously on the edge of the cliff. The church was originally located in the centre of the village, some 2km from the shore, but cliff erosion over the centuries caused the seafront to recede, finally leading to the collapse of most of the church in 1901. Some of the furnishings are displayed in nearby **REWAL**, a large popular resort with high cliffs and a good beach.

Church in Trzęsacz

A narrow gauge railway links Trzęsacz and Rewal with **NIECHORZE**, the best-known resort on this precipitous stretch of coastline, with a 19C lighthouse and wonderful views.

In Trzebiatów join road 102 to Kołobrzeg (49km).

Kołobrzeg

Kołobrzeg, one of Poland's oldest fortified coastal towns, is situated at the mouth of the Parsęta river. In summer, this popular resort is crowded with holidaymakers and sailing enthusiasts, but at other times visitors also come for the spa facilities. Whatever the season, you can always take a stroll along the promenade and pier.

■ **Practical information**

Hotels. ★★★★*Orbis-Solny*. Ul. Fredry 4, ☎ 354-5700. Located in the east of town in verdant surroundings, close to the beach. Fitness Centre, tenniscourts, swimming pool, garden, business services, car park, wheelchair access. 145 rooms with views over the park and forest.

Tourist information (***PAPT***). Ul. Wojska Polskiego 6c, ☎ 352-7939.
ORBIS. Ul. Dworcowa 4, ☎ 352-3689/352-3869/352-3272.
Telephone code: (0–94).

History

The first fortified settlement (9C), 3km to the south, thrived due to its rich salt deposits and abundant supplies of herring. Joined to the Polish state in 972, Kołobrzeg was the site of the first church in Western Pomerania, and had become a bishopric by the end of the millennium. In the 14C it joined the Hanseatic League. The Prussians, aware of Kołobrzeg's strategic significance, transformed the town into a fortress during the 18C. As much as 90 per cent of it was destroyed during the Second World War. When, after fierce fighting, the Polish battalions entered it in 1945, all they found was smouldering ruins.

The city centre

The few sights are all within short walking distance of the Main Square, whose centre is occupied by a Neo-Gothic **Town Hall,** built in 1832 to designs by Karl Friedrich Schinkel, who incorporated remnants of its 15C predecessor, such as the vaulted cellars, and the rare granite pillory embedded into the northeast wall. The interiors accommodate a **Cultural Centre** and an indifferent **Gallery of Modern Art** (open 10.00–17.00).

To the west of the town hall stands the imposing Gothic ***Collegiate Church of St Mary**. Begun in 1255, the first brick aisled hall consisted of a rib-vaulted nave, long chancel, and seven-sided apse (before 1331). In the early 15C, the apsed Chapel of Our Lady (south) was extended west to form a separate star-vaulted aisle, thus turning the building into a double-aisled hall (an extra star-vaulted aisle was added to the north). The west front, an extraordinary broad mass of red brick with windows in unlikely places, came into being when the two towers were amalgamated in the 15C; there is a viewing terrace at the top. The most interesting items inside are the extraordinary carved **wooden chandelier** (1523), depicting Mary and John the Baptist, the early Gothic bronze **font** with 26 Passion scenes in relief (1355), and the rare 4m-high seven-branched standing candelabrum (1327), with lions and dragon heads on its base. A finely detailed late Gothic triptych (1504), with a central scene of the *Last Supper*, forms the high altar. The engraved **canons' stalls** in the chancel date from c 1340.

Kołobrzeg's **Military Museum**, tracing the history of the Polish army, is contained in two separate buildings: the early 19C Brunszwicki's Palace on ul. Armii Krajowej 13 (open Mon–Tues, Thur–Fri 09.00–15.00, Wed 14.00–19.00), and a pavilion of the late Gothic **Schlieffen House** (15C, rebuilt c 1540) on ul. Emilii Gierczak 5, south of the church (open Thur–Sat 09.00–15.00, Wed 14.00–19.00, Sun 08.30–14.30).

On ul. Wąska, the 18C Neo-Renaissance building of the former College of Chivalry has been converted into a shopping arcade and beer hall. The remains of fortifications built by the Prussians (1630–1807) can be seen in the northern part of Salt Island (Wyspa Solna)—once the site of salt works—and just across the river by the fishing harbour.

Kołobrzeg to Słupsk

❖ Koszalin • Bukowo Morskie • Darłowo • Słupsk

Koszalin, which lies roughly midway between Szczecin and Gdańsk, is relatively poor in sights, but further east and north are the two pretty Pomeranian towns of Bukowo and Darłowo, the latter boasting a well-preserved castle with a good museum.

Leave Kołobrzeg on road 11 for **KOSZALIN** (43km), situated some 10km from the coast on the river Dzierżęcinka. During the 14C, it was one of the wealthiest Pomeranian towns, later rivalling Kołobrzeg as the chief ducal and ecclesiastical seat and centre of maritime commerce. Complete destruction during the Second World War, however, left few vestiges of Koszalin's rich and colourful past, and you will have to look hard amongst the mass of ugly modern concrete to find anything of interest.

Begin your tour at the **Cathedral of St Mary**, situated to the south of the main square (across the main thoroughfare). This Gothic brick basilica, owing much to the Hanseatic tradition, was built in 1300–33. It was partly reconstructed in 1842–45, when it was given a massive west tower. During the Reformation, the interior was covered in plaster; when much of this was removed in 1972, earlier Gothic elements were revealed underneath. The Gothic furnishings include figures of **saints** (1512), a **font** and a **crucifix** (14C). The 17C organ is sometimes used for summer concerts.

The Main Square has nothing to show but a fountain and an ugly monument, but going east along ul. Asnyka and right into ul. Grodzka, you will reach the small 15C **Executioner's House** by the park. After 1464, Koszalin had its own high court, and thus a special house had to be built for the resident executioner. Renovation in 1964 revealed fragments of Gothic wall on the front elevation. The building now houses a small theatre.

Backtracking along ul. Asnyka, notice to your right the **Orthodox Church**. Its Gothic portal on the park side is the sole remnant of the Cistercian convent (14C), destroyed during the Reformation. The church itself was once the chapel of a 16C Renaissance castle, which burned down in 1718 leaving only a single wing (now accommodating offices). Close by, bordering the river, is a fragment of the medieval **town walls** (1292–1310), which survived until the great fire of 1718. The sections you see today were integrated into houses before the war and thus could be faithfully reconstructed afterwards.

The **Regional Museum** in Koszalin has two branches. The first, situated close by on ul. Młyńska (Nos 27–29), adjoins a mini-skansen. The more interesting second branch, with a columned and pedimented entrance, is on ul. Piłsudskiego, which you pass on your way out of town. The permanent display, entitled 'From Gothic to Secession', presents a chaotic mix of sculpture, painting, furniture and craftwork.

From the centre of Koszalin follow the signs marked 'Gdańsk'. You should then turn left onto the 203, heading seaward in the direction of **Bukowo Morskie**, where a Gothic **church**, the only remnant of the 13C Cistercian abbey, scenically overlooks the still waters of Lake Bukowo.

Darłowo (10km) is a charming medieval town some 2.5km from the coast. Head straight for the *****Castle of the Pomeranian Dukes**, which lies southwest of the Main Square on ul. Zamkowa, overlooking the river. Built as a ducal seat by Bogusław V in 1352–72, the castle's medieval plan has been preserved despite numerous later modifications. The interiors currently house a **museum** (**open** 10.00–16.00), whose highlight is the star-vaulted **Knights' Hall** (1372–1624) on the ground floor, later used as the castle chapel (1639–1805), with a display of Pomeranian religious art. The main attraction here is the exquisite lime-wood **pulpit** (1639), decorated with figural sculptures and gilding. The doors of the pulpit are crowned with the armorial cartouche of the chapel's founder, the Duchess Elżbieta, wife of the last Duke of Pomerania. Upstairs, don't miss the large, finely detailed map of the Pomeranian Duchy, with vignettes of 49 towns, including Darłowo (Rügenwalde), drawn up for Filip II (1573–1618) by Eilhard Lubinus (Lubben) in 1618 (the present version is a 1925 copy). Outside, notice the reconstructed *dansker* (latrine) outside. Stocks, manacles and other instruments of torture can be viewed in the castle cellars.

Returning to the main square you pass the Gothic **Church of St Mary**, a standard brick basilica raised in the first half of the 14C and rebuilt many times. Today it is noted as the resting place of the Pomeranian Duke Erik I (1382–1459), briefly King of Denmark, Norway and Sweden, but later a pirate and outlaw, who spent the last 10 years of his life in Darłowo. The sepulchral chapel contains two more sarcophagi, those of the duchesses Elżbieta (1653) and Jadwiga (1650), both richly decorated and coated with tin. In the 1970s, medieval floral painting was discovered on the chancel vault, and a Gothic portal in the north wall.

The Main Square itself has a few historic houses built mostly after the fire of 1722, and a Baroque **town hall** of 1725 (rebuilt). Going north you reach the Gothic **High Gate**, with tall slender niches and a pointed-arch passageway. Beyond it, by the municipal cemetery, lies the remarkable 15C **Cemetery Chapel of St Gertrude**, founded by Erik I. The interior, often closed, consists of a star-vaulted centre surrounded by a dodecagonal ambulatory, buttressed from the outside.

At Sławno, join road 6 heading east for Słupsk (48km).

Słupsk

Słupsk (population 96,200), situated 18km from the Baltic coast, is a good base for excursions into the Słowiński National Park, best known for its remarkable 'shifting dunes'. Thanks to its inland location, Słupsk tends not to attract the summer crowds, and you can usually explore its preserved medieval centre in relative peace. In July and August, **organ concerts** are held each Thursday in the Dominican church of St Hyacinth; in September, you can attend the annual **Festival of Polish Piano Music**, with recitals held in the Knights' Hall of the castle.

■ Practical information

Hotels. ★★★ *Piast*. Ul. Jedności Narodowej 3, ☎ 425-286/7. Ideal central location. Good cuisine, car park. 25 rooms.

Tourist information (PAPT). Ul. Wojska Polskiego 16, ☎ 42-43-26.
ORBIS. Ul. Kołłątaja 31 (train station), ☎ 42-7014. There are also a couple of good travel agencies at ul. Wojska Polskiego 29.
Main post office. Ul. Łukasiewicza.
Telephone code: (0-59).

History

The earliest historical record of Słupsk reaches back to 1015, when it was captured by King Bolesław the Brave (Chrobry). By the 12C, Słupsk was rivalling Świecie and Gdańsk as the most important castellanship in Eastern Pomerania. Seized by the margraves of Brandenburg in 1307, the town later became a pawn in the political struggle between the West Pomeranian dukes and the Teutonic Order. The dukes repurchased the town in 1341–42 (a painting of the Act of Repurchase hangs in the town hall), and managed to hold on to it until the dynasty died out in the 1630s. The division of Western Pomerania under the Treaty of Westphalia (1648) saw Słupsk return to Brandenburg. This led to the increasing Germanisation of the region, particularly after 1720, when the Prussian state embarked on a colonisation campaign. As its forbears had done centuries ago, the still predominantly Slavic population of Słupsk resisted Prussian dominance, even turning to open revolt in 1848. Liberated by the Soviet army in 1945, Słupsk once again became part of Poland.

The city centre

Pl. Zwycięstwa marks the border of the Old and New Towns. On it stands the bulky, irregular, and anything but pretty Neo-Gothic **Town Hall** (1901). Across the square is the more interesting 14C **New Gate**, with a 16C Baroque crowning, and an adjoining fragment of 15C town fortifications. From the 17C onwards it served as a prison and a cloth mill, before being taken over by the military in the 19C. It is currently a gallery. Beyond the gate, heading northeast along ul. Nowobramska, you reach the Old Town Square, and just before it, the Gothic **Parish Church of St Mary**, a brick basilica built in the second half of the 14C. The star-vaulted interior contains a Baroque pulpit (1609) and a late Gothic Passion group (early 16C), at the east end of the north aisle.

Sections of **medieval wall** can be seen on ul. Jagiełły, which exits southeast off pl. Zwycięstwa. Further along, on the small square, stands the octagonal brick **Chapel of St George** (15C), hidden by trees. It is almost identical to the cemetery chapel in Darłowo (see above), with a Gothic entrance and steep roof rising to a wooden lantern. Turn left into ul. Dominikańska. Facing you is the **Dominican Church of St Hyacinth**, dating from the 15C. Originally a monastic church, it was rebuilt after a fire in 1602 as the castle church, and received late Renaissance furnishings, including the present high altar with a painting of *Christ on the Cross*, and the pulpit (left). Also dating from this ducal period are the sepulchral monuments of the Duchess Anna de Croy and her son, Bogusław Ernest Croy. Richly gilded tin sarcophagi of Anna and Bogusław were also discovered in the crypts (now in the museum). The decidedly odd interior of the church—two aisleless, star-vaulted rooms—had some Gothic elements restored during renovation work in 1875. The Baroque organ you see here is used during the summer festival.

The Castle

In the courtyard behind the church is a group of well restored buildings. Facing you is the **Castle of the Pomeranian Dukes**, begun by Duke Bogusław X in 1507 and rebuilt as a Renaissance residence in 1580–87. The castle's golden age ended in 1648, when it passed to the Hohenzollerns of Brandenburg, who removed all the furnishings to Berlin. It was subsequently used as a granary, armory and storehouse. Only the tower and one residential wing have survived to the present day. Since 1965, the castle has accommodated the **Museum of Central Pomerania** (open Wed–Sun 10.00–16.00). The display includes the two **tin sarcophagi** from St Hyacinth's church (mentioned above), Pomeranian art (14C–18C), Flemish Renaissance tapestries, Venetian majolica, and the largest national collection of **pastel drawings** by **Stanisław Ignacy Witkiewicz** (see p. 86), as well as many of his oil-paintings, sketches and portraits.

A regional ethnographical display on three floors can be seen in the half-timbered house opposite the castle (same opening times). This is the former **castle mill** (1310, rebuilt), one of the oldest examples of industrial architecture in the country. A wooden bridge leads across the stream and sluice-gate to the square brick **Mill Gate** (c 1400), which is gabled at both ends, but otherwise plain. Skirting the river north along ul. Francesco Nullo, you reach the **Witches' Tower**, another remnant of the medieval fortifications. During the 17C, women suspected of witchcraft were incarcerated here.

The Słowiński National Park

❖ Smołdzino • Smołdzinski Las • Kluki

This excursion takes you into the Słowiński National Park (186 sq km), a remote and beautiful area, which in 1997 was included on UNESCO's list of World Biosphere Reserves. It is the third largest National Park in Poland, comprising Lake Gardno (west), Lake Łebsko (east) and the protected stretch of coastline between them, with its famous 'shifting dunes'. The inland villages of Smołdzino and Kluki, see below) can both be reached by bus from Słupsk, but the best way to see the dunes is to drive to Smołdziński Las (see below) and continue on foot. The Park can also be visited from the town of Łeba (see p. 344).

Leave Słupsk northeast on road 213 (ul. Kaszubska); at Choćmirówko turn left onto minor roads for **SMOŁDZINO** (33km from Słupsk), a picturesque village situated at the foot of Rowokół (115m), the 'holy hill' of the early Pomeranians, the centre of a pagan cult. Ascend to the top for panoramic views. Smołdzino is also the birthplace of Anna de Croy's chaplain Michał Mostnik, a guardian in the 17C of the now extinct Slovincian dialect spoken by the native inhabitants of this region—a Slavic tribe related to the Kashubians. Despite Germanisation, the dialect was still in currency as late as the 19C.

The **Natural History Museum** (open Tues–Sat 09.00–17.00) contains a display of the rich variety of flora and fauna found in the Słowiński National Park.

About 5km after **SMOŁDZIŃSKI LAS**, you should turn left at the sign marked 'Czołpino'. Stop at the car park at the edge of the park and walk the remaining 2km (red trail) through woodland to the remarkable 'shifting dunes', up to 50m high, bordering a stretch of breathtaking coastline. Thereafter, the red trail continues for 25km to Łeba (see p. 344).

Kluki, 7km further on, is a hamlet enclosed by woods on the west bank of Lake Łebsko. This ancient settlement, lying within the bounds of the park, has a skansen (**open** Tues–Sun 09.00–15.00) of Slovincian culture, with original farmsteads, fishing and farming equipment.

Gdańsk to Toruń

❖   Tczew • Pelplin • Gniew • Piaseczno • Świecie • Chełmno • Toruń

This trip takes you upstream along the Vistula river (west bank), passing through areas exceptionally rich in cultural heritage. The highlights are Pelplin, with its splendid Cistercian Abbey and diocesan museum, the Teutonic castle in Gniew, also with a museum, and the picturesque, medieval town of Chełmno.

Leave Gdańsk on road 1 (E75) heading south. Tczew (34km from Gdańsk) has for centuries been associated with shipping and navigation. Poland's first naval academy was established here in 1920, later moving to Gdynia (see p. 331), yet the roots of this maritime tradition are much older. Settlements inhabited by the proto-Slavonic Wiślanie tribe began to emerge in the fertile Vistula basin as early as the 8C–9C.

The Wiślanie made remarkable 'logboats'—each dug out of a single tree trunk—and you can see examples of these at the **Vistula River Museum**, No. 4 ul. 30-go Stycznia (**open** Tues–Wed, Fri–Sun 10.00–16.00, Thur 12.00–18.00). The other permanent exhibition on the upper floor traces the history of navigation along the river. The museum building is itself of interest, erected in the late 19C for the Kelch Metal Goods factory, which the Nazis later used to produce bugging devices and anti-aircraft equipment. Emil Kelch established his first workshop in 1857, the very year that Lentze completed the iron truss bridge—at that time one of the longest in Europe (890m)—which still spans the Vistula on the Malbork road.

The Cistercian Abbey at Pelplin

From Tczew continue to Rudno, turning right onto the 229 for **Pelplin** (24km). This town on the Wierzyca river is famous for its ****Cistercian Abbey**, without doubt one of the most beautiful monuments of Gothic architecture in Poland.

> The Cistercians settled in Pelplin in 1276. Work on their brick church and convent began soon afterwards, lasting well into the 14C. Their patron, Duke Mszczuj II of Pomeralia, transferred the convent and its domains to the Teutonic Knights (see p. 334), who held on to it until their expulsion from the region in 1466. Destroyed during the Swedish Deluge (see p. 49), Pelplin came under Prussian rule after 1772. The Prussians dissolved the convent in 1823, and in the following year raised the church to the rank of a cathedral—the new seat of the expanded bishopric of Chełmno. Major renovation work was carried out in the late 19C, when the original Gothic appearance of the church, disfigured by later alterations, was restored.

Miraculously, the church was almost untouched during the Second World War—the only damage was a hole in the chancel vault made by a bomb which failed to explode.

Immediately striking are the fortress-like proportions of the church: a soaring mass of plain brick, 84m long, with great projecting aisled transepts. Decorative tracery and corbels in the form of busts—perhaps representing the builders of the church—adorn the east front. A frieze of plant motifs skirts the aisles, just above the large, three-step buttresses. Of the transepts, also gabled, most interesting is the north one (parallel to the road), with a richly moulded portal of c 1300, enlivened by stone sculpture. You may need to ask at the seminary building (see below) for permission to enter the church.

The predominantly Baroque **interior** is generally dark, with a few radiant spots on sunny days—such as the pretty net vaults (1557) arising from a slender octagonal pillar in the south transept. The aisles, half as broad and high as the nave, have elaborate star vaults, the best and oldest in the church, arising from corbels in the form of busts, atlantes and mythological creatures. The pulpit (1682) rests on a sculpture of Samson fighting a lion, executed with meticulous attention to detail. Lavishness of detail also characterises the group of beautifully carved Gothic stalls (1450–63)—the only surviving fragment of the medieval furnishings.

Of particular interest are the **stalls** in the north transept, with unconventional renderings of Catholic symbolism: the Holy Ghost, for instance, is shown as a youth holding a dove. Look out for the evil-looking man tied by his hands to one of the hundreds of little columns decorating the stalls.

The south transept uses the northeast corner of the cloisters as a support for an organ loft, which houses an elaborately carved organ (1674–80). The south aisle ends with the altar of St Mary—especially noteworthy for Hermann Hahn's (1574–1628) *Adoration of the Shepherds* (1618) in the predella, said to be one of the earliest examples of chiaroscuro in European painting. Other paintings by Hahn adorn the remarkable late Renaissance high altar (1623–24), the second largest in Europe. The admirable *Death of St James* (1640) in the altar of St James by the second pillar on the south side of the nave (counting from the east), is by Bartholomäus Strobel (1591–c 1660), court artist to King Władysław IV.

Adjoining the church to the south are the former monastery buildings with vaulted cloisters. The north cloister contains early 15C frescos, while in the east wing of the monastery (1272–76) there is a fine chapter house. Since 1864, its interiors have accommodated the **Chapel of the Holy Cross**, with 14C mascarons on the corbels flanking the recessed portal (1300).

Diocesan Museum

The museum on ul. Ks. Bp. K. Dominika II (**open** Tues–Sat 11.00–16.00, Sun 10.00–17.00) is one of the best of its kind in Poland. Its modern interiors contain over 50,000 exhibits, including the famous **Pelplin Tabulature for Organ**, one of the most voluminous hand-written musical relics of 17C Europe, discovered in 1957 in the theological seminary library, formerly located in the south refectory. There are also medieval illuminated manuscripts and many incunabula, the earliest dating from the 12C. Religious art is the dominant theme on the ground floor, with wooden sculpture, mostly painted, valuable gold and silver liturgical vessels (from Toruń, Gdańsk and Augsburg workshops), and liturgical vestments.

The highlight is a unique copy of the **Gutenberg Bible** (1435–55)—a printing error on page 46 of volume 1 allowed experts to measure the height of letter forms used by Gutenberg. Upstairs you will find a 14C Toruń polyptych from the church of St Mary, paintings of the *Flagellation of Christ* and the *Deposition*, both from the church of SS John the Baptist and Evangelist in Toruń, and many other items.

From Pelplin head south on road 230 marked 'Cierzpice', regaining road 1 for **GNIEW** (14km), a pleasant town overlooking meadows from the high Vistula spur, with narrow cobbled streets enclosed by partly preserved medieval walls. You should head straight for the Main Square (pl. Grunwaldzki), where there is a group of arcaded **burghers' houses** (15C, later rebuilt), unique in Pomerania. Just off the square is the **Parish Church of St Nicholas**, a small 14C brick aisled hall, reconstructed in 1870. Walking east from the centre you reach the Gothic *castle (Wzgórze Zamkowe 1).

> The Teutonic Knights acquired Gniew from the Cistercians of Oliwa (see p. 328) in 1276. Shortly thereafter, they began work on the castle, their first on the west bank of the Vistula, intended as the seat of the Komturei. To spur economic development and encourage German colonisation, an adjacent town was founded on Chełmno law (see below) in 1297. After the battle of Grunwald (see p. 417), the castle surrendered without a fight to Jagiełło's army, but soon returned to the Order. The Poles recovered it in 1464 after a rebellion by the burghers of Gniew against Teutonic misrule. Though it suffered extensive damage during the Swedish Deluge (see p. 49), the castle experienced something of a golden age when Jan Sobieski, the future king of Poland, was the local starost. Sobieski's wife, Maria Kazimiera, later added a hunting lodge and the Baroque Marysieńka palace to the south side (1667–69). Decline set in, though, after the Partitions, when the Prussians converted the castle into a warehouse and then a prison. It suffered again in 1921, when three-quarters of it burned down.

The castle is built on a regular plan, with four slender corner towers, and the base of a once huge keep in the northeast corner. Most striking are the deep pointed-arch windows of the chapel (east) and chapter house (west), set between stretches of red brick wall. The interiors, with permanent exhibitions devoted to archaeology, hunting and fine metalwork, can only be visited in the company of a guide. A number of cultural events are staged at the castle: a day in the life of a medieval town (first Sunday in **July**); a jousting and crossbow tournament (first weekend in **August**); a display of decorative metalwork techniques using medieval tools (end of **June**). There is also a riding school.

Tours begin on the hour from 09.00 to 16.00 on weekdays and every 45 minutes from 09.00 to 15.45 at weekends. For exact dates and details of events, contact: Zamek w Gniewie, Wzgórze Zamkowe 1, 83–140 Gniew; ☎ (0-69) 35-25-37.

Continuing south along road 1, you pass PIASECZNO, with its fine **parish church of** St Mary originally built by the Teutonic Knights; PIENIĄŻKOWO, with its 16C church; and NOWE, which has remnants of medieval fortifications wedged between houses, and two 14C churches: the **Parish Church of St Matthew**, and the **Franciscan church**.

Road 1 follows the Vistula south for a further 51km to ŚWIECIE, a bustling town with several buildings of interest. It is a convenient stopping point *en route* to Toruń. If you decide to stay, try the *Leśna Hotel*★★★ on ul. Bydgoska 1 (☎ (052) 14-372), bizarrely situated next door to a paper mill, but without doubt the best hotel in town.

The Baroque **parish church** on ul. Sądowa was built in 1692–1720. The walls and vaults of its nave are covered with *trompe l'oeil* painting (1800) depicting the bringing of the 'miraculous' painting of the *Virgin* to Świecie. A copy of this cult object has been placed at the Rococo high altar (1767), which fills the square apse. Adjoining the church are the monastery cloisters, with a gate-tower of 1741 and some fine Rococo paintings.

Heading southeast from the centre you reach the 'old town', set amongst meadows in the fork of the Wda and Vistula rivers. In the 19C, the town was moved up the hillside due to frequent flooding, and only two buildings were left behind: the 'water' castle of the Teutonic knights and the 'old' parish church. The **castle**, a ruin since the mid-17C, was built by the Teutonic Order in 1338–48, and later rebuilt as a Renaissance royal residence (1543–66). Preserved is a splendid round tower, some 40m high, with arched machicolations.

Return along ul. Zamkowa and then ul. PCK to the brick **parish church**, destroyed during the Second World War and renovated as late as the 1980s. It is enclosed by an L-shaped stretch of medieval town fortifications, with fragments of six towers and part of the Chełmno Gate. Work on the chancel began in the late 14C, with the nave, aisles and square gabled tower being added in 1526–66. In 1989, a copy of the famous Black Madonna of Częstochowa (see p. 267) was placed inside the church, each year attracting scores of pilgrims.

Chełmno

From Świecie, continue along road 1 for 7 km, across the river to **Chełmno**, one of the most beautiful towns in Poland, set in picturesque surroundings on the high embankment of the Vistula. The topographical features of the post-glacial landscape around Chełmno have, over the centuries, served as a natural system of defences, restricting the access of invading armies. For this reason, Chełmno can today boast a fully-preserved medieval town plan, a unique attraction. The chessboard of streets is surrounded by an almost unbroken ring of ***Town Walls**** (13C–15C), 2270m long, with 17 of the 33 towers preserved, as well as the Grudziądz Gate (northeast) defending what was once the only unprotected entrance to the city. Of the buildings, pride of place goes to the charming Renaissance town hall on the main square, but the six major churches should also not be missed.

If you are pressed for time, Chełmno can easily be visited on a long day-trip from Toruń.

History

Chełmno is mentioned in medieval chronicles as early as 1065. During the Middle Ages it was part of the Polish state, and later of the Duchy of Mazovia. In 1228, Konrad, the Duke of Mazovia, endowed Chełmno and its domains to the Teutonic Order, whom he had brought to Poland. Five years later, the Grand Master of the Order, Herman von Salza, granted Chełmno a municipal charter based on what would come to be known as 'Chełmno law', a legal model that later encompassed some 200 towns, among them Toruń. Until 1458, the court with jurisdiction over all the towns founded on this law (except Toruń) had its seat in Chełmno. Initially, the Teutonic Knights planned to make Chełmno the capital of their state, but Malbork was finally chosen instead.

Throughout the 14C, Chełmno remained the largest and most important city in the Order's realm after Toruń and Elbląg. Contacts with the Hanseatic League, of which it became a member, and the lucrative trade along the Vistula, ensured steady prosperity; a prestigious academy was even founded in 1386 to act as a Prussian counterweight to Kraków's Jagiellonian University. In 1440 the town joined the anti-Teutonic Prussian Union, consequently suffering much destruction, but did not return to Poland until 1479, well after the end of the Thirteen Years War.

Between 1505 and 1772, it was the property of the bishops of Chełmno, but wars and plagues, particularly during the 17C, led to its slow decline. After the First Partition of Poland, Chełmno came under Prussian rule. Frederick II established a cadets' college here in 1787. It encompassed barracks and 27 buildings, most of which can be seen on today's ul. 22 Stycznia.

The **Grudziądz Gate** (northeast) marks the entrance to the Old Town. The Nowe Planty, or park, skirts the town walls. In 1620, the gate was plastered, and expanded by means of a Renaissance chapel (park side), with a 15C *Pietà* in a niche halfway up the façade. On the other side of the gate, note the gabled **Burgher's House** at ul. Grudziądzka 36, originally 14C, whose present Baroque appearance dates from the late 18C. Nearby, in a courtyard off ul. Podmurna (No. 2) is an 18C timber granary (a similar one can be seen at ul. Wodna 24).

Ul. Grudziądzka continues southwest to the large MAIN SQUARE, which is dominated by the magnificent Renaissance **Town Hall*. Built in 1567–72, and modelled on its Poznań counterpart, the town hall remains Chełmno's finest secular building and, like no other, underscores the prosperity of the town's 16C heyday. The square, plastered block rises three storeys; a row of Ionic columns adorns the third, with a lively moulded parapet of flags and finials above. From its centre rises a lofty square tower (1584–96). Note the medieval measuring stick (4.35m long) embedded in the south façade. A **museum** (open Tues–Fri 10.00–16.00, Sat 10.00–15.00) displays period furniture and memorabilia, portraits of famous burghers, and the history of the Chełmno region from the earliest times until the 1945.

The houses surrounding the Main Square have modest 18C–19C façades, though the former residence of the Cywiński family (northeast, corner of ul. Rycerska), currently a furniture shop, is conspicuous for its sculpted Renaissance portal of c 1570, with the Cywiński crest in the tympanum and lions in relief at the sides.

Just off the square, at the corner of ul. Toruńska, stands the Gothic ***parish church**, its rows of narrow gables wedged between massive pinnacled buttresses. Most of this brick aisled hall was built in 1280–1333. Inside, the long nave has cross vaults supported on slender pillars, into which are set Gothic sculptures of the Apostles (c 1330–1340) under baldachins. **Murals** dating from the 14C–18C, some barely discernible, adorn the walls and vaults. A 13C Romanesque font stands at the east end of the south aisle, by the chapel. The other furnishings are all Baroque, except for the Rococo chancel stalls and shell-shaped pulpit. Note the coffin portrait of Marcin Kossenda (1705) on the south aisle wall, and the Mannerist relief figures of the Niemojewskis (c 1618) in the chapel of the Virgin Mary (end of the north aisle).

Back in the Main Square, walk north along ul. Rybacka, turning left into ul. Dominikańska, which brings you to the ***Cistercian Nuns' Abbey**. Founded in the late 13C, the abbey was later acquired by the Sisters of Charity of St Vincent a Paolo (1821), who are still there today. The early 14C church is concealed behind a 19C hospital building. Enter the courtyard at ul. Dominikańska 40 and proceed through the south portal (1619). Most striking is the two-tiered design of the interior: the upper gallery was used only by the nuns, who in this way had no contact with the lay believers attending mass, yet could see the Renaissance high altar and everything around it, such as the Pietà by Bartholomäus Strobel (17C) and the remarkable 16C organ loft to the left of the altar. Embedded in the west wall of the seminary chapel (north) is the memorial slab of Arnold Lischoren (1275). The upper tier of the church has star vaults adorned with ornamental bosses and large corbels and is circled by a broad painted frieze (c 1350) depicting religious scenes. At the gabled west end stands a slender brick tower (14C–17C) with a Baroque crowning of 1603. Close by are several buildings dating from the Teutonic period, including the present cloisters and the former stables, with granaries and servants' quarters above.

West of the church stands the **Mestwin Tower** (13C), the oldest element of the town fortifications, reached through a courtyard off ul. Klasztorna. This habitable tower, with a cross-vaulted room on the first floor, was probably part of the Teutonic Knights' residence. According to legend, the tower is named after the son of Duke Świętopełk, whom the Knights imprisoned here. Further west, overlooking the river, is the **Calvary Chapel**, which stands next to a large *Crucifix* (once 15m high). The chapel began life as the 13C Merseburg Gate. Inside it is a Gothic sculpture of the *Deposition*.

Opposite the Abbey on ul. Dominikańska is a grim brick building constructed as a lycée in 1865 on the ruins of the Franciscan convent. Right behind it is the 14C **Church of SS James and Nicholas**.

Looking east along ul. Dominikańska you will notice the distant stepped gable of the 13C **Dominican Church of SS Peter and Paul**. As you approach, another, smaller replica of the gable over the west porch becomes visible. Inside are fragments of 14C–15C murals, and a 13C Gothic memorial slab of Heidenryk, the first bishop of Chełmno.

Return to road 1 and continue south to Toruń.

Toruń

Toruń

Set in the broad Vistula valley, Toruń (population 197,000) is one of Poland's most beautiful cities, and if you are based in Warsaw or Gdańsk, a weekend trip here should be top priority. The unusually attractive Old Town, compact but not cramped, is the living centre of the city, with shops, cafés, restaurants, museums, the University and, above all, a wealth of original architecture ranging from the predominant Gothic, through Renaissance and Baroque, to Modernism. A tour through the medieval grid of streets will reveal that nearly every house is a historic monument, an echo of the illustrious past of this Hanseatic town which once rivalled Gdańsk and Kraków as Poland's greatest centre of commerce.

The Second World War was relatively kind to Toruń: with Chełmno (see p. 370) to the north, it managed to avoid the wide-scale physical destruction that befell so many other towns in the region. Today, Toruń has much more to offer than just the Copernicus Museum or the gingerbread for which it is has become famous. Attractive day trips can be made to Bydgoszcz (west) and the Brodnica Lake District (east), but if you are pressed for time, be sure to take the scenic Vistula route north towards Gdańsk, with its medieval towns, Teutonic castles and beautiful Gothic cathedrals.

Of the four grandest architectural monuments in Toruń, three are churches. Likewise, the tour of the Old Town is divided into three walks. **Walk 1** begins in the Old Town Square, with its magnificent Town Hall, and proceeds to the Church of St Mary, the first of the three. The **second walk** takes you to the Church of SS John the Baptist and Evangelist (the richest in works of art), but first visits the ruins of the Teutonic Castle and the Nicholas Copernicus Museum. The highlight of **walk 3** is the Church of St James.

■ Practical information

Hotels

★★★★

Orbis-Kosmos. Ul. Popiełuszki 2, ☎ 289-00, 270-85. Central location, close to the river. Car park, business services. 59 rooms overlooking the park and Vistula.
Orbis-Helios. Ul. Kraszewskiego 1–3, ☎ 262-44. Central location, close to the river. Car park, business services 108 rooms.
Wodnik. Ul. Bulwar Filadelfijski 12, ☎ 251-14. Car park, outdoor swimming pool, wheelchair access. 32 rooms.

★★★
Zajazd Staropolski. Ul. Żeglarska 10–14, ☎ 260-43. Superb location, just by the SS John the Baptist and Evangelist church. Quiet, comfortable, excellent service. 36 rooms.

Tourist information. Rynek Staromiejski 1, ☎ 237-46; PAPT, ul. Piekary 37/39, ☎ 621-0931.
ORBIS. ul. Mostowa 7, ☎ 225-53.
Post office. Rynek Staromiejski 12 (Old Town Square).
Telephone code: (0–56).

History
Initially an 11C settlement, *Toruń* (*Thorn*) was founded by the Teutonic Order, receiving a municipal charter in 1233. The oldest part, probably centred around the church of St John, soon proved too small, and a new town was founded in 1264 to accommodate the growing influx of artisans and journeymen. In 1454, the burghers, provoked by Teutonic misrule, launched a successful attack on the Order's 13C castle situated on the left bank of the Vistula. That same year, the old commercial district and the New Town were united to form a single metropolis. With the expulsion of the Teutonic Knights in 1466, Toruń returned to the Polish Crown; the castle was never rebuilt and under its new owners slowly fell into ruin. Conversely, the city entered a golden age, which would last throughout the 16C. Its most famous son—Nicholas Copernicus—was born here in 1473.

During the Swedish invasions of the 17C–18C (see p. 49), Toruń suffered less damage than most Polish towns, maintaining its role as an important cultural and religious centre until 1740, although in trade it was rapidly losing ground to Gdańsk. Annexed by Prussia during the Second Partition (1793), Toruń remained in German hands until 1920, except for the brief Napoleonic interlude (1807–15), during which it was incorporated into the Duchy of Warsaw. Since the last war, the city has grown a ring of grim housing estates and industrial wastelands around the irregular pentagon of the Old Town. The latter, though, with its broad streets sloping gently down towards the river, still preserves much of what the centuries have erased.

Walk One ~ The Old Town Square

The Town Hall
The centre of the Old Town Square is occupied by the ****Town Hall**, first erected in the mid-13C—the square tower dates from 1247. The renowned Gdańsk architect **Anthonis van Opbergen** modernised it in the early 17C, adding the third floor and four angle turrets, and giving the gables and window surrounds the characteristic touch of Flemish Mannerism. In 1703, the town hall was razed to the ground by a barrage of Swedish artillery. Rebuilt in 1737, it acquired late Baroque gables, but the interiors were never restored to their previous splendour. The Baroque west façade and many rooms were altered in the 19C and were not restored to their original form until 1957–63, when a **museum** (**open** Tues–Sun 10.00–16.00) was established inside. During the summer season visitors can climb the 42m Town Hall Tower for an

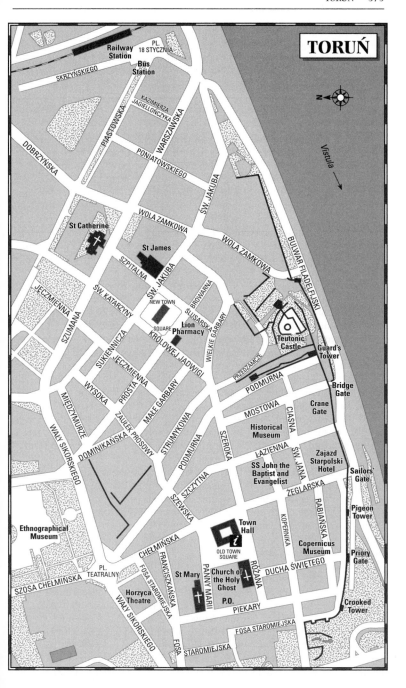

impressive vista over the surrounding city. The west wing of the town hall contains a restaurant, café, and tourist information centre.

The **Court Room** (to the right of the entrance) was used from the end of the 16C until 1973. It is adjoined by the Court Recess Chamber and the Gaol. A painting on the east wall of the Court Room shows the court in session. On the opposite wall hangs a portrait of the unfortunate J. G. Rösner, a mayor of Toruń sentenced to death in 1725 for his role during a bloody Catholic-Protestant conflict.

From the Court Room pass to the east wing, which houses a valuable collection of Gothic art. The most precious items are a 14C *Occursus Mariae*; a sculpture of St John the Evangelist moved here from the rood arch of the church of SS John the Baptist and Evangelist (see p. 380), works from the local St Wolfgang workshop (notably a figure of a king in the early 16C *The Homage of the Three Kings*, moved here from the church of St James, see p. 383); as well as excellent stained glass removed from the windows of several churches in Toruń and Chełmno. A display of handicrafts (14C–19C), including a collection of gingerbread art, for which Toruń is famous, occupies the west wing of the ground floor. A numismatics exhibition, with tools and other objects from the former Toruń mint, can be seen in the Weighing Room.

First floor. In the former **Chancellor's Room**, is a collection of gold, including the excellent 'Skrwilno Treasure', the largest such find made in Poland after the Second World War. It includes silver and gold jewellery (late 16C–early 17C) from the best Italian, southern German and Toruń workshops.

The **Great Burghers' Hall**, with a painted beamed ceiling, is adorned with 16C–18C portraits of eminent Toruń burghers. Among them is the famous 16C portrait of Nicholas Copernicus (anonymous) and a portrait of Mikołaj Hübner, painted in 1644 by Bartholomäus Strobel, the court artist of the Vasas. The room also contains some 16C coats of arms of Polish aristocratic families. The **Royal Room** is currently a portrait gallery of Polish monarchs (17C–19C), while the east wing of the first floor contains a collection of Polish painting (18C–19C) including works by Bacciarelli, Grottger, Matejko, Michałowski, Chełmoński and Gierymski; 20C paintings are displayed on the **second floor**.

The Baroque **Church of the Holy Ghost**, built by Andreas Bähr in 1753–56, is in the southwest corner of the square. Its columned late Baroque façade by Ephraim Schröger (a native of Toruń) is somewhat spoilt by an ugly west tower, (1897–99). In the north aisle is a tablet to the victims of Katyń—thousands of Polish officers murdered by the Soviets in 1940 (see p. 57).

South side of the square

Walking towards the Copernicus monument the first house you pass (No. 10) is the Neo-classical **commandery**, built after 1818 for the Prussian military commander of Toruń. **No. 9** is a medieval house, its two bays framed in tall pointed arches, with 15C Gothic brick arcades set into its pink wall. Passing the orange façade of the late Baroque **Meissner Palace** (No. 7), rebuilt in Neo-classical style in 1798, you reach the sumptuous, red-brick Neo-Renaissance **Artus Court** at No. 6. The present building was erected in 1889–91, replacing three former buildings, among which was the old Artus Court, an exclusive club for the city's wealthiest burghers, members of the Fraternity of St George.

Kazimierz the Jagiellon signed the second Peace of Toruń with the Teutonic Order in 1466 on this spot.

Until the 19C, the cellar of No. 5 served as the **Rafters' Inn**, where the initiation ceremony for rafters was held. A relief image of Bacchus in the façade is a reminder of those times (among the many humiliations, the candidate had to kiss the god's finger). Next door is the **Eagle Pharmacy**, originally Gothic, but rebuilt in Neo-classical style in the first half of the 18C. On the corner of the square and ul. Żeglarska is the Orbis travel agency, and close to that the **Copernicus Monument** (1853), with a Latin inscription on the plinth that translates: 'Nicholas Copernicus, Torunian, moved the earth, stopped the sun and the sky'.

East side of the square

The best building by far is No. 35, the **Star House** (1697), also known as the 'Haus Wendisch'. Its ornate grey Baroque façade is adorned with stuccowork and topped by a gabled roof. Inside is an impressive wooden spiral staircase, with carved lion motifs. The house is occupied by a **Regional Museum** devoted to the art of the Far East (**open** Tues–Fri 10.00–16.00, Sat–Sun 10.00–15.00). The ground floor contains ceremonial Japanese swords (18C–19C), Chinese Buddhas (stone and bronze) and carved statuettes of mythical creatures, 14C Chinese bronze bells, as well as swords, shields and sabres from India, Persia, Indonesia, the Caucuses and the Balkans. The first floor rooms, where fragments of 15C Gothic murals have been preserved, are devoted mainly to 17C–19C porcelain from the Far East.

North side of the square

On the north side of the square is the white Neo-classical **Three Crowns Hotel** at No. 21. The eponymous predecessor of this 19C building could boast such celebrated guests as Queen Maria Kazimiera (the wife of King Jan Sobieski), August II, and Czar Peter the Great. Further on, at **No. 20**, is a late Gothic house (15C–16C) with flaking brick, and a Gothic house at **No. 19** with Renaissance elements in its yellow and red-brick façade. The first house on the west side is **No. 17**, one of the oldest in town (14C), adapted in the 15C and 18C. A Mannerist portal of c 1630 leads to a hall with Renaissance painted decoration on the ceiling. Some Gothic murals are also preserved on the ground and first floors. Further south is the Neo-Gothic **Main Post Office** (1881–92).

The Church of St Mary

If you leave the square heading northwest along UL. PANNY MARII, you come to the huge brick ****Church of St Mary**, a fine example of 'Vistulian Gothic', with its characteristic east gable adorned by three octagonal turrets. The Franciscans arrived in Toruń before 1239 and erected the church of St Mary in 1263–1300. It was expanded into a high, star-vaulted aisled hall in 1343–70, and renovated in 1830. In 1898–1916 it was given new stained glass windows, made to resemble the 14C Gothic originals.

The **chancel** is dominated by a striking late Baroque main altar (1731) with a scene of the *Assumption* in the centre. A famous polyptych of 1380 stood here until it was plundered by the Nazis (recovered after the war, it is now in the National Museum in Warsaw). In the north wall of the chancel is an ornamented Rococo portal (1637), which leads to the mausoleum of King Zygmunt III's sister Anna Vasa, built in 1636, the year of her death. By the entrance to the sacristy is a late Gothic *Crucifix* (16C).

The **south aisle** contains frescoes of c 1370 (in poor condition), while a superb, richly carved Mannerist organ loft (1609) is in the **north aisle**. Below it is a pulpit (1605) with similar decoration. The early 15C oak stalls are among the most valuable of their kind in Poland.

All that remains of the former priory is part of its west wing, located in the yard behind the church. Until 1724 it accommodated a famous secondary school, where the 'Polish Noah Webster' S. B. Linde (1771–1847), author of the monumental *Dictionary of the Polish language* (1807–14), was a student.

Turn east into ul. Piekary and bear right into UL. FRANCISZKAŃSKA, passing the round brick planetarium. **No. 16** used to house the oldest printing press in Poland (1581–1829), established by Stanisław Reiss from Leipzig. On the left is **No. 12**, a 16C late Gothic gabled house with 14C cellars, a medieval chimney, and a giant stove. Currently a public library, it has a children's reading room on the top floor with a fine beamed roof. Further along on the left is a former **granary** with a partly preserved Gothic façade.

The street joins UL. CHEŁMIŃSKA. At its north end, on PL. TEATRALNY, stands the **W. Horzyca Theatre**, with two statues (1909) of the Muses *Melpomene* (Tragedy) and *Terpsychore* (Dance) in front. This Secessionist building is one of 48 theatre and concert hall buildings which the Viennese architects **Ferdinand Felner** and **Herman Helmer** built in cities as far apart as Hamburg and Odessa.

Continue along ul. Podmurna, which begins by the Neo-Gothic city council building (1901). No. 74 on the left is a 16C round brick tower known as the **Cat's Head**. Damaged in 1703, it was partly rebuilt in 1900 in Neo-Gothic style.

Turn right into ul. Szeroka (see Walk 3 around the New Market Square) and right again into ul. Szczytna, where there is a row of brick Gothic houses (Nos 11–17). **No. 14**, with a 14C Gothic façade, is a library and gallery for the disabled; **No. 15**, with a 15C façade, has 15C–16C murals inside.

Walk Two ~ The Castle and its environs

From the Old Town Square walk up ul. Szeroka (see Walk 3), turning right into UL. PRZEDZAMCZE. The street terminates at the ruins of the former **Teutonic castle**, visible beyond the gate and car park. The irregular, brick Gothic castle dates from the first half of the 13C. Toruń burghers conquered it in 1454, after which it was gradually dismantled over the centuries for building materials. Vaulted cellars from the upper castle and almost the entire ground floor, with its fragments of arcaded cloisters survive, as well as the foundations of a large, free-standing octagonal tower. Glazed floor tiles, and ornamented brick bearing fragments of painted decoration testify to the former splendour of the interiors. Several forecastles, mills, a bakery, brewery, granary, warehouses, coach houses, stables and smithies once surrounded the upper castle. The moat, equipped with a dam, afforded protection from the Old Town side, while a fish pond behind the east forecastle provided food.

Today, there is an exhibition in the ruins on the history of Toruń, as well as a café and wine bar. The terrace affords a fine view of the Vistula. To the right of the entrance is a stone slab erected in 1966 to commemorate the 500th anniversary of the Peace of Toruń; the inscription tells of the conflict between the town and the Teutonic Knights. Under the paving stones flows the Struga Toruńska— a brook which once turned the medieval mills.

The road bears left under the brick Castle Gate. Just before the gate is a low building—the **General's House**—where Wiktor Thommé commanded the defence of the Modlin stronghold against the advancing German troops in 1939 (see p. 150). This 18C late Baroque manor house presently houses the Toruń Cultural Association. Just after the gate, on the left, is the somewhat battered and abandoned former castle hospital, and past that, still on the left, the white **Tanners' Mill**, built in 1262. To the right is the former **Mill Gate**, now walled up, and adjacent to it the **Castle (Lower) Mill** (early 15C).

Walk down towards the river along a covered walkway supported on two arcades, which connected the **Dansker* (latrine tower) to the upper castle; the *dansker* is the only fully preserved part of the castle.

Follow BULWAR FILADELFIJSKI right along the riverbank, in between the 14C forecastle wall (right) and a 19C wall. Passing the 13C **Dam**, connected to the café by a gallery, you reach a 14C brick gabled **burgher's house**. The house is squeezed into the space between two of the forecastle walls and adjoins the **Guard's Tower** (which can be entered from ul. Podmurna, but is often locked); behind it was the former shooting gallery of the Fraternity of St George (see p. 376).

Walking further along the river you arrive at the **Bridge Gate**, erected in 1432. Next to it is the early 14C Gothic **Crane Gate**, which was used to draw water up from a well.

The next gate, at the end of UL. ŁAZIENNA, was demolished in the 19C. Nearby, closing UL. ŻEGLARSKA, is the 14C **Sailors' Gate**, extended in the 19C. The **Pigeon Tower** (next along) owes its name to a military aviary for homing pigeons; pocked with many niches, it is—amazingly—still inhabited. At the end of ul. DUCHA ŚWIĘTEGO stands the 14C **Priory Gate**, whose tall niche once housed a portcullis. Walk through it and turn immediately left along UL. POD KRZYWĄ WIEŻĄ, where, in the distance, the Crooked Tower will come into view. Walking towards it you pass a particularly fine Gothic **granary**, its well-preserved gable decorated with niches. Facing it on the corner of ul. Piekary and ul. Rabiańska is another **granary** (17C, late Renaissance).

The **Crooked Tower*, one of Toruń's most picturesque sights, was built in the first half of the 14C and soon began to lean as a result of subsidence. Adapted for residential use in the 19C, it now houses a political club-cum-café with inviting interiors.

Continue north along ul. Piekary and turn right into UL. KOPERNIKA. The Bankowa café occupies a Gothic house (**No. 38**) on the left. **No. 23**, also Gothic, at the corner of ul. Ducha Świętego, is currently an art gallery.

The Nicholas Copernicus Museum

Nos. 15 and **17** now form the Nicholas Copernicus Museum (**open** Tues–Sun 10.00–16.00). A display traces the life and work of the astronomer, who was born in this very house in 1473. There are two other permanent exhibitions, including one devoted to the astronomer Johannes Hevelius (1611–87; see p. 324).

It makes little sense to credit a single person with bringing the Middle Ages to a close, but if one were to name the man who had the greatest role in effecting this momentous revolution, it would be the Toruń-born Nicholas Copernicus (1473–1543).

Following the early death of his father, Copernicus was brought up by his uncle Lucas Watzenrode, the Bishop of Warmia. He studied at the Kraków Academy (see p. 221) and the universities of Bologna and Padua in Italy. In 1510 he became a canon and settled in Frombork (see p. 393), where he was able to pursue his astronomical investigations. At that time, astronomy, whose main practical function was the measurement of time and the preparation of calendars, was beset with difficulties that were growing in proportion to the precision demanded of it. Inspired by his Neo-platonic beliefs, Copernicus assigned the central place in the universe to the Sun, and determined that all the planets, including the Earth, revolve around it on circular orbits. This bold idea removed all the complications of the Ptolemaic system, but, ironically, failed to produce better predictions of the movement of the planets. Yet, it proved tenacious enough to survive the initial difficulties, and, bolstered by the genius of Galileo, Kepler and Newton, begot modern science.

Turn right into UL. ŻEGLARSKA. Inside **No. 7**, a public library, is a 14C brick Gothic house with a remarkable wooden spiral staircase decorated with sculptures (Baroque, 18C). Next to it, **No. 5** is a gabled late 13C brick Gothic house, rebuilt in the Mannerist style, with some fine 14C murals, currently the seat of the Toruń chamber orchestra. On the opposite side of ul. Żeglarska, the *Zajazd Staropolski* hotel occupies a row of original brick Gothic burghers' houses (Nos 10–14). Further south, towards the river, stands the **Academy of Fine Arts**—formerly the Palace of the Bishops of Kujawy. This striking Baroque edifice with a rusticated base and garlanded façade was erected for the Bishops of Włocławek in 1693.

The Church of SS John the Baptist and Evangelist
Turn back towards the imposing ****Church of SS John the Baptist and Evangelist** which has a valuable collection of religious art.

The construction of the Old Town's parish church started in 1250, making it one of the oldest religious buildings in the region. The present nave, rising to a staggering 30m, was built in 1468–73. About a century earlier, however, a fire created the opportunity to expand the church westward with the addition of an extra bay and a tower. Hastily built, the former collapsed in 1406 and a new one (which stands to this day) replaced it in 1407–33. It supports three bells, among them *Tuba Dei* (1522), the second largest bell in Poland, weighing 7238kg and measuring 2.27m across the base.

The nave. The aisled hall is entered through the north porch. As you walk along the nave towards the chancel, by the first pillar on the left, is the late Renaissance memorial slab of Kasper Frisius and his wife Anne (1584). Directly above it is that of Jakub Kazimierz Rubinkowski, the Royal Post-master, and his second wife. Rubinkowski also had two identical epitaph stones made for his son and daughter (on tower pillars). Two chandeliers hang in the nave (1580), adorned with figures of the Virgin and Child in the style of the 'Beautiful Madonnas' of the early 15C.

Attached to the second pillar on the right is a mid-18C Rococo pulpit with a Mannerist door and steps. On the same pillar is an early 18C Baroque altar with a sculpture of St Stanisław in the crowning. Opposite is a mid-17C Mannerist altar with a painting of the *Deposition*. The third pillar on the right carries a late Baroque altar of 1739 with a Gothic relief (c 1415) depicting the *Ecstasy of St Mary Magdalene* attended by six angels. On the same pillar is the Baroque memorial slab of Catherine Horlemens (d. 1633). Opposite is the late Baroque altar of the Holy Cross (1739), with a Gothic figure of Christ (c 1360).

The **chancel**, separated from the nave by a late Baroque wooden balustrade, is a modest rectangle of three bays. The high altar of St Wolfgang was made in Toruń in 1506, but contains earlier elements. Above it is a 14C Gothic *Crucifix* of the so-called 'dead Tree of Life' type. Rich Gothic tracery enlivens the postwar stained-glass window closing the apse, which incorporates some original medieval glass.

By the north wall of the chancel stands a white and gold Rococo throne, and a copy of a 15C 'Beautiful Madonna' (the original was stolen by the Nazis in 1944). Above the entrance to the sacristy adjoining the chancel on the north side is a 14C Gothic mural (in very poor condition), depicting the *Crucifixion* and scenes of the *Last Judgement*.

In the south wall of the chancel is the fine memorial slab of Mayor Jan von Soest and his wife, made in Bruges c 1360. To its left is a painted wing of a triptych (c 1480) showing the Archangel Gabriel. Leaving the chancel you pass two sculptures of Christ: a late Gothic *Christ Resurrected*, made in Toruń in 1497 and resting on a Baroque console (north), and a late Baroque work (south).

North aisle. To see the aisles and chapels, begin at the east end of the north aisle, where you will find an 18C Baroque altar. Its centrepiece is a late Renaissance *Annunciation* (before 1608), above which hangs a small Baroque organ (1688). In the chapel nearby is a Rococo altar (1753), with a 15C Gothic figure of Christ resting on the tabernacle. The painting of the *Last Supper* dates from the first half of the 18C, as do the other works on the wainscoting. The next chapel (west), the Chapel of Ignatius Loyola, is decorated with hardly discernible paintings on the wainscoting, dating from the end of the 17C. In the adjacent Chapel of St Joseph is a Rococo altar (after 1750) and paintings of saints. Passing a Renaissance memorial slab you come to the last chapel in the north aisle, founded by the Fishermen's Fraternity.

At the west end of the north aisle hangs a portrait of King Jan Sobieski. Pass to the south aisle and the chapel in which Nicholas Copernicus was baptised in 1473. Below a tablet in honour of the great astronomer (1589) is a late Baroque bust of Copernicus (1776). Against the south wall stands a Mannerist altar with a late Gothic relief depicting the *Dormition of the Virgin* (early 16C). In the centre of the chapel stands a bronze Gothic font (13C–14C). On the pillar opposite is a late Renaissance memorial slab with a painting of St Hieronymous based on a work by Dürer, and attributed to the Dutch painter Hans Michael of Amsterdam, who lived and worked in Toruń.

Further east, the Chapel of the Visitation of Mary contains a Rococo altar (after 1750), and, on the west wall above the wainscoting, a late 17C painting depicting the Jesuit Gwido Tachard with Siamese converts in audience with Pope Innocent in 1688.

On the wall just before the next chapel is the Rococo memorial slab of Stanisław Dutkiewicz (d. 1744). The chapel of St Stanisław Kostkahouses a late Baroque altar with figures of Polish saints (1719) and, on the west wall, the memorial slab of Sebastian Trost (d. 1578), with a Mannerist *Crucifixion*. The two Baroque epitaph slabs in the south wall date from the second half of the 17C. On the wall between the chapels is a coffin portrait of Paweł Działyński (d. 1649). The last chapel contains a late Baroque altar (18C) and a 15C late Gothic figure of Christ. On the west wall hangs a panel with three completely blackened coffin portraits (end of the 17C).

At the east end of the **south aisle** is a 17C Mannerist altar, funded by the Jesuits, who owned the church between 1596 and 1772.

Leaving the church, walk along UL. ŚW. JANA towards ul. Łazienna. The red-brick building opposite at No. 16 is the **Esken House**. Originally late Gothic (15C), with a Mannerist portal added in 1590, it was converted into a Neo-classical granary with a winding staircase at the turn of the 18C. Today it serves as the **City Historical Museum** (open Tues–Sun 10.00–16.00), with a display of modern Polish ceramics and painting, weaponry, and items connected with the Freemasons (mostly 19C).

Walking down ul. Ciasna, past a Gothic-Baroque granary (**No. 46**), you reach the late Baroque **Fenger Palace** at the junction with UL. MOSTOWA. Turn right for **No. 6**, which has a partly preserved wooden spiral staircase decorated with sculptures (1682). Three separate Gothic granaries were amalgamated in c 1520 to form this large complex with a single façade consisting of an attic and semicircular gables.

Return north along UL. PODMURNA, one of the city's most atmospheric streets, **No. 13** is a late Gothic burgher's house (c 1300) converted into a granary (currently accommodating a cultural centre). Beyond the Guard's Tower (see p. 379), is the entrance to the former seat of the Fraternity of St George (**No. 2**), a late Gothic brick house (1486). UL. PODMURNA takes you past the castle walls (right), a former granary (left)—now the University's archaeology and ethnography department—and, at the corner of ul. Ciasna, the two arches of the castle gate. Further up on the right are the remains of the moat and the Monstrance Tower. Turn left into ul. Szeroka and return to the Old Town Square for Walk 3.

Walk Three ~ New Market Square

From the Old Town Square walk up UL. SZEROKA, the commercial centre of Toruń. Built mainly between 1875 and 1914, it presents an array of architectural styles, from Secession to Modernism. **No. 38**, on the left, is a Gothic house with a square gable from the mid-15C, rebuilt in the 16C–19C. During adaptation work in the 1970s, fragments of 16C painted decoration were discovered on the ceilings.

At the fork, bear left into UL. KRÓLOWEJ JADWIGI, which brings you to the NEW MARKET SQUARE, surrounded for the most part by plain Renaissance houses. On the corner of ul. Królowej Jadwigi and the Square (*Rynek Nowomiejski*) is the *****Lion Pharmacy** (No. 13 Nowy Rynek). This 15C brick house, rebuilt in 1624 and 1830, is a handsome example of Romantic architecture superimposed on a medieval building, with elements of Neo-classical ornamentation. The name comes from the stone lion above the door. At the south corner of the square (by ul. Ślusarska) is the **Dappled Apron Inn** inside an 18C Baroque building, somewhat heavily renovated in 1957–58; the inn, said to have been established here in 1489, was allegedly visited by the monarchs Kazimierz the Jagiellon and Jan Olbracht. Another inn, the **Bricklayer's**, was located on the opposite side of the square in a 15C house (**No. 17**) rebuilt in Baroque style in the first half of the 18C. Today it is a gallery and a children's art centre.

From the square return along ul. Królowej Jadwigi and take the first right into ul. Małe Garbary, passing several houses with fine Gothic, Renaissance and Baroque façades. At the end of ul. Małe Garbary turn right into ul. Dominikańska, which ends at a boulevard. Across it, in a park (open daily until dusk), you will see a Neo-classical building of 1824. This is the former **city arsenal**, currently occupied by the **Ethnographical Museum**, which also runs a skansen in the vicinity. The interiors of the cottages here may be visited on Mon, Wed, Fri 09.00–15.00, and Tues, Thu, Sat–Sun 10.00–17.00. The museum possesses the richest collection of **traditional fishing tools** and equipment in Poland, supplemented by contemporary folk art and craft. Some of the better exhibits in the skansen include an early 17C house from a village in Bory Tucholske (south-west Poland), which was still inhabited in 1990 by a family of five. Instead of a chimney it has a hole in the roof through which smoke from an open fire inside the house would slowly escape. The revolving windmill (1896) from Wójtówka in Kujawy (north-central Poland) is still operational. The skansen also has a country inn-style café.

Go south along UL. PROSTA, passing several 19C houses. A particularly beautiful example of the Secessionist style can be found at **No. 10** (left). Turn right into ul. Wysoka and right again into UL. SUKIENNICZA, where **No. 26** is a partly reconstructed late Gothic 15C house, and **No. 20**, a former 18C inn. Ul. Sukiennicza leads back towards the New Market Square. Just before the square, turn left along ul. Św. Katarzyny to see the **Toruń printing press** at **No. 4**: a statue of **Johannes Gutenberg**, the inventor of printing, has been aptly placed on the eclectic façade. The street ends at pl. Św. Katarzyny, with a large, red-brick garrison church, built in 1893–97 and remarkable only for its tower—the tallest in the city. It stands on the site of a former chapel (1360). A group of nuns who reputedly settled next to the chapel used to bake gingerbread dubbed 'Katarzynki', now a local speciality.

Boss on St Mary's church, Toruń

Church of St James

Return to the New Market Square along UL. SZPITALNA. The Gothic ****Church of St James** is one of the three great churches in Toruń, and indeed one of the best examples of medieval architecture in northern Poland.

> The long rectangular chancel and sacristy were built in 1309–20, soon followed by the nave. Spring-vaulted chapels were gradually added

(1359–1424), and the aisles were covered with a roof that concealed the buttresses. The church had to be rebuilt after two fires (1391 and 1455), but since then it has survived in almost completely unaltered form.

The church is a basilica, with a tall, star-vaulted nave and chancel. A gallery of balconies runs around the nave, connected by a passageway hidden in the wall. The gallery was built in 1611 during the installation of the Mannerist organ loft at the west end of the nave (decorated with crests of Poland, East Prussia, and both old and new Toruń). On the tower pillars and arches are 14C murals, discovered in the 1950s. Opposite the Rococo pulpit (1770) is a Gothic sculpture of the *Virgin and Child* (14C, painted in the 18C). By the second pillar on the right stands the oldest Baroque altar in the church, dating from the mid-17C. At the east end of the south aisle you can see a fragment of a mural featuring St Mary Magdalene, and, before it, a huge, late 14C crucifix in the form of the Tree of Life.

In the **chancel**, Gothic murals from the late 14C have been preserved, albeit in poor condition. Just below the windows runs a frieze of glazed bricks with an inscription mentioning the foundation of the church in 1309. On the left hangs a large 15C Passion painting, in which the *Crucifixion* is shown against a background of medieval architecture and landscape. The choir above it formerly housed a small organ built in 1343. A painting of *St James* (1731) adorns the high altar. The low, highly ornamented rood beam (1733) supports a Passion group under a double-sided crucifix. The east side (seen from the chancel) is 14C Gothic.

Golub-Dobrzyń Castle and Szafarnia

The chief attraction of the medieval town of Golub is its Teutonic castle, restored since the last war and today housing a museum. The nearby village of Szafarnia would never have emerged from obscurity were it not for the teenage Chopin, who used to come here on his holidays. There is a small museum devoted to the composer, and concerts of his music are held twice a month.

GOLUB-DOBRZYŃ (42km from Toruń) was originally two towns on opposite sides of the Drwęca river. The Teutonic **castle** in Golub is just off the main road, which descends steeply into town (the driveway on the right is easy to miss). Leave Toruń going east on road 52, marked 'Olsztyn/Warszawa', thereafter following signs to Olsztyn. After Kowalewo Pomorskie, turn right onto road 554.

Begun in 1293 as a Gothic stronghold for the Komturei, the castle later passed to Anna Vasa, sister of Zygmunt III. The Duchess rebuilt it in the Mannerist style (1611–23), surmounting its plain brick mass with a decorative parapet wall, and adding small domed towers in the corners. The huge cannon which stands between the car park and the castle is not, as one might suspect, a relic of the Swedish Deluge (see p. 49), the Swedes having razed Golub to the ground in 1655: it is a gift from the Łódź film school and was purpose-made for the film *By Fire and Sword*, based on Sienkiewicz's famous novel (see p. 84) about this dark chapter in Poland's past. To the right, a viewing platform offers a fine vista of the castle and the town in the valley below. Clearly visible are the differing architectural styles of 14C Golub on the left and, across the river, the much later Dobrzyń, which after 1789 marked the border between Prussian and Russian Poland.

The castle fell into ruin during the 19C, but its picturesque mass, including the architectural elements introduced by Anna Vasa, has been restored since the war. Also preserved is the round Gothic keep near the southwest corner.

The interiors are somewhat disappointing, not least because the **Regional Museum** here (**open** 09.00–17.00) is sparse and absurdly commercialised—the exhibits have price tags rather than dates.

The compulsory guided tour begins on the ground floor with an 18C–19C ethnographical display. Stairs lead up to the first-floor chamber of Anna Vasa, who lived here from 1589 to 1625. Only the exterior walls are 17C; the decorations within, including a portrait of the Duchess (the original hangs in Warsaw's Royal Castle), are modern. The chamber is used for annual competitions and balls, the most popular of which are the Knights' Ball (1 July)—a historical fancy dress party during which inebriated guests are invited to buy what's left of the castle furnishings—and the incomparably tacky New Year's Ball when, at midnight, Miss Poland, masquerading as the 'White Lady' (the castle's resident ghost), emerges from behind the double doors. The adjoining conference room, with banners and inlaid wood panelling, was originally the castle hospital, strategically located so that patients could listen to the services in the chapel next door. It has Gothic star vaults and copies of armour and weapons used in the battle of Grunwald (1410). A hotel (50 rooms) occupies the uppermost storey of the castle. In the adjoining meadow, an annual jousting tournament is held on 22 July.

From the castle continue down the hill and then along the river, skirting fragments of the 14C town wall. A left turn at the junction with ul. Zamkowa brings you to the Main Square. Ignore the Neo-Gothic church there and proceed to the nearby **Parish Church of St Catherine**, shrouded by trees in a quiet side street. Built in 1293–1350, it was given a large Renaissance west tower after lightning destroyed the original in 1689. Inside, the nave has a flat beamed ceiling—the vaults fell after a fire in the 16C—but Gothic cross vaults have been preserved in the chancel. The heavily gilded high altar (1640) contains a late Gothic *Pietà*.

SZAFARNIA is 5km from Golub-Dobrzyń on road 534. After 5km, turn left along a minor road marked 'Płonne' and 'Szafarnia Muzeum', which brings you to a modest 19C manor house set in a pleasant park with a pond.

In the 1820s, the estate was owned by the Dziewanowskis, whose son was a close school friend of the young **Fryderyk Chopin**. In 1824–25, when he was 15, Chopin came on several occasions to spend his holidays in Szafarnia. It was here that he became fascinated for the first time by Polish folk music and patriotic songs, which would later exert an enormous influence on his own compositions.

The house contains a cultural centre with a small **museum** devoted to Chopin's life and work (**open** Tues–Fri 08.00–15.00, Sat–Sun 10.00–15.00). Concerts—mostly of Chopin music—are held twice a month, and the **International Chopin Piano Competition for Children** takes place on the last weekend in May each year.

Bydgoszcz

■ Practical information
Hotels
★★★★
City. Ul. 3 Maja 6, ☎ 22-52-66, 22-88-41. Very clean, modern and comfortable, a sheer delight. Central location, air conditioning, car park. 130 rooms.
Orbis-Pod Orłem. Ul. Gdańska 14, ☎ 22-18-61/69. Central location, surrounded by attractive gardens. Travel Office, car rental, car park, wheelchair access, Business Centre, Fitness Centre. 75 rooms.
★★★
Brda. Ul. Dworcowa 94, ☎ 22-40-61/69. Central location, car park. 250 rooms.

Tourist information (PAPT). Ul. Zygmunta Augusta 10, ☎ 22-84-32/22-53-50.
ORBIS. Ul. Gdańska 42, ☎ 22-96-34/22-84-80/22-16-27.
Post office. Ul. Jagiellońska 6.
Telephone code: (0–52).

The origins of Bydgoszcz date back to the early Middle Ages, when it was a stronghold and the seat of the castellanship. Its heyday began in the mid-14C, lasting until 1600. Large granaries were built to handle the town's extensive salt and wheat trade, and to store its famous beer. It even had its own mint, at first private, later royal. As elsewhere in Poland, the Swedish Deluge brought destruction and decline. Bydgoszcz fell into Prussian hands in 1772, and was not restored to Poland until 1920. The Prussians built the **Bydgoszcz canal**, linking the Vistula, Brda, Noteć and Warta rivers, thus establishing an east-west water route from Germany to Russia.

Today, though Bydgoszcz bears the scars of heavy post-war industrialisation, there are signs that cultural life is returning to the city. The triennial **International Festival and Congress of Early Music from Eastern and Central Europe**—'Musica Antiqua Europae Orientalis'—is held in the Pomeranian Philharmonia building on ul. Libelta, and each year the city hosts a **festival of Polish music**, in which the celebrated local group 'Capella Bydgostiensis' regularly takes part.

The city centre
There are frequent bus and train connections between Toruń and Bydgoszcz. If travelling by car you will enter the city through the sprawling industrial suburbs. Head straight for the OLD MARKET SQUARE south of the river. The Old Town is small, pleasant, and surprisingly free of pollution. Across the river via the Staromiejski bridge, at the intersection of ul. Gdańska and ul. Jagiellońska, is the **Poor Clares' Church and Convent**. The late Renaissance church, built in 1582–1602, consists of two gabled blocks and a west tower. An impressive carved stone portal leads to a sparsely furnished Renaissance-Baroque interior. The **convent buildings** are further up ul. Gdańska (No. 4). Built in 1615–18, and remodelled in the 19C, they currently house the **Wyczółkowski Museum**

(**open** Tues–Wed 10.00–18.00, Thur–Sat 10.00–16.00, Sun 10.00–14.00), with the largest collection in the country of works by the celebrated painter **Leon Wyczółkowski**. There is also exhibition of other Polish art.

Cross the river (ul. Mostowa) and turn left along ul. Grodzka. By the riverside, just before the Rybi Rynek (Fish Market), stand three timber granaries (ul. Grodzka, Nos 7, 9, 11), the oldest dating from 1793.

West of the Old Market Square, at No. 8 UL. FARNA, is the late Gothic **parish church**, built 1460–1502. This brick aisled hall is a particularly fine example of 'Vistulian Gothic' and a Gothic frieze adorns the chancel walls. Of the four original Renaissance chapels, only the **Chapel of the Holy Cross** (17C) has survived, and is closed off with a gilded iron grille. The Baroque high altar contains a painting of the *Virgin with Rose* (early 16C). Note the late Renaissance brass font (early 17C), with engraved images of SS Adalbert and Nicholas.

Turn left at the end of ul. Farna into the picturesque UL. PRZYRZECZE by the riverside. The group of historic 19C buildings here are known as the 'Bydgoszcz Venice'. Facing them is **Mill Island** (Wyspa Młyńska), nestled in an arm of the Brda. Cross over the bridge and continue right along UL. MENNICA to the late 18C half-timbered **White Granary** near the mill. Inside the granary a museum is **open** Tues–Wed 09.00–17.00, Thur–Sat 10.00–16.00, Sun 10.00–14.00.

Follow UL. MAGDZIŃSKIEGO from the Old Town Square, continuing past the Neo-Gothic church on pl. Kościeleckich. Across UL. BERNARDYŃSKA, near the roundabout, stands the late Gothic **Bernardine Church of St George** (now a garrison church). It was erected in 1545–52, but partly torn down and rebuilt in 1864, when the unharmonious tower was added to the stepped west gable. Diagonally opposite, by the east front, is a square 17C Renaissance bell tower. The Baroque monastic building abuts the church to the left. A small tomb of the Unknown Soldier from the Wielkopolska Uprising (the Uprising took place in 1919) is found in the small square nearby.

Toruń to Gdańsk

❖ Radzyń • Grudziądz • Kwidzyn • Sztum • Gdańsk

The lowlands between Toruń and Gdańsk east of the Vistula comprise three geographical regions—the Chełmno and Iława Lake Districts and the Vistula fens. There are many attractive medieval towns here, often with splendid Teutonic castles (such as the matchless Malbork castle, pp. 333–340, or the smaller castles at Radzyń and Kwidzyn). Grudziądz, the largest city of the region, has a very fine Old Town with medieval granaries overlooking the river.

Radzyń Chełmiński

Leave Toruń heading north on road 1, after 21km turning right onto the 551. Pass Chełmża, a medieval town with a Gothic parish church, and join the 534 in Wąbrzeźno. As you approach **RADZYŃ CHEŁMIŃSKI**, the ruins of the **Teutonic castle** will come into view. This massive brick structure, laid out on a quadrangular plan, with a decorative façade and spacious forecourt, was erected in the 13C–14C, and later destroyed by the Swedes. The south entrance consists of a tall arch over windows and a portal. Two square towers with battlements are preserved at the corners of the south wing. The remains of the *Dansker* (latrine tower) are situated in the moat by the west side.

Visible from the castle is the Gothic **Church of St Anne**, a 14C–15C brick structure, rebuilt from scratch in 1680. Its stepped gable is decorated with pinnacles and blank arches. Dominating the church is a massive tower (1340), which stands askew to the north of the chancel. The Mannerist funerary chapel of the Dąbrowski family, entered via an ornate gate (1587) from the south aisle, was added in the late 17C. Bartholomäus Strobel's *Coronation of the Virgin* (1643) is the centrepiece of the Baroque high altar.

Grudziądz

Grudziądz, some 20km further along road 534, is scenically positioned high on the bank of the Vistula. Bolesław the Brave (Chrobry) built a fortified settlement here as defence against Prussian attacks, and during the 13C the Teutonic Order built a castle. After the second Peace of Toruń (1466), Grudziądz was returned to Poland as a royal city. Following the Swedish Deluge (see p. 49), and plagues in 1709 and 1740, it fell into long-term decline, before coming under Prussian rule during the First Partition of Poland in 1772.

Begin your visit in the pleasant medieval MARKET SQUARE close to the river. The statue of the Unknown Soldier bears the inscription 'Has not died, will never die' (referring to Poland). Just off the square, on UL. RATUSZOWA stands the brick Gothic **Parish Church of St Nicholas** from the first half of the 14C. It still has its 15C star vaults in the nave, but all the Baroque furnishings were destroyed in 1945.

Close by is the former **Jesuit Church** (1648–1715), in front of which stands a monument to Nicholas Copernicus. The aisleless, late Baroque interior exhibits elements of Chinese-style decoration. Next door (opposite the parish church) is the Baroque **Jesuit College**, with a tower of 1648–1775. The plaque outside commemorates the town's first school—the 'Grudziądz atheneum'—which once occupied the building.

UL. ZAMKOWA leads from the Jesuit College along the bluff, ascending to the ruins of the Teutonic Order's castle on Klimek hill. Following destruction in 1945, all that remains of the castle is a round stump. On top of the mound is an observation point with a monument to the liberation of the town by the Soviet army on 6 March 1945, and a fine view over the Vistula valley.

Going south from the Market Square along UL. PAŃSKA you reach another square, at the southern end of which is the Baroque (formerly Gothic) **Benedictine Abbey**. The monastic building (17C) houses the **Museum and Gallery of Contemporary Pomeranian Art**; the former Palace of the Abbesses (1750) is used by a music school. The Church of the Holy Ghost, originally a 14C hospital chapel, adjoins the abbey to the east. The chapel was expanded and remodelled after 1659 and rebuilt in Baroque style after the war.

The southwest corner of the square is occupied by the 14C **Water Gate**, formerly part of the town walls (fragments are visible east of the museum), linking them to the granaries further north. Once equipped with a portcullis, the gate was one of the busiest places in town, providing access to the harbour and mill. Today it houses offices and, since reconstruction in 1659 and 1945, bears little resemblance to its original form. Pass through the gate onto the riverside, where you get the best view of the huge *granaries lining the bank of the Vistula. These brick, partly Gothic buildings provided the town not only with storage space, but also with an effective system of defences. Today, they house a **museum** (**open** Tues 10.00–18.00, Wed, Thur, Sat 10.00–15.00, Fri 13.00–18.00, Sun 10.00–14.00), with a display charting the history of the town.

Kwidzyn

Leave Grudziądz on road 16, joining the 514 heading 35km north for Kwidzyn, a town given a charter by the Teutonic Order in 1233. Soon after, it became the seat of the Pomeranian bishopric, with many bishops being members of the Order. The original church of St John the Evangelist was erected in 1235, but in 1310 a member of the Order was sent over from Italy to raise a new **cathedral**. He completed the chancel and an underground crypt for the bishops in 1343; the nave and huge west tower followed in 1350. The adjoining castle of the Pomeranian Chapter had already been standing for some 20 years. To commemorate the cathedral's consecration, Bishop Jan I erected a mosaic over the south entrance, all in red, gold and white, depicting St John in a cauldron of hot oil, as well as commissioning frescoes inside. The latter were plastered over in 1526 when the Protestants took over, and repainted in 1862–64 (remnants are still visible). In the early 16C, the cathedral acquired portraits of 17 Pomeranian bishops and three Grand Masters of the Order (found in the upper part of the Baroque high altar), and the exquisitely carved bishop's throne, which you can see in the chancel. The Gröben family tomb stands out as a particularly fine example of funerary sculpture. Notice, also, the Renaissance pulpit (1634), and the decorative Gothic corbels (1330–50), bearing images of people, animals and mythological creatures amid floral motifs. Apart from the west tower and south entrance, the most striking features of the exterior are the massive three-step buttresses, and the small towers in the southeast and northeast corners of the nave, adorned with triangular gables and brick spires.

The *castle, which now contains a **museum** (**open** Tues–Sun 09.00–16.00), originally had four wings, but those to the south and east were pulled down in 1798. Major renovation work was carried out in 1855–75. Currently, the cellars contain a display of torture instruments and items relating to the prehistory of the Kwidzyn region. The history of the castle is shown on the ground floor. More impressive is the **first floor**, where you may visit the well tower with an exhibition tracing the Polish-German struggle in the Kwidzyn region, the *dansker* (latrine tower, 1320–47), the former chapel, and the chapter house, with 15C–18C sculpture and painting. The **second floor** houses folk art and craft, while the top floor is dedicated to natural history. The gabled *dansker* is connected to the castle by a passageway resting on five soaring arches.

As you pass through the town of **Sztum**, 22km further north on road 514, a small brick **castle** of the Teutonic Knights will appear on the left. Built in 1326–35, and remodelled in the 19C, it was until recently a museum, but is now privately owned.

Continue north to Malbork (see p. 333) and pick up road 50 heading west across the river Nogat. The route cuts through the massive Vistula flood plain, giving an idea of just how wide the river once was. For Gdańsk, rejoin road 1 (72km).

Gdańsk to Frombork

❖ Elbląg • Kadyny • Tolkmicko • Frombork

This trip takes you across the lowlands near the mouth of the Vistula. The high-lights are the Vistula bay and the Ostróda-Elbląg canal, both of which can be visited by boat, and the town of Elbląg, with its Gothic Church of St Nicholas.

Leaving Gdańsk heading east on road 7 you soon enter the **Żuławy Wiślane**, or **Vistula fens**, a flat, treeless terrain, in places below sea level, and criss-crossed by streams, rivers and irrigation canals. To the north, the area is protected from the cold Baltic winds by an imposing wall of dunes stretching from Gdańsk along the Vistula spit to the Russian border and beyond. During the Middle Ages, Żuławy was chiefly swamp, interspersed with a few inhabited islands. Beginning in the 13C, land reclamation (polder) projects got under way, assisted by Dutch specialists. In time, a sizeable Dutch community emerged. Until 1939, the area was ethnically and religiously diverse, with Polish, Prussian and Dutch communities, Catholics, Protestants and Orthodox believers all co-existing in relative harmony. The Second World War and the mass depor-tations after it, changed all that. German armies flooded much of the area, and the indigenous culture was wiped out: the East Prussians who had inhabited Żuławy for centuries were expelled to make way for scores of Polish immigrants, many of whom had themselves been deported from the lost territories to the east.

Today, Żuławy has some of the most fertile soil (silt) in Poland, and is inten-sively farmed. Scattered around the area are a number of traditional **half-timbered farmhouses** of the 'bolt' type, their projecting porches supported on wooden posts occasionally sculpted in the rustic manner. There are good exam-ples in villages just off the Gdańsk-Elbląg road (7): Trutnowy (a Baroque half-timbered house, No. 4, 1720–26); Koszwały (a beautiful arcaded house, 1792); and Lubieszewo (No. 37, 1747) where you could also visit the nearby **Parish Church of St Elizabeth**, founded by the Teutonic Order in the 14C. Further south, as you enter Nowy Staw, you pass an arcaded house of 1820. Marynowy has five 19C arcaded wooden houses, the most interesting one at No. 55, with a porch (1803). Close by is the **Parish Church**, originally a Gothic hall. You regain road 7 at Nowy Dwór Gdański, where you turn right for Elbląg.

Elbląg

Elbląg is a good base for **boat trips** to Krynica Morska across the Vistula bay and to Kaliningrad (Königsberg) in Russia. Check the times at the ferry harbour by the riverside. Perhaps even more enticing is the Elbląg-Ostróda Canal (about 80km), part of a system of 19C waterways linking many lakes and navigable rivers. A canal trip takes you through the forested landscape of the Vistula valley and **Iława Lake District**. A unique attraction is its five dry slipways—the boats are carried across dry land on water-powered trolleys—and two locks, negoti-ating an overall difference in water level of almost 100m. Boats leave Elbląg at 08.00 (May 1–Sept 30; min. 20 passengers), arriving in Ostróda at 19.00, or Iława at 20.00.

Elbląg was founded in the 13C by the Teutonic Knights, who erected a brick castle (1237). After 1309, Hanseatic Elbląg became the Order's chief centre of government, a base for its conquests, rivalling Toruń and Gdańsk in wealth and importance. Unhappy with Teutonic misrule, the local population paid homage to the Polish King, Władysław Jagiełło, after the Order's defeat at the Battle of Grunwald (1410), with the city formally becoming part of the Polish realm in 1466. During the 16C, when it was still possible to sail between the gaps in the Vistula spit, Elbląg evolved into a key Baltic port; Zygmunt August built his war fleet here, while in 1577, following a dispute with Gdańsk, Stefan Bathory redirected the entire Baltic fishing trade to Elbląg. Decline set in after the Swedish invasions (see p. 49) and the gradual recession of the Vistula bay, causing the waterways to silt up. The town's inhabitants managed briefly to repel the army of Frederick II in 1772, but Elbląg soon succumbed to Prussian aggrandisement, and throughout the Partition period was reduced to the status of a Prussian provincial town.

The city centre suffered 60 per cent destruction during the Second World War, but many of the historic buildings in and around the vast central square have been restored.

On the MAIN SQUARE west of ul. Stary Rynek stands Elbląg's most remarkable monument: the grand Gothic ***Church of St Nicholas**, one of the few buildings that escaped complete destruction during the Second World War. The basilica lost its tower and elaborate 15C vaults during a fire in 1777 (only a fragment of the vaults has survived in a north aisle chapel). The valuable furnishings exhibit a range of styles (14C–18C). Most noteworthy are the crucifix (1410) above the high altar (1505); a Gothic lime-wood sculpture of *St Nicholas* (c 1410, to the right of the high altar) and other painted sculptures of the same period, depicting Christ and the 12 Apostles (on the corbels by the pillars facing the nave). The Maltsters' altar (after 1511) and the altar of St Mary (c 1520, both in the south aisle); a bronze font (1387) and two 16C Renaissance altars (in the north aisle), as well as a fine Mannerist pulpit (c 1588) are also of interest.

Facing the church on UL. MOSTOWA is a row of fine gabled **houses**, originally built c 1590, and faithfully reconstructed after the war. No. 17, connected to No. 18 by arches, is topped by a sculpture of St Nicholas. Walking further south through ŚCIEŻKA KOŚCIELNA—a narrow passageway which in the Middle Ages connected the town's three main churches—you will see on the right (ul. Św. Ducha) the ruins of the **Holy Ghost Church and Hospital**, the city's oldest building (13C), now used as a library. On the same street are more historic **houses**, such as the Gothic house No. 13 with ornamented niches, and the Mannerist No. 12 (c 1600).

Continuing along UL. ZAMKOWA you reach the site of the medieval castle, destroyed in 1454 after an anti-Teutonic uprising. Only scattered fragments of it remain: the former 14C brewery (now part of the museum); sections of wall (13C–14C) adjoining part of the former south wing; two partly preserved Gothic towers; and, within the former Protestant lycée (originally the castle granary), the main **museum** building (open 10.00–18.00). The display covers archaeological finds from the Old Town, and the history of Elbląg and its guilds. The highlights include part of a 13C late Romanesque stone font imported from

Gotland, 18C Baroque doors showing the *Dance of Death*, and a headless wooden sculpture of St John (15C).

North of St Nicholas, at the far end of ul. Stary Rynek, stands the brick Gothic **Market Gate**, the only remnant of the town fortifications, with a 14C base and a later superstructure of large arched niches and blank windows. Inside are two imprints of spades, recalling the legend of a baker's apprentice who managed to foil a Teutonic attack in 1521 by closing the gate in the nick of time.

To the left of the Gate stands the former **Dominican Monastery** (1238, Gothic) and **Church of St Mary** (chancel c 1250, nave 1320–30), two of the oldest examples of religious architecture in Prussia. The church was extended into an aisled hall after a fire in 1504, when net vaults were added to the nave. Severely damaged during the war, it has since been used as an art gallery. The low vaulted chancel, askew to the nave, still has discernible Gothic murals on the walls. The site is surrounded by a wall—the sole remnant of the Dominican cloister—with low pointed-arch niches containing epitaph stones, some commemorating the English timber merchants who settled here in 1579–1628.

Leave Elbląg along road 503, which skirts the bay to **KADYNY** (18km), an old Prussian settlement. A 700-year-old oak, named after the nobleman J. Bażyński, who bought Kadyny in 1431, is situated on the left of the main road as you enter. After 1898, the Kadyny estate was owned by the family of Kaiser Wilhelm II, whose stud farm and personal stables have survived. A celebrated ceramics factory, still extant, was established here in 1904. Today Kadyny's chief attraction is its Baroque **palace**. The interiors accommodate the commendable *Kadyny Palace Hotel* (☎ 0-55 231-6200). Next to it stands an orangery (1817). A walk through the leafy woods behind the palace brings you to the ruins of the **Franciscan Church** (1683), currently under renovation.

TOLKMICKO, further along the bay, is a quiet fishing village with a beach and ferry harbour. In the centre of the village stands a Gothic basilica, founded in 1376, with a late 19C chancel and transepts. The road behind the church leads northeast to the municipal cemetery (500m), with a Baroque chapel (1738). On the way you will pass a solitary brick tower on the right—the only remnant of the 14C town fortifications. Continue along road 503, joining the 504 at Pogrodzie for Frombork (16km).

Warmia and Masuria

North-eastern Poland is a sparsely populated region of great natural beauty. The major part of it is occupied by the **Masurian Lake District**, commonly referred to as *Mazury* in Polish. This undulating terrain, covered for the most part in dense pine forest, has earned the epithet of 'the land of a thousand lakes'. In fact, there are as many as 3000—vestiges of the last Ice Age—coming in all manner of shapes and sizes. Many of the lakes are connected by canals, making the area especially popular for sailing enthusiasts. Boat trips can be made along the Augustów and Elbląg canals, canoeing trips along the Krutynia and Czarna Hańcza rivers, while the largest lakes offer a variety of watersports: windsurfing, yachting, water-skiing, water-cycling, rowing, ice-boating and skating.

Stretching west of the Great Lakes is **Warmia**, an historic as opposed to a geographical region, occupying a triangle of land delineated by the towns of **Frombork** (north), **Olsztyn** (south) and **Reszel** (east). Warmia's strength lies less in its natural beauty than in its cultural interest. Its churches and castles, built in the characteristically austere brick Gothic style, preserve a discreet and undiscovered charm, at once attesting to the rich and varied past of a region where Copernicus once lived and worked.

The third region in north-eastern Poland is **Suwalszczyzna**, situated in the remote borderlands, and centred on the town of **Suwałki**. Travelling through the surrounding countryside you will find communities of Lithuanians, Tartars, Russians and Byelorussians, and villages where Polish is merely one of the languages spoken. Nature reserves have been established to protect the tracts of **primeval forest**, unique in Europe, where wild bison mingle with wolves, bears, wild swans, lynxes and many species that have long since vanished elsewhere on the European mainland. The **Suwałki Landscaped Park** and **Wigry National Park** are also attractive destinations.

Frombork

■ **Practical information**

Hotel. ★★★ *Kopernik*. Ul. Kościelna 2, ☎ 243-7285/6. Ideal central location. The best hotel in town. Car park. 32 rooms.

Ferries Passenger Quay. Regular summer service to Krynica Morska across the bay.

Telephone code: (0-55).

Frombork, a charming town situated on the shore of the Vistula bay, will forever be associated with the name of one man—Nicholas Copernicus (Mikołaj Kopernik, 1473–1543), the famous astronomer, who lived and worked here from 1510 to 1543. Copernicus was the chief administrator in the Warmian Chapter (a formal body of Canons), which had its seat at Frombork cathedral. It was here that he worked out the principles of his heliocentric theory, later set

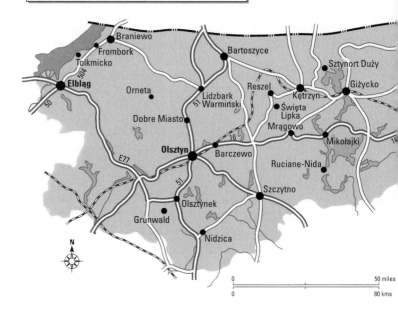

WARMIA and MASURIA

out in *De Revolutionibus Orbium Coelestium*, a work so radical for its time that it had to be published posthumously, and immediately earned its author an entry in the Papal Index (a list of books condemned by the Catholic church as dangerous to faith or morals) for many centuries to come. In 1626, the marauding Swedish army of Gustavus Adolphus pillaged anything of value in the town, including Copernicus' personal collection of astronomical texts and instruments, which were never recovered. The Second World War was also unkind to Frombork, with the historic centre suffering 80 per cent destruction at the hands of the retreating Wehrmacht.

Cathedral Hill

Today, Frombork is a small fishing town with a pier and beach facilities, offering regular summer cruises across the bay to Krynica Morska (see pp. 348–9). The main attraction, however, is ****Cathedral Hill**, five minutes' walk from the *Kopernik* Hotel.

From the main square, follow the lane which winds up the hill by the **Copernicus Monument**. On the right you will pass several 16C–18C **Canons' Houses**. You enter the cathedral grounds through the twin-towered south gate (late Gothic, c 1530), and the **cathedral** itself (open Mon–Sat 09.30–16.30) through its gabled west porch. A Swedish lime-wood portal framed in carved stone is followed by an inner portal, deeper and ornamented with blind tracery and a row of stone heads on the jambs. Remarkable stone figures and mythical creatures adorn the voussoirs. A stone frieze around the walls of the porch bears

an inscription indicating the date of completion (1388).

Interior. Built by the Warmian Chapter in 1329–88, the cathedral lost its Gothic interior when the Swedes destroyed it in the mid-17C. The broad eight-bay nave narrows to a deep, classically proportioned chancel, closed by a square apse. To the south are two chapels: the star-vaulted **chapel of St George** (the so-called Polish Chapel), adjoining the chancel; and, behind an elaborate wrought-iron grille of curly leaves, the square, domed, **late Baroque chapel of Christ the Saviour** (1732–35). The imposing black and white marble **high altar** (1750) is a copy of the high altar in Kraków's Wawel Cathedral. The previous high altar, a late Gothic polyptych made in Toruń in 1504, is in the west part of the south aisle. The church has many fine **side altars**.

North aisle. By the second pillar from the east, stands the wooden altar of St Anne (1639), in the form of a triumphal arch, with paintings, notably *St Anne* by Bartholomäus Strobel, the court painter to King Władysław IV. The next altar (1655) is painted and richly ornamented. Next to it is the altar of the Ascension (1642), surmounted by a sculpture of St Lodovicius. Rich oriental ornamentation adorns the westernmost altar of St Augustine, which has a Caravaggio copy for a centrepiece.

South Aisle. The fourth altar, dedicated to the Holy Cross, is one of the oldest in the church. By the sixth pillar stands the Copernicus altar, a 16C copy of the original owned by Copernicus. Close to it is the **tomb of Copernicus**, who is buried in the crypts beneath the cathedral. The chancel has inlaid **Rococo canons' stalls** (1730s), and earlier Mannerist ones.

The cathedral contains over 130 **memorial slabs**, mainly of bishops and canons, the oldest of which are Gothic (eg in the chancel). Better preserved are several Renaissance and Baroque ones, like the **tomb of Zacharias Szolc**, which depicts an engraved skeleton, its left hand resting on an hour-glass (by the penultimate north aisle pillar before the chancel). The present memorial tablet to Copernicus dates from 1735, as the original was destroyed. Located by the pillar adjacent to the central altar, it bears a portrait of the great astronomer.

The 61-voice **organ**, made in Gdańsk in 1694, is admired for its pure crisp sound. Organ recitals, often by first-rate performers, are held on Sundays during July and August. A short demonstration of the instrument's musical capabilities, as well as its moving parts, takes place every two hours or so, when the cathedral is open to visitors.

The Copernicus Museum

Bishop Ferber's 16C palace in the southeastern corner of the grounds, remodelled in Baroque style in 1727 and rebuilt after the war, now accommodates the Copernicus Museum (**open** Tues–Sun, 09.00–16.00).

The museum houses archaeological finds from the Frombork region, including 15C–16C household items which may have been used by Copernicus himself, and, upstairs, memorabilia connected with Copernicus—portraits, engravings, reliefs, medals, busts—as well as a copy of Jan Matejko's famous portrait (the original is kept at the Jagiellonian University in Kraków). An interesting detail among the many astronomical instruments depicted in this painting is the telescope, which Copernicus certainly never used, as it had not been invented at that time. The other objects on display include replicas of scientific instruments that Copernicus did use: a triquetrum, quadrant and astrolabe. There are also books belonging to him, copies of his letters, and fragments of his works, including a second edition of *De Revolutionibus*, published in Basle in 1566. Modern astronomical instruments and several large telescopes can be found in the last room on the first floor.

The **Copernicus Tower** in the northwestern corner of the grounds (**open** Tues–Sun 09.00–16.00) is the oldest building on Cathedral Hill. Its lower part and foundations date from the 14C; the upper section was rebuilt in the 15C–16C. Copernicus used the tower from 1510 until his death in 1543, but it is uncertain for what purpose. One room in the basement is open to visitors. Its centre is occupied by a Gothic table, whose top consists of lids that can be lifted to reveal small models of Italian cities. A portrait (copy) of Copernicus' father, astronomical instruments, a wardrobe, an hourglass and a travelling box complete the furnishing of the tiny cell.

The **Radziejowski Tower** in the southwestern corner of the grounds rests on an octagonal base, with walls that are in places a staggering 7.5m thick. Above it rises a square bell tower of 1685. Inside, a **planetarium** has been set up (**open** daily; programmes begin at 10.40, 12.20, 14.00 and 15.40), its ceiling (1973) modelled on the surface of the Moon. A Foucault pendulum demonstrating the movement of the Earth has been hung here for the benefit of school children. Ascend to the top of the tower for a breathtaking view of Frombork and its environs.

From Cathedral Hill, walk east along ul. Katedralna and then ul. Stara to reach the former 14C Hospital of the Holy Ghost, now a **museum** (**open** Tues–Sun 10.00–17.30), with items relating to the history of medicine, as well as 15C stoves, which supplied heat to the hospital's steam bath. In the late 15C, the hospital was integrated with a chapel of St Anne (1426–33), from which a Gothic mural depicting the *Last Judgement* has been preserved, albeit in poor condition. Next to the museum a herbarium has recently been established, where the curator hopes specimens of medicinal plants can be encouraged to grow.

Frombork to Olsztyn

❖ Braniewo • Orneta • Olsztyn

Braniewo

Braniewo is situated on the Pasłęka river, 10km east of Frombork (road 504), and a mere 8km from the Russian border.

The Teutonic Knights founded a settlement on the left bank of the Pasłęka in 1250. That same year Braniewo became the first seat of the bishopric of Warmia. The town rapidly grew into a medieval seaport specialising in linen trade with the Hanseatic League, and by 1340 had become the capital of Warmia. A New Town emerged on the right bank in 1342. It was in Braniewo that Cardinal Stanisław Hosius—leader of the Polish Counter Reformation—founded the first Jesuit college in Poland in 1565.

Braniewo was the scene of heavy fighting during the Second World War, with 85 per cent of the town centre being reduced to rubble. Today, it has a decidedly provincial flavour, and its few attractions deserve no more than a brief visit.

You enter Braniewo along UL. GDAŃSKA. On the right is the Gothic **Parish Church of St Catherine**, a brick aisled hall begun in 1346. Its chapels, vaults and tower date from the 15C. During the Second World War it suffered major damage, and was extensively rebuilt in the 1980s. The gabled north porch leads to a six-bay interior, immediately striking for its rich star vaults carried on octagonal brick pillars. Virtually none of the original furnishings have survived. A statue of St Joseph rests on a battered console at the entrance to the chancel, and there is a medieval triptych on the east wall of the north aisle.

The 13C Bishop's Palace has now vanished, but a remnant of it is found on UL. KOŚCIUSZKI, east of the church—a three-storey Gothic **Gate-tower**, adjoined by a section of medieval wall. On the opposite side of ul. Gdańska, partly concealed by trees, is the site of the famous **Collegium Hosianum**, founded in 1565. The present, late Baroque building was built for the Jesuits in 1743–71. Its west wing, connected to the nearby Klesza Tower, dates from 1904. Two more Gothic towers are found in the adjoining park, which descends to a small pond with an amphitheatre.

Continue along ul. Gdańska, which becomes UL. KRÓLEWIECKA across the river. On the left is the uninspiring Neo-classical **Church of St Anthony** (1830–3). Far better is the **Parish Church of the Holy Cross**, situated further from the centre on UL. ŚWIĘTOKRZYSKA, beside the river. Built on the plan of a Greek Cross in 1722–47, this late Baroque Church has a central dome topped by a lantern. The best of its late Baroque furnishings are the high altar (1739), pulpit (1745), musicians' choir (18C), two confessionals (18C), and the stone stoup (1728). The church is adjoined by a Redemptorist monastery.

Orneta

From Braniewo head 42km southeast on road 507 to Orneta. Close to the river, in the southwest corner of the Main Square (pl. Wolności), stands the **Parish Church of St John**, perhaps the most outstanding Gothic church in Warmia.

Originally built in 1340–1380 as a basilica on a cross plan, it was extended in late Gothic style during the 15C, receiving side chapels and new vaults for the nave. The body of the church was last renovated in 1899–1909, when the chapel gables, destroyed in 1520, were also rebuilt.

The lofty tower is flanked by two chapels, whose square gables are decorated with pinnacles, friezes and vertical rows of blind arcades. The exterior of the side chapels is similar. **Elaborate friezes**, especially on the north wall of the tower chapel (c 1480), have three layers of miniature arcades, busts, and vines.

The remarkable **interior**, covered with ornate ribbed vaults, contains a number of preserved murals (though heavily repainted in the 1900s): *The Holy Family* (1380), behind the altar; *The Wise and Foolish Virgins* (1420–40), by the first north pillar; *The Passion of St Sebastian* (early 16C) and *St Anne* (15C) in the chapels; and perhaps the best—*The Coronation of St Mary* (late 14C) by the second north pillar. The chancel seems almost too low for the black-and-gold high altar (1744), its three columned tiers densely packed with sculptures. Another piece of striking Baroque art can be found at the west end of the north aisle: an open-work font enclosure (c 1730–1740), with columns and a crowning supporting sculptures. The north chapel contains Renaissance councillors' stalls, beautifully inlaid and adorned with a portrait of Cardinal Stanisław Hosius (c 1570). Finally, in one of the south chapels, there is a two-tiered black-marble altar with alabaster statues and a relief of *The Last Supper* (1646).

Also on PL. WOLNOŚCI stands the Gothic **Town Hall** (1373), one of very few such buildings left in Warmia. It is a brick building with three pointed-arch windows in the façade, and gables at both ends. In the centre rises a Baroque clock tower containing the oldest bell in Warmia (1384).

Continue southeast (road 507) via Dobre Miasto (see p. 400), to Olsztyn.

Olsztyn

Olsztyn (population 154,900), situated on the river Łyna, is the main town of Warmia and Masuria. It is an ideal base for excursions into this naturally beautiful and culturally rich region. The town was established by the canons of the Warmian Cathedral Chapter, who raised a castle here in the mid-14C. In 1516–21, Copernicus administrated the Chapter from the castle, and was responsible for preparing its defences for the final showdown with the Teutonic Order (1519–21). Annexed to Prussia under the First Partition (1772), it later suffered an intense campaign of Germanisation, during which the Polish language was banned from schools. A plebiscite in 1920 saw it stay in German hands, and it remained part of the province of East Prussia until 1945. About half the city centre was destroyed during the Second World War, but today much of it has been restored to its original appearance.

■ **Practical information**
Hotels
★★★★
Park. Ul. Warszawska 119, ☎ 523-6604. Situated outside the town centre. Modern and well-run, the best in Olsztyn. Air conditioning, tennis courts, fitness centre, car park. 100 rooms.

Orbis-Novotel. Ul. Sielska 4a, ☎ 527-4081. Out-of-town location by Lake Ukiel. Business Centre, car rental, car park. 97 rooms.
Kormoran. Pl. Konstytucji 3 Maja 4, ☎ 534-5864. Car rental, car park. 97 rooms.

Tourist information (PAPT). Ul. Warszawska 13, ☎ 527-2807.
ORBIS. Ul. Dąbrowszczaków 1, ☎ 527-5793/527-4674.
Main post office. Ul. Piemiężnego 21.
Telephone code: (0–89).

The city centre

The Old Town begins at the Gothic **High Gate**—the only remnant of the medieval town fortifications—decorated with blind arcades and geometric patterns of glazed brick. During the second half of the 19C it was used as a prison—the gable and stair-tower date from this period. Behind the gate extends UL. STAROMIEJSKA, the axis of the Old Town, leading down to the Old Town Square. In the middle of it stands the **Old Town Hall** (1623–24), remodelled in the 18C–19C, and, like the square itself, rebuilt after the Second World War. It now houses a library. In the row of shops opposite the building, note the **Mayor's House**, which has retained its Gothic arcade. Most of the other arcaded houses around the square are post-war reconstructions.

St James' Cathedral

UL. ŚW. BARBARY leads off the northeast corner of the square to the **Cathedral of St James*, the last, and perhaps best, example of a Warmian hall church erected by the Teutonic Order.

Begun in 1370 as a Gothic aisled hall, the church received vaults in 1480–1510, and a huge brick tower (67m) with blind arcades in 1596. The aisles were later extended by means of vaulted chapels (1721), thus fully incorporating the tower into the rectangular ground plan. Napoleonic soldiers took refuge inside the church in 1807, after which it was briefly used as a prison. During major renovation in 1866–68 the church acquired its Neo-Gothic appearance.

The flat east end of the church is noted for its fine gable (reconstructed in 1866–68) with panels and diagonal turrets. Inside, the spacious six-bay nave is covered with 16C net vaults, with equally fine cellular vaults in the aisles. Most of the furnishings are Neo-Gothic, with a few notable exceptions: a black marble font (1715) to the left of the entrance in the north aisle, and, further on, a carved Gothic triptych with a central figure of the *Virgin and Child* (16C). The south aisle has a Neo-Gothic altar of the Holy Cross with a 16C triptych painted on wood. A 17C crucifix hangs from the vault at the far east end of the nave. There are also two fine chandeliers: one with a sculpture of the Virgin, the other in the shape of a deer's head (1598).

The Castle and Museum

Off the square on UL. ZAMKOWA stands the **Castle of the Warmian Cathedral Chapter*, situated on a spur above the Łyna river among greenery. From its inception, the castle served as a stronghold defending Warmia against the Teutonic Knights, who never managed to conquer it. The oldest north wing (Gothic, 1346–53), to the right as you enter the courtyard, has a covered arcade and rooms where Copernicus lived in 1516–21; the south wing, still Gothic, is slightly later, extended and rebuilt during the 16C; the east wing is Baroque (1756–58). A Prussian sculpture of a woman, originally found in Barciany, and probably as old as the 9C, stands in the castle courtyard. Only one of the towers (14C) has been preserved—its round superstructure is a later addition.

The oldest castle wing houses a **Museum of Warmia and Masuria** (open 09.00–17.00 in summer, 10.00–16.00 in winter) with a well-labelled display. You begin in the covered arcade, where, high up on the wall, is the most prized exhibit: a fragment of the original astronomical chart made by Copernicus to establish the precise date of the equinox, which he needed for his work on reforming the calendar. Further on are the cellular-vaulted chambers where Copernicus lived, with a display that gives us a glimpse into his life as an astronomer, and a diligent administrator of the Warmian Chapter. Around 1521 Copernicus made preparations to repulse an imminent siege by the Teutonic Knights, and a letter to the king has been preserved, in which he requests the shipment of state-of-the-art harquebus weapons. The long barrels of these formidable firearms are now on display in the arcade, along with some 16C infantry armour. Up some steep steps is Copernicus's private toilet. In addition to replicas of instruments used by the founder of modern science, you will find a copy of his major work, *De revolutionibus*. Begun in the castle, it was not published until 1543, the year of the author's death. The bold statement that revolutionised our civilisation is couched in rather unscientific terms: 'and so the sun as if sitting on a throne, manages the family of planets busying around'. The pride of the collection is an original book from Copernicus's private library, containing two medical works, and his *Treatise on the Coin*.

The second part of the museum, occupying the diamond-vaulted refectory, is devoted to temporary exhibitions. Each year the castle plays host to a July festival of poetry and song, with concerts in the afternoons and evenings, and the main event on Sunday.

Lidzbark Warmiński and Dobre Miasto

This excursion takes you north of Olsztyn to the Warmian town of Lidzbark (48km), with its famous Bishops' castle and museum. The other highlight is the collegiate church in Dobre Miasto (26km). Both towns can be reached by bus from Olsztyn.

Leave Olsztyn heading north on road 51, marked 'Bartoszyce'. **DOBRE MIASTO** (26km) was surrounded by a ring of walls with towers and gates until the 19C, but today only fragments remain, notably the round brick **Stork's Tower** by the river, which you pass on your way into town. Looming in the distance is the huge tower of the Gothic **collegiate church*, a typical Warmian hall, raised in 1357–89. The tower was built in stages during the 15C–17C, receiving its present roof and gables in 1895.

Interior. The grand seven-bay nave with no chancel rises to elaborate four- and eight-pointed star vaults carried on octagonal pillars of bare brick. Most of the furnishings are Baroque, including the **high altar** (1748), **font** (1630–85), richly sculpted **pulpit** (1693), and **stalls** (1673) with Gothic steps in the shape of lions. Two earlier triptych-like altars (of the *Virgin*, c 1430, and *St Anne*, c 1500) terminate the aisles. By the second pillar in the north aisle is an early 16C sculpture of the *Throne of Mercy*. Adjoining the church, by the mill on the canal, are the former collegiate buildings with first-floor Gothic cloisters around a courtyard.

Continue northeast on road 51, signposted 'Bartoszyce'. **LIDZBARK WARMIŃSKI** is located in a picturesque setting at the confluence of the Symsarna and Łyna rivers.

Established in 1240 on the site of a Prussian settlement, Lidzbark received a municipal charter in 1308. Its prosperity began in 1350, when the bishops of Warmia moved their episcopal seat here from out-of-the-way Frombork, and commissioned the construction of a castle, completed in 1401. With Warmia's annexation to the Polish crown (1466), Lidzbark became a remarkable centre of intellectual and cultural life, from the 16C a bastion of the Counter Reformation. Among its most eminent residents were Copernicus, and Bishop Ignacy Krasicki, whose 30-year tenure at the castle inspired him to write the satirical poems *Monachomachia or War of the Monks* and *Anti-Monachomachia* (see p. 82). Copernicus lived in the castle from 1503 to 1510, working as a secretary and physician to his uncle Bishop Watzenrode. Towards the end of the 16C, the castle lost its military significance and became a luxurious ducal court.

After Ignacy Krasicki, the last Warmian prince-bishop, was ousted from the castle in 1795, it fell into decline. Damaged during the Napoleonic wars, it was renovated by the Prussians and converted into an orphanage and hospital. The first conservation work got under way in 1927, and in 1963 Lidzbark entered UNESCO's World Heritage List.

The Bishop's Castle and Museum

The **Bishops' Castle, situated at the end of UL. ZAMKOWA, is a masterpiece of medieval secular architecture, second only to Malbork (see p. 333). First you enter the forecastle—a courtyard surrounded by a horseshoe of buildings, all remodelled in the 18C. Most impressive is the **east wing**, converted into a late Baroque palace in 1741–66 by Bishop Grabowski, who also sponsored the statue of St Catherine in the courtyard (1756, Pierre Coudray). Note, also, the round 16C tower in the southeast corner. The south wing is nondescript, except for the arched 14C gate through which you enter. To the south and east the forecastle is bordered by the former moat.

To the north rises the castle proper, a square fort, with a bulky northeast tower, and large turrets (1442) in the corners. A tall entrance niche leads to the castle courtyard, surrounded by charming cloisters (1380). You begin the tour of the **museum** (open Tues–Sun 09.00–16.00) in the courtyard by ascending the 17C stairs to the first-floor cloisters, with an abundance of frescoes, coats of arms, late Renaissance marble and sandstone portals, and a sun-dial (1746) on the north wall. The first room is the star-vaulted **Chapel** (south wing, east end), with mid-18C Rococo furnishings. The pulpit, altar and organ loft are all lavishly gilded. Also mid-18C are the murals on the aisle arches, depicting Old Testament

scenes: *Three Angels at the House of Abraham*, *The Sacrifice of Isaac*, *The Meeting with Rebecca*, *Jacob's Ladder*, *Joseph's Dream*, and *Joseph as the Ruler of Egypt*.

The **Great Refectory**, the largest and most impressive room in the castle, occupies the entire east wing. The 14C appearance of the room is a 1930s reconstruction. It contains an exhibition of medieval art from Warmia and Ducal Prussia. Next along is the **private chapel** of Bishop Watzenrode, actually part of the tower, with paintings commissioned by him. In the passageway to the chapel is the entrance to the **dungeon**, dubbed the 'Chamber of Forgetting'. The square Audience Chamber and **Library**, with a vault of five interlocking stars (1497), displays 17C–18C Warmian religious painting. In 1749, the chronicle of Gallus Anonymous was discovered in the library. The Bishops' Apartments (north wing) include a dining room with floral designs on the ceiling and 18C fresco landscapes. The **Small Refectory** (west wing) displays silverware, pewter-ware, bells and liturgical items (17C–20C). In the Chapter House (conference hall) there are fragments of 14C frescoes and a portrait gallery of Warmian bishops (15C). The large **Summer Chamber** (south wing, west end) has an elaborate six-pointed star vault.

Foregate, Lidzbark Warmiński

Second floor. The exhibitions on the top floor of the castle include 20C Polish art and a collection of 72 well-preserved Russian icons from the Old Believers' Convent in Wojnowo (see p. 410). Dating from the 17C–20C, the icons present images of *Christ*, the *Virgin* and the *Archangel Michael*, full of Byzantine severity, as well as biblical scenes, including the *Annunciation*, *Baptism* and *Crucifixion*. In some cases the figures wear repoussé silver robes. All the icons carry explanatory inscriptions in Old Church Slavonic, the liturgical language of the Russian Orthodox Church.

Ground floor. The former armoury (south wing), has low cross vaults and an art gallery. From the east wing you can enter the rib-vaulted cellars, parts of which are accessible to visitors. The cellars house a collection of medieval weaponry.

Across the river on UL. MIKOŁAJA REJA stands the Gothic **Parish Church of SS Peter and Paul**, begun in 1315 as a basilica, but completely destroyed by fire in 1497, and rebuilt thereafter as a five-bay hall with elaborate star vaults. After damage caused by lightning in 1698, the tower was extended and given a Baroque triple lantern, but its lower sections and flanking chapel gables are still 14C. The chancel, north and south porches, and most of the furnishings were added during restoration work in 1891–93. Inside the large, musty hall are two late 17C altars, the south one with a painting of *St Mary of the Rosary*; a fine Renaissance **bronze epitaph**; and a Rococo pulpit and confessionals. The Treasury (often closed) has a valuable Gothic reliquary of St Ida (c 1425), with a bust of the saint.

Walking west of the Main Square along UL. POWSTAŃCÓW WARSZAWY you reach the late Gothic **Foregate**, a massive brick structure flanked by two solid round towers. It was originally part of the High Gate, now vanished, to which it was connected by a covered passageway. From the mid-19C, the foregate—rebuilt in Neo-Gothic style—served as a prison. Today, the building is used as a hostel and tourist office. Beyond it, on ul. Wysoka Brama, stands a former **Lutheran church** (now Orthodox), attributed to the Prussian Karl Friedrich Schinkel (1821–23).

The Church of Święta Lipka and Hitler's Bunkers at Gierłoż

❖ Barczewo • Reszel • Św. Lipka • Kętrzyn • Gierłoż • Sztynort Duży

This long but fascinating trip takes you east of Olsztyn towards the Masurian Lake District. The highlights are the medieval town of Reszel, the pilgrimage church at Święta Lipka, and Hitler's bunkers in the forests around Gierłoż. All these places are well worth visiting, but you should leave early if you intend to see them all in a single day. By public transport it is best to take the train or bus to Kętrzyn (102km), a good base for exploring the region, with bus connections to all the sites listed in the itinerary.

Head east from Olsztyn on road 16 to Barczewo (16km) described on p. 408. Continue to Biskupiec; from there, drive (83km) northeast on road 596 to RESZEL, a charming, peaceful town on the banks of the river Sajna.

Reszel was founded in the 13C on the site of the much older Prussian settlement of Resl. From 1254 until the Prussian takeover in 1772, it was directly administered by the Warmian Chapter, and marked the eastern border of the bishops' domain.

Reputedly (or disreputably) it was the site of the last witch-trial in Europe: during the Napoleonic wars a woman was accused of witchcraft and arson; thanks to a merciful 'pardon' granted her by King Frederick William of Prussia, she was first choked to death, and only then burnt at the stake. A document confirming the event is preserved in the castle (see below).

In the wake of Operation Wisła (see p. 254) after the Second World War, many Ukrainians were settled in Reszel. Even today they constitute almost half the town's population, a fact which, for political reasons, the Communist authorities never acknowledged. Consequently, as Uniate believers (see p.253), the Ukrainians could not practise their faith openly, but were forced to celebrate mass covertly in the former Lutheran church in the castle, and in the former Jesuit church (see below).

All of Reszel's attractions are found in the vicinity of the small Market Square, which has 19C houses and a Neo-classical **Town Hall** (1815) built on medieval foundations. The urban plan of the town as well as its watersupply and sewers are medieval (14C), though the latter are now only used for cellar drainage. Many of the buildings were damaged when the sewers recently caved in, but the showpiece castle was fortunately unscathed.

UL. WYSPIAŃSKIEGO leads off the square to the Gothic **Parish Church of SS Peter and Paul** (c 1350), a rectangular brick aisled hall of five bays, with later star vaults (1475–76). The huge eight-storey west tower was renovated in the 15C, with the upper section and lantern being added in 1837. Also 15C are the gables of the star-vaulted sacristy and vestibule to the north. The wooden door to the sacristy has iron bars and original medieval metalwork, including a lock and bolt. To the east, the church is adjoined by a library, now a storeroom, with tunnel vaults of 1471. The pointed-arch portals leading into the church have richly carved jambs (c 1350). You enter through the vestibule, which has a late Baroque Passion group in a niche above its portal. Most of the furnishings are Baroque-Classical and Empire style (1820–44).

The Castle in Reszel

From the church, walk east along UL. SŁOWACKIEGO to the impressive *Bishops' Castle.

> The castle was built c 1350 by Heinrich von Meissen, who sought to defend the property of the Warmian bishops against Lithuanian raids. It was extended during the 16C–17C, and in 1783 converted into a prison. In 1807, rioting prisoners began a fire, causing extensive damage. Major renovation work was undertaken in 1822, when Frederick William III gave the castle to the Lutheran community. The south wing, encompassing the keep, was rebuilt as a Protestant church.

The castle is situated on the high bank of the Sajna, which in the Middle Ages served as a natural moat. You enter through a tall arched recess in the gate-tower (west). To the left rises the huge protruding keep with loopholes and an arcaded frieze in its upper section. Between the two towers is a great rarity: a 16C machicolated passage on top of the wall: defences of this type were usually built of wood, but this one is of brick and stone. During the 16C, the castle was surrounded by an outer wall, of which only the north section survives. One of its semi-circular turrets (still extant) served as a latrine tower, or *dansker* (1505), connected to the north side of the castle by means of a covered passageway.

The timber courtyard and original interiors of the castle were destroyed over the centuries, but since renovation in 1976–85 an **archaeological museum** has been opened in the keep, while the former Lutheran church accommodates a **gallery of modern art**, staging various temporary exhibitions. The remainder is used for most of the year as a cultural centre and workshop for artists, who live on site. If there are vacant rooms (ten singles and doubles with modern bathrooms), tourists can also stay. It is a popular venue for festivals, plays and concerts, with participants from many countries. The friendly management team contributes much to the homely, informal atmosphere of the place (**open** Tues–Sun 10.00–17.00, and at other times by arrangement with the curator Bolesław Marschal, ☎ Kętrzyn 39-49).

The **keep** displays archaeological finds from the castle and its environs. Below it is the former **prison**, unused since 1822. On the wall close to it, you can see crosses scratched by prisoners with their fingernails. Still deeper, underneath the prison, is a small room entered by a tiny hole (40cm by 40cm), which was used as a waste storage area, and completely blocked off in the 14C. Consequently, many items from the period were discovered inside, fully preserved. Along the passageways leading off the keep are medieval wooden water and sewage pipes. As you climb the keep, you will pass a window, inaccessible since its construction, in which, under a thick layer of bird droppings, a beer tankard forgotten by the stonemasons was discovered. The upper rooms contain a large collection of cannons and cannonballs, found in the courtyard well. From the top you get a fine view over the town.

To the north of the castle on UL. PODZAMCZE stands the former **Jesuit Church** (Baroque, 1799–1800), which has recently been turned over to the Uniate community. Next door are the buildings of the former Jesuit college, partly rebuilt in Neo-classical style after a fire in 1865 (now a secondary school). Opposite the church on ul. Spichrzowa is a large, disused wooden **granary** (18C), with fragments of the medieval town fortifications close by. Continue along ul. Podzamcze to the three-tiered, arcaded Gothic **bridge** (14C), spanning the Izera river. In the past it was also used as an aqueduct, and—during the 19C—the tiny rooms below it housed a prison.

The Pilgrimage Church in Święta Lipka

From Reszel, head southeast for about 5km on road 594, signposted 'Kętrzyn'. In the village of ŚWIĘTA LIPKA, the silhouette of the Baroque ****pilgrimage church** will come into view on the right. The name of the church, as of the village itself, derives from a legend about a lime tree and a miraculous figure of the Virgin ('*święta lipka*' means 'holy lime'). Historical sources confirm that a chapel existed here as early as 1320. After 1631, the pilgrimage site was run by the Jesuits, who in 1687–93 commissioned Georg Ertly from Vilnius to erect the present church, the earliest of its kind in Warmia, and without doubt one of the best in Poland—a beautifully preserved example of Baroque architecture.

The legend of the holy lime

Considering its fame and grandiose proportions, the church's location might seem rather strange and unprepossessing. It stands far from any town (even the village was established later than the church), and is not even on a hill, but hidden in a valley among trees, partly on a marsh.

Perhaps the legend provides an explanation: a prisoner incarcerated in Kętrzyn castle had a visitation from St Mary the night before his execution, in which he was told to carve a wooden sculpture. Though he had never sculpted before, by dawn he had managed to create a work of great beauty. His captors understood this as a divine pardon, and promptly set the man free. The sculpture of St Mary was hung from a lime tree by the road to Reszel, and soon became famous for its miraculous workings. On three occassions it was moved to the parish church in Kętrzyn, but each time it miraculously returned to the tree. Finally, a chapel and then a grand church were built at the spot, becoming a place of pilgrimage.

The striking twin-towered **façade** (1730), decked out in bright yellow and white plaster, has an abundance of stone detailing creating a complex interplay of light and shade. Below the Baroque gable is an arched recess containing a sculpted scene of the Virgin on the Holy Lime-tree (1730). The rectangular cloister (1694–1708) is polychromed on the inside, and has domed corner chapels; on the balustrade are 44 Baroque sandstone sculptures of saints. In the first chapel, as you walk clockwise around the cloister, note the fine *trompe l'oeil* frescoes (1733–37). Most impressive of all, however, is the entrance gate (1734)—a splendid maze of metal vines and leaves.

The six-bay interior is a basilica with galleries fronted by gilt-edged balustrades over the aisles, fluted pilasters with similarly gilded Corinthian capitals along the nave, and no transepts. The three-tiered 18C high altar (19m) includes a painting of *St Mary* (1640) with a repoussé silver gown. Opposite the chancel there is a silver figure of the Virgin (1654) on a wood-carved lime-tree (1728) with gypsum branches and metal leaves (it is said to mark the spot of the original 'holy lime tree'). There is a late 18C painting of *Occursus Mariae* by Sobieski's court painter Martin Altomonte on the left (north), just before the high altar. The ornate Baroque **pulpit** on the right (1700) is decorated with fine sculptures. Murals on the cross-vaulted ceiling depict scenes from the life of the Virgin and the Passion of Christ. The organ (1719–21) is a fantastically ornate Baroque instrument by Mosengel of Königsberg. Renovated in 1965, it comes complete with tacky moving parts, bells and angels among them. Organ concerts are held in the church on Fridays in summer.

Road 594 continues 14km east to **KĘTRZYN** (population 29,600), an appealing town whose origins date back to 1329, when the Teutonic Knights built a castle here next to the Old Prussian village of Rast. From the 16C it acquired the name of Rastenburg. Most of the Prussian population died during the Second World War, or was expelled after 1946, when Rastenburg (now a Polish town) was renamed after the historian and activist **Wojciech Kętrzyński**, whose monument stands on the Main Square.

Walk south off the Square along UL. MICKIEWICZA where, at No. 1, there is a former **Masonic Lodge** (1810), a Neo-Gothic building on a rectangular plan with four octagonal turrets, one of very few preserved examples of Masonic architecture in Poland. The interior houses a cultural centre with a library and small **museum** offering temporary exhibitions, mainly sculpture, painting and weaving. Note the gold- and platinum-plated pendulum bearing Masonic symbols.

Continue south along UL. STAROMIEJSKA, past a glass pavilion, to the Gothic **Collegiate Church of St George**, built in stages, initially as an aisleless hall with a flat roof (1359–1407). It was extended after 1470 into its present form of a pseudo-basilica with huge octagonal piers, arcades, and a small chapel. Following a fire in 1500 it received a three-bay chancel, a gabled sacristy and porch to the north, and an impressive honeycomb of **cellular vaults** on star plans (1517) were added. The sparse furnishings include a late Renaissance pulpit (1594), an altar (1609) in the south aisle with a painting by Rosenfelder of Königsberg, 16C epitaph slabs, also in the south aisle, and chandeliers in the form of wheels symbolising the torture and martyrdom of St George.

Next to St George's stands the **Lutheran church**, initially built in 1480, extended during the 16C–17C, and remodelled in Neo-classical style in 1817–27. From the second half of the 16C it schooled candidates for entry to Königsberg University. The Polish community also used it for christenings, and it thus became known as the 'Polish church'.

Walking down UL. ZJAZDOWA you reach the former **Teutonic Castle** (c 1360–70) on pl. Zamkowy. The building was reconstructed from scratch after the Second World War, and today it consists of three wings connected by a curtain wall. Inside is a library and **museum** (open Tues–Fri 10.00–17.00, Sat–Sun 09.00–16.00), with permanent exhibitions devoted to local flora and fauna, the life of Wojciech Kętrzyński, the history of Kętrzyn, and the archaeology and geology of the region.

The Wolf's Lair ~ Hitler's bunker

Better known than Kętrzyn itself is the ***Wolf's Lair** in the village of **GIERŁOŻ**, 9km to the east (take road 592 marked 'Giżycko', turning left at Karolewo; alternatively, bus No. 1 from the city centre will take you to the site).

The Wolf's Lair, or *Wolfsschanze*, is the name given to a grim complex of bunkers built by the Nazis in 1940–44, which served as the main command centre of **Operation Barbarossa** (the invasion of the Soviet Union). It is said that the Wolf's Lair was one of the few places in Europe where Hitler actually felt secure. He certainly preferred it to Berlin, and, with few interruptions, lived here between 24 June 1941 and 20 November 1944. The system of defences was indeed formidable: the reinforced concrete bunkers, 1–6m thick, were covered with imitation foliage nets that merged imperceptibly with the surrounding forest. A 10km ring of minefields and concealed anti-aircraft guns protected the site against potential attack by aircraft or infantry and a small railway station and airfield provided emergency escape routes. Hitler's own windowless bunker had an 8m thick roof, and was equipped with a direct telephone link to Berlin. In total, there were some 80 buildings on site, including officers' messes, barracks and special bunkers for the Nazi top brass. The Allies searched in vain for the hide-out, finally discovering it in 1945, when its inhabitants had fled.

Paradoxically, it was in the Wolf's Lair that the Führer literally came within an inch of death. On 20 July 1944, Colonel Claus Schenk von Stauffenberg, in collaboration with other members of the German High Command, planted a bomb in Hitler's bunker which went off a fraction too late. The conspirators realised that continuation of the war was madness, and in the event of success had intended to sue for peace, which would have saved millions of lives and spared Europe the mass destruction of the final year of the war. As it turned out, Stauffenberg and his associates were caught and summarily executed. The Wolf's Lair was eventually destroyed by the retreating Germans in January 1945. A staggering 8–12 tonnes of explosive were required to blow up a single bunker. The Red Army did not enter the site because of the mines, and it was not until the 1950s that its secrets could be uncovered.

Today, what remains of the Wolf's Lair has been opened to the public as a **museum** (open 09.00–dusk). Most of the bunkers are the way the Germans left them in 1945—massive concrete blocks pierced by twisted bits of steel, or dark, hollow shells now filled with mud and litter. Some, though, have been restored to house displays connected with the rise and fall of Nazism, and the history of the Second World War. The red trail takes you round the site, and German- and

English-speaking guides are available. Visitors wishing to stay longer in Gierłoż could try the modest on-site hotel, located in the former officers' rooms.

The palace at **Sztynort Duży** on Lake Sztynorckie is still well worth visiting for its gardens and a glimpse of the palace exterior (interior closed to the public). Continue east and northeast from Gierłoż along minor roads for about 20km. The **palace** was, from the 15C until the Second World War, the home of the Prussian Lehndorff family. Its last owner, Heinrich Lehndorff, was hanged for his part in the Bomb Plot against Hitler (see above). Built in 1690, the palace owes its present form to 19C remodelling, when two Neo-Gothic wings, a tower and annexes were added. Surrounding it is a beautiful formal garden and landscaped park, also mid-19C, with lime-tree alleys and moats.

Olsztyn to Suwałki ~ the Great Masurian Lakes

❖ Barczewo • Mrągowo • Mikołajki • Wojnowo • Pranie • Giżycko • Olecko Suwałki

This trip takes you into the heart of the Masurian Lake District, a beautiful region centred on the resorts of Mrągowo, Mikołajki and Giżycko. With accommodation plentiful, all these towns are good places to break your journey. Among the cultural highlights of the trip are the Old Believers' Convent at Wojnowo and the idyllically set cottage of the writer Gałczyński in Pranie. The main attraction is the countryside, with its numerous lakes, forests and nature reserves. Getting around the region by public transport is not easy. The train network is hopelessly slow; buses are infrequent, but still the best way of getting between the major towns.

Barczewo (16km east of Olsztyn on road 16) is a small town chartered in 1364, and the birthplace of the composer of the Polish national anthem Feliks Nowowiejski (1877–1946). The house at ul. Mickiewicza 15 has a modest **museum** (open Tues–Fri 10.00–17.00, Sat–Sun 10.00–15.00), devoted to his life and work.

Two churches in the town deserve a visit. The Gothic **Parish Church of St Anne**, located on UL. KOPERNIKA, off the Main Square, is an aisled hall begun in 1387, and covered with star vaults in the 1540s. Inside, the highlights are a Gothic crucifix (c 1500) in the sacristy, a statue of St Anne (Baroque, mid-18C) in the chancel, and a Baroque organ (c 1700).

More impressive is the former ***Franciscan Church of St Andrew** on UL. KLASZTORNA (through the arch off the Main Square). The monks were brought to Barczewo in 1364 and built their church and monastery in 1380–90. During the Reformation the monastery was abandoned, but in 1594 Bernardine monks settled here at the invitation of Cardinal Andrzej Bathory, the Bishop of Warmia, who re-vaulted the church and gave it a new Baroque façade. In 1598, Cardinal Bathory entrusted the design of his **funerary monument** to the accomplished Gdańsk sculptor Willem van den Blocke (see p. 311), who created what is now regarded to be one of the finest works of

Mannerism in Poland. The monument is in the south chapel of St Anthony and shows the Cardinal kneeling at an altar. Below him is a reclining figure of his armour-clad brother, Balthasar. Other works of interest include the Dutch Mannerist **stalls** in the long chancel (early 17C), a carved Rococo **pulpit** (late 18C), and a **high altar** of c 1730.

The Prussian authorities dissolved the nearby monastery in 1810, and later converted it into a prison. During the 1980s, the prison achieved notoriety when many of Solidarity's leaders were incarcerated there. Today, it remains one of Poland's toughest penal institutions.

Continue along road 16 to **MRĄGOWO** (48km), a resort set between LAKES JUNO and **Czos**, popular among yachting enthusiasts. It was formerly called Ządzbork, but in 1946 the authorities changed the name in memory of K. C. Mrongowiusz (1764–1855; see p. 416), an indefatigable champion of the 'Polishness' of Masuria. In fact, Mrągowo had been chartered by the Teutonic Knights (1404–07), and for centuries remained Prussian. The town is a good base for trips to the surrounding lakes and the beautiful Pisz Forest to the south. If you wish to break your journey here, excellent accommodation is provided at the ★★★★*Orbis Mrongowia Hotel* (ul. Giżycka 6, ☎ 0-89-741-3221), scenically located near Lake Czos.

On the corner of the Main Square (pl. Kajki) and ul. Ratuszowa stands the 19C **Town Hall**. The **Regional Museum** inside (open Tues–Sun 09.00–16.00), has a display tracing the prehistory of the region. The public gardens opposite the building lead down to a lake. Just off the Mały Rynek, on ul. Kościelna, is a former Protestant **church** (Baroque, 1734), which was thoroughly remodelled at the beginning of the present century; its modern interior is rather plain.

Further east along road 16 is the resort of **MIKOŁAJKI**, one of the most popular Masurian resorts on account of its proximity to LAKE ŚNIARDWY, the 'Polish sea' (11,383ha, 10–23m deep). Tour operators in town run boat, kayak and yacht excursions to Lake Śniardwy and the Great Lakes, many of which are joined by canals. Boats can also be rented by individuals if you prefer not to travel in a group. Ask at the *Wioska Żeglarska* on the waterfront for information. Lake Śniardwy has low, treeless banks—except in the southwest, where it borders the Pisz Forest—and numerous peninsulas, bays and islands. It is so vast that even on a clear day the far banks may be invisible. Birdwatchers might want to see the Czapliniec heron reserve on Śniardwy, although nearby LAKE ŁUKNAJNO (709ha, 3.2m deep), 4km to the east of Mikołajki, is more enticing. Łuknajno has been entered on the world list of biosphere reserves and is therefore largely protected from human interference. It is home to many species of rare water fowl (including wild swans, being the largest breeding ground of this species in Eastern Europe). To the north of Mikołajki stretches the elongated LAKE TAŁTY (1160ha, 44m deep). You can get a beautiful view of the town and its environs from Olszowy Róg, a small peninsula located on the west bank of the lake.

Mikołajki preserves a discreet charm despite attracting scores of holiday-makers. The tourist infrastructure is well developed, but the only (dubious) cultural attraction is a **Museum of the Reformation** (open 10.00–17.00), situated in a broad building on the left as you enter town. According to the earnest curator, the aim of the museum is to demonstrate that Reformation fostered tolerance, and to show that Warmia, Masuria and other disputed regions have always harboured their essential Polishness. This two-fold purpose is served by a display of various editions of the Bible (some in photocopy), a map of Europe showing the gradual proliferation of vernacular versions of the Scriptures, and a map of Central Europe showing the distribution of Polish nationals in 1910.

Head south (19km) from Mikołajki on road 609, which follows the course of the Krutynia river to Ukta. Here you should join a minor road to **WOJNOWO**, set on the shores of a small lake. Once in the village, follow the signs to 'Zabytkowy Klasztor Starowierców'. The **Old Believers' Convent** will come into view at the end of a dirt track.

> The **Old Believers**, also called the Philipons, fled Russia after they were persecuted for resisting the reforms introduced in the 17C by Nikon, the patriarch of the Russian Orthodox Church. Their monastery in Wojnowo dates back to 1836, when the monks were given land by Frederick III of Prussia and proceeded to build wooden hermitages and a church by the lakeshore. The monastery flourished 1852–67, when Piotr Ledniew, also called Paul of Prussia, was its elected hegumen (prior). It fell into decline, however, when he converted to a brand of Russian Orthodoxy known as *yedinovyerye* (literally 'one faith'). Many of the monks followed suit, and the monastery lay abandoned until a young nun by the name of Eupraksiya came to Wojnowo in 1885. She founded a convent with a very strict rule, which included 200 days of fasting per year. One of the nuns vowed to spend her entire life wearing chainmail and sleeping on bare stone.

The convent is run by two sisters, the only Old Believers left in Wojnowo. Their temple, or *molena*, is really just a small room, sparsely furnished. It has a 19C iconostasis across the far wall, although for safety reasons the most precious icons have been moved to the museum in Lidzbark Warmiński (see p. 401). The other items include: a silver chandelier (18C), with as many candles as the wife of the donor had years when she died; a 12 volume book in Old Church Slavonic, containing the rule of the order, and allegedly dating from 1645; and a hymn book written in *krukaviye* (old-style notation without staves) for sung and spoken hymns. The convent cemetery can be visited nearby. There is also a wooden **Russian Orthodox church** in the village, built in 1922–27 initially for the followers of *yedinovyerye*.

Drive on through Wojnowo and turn left onto the 611 for **RUCIANE-NIDA** (9km), a resort situated in the Pisz Forest at the north end of the sickle-shaped **LAKE NIDZKIE** (1734ha). Popular **boat trips** across the Great Lakes to Giżycko begin in Ruciane, but otherwise there is little reason to stop here. You should proceed straight to the village of **PRANIE**, which lies to the southwest: drive to Nida and turn right into ul. Gałczyńskiego. Just after crossing the railway lines, follow the signs to 'Pranie' and '*Hotel Mazury*'. Continue along the black dirt road through dense spruce forest for about 3km and then turn left down an incline, signposted 'Pranie'.

The ****Gałczyński Museum** (open Wed–Sun 09.30–17.00; about 200m from the car park) occupies a forester's house, in a beautiful setting on the high bank of Lake Nidzkie. It is devoted to the life and work of the poet **Konstanty**

Ildefons Gałczyński (1950–53), who drew much inspiration from the beauty of the region (see p. 85) and even wrote a poem about the house where he lived, entitled *Leśniczówka Pranie* ('*The Pranie Forester's House*'). Among the exhibits are photographs, manuscripts, first editions, letters, books from his personal library, quotations from his verse, and a reconstruction of his room in Warsaw. In July and August, concerts and poetry readings (in Polish) are held on Sun at 11.00. Accommodation is available at the Hotel *Skorpion* in nearby Krzyże, 3km from Pranie. Even if you are not a connoisseur of Gałczyński's verse, the beautiful surroundings and famously clean air will more than compensate you for the journey. The museum can be reached by boat from Ruciane-Nida, or on foot along the blue trail (10km). From the garden, a long flight of steps descends to the peaceful waters of Lake Nidzkie. A large **heron reserve** occupies the Zamordeje peninsula across the lake.

North of Mikołajki

Return to Mikołajki and continue north on roads 16 and 643 through scenic landscape to **GIŻYCKO** (32km), which lies at the heart of the Great Masurian Lakes. This is the most popular Masurian resort, and tends to become very crowded in summer. It is an ideal base for **boat excursions** to **LAKE NIEGOCIN** to the south and **LAKE MAMRY** to the north (ask for information at the tourist office on ul. Warszawska 7).

The Teutonic Order built a castle here in 1340, around which there emerged a bee-keeping settlement. Destroyed during the Thirteen Years War, the town was eventually chartered in 1612 as Lötzen (formerly Leczenburg). In the mid-19C, the Prussians erected the massive **Boyen Fortress** to guard the border with Russia (see below) and the first steamships began carrying passengers across the Great Lakes. The Polish authorities renamed Lötzen 'Giżycko' in 1946, after the pastor Gustaw Gizewiusz (1810–48), an ardent supporter of the 'Polishness' of Masuria.

The Main Square (pl. Grunwaldzki) has a Neo-classical **Lutheran church** (1827) at its east end, remodelled in 1881 as a hall with a gallery. Organ concerts are held here on Sun at 19.00.

Ul. Olsztyńska leads west off the square and merges with ul. Moniuszki. On the left, just after the canal with its revolving bridge, is a gabled wing of the former **Teutonic castle**. The building was remodelled in Renaissance style in 1560, becoming a spartan country residence in 1614. During the 19C, it was converted into living quarters for the commander of the Boyen Fortress (see below); Gen. Hindenburg later set up his HQ here. Since the Second World War it has been used as a motel.

Turn left and walk along the canal to the shore of Lake Niegocin (2604ha), the third largest lake in Masuria, where you could stop at one of the numerous bars on the waterfront offering freshly caught fish. Returning to the bridge, continue west along ul. Moniuszki. The road winds up the hill through a small wood. Beyond the red-brick arch stretches the vast **Boyen Fortress** (1842–55), named after the Prussian war minister, General von Boyen. The stronghold, protected by ramparts, towers and a moat, was extended and modernised right up until 1939. German Intelligence used it as a training centre for spies during the Second World War. It was defended by General Hossbach's army, but abandoned in 1945 without a fight, before the advancing Soviets. Today, the fortress is partly in ruin and partly used for commercial purposes.

From Giżycko head east on road 655 to Olecko, a run-of-the-mill town, whose only point of interest is its vast Market Square (5.5ha), laid out in the 16C, and even larger than Kraków's. Today it is a pleasant park with an abundance of trees and shrubs and a **monument** to the Red Army soldiers killed during the liberation of the town in 1945. From Olecko, road 653 (east) takes you to Suwałki.

Suwałki

Suwałki (population 55,900) is a provincial town that lies at the heart of Suwalszczyzna, a sparsely populated region in Poland's northeast borderlands. It is an area of great natural beauty, unsullied by industry, whose clean air and rural charm attracts those eager to escape the noise and fumes of the city. Yet it is never swamped with tourists, as the summer crowds tend to flock to the Great Lakes, which offer more in the way of facilities and accommodation. Travelling north and east of Suwałki, you enter a landscape of hills cut by ravines and valleys, clear streams and rivers, and an abundance of small lakes.

About 1km east of the village of Gulbieniszki (17km north of Suwałki) lies **Cisowa Góra** (258m), an intriguing hill, dubbed the 'Polish Fujiyama', with a beautiful view over **Lake Kopane** in the distance. The Czarna Hańcza river flows north through Suwałki and empties into **Lake Hańcza** (304ha), the deepest lake on the North European Plain (108.5m), with steep banks and a nearby nature reserve.

Thanks to its borderland location, Suwalszczyzna is a region of rich ethnic diversity. In Puńsk to the northeast, you will hear as much Lithuanian spoken as Polish. The town is a vibrant centre of **Lithuanian culture**—the community has its own schools, music, newspapers, folklore and handicrafts. A good time to visit is on the **feast of SS Peter and Paul** (29 June), or other local holidays, when the grounds of the parish church are crowded with women wearing lavishly embroidered regional costume.

Gołdap, which lies to the northwest, a few kilometres from the Kaliningrad enclave, likewise has a multi-ethnic heritage. Colonised first by the Lithuanians, and later, after the plague of 1710, by German settlers, it is now home to both Russians and Poles. To the south and east, beyond the **Augustów Forest**, Byelorussian communities are common, with many small-time traders arriving on market days from the once-Polish town of Grodno across the border. Mention should also be made of the **Old Believers**, a religious sect of Russian origin, who made their home in the villages around Suwałki from as early as the 17C. You might visit their church in Wodziłki, northwest of Suwałki, but their monastery in the Masurian village of Wojnowo (see p. 410) should not be missed.

Suwalszczyzna has an ancient history that is unique in Poland. During the 3C–4C, the native inhabitants were a tribe known as the Jatzvingians. Their culture vanished when the Teutonic Order swept eastwards in the 13C, but archaeologists have discovered **burial grounds** in two main sites: **Osowa**, 8km to the northwest of Suwałki, and **Szwajcaria**, 5km to the north. Many of the finds can be seen in the regional museum in Suwałki (see below).

Suwałki itself was a village until 1690, owned by the Camaldolese monks from Wigry (see p. 414). Chartered in the early 18C, it joined the Kingdom of Poland in 1815, later evolving into a provincial capital. During the first half of the 19C, most of the city centre was remodelled in Neo-classical style, a legacy that has survived to the present day. Significantly, Suwałki remained Polish after 1918; it has thus preserved an identity which sets it apart from the formerly East Prussian territory of Masuria to the west.

■ Practical information

Hotels. ★★★*Dom Nauczyciela*. Ul. Kościuszki 120, ☎ 66-69-00. 30 rooms.
Tourist information (PAPT). Ul. Kościuszki 71, ☎ 66-54-94/66-58-72.
ORBIS. Ul. Noniewicza 48, ☎ 66-38-38/66-59-16.
Main post office. Ul. Sejneńska.
Telephone code: (0–87).

The city centre

Suwałki is a good base for exploring the countryside of the northeast, but the town itself is not particularly arresting. The streets converge on PL. PIŁSUDSKIEGO, which encompasses the municipal park, laid out in 1820. On the north side of the square stands the Neo-classical **Parish Church of St Alexander** (1820–25). Inside, there are several 18C paintings by the Wilno (Vilnius) artist Franciszek Smuglewicz. Across the square stands the smaller **Church of the Holy Heart of Jesus** and a group of Neo-classical buildings: a **Town Hall** (1843) with a former guardhouse (1834), and the *lycée* building of 1845.

Walk north from the square along ul. Kościuszki to the **Regional Museum** at No. 81 (**open** Tues–Fri 08.00–16.00, Sat–Sun 10.00–17.00). A display focuses on the prehistory of the Suwałki region, particularly Jatzvingian and Lusatian culture. There are also some good 19C–20C Polish paintings, and a small section on Polish and European applied art.

South of the square on ul. Kościuszki is a manor house at No. 31, where the poet **Maria Konopnicka** (1842–1910) was born. The building is now a **museum** with a display covering Konopnicka's life and work.

Excursions from Suwalki

Thirty-one kilometres south of Suwałki on road 19 is the provincial town of AUGUSTÓW, scenically located between three lakes (Necko, Białe, Sajno) at the edge of the Augustów Forest. The Netta river, which flows through the town, once marked the border between Poland and the Grand Duchy of Lithuania. During the 19C, following the construction of the **Augustów Canal** (see below), the town evolved into a major centre of the timber industry.

You enter the town along al. Wyszyńskiego, which becomes UL. 29 LISTOPADA. At No. 5a, on a peninsula between two canals, is the **Augustów Canal Museum** (**open** Tues–Sun 09.00–16.00), which occupies a low wooden building resembling a hut. This is, in fact, a remnant of the 19C manor house of General I. Prądzyński, designer of the Augustów Canal, built 1824–39 to give Poland alternative access to the Baltic. The engineers successfully managed to link the Vistula, Biebrza and Narew rivers with the Niemen to the east, but the Russian part of the project was never completed. In summer, **boat trips** lasting two, three and nine hours can be made along the Polish section of the canal, which is 82km long and has 14 locks. On the way you will travel through many beautiful lakes. The harbour is situated on the wharf slightly further back along ul. 29 Listopada. Check there for departure times and prices.

Continue along ul. 29 Listopada and turn right at the roundabout into ul. 3 Maja, which leads to the MAIN SQUARE (Rynek Zygmunta Augusta). First, though, turn left into ul. Hoża and drive to the end of the street, where there is a **Regional Museum** (open 09.00–16.00) inside the library building, with an ethnographical display.

As much as 75 per cent of Augustów was destroyed during the Second World War, so there is little else in the way of sights. Returning back along al. Wyszyńskiego, you could turn left into the road opposite ul. Tytoniowa, which will bring you to the shore of LAKE NECKO. Overlooking the beach is a former PTTK hostel (1939) designed by M. Nowicki, co-designer of the UN building in New York.

To the east of Augustów is the **AUGUSTÓW FOREST** (Puszcza Augustowska), the largest expanse of uninterrupted forest in Poland (100,000ha), occupying the area between Lake Wigry to the north and the Biebrza river to the south. The terrain is predominantly flat, with marshes, heathland, and numerous lakes linked by rivers and streams. The dense tracts of ancient spruce and pine provided ideal cover for the insurrectionists of 1831 and 1863, and for Polish partisan units during the Second World War. Much of it can be visited by kayak or boat (for details ask at the PTTK building at ul. Nadrzeczna 70a in Augustów). A particularly attractive route is along the Augustów Canal, which cuts right across the forest from east to west, and then along the Czarna Hańcza river. Aside from its breathtaking beauty, the area is noted for its microclimate and especially clean air. It is also rich in flora and fauna.

Lake Wigry and environs

Scenically set on a peninsula (formerly an island) amid trees is the former *Camaldolese Monastery*. The buildings are spread out over terraces, which rise up to an imposing Baroque church, with beautiful views over the lake.

From Suwałki go east (14km) along ul. Sejneńska (road 660), and follow signs to Sejny. After the village of Krzywe, the route enters the Wigry National Park (14,840ha), a forested area with 45 small lakes. Lake Wigry (2170ha, 73m deep) lies at its centre. In Stary Folwark, turn right at the sign marked 'Wigry' and 'Klasztor Kamedułów'. The road skirts the edge of the lake.

Zygmunt August built a royal hunting lodge on the island in 1559, using it as a base for forays into the nearby Augustów Forest. Jan Kazimierz later gave the property, together with tracts of land, to the Camaldolese monks. In 1704 they commissioned a church, completed in 1745. The monks amassed considerable wealth from colonisation and industrial exploitation of the Augustów Forest. At the turn of the 17C they owned 14 ore mines and 13 wood distilleries.

In 1796, the Prussians seized the entire estate, which by then covered an area of 300 sq. km, and included 11 farms and 56 villages. Four years later the monastery was dissolved and the monks moved to Bielany near Warsaw, where they have remained to the present day. Thereafter, their church was made into a cathedral; in 1829 it was renovated and stripped of most of its treasures. It was rebuilt in 1929, and again in 1945–49.

Despite its grand appearance and beautiful setting, the church is modestly furnished. The former monastic buildings, including hermitages, refectories, and a building with a clock tower, also merit a visit. Today, they provide refuge for writers and artists, though rooms are also available to tourists (Dom Pracy Twórczej; Centre for Creative Works, ☎ 67-97-48).

Return to the main road and continue to **SEJNY** (18km), a market town with a large Lithuanian community. It was founded by J. Grodzieński (1593–1602), who gave the property to the Dominicans from Wilno (Vilnius). Their former **church and monastery** (1610–19) stands on an incline at the north end of town. The recently refurbished basilican interior has **Rococo stuccoes** and a 15C lime-wood sculpture of the Madonna, an object of cult (south transept).

Walk back along the main street, still called ul. Armii Czerwonej (Red Army Street), which has a few 19C houses. The interiors of the former **synagogue** (1885), a large eclectic building on a square plan with a Neo-classical cornice, were destroyed by the Nazis, who stationed the local fire brigade here. Renovated in 1978–87, the building now contains an art gallery and hosts cultural events. You can still see the recess where the scrolls of the Torah were once kept.

Thirteen kilometres northeast of Sejny lies **OGRODNIKI**, the border crossing to Lithuania.

Olsztyn to Warsaw

❖ Olsztynek • Grunwald • Nidzica • Opinogóra • Warsaw

The highlight of this trip is the medieval battlefield at Grunwald, 44km southwest of Olsztyn. You can get there directly by bus from Olsztyn. Alternatively, take the train to Olsztynek, where there is an interesting skansen of folk architecture, and then continue by bus to Grunwald. The last stop on this trip, the Romantic manor house at Opinogóra, can also be done as a day trip from Warsaw (train to Ciechanów, followed by local bus to Opinogóra).

From Olsztyn, head 25km south on road 51 to **OLSZTYNEK**, which lies on the Jemiołówka river.

Founded in 1359 by the Teutonic Order, Olsztynek was occupied by the Poles on several occasions during the 15C, but remained part of Ducal Prussia after 1525. French armies under the command of Marshal Ney were quartered here in 1807. The bacteriologist E. Behring (1854–1917), who discovered a vaccine for diphtheria and later won the first Nobel Prize for Medicine, was a graduate of the local secondary school.

By the main road into town is a rather good **Skansen of Folk Architecture** (**open** Tues–Fri 09.00–17.00, Sat–Sun 09.00–18.00 in summer; Tues–Fri 09.00–15.00 in winter), with a collection of 18C–20C wooden buildings from the Warmia, Powiśle and Masuria regions and Prussian Lithuania (some of them copies). The 40 or so exhibits include a watermill, a Masurian farmyard, thatched cottages, inns, windmills, as well as farm equipment, furniture and regional costume. The highlight is an excellent copy of the 18C wooden church in nearby Rychnowo.

Continue to the Market Square, by which stands a 14C Gothic church, formerly Protestant. Gutted in 1945, it has since been converted into a **museum** (open Tues–Sat 09.00–17.00 in summer, 09.00–14.00 in winter) holding temporary art exhibitions. In a house behind the church you can browse through a display devoted to the philosopher, writer and translator **Krzysztof Celestyn Mrongowiusz** (1764–1855), born in the house, and best known for his Polish-German dictionary. The small beamed room on the ground floor has various items of Mrongowiusz memorabilia; upstairs is a display of objects salvaged from the Stalag 1B Hohenstein near Olsztynek, where French POWs were imprisoned.

To the right of the church stands a former **Teutonic Castle**, raised in the mid-14C. It later served as an arsenal, before being converted into a school in 1847–49. Preserved from the Gothic period are vaulted cellars, presently inaccessible, and parts of the walls. The red-brick exterior, with stepped gables and a courtyard, is topped by a banner with an eagle and the date 1410.

The Hindenburg Mausoleum
About 1.5km west of town (road 7), on a hillock close to the village of Sudwa, scattered masonry foundations mark the spot where the Hindenburg Mausoleum stood before the war.

The mausoleum was built in the years 1927–35, initially to commemorate the crushing victory of Hindenburg's German Eighth Army against Samsonov's Russian forces in August 1914, which the German authorities dubbed the 'second battle of Tannenberg'. Indeed, the hostilities had taken place near Tannenberg (Stębark, 16km southwest of Olsztynek), where, half a millennium earlier, the Teutonic Knights had suffered their heaviest defeat at the hands of the combined Polish, Lithuanian and Ruthenian armies (to Poles this battle is known as the Battle of Grunwald—see below.)

During the 1930s, nationalist fervour was whipped up when Nazi-inspired rallies and demonstrations were held at the mausoleum. Hindenburg's body was moved there in 1935, after which the site was declared a national monument, attracting pilgrims from the furthest corners of the Reich. The Germans managed to remove Hindenburg's remains before the Red Army blew up the mausoleum in 1945. During the 1950s, the Polish Communist authorities dismantled what was left of the building, using the granite blocks to build, among other things, the Communist Party Headquarters in Warsaw.

For Grunwald (19km), head south from Olsztynek (road 7), following signs to Warsaw. At Pawłowo, turn right onto a minor road; after Stębark (10km), follow the white signs marked 'Grunwald Pole Bitwy'. A group of tall masts with metal pennants will come into view as you approach *GRUNWALD.

In 1960, a monument commemorating the 550th anniversary of the Grunwald victory was unveiled on the battle site. It consists of three parts: a granite obelisk (8m) bearing bas-relief images of Jagiełło's soldiers; 11 flagstaffs (30m) with

The Battle of Grunwald

On 15 July 1410, in a field near the village of Grunwald, 60,000 soldiers fought one of the greatest and bloodiest battles of the Middle Ages, an event described by Henryk Sienkiewicz (see p. 84) in his novel *The Teutonic Knights*. On one side stood the combined Polish-Lithuanian army led by Władysław Jagiełło, the Polish king, and Duke Vytautas, the regent of Lithuania; on the other—the Teutonic Knights under the command of the Grand Master, Ulrich von Jungingen, aided by monastic regiments from western Europe.

With 29,000 cavalry and 5000 infantry, Jagiełło had the numerical advantage. His forces included Ruthenian, Czech and, crucially, Tartar regiments. The latter were expert horsemen, swift and cunning, adept at evading the blows of the cumbersome, armour-clad Knights. Indeed, it was tactics that won the day. Recklessly brave, the Knights were outflanked, unable to withstand the repeated onslaughts of their adversary. The fighting lasted six hours, during which half the Order's army, almost all of its officers, and the Grand Master himself, perished in the field. The Grunwald battle was a key event in East European history. It broke the backbone of the Order, despite that fact that Jagiełło imposed remarkably lenient peace terms on the Knights, making only modest territorial demands.

metal pennants symbolising the ensigns of the respective armies; and an amphitheatre with a relief map showing positions of the armies before the battle. A small **museum** (**open** May–Sept 08.00–16.00) exhibits items connected with the battle and its aftermath, including a skull with sword wounds, found in a grave near the chapel (about 700m to the west). Built by the defeated Knights in 1411–13, the chapel is the only surviving landmark allowing delimitation of the battlefield. Originally a stone hall (23m by 12m) supported by eight buttresses, it fell into ruin during the 16C, before being dismantled by the Prussians in 1720. Now only the foundations remain. Postwar archaeological excavations have uncovered two graves containing the remains of 20 men with battle wounds. Nearby, a commemorative stone (1901) marks the spot where the Grand Master is said to have died. About 1.3km southeast of the amphitheatre, a mound indicates the place where Jagiełło and Vytautas had their command post during the first phase of the battle. Walking from the amphitheatre back to the car park, you will pass a group of 265 granite boulders. These are the remains of the former Grunwald monument in Kraków (see p. 204), erected in 1910 and later destroyed by the Nazis.

Return to road 7 and continue south (36km). NIDZICA, situated on the Nida river, is dominated by the *Teutonic Castle, which overlooks the town from a hill. Built in 1370–1400 on a rectangular plan, this brick Gothic castle was occupied by Jagiełło's army in 1410, and again in 1454 by the burghers, who turned it over to Polish troops. Recovered by the Order in 1466, it was adapted in the early 16C to withstand attack from firearms, receiving, among other things, a forecastle (1517). By the 19C, plagues, fires and the Napoleonic wars had left the castle in ruins. It was rebuilt in 1828–30 for use as law courts, and reconstructed after the Second World War. Today it houses a library, cultural centre, hotel and café. There is no museum as such, but individual guided tours of the building are available. You enter the narrow courtyard through the gate-house in the east wing, which is flanked by two five-storey towers. Most impressive is the square west wing, with pinnacled gables, a star-vaulted refectory and chapel. Preserved in the latter are Gothic murals dating from c 1400.

On the pleasant green below the castle are remnants of the medieval town fortifications—two stone **towers**, one housing a shop. Just off the green (south-east) stands another Gothic building (14C), currently an archive. Beyond the 19C **Town Hall** is the Gothic **Parish Church of St Adalbert**, rebuilt in 1818 and 1920–24.

Continuing south on road 7 you will pass Mława, a drab town where you should join the 544, following signs to Przasnysz; after 3km turn right onto road 615, marked 'Konopki'. CIECHANÓW has little to offer in the way of sights, though Opinogóra (8km), is well worth a visit.

If you want to break your journey to Warsaw (114km) here, convenient acco-modation is provided in Ciechanów at the ★★*Olimpijski* Hotel (ul. 17 Stycznia 60a, ☎ 0-23-672-2012). The ruins of the **Mazovian Dukes' Castle** (15C) are situated in a boggy meadow north of the Main Square, across the river; a modest Regional Museum (**open** Tues–Sun 10.00–16.00) is found on ul. Warszawska 61.

To get to OPINOGÓRA, head east from Ciechanów on road 60, turning left after about 5km onto a minor road. The village was initially owned by the Mazovian dukes, and later by the Krasińskis, who in the 1820s built a delightful Romantic *manor house comprising a single storey of rib-vaulted rooms running to an octagonal southeast corner tower with windows and balconies. You enter through a gabled porch on steep stone arches. Inside is a **Museum of Romanti-cism** (**open** Tues–Sun 10.00–16.00), embellished by period furnishings. The house, rebuilt since the war, is set in a pleasant landscaped park; check the map by the entrance for a key to all the points of interest. Also in the castle grounds is a Neo-classical **parish church** (1825), with tombs of the Krasiński family, inc-luding the **tomb of Zygmunt Krasiński** the great Romantic poet (see p. 83).

From Ciechanów, drive south along road 617 marked 'Płońsk', where you should rejoin road 7 heading south to Warsaw.

Silesia

Silesia is a region of stormy history and great contrasts. On the one hand, its east part, or Upper Silesia, is by far the ugliest region of Poland—polluted, industrialised, with almost nothing in the way of tourist attractions. On the other hand, Lower Silesia, with Wrocław its capital, is more densly filled with historic monuments, fascinating towns, splendid churches, castles and wonders of nature than any other region of Poland. Day-trips can be made to the impressive **Cistercian monasteries** at Trzebnica, Oleśnica and Lubiąż. Within easy reach, too, is the mountain of **Ślęża**, with its pagan statues and magnificent views. Going further afield, the **Karkonosze Mountains** are second only to Tatras in their beauty, and far less crowded. The Kłodzko region combines natural charm with elegant 19C spa architecture. South of Wrocław are the splendid **abbeys** at Henryków and Krzeszów. Further north lie the towns of Legnica (west of Wrocław), Brzeg and Opole (east), all worth a visit.

Wrocław

Wrocław (population 650,000), Poland's fourth largest city, lies on the Odra (Oder) river in the centre of the elongated Silesian Lowland. For centuries it belonged to the German-speaking world—first under the Habsburg dynasty as part of the Austrian empire, then under Prussian rule. After the Second World War it suddenly became home to thousands of settlers from Lwów, Poland's major city in the southeast, which Stalin incorporated into the Socialist Republic of Ukraine. Whether it preserved the best or worst of both worlds, it certainly owes much of its vitality to this unusual blend of reliable, if somewhat pedantic German *Ordnung* and the relaxed, amiable attitude so characteristic of the eastern provinces, or *kresy* (literally, the borderlands). In architecture, the Germanic legacy has remained particularly strong, and even today echoes of pre-war Breslau are everywhere in evidence.

With a dozen or so institutions of higher education, libraries, theatres, a concert hall, opera house, a film company, local radio and TV stations, Wrocław is a thriving cultural centre. The **international music festival** *Wratislavia Cantans* is ranked alongside the Warsaw Autumn as the most important annual music event in Poland. Wrocław's choir *Cantores Minores Wratislavienses* is also one of the finest in the country. In the dramatic arts, Jerzy Grotowski's avant-garde **Laboratory** theatre acquired worldwide fame. The monthly *Odra* was one of the most influential and relatively independent journals in the People's Republic.

Wrocław is rightly seen as one of Poland's most attractive cities. It has a picturesque Market Square that bustles with activity until late into the night. Beyond the surrounding maze of medieval streets lies the ecclesiastical centre of Ostrów Tumski and Piaskowy—an enclave of silence amid the roar of the city—with its grand churches and peaceful atmosphere. Neglected and underfunded for decades, Wrocław's Old Town was lavishly renovated in preparation for the

World Eucharistic Congress and the Pope's visit in 1997. A few weeks later all this painstaking work was nearly destroyed when, after unprecedented rains, the Odra river flooded town after town in Lower Silesia, eventually reaching Wrocław. The historic centre was saved by volunteers, who, during the critical hours, lined the riverbank with makeshift barricades. The suburbs, however, as well as many other Silesian towns, were not so lucky, and a government-sponsored rebuilding programme is still under way.

Walks around the city

Wrocław's best sights lie within walking distance of the Main Market Square (described in **walk 1**). **Walk 2** explores the Old Town to the north and east of the square, except for the islands of Ostrów Tumski and Piaskowy, which are covered in **walk 3**. **Walk 4** goes south of the square to the leafy New Town and returns to it via the western part of the Old Town.

■ Practical information

Hotels
★★★★

Orbis-Wrocław. Ul. Powstańców Śląskich 5/7, ☎ 61-46-51. Highly recommended, very modern and comfortable, not far from the Old Town. Air conditioning, Business Centre, car rental, storeyed parking, petrol station, car wash, indoor swimming pool. 291 rooms.

Orbis-Panorama. Pl. Dominikański 8, ☎ 44-36-81. Older and smaller than Orbis-Wrocław, and not quite the same standard. Located in the city centre. 110 rooms.

Orbis-Novotel. Ul. Wyścigowa 35, ☎ 67-50-51/9. Out of town location. Wheelchair access, car rental, car park, outdoor swimming pool, business services. 145 rooms overlooking a park.

Dwór Wazów. Ul. Kiełbaśnicza 2, ☎ 72-34-15. Stylish, rather pricy, but a good, central location. Car rental, car park. 28 rooms.

★★★

Hotel Zaulek. Ul. Odrzańska 18a (entrance from ul. Garbary), ☎ 40-29-45. Small and quiet, excellent central location, but often fully booked. 12 rooms.

Orbis-Motel. Ul. Lotnicza 151, ☎ 51-81-53. Out of town location. Wheelchair access, car park. 76 rooms overlooking the garden.

Orbis-Monopol. Ul. Modrzejewskiej 2, ☎ 343-7041/9. Art Nouveau building in the city centre. Car park. 71 rooms overlooking the Opera House.

Restaurants

Exclusive

Belle Epoque, Rynek 20/21. International.

La Scala, Rynek 38. Italian.

Spiż, Rynek-Ratusz 9. European.

Medium-priced

Guiness, pl. Solny 5. Irish pub and restaurant.

Pastelowa, ul. Ruska. Crêpes, galletes.

U Szwejka, ul. Odrzańska 17. Czech.

Academia Brasserie, ul. Kuźnicza 65/66. International (mostly French).

Medium-priced
Zaułek, ul. Ordrzańska 18a (inside the Zaułek Hotel). International.
Piwnica Pod Złotym Psem, Rynek 41. International.
Wratislava, ul. Kiełbaśnicza 20 (inside the Art Hotel). Polish, Italian.
Królewska, Rynek 5 (owned by the Dwór Polski Hotel). Polish.
Karczma Piastów, ul. Kiełbaśnicza 7 (owned by the Dwór Polski Hotel). Polish.
Armine, ul. Bogusławskiego 83. Armenian.
Da-Lat, ul. Piłsudskiego 74. Vietnamese.
Royal Ginseng, pl. Hirszfelda 16/17. Chinese.
Sajgon, ul. Wita Stwosza 22/23 (inside the Saigon Hotel). Vietnamese.

Splendido, ul. Świdnicka 53. Italian.
Tutti-Frutti, ul. Świdnicka 41. European.

Cheap eateries
Vega (vegetarian), Rynek-Ratusz 27a. (The best milk bar in town).
Bar Wzorcowy, ul. Piłsudskiego 86.
Bar Miś, ul. Kuźnicza 48.
Bar Jacek i Agatka, pl. Nowy Targ 27.
Bar Krab, pl. 1 Maja (fish and chips).

Cafés
Kawiarnia Czwartkowa, Rynek 5 (owned by the Dwór Polski Hotel).
Pożegnanie z Afryką, ul. Igielna 16.
Pod Kalamburem, ul. Kuźnicza 29a.
Uni, pl. Uniwersytecki 11 (Wrocław university café).
Pod Gryfami, Rynek 2.

Savoy. Pl. Kościuszki 19, ☎ 40-32-19. Quiet, central location. 34 rooms.
Tourist Information (PAPT). Rynek 14, ☎ 44-31-11 (open Mon–Fri 09.00–17.00, Sat 10.00–16.00).
ORBIS. Rynek 29, ☎ 44-41-09 (air tickets, hotel reservations), ☎ 44-44-08 (train, coach and ferry tickets), ☎ 343-2665 (international travel), ☎ 343-4780 (domestic travel).
Main railway station. (Wrocław Główny) ul. Piłsudskiego 105, ☎ 343-6031 (train information). The Market Square (Rynek) is a 10 minute walk north.
Main coach station. Ul. Sucha, ☎ 61-81-22 (coach information). Close to the main railway station.

Airport. Starachowice, ul. Skarżyńskiego 36 (10km from the city centre) ☎ 358-1100/57-07-34
LOT. Ul. Skarżyńskiego 36 (airport), ☎ 358-1202. Flight information ☎ 952.
Disabled travellers. Taxi Serc runs a transport service for disabled travellers ☎ 363-3737. A trip costs 4.20 PLN + 0.70 PLN per 1km. Sundays and holidays 50% more. The office takes calls 24 hours. For information, contact the Wrocław Information Centre for the Disabled, ul. Włodkowica 8, ☎ 44-17-34.

Main post office. ul. Krasińskiego 1. Telex, fax, poste restante, and 24-hour telephone service.
Telephone code: (0–71).
Taxis. ☎ 919.
Lost property. For property lost on trams and buses, ☎ 21-58-92; for property lost on trains, ☎ 68-53-28.

Major festivals. 'Jazz on the Odra' (**May**); 'Wratislavia Cantans' International Festival (**June**); Wrocław Summer Organ Music Festival (**June–August**); International Puppet Theatre Festival (**October**); Chantey and Folk Music Festival (**December**).

History

Evidence of a human settlement in Wrocław dates from the early Stone Age (2500–1700 BC), but the first written record of the city is from 1000 AD, when a bishopric belonging to the See of Gniezno was founded. The settlement originally occupied what later came to be known as Ostrów Tumski—'Cathedral Island'—and another island, Ostrów Piaskowy. Following an invasion by the Czech prince Bretislav (1005?–1055) in 1039, a new town was built by **Kazimierz the Restorer**.

During the 12C, the city centre moved to the left bank of Odra in response to shifting trade routes, and soon the Market Square, with a typical medieval grid of streets appeared. Religious architecture flourished, though the only surviving example of this period is the portal from the Benedictine monastery in Olbin, which has lodged in Wrocław's church of St Magdalene since the 16C (see p. 436).

Henryk the Bearded, who reigned in Wrocław at the beginning of the 13C, thoroughly modernised the city and its institutions, greatly contributing to its economic prosperity, and strengthening its links to West European trade and culture. The Tartar invasion of 1241 did not interrupt the growth of the city, which, by the mid-14C, had 13,000 inhabitants, many of whom were settlers arriving to engage in crafts and trade: Jews, Germans, Dutch and French.

In 1335 Wrocław came under the rule of the **Luxembourg dynasty**, and the German burghers slowly gained supremacy. This was a time of social and ethnic conflict, exacerbated by a major fire in 1342. In 1339, the **Apprentices' Rebellion** broke out; four years later, weavers tried to resist the authority of the City Council; and in 1349, a *pogrom* drove the Jews out of town. The most violent events took place in 1418, when the mob stormed the Town Hall and lynched seven members of the Council. The first half of the 15C was also marked by religious strife, with the patriciate fiercely opposing the Hussites and refusing to acknowledge the Czech king, Jiři of Podebrad, himself a Hussite.

Under Habsburg rule

The early 16C was marked by the onset of the **Reformation**, which reached Wrocław during a brief interlude of Jagiellon rule in the city (1490–1526) and continued to exert powerful influence on the population despite the Counter Reformation backlash. The latter was supported by the Austrian Habsburgs, who ruled the city for 200 years following the death of Ludwik the Jagiellon in 1526.

Despite the political vicissitudes, economic links with Poland remained strong, and were mostly dominated by the export of handicrafts, and the import of food, raw materials and salt. Burghers had to know Polish, and even if the language did not thrive, it was certainly here to stay. The earliest print containing Polish text—traditional prayers included in *Status Synodalia episcoporum Wratislaviensium*, a church document—was published in Wrocław by Kacper Elyan in 1475. Numerous Polish-German dictionaries and textbooks appeared; the first newspaper started circulation in 1622. In religious architecture, Baroque was predominant, with ideas permeating from Catholic Vienna and Prague. Unlike Gothic and Renaissance architecture, Baroque buildings survived fairly well into the modern period, and even today they largely determine the overall look of the Old Town. The ruined castle on the left bank of Odra passed to the Jesuits, who erected the Church of the Holy Name of Jesus and the Jesuit Academy (never completed). In the late 17C, the Monastery of the Knights Hospitallers of the Red Star arose nearby. Many burghers' houses were also rebuilt in the Baroque style, and several magnificent palaces went up.

These were times of relative peace, interrupted only by the **Thirty Years War** (1618–48) which greatly depopulated Wrocław (mostly because of plagues), prompting the construction of new fortifications. Dutch-style earth ramparts proved cheaper than the earlier Italian-style brick walls, and a new ring of Dutch defences was raised at the end of the 17C.

Under Prussian rule

Austrian rule over the city was brought to an end in 1741 by the army of **Frederick the Great**. Wrocław's fate was sealed in 1763 with the signing of the Treaty of Hubertsburg, which gave Prussia a large part of Silesia. The appearance of a new building on the Market Square—the Guardhouse—and the conversion of the Academy into a barracks, were ominous and poignant signs of the new times. Any traces of autonomy were wiped out, and Germanisation became ever more aggressive. But rather than eradicate Polish language and culture, it only nurtured hatred towards the Germans. Unsurprisingly, Napoleon's army received an enthusiastic welcome in 1807. The French did not hold out for long in Wrocław—in fact, by 1808, the city had already become a major centre of anti-Napoleonic opposition—but they left a lasting legacy: on Napoleon's orders, and with the eager cooperation of Wrocławians, the Prussian fortifications were dismantled with a thoroughness that today may seem regrettable. Parks and promenades replaced the former moats and ramparts, and all the medieval gates were pulled down in the process.

New currents in architecture appeared towards the end of the 18C. The most prominent architect was Carl Gotthard Langhans, whose Neoclassical edifices significantly changed the city's appearance. However, the greatest changes occurred during the second half of the 19C, especially after France had paid reparations to Prussia after the war of 1870. The money fuelled the Prussian economy, leading to the demolition of many historic buildings in the Old Town to make room for offices and shops. Neoclassicism was superseded by Romantic currents and the Jugendstil which dominated the fin-de-siècle period. In 1842 citizens celebrated the departure of the first passenger train in Silesia, and soon the city's train station, Wrocław Główny, designed in 1856 by W. Grapow and later rebuilt in English Neo-Gothic, became one of the busiest in Europe.

The First and Second World Wars

The First World War had little impact on life in Wrocław, and after 1918 it quickly rose to prominence as one of Germany's largest and most densely populated cities. During the **Second World War** it was spared major damage until the very last stage, when the Nazis turned it into a stronghold ('Festung Breslau'), to be defended at all costs. Indeed, it capitulated four days after Berlin, but before that it was turned into a smoldering mass of rubble. It was the second most damaged city in post-war Poland (after Warsaw). Its population also changed dramatically. The new borders delineated for Poland by Churchill, Roosevelt and Stalin left Lwów—one of Poland's major cities during the inter-war period—outside Polish territory. Now Wrocław, from which thousands of Germans were forcibly expelled, was resettled with Lwowians who had suffered an analogous fate. Thus, Wrocław became the most 'eastern' of Polish cities, and even today the soft, melodious accent of Eastern Galicia is not at all uncommon here.

Under Communist rule

In 1980 the city became an important Solidarity stronghold, but it was really after the imposition of Martial Law in 1981 that it gained a reputation for fierce anti-Communist resistance, which sometimes took on highly original forms. The 'Orange Alternative' succeeded in elevating political demonstrations to the status of art. On one occasion, in a mock-celebration of the 70th anniversary of the October Revolution, actors dressed up as Lenin, Trotsky, Stalin and other heroes of 1917, marched up and down ul. Grabiszyńska amid torrents of abuse from the onlooking crowd. The police were at a loss what to do: who would have dared to strike Lenin with a truncheon, let alone arrest him? But to condone the audacious pranks would have been equally unacceptable.

Walk One ~ The Market Square

The walk takes you round Wrocław's Main Market Square. It is the second largest market square in Poland, yet it has nothing of the vastness of its Cracovian counterpart, its centre being occupied by a large group of buildings cut across by three streets: the Ironmongers', Cloth Merchants' and Potware Sellers' Passages.

The Town Hall

Certainly the most ambitious building on the square is the **Town Hall.

The first written record of the Town Hall dates back to 1299. Its predecessor—the single-storey *Domus Mercatorum*, or a Merchant House—was already used as a municipal seat, and boasted a tower. The Officials' Chamber and Councillors' Chamber were added at the turn of the 13C, followed by an upper storey and ornamental vaults, particularly in the Officials' Chamber, to reflect the growing prosperity and importance of the Silesian capital. The originally double-naved building received the south nave with its characteristic oriels and decoration at the turn of the 15C.

At the end of the 19C various Neo-Gothic elements were introduced, and parts of the painted decoration were removed. Though hit by a bomb in 1945, the building survived relatively intact, preserving the original Gothic-Renaissance form one sees today.

Gables subdivide the **east façade** into three parts, each suggestive of a different period in the Town Hall's history. The oldest part (14C), with characteristic early

Gothic pointed arch windows on the ground floor and ogee windows above, adjoins the Cloth Hall to the right. The brickwork is patterned in the so-called 'Polish style'. A triangular gable adorned with 4 m high pinnacles and filled with tracery rises above the middle part of the façade. Below is a **sundial** (1580) with symbols of the Sun, Moon and seasons of the year. Lower still is the chapel oriel, flanked by windows with tracery. Small, quaint sculptures—two heads, a bitch with her puppy—sit on the windowsills. The leftmost and earliest part of the east façade has an intricately carved oriel of white stone. The portal (1328) is the oldest Gothic portal in Wrocław. By the stairs is a slab (1492) which shows in relief a town messenger holding a scroll.

The Gothic-Renaissance **south façade** is subdivided by three oriels. Here the richness of stone decoration is quite

Town hall

striking: on the first floor, the window heads have pinnacles and ogee arches bearing coats of arms; between the windows, resting on consoles, are sculptures of burghers, craftsmen, a monk, a nobleman etc. Two carved **friezes** further amplify the visual effect. The one over the first floor depicts St George fighting the dragon, and jousts between representatives of the various estates; the one above the ground floor shows more mundane activities: a fist-fight, a game of draughts, beer-drinking, music-making and other pastimes favoured by the burghers. Lower still, just above the entrance to the Świdnica Cellar are two sculptures: a drunken apprentice raising a wine pitcher, and a woman (the master's wife perhaps) brandishing a slipper. The cellar, which is mentioned as early as 1331, still serves its original function (a wine bar).

The **west façade** is the most austere. To the left rises the tower bearing four clock faces with gilded hands and digits. The first **mechanical clock**, the oldest in Poland, was installed here in 1368—earlier than in Kraków, Prague or Gdańsk. A handsome Renaissance two-tiered crowning completes the tower.

The **Historical Museum of the City of Wrocław** (open Tues, Wed, Fri, 10.00–16.00, Sat–Sun 10.00–17.00) occupies the ground and first floors of the Town Hall. First comes the spacious twin-aisled **Burghers' Hall**, subdivided by pillars. It used to house merchant stalls, but has since been rebuilt many times. At present, it is mainly used for temporary exhibitions. East of the Burghers' Hall is the **Officials' Chamber**, built in 1299 and star-vaulted in 1450–60. The court would assemble here, with the jury sitting on the raised pedestal to the left.

The Mannerist portal in the south wall (right) leads to the **Green Room**. On the opposite wall is one of Wrocław's oldest Renaissance portals, made in 1528 *ex voto* Henryk Rybisch. Continue to the **Councillors' Chamber** which dates from 1328. A Baroque stove, remnants of Renaissance painted decoration, and two paintings—*Paradise* and *Flight from Egypt*—by Michael Willmann

(1630–1704) are all that remain of this once splendid hall. A gruesome story is connected with a small wooden door in the southwest corner; rebels broke through it and into the room during a violent uprising in 1418, slaughtering seven councillors. The next room—the **Municipal Scribe's Office**—is entered through a late Gothic carved portal (1428). Here, the late Gothic net vaults (c 1490) have nine painted bosses ornamented with motifs borrowed from the Wrocław coat of arms.

First floor. The ***Refectory**—the largest and most exquisite room—consists of three aisles separated by arcades. The north and middle aisles were built in the 14C, with the south aisle and vaults being added a century later. They are adorned with uncommonly rich, imaginative, and often fanciful **bosses** and corbels. Equally impressive is the **oriel** adjoining the south aisle; its entrance is guarded by two monkeys and knights clad in plate-mail armour. In the tympanum of the east wall portal, two burly savages with an abundance of body hair support the coat of arms of the Hungarian King Matthias Corvinus. The square, star-vaulted room is distinguished by its pretty wainscotting of ash and oak (reconstructed in 1934–35; only the wardrobe door, to the right of entrance, is original). The large painting (1668) hanging on the east wall shows the Councillors' Chamber as it looked centuries ago, with all the stern councillors and jurors assembled. Pass through the repoussé door on the right to the **Council Elders' Chamber**, which contains silverware, including ceremonial sceptres of the Wrocław Academy. The next room (1450) and adjoining oriel used to serve as the **Town Treasury**. They now contain an exhibition of coins and coin-minting tools. North of the Treasury is the Prince's Room (1345), reached through a late Gothic portal of 1490. The oldest portal (1357) leads to the refectory; over its pointed arch is a tympanum with elements taken from the Wrocław coat of arms.

West of the Town Hall, opposite the museum entrance stands a **statue of Aleksander Fredro** (see p. 84), with the playwright seated on a simple plinth. It was carved by Leonard Marconi in 1897 and unveiled in Lwów, where Fredro died in 1876. In 1956 the Soviet authorities returned it to Poland, and it was only natural to bring it to Wrocław where many natives of Lwów were resettled after the war. Fredro's monument is shaded by a tall poplar planted by the Mayors of Wrocław and Brno as a token of Polish-Czechoslovak friendship. On its southeast side stands a copy of a 15C **Pillory**.

Directly adjoining the Town Hall is a cluster of buildings in various architectural styles, ranging from Renaissance to Modernism, with three passageways cutting through. Go down the **Cloth Merchants' Passage** (nearest the Town Hall). Jerzy Grotowski's famous experimental theatre used to occupy the building at **No. 27**. After the theatre's closure in 1984, a centre devoted to the study of Grotowski's work was opened here.

Around the square

A tour of the square is best begun in its northwest corner, where you will notice the unmistakable **Jaś and Małgosia** (Johnny and Mary), two miniature houses, whose toy-like appearance is heightened against the background of the huge, imposing mass of St Elizabeth's Church (see p. 444). They are the only surviving Altarists' Houses, which used to stand in the church graveyard to provide accommodation for sextons employed at St Elizabeth's. Built in the 16C and 17C respectively, they are connected by a late Baroque arched gate (1728) with putti supporting a medallion, which bears the Latin inscription '*Mors ianua vitae*' ('Death is the gate to life'). The inscription was carved to commemorate the dramatic events of 1418, when, in the aftermath of a ruthlessly crushed guild rebellion, the leaders were executed and their bodies thrown into the passage for people to tread upon. A café, conveniently located in the cellar of Małgosia, allows the philosophically-inclined tourist to ponder the meaning of life and death over a glass of Coca-Cola.

North side

Along the north side of the square, the house at **No. 58** (1905), currently a public library, is remarkable for its single-pillar hall and a curious, macabre mural which covers the ceiling. At **No. 52** a passage leads through to ul. Więzienna (Prison Street), where a pleasant surprise awaits you at **No. 6**: behind the arched gate lies a charming cobbled courtyard overlooked by wooden galleries on its east side (reconstructed in the 1970s) and shaded by a large ash tree. The sturdy Gothic brick building served appropriately as the city prison after the Town Hall proved too small to accommodate a rapidly growing clientele. Currently, it houses the Institute of Archaeology and Ethnology of the Polish Academy of Sciences.

Back in the Market Square, a reconstructed Baroque house at **No. 51** is distinguished by a pretty cream-coloured sandstone portal replete with subtle floral motifs. The **Golden Deer House** (No. 44), named after the sculpture above the portal, was formerly a pharmacy. In the hall, a stone tablet (1624) with a Latin inscription has been preserved.

East side

No. 32 at the corner of Kurzy Targ (Poultry Market) is a large fin-de-siècle house (1904) with a light sandstone façade and a peculiar copper dome surmounted by a balustrade. At No. 30, the **Old Town Hall** has a rusticated façade with Ionic pillars and carved window heads. The name is somewhat misleading, as the original 13C building, indeed used by the municipal authorities, was replaced in 1714 by an inn. The latter, which received its present form in 1904, was patronised by many celebrated guests, among them Poland's Saxon rulers of the 17C–18C, *en route* between Dresden and Warsaw. The **Golden Crown House** at No. 29 derives its name from an object resembling a crown, attached to the corner. Originally the plot was occupied by an Italian Renaissance house (c 1521–28), which had the oldest parapet in Silesia. It was almost completely destroyed in 1945, and has been partly reconstructed since.

South side

This suffered severe damage during the Second World War. Beyond an elaborately carved portal with floral decoration and the date 1689 is the *Belle Epoque* restaurant. The **Gallows House** (No. 19), owes its name to the gallows that once stood in front of it. The ground and first floors accommodate the *Herbowa* tea-room. It has an even more ornate portal with Corinthian fluted columns

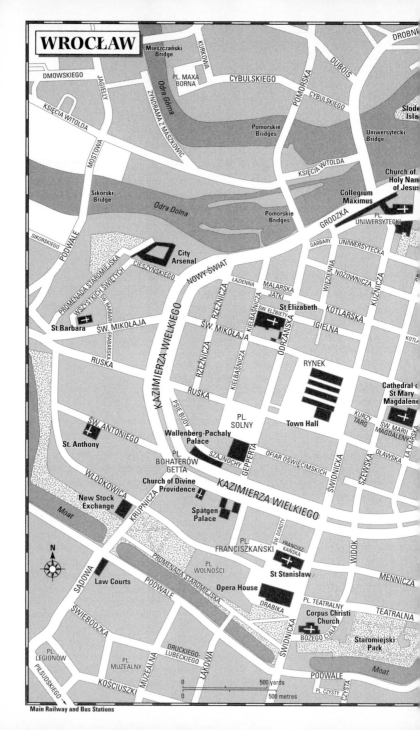

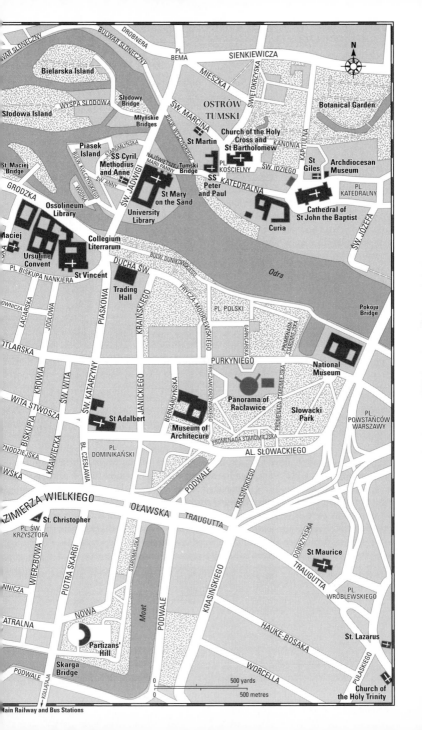

supporting a pediment, a coat of arms and, below, reliefs of a naked couple. **No. 16** has a stylish Gothic wine cellar (*Bacchus*), in which 13C pillars have been preserved. **No. 13** is an Art Nouveau building of 1903, faced with sandstone and adorned with sculptures. The second-floor balcony, which imitates a sea-shell, is flanked by two sculptures of children holding an anchor and a hammer.

West side

The west side suffered least damage in 1945. On the corner stands a tall, rein-forced-concrete office building erected in 1930–31. No. 8, next door, is the **Seven Electors' House**, whose façade is covered with illusionist painted deco-ration and fragments of 17C murals depicting emperor Leopold I and the Arch-dukes-Electors. It was originally built in the 13C, and still has preserved 14C–15C fragments. In the **House of the Golden Sun** (No. 6) is the Museum of Medal Engraving (**open** Wed–Sun 10.00–17.00) with an extensive collection of coins and medals. The museum occasionally stages classical concerts. The rich portal, with undulating lines and relief floral decoration, was commis-sioned in 1727 by Karol Exner, who rebuilt the house in Baroque style. **No. 5**, with a simple sandstone portal and stuccoed window surrounds, houses a mead and wine cellar, as well as a café. The **Golden Eagle House** at No. 4 has two interesting portals: an early 18C Baroque one outside, and another one inside, in the Gothic style. The pretty Renaissance portal leading to the neighbouring house at **No. 3** was made in 1580. The most impressive building on the Market Square is the **Griffin House** (No. 2), a sumptuous Dutch Mannerist residence built by Friedrich Gross and Gerhard Hendrik in 1587–89. Over the elaborately reliefed portal with fluted columns and niches are two coats of arms. The tall gable is decorated symmetrically with lions, griffins, eagles and pelicans. The house has an inner courtyard surrounded by a gallery.

Following the west side of the Rynek towards the John Bull Pub on the corner, you will reach the adjoining **Salt Market**.

Now mostly a flower market, this adjunct to the Main Market Square, founded in 1242, was used for selling salt, wax, honey, furs, leather goods and other commodities imported from Małopolska (hence its original name of Polish Market, later changed to Salt Market). It was here in 1453 that crowds were driven to religious frenzy by the sermons of St John Capistrano. The last salt stalls were removed in 1815; soon the market was renamed Gebhard Blücher Platz and received a statue of the eponymous Prussian general, which survived until 1945.

The largest building on the Salt Market is the Neo-classical **Old Stock Exchange** (No. 16), built by Carl Ferdinand Langhans in 1822–24. Its centre is dominated by a large portal with a portico supported on massive fluted Corinthian columns. Above it rises a tri-partite window topped by figures of two seated females and a coat of arms. The mezzanine windows above the rusticated ground floor are interspersed with garlands, additionally decorated with eagles on the east side (facing ul. Gepperta). Nearby, at ul. Ofiar Oświęcimskich No. 1, stands the **Rybisch House**, whose splendid Renaissance portal (c 1531) has a lion in a niche supporting a coat of arms, and—in the upper part of the columns—curious reliefs showing women giving birth.

Walk Two ~ The University Quarter

The area north and east of the market square is designated here as the University quarter, although in fact it includes many more sights than just the University buildings. The walk includes the showpiece Aula Leopoldina, but also the superb National Museum, the rotunda housing the famous *Panorama of Racławice*, and several fine churches.

Take UL. KUŹNICZA from the northeast corner of the Market Square. In the Middle Ages this street seethed with activity as craftsmen's workshops spilled out onto the pavement. Several smithies at the far end catered to the needs of itinerant merchants, while the merchants themselves found shelter at one of the street's many inns and hostels.

Passing the gabled 18C **Silver Helmet House** at No. 12 (right), with Rococo garlands and sculpted panoplies, and the **Golden Sceptre Inn** at No. 22 (left), you will arrive at the **Steffens House** (No. 33), erected for the Jesuits in 1734–35, and now housing the University's Department of Anthropology. The pleasant courtyard has two fountains, a miniature labyrinth and a Baroque statue of St Catherine, the patron of philosophers. On weekdays, visitors are allowed into the Refectory, which has sumptuous Baroque stuccoes, with more in the corridors.

Ul. Kuźnicza is closed off by the **Church of the Holy Name of Jesus** (also known as the University Church, or Church of St Maciej), which is **open** daily 07.00–09.00 and 17.00–19.00 (if you are with a group of more than 15 people, ask for the key at the priory on pl. Nankiera 17). The interior, designed by Krzysztof Tausch (1673–1731), is a model of Baroque sophistication. In contrast to most Wrocław churches, the walls are almost entirely covered with rich, superabundant decoration. The Viennese painter J. M. Rottmayr, famed for his murals in Melk (Austria) and Vranov (Moravia), was responsible for the illusionist painting on the vaults (1703–06). The high altar, designed by Tausch in 1722–24, fills the apse at the end of a short chancel.

The Collegium Maximus

To the west of the church stands the main University building, the Collegium Maximus.

> In the late 12C, when Ostrów Tumski ('Cathedral Island') lost its importance and the left bank of the Odra became the new town centre, the Silesian dukes erected a castle roughly on the site of today's University. It fell into decline with the end of Piast rule in Wrocław, and was turned over in 1659 to the Jesuits, who opened a college there. The castle soon proved inadequate for the society's growing needs, and was pulled down (the only remnant is the present sacristy). At the turn of the 17C, the Church of the Holy Name of Jesus was erected on the site, followed by a new Baroque edifice in 1728–42 (after the College had been promoted to the rank of Academy).
>
> The Academy survived the dissolution of the Jesuit order in 1773, but its religious status changed in 1811, when the Prussian King Frederick William III ordered the closure of the university in Frankfurt on the Oder, and the transfer of its three faculties—Protestant Theology, Medicine and Law—to Wrocław, which thus became a major centre of German Letters.

The ascent of Nazism effectively wiped out the University: research was sacrificed to ideology, Jewish professors were expelled, students were selected on racial criteria. Collegium Maximus itself suffered a direct bomb hit in 1945. The first post-war rector was brought in from the University of Lwów; most of the staff also came from Lwów (including the world-famous mathematician Hugo Steinhaus), as well as from Wilno, Warsaw and Kraków.

Viewed from pl. Uniwersytecki, Collegium Maximus looks cramped: the enormous length of the façade and the narrowness of the street are somehow incongruous. It is better seen from the other side, from the far bank of the Odra. The Mathematical Tower, tiny against the bulky edifice, rises above the roof and a raised terrace. In the corners stand allegorical sculptures by Franz Josef Mangoldt (1753) depicting Astronomy, Medicine, Theology and Law. Other figures, by J. A. Siegwitz (1736), representing Justice, Wisdom, Courage and Restraint adorn the main entrance (from pl. Uniwersytecki). The staircase, stuccoed and painted in 1734, leads upstairs through a richly carved oak door to the renowned ***Aula Leopoldina**, named after emperor Leopold I. Its magnificent sculptural and painted decoration is rightly held up as the finest example of Baroque in Wrocław. The low ceiling over the trapezoid room is made to look higher by J. K. Handke's illusionist painting (1732), which shows allegories of the academic disciplines, as well as Evangelists and Fathers of the Church. The fine stuccoes are the work of J. Provisone. Around the room hang paintings in gilded oval frames depicting various benefactors of the University. Window jambs bear the portraits of great philosophers, scientists and prophets of the past. An effigy of emperor Leopold I, the founder of the Jesuit Academy, sits on a throne just below the ceiling at the far end of the room, surrounded by allegorical figures. The gallery—actually the musicians' choir—at the back of the room, bears the crest of Count Schaffgotsch, the starost of Silesia.

Leaving allegorical stone sculptures of the four seasons on PL. UNIWERSYTECKI, and passing H. Lederer's statue of a *Fencer* (1904), go towards Tamka Island to get a good view of the **Ossolineum Library**, whose two convex gables at the west and east ends are connected by a balustraded wall with a dome in the middle. Originally a monastery of the Knights Hospitallers of the Red Star (1675–1715), it now houses the Ossoliński library, founded in 1817 in Lwów by Count Józef Maksimilian Ossoliński. The library has a valuable collection of manuscripts, old prints, etchings and drawings. The entrance on ul. Szewska leads through to an inner courtyard shaded by a chestnut tree, its walls overgrown with vine, and wide arched windows on the ground floor. The quiet charm of the place attracts art students, who often come here to practise sketching and watercolour.

You might take a detour to the University's **Geological Museum** (open Mon–Fri 10.00–15.00), which has one of the richest collections of minerals in Europe (though only a small part is displayed to visitors). To get there cross the Uniwersytecki Bridge, turn left into UL. CYBULSKIEGO and continue to PL. MAXA BORNA.

Alternatively, continue south along ul. Szewska to the **Church of St Maciej**, built by the Knights Hospitallers of the Red Star in the second half of the 13C. South of the church, guarded by two chestnut trees, is a **statue of St John Nepomuk** (1713).

Turn left into UL. NANKIERA. No. 16 (left) is the **Ursuline Convent** (currently housing a girls' secondary school and a University dormitory). You may have to ask the reception for admittance to the adjoining **Church of St Clare**.

> After the death of Henryk the Pious in the disastrous battle of Legnica (see p. 467), his widow decided to found a convent in Wrocław. She invited the Nuns of St Clare from her home city of Prague in 1257, and began construction of a brick convent and church, which was consecrated three years later. Soon it was enlarged with the addition of the Chapel of St Jadwiga to the south, where, in the late 14C, the tomb of Henryk VI Probus was placed. In the late 17C, Jan K. Knoll extensively remodelled both the convent and church in Baroque style. The nave, however, was so badly damaged in 1945 that its Baroque layer had to be stripped, revealing the Gothic remnants beneath (now partly reconstructed).

Under a low, reinforced-concrete ceiling covering the nave stands Henryk VI's tomb with a reclining figure (c 1350) of the king. Embedded in the walls are epitaph slabs of other Piasts from Wrocław and Opole. The best is a mid-14C sandstone slab in the north wall to the Duchess Anna, which shows the Piast eagle surrounded by an inscription. The adjoining Chapel of St Jadwiga suffered less damage during the war and was restored in Baroque style, except for the Gothic east wall. Inside are 18C portraits of St Jadwiga and her husband Henryk the Pious, Duchess Anna, as well as Anna's crypt in the floor by the north wall. Opposite is another similar slab, marking the probable burial place of the Piast dukes. Above the entrance is a memorial to the Duchess Karolina, consisting of a silver urn adorned with eagles.

If you continue along ul. Nankiera, you come to the **Church of St Vincent**, built in 1240–70. Severely damaged in 1945, it lost nearly all its furniture and decoration, except for statues of saints by Jan Jerzy Urbański, which decorate the Hochberg Chapel.

Across the street stands the late Romanesque **House of the Nuns of Trzebnica**, discovered in 1959. It once served as residence for the abbesses of the Cistercian abbey in Trzebnica (see p. 445) visiting the city. Integrated in a peculiar fashion with an ugly modern block of flats, and visible behind large windows, are fragments of wall several metres below ground level. The concrete box protecting the walls is also used as a photography gallery.

Adjoining the Church of St Vincent to the northeast is the **Collegium Literrarum**, a former Premonstratensian monastery. Originally Gothic, it was rebuilt in 1682–95 in early Baroque style. It has an untidy inner courtyard surrounded by pedimented windows with rather crude decorative window heads.

Crossing the busy ul. Piaskowa you will come to the **Trading Hall**, built by R. Plüddemann in 1908 on the site of a former arsenal (hence the cannon balls set into the façade). Through an ornamental stone portal you enter a spacious hall, lit by what in a basilican church would be the clerestory windows. The hall was renovated in 1983 and presently serves as Wrocław's main shopping centre, with well-stocked fruit and vegetable stalls. Passing through the hall you emerge onto UL. KRAIŃSKIEGO. Turn right to view remnants of the **medieval walls** with a squat brick tower, and then return to the river. Walking along XAWERY DUNIKOWSKI BOULEVARD, look back on the north façade of the Trading Hall with its towers and gables, and across the Odra to Ostrów Tumski and Piaskowy, with the twin spires of the Cathedral (see p. 439), the large white building of the University Library (see p. 437) partly concealing the Church of St Mary (see p. 438), and the steep roof of the Holy Cross Church (see p. 438), with a row of flamboyant little gables.

National Museum

The excellent *National Museum (**open** Tues, Wed, Fri–Sun 10.00–16.00, Thur 09.00–16.00) is along the boulevard past the Polish Hill (see below). Statues of Albrecht Dürer and Michelangelo Buonarroti (1881–82) guard the entrance to the Neo-Renaissance building. Unlike many museums in Poland, this one is run in a modern, tourist-friendly way. A tiny café, well-stocked bookshop, and comfortable armchairs amidst potted plants, contribute to the pleasant and relaxed atmosphere of the place. There is also a small concert hall in the inner courtyard with a gallery below a glass roof. The rooms on the **ground floor** display Silesian stone sculpture, a tomb slab of Duke Bolesław III from Lubiąż (1352), a 12C tympanum from the Ołbin monastery (see p. 436), the sarcophagus of Henryk Probus (1300), and a memorial slab of Henryk the Pious, with the king shown resting his feet against a cowering Tartar (in fact, the Tartars convincingly defeated Henryk the Pious at the battle of Legnica in 1241). Among the exhibits displayed on the **first floor** are 16C paintings moved here from Wrocław churches, a portrait of **Martin Luther** by Lucas Cranach (1540), several paintings by the greatest Silesian artist of the Baroque period, Michael Willmann (1630–1712), and extraordinary larger-than-life wooden sculptures of saints by Thomas Weissfeldt (1630–1712), a Norwegian-born artist who greatly influenced Silesian Baroque sculpture of the early 18C. The **second floor** contains modern Polish art, with works by Chwistek, Makowski, Witkacy, Brzozowski, Jarema, Tchórzewski, Lebenstein, Kantor, Hasior and Abakanowicz.

South of the National Museum rises the Polish Hill, opposite which stands a rotunda with the ***Panorama of Racławice**, a curious 19C attempt at virtual reality.

> The idea was put forward by Jan Styka, a third-rate painter, but an indefatigable organiser, always on the lookout for opportunities to capture the public's attention. Panoramas, so popular in the 19C, became his main genre, and he travelled around the world soliciting orders. The *Panorama of Racławice* was perhaps his most successful project, largely because he managed to win the cooperation of a decent battle-scene painter, Wojciech Kossak, the son of Juliusz, and because the subject-matter was so laden with themes of national glory (see p. 51). It took the artists nine months to cover over 1700 square metres of canvas with realistic imagery, and on 5 June, 1894, the work was put on display in a specially constructed rotunda in Lwów. It was an immediate and resounding success. The investment was quickly paid off and this precursor of modern cinema was even bringing profits to the city until the outbreak of the First World War. Slightly damaged, it was restored by Kossak himself in the late 1920s. During the Second World War it was damaged more seriously and spirited away by the Soviets, who had no intention of displaying such an 'anti-Russian' work, returning it to Poland in 1946. They advised the Polish authorities against

showing it to the public for fear that it might 'stir anti-Russian sentiment'. Eventually, the Gierek regime (1970–80) mustered up the courage to display it—neither in Kraków's Barbican, nor in Racławice, nor even in Warsaw, but in Wrocław. It took another five years to finalise the project, build the rotunda and hang the enormous painting inside.

Viewers are admitted to the rotunda in groups at set times (daily, every half-hour). Inside, as you ascend the winding staircase, you may think the weather has suddenly changed—so strong is the illusion afforded by the painted sunny sky and scattered clouds. You circle the rotunda along a special promenade, successively passing chronologically arranged scenes illustrating the progress of the five-hour battle that took place on 4 April 1794, near the village of Racławice.

From the Rotunda walk across JULIUSZ SŁOWACKI PARK, where a bronze **statue** of the great Romantic poet was unveiled in 1984. The former Dominican complex on the edge of the park and at the corner of PL. DOMINIKAŃSKI is now home to the **Museum of Architecture** (open Tues–Thur 10.00–15.30, Wed, Sat 10.00–16.00, Sun 10.00–17.00). The church is used as an exhibition hall, the vine-clad monastic building (No. 5) as offices.

> The Bernardine monastery was founded after 1453 by the Italian religious fanatic, St John Capistrano, following his enormous success in Wrocław as a preacher. A Gothic aisled basilica, with star and cross vaults and a south chapel, was consecrated in 1502, preceded by a monastic building of four wings surrounding an inner garden. In 1517 the south wing was extended, forming a second enclosed garden. The city council ordered the Bernardines to relinquish the monastery in 1522; a hospital was set up inside, while the church became Protestant. It went through the usual cycle of fires, renovation and remodelling, before suffering severe damage in 1945. During the 1960s and 1970s it was once again raised from a state of ruin, and turned into a Museum of Architecture.

Both the church and cloisters contain several permanent exhibitions, as well as temporary ones. The core of the collection consists of authentic fragments of buildings recovered in Wrocław during post-war conservation work—capitals, bosses, portals, window surrounds, stuccoes, stained-glass, stoves and floor tiles as well as documentation relating to Wrocław's architecture.

Continue west to pl. Dominikański. At the corner of ul. Św. Katarzyny stands the ***Church of St Adalbert**.

> The first church on this site was built before 1112 for the Augustinians, but nothing of it has survived. Its successor appeared in c 1226 with the arrival of the Dominicans led by Czesław Odrowąż from Kraków. During a Tartar siege in 1241, Odrowąż is said to have miraculously turned back the missiles hurled at the city by the enemy, thus saving it from total destruction. The Baroque **Chapel of Blessed Czesław** was built in 1711–18 to celebrate Odrowąż's beatification (a tablet commemorating the event is found in the south porch).

Viewed from the outside, the church is grim, almost black, and even the brick frieze and the west gable with its delicate moulding do not dispel this impression.

A slender octagonal tower with a sharp spire (a reconstruction) rises above the chancel. The massive transept looms over the domed Chapel of Blessed Czesław to the south. Red stained glass fills the interior of this chapel with a warm radiance, highlighting the alabaster sarcophagus, on which a cycle of reliefs narrates the life of Blessed Czesław. The pallor of J. L. Weber's sculptures contrasts with the blacks and grays of the marble finish. In the altar, the figures supporting the mensa represent Courage, Wisdom, Justice and Restraint. In between, the struggle against evil forces is shown through allegorical sculpture. An angel, kneeling and breaking the crescent, the symbol of Islam, is below the Blessed Czesław in a niche. Large paintings by J. F. de Backer of Antwerp, showing the patron of the chapel and his missionary work among the Tartars, hang on the east and west walls. The long chancel ends in an apse typical of Dominican architecture, with a rose window and stained glass.

Proceed along UL. WITA STWOSZA. At the corner of ul. Św. Wita (**Nos 33–35**) stands an Art Nouveau building (1889) (currently a bank). Across the street, the Neo-classical **Geissler House** (1802–4) has a twin-columned portico topped with a balcony, flanked by columns, and figures in relief in the tympanum. Formerly the Filippi winehouse, it is now a café, with a quaint spiral staircase. Further down the street is the former **Hatzfeld Palace** built by Carl Gotthard Langhans in 1765–75. The house is currently an art gallery.

Turning left into UL. ŁACIARSKA you will come to the **Cathedral of St Mary Magdalene**, whose walls are dotted with numerous memorial slabs. The single most precious item in this church, however, is the Romanesque portal in the south wall, one of the finest in central Europe.

> St Mary Magdalene's dates from the early 13C, when the Dominicans from Kraków (see above) took over the existing parish church of St Adalbert. Both the first edifice, as well as its much larger successor (after 1342), were sponsored by Wrocław burghers. Construction of the chancel, nave, aisles and towers took 20 years, and was supervised by Master Pieszko (d. 1371), who designed the unusual two-bay chancel ending in a square apse. In subsequent years, the church was remodelled several times (the towers in particular) and later became Protestant. Disaster struck in 1945, when the south tower split along its entire length, causing damage to the vaults and the west façade; a fire completely gutted the interior.

Exterior. Along the south wall, under a triangular gable, stands the famous sandstone ***portal**, brought here in c 1546 from the Benedictine monastery in Ołbin. It was carved in 1150–75, clearly under the influence of medieval French art. Floral, geometric and figural bas-reliefs adorn the columns and arches. Especially noteworthy are scenes from the life of Jesus on the archivolt. The tympanum, showing the *Dormition of the Virgin*, is in the National Museum (see p. 434).

Further west is another portal (Mannerist, 1578), with a pediment supported on Corinthian columns and shallow relief decoration. Of the many epitaphs, most striking perhaps is the 16C *Deposition* at the east end of the south wall.

Inside the church is a richly carved Mannerist stone pulpit (1579), a 16C font enclosed in a wrought-iron Baroque grille, a 15C polychromed stone tabernacle, many fragments of original Gothic stonework, and some good 15C–18C memorial slabs.

On the east side of the square is the former Hohenlohe palace, with a peculiar bulging façade decorated with two reliefs placed between the first and second floors.

Walk south along ul. Szewska to the junction with UL. OŁAWSKA. Before the war, the corner house was the famous **Petersdorf shop**, whose 'Expressionist' design, the work of Erich Mendelsohn (1927), must have seemed very avant-garde. Rows of windows make up horizontal brass-framed strips forming a curved projection at the corner, so full of dynamism it could almost be a tightly-wound spring.

Walk Three ~ Ostrów Tumski and Piaskowy

This walk leaves behind the hectic activity of the Market Square and university area, taking you across the river to Wrocław's enchanting ecclesiastical island, with its magnificent religious architecture.

The oldest traces of human settlement on Ostrów Tumski date from the 7C–8C. It must have been a convenient site: an island on the Odra river, sufficiently large and elevated to be safe from flooding, yet easy to fortify and defend. It also lay on the important south-north trade route from Moravia to the Baltic coast. Equipped in the 10C with earth-and-wood ramparts characteristic of the Slavonic tribes, its population grew to more than 2000 inhabitants in the following century.

After the momentous meeting in Gniezno between Emperor Otto III and King Bolesław the Brave (see p. 522) in 1000, Ostrów Tumski was decreed a bishopric. Growth was temporarily halted following an anti-Christian rebellion and the invasion of the Czech prince Bretislav in 1038–9. From 1257 onwards, Ostrów Tumski was gradually taken over by the church, the process reaching completion in 1439, when the castle formally became the property of the Chapter.

From the Main Market Square, walk north along ul. Szewska or ul. Kuźnicza, and then cross the PIASKOWY BRIDGE to Ostrów Piaskowy. In the mid-12C, the small island on the north-south trade route became the seat of the Order of Canons Regular, founded by Piotr Włostowic.

Piotr Włostowic, a palatine in the service of Bolesław the Wry-Mouthed and a man of fantastic wealth, was given to rashness and generosity in equal measure. He made his fortune in Denmark, and later during several successful campaigns against the Pomeranian cities. It is said that after he kidnapped the duke of Przemyśl, Włostowic was ordered by the bishop to build seven churches as penance. He vowed to erect a staggering seventy-seven, among them three in Wrocław. He died in 1153 and was buried in the Ołbin monastery.

Of the Romanesque basilica of St Mary, only fragments of granite foundations and the tympanum (c 1175) have survived. The monastic building south of the church is also long gone. Today, the spot is occupied by the Baroque building of the **University Library**, erected in the 18C and much damaged in 1945, when the Nazis set up the headquarters of 'Festung Breslau' ('Fortress Breslau') in the cellars.

From a pleasant courtyard shaded by trees you can observe the pointed arch windows with trefoil and quatrefoil tracery in the south wall of the **Church of

St Mary on the Sand. The construction of the church was continued after the death of its sponsor, Piotr Włostowic, by his widow and her son Świętosław. The pious woman is portrayed in the original sandstone **tympanum** (presently in the south aisle) showing a small model of the church to Mary and Jesus. In the north aisle is the kneeling figure of her son Świętosław. The church was not destined to survive for long, and by 1334 construction of a new Gothic hall had already begun. It took almost a hundred years to complete and over the centuries it accumulated rich decoration, most of which was destroyed in 1945.

The dominant mood of the **interior** is one of space and light, emphasised by the ribbed star vaults of the nave, resting on original corbels with remnants of painted decoration. Hanging high up on the pillars and facing the nave are figures of the Apostles. Gothic triptychs brought here from other Wrocław churches (among them the altar of St Hieronimus, c 1505) have been placed at the pillar bases. The apse, aglow with warm, red-and-yellow hues emanating from the excellent **stained glass** by T. Reklewska (1966), contains a small triptych with a statue of the Virgin and Child. At the west end of the north aisle stands an octagonal late **Gothic font** (c 1450) with reliefs depicting scenes from the life of Christ, the Virgin and St Jadwiga.

On the opposite side of ul. Św. Jadwigi is the former church of St James, now the **Orthodox Church of SS Cyril, Methodius and Anne**. Built in the Baroque style in 1686–90, it was much damaged in 1945. The gable is decorated with sculptures of saints placed in niches flanked by pilasters.

Further north is the building of a former **Augustinian convent** (1705–15). The ogival gable at No. 11 belongs to the former **Hospital of St Anne**, currently a Salesian convent, which is followed by two Neo-classical houses (**Nos 10 and 9**) with similar window decoration, pilasters and portals. Both were designed by K. G. Geissler at the turn of the 18C. **No. 9**, once a pharmacy, has a sculpture of King Solomon seated in a niche between the first floor windows.

Continuing north you come to the Mill Bridge, from which you can see the **Mill of St Mary**—originally 14C, today privatised and operational (the water wheels have been replaced by electricity). Crossing the bridge you enter Ostrów Tumski, an island proper until 1824, when it was connected to the east bank of the Odra.

Turn right into pl. Kościelny, past a **statue of Pope John XXIII**, built of roughly-hewn granite blocks (1968), to the **Church of St Martin**, originally the castle chapel, and probably sponsored by the ubiquitous Piotr Włostowic. The present church is a post-war reconstruction of the late 13C structure which replaced the first Romanesque chapel.

A Baroque **statue of St John Nepomuk** stands on a high plinth surrounded by putti in the centre of pl. Kościelny. Reliefs on the plinth depict scenes from the life of the saint. Dominating the square is the two-tiered ***Church of the Holy Cross and St Bartholomew**.

The church was sponsored by King Henryk Probus, whose sarcophagus was placed in the chancel of the **upper church** in c 1300 (it is now in the National Museum, see p. 443). The **lower church** was on occasion used as a warehouse, stables, and even a shelter. Today it belongs to the Ukrainian Orthodox community.

Over the entrance in the north aisle is a tympanum commemorating the foundation of St Bartholomew's, with reliefs of King Henryk Probus and his wife kneeling before God the Father holding the crucified Christ. A 15C triptych brought here from Świny serves as the high altar. The lower church, 7m high and built on cruciform plan with three-sided apses and cross vaults, contains epitaph slabs of bishops Nankier and Lubusz in the north aisle, a Renaissance font and epitaphs in the south transept, and a stone altar with a *Crucifixion* in the south transept. The porch vault has a 15C reliefed boss depicting St Jadwiga.

West of the church, at No. 4, is a former 18C **Orphanage**. Note the broken-pedimented portal with plain pilasters topped by ornate capitals and the protruding coat of arms of the sponsor, Archduke Franciszek Neuburg. West of the Orphanage you come to the Gothic **Church of SS Peter and Paul**, a 15C brick building, devastated by fires in the 17C–18C, and again hit in 1945. Restored in 1951–52, it is now usually closed.

Further east along ul. Katedralna, an early 17C house (**No. 5**) has a stone portal with geometric motifs that are echoed on the wooden door. A similar Renaissance portal adorns the house at **No. 9**, which bears Latin aphorisms and a garlanded and crowned circle with an engraved star. The **Archbishop's Palace** at No. 11 is a rather plain house with the date 1794 inscribed over the entrance. Further east, at No. 15, is the **Curia** (former Archbishop's Palace), whose heavy pedimented porch rests on two pairs of Ionic columns and has two empty niches that look like imprints of a gigantic egg.

Cathedral of St John the Baptist

Ul. Kościelna ends at pl. Katedralny, which is almost entirely occupied by the huge ****Cathedral of St John the Baptist**.

> The Cathedral owes its existence to the meeting of Bolesław the Brave and Emperor Otto III at Gniezno in 1000 (see p. 522), when it was decided to establish bishoprics at Kołobrzeg, Kraków and Wrocław. The first Cathedral was destroyed by the Czech prince Bretislav in 1038, and was replaced by a new one in the second half of the 12C. The Gothic version that you see today is later still—the chancel was finished in 1272, the nave some 50 years later. Over the centuries chapels were added, including St Mary's built in 1354–61 by Master Pieszko. The west crowning of the towers (1416) changed several times. In 1945 the Cathedral was damaged so extensively that there were even plans to pull it down altogether.

Interior

Enter the dark and cold interior of the Cathedral through the west porch (1465–68) with several Gothic sculptures, restored after the war. By the right-hand pillar, supporting the musicians' choir, is Urbański's relief (1732) showing Bishop Nankier (1270–1341) in the act of excommunicating King John of Luxembourg. On the last south pillar of the nave, before the entrance to the chancel, is the **altar of St Vincent of Saragossa**: a broken pediment topped by putti with Corinthian columns flanking the splendid Mannerist **bronze relief** by Adriaen de Vries (1614). Gilded sculptures depicting *Gregory the Great* and *St Hieronimus*, both by Jan Jerzy Urbański (c 1727), guard the entrance to the chancel. The Gothic **high altar** (1522) was brought here from a church in Lubin after the war. The relief in the central part of the triptych shows the *Dormition of the Virgin*, and is flanked by Biblical scenes. On both sides of the chancel are richly

carved oak stalls, transferred here from the church of St Vincent. The memorial slab of Bishop Jerin (c 1590) is by the Dutch sculptor, G. Hendrik.

Return to the west end of the south aisle. The domed **Chapel of the Holy Sacrament** is fronted by a 17C Baroque wrought-iron grille and richly decorated. From the ambulatory, a sandstone portal leads to the sacristy. Designed in 1517, it is one of the earliest examples of Renaissance art in Silesia. In the tympanum, a relief shows the decapitation of St John the Baptist.

The **Chapel of St Elizabeth** (1680–1700) stands at the southeast end of the ambulatory. Above the entrance is the bust of the chapel's founder, Cardinal Frederick of Hasse von Darmstadt, attributed to Gian Lorenzo Bernini. Inside is the kneeling figure of the Cardinal, carved by Bernini's pupil, Domenico Guidi. The altar opposite has a statue of St Elizabeth by E. Ferrata, another student of Bernini.

The **Chapel of St Mary**, situated along the west-east axis of the church, dates back to 1354–65. Its narrow chancel is covered with tripartite Piast vaults. In the centre stands Bishop Przecław's red marble sarcophagus. Embedded in the south wall is a bronze memorial slab to Bishop Johannes Roth (d. 1506) from the famous Vischer workshop in Nürnberg.

The **Corpus Christi Chapel** is placed symmetrically to St Elizabeth's. This masterpiece of Baroque art was designed and built in 1716–21 by the Viennese architect Fischer von Erlach as the funerary chapel of Cardinal Franz Ludwig Neuburg, Archbishop of Mainz. Several outstanding artists contributed the interior decoration: Ferdinand Brokoff (sculptures), Santino Bussi (stuccoes), Carlo Innocenzo Carlone (murals), J. F. Backer (paintings). The altar consists of a gilded tabernacle flanked by statues of Moses and Aaron. Facing it are Cardinal Neuburg's portrait and a commemorative slab. Backer's paintings—(*Abraham Welcomed by Melchizedech, King of Salem* and *The Last Supper*)—as well as other decoration evoke ideas proper to a funerary chapel: Death, Paradise and Hell, the Final Judgement. The unity of the interior, achieved by a subtle manipulation of colour, and the serene yet intense mood engendered by the sculptural and painted detail brought out by sophisticated lighting effects, rank the chapel among the best Baroque architecture in Silesia.

Next along, in the north wing of the ambulatory is the **Chapel of St John the Baptist** (1408), whose chief attraction is the **tomb** of Bishop Jan Turzon (d. 1520). The Renaissance figure of the bishop was carved in alabaster c 1537. On the ambulatory wall, above the entrance to the tower, are fragments of fine 15C painted decoration. Walking west along the north aisle you pass the red marble Renaissance **tomb** of Bishop Weisskopf (d. 1605) to the right of the side entrance. The westernmost domed **Chapel of the Dead** dates from 1749. Its Baroque interior contains post-war murals by W. Taranczewski.

North of the Cathedral stands the small **Church of St Giles**, Wrocław's oldest surviving church (c 1218–30), with an austere Romanesque portal in its south wall. Further east, at pl. Katedralny 16, is the entrance to the *****Archdiocesan Museum** (open Wed–Sun 10.00–17.00), one of the oldest of its kind in Poland, and particularly rich in Gothic art. The most treasured items include a 12C Romanesque figure of *St John the Baptist* (slightly damaged—a copy is hung over the north entrance to the Cathedral), two 3C reliefs from Damascus, and a 15C 'Beautiful Madonna'.

Leaving the museum, return to St Giles' and walk under the arch connecting it to the late Gothic Chapter House (c 1520). Continuing along ul. Kapitulna, with the Neo-Gothic museum building to the right, you will come to the **Botanical Garden**. If the weather is fine, this is an ideal place to absorb the peaceful, unhurried atmosphere of Ostrów Tumski. The garden (a detailed map is available at the ticket office) was founded in the early 19C and has some 7000 species of plants, including the largest collection of cactuses in Poland. You can continue your exploration of natural history at the university's **Natural History Museum** (entrance from ul. Sienkiewicza 21; **open** Tues–Wed, Fri–Sat 10.00–15.00, Thur, Sun 10.00–18.00).

Walk Four ~ The New Town

This walk takes you to the New Town (*Nowe Miasto*), once an independent entity with a separate municipal charter, merged with Wrocław in 1327. After its almost complete destruction in 1945, only some of the buildings were reconstructed, and the vacated plots were converted into pleasant parks. The itinerary leads back to the Market Square via the western part of the Old Town, on the way stopping at Wrocław's most conspicuous church, St Elizabeth's.

From the southeastern corner of the Main Market Square walk south along UL. ŚWIDNICKA until you come to the Franciscan **Church of St Stanisław** (right) which, dark and gloomy, contrasts strongly with the Lego-like pastel-coloured shopping centre next door.

> The church was built to commemorate a meeting between King Kazimierz the Great and Emperor Charles IV in 1351, and to serve as a guarantor of good relations between the various ethnic groups living in Wrocław. Initially, the church had three dedicatees: the Polish St Stanisław, the German St Dorothea, and the Czech St Wenceslaus, and it was only in 1946 that the last two saints were removed from its official name. After a major fire in 1688, the whole church was rebuilt in Baroque style. During later times it was briefly used by troops as an arsenal and a prison, but it survived the ordeal and the last war relatively unscathed.

The west façade is impressive, but more for its sheer size than aesthetic appeal. Equally monumental is the vaulted interior. Its pillars, wider at the bottom than the top, create an impression of lightness and solidity combined. The highlight of the church, found in west end of the north aisle, is a memorial to baron Gotfryd von Spätgen, made in 1752–53 by Franz Josef Mangoldt.

Further south along ul. Świdnicka stands the Neo-classical **Opera House** designed by Carl Ferdynand Langhans in 1837–41, and rebuilt in 1871 after a fire. This large white building has rows of fluted Corinthian pilasters on the north and south sides, thick columns in the west façade, and a large portico on the east side.

Across the street, further south, is the **Corpus Christi Church**, an early 14C work by Master Pieszko.

> The church was built for the Knights Hospitallers of St John of Jerusalem. After the dissolution of the order in the 16C, the church served as a warehouse, before being returning to the Catholic community in 1700. Napoleonic soldiers later used it as a granary and a hospital. Much damaged in 1945, it was reconstructed in 1955–62.

The church has a splendid 'Vistulian Gothic' **west façade** with a protruding porch, a tall pointed arch window with tracery, and a stepped gable elaborately decorated with frills and mesh patterns of brick. The **interior** looks rather barren, as all the Gothic and Baroque furnishing and decoration was lost during the war. Note the unusual **high altar**: a painted sculpture of Jesus (20C) framed in a superabundance of putti, wreathes and acanthus leaves. An impression of restless movement is created by the aisles, much lower than the nave, which have remarkable tri-partite Piast vaulting. A fine Gothic crucifix rests on the rood arch, difficult to see in detail because of the bright light entering through the apse window.

South of the church is a small 18C **Guardhouse**, currently an art gallery. To the east, next to a bank painted in garish pinks, greens and yellows, stands a Neo-Renaissance building housing a Puppet Theatre. Continue east across the park, past a statue of **Pegasus** mounted by Amor (which local anarchists like to spray-paint with tasteless graffiti) and a monument to Copernicus, to arrive at Partizans' Hill.

> By the 14C, the hill was an important element of the city's defences. At the turn of the 16C, the Swiss engineer Hans Schneider von Lindau built a bastion with underground corridors. Modernised and expanded by the Prussians, the bastion was then dismantled on Napoleon's orders. In 1866–7, the industrialist Adolf Liebich erected a tower with a terrace, restaurant and other attractions, destroyed in 1945. Today, the site consists of a fountain accessible by a broad flight of stairs and surrounded by a semi-circular colonnade.

Either return to ul. Świdnicka and cross the moat there, or walk back along the other side (ul. Podwale). At the junction of ul. Świdnicka and Podwale stands a shopping centre. Go south to pl. Kościuszki, which offers a good example of Socialist-Realist architecture from the 1950s. The west side is occupied by a Neo-Renaissance bank (1910), which could almost pass for a Stalinist building: roughly hewn stone in the lower part, huge Ionic half-columns supporting a pediment topped by a statue of a woman.

Return to the Opera on ul. Świdnicka, and turn left just before it into a small park with a recent **monument to the victims of Stalinism**, consisting of several slabs of granite surmounted by a crown of stylised barbed wire. Walk across the park and further north to the busy UL. KAZIMIERZA WIELKIEGO. At the corner of ul. Św. Doroty is the former **Selder Palace** (early 18C) currently a hotel. No. 33–35 is the former Spätgen Palace.

Spätgen Palace

The Spätgens built a Baroque palace in 1719, which they sold to King Frederick II when Wrocław came under Prussian rule. The Prussian monarch expanded the palace, adding a south wing (destroyed in 1945), and later commissioning Carl Gotthard Langhans to build the two Neo-classical wings facing ul. Kazimierza Wielkiego, thus forming a large court. Badly damaged in 1945, it was reconstructed in the 1960s.

■ The palace houses two museums: the **Archaeological Museum** (open Tues, Wed, Fri 10.00–16.00, Thur 09.00–16.00, Sat, Sun 10.00–17.00), and the

Ethnographical Museum (open Wed–Sat 10.00–16.00, Tues, Sun 11.00–18.00).

The **Archaeological Museum** has an exceptionally varied collection of items, mostly from Silesia, but also from Africa and southern Europe. It traces the history of Silesia from the Stone Age (especially the Neolithic period) through the Middle Ages to the 17C. Among the most treasured exhibits are stone tools used by *Homo Erectus*—the oldest in Poland—including a Neolithic flint tool (4500–1800 BC), discovered in Trzebnica in 1989. There is also a stone sculpture of a ram, an ancient deity worshipped in Lusatian culture. Painted ceramics from the early Iron Age, iron swords, a cult chariot, items discovered in 4C graves in Zakrzów, an amber treasury from a prehistoric trading settlement (2570 kilograms of raw amber), and 11C pagan cult objects are also displayed. The second part of the exhibition is devoted to the Middle Ages.

The neighbouring but independent **Ethnographical Museum** has a standard display enlivened by some interesting beehives and paintings on glass. The first floor is devoted both to indigenous Silesian culture and to the culture of the new settlers who arrived from the east after 1945. On the second floor you will find folk art, weaving, embroidery and costume from the pre- and post-war periods.

Further west along ul. Kazimierza Wielkiego is the Protestant **Church of Divine Providence**, which the Calvinists raised soon after Wrocław was annexed by Prussia. It was rebuilt after an explosion at a nearby gunpowder tower that wiped out the almost finished first version. The elliptical interior, usually closed, is circled by two-tiered galleries.

Across ul. Kazimierza Wielkiego stands a Neo-classical building, formerly the **Wallenberg-Pachaly Palace**, now the University Library. It was built by Carl Gotthard Langhans in 1785–87 and expanded (west wing) by his son, Carl Ferdinand. Inside is an elliptical winding staircase. Part of the library collection was inherited from the **Rehdiger Library**, which used to occupy the neighbouring Neo-Gothic building, whose sombre red brick bristles with towers and turrets.

On PL. BOHATERÓW GETTA, by the Rehdigeranum, a small plaque commemorates the Warsaw Ghetto Uprising. From the square you get a good view of the Old Town and the tower of St Elizabeth's Church (see below). An arched passage nearby leads to the **Salt Market**. Looking south along ul. Krupnicza you will notice, at the junction of ul. Krupnicza and ul. Włodkowica, the **New Stock Exchange** (now a sports club) where a plethora of turrets, balustrades, pointed arches with tracery, sculptures on consoles all contribute to a picturesque if tasteless burst of Neo-Gothic. Further south, across the street, notice the red-brick **law courts** (1845–52), with two octagonal crenellated towers imitating English Gothic.

From the junction of UL. KRUPNICZA and ul. Kazimierza Wielkiego continue east along ul. ŚW. ANTONIEGO. On the left, sandwiched between two houses, is the early Baroque **Church of St Anthony**, raised by the Reformed Franciscans in the late 17C. The façade is decorated with pilasters carrying a prominent cornice, a sloping gable with two thick pinnacles on both sides, a pedimented window in the centre, and an oval one above flanked by niches with shell-like ornaments. A figure of St Anthony has been placed inside the portal's broken pediment.

Continue along ul. Św. Antoniego and then ul. Włodkowica to PL. 1 MAJA. On the left, opposite a modern hospital building, stands the Music Academy (formerly student lodgings), with rounded corners and a clock. The fountain in the centre has two allegorical figures (1905): a man taming a lion (left), and the lion already tamed, with the man astride (right).

Close to pl. 1 Maja, on UL. ŚW. MIKOŁAJA, is the Orthodox **Church of St Barbara** (mass in Old Church Slavonic is held daily at 09.30). An excellent figure of St Barbara which used to stand on one of the tower buttresses, has been replaced with mosaic. Likewise, the 15C painted altar of St Barbara has been removed and is presently on display in the National Museum in Warsaw (see p. 125). As compensation of sorts, the church has recently acquired murals by one of the best-known contemporary Polish painters, Jerzy Nowosielski from Kraków.

Continue along ul. Św. Mikołaja and turn left into UL. NOWY ŚWIAT for the large, brick building of the former **City Arsenal**, now the Museum of Banners and Weaponry (**open** Tues, Thur–Sun 10.00–16.00).

> A Gothic granary was built in 1459, a large, rectangular building adjoining the city walls (a fragment of these walls and a square tower are still visible). It was converted into an arsenal in the 16C, when the north wing (now the oldest) was erected, and after the incorporation of Wrocław into Prussia, it was used as a warehouse. Today, it is one of the oldest extant buildings of its kind in Europe, predating the arsenals of Kraków, Berlin and Vienna.

The museum is not rich in exhibits, and the complex is still undergoing archaeological excavations and renovation work. A fragment of a column from the Ołbin monastery is displayed in the main hall; in the courtyard is the original well, and in the east wing preserved wooden ceilings. The portals are also Gothic originals.

Visible from ul. Nowy Świat is a row of pretty gabled houses on UL. BIAŁOSKÓR-NICZA, which runs parallel to it. The name (*'biała skóra'* means 'white leather') derives from the tanners who used to have their workshops here. Walk down UL. ŁAZIENNA. At the corner of ul. Kiełbaśnicza is the former **Baumann Printing House** (No. 20). Its pedimented portal bears the date 1800, when the original 15C house was extensively remodelled. Close by, at the west end of UL. MALARSKA (No. 30), is the **Artzant House** (c 1690), named after its original owners, with a Baroque curly gable and putti amid floral decoration. A pedimented portal occupies the centre of the façade. Inside is a cosy café. Parallel to ul. Malarska runs UL. JATKI, named after the butchers' shops that once stood here (13C–19C), and which today have given way to galleries and art shops.

From a distance you will have noticed the soaring tower of **St Elizabeth's Church**.

> The present church was built in the 14C–15C, receiving its tower—one of the tallest brick Gothic towers in Europe—in 1450–56. The steeple, which together with the tower rose to a height of 130m, was destroyed by lightning in 1529. The Renaissance crowing which replaced it was lost in a fire in 1975. The following year a more serious fire completely gutted the whole church, melting down its superb Silbermann organ, the finest in Poland. The church was reopened in 1997, but the flames had consumed almost all the furnishings and works of art.

The best surviving works have been moved to museums (notably the Warsaw National Museum, see p. 125). However, the aisles and chancel still contain some excellent examples of Renaissance and Mannerist **sepulchral art**. Among the countless memorial slabs and monuments to Silesian nobility and wealthy burghers, the best are by Gerhard Hendrik of Amsterdam and Friedrich Gross. The tower (83m; **open** 10.00–12.00 and 14.00–16.00) can be climbed for breathtaking views of the city and—weather permitting—Mount Ślęża (see p. 447).

Excursions from Wrocław

❖ Trzebnica • Oleśnica • Sobótka • Mount Ślęża • Lubiąż

This excursion takes you north of Wrocław to the Cistercian abbey at Trzebnica. The second stop is Oleśnica, with its fine 14C castle. Both places can be easily reached by bus from Wrocław. If travelling by car, drive north on road 5 (E261), signposted 'Poznań'.

TRZEBNICA (24km), originally a small trading settlement, gained religious and cultural importance in the early 13C when King Henryk the Bearded and his wife Jadwiga chose it as the site of a Cistercian abbey, the first convent in Silesia.

A late Romanesque basilican church, with a crypt below the chancel, was erected in 1203–40. After Henryk's death, Jadwiga entered the abbey and spent the rest of her life there in solitude. She was canonised in 1267.

The **church**, Trzebnica's only monument of note, is easily found in the town centre. It was remodelled in Baroque style in the second half of the 17C, and again in the early 18C. The square neo-classical tower of three storeys was built in 1780–85. Inside, the long cross-vaulted nave consists of four broad bays subdivided by pillars, with an altar by each. By a north pillar (on its east side) is a relief-carved marble tablet to St Jadwiga (see below). Two portals (c 1220) with carved tympana have survived from the Romanesque period: one lies to the left of main entrance, partially hidden by the tower; the other is by the north façade. Franz Josef Mangoldt designed the ornate high altar (1740), as well as the pulpit (1739–45).

At the east end of the south aisle is the showpiece **chapel of St Jadwiga** (1268–69), where you will find the queen's black marble and alabaster tomb (1680), adorned with sculptures and a fine wooden crowning. The chapel also contains an early Baroque **pulpit** (1685), a Baroque **altar** (1730) with a painting by T. Hammermacher (1653), and a Gothic portal with a carved tympanum. The far more modest tomb of Jadwiga's husband, Henryk the Bearded (1685) stands in the chancel. Adjoining the church is the convent with two late Baroque cloister gardens (1697–1726), redesigned at the turn of the 19C.

From Trzebnica, pick up road 340 signposted 'Oleśnica' (east).

OLEŚNICA (28km) is first mentioned as an 11C trading settlement on the Amber Route. It was ruled by the Piasts until 1492, later passing to the Podebrad dynasty (until 1647), the dukes of Württemberg (until 1742) and finally to Prussia. Incorporated into Poland after the Second World War, it is now a small market town.

Entering Oleśnica along ul. Wrocławska, you will pass a section of the 14C brick fortifications, which include the Gothic **Wrocław Gate**, square and

SILESIA

Głogów
Odra
Lubin
34
344
E261
Trzebnica
Legnica
Lubiąż
E67
E40
Lwówek
Złotoryja
E40
Oleśnica
WROCŁAW
Zgorzelec
Wleń
Jawor
Legnickie
Pole
5
Jelenia Góra
Strzegom
Bolków
E65
367
E67
Oława
Brzeg
Szklarska Poręba
E65 Kamienna Góra
Świdnica
Sobótka
Lck.
Turaws.
Karpacz
Wałbrzych
Henryków
Opole
Krzeszów
Ząbkowice Śl.
Ziębice
Grodków
E40
381
Niemodlin
Wambierzyce
Góra Świętej An
Kudowa-Zdrój
E67
Paczków
Otmuchów
Nysa
411
367 Głogówek
Duszniki-Zdrój
Kłodzko
Lądek-Zdrój
Prudnik
Kedzierzyr
Polanica-Zdrój
Stronie Śl.
Koźle
Bystrzyca Kłodzka
Międzylesie
Racibór.

N

0   50 miles
0   80 kms

turreted, with a 16C superstructure. You can park at the market square, close to which stands a large, quadrangular **castle** sporting gables, angular turrets and ornate portals. Raised by the Dukes of Oleśnica in the early 14C, it was extensively rebuilt in 1542–61 and 1586–1608 by the Podebrad family as a splendid Renaissance residence. It is entered through a double gate with coats of arms in relief, supported by lions. Sgraffito decoration covers the octagonal tower and walls. The interiors are used as offices and are closed to tourists.

Northeast of the castle, connected to it via an arcaded passageway of 1616, is the 14C–16C late Gothic **Church of St John the Evangelist**. The south portal, with tracery in the tympanum, is flanked by stone sculptures of a lion devouring a lamb, and an eagle doing the same to a quail. The interior, rebuilt in Baroque style at the turn of the 17C, underwent major reconstruction in 1906–08. Wooden galleries echo the church's distant Protestant past. Decorative bosses, corbels and the brick ribs of the star vaults stand out against the whitewashed background. The uncramped, airy space of the church is filled with light entering from three large stained-glass windows in the apse. Sculptures and a three-tiered baldachino decorate the pulpit (1605). In the north wall of the chancel are several 16C Renaissance tombs, and on the opposite wall is a pedimented entrance to the Baroque chapel of the Dukes of Würtemberg (1698).

Mount Ślęża

The town of **SOBÓTKA** has little to offer, but the nearby forested Ślęża mountain (718m), with its scenic view of the **Sudeten mountains**, makes it a popular destination for day-trippers from Wrocław. The excursion is best made on a clear, sunny day, but beware that in spring or summer the place is usually invaded by school parties. Drive south west across the flat Odra plain on road 5 and then along minor roads for Sobotka (33km).

MT ŚLĘŻA was an important centre **pagan cult** from the Bronze Age (c 1700 BC) until the adoption of Christianity in Poland during the 10C. Traces of the mysterious religious practices have survived in the form of several curious stone sculptures of uncertain age, notably a 'bear' at the top of the mountain, and—on the north slope—a headless woman clutching a large fish. A third sculpture, known as the 'mushroom', is found by St Anne's church (not the Romanesque parish church) in the centre of Sobótka. Also at the summit is an oblong stone dyke of unknown cult significance.

From the car park it is a brisk one-and-a-half hour walk to the top of Mt Ślęża. Six marked trails ascend the hill, the yellow one being the most direct. Along the way you will pass several of the ancient sculptures. The summit, which on a clear day offers a fine view over the surrounding region, is somewhat marred by the inevitable refreshments bar (often teeming with schoolchildren), and an unseemly TV tower with a loud electric generator. The stone 'bear', mentioned above, lies at the foot of the church, built in 1702 by the Augustinian abbot Jan Sivert, and later remodelled in ugly Neo-Gothic.

The Cistercian Abbey at Lubiąż

The Cistercian abbey in **LUBIĄŻ**, one of the finest examples of monastic architecture in Poland, lies 51km west of Wrocław. It is best reached by car, as buses to and from the village are very infrequent. Head west from Wrocław along road 344, turning right in Kawice (46km) for Lubiąż (road 388). The abbey founded in 1163 by Bolesław the Tall, is one of largest in central Europe. With its 40ha of land, and roughly 3ha of buildings, it is even larger than the vast Teutonic castle at Malbork. Most of it is undergoing renovation, which is likely to continue for many years, due to both lack of funds and the enormity of the task at hand. At present, only the Abbot's Refectory is open to tourists.

The ***church**, a truly astonishing edifice of brick and stone, originally dates from the early 14C. It was then that a Gothic basilica with a square apse, an ambulatory, chapel and transept was raised on the ruins of a former 12C Romanesque church. Destroyed by Hussites (1432), and then the Swedes (1642), the abbey was rebuilt in the 17C–18C as a magnificent Baroque residence. Today, however, the massive main building presents a sorry sight, and much-needed renovation work has been indefinitely suspended.

The cross-vaulted nave is lit by tall clerestory windows with tracery. In front of the high altar are **tombs** of Piast dukes (14C). The ducal chapel (1312) at the east end of the north aisle has murals covering the ceiling, and the round domes in the ambulatory behind the chancel have painted and stuccoed decoration. The west part of the north aisle is separated from the rest of the church by a wrought-iron grille bearing the date 1701. Outside, the Baroque north porch (1681–1700) has Corinthian columns, sculptures in niches, and a relief in the tympanum. The aisle and ambulatory vaults, and the twin-towered west façade date from the same period.

The church divides the uniform Baroque façade of the monastic building into two equal parts. To the left is the two-winged **Abbot's Palace** (1690–1700) where, in the Refectory and the adjoining rooms, there is a small museum (**open** Wed–Fri 10.00–14.00, Sat–Sun 11.00–17.00) with paintings by Christian Philipp von Bentum, wooden sculptures from various Silesian churches (including several extraordinary figures by Thomas Weissfeldt), fragments of church masonry and decoration, Silesian furniture, and coats of arms. The greatest attraction is the large **rectangular plafond** in the Refectory, with one of the best **murals by Michael Willmann** (1630–1712) framed in sumptuous stuccoes. Willmann, the greatest Silesian painter of the Baroque period, lived in Lubiąż, but his works were also admired and sought after outside Silesia.

In the same part of the building, be sure not to miss the stunning ***Ducal Hall**, whose entrance is guarded by two statues of Moors supporting the tympanum. Inside, the square hall has splendid painted decoration by Bentum and an astounding collection of sculptures by Franz Josef Mangoldt.

The quadrangular **monastery** (1690–1720) to the right of the church houses the oval **Summer Refectory**, with a ceiling mural (1733) by Felix Anton Scheffler. In the deep window jambs, empty and dusty niches await the return of the sculptures they used to hold. Above the Summer Refectory, on the first floor, is a **library** with a gallery and fading illusionist murals (1734–38) on the ceiling, again by Bentum. The corridor next to the library leads to the monks' living quarters.

Spread out around the abbey grounds are a number of other buildings (see the map in the museum), including the church of St James, the chancellery, a bakery and brewery, farm and administration buildings, three gardens and an orchard. Most were constructed between 1681 and 1739, the heyday of the abbey, which began to decline after the incorporation of Silesia into the Prussian state (1740). Frederick the Great (Hohenzollern) looked askance at the enormous wealth amassed by the Catholic monks and finally, the Order was dissolved in 1810. Most of the works of art that could be moved were taken away (including 63 paintings by Willmann), while the spacious buildings were converted into stables, an arsenal, and an asylum. During the Second World War a small armaments factory was set up in Lubiąż, and in 1944 the remaining works of art were removed. Rumour has it that some of the treasures are buried in the abbey grounds.

There are plans to turn the complex into a major conference and recreation centre. The calm and peaceful surroundings do indeed seem ideal for this. If fully restored to its original splendour, Lubiąż may yet become one of Poland's greatest tourist attractions. Even in its present state, the richness and sheer size of this Cistercian wonder are quite remarkable.

Kraków to Cieszyn

❖ Lanckorona • Kalwaria Zebrzydowska • Wadowice • Pszczyna • Cieszyn

This route begins in Małopolska with one of the most popular pilgrimage spots in Poland—Kalwaria Zebrzydowska. It then continues to Wadowice, the birth-place of Pope John Paul II, before entering Silesia. The chief attraction of this part of the trip is the sumptuous Promnitz Palace in Pszczyna, today an excel-lent museum of interiors.

Leave Kraków south on ul. Zakopiańska. After about 20km take the right fork signposted 'Bielsko Biała' (road 96). After Izdebnik turn onto a narrow winding road which takes you across hilly forested landscape to the charming village of **LANCKORONA**, situated on a steep hill. The sloping, cobbled Market Square is lined with traditional 19C wooden houses, of which one (by the bus stop) contains a **Museum of Folklore** (tools, household items, handicrafts). Follow ul. Św. Jana up the hill to the Gothic **Church of St John the Baptist** (1336), beautifully set, but unfortunately accessible only on Sundays. Higher up are the ruins of a 14C **castle**, surrounded by a park.

The Monastery at Kalwaria Zebrzydowska

From Lanckorona either return to the main road (96), or continue (4km) to Kalwaria Zebrzydowska, where you should watch out for the white signs marked 'Do Klasztoru' (to the monastery). Ascending the hill you will reach a square with a row of one-storey houses with balconies along the north side. To the west stands the huge Baroque *monastery church (1702). It is separated from the square by a row of stone statues of saints (1823) and a yard—the Paradise Square, with cloisters on its north and south sides. The majority of the monastic buildings are behind the church. They were built between 1603 and 1609 by Giovanni Maria Bernadoni and P. Baudarth, and are surrounded by partly preserved fortifications, two towers of which have been converted into chapels (the chapel of St Anne is the low, square tower with a red tiled roof and lantern).

The broad, pedimented **façade** with niches holding statues, is dominated by two symmetrically placed towers. Three domed chapels adjoin the church on the north side. Baroque art and architecture hold sway inside the church.

The spacious vaulted hall is lit by large plain glass windows, providing a sharp contrast to the dark, narrow and much lower chancel.

Beginning in the northeast corner of the nave and walking west, you pass a Baroque side altar with a painting of *St Mary Magdalene*, and the altar of St Catherine, followed by the entrance to the chapel of the Immaculate Conception. The 17C organ loft is flanked by murals depicting the 17C Cossack leader Chmielnicki on a horse (north) and the Blessed Simon of Lipnica (south).

Be sure to walk behind the high altar to see the finely carved 17C **wooden stalls**. The altar itself is a bulky, rectangular structure, with four twisted columns supporting large pedestals on which frolicking angels are perched. The central painting of *St Francis* conceals a figure of St Mary, who is also portrayed in garish murals covering the walls of the chancel. Another painting further east shows *King Władysław IV*; on the north wall, *Emperor Francis I* is shown attending mass at this very church (1817). The stuccoed **Zebrzydowski chapel**, whose cream-coloured stone is enhanced by the mellow light entering through the large plain-glass window in the elliptical dome, has a marble altar with a miraculous painting of the *Virgin and Child* (17C). A door in its east wall leads to the **chapel of St Anthony** (1686), with a 17C painting of *St Anthony of Padua* in its altar.

Kalwaria is a popular pilgrimage spot, where thousands flock at Easter to watch the traditional 'Golgota' play, in which peasants from local villages act out the Crucifixion. The origins of this custom reach back to the early 17C, when Mikołaj Zebrzydowski, struck by the similarity of the hills around Kalwaria to the landscape of Jerusalem, attempted to recreate the atmosphere of the Holy City by erecting 46 chapels and churches. His **Way of the Cross**, a pleasant walk through woodland, begins at pl. Rajski and goes west before turning full circle back to the monastery. Passing over the Mount of Olives, Mt. Zion and Mt. Moriah, it ends on Mt. Calvary, upon which stands the **Church of the Crucifixion**, its interior (usually closed) adorned with paintings by F. Lekszycki (1600–1). Some of the stations are tiny stone cubicles; others are churches in their own right, mostly Mannerist.

Return to the centre of Kalwaria and join the road heading north, later marked 'Skawina'. It soon turns west, bringing you to **Wadowice** (14km), a forgettable town, but famous for being the **birthplace of Karol Wojtyła**, alias Pope John Paul II. The Wojtyłas' house is just off the Main Square, to the right of the church. Inside is a small **museum** (open Tues–Sun 09.00–12.00 and 14.00–17.00) with a collection of photographs and sundry items connected with the life of the Pope.

Continue along road 96 heading west. In Bielsko, join road 1 (E-75) heading north to **Pszczyna** (57km). The spacious Market Square has a newly-renovated Baroque **Town Hall** (1658) that adjoins a church with green onion domes, and small single-storey painted houses, the most noteworthy of which is an 18C burgher's house at **No. 3**. Around the square extends a maze of narrow one-way streets.

Promnitz Palace

Walking west of the square you reach the *Promnitz Palace, set in a delightful landscaped park (18C–19C), with pavilions, ponds and bridges, covering an area of 84ha. The palace, comprising three wings (1743–67), incorporates some

Gothic elements (1424–49). It was refashioned in 1870–74 for a family of German magnates—the fabulously wealthy Hochberg von Pless—who kept it until 1945. The excellent **museum** (**open** Wed–Fri 09.00–15.00, Sat–Sun 10.00–15.00) inside features sumptuous interiors reconstructed in their original period style.

Begin on the ground floor with a series of connected rooms containing impressive fireplaces, Japanese, Persian and European armoury and weaponry, and some good pieces of furniture, including an elaborately carved and inlaid chess and backgammon table. The penultimate room on the ground floor contains a 16C Gobelin tapestry from Flanders showing Hercules killing the Nemean lion; the last is a Renaissance bedroom, with an English four-poster bed from the reign of Elizabeth I.

Broad stone stairs with fine stuccowork and a huge tapestry, a gift from Catherine the Great, the Russian Czarina, lead up to the bedchambers and reception rooms.

The **first floor** begins with a gallery of 19C mirrors and crystal chandeliers. On the right is perhaps the grandest room of the palace—the **Hall of Mirrors**, named after the two enormous mirrors placed on facing walls, thus infinitely enlarging the room. Every square inch of the walls is covered with fabulous frescoes and stuccowork. The vault is covered by a *trompe l'oeil* azure sky resting on a frieze of flowers. Below it, 19C allegorical paintings represent the four seasons and the signs of the Zodiac. The room rises through two storeys, and can be surveyed from the balconies above. It is furnished with a grand piano and chairs—a three-day **Telemann festival** is held here each October, in memory of the composer, who worked here from 1704 to 1708. Further on are bedrooms, salons, a library, study and dressing room. Right at the very end are the private rooms of Princess Daisy, an English heiress who owned and inhabited the palace at the beginning of the 20C.

The **second floor** has a hunting gallery and a billiard room. You can also ask to see the collection of miniatures, usually closed.

Return south along road 1 (E-75), continuing to Cieszyn (49km).

Cieszyn

Cieszyn is a border town with a history of territorial and ethnic disputes. From the 13C to the 17C it was ruled by Silesian dukes loyal to the Bohemian crown; then it became part of the Habsburg empire. In 1918, following the collapse of the Central Powers, Cieszyn became the first Polish city to regain independence after 150 years of Austro-Hungarian rule. The local Polish and Czech councils divided it between the two states, but a Czechoslovak invasion a few months later broke the agreement. The dispute was ostensibly resolved at the Paris Conference in July 1920, when the Olza river was chosen as the border. Yet in 1938 the Polish army launched a sudden attack on the Czech part—a strategic mistake given the more pressing threat posed by Nazi Germany—and all to no avail, for in 1945 Cieszyn was once again divided, this time by Stalin, and remains so today. It is the busiest border crossing between Poland and the Czech Republic, as well as a thriving cultural centre, hosting several festivals.

■ Practical information

Hotel. ★★★★*Orbis-Motel*. Ul. Motelowa 21, ☎ 852-0451. Good facilities, helpful staff. Car park, business services. 77 rooms overlooking gardens.
Tourist information. Ul. Głęboka 56, ☎ 852-3050.
ORBIS. Rynek 19, ☎ 852-1240.
Main post office. Rynek 13.
Telephone code: (0–33).

Major festivals. Viva il Canto (last week of **August**), featuring open-air performances in the Market Square and more in the municipal theatre; Three Brothers Festival (end of **June**), named after the legendary founders of Cieszyn and organised in co-operation with the Czech part of the town (it is rather low-brow compared to the Viva il Canto and features raucous events, beer drinking etc); On-the-Border Theatre Festival, run by the Polish-Czech Solidarity organisation in **October**, and showing the best theatre productions of the year; Beskidy Cultural Festival in Wisła near Cieszyn.

The city centre

The Market Square acquired its present form and appearance in 1789, when, after a major fire, it was rebuilt in Neo-classical style. It is dominated by a Baroque-Classical **Town Hall**. In 1816 a theatre was added at the back, which proved an ill-fated move: a fire in 1832, started by the reckless actors, reduced the building to rubble. The former arcades were replaced by today's colonnade, and a plain pediment was added, adorned only with the coat of arms of the Silesian Piasts. The 16C **well** in the middle of the square used to supply the town with water. Some of the arcaded houses on the west side date from the same period, since then rebuilt many times and reduced to a mixture of styles. On the north side is the eclectic, onion-domed **National House**, opened in 1901. The plaque commemorates the National Council of the Duchy of Cieszyn, which declared independence in 1918.

From the north side UL. MATEJKI descends steeply to the **Holy Trinity Church**, its thick-spired tower (1864) lurking above chestnut trees. The façade of the 16C church, late Gothic with a Renaissance gable, is rather plain, almost devoid of ornamentation. Victims of the plague of 1585 are buried around it. The first wooden church was built as an expression of gratitude for the ending of the plague, and was replaced in 1594 by the present brick one.

Discernible on the east side of the Market Square are the former arcades, walled up after a fire in 1789. One of the houses (**No. 18**) contains a passable café. Next to it is ul. Szersznika, which brings you to the **Holy Cross Church**, built by the Jesuits in 1707. It was reconstructed after a fire by the Jesuit Leopold J. Scherschnick (1747–1814), a Prague-educated native of Cieszyn, who also founded a museum (see below), and one of the first public libraries in Poland. The **library** has been preserved almost intact, along with the original bookcases and cataloguing system. A small portion of it—including prints from the Kroberger, Altmanciusz and Elzewir publishing houses, Bleau's World Atlas, a 14C parchment copy of a work by St Augustine, and a 1418 Hussite Bible—is on display at the **Municipal Public Library** (No. 18 Market Square) **open** Mon–Wed, Fri–Sat 08.00–15.00, Sun 10.00–14.00.

Further along the east side of the Square is the former **Brown Deer Hotel**, a

Secessionist edifice erected in 1912 by Kilian Köhler. It was the most luxurious hotel in Cieszyn at the turn of the century, and offered such ultra-modern facilities as lifts, electricity, and English bathrooms.

From the southeast corner walk along UL. REGERA to the **Regional Museum** (**open** Tues–Fri 10.00–14.30, Sat–Sun 10.00–13.30), the oldest museum in Poland, established in 1802 by Scherschnick (see above). From 1794 the building was the residence of Count Johann Larisch-Mönnich, and is now known as the Larisch Palace. The museum is undergoing a long process of renovation, which, according to the curator, will probably outlast him. The collections, held in the building at ul. Srebrna 1 around the corner, are mainly devoted to the history and culture of the Cieszyn region.

Return to the square and walk down UL. GŁĘBOKA, the city's main thoroughfare and shopping area, which leads down to the border crossing at ul. Zamkowa. On the left is the **Parish Church of St Mary Magdalene*, completed in 1289 by the Dukes of Cieszyn, many of whom are buried here. In the course of many alterations, the church has acquired a predominantly Baroque character; only some of the windows in the nave have Gothic tracery, uncovered during renovation work in 1962. The **tombs of Piast dukes** are found in the crypts underneath the church. The best chapel is in the southwest corner; built in 1660 by Jan F. Larisch, it is topped with a dome and lantern.

Continuing along ul. Głęboka, turn left into UL. SEJMOWA, and then right into UL. TRZECH BRACI (Three Brothers), which descends steeply towards the river. On the left is the **Three Brothers' Well**, allegedly the place where the three brothers—Bolko, Leszko and Cieszko—met in 810 after many years of separation. To commemorate their joyful meeting, so the legend goes, the brothers founded a city called Cieszyn (from the Polish '*cieszę się*'—I am happy). Walk down the steps and turn right into UL. PRZYKOPA. To the left is the former watermill. The millstream follows the road on the left; on the right, rising above the stone wall, is the crimson half-timbered back of an old brewery.

You emerge on UL. ZAMKOWA, which ends at the busy border crossing. On the opposite side of the street rises the castle hill, once the site of a prehistoric settlement (5C BC). Nothing remains of the original Gothic castle, which was destroyed by the Austrians in the 1840s to make way for a Neo-classical summer residence for the Habsburgs, designed by the renowned Viennese architect **Joseph Korhäusel** (it is now a music school). Enter through the central passageway, inside which is the café *Baszta*. You emerge onto a grassy courtyard that leads up to the Romanesque rotunda and Gothic tower. The limestone rotunda is actually the **Church of St Nicholas**, the oldest in Cieszyn (11C). It was first mentioned in 1223 by Bishop Lawrence, and originally run by the Benedictines. Rebuilt in the 14C and 19C, it now consists of a cylindrical nave and adjoining vaulted semi-circular apse; the wall is 1m thick and pierced by six arched windows. Opposite the chancel is a gallery supported on six Romanesque sandstone columns. The Gothic stone tower (29 m) with brick crenellations and a roof, was given a clock in the 19C. It is empty inside, save for steep stairs leading up to a platform offering a panoramic view over Polish and Czech Cieszyn and the Beskidy Mountains in the distance. In the northwest corner of the castle courtyard is a pile of artificial ruins (sic) from 1916, now apparently the subject of archaeological enquiry.

Return to ul. Głęboka and take the first left to PL. TEATRALNY, on which stands the **Municipal Theatre**, a Secessionist building designed by the Viennese architects Ferdinand Felner and Herman Helmer. Opposite, on the curve of UL. MENNICZA, is the **Old Mint**, established at the end of the 13C and closed in 1655 (coins made at this mint can be seen in the Regional Museum). The present Neo-Rococo façade dates back to 1902, and is badly in need of renovation. Continue along ul. Mennicza back to the Market Square.

On PL. KOŚCIELNY, off ul. Wyższa Brama in the south part of Cieszyn, is a large 18C Baroque **Protestant Church**, one of the six that Emperor Joseph I, under pressure from the Swedish King Charles XII, granted to the Protestants after they had lost all their churches in the wake of the Counter Reformation. To the right of the altar is a bronze bust of Charles XII (1933), a gift from Sweden. The 33-voice organ is used during two **10-day music festivals**, held during spring and autumn. Mass, announced by three steel bells from Westphalia, can be attended by up to 7000 believers, with 3500 seated.

Cieszyn to Nysa

❖ Racibórz • Głogówek • (detour: Moszna) • Prudnik • Nysa

The highlight of the trip is the picturesque town of Głogówek, with its two remarkable churches. A detour can also be made to the fairy-tale castle at Moszna, conceived as an architectural joke.

Leave Cieszyn on road 938 marked 'Katowice'. After 6km join the 937 heading north. At Jastrzębie Zdrój pick up the 933 going northwest and follow signs to Racibórz. You will be passing through landscape peppered with mines, the odd slag heap, and unremarkable houses, all darkened with smog and smoke.

In **RACIBÓRZ** (61km), most of the monuments are centred on the Main Square. The Gothic **Church of the Ascension** has a heavy tower (1574–80) and a chancel (c 1300) covered with mid-16C vaults; The early 14C **Dominican Church of St James** in the northeast corner has a finely stuccoed early Baroque Gaschin chapel. Behind the Dominican church is a bustling market, most busy on Thursdays, when some traders come decked out in local Racibórz dress.

Follow UL. CHOPINA off the Market Square to the house at **No. 12**, where Liszt performed Chopin's music in 1846, and where concerts are occasionally held. The **museum** on nearby ul. Gimnazjalna 1 is contained within the ivy-clad walls of the former Dominican Nuns' Church (14C). The display focuses on **Silesian religious art**, armour and weaponry, and archaeological finds, including a Celtic kiln from Nowa Cerkiew (125 BC).

Leaving Racibórz west along road 416 the landscape suddenly changes into unrelenting flat fields dotted with houses.

In **GŁOGÓWEK** (58km) the cobbled Market Square has a fine late Renaissance **Town Hall** (1608), partly rebuilt in 1880. The northwest corner of the square is occupied by the Franciscan monastery, founded in 1264.

The adjoining **church** is one of the finest and oddest in the region, built in Gothic style in the 15C, but significantly altered in 1628–37, when the transept, tower and Loreto shrine were added, and the whole was remodelled in early

Baroque style. Franz Sebastini and Johann Schubert were responsible for the late Baroque and Rococo painted decoration and furniture (1770). An exceptionally ornate **high altar** with statues of saints and angels fills the apse. The south transept contains the church's chief attraction—the **Loreto Shrine**, a rectangular 'house', with rough frescoes on its exterior walls, filling the entire transept. Inside the bare brick tunnel-vaulted room is a sombre and quiet shrine to the Madonna of Loreto behind a gilded, regular grille.

The *parish church of St Bartholomew**, in the southwest corner of the Main Square, was built in 1380–1463 as a Gothic basilica. However, its interior decoration (stuccowork by Johann Schubert, murals by Franz Sebastini, both 1777–81) is glorious Baroque and Rococo. The long and deep lunettes and *trompe l'oeil* murals make the nave vaults look like a huge sea shell. The 15C–16C vaults in the chancel are equally remarkable, as are the pulpit, and especially the font, which abounds in sculptures. Most conspicuous, however, is the large tabernacle in the form of an octagonal columned pavilion. The Gothic **Oppersdorff chapel** (before 1419) by the chancel has an early Baroque tomb (1634) by Sebastiano Sala. The west façade of the church sports twin Baroque towers and a mock tower in between—just a flat front, covered with *trompe l'oeil* decoration to create an impression of cylindrical shape.

Further north is the Renaissance/Baroque **Oppersdorff Castle** (1561–71 and 1584–1606), set in a pleasant landscaped and formal park (17C). A small stone **monument** to Beethoven stands by the road, just before the castle. The composer stayed here in 1806 after completing his 4th Symphony, and began work on the 5th (there is a Beethoven memorial room in the castle museum). Further along, the road passes underneath the Baroque castle gate (c 1700). Nearby is the Gothic prison tower, currently a small café. The **lower castle** (southeast wing) contains a **museum** (open Tues, Thur–Sun 10.00–15.00, Wed 10.00–17.00), with an exhibition devoted to the painter **Jan Cybis** (1897–1972).

Walking south of the Main Square you come to the **Water Gate** on ul. Młyńska (1597). From here the town cemetery ascends to the agreeably situated **Cemetery Church** (1705), half-timbered, with 17C–18C sculptures.

In Głogówek, join the 408 heading west towards Prudnik.

Detour to Moszna Castle

Just after Lubrza (19km) you could take a detour (36km there and back) north along the 414 to the extraordinary **Castle** at MOSZNA. Turn left down an unmarked road by the large white stud-farm building just before the village, and follow the signs marked 'Sanatorium' (guided tours in high season only, Sat–Sun 10.00–12.00, 14.00–17.00). This amorphous and rambling mass of towers, turrets, spires, gables and monumental façades, of anonymous design, was erected after 1896. The castle, set in an 18C English park, was nationalised after the war, and is now a sanatorium for patients suffering from nervous disorders.

The centre of the Market Square in PRUDNIK is occupied by a **Town Hall** (1782), which lost its original Baroque appearance during reconstruction in 1894–96. Around the Square are some houses with late Baroque façades. The **Parish Church** on ul. Farna, originally Renaissance (1612), was remodelled in

Baroque style after a fire in 1735. The fondness for symmetry so characteristic of that era has been carried so far here that the ornate pulpit on the left has a twin on the opposite side, with a statue of a priest giving a sermon.

South of the square stands a solitary stone tower, round at the base rising to octagonal, the only remnant of the **Castle of the Dukes of Opole** (13C–14C), dismantled by the Prussian authorities after a fire in 1806.

On ul. Opolska, north of the square, is the Gothic **Lower Gate Tower** (15C), a fragment of the town fortifications, which was merged in the 19C with the adjoining buildings. The upper part, with loopholes and arched windows, is surmounted by crenellation in the form of a parapet. The weathervane bears the date 1580.

East of the square, at ul. Chrobrego 11, is the former armoury, abutting medieval walls and towers, and housing a **museum** (open Tues, Thur–Sat 10.00–14.00, Wed 11.00–17.00, Sun 10.00–14.00). The collections are rather poor, and mainly seek to prove the Polishness of the region. One of the towers contains a display of armour and weaponry, mostly from the Napoleonic period.

After Prudnik, stay on the 408 for Nysa (27km).

Nysa

Nysa (population 45,900) is ancient indeed, but somewhat overrated as a tourist attraction. It began life as a 12C ducal stronghold, later evolving into an important religious centre, particularly during the Counter Reformation. Two of Poland's 17C monarchs—**Jan Sobieski** and **Michał Korybut Wiśniowiecki**—were educated at its renowned Jesuit college. Nysa suffered severe destruction during the Second World War. Today, the best monument is the 15C *Parish Church of St James**, on the Main Square. Its huge tiled roof—one of the tallest and steepest in Europe—required an entire forest to be felled for building material. A tiny bright green lantern sprouts from the middle like the tip of a pencil. Inside, two rows of octagonal pillars support the huge brick cross vaults. A wreath of 16 Gothic chapels (and three Baroque) circles the body of the church. The octagonal, domed **Chapel of the Dead** (now the baptistery) is entered from the left of the apse through a wrought-iron gate. A flight of stairs leads down to the crypts. Nysa was once the capital of the Dukes of Wrocław, and six of them are buried inside the church.

■ Practical information
★★ *Hotels*
Lazurowy. Ul. Otmuchowska, ☎ 33-40-76. On the Kłodzko road, close to a lake. Car park. 25 rooooms.
Piast. Ul. Krzywoustego 14, ☎ 33-40-84/5. Central location. 40 rooms.

Tourist information. Ul. Bracka 4.
ORBIS. Ul. Wrocławska 14.
Telephone code: (0–77).

The Town Museum
From the square walk south along UL. BISKUPA JAROSŁAWA to the *Town Museum at No. 11, which occupies the former Palace of the Bishops of Wrocław (open Tues–Fri 10.00–15.00, Sat 11.00–14.30, Sun 11.00–15.30). This quad-

rangular edifice with an inner courtyard was built in Italian Baroque style in the 17C–18C (rebuilt since the war). Its three floors accommodate an exceptionally rich and worthwhile display of items from the region and indeed from all over Europe. The archaeology section has objects found in the Nysa and Grodków regions from the Mesolithic era to modern times, with a particularly fine collection of **medieval glass**. The 15C–19C **European Painting** section has over 240 works, mostly Flemish and Dutch, but also Italian, French and German, including canvases by Lucas Cranach the Elder, Hugo van der Goes, Francesco Bassan, Bartholomeus van der Helst and Antonio Palamedes. In the **Graphic Art** section you will find Albercht Dürer's *Melancholy* cycle from 1514. Other sections cover sculpture, 16C–19C **furniture**, 15C–19C **pewterware** from Silesian workshops, photographs and etchings showing Nysa in former times (revealing just how much was destroyed during the Second World War), weaponry, including a Renaissance sword allegedly used in the decapitation of Duke Nicholas II on the square in Nysa, and 19C Silesian painting.

Return to the parish church and walk southwest across the square, passing a gabled **weighing house** (Mannerist, 1604), currently a public library, with sculptures and sgraffito on the façade. Opposite are a number of historic houses: of particular interest is the gabled **No. 23**, with remnants of Renaissance sgraffito decoration from the 16C–17C. Further southwest, at the corner of UL. BRACKA and UL. CELNA, is the Baroque **Triton Fountain** (1700–01), a copy of Bernini's famous Roman monument, with carved fish and a Triton swigging from a goblet.

Continue along ul. Bracka to the 18C **Church of SS Peter and Paul** of the Canons Regular of the Holy Sepulchre, its twin green-topped towers visible from the square. Its fine stuccos, fanciful ornamentation, cornices, arcades, balustrades, *trompe l'oeil* painted decoration—all the work of the **Scheffler brothers**—constitute **Silesian Baroque art** at its best.

Between the Main Square and the river (west) stand two brick towers, once part of the town fortifications (mid-14C, expanded in the 16C): the **Ziębice Tower** on ul. Bolesława Krzywoustego, and the **Wrocław Tower** on ul. Wrocławska.

Nysa to Kłodzko

❖ Otmuchów • Paczków • Kłodzko

This route leads to the prettiest part of Silesia—the Kłodzko valley (*Kotlina Kłodzka*)—passing on the way the beautifully preserved medieval town of Paczków. Leave Nysa along road 408 heading west. The sloping Market Square in **OTMUCHÓW** has all the monuments of interest within easy walking distance. At its lower end stands the Renaissance **Town Hall** (1538), with an early 17C tower (rebuilt in 1827), square rising to octagonal, and Renaissance sgraffito decoration—notably a sundial of 1575 on the northeast corner wall. Adjoining the Town Hall are several Baroque **Houses** (Nos 2, 3 and 4, 17C–18C).

The square ascends to the late 17C **parish church**, surrounded by a stone wall, with murals by Karl Dankwart and paintings by Michael Willmann inside. At the foot of the Castle Hill (on the left, if you face the church) is a small

Baroque palace (rebuilt in 1927). It was once known as the **Lower Castle**, and served as the second residence of the Bishops of Wrocław; it is now the seat of the City Council.

Walk up the hill (246m) to the **Castle of the Bishops of Wrocław**. Originally 13C, it was rebuilt many times over the centuries, acquiring a late Renaissance character in the 16C–17C. To the left of the entrance, beyond a circular portico resting on pillars, is a large **Baroque staircase** of 1638, recognisable by the slanting lines and oval windows in the wall. The stairs were adapted for horses, as Cardinal Ferdinand Vasa, an amateur equestrian, wished to be able to ride to his apartments in the north wing on horseback; he even had stables made for his (and only his) horses on the first floor. You approach the castle via a Gothic gate, which leads to a cobbled courtyard with a deep medieval well protected by a Neo-classical enclosure. Notice the remnants of 16C fortifications, and the sgraffito covering the castle walls. Weather permitting, the north tower is a good viewpoint (no fixed opening times). Set in a pleasant landscaped park and shrouded by trees, the castle is separated from the parish church by a lush ravine.

Walk to ul. Nyska (on the left as you enter the town) to see the Gothic **Sparrow Tower**, with a Renaissance superstructure (1566), once part of the medieval town fortifications.

Continue along road 408, following signs to Kłodzko. Just after you leave town, you could take a short detour right to the artificial LAKE OTMUCHOWSKIE (13km) behind a high embankment, along which runs a promenade. The lake is a watersports centre, with a modest campsite on the shore.

PACZKÓW (13km from Otmuchów), though not quite deserving its epithet of the 'Polish Carcassone', does indeed have one unique feature: an almost entirely preserved ring of medieval town walls with 19 towers. It was originally built in c 1350, and expanded in the 15C–16C to meet the demands of changing warfare technology. Additionally, there are three late Gothic towers adjoining the town's three main medieval gates: the 15C **Kłodzko Gate** (ul. Narutowicza, off the Market Square), with a Renaissance parapet of 1595; the 14C **Wrocław Gate** (ul. Wrocławska, off the Square); and the 15C **Ziembicka Gate** (ul. Świerczewskiego), also with a Renaissance decorative parapet (late 16C).

In the Main Square is the 19C **Town Hall** with a Renaissance tower (1550–52) surmounted by an octagonal turret, and several gabled houses, mostly late Baroque and Renaissance (**Nos 3, 22–27, 35** and **36**).

The fortress-like ****Parish Church of SS Mary, John the Evangelist and John the Baptist** looms above the town on PL. KOŚCIELNY (south). Indeed, the Gothic aisled hall, built originally in 1361–89, was altered in 1529–40 to fulfil a defensive purpose: the architects lowered the roof, added a 4m-thick parapet with loopholes for cannons, and drilled a well inside. Equally commanding is the 64m tower, with its hefty buttresses and squat, octagonal crowning. The 14C Gothic portal in west façade (renovated in 1577) is decorated with sculptures showing, among others, a henchman in chain-mail holding the crest of Bishop Przecław. Stairs were built in 1472, and the graceful Renaissance galilee in 1548–62. The church is a veritable museum of vaults: spring vaults (14C–15C) in the aisles and sacristy, star vaults in the nave and net vaults in the chancel and southeast Maltitz chapel (in the latter, of a rare variety, decorated with bosses in the form of little faces). Gothic figures of the Virgin and St Lawrence

(15C) rest in the apse to the left of the Neo-Gothic high altar. At the west end of the south aisle is the so-called Tartar Well, used in times of siege. It is covered by a wooden lid and surmounted by a wrought-iron structure supporting the bucket. The **Gothic Maltitz** chapel (mentioned above), built in 1447 and remodelled in 1588, holds a remarkable late Renaissance **altar** made of intricately carved sandstone. Its sculptures and reliefs depict Passion scenes.

Continue for 32km along road 408 to Kłodzko.

Kłodzko

Kłodzko lies at the centre of the **Kotlina Kłodzka**, a knot of land, bordered by mountains, which juts into the Czech Republic. The region offers varied landscape, and a rich assortment of spas and resort towns. It used to be a separate county under Bohemian protectorate, before passing into Austrian (1526), and then Prussian (1742) hands. During the 19C, the Prussians completed the massive **fortress**, today an imposing reminder of imperial rule and one of the town's chief attractions. Once an important medieval trading town, much of its 14C plan has been preserved, with a web of sloping streets spread out over a hillside.

■ **Practical information**

Hotel. ★★*Astoria*. Pl. Jedności 1, ☎ 67-30-35. Central location. Car park. 17 rooms.
Tourist information (PTTK). Ul. Wita Stwosza 1, ☎ 67-37-40.
ORBIS. ul. Grottgera 1, ☎ 67-40-59 (actually a private travel agency licensed by Orbis)
Main post office. Pl. Władysława Jagiełły 2.
Telephone code: (0–74).

The city centre

In the sloping Market Square (pl. Chrobrego) is a figure of St Mary, funded by the city council in 1644 after a bout of the plague; a municipal well with fish and a crowned lion, all carved in stone. The square is bisected by the **Town Hall** with a late Renaissance tower and gallery (1653–55). There are several good 16C–18C **burghers' houses**, particularly **Nos 5, 13,** and **34-36**, and more on ul. Armii Krajowej and ul. Czeska.

The **Parish Church of the Ascension** occupies PL. KOŚCIELNY at the end of UL. KOŚCIELNA. It was erected in late Gothic style (1344–1490), with the work being supervised by pupils of **Peter Parler**, the architect of St Vitus's Cathedral in Prague. The Jesuits, who acquired it in 1624, remodelled it in Baroque style (1673–75), adding galleries, stuccoes and sculptures. Christoph Tausch (1673–1731) raised the chancel vaults, decorating them with a mural of the *Ascension*, and built the high altar in 1727–29. Its centrepiece is the 13C *Beautiful Madonna of Kłodzko*, carved in cedar wood.

The rich, **Baroque interior** abounds in sculptures, paintings and ornaments. In the upper part of the nave are 14 **busts** of the patrons of Kłodzko; between the bays, murals and marble figures of the twelve Apostles; and on the pillars, paintings showing the saints of the Jesuit order in ornate frames. The pulpit, confessionals and organ are all the early 18C work of **Master Michał Klahar**. In the north aisle, just before the chancel, kneels the sepulchral stone figure of Bishop Ernest of Pardubice, hanged for keeping the secrets of the confession (Gothic, second half of the 14C). Next to the church, the Jesuits commissioned Carlo Lurago to build a College in 1655–90.

The town is dominated by the huge **fortress**, rising north of the square upon the site of an ancient fortified settlement and castle, built in 1680–1702 and later expanded. During the 19C, the fortress was used by the Prussians as a prison, and later by the Nazis as a POW camp. The fortress **museum** (open 09.00–16.00) is rather uninspiring, consisting of a series of dark, dank rooms with mediocre to poor exhibits, while the Fire Brigade Museum is no more than a row of fire engines stacked away in the corner of a yard. Modest, too, is the Lapidarium, which has a ramshackle collection of bits and pieces from dismantled buildings in the Kłodzko region. The high point of the tour is the **panoramic view** of Kłodzko, with its mass of construction sites and smoky chimneys bordered by the river to the east, and some vast ugly housing estates to the west.

Unless you suffer from heart disease or claustrophobia, you could also brave the labyrinth below the fortress: this maze of stuffy brick tunnels and passageways can only be visited with a guide (tours begin on the hour), but for those wanting just a taster, there is a shortened version—a 400m **Underground Tourist Route** in honour of the '1000th anniversary of the Polish state', which begins at the fortress and emerges by the parish church, and takes about 15 minutes.

From the church, walk along UL. ŁUKASIEWICZA to the commendable ***Regional Museum** at No. 4 (**open** Wed–Fri 10.00–17.00, Tues 10.00–15.00, Sat–Sun 11.00–17.00). The standard 'history of the town' display is supplemented by an excellent collection of clocks—everything from small ornamental ones to English long case clocks and huge church and town-hall tower clocks. The exhibition has been planned and designed with care and is far from tedious. The museum has a small concert hall, which occasionally hosts concerts, such as Chopin piano recitals coinciding with the Chopin festival in Duszniki Zdrój (see below).

A stone **Gothic bridge** (1390) spans the canal south of the Market Square. This small replica of the Charles Bridge in Prague is decorated with six late Baroque statues from the first half of the 18C. Between the bridge and the river stands the **Franciscan Church and Monastery**, completed in the second half of the 17C. The interior is standard Baroque, with chapels flanking the nave, a very short chancel, *trompe l'oeil* decoration, a Passion group and an organ, whose shiny gold ornamentation looks like molten wax trickling down a candle. The Monastery refectory has murals (1744) by Felix Anton Scheffler.

Spas at the foot of Table Mountains

❖ Polanica Zdrój • Duszniki Zdrój • Kudowa Zdrój • Karłów • Radków •
  Ratno • Wambierzyce

The region west of Kłodzko is rich in beautiful landscapes and dreamy spas. The highlight of the excursion are the fairy-tale Góry Stołowe (Table Mountains), reached along the 'Road of a Hundred Bends'. From Kłodzko head west on road 8 to **POLANICA ZDRÓJ** (12km), an attractive resort with the **Spring Pavilion** set in a large park, where you can sample the delicious local waters.

The next stop, **DUSZNIKI ZDRÓJ** (9km), is the oldest and grandest of the spas. To get there, follow signs to Szczytna along a minor road, which climbs through beautiful forested hills. As you enter town, you will see an old wooden paper mill to the left of the road, still partly operational, housing the **Museum of the Paper Industry** (open Tues–Sun 09.00–15.00). Built in 1605, the mill produced high quality paper until 1938. On weekdays you can observe the traditional paper-making process. The products—writing paper, envelopes, etc.—all hand-made, can be purchased at the ticket office.

Dusznki Zdrój consists of the town, with a number of historic houses on the Main Square, and the spa,

Paper mill, Duszniki Zdrój

a kilometre or so further west. The road to the spa passes several grand villas, which lend the place a somewhat stately air, though the site of the house where Chopin lived in 1826 is disappointing—only a plaque on the wall of a plain modern house. Each August, a Chopin Music Festival is held in the old theatre to commemorate the composer's stay here.

KUDOWA ZDRÓJ (14km), the largest spa town in the region, is an excellent base for excursions into the **Table Mountains** (Góry Stołowe), and offers good, inexpensive accommodation in Hotel *Kosmos* on ul. Buczka 16 (☎ 66-15-11/2). Be sure to try the waters in the elegant **Spa Park**.

Chapel of the Skulls

From the town centre, follow the white signs to 'Kaplica Czaszek'—the **Chapel of Skulls**, situated a few kilometres outside Kudowa, by a village church. The chapel (open Tues–Sat 10.00–17.00, Sun 14.00–17.00) was founded in 1776 by Father Tomaszek, who probably got the idea whilst visiting the catacombs in Rome, or modelled it on the famous Church of Skulls in Kutna Hora in the Czech Republic. For 18 years, Tomaszek collected the bones of the victims of the Thirty Years War and the plagues that followed. In total he amassed 24,000 items, of which 3000 are used in the chapel as decoration, and the rest are stored away in the crypt. Among the skulls and bones lining the chapel's walls and ceiling are two sculptures of angels, one holding a trumpet with the inscription 'Arise from the dead', the other holding scales marked 'Thou shalt be judged'. In the middle stands a small Baroque altar. Glass cases hold the more interesting items from this morbid collection, such as the skull of a syphilis victim, Mongolian and Tartar skulls, the skull of Father Tomaszek himself (for some reason the only one with its back turned to visitors), and Langer's, a gravedigger who helped Tomaszek.

Detour to the Crib at Czermna

Continue up the road to **CZERMNA**. In the green-gabled house at No. 101 (left), you can examine a fantastically intricate **mechanical nativity crib** (*szopka*), which Franciszek Stepan (b. 1888) carved during 20 years of painstaking work. With similar persistence, its 250 small lime-wood figures go through their motions—a chimney-sweep pushing his brush up and down a chimney, a smith hammering the same horseshoe, wafer-thin by now, a procession of pilgrims never reaching its destination, a drunkard trying in vain to empty an already empty jug into his gaping mouth, and scores of others, all powered by a noisy electrical engine (installed in 1927), which thankfully can be turned off. In 1930, the same artist, grandfather of the present owner of the house, began construction of another wonder: a wooden organ. Completed in a mere 8 years, it has 270 voices and 10 registers. Unfortunately, Stepan's granddaughter cannot play it, and visitors may appreciate only its visual qualities.

Return to Kudowa (2km) and join road 387, popularly known as the **Road of a Hundred Bends**. After a few kilometres, turn left at the sign marked 'Błędne Skały' (sandstone labyrinth). To avoid cars travelling in the opposite direction along this narrow and winding road, you should enter it only at the times specified on the billboard (this is possible at least twice every hour).

The walk begins at the car park. Ascending the hill (3.5km from the road), you enter the ***Góry Stołowe National Park**, a lush terrain of extraordinary rock formations caused by the erosion of the sandstone hills over many millions of years. Were it not for the marked trail, one could easily get lost in the spectacular labyrinth of rocks, 6–8m high. The walk leads through cracks in the gigantic sandstone boulders—some are quite narrow, so you might have to sqeeze through. On the way back you can take a shorter trail, which skirts the labyrinth. Several other trails leading to the nearby peaks begin from the other side of Błędne Skały. Approximate walking time is given on the signposts.

Return to the Road of a Hundred Bends and continue 13km to **KARŁÓW**. You will see a range of rocky hills in the distance, a bus stop, and a large building with a car park by the side of the road. Stop here and follow the gravel path next to the shelter up a long flight of stone steps (682 in all). On top of the hill (refreshments available) you enter the Szczeliniec range (919m). Contrary to Błędne Skały, you can walk across the top of the peak, enjoying the views, and descend into the bottom of narrow fisures, which have been quaintly dubbed 'Little Hell', 'Devil's Kitchen' etc. One of the main attractions is the sandstone boulders shaped by erosion to resemble people, animals and other creatures, both mythical and natural (approximate sightseeing time 1hr).

Eleven kilometres along the Road of a Hundred Bends you come to **RADKÓW**, where the stone **Church of St Dorothy** (16C–18C) will come into view. The elegant portal, with its protruding pillars and pediment, is enticing, but the interior, cheap and garish, is hardly worth a visit.

Drive on to **WAMBIERZYCE**, passing **RATNO DOLNE** on the way, where you can stop briefly for a view of a 15C–16C hilltop **Castle**, with a tower, turrets, an arcaded wall and parapets typical of Silesia.

The Pilgrimage Church

The *Pilgrimage Church in Wambierzyce is approached by a long, broad flight of 33 steps (1693–1710, rebuilt in 1715–20), flanked by stone statues with brass flames above their heads and animals at their feet. The two-storey **façade** overflows with ornaments: pilasters, blind arches, pinnacles, sculptures, terraces and balustrades—only the towers are conspicuously absent. The **cloisters**, entered through the door on the left, contain a series of rather murky and austere chapels, housing the **Stations of the Cross**—one of the main pilgrim attractions of Wambierzyce. A large painting by L. Bittner (1825) shows the legendary Jan of Raszów being cured of blindness by a small wooden statuette of St Mary in c 1200. Crutches displayed nearby are said to have been joyfully cast away by cripples, likewise cured by the miraculous statuette. Next is a 13C stone altar, stoup and candelabra, followed by a garish painting (1775) of a party of angels building the church. Several religious paintings in the naive style, by anonymous artists, are protected by a large glass panel. Eventually you come to a vaulted porch on the west side of the church, with four sculptures supported on consoles, among them St Elizabeth. Continuing along the cloister, you will pass more religious paintings and frescoes, as well as niches with sculptures illustrating the life of Jesus.

The church **interior** is quite extraordinary: the round nave, covered with an elliptical dome bearing a large mural, is crowded with pilasters surmounted with gilded capitals and a prominent cornice. The furniture seems almost dripping with gilded ornaments, tassels, wreaths and sculptures forming a swirling mass of cherubs, saints and other figures. On the north and south walls, placed symmetrically as befits a perfectly Baroque interior, are panels of three paintings each. The tiny organ on the west side of the gallery looks like a miniature toy amid the elephantine surroundings. The chancel, covered with a handsome elliptical dome, is separated by a very elaborate wrought-iron rood screen, with bouquets of iron flowers in the upper part. Framed murals line the dome. It is lit by a lantern, which looks like a miniature church in itself, complete with columns, windows, and a mural above. Sculptures of SS *Hieronimus*, *Gregory*, *Augustine* and *Ambrose* (going clockwise from the northwest corner) inhabit niches in the chancel wall. The high altar columns enclose a tabernacle with the miraculous figure of St Mary.

A pleasant walk can be made to the **Calvary**, whose chapels are scattered over the nearby hills. This was the 18C brainchild of Daniel Paschasius von Osterberg, who planned it as a sort of Silesian Jerusalem. The ascent to the final Station begins opposite the church and leads through the Gate of the Judgement, resembling a triumphal arch.

Mt Śnieżnik and the Bear's Cave

❖ Bystrzyca Kłodzka • (detour: Międzygórze • Międzylesie) • Stronie Śląskie • (detour: Kletno) • Lądek Zdrój

Head south from Kłodzko on road 381, marked 'Międzylesie'. From Bystrzyca Kłodzka (22km) continue east to the crystal glass factory at Stronie Śląskie (see below), or take a detour (18km) to the mountain resort-cum-spa of Międzygórze and the spa town of Międzylesie (road 381). For **MIĘDZYGÓRZE** turn left at Wilkanów. The resort is set in a lush valley with a stream that tumbles into the Wilczki waterfall (27m; on the left as you enter). The village is noted for its almost entirely wooden architecture, with most of the Swiss- and Norwegian-style villas dating from the 19C. It is also a good base for excursions into the mountains. Trails start from the small car park beyond the parish church (18C) leading to the mountain shelter of **Maria Śnieżna**, a former inn (1h 15 min.), and to Mt. Igliczna (1h 30 min.), on the summit of which stands the **Church of Our Lady Śnieżna** (1781–82). Further up the hill another trail begins to **Mt. Śnieżnik** (1h 30 min.), the highest peak in the region (1425m).

Return to the 381 and continue south to the spa town of **MIĘDZYLESIE**. The main monuments are concentrated near the long square: the **Parish Church of Corpus Christi**, and a 17C Baroque **Palace**, with a passageway connecting the two. Behind the palace stands a 16C Renaissance **castle**. Walk the length of the square to a wooden gabled house with an arcade—a remnant of the 18C weavers' quarter.

To continue the main route follow the 393 from Bystrzyca Kłodzka, signposted 'Stronie Śląskie' (23km). The road climbs steeply along hairpin bends, with fine views from the **Puchaczówka Pass** (864m; there is a walking trail from here, 1h 30 min., to **Mt. Igliczna**), eventually descending to Stronie Śląskie. The country-side—hills and forest merging with undulating meadows—is very pretty.

STRONIE ŚLĄSKIE (23km) is a town that would probably not exist were it not for its renowned **Crystal Glass Factory**, built in the mid-19C, and nationalised after the war. The PTTK bureau in the office block next door can arrange a guided tour of the site (also in English), where you can observe the antique production process—from molten glass being hand-moulded by glass blowers in the traditional way, to the finished product of fancy crystal vases, bowls and other fragile vessels, packaged and ready for export. The items can, of course, be purchased on site. Next to the factory is the mansion of the former owner: a veritable storybook castle with a round tower and a curious array of gables, parapets and turrets.

The Bear's Cave

From Stronie, a short and worthwhile detour south along a minor road takes you to the *Bear's Cave, just beyond the village of **KLETNO** (14km) (follow the white signs to 'Jaskinia Niedźwiedzia', initially along a cobbled road). The road ends at a car park near a quarry (trails start from here to Mt. Śnieżnik), leaving the remaining 1km to be covered on foot.

■ **Open** Mon, Wed, Fri–Sun 09.00–16.30; closed Dec–Jan.
In order to protect the unique atmospheric conditions inside, no more than 300 people are allowed to visit the cave each day (guided tours only). It is best to pre-arrange a visit (☎ Stronie Śląskie 14-12-50).

English is likely to be spoken, as, in addition to bats, the cave is presently inhabited by scientists. Unlike many similar caves, especially in the neighbouring Czech Republic, this one is still 'alive': the stalactites and stalagmites are growing, the marble is being washed away, geological eras are rushing by. Discovered accidentally in 1966, the cave was so named on account of the tens of thousands of bear bones found inside. To the invariable disappointment of younger visitors, no bear ever lived here; the bones were merely washed inside by stream waters.

Return to Stronie and regain road 392 heading north to LĄDEK ZDRÓJ (7km), a tranquil and hilly spa town set at the foot of the Golden Mountains (Góry Złote), with less tourist traffic compared to other spas in the region. The waters at Lądek were put to medicinal use as early as the 15C, and later the bath houses were frequented by Prussian royalty. On PL. MARIAŃSKI is the much-photographed 'Wojciech' Spa Pavilion (1678)—the symbol of Lądek. Round, covered with a lanterned dome, and decorated with pillars, reliefs, and sculptures, it looks truly grand after recent renovation. Inside is an enormous tub for mud baths. At No. 2 ul. Ostrowicza you will find the 'Jerzy' Sanatorium, built as early as 1459. About 1km further on is the Main Square, with arcaded 16C–17C Houses (north), a row of pretty Baroque gables (west), a 17C sculpture depicting the Holy Trinity, and a 19C Town Hall decorated in yellow and white.

Kłodzko to Wrocław

❖ Ząbkowice Śląskie • Ziębice • Henryków • Wrocław

From Kłodzko take road 8 northwards to ZĄBKOWICE ŚLĄSKIE (23km). The Neo-Gothic Town Hall on the MARKET SQUARE was built in 1862–64. It is most conspicuous for its tall, slender clock tower, and, on the left, an ornamental stone façade with a gable, pinnacles and small mascarons along the gable edge. Over the portal hangs the crest of Ząbkowice, flanked by the Auersperg and Podebrad coats of arms.

From the southwest corner of the square walk west along UL. ŚW. WOJCIECHA. In the distance you will see the brick Leaning Tower of Ząbkowice (34 m), built in the early 14C, probably as part of the nearby castle. A local earthquake in 1598 caused it to lean 1.52m off the vertical, and a fire of 1858 destroyed the crowning (the present Silesian-style parapet is a later addition). It is possible to climb the tower for a good view of the town (ask for the key at the museum on ul. Ciasna 1, see below).

Further west is the Gothic Church of St Anne, erected after 1351. Note the many epitaph slabs, most with reliefs, and the paintings on wood on the walls and buttresses. The interior—a short nave and long, narrow chancel—is rich in sculptures; some adorn the Mannerist sandstone pulpit (1619) on the right. The most valuable are St Anne (1493), the Virgin and Child (1507), and a Pietà (1500). The south chapel contains the Gothic tomb of Charles I of Podebrad (Ziębice) (d. 1536) and his wife Anna of Żagań (d. 1541), as well as the tomb of his courtier, Zygmunt Kaufung. By means of robbery and assault, Kaufung quickly amassed a considerable fortune, but was eventually banished to Bohemia and later decapitated in Vienna. His wife paid a heavy ransom for his head and also for the right to bury him in the Ząbkowice church in 1573. His residence, known as the Knight's House (1526), stands a short distance further south, and is currently a museum, established in the 1950s by a local teacher. The collection consists almost exclusively of individual donations, and this is reflected in its somewhat haphazard character. On the ground floor is perhaps the most interesting item: an internal well 25m deep, with a horizontal corridor in its lower part. The well once saved Kaufung from being lynched: he hid in the corridor when a crowd of angry burghers wanted to rid the town of him. The oldest part of the building is the chapel on the first floor.

Walking further down UL. CIASNA you will come to the **Castle of the Dukes of Ziębice**, a ruin now inhabited only by swallows. The stone structure on a square plan with an inner courtyard is equipped with two angle rondelles and a gate tower. A conspicuous detail amid the rubble is a coat of arms over the portal, bearing three eagles' heads. Charles I of Podebrad (Ziębice) commissioned the celebrated Prague architect **Benedikt Ried** to reconstruct a former castle on this site in Renaissance style in 1524–32. The parapet crowning the tower gate and the south wing became models for many other buildings of the time. During the Thirty Years War the castle suffered much damage, particularly at the hands of the Swedes. Rebuilt in 1651–61, it fell into ruin after devastation by fire in 1784.

From Ząbkowice take road 385 to **ZIĘBICE** (19km), where you can see several good 17C–18C town houses around the Market Square. In the centre stands the Town Hall, with a curious **Museum of Household Items** (open Wed–Fri 10.00–15.00, Sat–Sun 10.00–17.00), including a room entirely devoted to irons!

The medieval town walls with towers are only partly preserved: on ul. Grunwaldzka, off the square, stands the early 15C **Paczków Gate**, the only survivor of five; its crenellation, with a 16C brick superstructure, is a rarity in the region.

From Ziębice join road 395 heading towards Wrocław. After about 10km you will reach **HENRYKÓW**, by far the most attractive stop on the route.

The Cistercian Abbey

The tower of the Cistercian ** **Abbey Church** comes into view on the right of the road as you approach Henryków.

> Founded in 1225–27 by Henryk the Bearded and his wife Jadwiga, Henryków is one of the oldest Cistercian abbeys in Poland, combining Romanesque, Gothic and Baroque architecture and decoration. The chancel, with its ambulatory and chapels, dates back to 1241–60; the Gothic basilican body proper went up in the first half of the 14C. In 1506 and c 1560 two late Gothic chapels were added, followed by the tower in 1608. In 1692 the whole church was rebuilt, with Baroque elements being introduced in the three chapels behind the chancel and in the façade and galilee.
>
> From its inception until the mid-18C, Henryków was an important Silesian cultural and religious institution. The Abbey chronicle, the *Liber Enricianus*, spanning the years 1268–73 and the early 14C (the original is kept in the Archdiocesan Archive in Wrocław and cannot be viewed), contains the oldest written sentence in the Polish language: 'Let me turn the wheel while you rest', attributed to a certain Boguchwał, who spoke these memorable words to his peasant wife as she sweated over a millstone.

The furniture of the church is uniformly Baroque, dating mostly from the late 17C. In the centre of the 17C high altar is *The Birth of Christ in the Vision of*

St Bernard of Clairvaux, a painting by the renowned Silesian artist Michael Will-mann (1630–1712). It is flanked by figures of saints, three on each side, with the founders of the Abbey, Henryk the Bearded and St Jadwiga, above. The Renaissance stalls (c 1560) have sumptuous Rococo decoration in limewood and oak (1702–12), depicting the Way of the Cross. Above the stalls hang paint-ings by Jan Bonoro (1729), narrating the *Life of St Bernard*. In addition to the main organ at the west end, a smaller one, meant to accompany the Gregorian chant cultivated by Bernardine and Cistercian monks, has been added to the south wall over the stalls. The characteristically Baroque love of symmetry required the placement of a mock organ on the north wall. In the north transept stands the 18C stuccoed altar of St John Nepomuk; the carving above the portal shows his execution: he was thrown into Vltava river from the Charles Bridge in Prague for keeping the secret of the Confession. The central chapel entered from the ambulatory is a **mausoleum of the Silesian Piasts** with a Gothic sarcoph-agus (1341) of Duke Bolko II of Ziębice and his wife, Jutta. In the south aisle, note the paintings by Michael Willmann and the epitaph slabs of Cistercian abbots. The sacristy, itself Romanesque, is furnished in the Baroque style. Adjoining the church is the Baroque monastic building (seminary and priory, with angle towers), erected in 1681–1702.

Continue north along road 395 to Wrocław (60km).

Wrocław to Jelenia Góra

❖ Legnickie Pole • Legnica • Złotoryja • (detour: Grodziec) • Jelenia Góra

Legnickie Pole

Leave Wrocław on the motorway (E40) south of the city centre and turn left for Legnickie Pole some 56km later. The most commanding sight in the village is the huge *Benedictine Abbey* (18C), with its Baroque church of St Jadwiga. To enter, you should buy a ticket at the museum in the nearby Gothic church (see below). The abbey is the work of **Kilian Ignaz Dienzenhofer**, an architect known for many buildings in Prague.

Soft in appearance, the yellow façade of St Jadwiga's church has twin towers and Corinthian pilasters flanking a bulging two-tiered fronton with two broken pediments; note also the ornate stone carved portal sandwiched between two lesser ones. The fabulous **interior**, both graceful and rich, consists of an oval aisleless nave leading to a short chancel, very white and bright. Ornately carved white Corinthian pillars support vaults covered with superb **frescoes** (1733) by Cosmas Damian Asam, most depicting biblical scenes, except above the organ loft, where the Tartars are shown celebrating their victory (see below). The monastic buildings rise symmetrically on both sides of the church. After 1810, the buildings housed a Prussian military academy; Paul von Hindenburg was one of its graduates.

Opposite the abbey is the Gothic **Church of the Holy Trinity and St Mary**. According to popular legend, it was erected on the spot where the decapitated body of King Henryk the Pious was found after the Polish army's disastrous defeat at the hands of the Tartars in 1241. In 1961 the church was converted into a **museum** (**open** Wed–Sun 11.00–17.00) to commemorate the 720th anniversary of the famous battle. Jan Matejko (see p. 72) portrayed the event in his *The Defeat at Legnickie Pole in 1241* (now in the National Museum in Warsaw) and *The Departure of Henryk the Pious from Legnica* (now in the National Museum in Poznań).

Legnica

From Legnickie Pole you can avoid the motorway by taking a minor road to LEGNICA. The town is something of a let-down considering its rich and varied history. Initially the capital of a Piast duchy, it passed to the Bohemian crown in 1329. The first Lutheran university in Europe was established here in 1526. With the extinction of the Piast line in 1675, it passed to the Habsburgs. A period of slow decline was finally checked in the 19C, when, under Prussian rule (after 1742), it became an important industrial centre.

The centre of the drab Market Square, largely dominated by modern tenements, is occupied by a Baroque **Town Hall** and adjoining 19C theatre. Slightly further along are the delightful Renaissance **Herring Stalls** (Nos 24–31), narrow and gabled, each one a different colour, and some (Nos 26–27) with sgraffito decoration (c 1560). Close by, facing the passageway next to the Town Hall, is the exquisitely sgraffitoed **'By the Quail's Nest' House** (16C), the town's finest house.

At the far end of the Square (pl. Najświętszej Marii Panny) stands the twin-towered **Church of SS Peter and Paul**, dating back to the 14C. The interior was heavily remodelled in 1892–94, stripping it of many Gothic elements. Note the rare spring vaults in the aisles, the 13C bronze font in the chancel, and the Piast sarcophagus in the south aisle. The high altar (1738) and many epitaph stones are Baroque, but the stone pulpit and wooden stalls are Renaissance. The tympanum of the north portal (visible from the outside) holds a 15C Gothic carving depicting the *Adoration of the Magi*.

From the Market Square walk along UL. CHOJNOWSKA; on the right you will pass the **Military Academy** (1726–35), now a public library and cultural centre, and, further down, at the corner of ul. Bohaterów Getta, the rather forlorn **Chojnów Tower** (14C) with plain windows. A small monument on the square next to it commemorates the victims of the Warsaw Ghetto.

Continue along UL. BOHATERÓW GETTA and turn right into UL. PARTYZANTÓW, which leads up to the castle (see below). First you might visit the **Regional Museum** (open Wed–Sun 11.00–16.30) inside the late Baroque Palace of the Abbots of Lubiąż (ul. Partyzantów 3), featuring exhibits connected with the history of Legnica and a curious display entitled 'Dangers, Threats and Environmental Disasters', and numerous paintings by Józef Łukomski.

Opposite the museum stands the twin-towered **Church of St John** (late Baroque, 1714–30). The adjoining circular domed chapel serves as the **mausoleum of the Legnica and Brzeg Piasts** (open Tues–Sat 10.00–16.00). Its sepulchral and painted decoration continues the Piast theme.

Continue along ul. Partyzantów to the **castle**. Its stuccoed gate (1533) is the sole remnant of its Renaissance period.

> The first wooden castle on the site, dating back to the 11C, was replaced with a brick one in the early 13C. Two round stone towers and the palatium

along the south side were added. Next to the palatium, a dodecagonal chapel was erected in the courtyard. During the 16C the castle was re-designed in Renaissance style, receiving ramparts, bastions and a moat. In 1674, a gallery with a clock tower was built, dividing the spacious courtyard into its west and east parts. A fire in 1711 destroyed the north wing; another in 1835 led to renovation work carried out by the celebrated architect, Karl Friedrich Schinkel. The castle again suffered heavy damage in 1945.

A glass pavilion has been erected on the site of the former chapel; inside, frag-ments of it have been put on display (**open** Tues–Sat 10.00–16.30). Even when the pavilion is closed, the windows offer a good view of the interior. The wall that cuts the courtyard in two is pierced by a portal bearing the Piast eagle. An arched passage leads through to the west part of the courtyard, where you can see the round brick tower of St Jadwiga with its crenellated 'cuff', above which rises an octagonal extension topped by a red-tiled spire.

From Legnica follow signs to **ZŁOTORYJA** (19km) along road 364. The town's name recalls the times when gold was mined in the Kaczawa river (*złoto* means gold in Polish). Later, in the 16C, copper was discovered in the surrounding hills. Old shafts (padlocked) still exist by the river. The sloping Market Square has a number of historic **Burghers' Houses**, particularly Nos 5–15, some gabled and most in need of renovation. At the upper end of the Square is the Romanesque-Gothic **Parish Church of St Mary**, with many epitaph slabs, some quite ornate, embedded in its walls.

From Złotoryja, you could take a 24km detour along minor roads to the impressive **Castle of the Dukes of Legnica** in Grodziec. Perched high on a basalt hill (390m), the castle was expanded in late Gothic/Renaissance style in 1522–4. Though heavily remodelled in the 19C–20C, some older elements have been preserved, such as the vaults in the hall and the 16C tower and gatehouse.

Return to Olszanica and turn right for Złotoryja, where you should join road 370 marked 'Jelenia Góra-Karczów'. Road 365, forking right after 2km after Świerzawa, winds its way through forested hills to Jelenia Góra (37km).

Jelenia Góra

At the foot of the Karkonosze mountains, Jelenia Góra is a large regional capital with over 90,000 inhabitants, its history dating from the 11C. The initial settle-ment was founded at the confluence of the Bóbr and Kamienna rivers, the area occupied by today's Old Town. For **King Bolesław the Wry-Mouthed** it was an important border stronghold in his struggle against the Germans, as evidenced by the huge ramparts on the Hill of Bolesław Krzywousty (the Wry-Mouthed) west of the Old Town and the numerous archaeological discoveries made there. Jelenia Góra received a municipal charter in 1288 and enjoyed the status of an economic and regional capital during the Piast period, which lasted until 1392.

Later, under Bohemian rule, it first specialised in glass production, and then, during the 16C, in the cloth trade, becoming the largest exporter of cloth in Silesia, with buyers in places as far away as Africa and America. It suffered complete destruction during the Thirty Years War, and thereafter suffered economic decline. The tragic fate of the city's weavers in the 17C was described by J. G. Hauptmann in his Nobel Prize-winning novel *The Weavers*. It was also at that time that the Renaissance-Baroque character of the Old Town took shape.

After the Prussians took over in 1741, Jelenia Góra gradually lost significance, though during the late 19C it experienced a minor revival thanks to the development of industry and tourism. Today, much of the city is tainted by heavy industry, and despite efforts to keep pollution out of the centre, a thick layer of smog seems to hover permanently above it. Visitors arriving in summer might want to catch the **Street Theatre Festival** in August, the **Theatre Festival** in September, or the **Antiques Fair** on pl. Ratuszowy (the last Sunday in September). A fine panoramic view of the city can be had from the viewing tower on the Hill of Bolesław Krzywousty.

■ Practical information
Hotels
★★★★ *Orbis Jelenia Góra*. Ul. Sudecka 63, ☎ 764-6481. Central location, very helpful staff. By far the best hotel in town. Car park, swimming pool, business services. 188 rooms with views over the park, woods or Karkonosze Mountains.
★★ *Cieplicka Harenda*. Ul. Francuska 2a, ☎ 755-2030. In the neighbouring spa suburb of Cieplice Śląskie-Zdrój. 12 rooms.

Tourist information (PAPT). Ul. 1 Maja 42, ☎ 752-4054/752-5114.
ORBIS. Ul. 1 Maja, ☎ 262-06.
Main post office. Pocztowa 9.
Telephone code. (0–75).

The city centre
Begin exploring the city at the Main Square (PL. RATUSZOWY), unique in Silesia for its ring of whitewashed 17C–18C Renaissance and Baroque **houses**, 55 in all; the arcades, preserved in their entirety, were once used for cloth fairs. The houses have been reconstructed since the war, mainly for residential purposes, losing much of their original stucco. In the middle of the square stands the **Town Hall**—a stone Neo-classical building from 1744–49, with a Latin inscription over the entrance referring to the founding of the town by **Bolesław the Wry-Mouthed** in 1108. The **Neptune Fountain** is supposed to symbolise the town's international trade, which thrived under Habsburg rule. West of the Square along UL. JASNA is the 16C **Castle Tower**, rebuilt in the 19C. Apart from the Wojanowska Tower (see below), this is all that remains of the town's medieval fortifications.

Walk east from the square along UL. KONOPNICKIEJ, the city's main thoroughfare, which eventually becomes ul. 1 Maja. Just off it on the left (ul. Boczna) is the **Church of SS Erasmus and Pancras**, a late Gothic basilica (14C–15C) with a 70m tower. Two **burghers' tombstones** in the west wall bear symbols of the crafts their owners were engaged in: a baker's bun and a tailor's scissors. Other tombstones, especially those in the south wall, display full-size figures in relief.

Further along ul. Konopnickiej is the **Chapel of St Anne** and **Wojanowska Tower**. The tower was given a bastion in 1514, which, at the beginning of the 18C, was covered with a roof and turned into the chapel of St Anne, though the loopholes in the wall still testify to its former defensive function. The tower, in turn came to serve as the chapel belfry.

Further along UL. 1 MAJA is the **Orthodox Church of SS Peter and Paul**. This Baroque edifice of 1737 was given to the Uniates after the war to accommodate believers resettled from the eastern part of pre-war Poland.

Nowadays, an Orthodox priest from Legnica comes in every week to say mass. On the outside north wall are two penitentiary crosses.

> During the Middle Ages, when depopulation was often a major problem, instead of being hanged, murderers would sometimes be sentenced to work for and support the family of their victim, to pay the church a hefty fine for absolution, and carve a stone cross bearing an image of the weapon they used to commit the crime. These so-called '**penitentiary crosses**' can be found in many places in Silesia.

Continue along ul. 1 Maja to the garrison **Church of the Holy Cross** (formerly Lutheran), built in 1709–18 and modelled on St Catherine's in Stockholm. It has a central cruciform design and wooden galleries for 4000 worshippers. Behind the altar is one of the largest organs in Silesia, the focus for concerts, which are often held in the church, particularly in September. The spacious grounds, shaded by sparse trees, are criss-crossed with pathways and surrounded by a wall lined with many 18C sepulchral chapels closed off by grilles, where rich cloth merchants were buried (most of the chapels are in poor condition).

Though outside the Old Town centre, the **Regional Museum** on UL. MATEJKI is one of Jelenia Góra's more attractive sights (**open** Tues, Thur, Fri 09.00–15.30, Wed, Sat–Sun 09.00–17.00). The permanent display is devoted to the history of glass, with special emphasis on the 19C–20C, and on local manufacture. The finest examples are of the Biedermeier and Art Nouveau styles. All items are labelled in English.

A pleasant park stretches southeast from the museum, rising up to Kościuszko hill. Close to the cemetery is a model showing the geology of the Karkonosze mountains in cross-section.

Cieplice

The spa town of Cieplice, about 6km south of the centre, became a suburb of Jelenia Góra in 1976.

> According to legend, the origins of the spa date back to 1175, when **Bolesław the Curly**, son of Bolesław the Wry-Mouthed, discovered a warm spring while chasing an injured deer. Historical documents confirm only that in 1281 Duke Bernard Lwówecki gave a large tract of land and 'warm springs' to the Knights Hospitallers of St John of Jerusalem, which proves that the healing properties of the springs were already known at that time. In 1403, Count Schaffgotsch funded a benefice for the Cistercians from Krzeszów, who took care of the spa until 1810.
>
> In the 17C–18C the town became an important centre for glass-making.

Today, Cieplice Spa, with its modern sanatoria, is hardly a place—its name notwithstanding—where you would come to convalesce. The Market Square is too drab and devoid of life to compensate for the sprawling conglomeration of industrial suburbs. The main thoroughfare—PL. PIASTOWSKI—is closed off at its northeast end by an 18C Baroque Protestant church and, at its southwest end, by the slightly more interesting Catholic **Parish Church of St John the Baptist**, built in the 18C, with a rich Baroque interior, including a painting by Michael Willmann at the high altar. Close by are 16 **knights' tombstones** from the 16C–17C, and a modest four-wing 16C Cistercian abbey with a spa pavilion.

About half-way along pl. Piastowski is the imposing late Baroque **Schaff-gotsch Palace** (1784–88), which overlooks the Spa Park. It is decorated with the Schaffgotsch coat of arms bearing Piast eagles. The one hundred or so rooms, decorated in the Empire and Neo-classical styles, have been given over to a branch of the Wrocław Technical University and are usually closed to visitors. The **Spa Park**, designed in 1748 as a French garden for the Schaffgotsch Palace, and remodelled as a landscaped park in 1819 and 1838, contains two buildings of note: the whitewashed Neo-classical **Spa Theatre**, equipped in 1836 with a stuccoed pediment, and, further down the alley, the **Spa Cultural Centre**— another Neo-classical building (1799). On the west edge of the park by ul. Cervi is a **Martyrology Monument** in the shape of a totem pole carved in wood (1967). Inscribed on it are the names of places memorable for their role in Polish history, and showing the dark side of Polish-German relations—Psie Pole, Grunwald, Auschwitz etc.

Further south, across UL. CERVI and the Podgórna river, is the **Norwegian Park**, with a wooden Norwegian Pavilion overlooking a pond. The building houses a **Natural History Museum** (ul. Wolności 268, **open** Tues 09.00–14.00, Wed–Fri 09.00–15.00, Sat–Sun 09.00–16.00), with an uninspiring exhibition of stuffed birds and butterflies that falls short of the superb zoological collection owned by the Schaffgotsch family—even the curator admits the present display is a far cry from the original.

From the museum follow ul. Cervi and then UL. CIEPLICKA into the village-cum-suburb of Sobieszów. Upon a high hill overgrown with trees stands **Chojnik Castle** (a 40 minute climb from the car park). Built by Bolko II of Świdnica in 1353–64 on the site of a former hunting lodge, it was later owned by the Schaffgotsch family. In 1675 it burned down after being struck by lightning. Though conservation work was carried out in 1965–69, it is mostly in ruin, with a restaurant, rather spartan accommodation and jousting tournaments, usually in September. On the west side, huge granite boulders form a precipice (627m) with an agreeable view over Sobieszów.

Drive uphill (south) along UL. KARKONOSKA, turning right when you reach Jagniątków. As the road levels off, watch out for the sign marked 'Hauptmann Haus' pointing right. The house, about 100m from the road, is the **birthplace of Gerhart Hauptmann**, the Nobel Prize-winning German writer, best known for his novel *The Weavers* (1892), in which he describes the life of weavers in Jelenia Góra after the Prussian takeover of Silesia. The sprawling and irregular house (currently a

Chojnik Castle

children's home) from the **Jugendstil period** has a red-tiled roof and a curious round tower with a pointed top looking rather like a traditional Prussian helmet.

The Karkonosze Mountains

❖ Karpacz • Szklarska Poręba

South of Jelenia Góra are the resort towns of Karpacz (19km) and Szklarska Poręba (29km), both ideal bases for excursions into the Karkonosze mountains, which form the border with the Czech Republic. In winter, the region gets plenty of snow and the often steep, winding roads may be difficult to pass (snow chains are strongly advised).

Leave Jelenia Góra along ul. Sudecka (road 367) and follow signs to Karpacz; the route passes through the village of MYSŁAKOWICE (9km), with a group of 60 or so Tyrol-style houses on either side of the road, built in the 19C by Protestant refugees escaping catholicisation in the Tyrol.

KARPACZ has an affluent, unspoilt feel to it. The clean air and elegant 19C–20C houses provide refuge for scores of tourists on their winter break from the industrial heartlands around Jelenia Góra and beyond. Most of the buildings are clustered around the main road—ul. 1 Maja—which winds its way up through the town to the *Biały Jar* hotel.

Further on, just before the village of Bierutowice, is one of Karpacz's chief attractions—the **Wang Chapel**, a unique example of Scandinavian Romanesque architecture. This small, almost entirely wooden 13C church (not a single nail was used in its construction) was purchased in 1841 by the King of Prussia, Frederick William IV, dismantled, and brought to Karpacz from its original site on Lake Wang in southern Norway. The gables are topped with striking pinnacles in the form of gaping dragon mouths—a curious link between paganism and Christianity.

Many elements of the **interior** date back to the Viking era: the columns with carved capitals bearing mascarons that separate the nave from the chancel; the north and south inner portals with allegorical and floral motifs, including faces of Vikings with forked tongues and the trefoil window over the south portal—carved in glorious Norwegian pine. Among the later additions are the intricately carved wooden Baroque font, two candle-holders—used only during wedding ceremonies—standing on either side of the altar, and the *Crucifix* by Jakub of Janowice, carved from a single piece of oak.

To protect the church against strong winds, a stone bell tower was built in the 20C. (A taped

Wang Chapel, Karpacz

commentary about the church is available in many languages, including English.)

In a former holiday home in Upper Karpacz is the **Toy Museum** with a collection donated by Henryk Tomaszewski, founder-director of the Wrocław Pantomime Theatre.

Walking trails

The *Biały Jar* hotel is the starting point for a number of hiking trails into the mountains. Most popular is the **blue trail**, which rises to the summit of **Mt Śnieżka** (1602m), the highest peak in the Karkonosze. If the three-hour ascent is too daunting, you could take the chair lift to **Mt Kopa** (1325m) (follow signs to 'wyciąg' between the *Biały Jar* and the Wang church): from there, Mt. Śnieżka can be reached in 45 minutes along the black trail. For more serious climbers, mountain bikes and climbing equipment can be rented from the PTTK Mountain School on ul. Obrońców Pokoju 6. The picturesque **Łomnica Waterfall** is close to the chair lift to Mt Kopa (west).

Continue past the Wang church along a good mountain road to Sosnówka; then turn left, and continue through to Sobieszów, joining the E65 south at Piechowice. On the left of the main road (ul. Jeleniogórska) just before you enter Szklarska Poręba, there is a **Turbine Museum** (open Tues 09.00–12.00, Wed–Thur 11.00–14.00). Apart from being a tourist resort, the town is best known for its **Julia glassworks** and grindery, which are spread out along the banks of the Kamienna river to the west. The oldest glass-works in Silesia was established here in 1366. Today, the main complex can be visited on a guided tour (no fixed opening hours); items of crystal glass produced there can be bought at the factory shop in the city centre. A 20-minute walk from the glassworks (red trail) will bring you to the **Kamieńczyk Waterfall** (27m)—the largest on the Polish side of the Karkonosze—in a beautiful woodland setting.

Like Karpacz, Szklarska Poręba is an excellent base for excursions and hiking trips into the Western Karkonosze and Izerskie hills. From ul. Turystyczna (a suburb of Marysin) in the south part of town, there is a two-stage chair lift to the summit of **Mt Szrenica** (1362m), from where you can make the 1 hour 30 minute ascent to the peak of **Śnieżne Kotły** (1509m).

From Szklarska Poręba a mountain road winds its way through the Izerskie hills to the spa town of Świeradów-Zdrój further west. On the way, there is a treacherous hairpin bend—'the Bend of Death'—perched above a precipice, with a breath-taking view over the Karkonosze and Izerskie mountains. According to local tradition, a gypsy train fell down the precipice during heavy fog—hence its name.

Karkonosze Mountains

Road E65 continues through Szklarska Poręba to the border crossing with the Czech Republic at Jakuszyce, a town otherwise known for winter sports, in particular the Piast international ski-run, and a number of excellent trails for cross-country skiing.

The Cistercian Abbey at Krzeszów

❖ Kamienna Góra • Krzeszów • Chełmsko Śląskie • Jelenia Góra

From Jelenia Góra take road 367 to **KAMIENNA GÓRA** (41km), a small town with weaving traditions reaching back to the 16C. The history of weaving in the region is documented in the **Museum of the Textile Industry** under the arcades on the Market Square (pl. Wolności No. 11; **open** Tues, Fri–Sun 10.00–16.00, Wed–Thur 10.00–16.00). The Square has a few fine houses, particularly **Nos 12/13**, **No. 6** in the northwest corner, with a stone portal and balcony, Corinthian pilasters and a gable decorated with sculptures, and **No. 18** on the east side, small, with stuccowork and a tall, pinnacled gable.

The Cistercian Abbey at Krzeszów

From Kamienna Góra take a minor road 7km south to **KRZESZÓW**, a small village entirely dominated by its imposing ****Cistercian Abbey**. The Cistercian monks, settled here by Duke Bolko I in 1292, experienced their golden age in the late 17C. It was during this period that they built the church of St Joseph (see below) and the **32 Calvary Chapels** to the west. The first abbey church was pulled down in 1728 to make way for the present Baroque **Abbey Church of St Mary**, built in 1728–35 and set in a garden at the end of a tree-lined driveway. The twin towers topped by green lanterns create an impression of small detail magnified many times. Corinthian columns and sculptures by the Prague sculptor **Ferdinand Brokoff** adorn the west façade.

The **interior** of this huge cruciform church is dominated by *trompe l'oeil* **murals** by Georg Wilhelm Neunhertz (1733–36), which entirely cover the ceiling. Scenes from the life of the Virgin are arranged in a cascade of plans, creating a shocking impression of exaggerated depth. The original frescoes by Michael Willmann, the greatest Silesian artist of the Baroque period, are no longer. In the high altar, completely filling the apse and richly decorated with sculptures, is the famous Gothic painting of *Our Lady of Krzeszów* (early 15C), hanging below a huge canvas depicting the *Ascension* by P. Brandl (1731). According to oral tradition, when the Hussites raided the monastery in 1426 and burned down the church, one of the monks managed to hide the painting of Our Lady of Krzeszów, but was then killed, taking his secret to the grave. It was 196 years before the painting was discovered in an oak box hidden under the floor in the sacristy. The transepts are closed off by stalls with painted backs; a veritable crowd of jostling sculptures is perched on top. Altars in the side chapels contain several valuable paintings. The large, ornate **Rococo organ** at the west end of the nave, one of the best in Silesia, was made in 1732–36 by M. Engler, and is also richly decorated with sculptures.

Behind the abbey church is the **Piast Mausoleum** (Baroque, 1735–47), its two domes covered with frescoes (1736–38), again by Neunhertz. It can be reached through the south transept, or, if this is closed, from the entrance outside. The Baroque tombs of the Piast dukes, buried in copper coffins placed in a common sarcophagus, are set against the west wall. On both sides of the marble monument to Bernard of Świdnica are slabs from the **Gothic tombs** of Bolko I (d. 1301) and his grandson, Bolko II (d. 1368). Opposite the tombs are figures of the dukes' wives.

Michael Willmann's remarkable frescoes did survive in the **Church of St Joseph** (1690–96), which stands next to the abbey church. One monumental cycle (1692–1695) pays homage to the Counter Reformation cult of St Joseph; others, covering the ceiling, depict biblical scenes.

From Krzeszów continue 8km along a minor road to the village of **CHEŁMSKO ŚLĄSKIE**. On ul. Sądecka, beginning in the northeast corner of the square, is a line of wooden **weavers' dwellings** from 1707, the so-called Twelve Apostles, though oddly there are only 11 (perhaps zealous locals had Judas removed). They have overhanging gables which create a kind of gallery protecting the entrances, and are all still inhabited. You can rejoin the road back to Kamienna Góra at the nearby village of Lubawka, where there is a border crossing to Kralovec in the Czech Republic.

North of Jelenia Góra

❖ Siedlęcin • Wleń • Lwówek Śląski

The main attraction of this trip is the charming town of Lwówek Śląski, with several examples of Silesian Gothic architecture. A tower with unusual 14C frescoes can be seen in Siedlęcin, on the way to Lwówek.

From Jelenia Góra follow the signs marked 'Wleń/Bolesławiec'; at the fork, follow the green sign to Siedlęcin (4km), turning sharp right just before the bridge.

In **SIEDLĘCIN** you will notice a large rectangular stone **tower** covered with a shingled roof. The key is kept in the adjacent building (knock on the green door). The tower, built around 1300, is an example of the defensive architecture that emerged in Silesia at the turn of the 13C after the feudal lords had banned the construction of castles. Originally, the roof was concealed by a crenellated parapet, which was removed in the 15C when a third storey was added. The rooms on the ground and third floors, now empty, were used to store farm equipment, while the second floor was the so-called **Knights' Hall**, beamed and decorated with remarkable **frescoes** (1320–40), some of which are still preserved. What makes them unusual is the secular subject matter—indeed, they are the oldest secular murals in Poland. The themes shown on the south wall are (from the left): *Life and Death*, symbolised by human figures, either standing or coiled in tombs; *St Christopher*; the *Founding of a Cistercian monastery by Bolko I in 1292* (probably Krzeszów; see above) and, below, an unfinished epic tale of Sir Iwain's search for *aqua vita*.

Return to the main road and follow signs to Bolesławiec. Just before Pilchowice you will pass a lake and a pre-war dam. The road runs alongside the Bóbr river to the village of **WLEŃ** (16km). On the Main Square a statue of a girl with two pigeons commemorates the pigeon market held here in 1914. Cross the railway lines and proceed to the **castle**, which comes into view on a hill to the left. Built anew in 1470 and remodelled in 1568, it is now a well-preserved and little visited ruin. The greatest attraction is the splendid view from the tower. Looking south you can see an 18C palace in the distance. Rejoin the main road and turn left; then pick up the 297 marked 'Bolesławiec'.

In **Lwówek Śląski** (17km), the centre of the rectangular Main Square (pl. Wolności) is occupied by a particularly fine Gothic **Town Hall**. It was raised in the 13C, but the oldest parts visible today date from 1480. Its characteristic tower dates from 1500–4, and used to contain a torture chamber and starvation cell. The interiors, in Gothic/Renaissance style, date from 1522–46. Enter and turn left at the end of the vaulted corridor: in the wall is a curious **Gothic tombstone** of an unidentified duke and his wife, unusually depicted lying side by side and holding hands. There is another good memorial slab—of Duke Henryk Jaworski and his wife Agnieszka (Gothic, c 1350)—on the first floor.

The **Church of the Assumption**, which stands west of the square on UL. Kościelna, was founded by Henryk the Pious in 1238, but all that remains of the original building is the late Romanesque west façade. A bas-relief of the *Coronation of the Virgin* (c 1300), one of the oldest in Silesia, adorns the tympanum of the portal. Next to the church (ul. Kościelna 29) stands the Baroque former **Commandery** of the Knights of St John of Jerusalem (c 1760). Also close by are fragments of the town fortifications, reconstructed in 1935, complete with a guards' passageway along the top. The **Lubańska Gate** (13C–14C), one of Lwówek's three gatetowers, was remodelled at the turn of the 18C. North of the square on ul. Chrobrego is the 13C Gothic **Bolesławiec Tower**. It fell into ruin after a fire in 1752; the new crowning it received in 1983 is faithful to its original appearance.

Jelenia Góra to Wrocław

❖ Bolków • Jawor • Rogoźnica • Strzegom • Książ • Wałbrzych • Zagórze Śląskie • Świdnica • Wrocław

The most important sights along this route are the enormous castle in Książ near Wałbrzych; the former concentration camp in Rogoźnica (Gross-Rosen), and several examples of Silesian religious architecture in Strzegom, Jawor and Świdnica.

Leave Jelenia Góra on road 3 heading east (32km). In **Bolków** go past the early Gothic Church of St Jadwiga (c 1300) on the sloping Market Square, and turn right into UL. Bolka. Passing a Baroque chapel on the left, you ascend to the **castle**, now a **Museum** (open Tues–Sat 09.00–15.00, Sun 09.00–16.00).

The huge, oddly shaped tower and part of the adjoining living quarters date from 1297–1302, when Bolko I, Duke of Świdnica-Jawor, erected the castle. It was extended in 1326–1368, becoming the largest Piast stronghold in Silesia, and again in 1540–1593. The Cistercians from Krzeszów (see p. 475) owned the castle from 1703 until 1810, after which it fell into ruin. On display in the museum are maps, photographs and plans of the castle from various epochs, as well as furniture, and—on the upper floor—Lower Silesian folk art from the end of the 17C to the mid-19C.

Continue on road 3 to **JAWOR** (19km). Along the south side of the Market Square several arcaded **houses** with 18C Baroque façades have been preserved. Its centre is occupied by the **Town Hall** (1897) with a 14C Gothic tower. From the southeast corner of the square walk to the former Franciscan monastery, built at the turn of the 15C, and currently a **museum** (**open** Tues–Sun 09.00–15.00), featuring a **16C mural** in a corridor lined with hunting trophies, a room devoted to the Piast dukes of the Świdnica-Jawor line, Lower Silesian folk art, and a small display commemorating Goethe's trip to the region.

Taking UL. GRUNWALDZKA from the square and turning right along UL. ZAMKOWA you will come to the **Parish Church of St Martin**. The initial Gothic building was built in 1267–1290, but what you see today dates from the 14C, and—in the west parts—from 1446 and 1573. Near the main south entrance to the chancel is the best portal, with a 16C sculpture over it depicting St Martin on a horse.

Continue along ul. Grunwaldzka to pl. Wolności, where the **Protestant Church of the Holy Ghost** is visible through a gate leading to the Park of Peace. The Baroque church, with rustic painted decoration, was built of timber by Albrecht von Säbisch in 1654–56. It is one of three 'Churches of Peace' that the Silesian Protestants were allowed to build under the Peace of Westphalia in 1648. At the beginning of the 20C the half-timbered walls were faced with planks of wood.

Leave Jawor on road 374 signposted 'Wałbrzych'. In **ROGOŹNICA** (8km), turn right at the white sign marked 'Gross-Rosen'. Not much has been preserved of the **Nazi concentration camp**, which was cleared of prisoners before the Soviet army moved in. There is the gate and guardhouse, bearing the infamous inscription 'Arbeit macht frei' (work brings freedom), the SS canteen, sections of barbed wire, the foundations of the barracks, and wooden posts which served as a bell tower, used to summon prisoners to daily roll-call and to announce executions. The canteen—on the right as you enter the site—is the main museum building. Inside is a narrative display consisting of blown-up photographs, reproductions of documents and quotations. Items more directly relevant to Gross Rosen can be found in the guardhouse further down the cobbled road. A video on the history of the camp (available in foreign languages, including English, German and Hebrew) is shown in the canteen. The camp, though not big, conveys a sense of the prisoners' loneliness and abandonment even more poignantly than the carefully arranged displays at other camps, such as Auschwitz or Treblinka.

The Gothic *Parish Church of SS Peter and Paul** in nearby Strzegom (7km), a cruciform basilica dating from the second half of the 14C, is one of the largest and best in lower Silesia. The external decoration was carved in sandstone, while granite and basalt mined in local quarries was used as the main building material. Two towers were planned for the west façade, but only the north one was completed in the 15C. The church has three Gothic carved portals from the second half of the 14C and c 1400 with richly sculpted tympana. The Gothic corbels supporting the aisle vaults are decorated with figures of prophets, the

Wise and the Foolish Virgins, and plant motifs. The valuable epitaph slabs (16C–17C) include full-size, figures in relief, which adorn the Seidlitz slabs.

After Strzegom, stay on the 374 and either bear left along the 382 heading straight for Świdnica (see below), or continue for 17km to Książ and Wałbrzych.

Książ Castle

The third largest castle in Poland after Malbork and Wawel, it is set majestically on a high bluff overlooking the Pełcznica river, surrounded by forest.

Built in 1288–91, the castle initially served as a residence of the Piast Duke Bolko I of Świdnica. After changing hands several times, it was purchased by the Hochbergs of Meissen, who held it until the Second World War. Conrad Ernst Maximilian Hochberg, owner of the castle from 1705 to 1742, added the Baroque east wing with a lavishly decorated marble hall on the first floor.

In the 19C, Książ witnessed many illustrious visitors. It was here in 1821 that the **Prussian Prince Wilhelm**, later to become German Emperor, met the Polish Princess Eliza Radziwiłł and fell in love. Though the Princess was related to the Hohenzollerns, the planned marriage was deemed a misalliance by the Berlin government and prevented. The affair became the subject of much press speculation and even several books. In 1838, the Russian **Czar Nicholas I** stayed in Książ—under considerable security—when undergoing treatment with mineral water from the 'Mieszko' spring.

After 1846, the owners of Książ inherited the palace in Pszczyna (see p. 450), assuming the name of Pless and becoming one of the richest and most powerful families in Prussia. To make the castle worthy of their distinguished guests, they expanded it with the addition of a Neo-Renaissance wing. One of the visitors in 1906 was the British statesman-to-be **Winston Churchill**, whose stepfather was the brother of Princess Daisy von Pless. The Princess, née Cornwallis West, was unhappily married to Prince Hans Henry XV von Pless. The marriage finally ended in divorce, after which Daisy published her memoirs—*Dance on a Volcano*—in which she gave vent to her contempt for everything Prussian. In 1938 the castle was confiscated by the Nazis, who in 1941 began its reconstruction—or rather destruction. Many of the Nazi High Command visited Książ: **Hitler**, **Frank**, **Goebbels**, **Göring**, **von Braun** (creator of the V1 rocket). The castle was to become part of a large complex of military installations, including an atomic plant in the Sowie Mountains fuelled by uranium mined in Wałbrzych, but a Soviet offensive thwarted these plans. The deep underground tunnels and chambers which the Nazis drilled into the mountains, using slave labour, stretch for an astonishing 170km. V1 rockets were tested in the deep shaft next to the castle (and 4 more in the Sowie mountains). Today, the tunnels are used for seismographic research, and there are plans to open some of them to the public. Ironically, the castle only suffered major damage after the war, when the Soviet army used it as a barracks until 1949.

The outbuildings house a unique and atmospheric hotel (☎ 250-17), while the rest of the castle is a **museum** (open May–Sep, Tues–Sun 09.00–17.00; Oct–Apr, Tues–Sun 09.00–15.00), much in need of restoration, for which funds are sadly lacking. The valuable collection of Polish post-war porcelain was largely sold off to raise funds and make space for the more profitable hotel business. What was saved by the valiant and understandably rather bitter museum curator is now on display on the second floor, alongside ceramics, both mass produced and artistic (one of only two such collections in Poland), glass-work and 18C–19C Silesian painting and sculptures. The other parts of the castle worth seeing are the 18C east wing (1705–35) and the so-called High Castle, encompassing a 13C stone tower and two Renaissance wings (best seen from the upper floors or from the tower). The west wing, whose rich decorations and sheer size attest to the great ambitions of the owners, was built in 1908–23. It is entered through the Tower of George and the Chestnut Terrace. From the east and south sides, the castle is adjoined by a total of 12 terraced gardens. Nearby is a stud farm (riding holidays available ☎ (0–74) 41-16-44).

The neighbouring city of **Wałbrzych** (6km) is a grimy, drab mining town; one of the ugliest and most polluted in Poland, if not in Europe. It offers very little in the way of sights except a Neo-classical **Lutheran Church** (1785–88) and the **Regional Museum** nearby, on ul. 1 Maja 9 (open Tues–Fri 10.00–16.00, Sat–Sun 11.00–17.00). The exhibits are divided into four sections: mineralogy, with a collection of impressions of plants in Carboniferous shale, and 'terra sigillata' pills (a 17C medicine made from Strzegom clay, also popular in the south of Italy at that time); porcelain from local and European factories; the history of Wałbrzych, especially mining; and Polish painting. There is also a folk art branch of the museum in Pstrążna (a skansen), and an archaeology branch in Kamieniec Ząbkowicki.

Leaving Wałbrzych on road 381, turning left for **Zagórze Śląskie** (8km). Follow the trail marked 'Zamek Grodno' from the small car park at the foot of the hill. The **castle** (open Tues–Fri 10.00–15.00, Sat–Sun 10.00–17.00) stands on a steep bluff (450m) above the Bystrzyca river.

A military outpost was established here in 1198, but the construction of the castle probably did not begin until the late 13C. It came under the direct control of the royal court in Prague in 1392, and in 1443–50 was used as a base by robbers. The upper Gothic part was enlarged in 1545–67, and the foregate with tower was added. Twenty years later the lower castle was built, including farm buildings, a bakery, baths and dwellings, and a ring of walls with rondelles and a gatehouse. Damaged during the Swedish Deluge (see p. 49), the castle was finally abandoned in 1774. Renovation work began in 1823–29, when the foregate was rebuilt in Neo-Renaissance style.

The entrance to the lower castle leads through an arched and pedimented portal with a fine sgraffito depicting two griffins. In the courtyard, beside a cannon— donated to the castle by the anti-Nazi General von Moltke—grows a 600-year-old lime tree, named 'the tree of justice' on account of local trials that were held under it.

In the passage to the upper castle are two penitentiary crosses from the 14C and 16C (see p. 471). Further along, an iron grille marks the entrance to the dungeon, where some bones and two human skulls have been put on display to illustrate the gruesome, albeit hackneyed castle legend, involving thwarted love, imprisonment and decapitation. The upper floor contains a number of fine stone portals, portraits of Duke Bolko and other owners of the castle, instruments of torture, furniture, maps, royal seals, armour, medieval siege equipment, and some poorly preserved fragments of murals. You can also climb the tower to enjoy the view over the woods and river below.

Head back towards Wałbrzych and join the 379 for Świdnica (20km), which in the Middle Ages rivalled Wrocław as Silesia's wealthiest and most important town. The Town Hall (c 1710), standing somewhat off-centre, houses a **Museum of Silesian Trade** (open Tues–Fri 10.00–15.00, Sat–Sun 11.00–17.00), with a good collection of old scales and measures. The hall itself, originally late Gothic (early 16C), was rebuilt in the first half of the 18C, when it acquired Baroque elements. The four ornate fountains nearby are also Baroque. From the square walk north along ul. Bohaterów Getta and then ul. Kościelna. Through an arcaded gate on the left is the **Protestant Church of the Holy Trinity**, set in cemetery grounds (open Sat 09.00–13.00, Sun 15.00–17.00). This is one of the 'Churches of Peace' (see p. 478), built in the 1650s. Its south wall, lined with epitaph slabs, has a triangular gable with a clock. Several octagonal porches and chapels cling to the main body of the building like wasps' nests. The cruciform interior, with tiers of galleries, is furnished and painted in rustic Baroque style.

On ul. Długa (northeast of the square) is the enormous, 14C brick *Basilica of SS Wenceslaus and Stanisław, with the tallest tower in Silesia (103m), finished in 1570 and later crowned with a Renaissance spire. The west façade, blackened and grim, with huge, traceried pointed-arch windows and four portals with pinnacles, pillars and statues (including a late 15C St Anne, and 15C figures of the church's patrons) is truly overpowering. Inside, the Baroque furnishings and decoration (1690–1735) are dominated by the intricately carved **high altar** (27m wide, 71m high). A huge early 18C canvas by Michael Willmann hangs high up in the chancel. The Renaissance style is represented by a sculpted sandstone font (1580), found in the last chapel in the north aisle behind an iron grille, while the Gothic elements include a 15C stone choir resting on arcades, a large early 15C *Pietà* in the north aisle by the choir, and a south chapel altar, originating from the school of Veit Stoss, with a polyptych depicting the *Dormition of the Virgin* (1492).

In Świdnica, join road 5 heading northeast (51km) to Wrocław.

Wrocław to Opole

❖ Wrocław • Brzeg • Opole

From Wrocław take road 456 southeast to **Brzeg**, a town chartered in 1245, and from 1311 to 1675 the capital of the Legnica-Brzeg Duchy. It shared the fate of other Silesian towns, passing from the Bohemian crown to the Habsburgs in the 17C, before being annexed by Prussia in the mid-18C. Its main attraction is the *Castle of the Dukes of Brzeg in the northwest of town (pl. Zamkowy).

The first castle was built at the end of the 13C, and the square Lwów Tower dating from that period survives. **Duke Bolesław III**—the first of the Brzeg Piast line—used the castle as his main residence from 1342 onwards, as did his successors, until their extinction in 1675. In the 16C, major reconstruction was undertaken to transform the Gothic castle into a Renaissance palace. Most important were the years 1547–60, when the Italian architects **Giacomo and Francesco Parr**, and **Bernardo Niuron** worked on the south and west wings. The three-tiered arcades around the inner courtyard date from this period, as does the gatehouse with its exquisite portal bearing busts of Piast rulers. Its **façade**, decorated by **Andreas Walther**, **Kaspar Khune** and **Jakob Werter**, is often mentioned along with Wawel's Zygmunt Chapel (see p. 216) as the most valuable example of Renaissance sculpture preserved in Poland. The lowest tier consists of two entrances flanked by pilasters with intricate Renaissance carving. The middle tier features statues of Duke Jerzy II and his wife Barbara, and cartouches held by henchmen. Above are two storeys of rectangular windows, separated by two friezes containing 24 sandstone busts of Piast kings and dukes, the predecessors of Jerzy II. Arguably, no other European dynasty of this period can boast such a splendid gallery of sculpted portraits. The façade is crowned with a balustrade; in the centre, note the coat of arms of King Zygmunt August, with the familiar Jagiellon eagle. The castle is currently a **museum** (**open** Tues–Sun 10.00–16.00, Wed 10.00–18.00), with a display related to the Silesian Piasts, and 15C–18C Silesian art.

Adjoining the castle on the left is the small Gothic **Church of St Jadwiga**, with ornamental vault bosses, Rococo furniture, and a north chapel containing a gilded sarcophagus of St Jadwiga behind a grille. Fragments of painted decoration are preserved on the south gallery, while a *trompe l'oeil* mural covers the apse wall.

Close by on pl. Zamkowy is the late Baroque **Church of the Holy Cross**, built for the Jesuits in 1734–45. The vaulted ceiling is covered with *trompe l'oeil* painted decoration and images of saints in adoration of the Cross. In front of the church stand two stone statues of SS Thaddeus and John Nepomuk (1722). Nearby, still on the square, is a stone sculpture of the *Holy Trinity* (1731).

Walk to the MARKET SQUARE, whose Renaissance **Town Hall**, one of the best in the region, was designed and built in 1570–77 by Bernardo Niuron and Giacomo Parr. Two square towers in the west façade, lower than the roof, are connected by a passageway supported on slender round columns and arches. The east façade also has a tower with a Renaissance crowning. Notice the moulded window surrounds and Renaissance portals, the most ornate one being found in the south wing. The late Baroque interior (c 1747) features the **Ceiling Room**, named after its splendid larch ceiling (1646), and the **Council Chamber**, with an 18C stucco plafond and wardrobes with painted doors.

There are several fine **burghers' houses** around the Square, particularly **No. 13** with an elegant portico; **No. 18** with a newly-renovated Renaissance façade featuring a ridiculously tall parapet and geometric decoration that could pass for pop-art; and **No. 5**, recognizable for its tall triangular gable.

Continue for 26km to Opole along road 4.

Opole

Opole lies in the Silesian Lowland on the Odra river. Archaeological finds on Pasieka Island (see below) suggest that an ancient Slav town existed here as early as the 8C. This was probably one of the 20 settlements of the **Opolanie** tribe mentioned by the so-called 'Bavarian Geographer' (his real name is not known) in the mid-9C. The town on the right bank of the Odra received its charter before 1217, and was surrounded with earth-and-wood ramparts. A century later it already had a ring of walls and its first brick church. Though the town developed rapidly under the Silesian Piasts, prosperity came to an end when the Habsburg dynasty took over in the 16C. Like other towns in the region, it fell into Prussian hands in the mid-18C, remaining under German influence until 1945, when, with the rest of Silesia, it was incorporated into Poland.

Today, Opole is chiefly known for its **Song Festival** in June, when crowds converge on the city to hear the latest offerings of Poland's vibrant pop culture. Whilst lacking the international flavour of Sopot (see p. 331), the Opole Festival remains the most important event in the country's pop music calendar. Established in the 1960s, it was for many years heavily promoted by the Communist propaganda apparatus. However, it also launched the careers of many of the biggest names in the business, and today few budding stars would eschew the opportunity of playing here to a nationwide TV audience.

▪ Practical information
Hotels
★★★
Olimpijski. Ul. Oleska 86, ☎ 55-60-11/17. Air conditioning, car park. 60 rooms.
Weneda. Ul. 1 Maja 77, ☎ 53-65-13. Recently refurbished. Car park. 30 rooms.
★★
Zacisze. Ul. Grunwaldzka 28, ☎ 53-95-53. Comfortable, recently modernised.

ORBIS. Ul. Krakowska 31, ☎ 53-97-30/54-55-07/54-33-63.
Tourist information. Ul. Książąt Opolskich 22, ☎ 54-54-80.
Post office. Ul. Korfantego.
Telephone code. (0–77).

The city centre
The centre of the Main Square is occupied by the **Town Hall** (1936), modelled on the Palazzo Vecchio in Florence. It is a heavy building consisting of several rectangular blocks and a tower. A parapet adorns the main wing, mirrored by similar decoration on the tower. The late Gothic and Renaissance **Burghers' Houses** around the square have been rebuilt and reconstructed on many occasions. Most have late Baroque façades (18C) with curly gables, ornamental portals and stuccoed window heads. The **Eagle Pharmacy** in the northeast corner was founded in 1824.

North of the Square, on UL. KATEDRALNA, stands the **Church of the Holy Cross**, a cathedral since the war. The Gothic, brick aisled hall was erected in the first half of the 15C, and later surrounded with chapels. Embedded in the outside walls are several epitaph slabs of the Oppersdorff family, made in the 15C in an iron mill in Kluczbork, one of oldest in Europe. The furniture includes a dark, single-tiered Baroque high altar (1773); a wooden late Renaissance pulpit (1653); and, closing the south aisle, an 18C altar with a painting of the *Madonna of Piekary* (c 1480), famed for its miraculous powers. In 1680, the painting was sent to Prague to quell a plague, and again in 1741, to Olomouc. Inside the Piast chapel, entered from the south aisle, is a 1591 triptych and a red marble **Renaissance tombstone** (1532) of the last **Opole Piast, Jan the Good**.

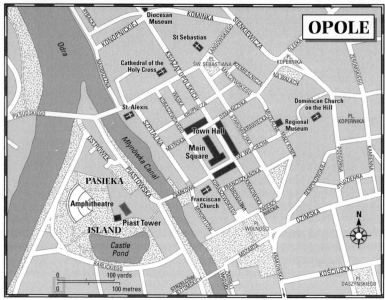

West of the Cathedral and across the square on UL. NADBRZEŻNA you will find remnants of Opole's brick fortifications. Close to the river, on ul. Katedralna, just before the bridge, is the **Hospital Chapel of St Alexis** (Gothic, 1421–c 1450). The hospital was built before 1800, and later expanded in Neo-classical style.

Turn north from ul. Katedralna into UL. KSIĄŻĄT OPOLSKICH, and then right into UL. KARDYNAŁA KOMINKA. At No. 4 is the modern building of the **Diocesan Museum** (**open** Tues–Thur 10.00–12.00 and 14.00–17.00), featuring religious art from the Middle Ages to the 20C, mostly from Silesian churches.

Return to ul. Katedralna and cross the bridge; strolling along the boulevard, you get an attractive view of the houses lining the river bank, one of them conspicuous for its unusual gable of brick arches. Turn into UL. OSTRÓWEK; passing under the building of the Provincial Governor's Office, you will find yourself on **PASIEKA ISLAND**, the oldest part of Opole, where archaeological excavations unearthed the remnants of an 8C Slav settlement. The **Amphitheatre** here is well-known to fans of Polish popular music, as it is the venue of the annual Opole Song Festival (**open** Tues–Sun 09.30–17.30). Nearby stands the 14C Gothic **Piast Tower** (same opening times as the amphitheatre): a round structure, slightly leaning, with a conical roof, originally wooden, but now also made of brick. The tower formerly belonged to the castle of the Dukes of Opole, one of the oldest examples of Polish defensive architecture, which was demolished by the Germans in 1928–31.

Cross the millstream back to the east side. Off the southern corner of the main square stands the **Franciscan Church** and monastery, raised by Duke Bolesław I in 1280–1329. It suffered major damage during the religious wars of the 16C–17C, and its nave was rebuilt in Renaissance style after a fire in 1739. The chancel, dating from 1280, has preserved its Gothic ribbed vaults, but most of the decoration is Baroque—particularly good on the organ and organ loft. Half way along the south aisle is the entrance to the **chapel of St Anne** (1309), its portal surmounted with a Piast eagle (on the outside) and a scene in relief of Władysław I founding the monastery in 1248 (on the inside). The **15C star vault** is decorated with 18C medallions and 14C Piast coats of arms. In front of the altar stand four huge **tombs of the Piast Dukes** (c 1380). Another chapel of note—the **chapel of the Sacred Heart**—is covered with a 16C Renaissance dome, the oldest in Silesia. It is separated from the north aisle by a fine wrought-iron grille. Inside the crypt (**open** 10.15–11.30, 14.00–16.30; ask at the office on pl. Wolności 2 beforehand for groups of less than ten) is a valuable Gothic fresco of the *Crucifixion* (c 1320) and wooden tombs of the dukes of Opole. The **monastery**, which adjoins the church to the south, is entered through a fine 18C carved portal. The foyer corridor is covered with a 15C Gothic cellular vault.

Return to the Main Square and walk up UL. WOJCIECHA towards the Church on the Hill (see below), which closes the far end of the street. On the left you will pass the former Jesuit College; the amalgamation of two late Gothic/Renaissance burghers' houses, rebuilt in late Baroque style after fires in 1739 and 1762. Inside is a **Regional Museum** (**open** Tues–Fri 09.00–15.00, Sat–Sun 10.00–15.00) with a display of 19C–20C Polish painting in addition to the usual sections on archaeology, history, folk culture and natural history. The museum has the largest collection of works by Jan Cybis (1897–1972) in Poland.

Walk up the steps to the **Dominican Church on the Hill**. According to legend, St Adalbert stopped here in 984 on his journey to convert the heathen Prussians. The painting at the high altar depicts his alleged meeting with Duke Jerzy in 984. Originally Gothic, the church was reconstructed in Baroque style c 1740. The Neo-Romanesque west façade dates from the 1930s.

The Skansen in Opole-Bierkowice

The **Skansen** (**open** Apr–Oct Tues–Sun 10.00–15.00) located on ul. Wrocławska 174 in the suburb of Opole-Bierkowice, is best reached by car or by bus No. 5 from the city centre. On display are several wooden buildings (17C–19C) transferred here from various Silesian villages. They include complete farmsteads, granaries, watermills and windmills, a smithy, a church (1613) and a school building.

Opole to Kraków

❖ Góra Świętej Anny • Toszek • Tarnowskie Góry • Katowice • Będzin • Kraków

This route passes through some of the most heavily industrialised and polluted regions of Poland. There are few sights of historical significance, but driving through the vast conurbation may afford an interesting glimpse into Poland's recent past.

Leave Opole south on road 4, turning right onto the 426 in the town of Strzelce Opolskie. In the village of **GÓRA ŚWIĘTEJ ANNY** (47km) the Gaschin family founded a Franciscan monastery after 1655. The earlier **Pilgrimage**

Church of St Anne, remodelled by the Gaschins, stands on the summit of **St Anne's Hill** (410m), on whose slopes numerous **Calvary chapels** (1700–64) are scattered. Several chapels built in the form of artificial limestone caves surround a yard, to which you descend by a flight of stairs. The centre of the yard is occupied by the chapel of St Rafał.

West of the village is an **Amphitheatre** (1934–38), with seating for 60,000, and Xawery Dunikowski's **monument** commemorating the Third Silesian Uprising in 1921 (St Anne's Hill was an important battlefield during the Uprising).

Return to Strzelce Opolskie and head east on road 4, joining the 903 for Toszek (30km). The ruined **Castle of the Dukes of Racibórz and Opole** commands the town from a hill, where traces of human settlement dating from as early as 8000 BC were discovered. Giovanni Seregno expanded the mid-15C castle for the Colonna family in early Baroque style in 1650–66, but it was gutted in 1811, never to be rebuilt.

Continue along the 903, turning left at Wieszowa onto the 908. In **Tarnowskie Góry** (30km) watch out for the white signs marked 'Kopalnia Zabytkowa', which lead to a historic coal mine, now a **museum** (No. 52 ul. Sześć Boże; **open** Wed–Mon 08.30–14.00). The tour takes about an 1.5h. Those wishing to see more may continue to the **Black Trout Mine**, following white signs to 'Śląskie Centrum Rehabilitacji'. A half-hour walk from the car park along the blue trail will bring you to the Ewa shaft (open only during summer on Sun and public holidays 12.00–16.00), where you descend some 20m underground to begin your journey by boat along a narrow 600m tunnel, one of the mine's former drainage channels. Be warned that the temperature below ground is very low. You emerge on the surface through the Sylwester shaft. The tours start at different times from each shaft (there is also a third one). The ribald commentary fails to enliven this rather monotonous experience, and it takes some scouting acumen to find your way to the right car park afterwards.

Heading southeast from Tarnowskie Góry you enter the heart of **Upper Silesia**, a sprawling, densely populated industrial conurbation, which is a vast labyrinth of poorly marked roads, a real motorist's nightmare.

> During the Communist period, the area enjoyed special privileges: shops were better stocked than elsewhere, and miners' salaries were much higher than the national average. Coal was a precious export commodity, and the image of the proud and stubborn miner was ideally suited to the needs of Communist propaganda. This has all changed since 1989. The proletariat is no longer in vogue; demand for coal has plummeted, and unfavourable exchange rates have made export difficult. Suddenly, Silesia has lost more than its privileged status: economically, it has sunk well below many other Polish regions. As the mines and steel mills fall deeper into debt, so their chances for survival in the new market conditions become slimmer. Unemployment is already high and rising, and politically the region is very unstable, under constant threat of mass strikes. The bitterness and anger felt by the miners is hardly surprising, considering their enormous role in bringing down the Communist regime in Poland. The workers from the Wójek mine who were killed by army bullets in 1982 have become as much

a symbol of Solidarity's tragic resistance under Martial Law, as the Gdańsk shipyard is a symbol of its joyous infancy in the heady days of 1980–81.

For the tourist, Upper Silesia has very little to offer in the way of sights. Even as a transit area, it is far better avoided. The central part is known as the Upper Silesian Industrial Region (Górnośląski Okręg Przemysłowy), which encompasses 14 large towns, each as ugly and depressing as the next. With over 50 collieries, several steel mills and coking plants, this is the most industrialised region of Poland, which even the last Communist government proclaimed an 'environmental disaster area'.

KATOWICE merges imperceptibly with the neighbouring towns of Tychy, Chorzów, Bytom, Ruda Śląska, Zabrze, and, further to the east, the slightly greener and less polluted Gliwice. The space between these towns, filled with antiquated industry and vast housing estates, offers no respite from the fumes and ugliness.

In Katowice, the **Museum of Silesia** (open Tues–Sun 11.00–14.00) at al. Korfantego 3 has a large collection of Polish 19C–20C art, including a fine **Witkacy self-portrait**. Close by is the modern **Sports Hall** (1971), a huge concrete building that looks like some futuristic spaceship. Opposite stands a **Monument to the Silesian Uprisings of 1919–21**; the clipped wings symbolise the three thwarted attempts by the local Polish community to gain re-inclusion into the new Polish state. In the nearby Kościuszko Park there is a wooden **Church** of 1510, transferred here from a Silesian village. The more famous **Park of Culture and Recreation** (actually in Chorzów) occupies an area of 5 sq. km. Its two highlights are a **Skansen** of local rural architecture (**open** 10.00–dusk) and the **football stadium**, where, as Poles wistfully recall, the national team scored its historic 2:0 victory over England in 1973.

In **BĘDZIN**, 14km north of Katowice, a small **castle**, visible from the road, is incongruously situated on a hillock overlooking the grey tower blocks and smog of Sosnowiec. Inside is a **museum** (open Tues, Thur–Fri 09.00–15.00, Wed 11.00–17.00, Sat–Sun 10.00–15.00) on three floors, with a weaponry and armoury display and some regional folk art and costume. You may also climb the 13C–14C tower. The original castle erected by Kazimierz the Great was rebuilt in the Neo-Gothic style by Francesco Maria Lanci in 1834, and partly reconstructed after the war.

Return to the roundabout on the main road and turn right. The Mieroszewski Palace will soon come into view. This Baroque building from the early 18C, rebuilt in the 18C–19C, contains a decent **museum** devoted to the history of the Będzin region from pre-historic times until the Second World War (**open** Tue, Thu–Sun 10.00–15.00, Wed 11.00–17.00).

Return to Katowice and pick up the A4 motorway east to Kraków (72km).

Wrocław to Zielona Góra

❖ Lubiąż • Głogów • Bytom Odrzański • Zielona Góra

Leave Wrocław on road 344 heading west; 14km past Środa Śląska you could turn right onto the 338 for a worthwhile detour (51km) to **LUBIĄŻ**, described elsewhere in the guide (see p. 447). Join road 3 in Lubin, turning off after 24km onto the 329 for Głogów.

GŁOGÓW (68km) is one of the strangest towns in Western Poland, mainly because post-war reconstruction seems to have completely by-passed it. The retreating German army declared it a fortress in 1945, and as a result it was utterly destroyed. The old pre-war centre abounds in vast ruined buildings which the local authorities have done little to preserve. The Main Square is just a dusty space with no shops, and a two-columned grand entrance to what was once the **Town Hall**.

Around the corner, facing an 'L' of gabled houses, is the astonishing ruin of the **Parish Church of St Nicholas**, abandoned in a wasteland. It seems not a brick has been moved since the Germans destroyed it in 1945. St Nicholas's was formerly a Gothic aisled hall, with a square panelled tower, and a Loreto chapel (1429) rebuilt in Baroque style during the 17C–18C.

Close to the Square stands the **Jesuit Church** (1694–1724), built in late Baroque style by Giulio Simonetti, and reconstructed after the war. Inside, note the fine stuccoes on the rood beam. At the back, the church overlooks a crumbling Jesuit college.

The small Baroque castle, which lies by the iron bridge on the Odra river, was first built in 1652–69. Destroyed during the Second World War, it has been reconstructed since, and presently houses a **Museum of Mining and Non-ferrous Casting** (open Tues–Sun 10.00–15.00). Of greater interest is the curious **park** next to the castle, with a miniature maze, and a concrete monument dedicated to the children of Głogów taken hostage by the troops of Emperor Henry V when he laid siege to the town in 1109. In illustration of this harrowing story, their contorted faces are depicted at the end of a long shaft—perhaps the battering ram to which they were tied.

Cross the river to see the ruins of the **Collegiate Church of St Mary**. This brick aisled hall (late Gothic, 1413–66), with a slim octagonal tower and remnants of an earlier Romanesque church, was destroyed during the Second World War, and is currently undergoing renovation.

Road 292 from Głogów follows the Odra downstream (northwest) to **BYTOM ODRZAŃSKI** (21km), a small, peaceful riverside town. Worthy of note is the charming Market Square with a late Renaissance **Town Hall** (1602–09), and some pretty gabled houses along the east side. The late Gothic Parish Church (1584–86) stands on an adjoining, smaller square.

From Bytom, return to road 3 for the quickest way to Zielona Góra (40km); alternatively, cross the river on the car ferry and make a short detour via **SIEDLISKO**, where there is a 16C–17C Mannerist **Palace**, partly in ruins.

Wielkopolska

Compared to other regions of Poland, the vast plain of Wielkopolska has relatively few tourist attractions, despite its ancient history. Most lie to the east of Poznań. Yet, despite the large distances separating interesting sites, there are certainly places well worth travelling to. **Gniezno**, the first capital of Poland, should be mentioned above all (see p. 521), as well as the prehistoric Slav settlement in **Biskupin** (see p. 524). **Ostrów Lednicki** was also the site of an ancient Slav settlement, and there is currently much speculation among historians as to its role in early Polish history (see p. 525). Wielkopolska's most important monuments of religious architecture include the Romanesque stone basilica in **Trzemeszno** (see p. 521), and the Cistercian abbey in **Ląd** (see p. 526). In the pleasant town of **Kruszwica** (see p. 519) on lake Gopło you will find the ruins of Kazimierz the Great's castle, but an even more picturesque sight is the extraordinary town of **Łagów** (see p. 533), wedged between two lakes.

Of all Polish cities, Poznań can lay greatest claim to being the cradle of the Polish state. It was here in the 10C that the Polanian prince Mieszko I established his royal seat, adopting Christianity, and turning his demesne into a bastion of the Roman Catholic Church for the next millennium. The Prussians left an indelible mark: the prevailing stereotype of Poznanians is that they are diligent, punctual and thrifty, if a little stiff and lacking in humour. Their city still enjoys a reputation for cleanliness and order, and when the formidable team of Hanna Suchocka (Prime Minister, 1992–93) and Prof. Skubiszewski (Foreign Minister, 1989–93), both from Poznań, took the reins of government, it was said that at last some order would be brought to the mess created by the sloppy Varsovians.

Poznań

Today, the capital of Wielkopolska (accounting for one sixth of Polish territory) has 600,000 inhabitants and a thriving cultural and academic life. It is perhaps best known abroad for the many international trade fairs held every year, a tradition going back to the 1920s. But for the many new hotels built after 1970, it would indeed be difficult for the tourist to find accommodation during trade fairs when scores of business and trade people invade the city.

Every five years, a prestigious international violin competition takes place in the University Auditorium; during the intervening years, the city suffers from no shortage of excellent music. The **chamber orchestra** of Agnieszka Duczmal is one of the best of its kind in Poland; so is the **Boys' Choir**, for many years led by Stefan Stuligrosz (currently by Wojciech A. Krolopp). The celebrated **Theatre of the Eighth Day** has achieved both domestic and international success, winning numerous awards including a prize at the Edinburgh Festival.

Walks around the city

Though considerably damaged in 1945, the Old Town has been meticulously rebuilt, while a few ancient buildings managed to survive almost intact. There are actually two separate old centres: one is the Main Market Square (**walk 1**) with its famous Town Hall; the other is the island of Ostrów Tumski, the Bishop's domain (**walk 2**). Poznań's more recent history is explored in **walks 3 and 4**. If you are travelling by car, there are several excellent excursions to be made, most notably to Kórnik Castle and, further west, to the Raczyński Palace in Rogalin.

■ Practical information
Hotels
★★★★

Orbis-Poznań. Pl. Andersa 1, ☎ 833-2081. Modern, very comfortable, close to the centre. Car rental, car park, business services, accomodation office, wheelchair access. 495 rooms overlooking the city centre. If you are staying at the *Orbis-Poznań* you cannot miss the **Monument to the Wielkopolska Uprising**: a stone obelisk guarded by two soldiers dressed in the uniforms of 1919 insurrectionists. On the obelisk are carved several images depicting episodes from Polish history, symbols of the nation's struggle for independence.

Orbis-Polonez. Al. Niepodległości 36, ☎ 869-9141. Somewhat older than the *Orbis-Poznań*, and further from the centre. Car rental, car park, business services. 391 rooms overlooking the city and park.

Park. Ul. Majakowskiego 77, ☎ 879-4081. Excellent modern hotel situated by a lake. Car park, business services. 99 rooms.

Orbis-Merkury. Ul. Roosevelta 20, ☎ 855-8000. Located in the city centre, close to the International Fair Ground. Car park, car rental, business services. 314 rooms.

Orbis-Novotel. Ul. Warszawska 64/66, ☎ 877-0011. Situated outside the city centre, next to a leisure and sports complex. Easy access to the Berlin-Warsaw motorway. Business Centre, car park, outdoor swimming pool, tennis courts, all-year skiing facilities. 150 rooms overlooking a park and lake.

★★★

Wielkopolska ul. Św. Marcin 67, ☎ 852-7631. Located in the city centre. 107 rooms.

Dworek Pod Platanem ul. Sypniewo 10, Poznań-Głuszyna, ☎ 878-8684. Outside the city centre. Good restaurant, car park. 17 rooms.

★★

Dom Turysty Stary Rynek 91, ☎ 852-8893. Located at the heart of the historic city centre. 44 rooms.

Recommended restaurants

Exclusive
Cztery Pory Roku, ul. Winogrady 9. International.
Delicja, ul. Mostowa 22, Oborniki (outside Poznań). Polish.
Meridian, ul. Litewska 22. International.

Medium-priced
Africana, ul. Zamkowa 3, West African.

Andriusza, os. Pod Lipami 104. International.
Arirang, ul. Ratajczaka 44. Korean.
Bambus, Stary Rynek 64/65. Chinese.
Bumerang, ul. Chojnicka 72, Kiekrz (outside Poznań). International.
Dom Turysty, Stary Rynek 91. Polish.
Dworek Pod Platanem, ul. Sypniewo

Medium priced (cont'd)

10, Poznań-Głuszyna, Polish.
Figaro, ul. Ogrodowa 10. Pizzeria.
Kresowa, Stary Rynek 3. Polish,
International.
Laguna, ul. Nowowiejskiego 6.
Polish.
Lorenz-Gallery, ul. Ślusarska 16,
International.
Mat's, ul. Bułgarska 115. Polish,
French.
Mexican Grill, ul. 27 Grudnia 19.
Mexican.
Pekin, ul. 23 Lutego 33. Chinese.
Rani, ul. Kantaka 8/9. Indian.
Ratuszowa, Stary Rynek 55. Polish.
Sphinx, ul. Św. Marcin 66/62,
Arabic.

Cheap eateries

Avanti, Stary Rynek 76. Salad bar.
Fast food.
Bar Mleczny Apetyt, pl. Wolności 1.
Polish.
Bar Mleczny Pod Kuchcikiem, ul.
Św. Marcin 75. Polish.
Chochlik, ul. Błękitna 1/7. Polish.
Maltańska, ul. Warszawska 25.
Polish.
Piccolo, Stary Rynek 49. Italian.

Cafés

Café Glos, Ratajczaka 39.
Chimera, Dominikańska 7.
Kamea, ul. Żydowska 2/3.
Pożegnanie z Afryką, Stary Rynek 50.
U Rajców, Stary Rynek 93.
Sukiennicza, Stary Rynek 98.

Wielkopolski Tourist Information Centre. Stary Rynek 59, ☎ 852-6156 (open Mon–Fri 09.00–17.00).
Tourist Information Office (PAPT). Ul. Kramarska 32, ☎ 852-9805 (open Mon–Fri 09.00–16.00).
ORBIS. ul. Marcinkowskiego 20, ☎ 853-2052.

Main railway station. (Poznań Główny) ul. Dworcowa 1, ☎ 866-1212. The station has all the usual facilities, including money exchange, left luggage, restaurant and tourist information. The Main Market Square (*Stary Rynek*) is about a 20 minute walk.
Main coach station. Ul. Towarowa 17, ☎ 833-1212 (open Mon–Fri 06.30–21.00, Sat–Sun 08.00–16.00).
Airport. Ławica (7km west of the city centre).
LOT. Ul. Piekary 6/1, ☎ 952 (09.00-18.00) for reservations and enquiries.

Main post office. Ul. Kościuszki 77 (open Mon–Fri 08.00–20.00, Sat 08.00–14.00, Sun 09.00–11.00), telex, fax, poste restante, and 24-hour telephone service.
Telephone code. (0–61).

Taxis. Two of most reputable 'radio taxi' companies in Poznań are ☎ 919 and 951.
British (Honorary) Consulate. ul. Kramarska 26, ☎ 853-2919/851-7290 (open Mon–Fri 09.00–15.00).
Disabled travellers. There is a special 'radio taxi' service for disabled travellers, ☎ 919. A trip costs 1 PLN per 1km. The office takes calls 24 hours.

Major festivals. 'Malta' International Theatre Festival (**June**); International Jazz Festival (**May**); Biennale of Polish Photography (**April–May**; next in 2000);

'Ars Baltica' Triennale (**November-December**; next in 2000); International Celtic Festival (**May-June**).

History

The origins of the city are closely intertwined with the birth of the Polish state. In the 9C, Poznań was a fortified settlement on the banks of the Warta, inhabited by a tribe known as the **Polanie** (Polanians), literally 'people of the fields'. It was then that a unification movement began among the Slavic tribes under the leadership of the Polanian dukes, with **Mieszko I** rising to power as the Prince of Gniezno and Poznań in 960. Mieszko took a Christian wife—the Bohemian Princess Dobrava—and had himself baptised in 966. Poznań flourished under Mieszko's reign, attaining a status almost equal to that of Gniezno, the official capital.

Poznań became the seat of the **first bishopric** in Poland in 968; soon afterwards, construction of the cathedral began, and it was here that Mieszko was buried in 992. His son Bolesław the Brave continued the policy of opposing the Germans with even greater success, culminating in 1000, when Emperor Otto III was persuaded to visit Gniezno. Otto died in 1002, leaving Bolesław's German policy in disarray, and in 1005 the troops of Emperor Henry II were at the gates of Poznań, though the sturdy fortifications dispelled any plans of a siege. A little more than 30 years later the town succumbed to the Czech prince Bretislav (1005?–1055), whose troops plundered and destroyed the town and its cathedral.

In the 13C Poznań was founded anew on Magdeburg law, after the island of **Ostrów Tumski**—the initial settlement site—had been turned over to the bishop. The town centre moved to the left bank of the Warta. This traditional independence of Ostrów Tumski from secular rule lasted until the 20C; during the Partitions, when the Prussian authorities subjected Poznań to a vehement campaign of Germanisation, it remained an enclave of Polishness.

The town thrived economically in the 14C–16C; trade and crafts were the main sources of income, with the Fair of St John held every year in June attracting merchants and visitors from all over Europe. Minor and major disasters, such as two catastrophic fires in 1447 and 1536 (many of the historic buildings one sees today were seriously damaged in those years), were quickly dealt with and even accelerated progress. Two institutions of higher education were founded: the Lubrański Academy in 1519 and the Jesuit College in 1573. As elsewhere in Poland, these halcyon days were brought to an end by the **Swedish invasions** from the mid-17C onwards. The Northern War of 1703, natural disasters, and the unsuccessful Confederation of Bar directed against Prussian influence in Poland (see p. 49) were the final blows to Poznań's prosperity.

In 1793, the country was carved up by the three partitioning powers—Austria, Prussia and Russia. Poznań, under the rule of the **Hohenzollerns**, became the capital of the new province of Southern Prussia. The Prussians did much to bolster Poznań economically, though their diligence was not always accompanied by imagination and foresight: the fast-growing city was confined within a series of fortifications and embankments, with an absurdly small number of narrow and inconveniently situated gates. It was at that time that the Citadel (see p. 513) was built north of the Old Town.

When, in the aftermath of the First World War, Poland regained independence, an armed uprising in Wielkopolska determined the fate of Poznań as a Polish city. The **University of Poznań** was opened in 1919, and two years later the local Polish radio station began broadcasting. In 1929, Poznań hosted a much-publicised exhibition seen by nearly five million people: the aim was to show the accomplishments of the **Second Republic of Poland** during the first decade of independence. There was only one more decade to go before Hitler's troops entered Poznań on 10 September 1939. The liberation brought by Stalin's Red Army in 1945 turned 65 per cent of the city into smouldering rubble, commencing the grim and grotesque period of the **People's Republic** (1945–89). The most significant, as well as the most tragic year in the city's post-war history was without doubt 1956, when the 'thaw' following Stalin's death inspired people's political aspirations and led to **pro-democracy demonstrations**, ruthlessly crushed by the authorities (see p. 510).

Walk One ~ The Old Town

The walk begins on the Main Market Square, and then takes you on a tour around the medieval Old Town. The highlights are the picturesque Town Hall, several good museums (including the excellent Museum of Musical Instruments), and the monumental Church of St Mary Magdalene.

Once Ostrów Tumski had become the sole property of the bishop, a new town was founded in 1253 centred on the Old Market. The latter was disproportionate to the rest of the town—almost 20,000 sq. m in area, making it the third largest market square in Poland, after Kraków and Wrocław. The newly-founded settlement was quickly encircled with massive fortifications and acquired a town hall, cloth hall, and municipal weighing house.

Undoubtedly the most grandiose building in the **Market Square** is the ****Town Hall**; some would even say it is one of the best examples of the secular Renaissance style in Central Europe. Its classical tower, octagonal, with a striking crowning and a square, Gothic-looking base, rises above an ornate box bristling with turrets, sculptures, friezes and rustication. The most magnificent part is the parapet, or rather the entire east façade with its three-tiered loggia.

The original Gothic Town Hall—a modest single-storey building on a square plan—was erected in late 13C or early 14C. A tall tower was added at the turn of 15C, followed by remodelling in 1508. The catastrophic fire of 1536 almost completely destroyed the building. The town authorities drew up a contract (preserved to this day) with the Italian architect **Giovanni Battista di Quadro**, at that time active in southern Poland. Work commenced in 1550 and took ten years; evidently, the councillors were satisfied with the result as they rewarded di Quadro with the title of the city's chief architect. Most of his work survives: the façades, particularly on the east side (one of the first columned façades of this kind in Europe), the parapet with pinnacles and palms, the second storey, and some of the rich interior ornamentation on the first floor.

The tower was less fortunate: it was struck by lightning in 1690 (rebuilt in Baroque style), then damaged in 1725 during a heavy storm (rebuilt in classical style), and finally burned down in 1945, after which its classical form was restored. Only the huge eagle (1783) on top of the spire is original.

If you happen to be in the Market Square at noon, do not miss the famous 'Poznań Goats', a marvel of 16C technology (reconstructed), which pop out from behind a small door in the attic above the Town Hall clock. The goats have become a symbol of the city. Below, covering the attic, are murals showing the Jagiellon kings (painted in 1954, but probably not unlike the original 16C decoration). Murals, reliefs and sgraffito adorn the three-tiered loggia; notice the images of heroes of antiquity, allegorical figures, and quotations from Polish writers of the past (mostly on the sides).

After post-war reconstruction, the Town Hall was converted into a **Museum** (**open** Mon, Tues, Fri 10.00–16.00; Wed 12.00–18.00; Sun 10.00–15.00). The **cellars**—the only surviving Gothic part of the building—have cross vaults carried on a single pillar and decorated with large bosses, where the motif of a lion and crossed keys (the heraldic emblem of Poznań) is discernible. Various archaeological finds from the region have been assembled here, the best is a 13C statue made in Marburg of Princess Salomea, sister of Przemysł I, duke of Wielkopolska; there is also the original pillory from the Market Square (see below); fragments of decorative architecture; documents relating to the town's history from the 13C onwards (including the town seal, 1344), a model of the settlement on Ostrów Tumski in the 10C; precious 11C–14C liturgical items from Limoges discovered in the Cathedral, and the ring of Bishop Boguchwał, mid-13C.

The costs of erecting the pillory (1535)—once used to flog and brand criminals—were covered from fines levied by the Town Council on female servants who had the audacity to appear in public dressed more expensively than their mistresses. On top is the figure of an executioner, solemnly holding a sword, the symbol of capital punishment. The copy that now stands on the Market Square was made in 1925.

The **ground floor** has a collection of coffin portraits and other paintings, ceramics and pewterware, as well as a rare wrought-iron grille, probably made in Toruń c 1400, one of the oldest objects of this kind in Poland; a bell that used to announce executions at the pillory, and various objects connected with the guilds (among them a leather whip, known as 'Good Manners', used in the Middle Ages to punish unruly apprentices).

The *Great Hall on the **first floor** is the grandest and largest of all the rooms in the Town Hall. Magnificent vaults, resting on corbels and two square sandstone pillars with Renaissance bas-relief, are covered with decorative coffers. You can find here images of animals, both real and mythical, Biblical characters, deities and heroes of Antiquity, astrological symbols and figures, and the crests of cities, countries and royal families. The date '1555' testifies to the completion of the work in that year. Slightly older are the two Gothic-Renaissance portals, bearing the date 1508, with remnants of original paintwork discovered in 1954.

In the northeast corner of the Hall is a staircase leading to the upper storeys. A large 17C globe has been placed between the windows in the north wall; busts of Roman emperors display an air of philosophical resignation. Through the portal on the left you enter the **Royal Chamber** with portraits of monarchs (hence the name), items illustrating the cultural history of Poznań, a 1541 fireplace moved here from the Municipal Weighing House, a table clock made in Poznań in 1580, and a portal of 1536, above which hangs a painting of the *Crucifixion*. On the **second floor** landing are objects connected with *Bractwo Kurkowe*, a medieval rifle guild; the next two rooms trace the history of the city in the 19C–20C (including, notably, drawings and watercolours by Leon Wyczółkowski).

As you leave the Town Hall, you will see the **Proserpine Fountain** on your left and pillory to the right. The Rococo fountain was made in 1766 by Augustyn Szeps, and depicts the abduction of Proserpine by Pluto. The house at No. 37 opposite the Town Hall, on the corner of ul. Wielka, has been known since the 16C as the **Red Pharmacy**. The portal and façade date from 1652–54, when the building was remodelled by Tomaso Poncino. No. 41 was also a pharmacy,

Town Hall, Poznań

known as the **White Eagle** to avoid confusion with the other one. Designed in 16C Gothic style, it has survived till the present day relatively unscathed; there are original vaults on the ground floor, as well as a Renaissance coffered ceiling on the first, where a modest **Museum of Pharmacy** was set up in 1989 (**open** Wed 14.00–17.00, Fri 10.00–13.00).

The Museum of Musical Instruments

Three adjacent houses beyond ul. Woźna, Nos 45–47, are occupied by the **Museum of Musical Instruments* (open Tues 11.00–17.00; Wed–Fri 10.00–16.00; Sat 10.00–17.00; Sun 10.00–15.00), unique in Poland and one of the best of its kind in Europe. The ground and first floors are devoted to professional instruments from all over Europe, while the second floor houses a collection of folk and exotic instruments.

The first room, to the right of the entrance, contains music machines rather than instruments—a pianola, musical boxes, jukeboxes, positives, Edison's gramophone of 1903, hurdy-gurdies, other old gramophones, and even a typewriter for typing musical scores. Left of the entrance is the piano room, with various mutations of the piano, the positive and the organ. Woodwind and brass instruments dating from the 17C–20C occupy the remaining rooms on the ground floor; amongst them is a Celtic carnyx, 2C–1C B.C. (a great rarity, one of only four in the world). Another curiosity is a walking-stick flute, made by G. Amman in 1750.

The **first floor** is dominated by stringed instruments, particularly the violin, with many examples by renowned craftsmen. (Every five years, an international violin makers' competition is held at the museum as a companion event to the

Wieniawski Violin Competition). There are some non-orthodox variants as well: bizarre Siamese violins (two joined at the back—French, 19C), and a jazz violin (1930) from Częstochowa, which has an amplifying tube (as in an old gramophone) instead of the usual resonance box.

Apart from folk and exotic instruments, divided geographically into three sections–Poland, the rest of Europe, and other continents–the **second floor** also features a room devoted to Chopin, containing the piano on which he played in Antonin in 1827 and 1829 (see p. 529), a rather macabre gypsum cast of the master's own hand, and a death-mask. The museum's collection of pianos alone would merit a visit: it comprises about 160 items, showing the enormous variety and the evolution of this most versatile of instruments.

Left (south) of the Town Hall, opposite the Museum, is a row of dainty arcaded **Market Traders' Houses**, once belonging to the Market Traders' Guild. These were an integral part of the commercial section of the Market Square to the south of the Town Hall and the Municipal Weighing House. Precursors of the present houses—wooden herring stalls—existed on this spot as early as the 13C. Brick houses began to appear in the 15C, receiving their present form with Renaissance arcades in the first half of the 16C. The columns supporting the arcades have retained some of the original Late Gothic and Renaissance decoration. **No. 17** bears the sign of the Market Traders' Guild—a herring and three palm trees. The herring stalls have of course been supplanted by art and trinket shops.

Continue along the east side of the Market Square to **No. 48**. This house, as well as the one directly behind it, from which it is separated by a small courtyard, was built in the Gothic period and still has 13C vaulted cellars, the oldest in the square. In the 17C it belonged to the Mayor of Poznań, Kasper Goski, a famous mathematician, whose achievements in science earned him a statue (still extant) at the Venetian Academy. The adjoining house, **No. 49**, also belonged to a renowned scientist, Jakub Ligenza, physician to King Jan Kazimierz. No. 50, known as the **House Under the Roof**, takes its name from a small roof above the portal, which is reputed to have saved the life of King August II, when he fell out of the window during a banquet in 1716 (notice also a sign by the portal marking the water level during flooding in 1736). The house at **No. 51** used to belong to Filippo Buonaccorsi, otherwise known as Callimachus.

> Filippo Buonaccorsi (1437–96) had to flee Rome in 1468 after participating in an attempted assassination of Pope Paul II. From 1474 he resided at the court of King Kazimierz the Jagiellon, tutoring the king's sons, serving as secretary and carrying out diplomatic missions abroad. He wrote Latin poetry and political treatises, and is credited with the authorship of *The Advice of Callimachus*, a text offering ways to redress the crumbling power of the Polish state.

The former owners of **No. 52**—the Ridt family—were one of the richest merchant clans in Poznań, possessing, in addition to several houses in the city, a number of ships and buildings in Gdańsk where they based their cloth trade. The present house, mentioned already in 1472, was rebuilt in 1573, probably by the ubiquitous di Quadro (see p. 493).

On the south side of the square, the house at **No. 55** has a vaulted Gothic

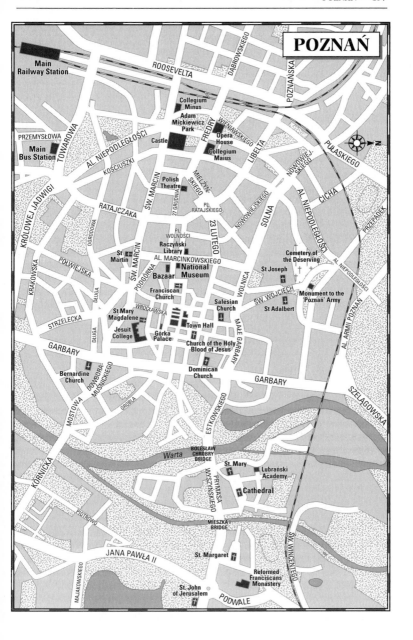

POZNAŃ

cellar, now a wine bar. **The Golden House**, next along at No. 56, is mentioned as early as the 15C; today it is used by the Polish Society of Architects (hence the decoration: bas-relief allegories of Painting, Sculpture and Architecture).

Turn towards the centre of the Square. **No. 10**, which backs onto the Market Traders' Houses, was built in 1538 by the municipal authorities as the residence and office of the city scribe. It is currently home to the Friends of Poznań Society and often has temporary exhibitions.

Further west, parallel to the Market Traders' Houses, is the former **Cloth Hall**, now the **Military Museum of Wielkopolska** (open Tues 12.00–18.00; Wed–Sat 09.00–16.00; Sun 10.00–15.00; closed Mon and Thur). The ground floor section features a 10C boat, helmets and arrowheads from Lake Lednickie (see p. 525), much medieval and early modern weaponry, as well as armour worn by the famous Polish hussars. The first floor is devoted to 20C history of the Polish army. Between the Military Museum and the Arsenal further west is a Baroque statue of St John Nepomuk, 1724, surveying the market square from his high stone pedestal.

Walk down UL. RÓŻANA, between the Cloth Hall and the Arsenal, to another statue, this time of a young woman, otherwise known as the **Monument to the Bamberg Girl**.

> Colonists from Bavaria arrived in Poznań in the early 18C after an exchange of correspondence between the Bishop of Poznań and the Bishop of Bamberg, in which the two men addressed the calamities that had befallen their respective regions: depopulation of Wielkopolska following the wars waged by Sweden, Saxony and Russia on Polish soil, and overpopulation and famine in Bavaria. The settlers were especially welcome in largely Catholic Poznań as they came from the like-minded bishopric of Bamberg. They were quickly polonised, and even took part in the national uprisings against the partitioning powers in the 19C. Yet, they preserved many of their native customs, such as the traditional pastel-coloured dresses and lavish headgear worn by the women (you can see the dresses in the Ethnographical Museum, p. 511).

To the left is the **Municipal Weighing House**, erected soon after the founding of the Market Square to provide a much-needed service to merchants doing business in its south section. It was replaced by a new weighing house in 1532–34, which di Quadro then remodelled in the Renaissance style. The Prussian authorities dismantled the building and put up a bulky Neo-Renaissance edifice in its place, which was completely destroyed in 1945. After much deliberation, the city council decided to reconstruct di Quadro's work and carried out the project in 1958–60. It currently houses a registry office.

On the west side of the square, in the corner house at **No. 84**, is the **Henryk Sienkiewicz Museum**, founded by Ignacy Moś, who donated most of the exhibits and who—when available—is eager to show visitors round. The building itself belonged to the architect di Quadro (see p. 493), and its Gothic walls and a splendid 17C wooden coffered ceiling on the first floor are preserved. The 18C façade was carefully restored after the war and decorated with sgraffito. The **museum** (open Mon–Fri 10.00–17.00) displays innumerable editions of Sienkiewicz's books in as many languages, attesting to the universal popularity of the Nobel Prize-winning novelist (see p. 84). Drawings, illustrations, busts of the writer, Biedermeier furniture (including the very desk on which he used to write) complete the collection of memorabilia.

Other celebrated Poles are commemorated further south: sgraffito portraits of Nicolaus Copernicus, Marie Curie-Skłodowska, political reformer Stanisław Staszic, and the scientists Jan and Jędrzej Śniadecki grace the façade of the restored Gothic house at **No. 79**.

Most impressive of all the houses around the square is the *****Działyński Palace** at **No. 78**, now a library of the Polish Academy of Sciences. Built in 1773–76, it was acquired by the wealthy Działyński family in 1808 (see p. 515). The pediment is somewhat dwarfed by the 18C parapet, bearing a stone eagle about to soar into the sky and flanked by Roman helmets, spears, swords and banners. Roman scenes are depicted on the attic, and two reclining figures on the pediment are blowing horns; in the centre is the Działyński coat of arms. The first-floor balcony, with a Baroque balustrade, belongs to the **Red Hall**, the most sumptuous and historic room in the palace. This is where Polish insurrectionists conspired against the partitioning powers in 1830 and 1863.

Turn towards the centre of the Market Square. To the right of the Municipal Weighing House is the **Guardhouse**. This low, classical pavilion was constructed in 1783–87 to the design of the Warsaw architect Jan Chrystian Kamsetzer. Stone crests and sculptures adorn the tiny attic resting on four columns. The building used to house the Museum of the Proletarian Movement, replaced soon after 1989 by the **Museum of the History of Wielkopolska** (**open** Tues–Sat 10.00–18.00; Sun 10.00–15.00). There is no permanent exhibition. Past the corner with ul. Franciszkańska is an originally 15C house, heavily rebuilt in the 19C, where you can find the **Tourist Information Centre** (No. 59).

The Franciscan Church

From the south side of the Market Square, walk up UL. PADEREWSKIEGO and take the first right, UL. LUDGARDY. On the left you pass the painted back wall of the National Museum (the sgraffito depicts the 'three kingdoms': mineral, plant and animal). On the right, standing on a high pedestal by the Franciscan church, is the **Monument to the Ulani of Wielkopolska Regiment**, erected in 1927, destroyed by the the Nazis, and not reconstructed until the Solidarity period (1982). The Franciscan Church is round the corner, just past the monument.

> The Franciscans arrived in Poznań in the 17C and got permission to built a priory in 1668. Construction began in 1674 and took more than half a century to complete. Little remains of the priory, most of which was pulled down by the Prussians to make room for a bank, but the church has survived, and even fighting in 1945 left it relatively unscathed.

Tuscan pilasters and cornices decorate the rather plain, twin-towered Baroque façade, elevated above street level (the stairs leading up to the entrance were added in the 19C when ul. Franciszkańska was lowered). The interior of the basilica is adorned with rich Baroque stuccowork and murals by **Adam Swach**—a local Franciscan monk whose name crops up in churches all over Poland. His brother Antoni made the two-tiered high altar filling the apse, and the chancel stalls, intricately inlaid with floral and fantastical motifs. The main showpieces of the brothers' combined skills, however, are the **domed chapels** in the transept, entered through broad arches and filled with stuccoes, sculptures and painted decoration. The black wooden altar in the east Chapel of the Virgin Mary makes a good background to a small painting of the *Madonna* (1666) made in Poznań, while the west chapel, slightly later and modelled on the first, has statues of Franciscan saints, a good memorial slab with a portrait of the philosopher and theologian Ludwik Miski (d. 1768), and a portrait of the founder of the monastery, Wojciech Zawadzki (d. 1680). Opposite the 18C pulpit is a large memorial sculpture (1736).

The Franciscan church stands at the foot of **Przemysław Hill**, on which a small castle was built in the 13C as part of the fortifications defending the settlement on the left bank of the river; parts of the town walls survive to this day. Later expanded and rebuilt, the castle suffered near-complete destruction by the Swedes, and became a ruin. It was (partly) rebuilt in neo-classical style in 1783, incorporating the surviving Gothic cellars.

It was reconstructed in this form after 1945 and turned into a **Museum of Applied Art** (open Tues, Wed, Fri, Sat 10.00–16.00; Sun 10.00–15.00). From the hall (items connected with Judaism) pass to a room on the left covering the 13C–17C; of greatest interest are enamelled Romanesque objects from Limoges, a curious vessel for hand-washing in the form of a lion, Gothic furniture and goldwork, Renaissance majolica, clocks and sundials. The second room is devoted to Baroque art, including furniture, gold, silver and pewterware, clocks and sundials (mostly from Augsburg), decorative fabrics, glass and porcelain, both Eastern and European. Interesting items are a large tankard studded with 1C–2C Roman denarii found in Korzkiew near Kraków in the 18C, and an early 18C cut-glass tankard from the Silesian workshop of Fryderyk Winter, with decoration depicting two naked boys engaged in a fistfight. The **upper floor** displays more furniture and porcelain, including a few items from the famous 2200-piece Meissen 'Swan' set, made in 1737–43 for Count Brühl, the Minister of King August III. The following rooms cover more recent periods, from the Rococo, through Biedermeier and Art Nouveau, to the 1980s.

Walk along UL. GÓRA PRZEMYSŁAWA, then UL. ZAMKOWA and UL. MASZTALARSKA. On the way, crossing ul. 23 Lutego, you pass (left) the remains of a medieval tower, the only surviving part of the outer ring of fortifications. Another tower, belonging to the inner ring of walls and situated in the yard of the **Salesian Church**, is further down ul. Masztalarska. Originally open on the town side, the tower was incorporated into the Dominican monastery in 1503 and largely destroyed by the great fire of 1536. The coffered Renaissance ceilings preserved to this day (usually inaccessible to visitors) were made after the fire. The church, originally Dominican, now Salesian, was built in 1404, and—like the adjoining tower—gutted in 1536. The fine Gothic east gable with blank arches filled with a filigree net of moulded brick was built afterwards, as were the rare Piast (tripartite) vaults of the small chancel.

Turn left into UL. WRONIECKA. Walk a short distance along UL. STAWNA, turning right into UL. ŻYDOWSKA and then left into UL. DOMINIKAŃSKA. The west façade of the former **Dominican Church** (now Jesus church) comes into view. In contrast to the austere brick wall, the pointed-arch portal (c 1250), is richly decorated with moulded and glazed brick, combining Gothic and Romanesque.

This is the oldest church on the left bank of the Warta, dating from 1244–53. It acquired two chapels—of the Virgin Mary of the Rosary and of St Hyacinth—in the 16C and 17C. During floods in 1698 the pillars and the vaults collapsed and the church had to be rebuilt. This task was undertaken by Giovanni Catenaci, who also built the Baroque west tower. Fires, hostile armies, and authorities bent on demolishing old buildings continued to plague the church, but by some quirk of fate 1945 left it almost intact.

The aisleless **interior** (open daily 06.30–08.45 and 17.30–19.00) is tall and long, with whitewashed walls divided by inner buttresses framing side chapels; the Baroque decoration and furnishing date back to the reconstruction by Giovanni Catenaci. Note the 17C Mannerist stalls in the chancel, a fine pulpit (1714–15), and a late Gothic stone font with relief decoration. Fragments of 18C painted decoration were uncovered on the walls in 1963. The large, rectangular, star-vaulted Chapel of St Mary of the Rosary, built in the early 16C, is accessible through a 17C ironwork grille. Adjoining the chapel are the surviving parts of the monastery, with Gothic cross-vaulted cloisters. The Chapel of St Hyacinth (1622) is above the sacristy.

Return to ul. Żydowska and turn left. On the corner of ul. Kramarska is the two-storey **Church of the Holy Blood of Jesus** (open Sun only 08.00–10.00), built by the Carmelites in 1702. Above the main portal, flanked by two tiny side portals, is a 15C Gothic sculpture of the *Virgin*. Another Gothic sculpture, a 16C *Pietà*, stands by the south wall inside. The interior walls of the upper storey are decorated with murals by Adam Swach; the rest of the decoration and furniture is Baroque, 18C.

Continue towards the Market Square, turning left into UL. WIELKA and then right into UL. KLASZTORNA (Priory Street). This is where in the 19C down-market prostitutes used to ply their trade and several rowdy establishments were located. Walking towards the Jesuit church tower at the end of the street you arrive at the **Górka Palace** (corner of ul. Wodna) entered through a graceful Renaissance portal bearing the date 1548, beyond which is an arcaded court-yard, c 1545. The palace was built in 1545–49 by **Andrzej Górka** and became one of the most sumptuous residences in Poznań. Following the extinction of the powerful Górka family, the building was taken over by Benedictine Nuns, who remodelled it in 1609. It subsequently became a school and a tenement house, before its final destruction in 1945. After restoration in the 1960s, the building became the seat of the **Archaeological Museum** (open Tues–Fri 10.00–16.00; Sat 10.00–18.00; Sun 10.00–15.00). Heavily didactic and geared towards school parties, the museum is hardly worth a visit.

Continue along ul. Klasztorna to the parish church, passing the long and narrow Gothic **priest's house** with a gable and a 16C figure of the *Virgin and Child* at the corner. Gothic star vaults have been preserved in one of the rooms (usually inaccessible to visitors).

The Jesuit Church of St Mary Magdalene
The Jesuits arrived in Poznań in 1570, intending to establish a major centre here, covering all of northwest Poland. They were given a small church by the town walls (no longer extant) but soon decided they needed something larger.

A new church went up in fits and starts between 1651 and 1732. When the collegiate church on nearby Plac Katedralny was completely gutted in 1870, the Jesuit church was taken over by the parish (the Jesuit order had already been dissolved in 1773).

During the Second World War the church was turned into a warehouse and suffered damage, but the original architecture and much of the interior decoration have luckily been preserved.

The ornate façade of the Jesuit **Church of St Mary Magdalene**, facing ul. Świętosławska, flanked by low copper-domed twin-towers built by Catenaci, is divided horizontally by conspicuous cornices and framed in double pilasters on both sides. Niches hold sculptures of SS Ignatius Loyola, Stanisław, Adalbert, Francis Xavier and Francis Borgia. **Pompeo Ferrari's** columned portal leads to a truly monumental **interior**: elephantine fluted columns of artificial red marble conceal the real pillars supporting the stuccoed tunnel vaults in the nave. The heavy cornice, decorated with mascarons, supports figures by **Giovanni Battista Bianco**, who was responsible for most of the splendid stucco and sculptural decoration in the church. The **murals**, no less impressive, are by the Silesian master **Karl Dankwart**. Typically Baroque ingenuity in the use of light amplifies the effect: the plain-glass windows illuminate the dark-red artificial marble of the walls and columns, creating complex patterns of light and shade. Ferrari's expressive sculptures fill the retable of the high altar, emphasising the dramatic effect of the large central painting by Szymon Czechowicz, the *Resurrection of Piotrowin* (c 1756). Below it glows a gold- and silver-plated Rococo tabernacle (1750). Two large altars stand in the wings of the short transept: the one to the left is devoted to St Ignatius Loyola, the founder of the Jesuit order, the other to St Stanisław Kostka. At the intersection of the transept and the nave is an illusionist dome painted in 1948–9. The aisles, narrow, low and cross-vaulted, contain six Baroque altars of artificial red marble and a Gothic figure of Christ (c 1430), in striking contrast to the Baroque surroundings.

Adjacent to the church on the left is the former **Jesuit College**, founded in 1573. The building you see today is an early 18C work by Catenaci, a large, L-shaped edifice, with a solemn air about it, appropriate to both its original and present purpose (offices of the President of Poznań). The wing adjacent to the church has a tall bell-tower, and there are partly-preserved cloisters which used to surround an inner garden (in the centre of which is a post-war sculpture by Edward Haupt entitled *Maternity*).

> The College, whose first rector was Jakub Wujek, the author of an epoch-making translation of the Bible (see p. 81), was so successful that it could easily compete even with the Lubrański Academy, founded some fifty years earlier (see p. 506). After the dissolution of the Jesuits in 1773 the two institutions were merged, and the College building was turned over to the newly-founded National School. In the 19C it became the seat of the Governor of the Grand Duchy of Poznań. Several celebrated people set foot here: Napoleon stayed for as long as three weeks; Chopin only for the duration of a concert.

On the opposite side of UL. GOŁĘBIA the Jesuits built a **lycée** at the beginning of 18C. It has a charming, small arcaded courtyard in Baroque style (reputedly to

Catenaci's design). A graceful stone staircase invites you to ascend to the first-floor loggia, now closed with windows. The building is now used by a ballet school, which somehow befits the architecture.

Walk Two ~ Ostrów Tumski

This walk takes you to the oldest part of Poznań, the island of Ostrów Tumski. Its main attractions—apart from the pleasantly relaxed atmosphere—are the Cathedral with many excellent works of art, and the rich, if somewhat chaotic, diocesan museum. The word '*ostrów*' actually means 'island on a river over-grown with vegetation', while 'tum' is a word of German origin signifying a cathedral. A cathedral was indeed built soon after the adoption of Christianity by Mieszko I in 968, though a defensive settlement on the island had existed at least as early as the 9C. A new stronghold, surrounded by 10m tall earth-and-wood ramparts, was built for the duke and his court in the mid-10C. The site was chosen for its defensive potential and the fact that it lay at the intersection of several important trading routes. A palatium with a chapel soon appeared, followed somewhat later by a stone Romanesque cathedral.

The Cathedral

Setting off from the Market Square, either go north to reach PL. STAWNY, where ul. Garbary joins ul. Małe Garbary and ul. Estkowskiego, or go east to cross UL. GARBARY and then walk through CHWALISZEWO. Either way, you will eventually reach the BOLESŁAW CHROBRY BRIDGE (a 15 minute walk from the Main Market Square). Cross over to Ostrów Tumski and turn left into UL. MIESZKA I, which takes you right to the ****Cathedral**.

The Cathedral was built after the first Polish bishopric had been founded in Poznań in 968. It was located on the site of a baptistery that may have been used by Mieszko I himself. Largely destroyed by the Czech prince Bretislav in 1038, it had to be rebuilt from scratch. This second, Romanesque version, twin-towered, was remodelled several times during subsequent years, first in the 13C, when cracks appeared in the walls and vaults. The Gothic chancel dates from that period, while the nave was Gothicised a century later. The chapels and three towers rising above the chancel were added in the mid-15C.

In the 17C, various disasters befell the church, such as fires and violent storms, causing it to be closed down in 1755. It was reopened after much remodelling and modernisation, which gave it a decidedly Baroque flavour with a few classical elements. The work was carried out by **Ephraim Schröger** and **Bonawentura Solari**. It was this building that the 19C Baedeker declared 'architecturally uninteresting'. The Gothic form, except for the chapels, was restored after war damage in 1945. Many fragments of the pre-Romanesque and Romanesque walls were also discovered and can now be seen in the underground crypt.

The west **façade** is dominated by two tall, bulky towers, nearly crushing the stepped gable squeezed in between. Above the moulded portal of glazed-brick is an immense quadri-partite pointed-arch window with a rosette in its upper part and post-war stained-glass. Viewed from the east, the building is a cluster of towers and turrets, with the dome of the Golden Chapel (see below) at the easternmost end, topped with a royal crown and carrying stone statues in its corners. Above the flat roof over the aisles stretch flying buttresses, a rarity in Poland.

Enter the cathedral through a bronze door depicting scenes from the life of SS Peter and Paul. Inside, one is immediately struck by the vast expanse of brick rising above the pointed-arch arcades and interrupted only by vertical moulding. In the chancel, under a triforium, stands the high altar: a late Gothic gilded triptych (16C), brought here from Silesia in 1952. The centrepiece holds sculptures of SS Mary, Barbara and Catherine, with 12 other saints in the wings and a painting of the *Last Supper* on the predella. The finely carved late Gothic stalls in the chancel are also of Silesian origin, as is the Baroque pulpit (1720), decorated with reliefs, sculptures and floral patterns, and the font, opposite.

At the northwest corner of the cathedral, you descend to the **crypt**. Here you can examine the uncovered fragments of the original pre-Romanesque cathedral, its Romanesque descendant, the 10C baptistery, as well as the **tombs of Mieszko I** and his son **Bolesław the Brave**, a lapidarium, and a bishops' crypt (usually closed).

By the entrance to the crypt is the 15C memorial slab of canon Adam Dąbrowski, with his figure in bronze. The **Chapel of St Martin**, the first of the 12, contains an early Baroque tomb of bishop Wawrzyniec Goślicki, author of the once popular *De optima senatore*, published in Venice in 1568. In the altar is a painting of St Martin (1628) by Krzysztof Aleksander Boguszewski, a talented painter from Wielkopolska (d. 1635). The following **Chapel of St Joseph** has two modern sculptures: a 1964 monument to Catholic priests murdered by the Nazis, and, by the west wall, the tomb of Cardinal Ledóchowski (1902), imprisoned by the Prussians for resisting Bismarck's *Kulturkampf* (policy of germanisation). In the **Chapel of St Cecilia** stands a Renaissance tomb commemorating archbishop Teofil Wolicki, founder of the Golden Chapel (see below). A Baroque double tomb by the west wall features two figures of kneeling men beside suits of plate armour. Opposite, the alabaster sculptures and reliefs of the Baroque high altar contrast delightfully with the dark background of the central painting showing *St Cecilia*, by the 17C Italian master Giovanni Francesco Barbieri. The **Chapel of St Francis Xavier** is remarkable mainly for the exquisite 15C Renaissance frame surrounding a painting depicting the Virgin. The frame contains small elliptical medallions representing the Mysteries of the Rosary. Under the window is a kneeling figure of Cardinal Hlond, Primate of Poland, who was succeeded in 1948 by Stefan Wyszyński. The **Chapel of the Holy Sacrament**, just behind a memorial slab in the aisle wall, is closed off by a wrought-iron grille. By its west wall stands the Mannerist tomb of the Górka family by Girolamo Canavesi (1574).

From here you pass under a curious pentagonal lantern with prominent squinches (seen from the outside, it is one of the three towers above the chancel) which provides light to the otherwise dark ambulatory. A 17C tomb and a collection of coffin portraits of Poznań canons hanging above the entrance to the **sacristy** are followed by the graceful Mannerist tomb of bishop Benedykt Izdbieński, designed by Jan Michałowicz of Urzędów, the 'Polish Praxiteles'.

Finally, at the east end of the cathedral, you come to the **Golden Chapel**, covered with a shallow gilded dome. It is adorned with a 19C mosaic set into the floor, and niches all around. In its present form, the chapel represents a 'Byzantine' style, in the Romantic manner of the 19C. To the right are the sarcophagi of

Mieszko I and Bolesław the Brave; a painting above shows the latter and Emperor Otto III by the tomb of St Adalbert. On the opposite side of the chapel stand bronze statues of the first two Polish kings, made by Chrystian Rauch, and placed here in 1841. The mosaic on the altar (1838) is based on Titian's *Assumption*.

In the ambulatory, opposite the entrance to the Golden Chapel, is the Baroque tomb of bishop Adam Nowodworski, by Wilhelm Richter of Gdańsk. The **Chapel of Our Lady of Częstochowa and St Stanisław Kostka** has twin domes bearing modern painted decoration (1962); in the altar is a copy of the Black Madonna of Częstochowa, and, under the window, a Renaissance tomb of the Powodowski family. The stuccoed Chapel of the Heart of Jesus, closed off with an ornate bronze door (1905) has modern furnishing. Under the pentagonal lantern, in the aisle wall, is the oldest memorial slab in the cathedral, discovered in 1954: it commemorates the dean of the Poznań Chapter, Teodoryk Pradel (d. 1383). Continuing west you cross the door leading to the archbishops' crypt and pass a fragment of a 16C Gothic mural depicting St Anne, discovered during post-war renovation. Other fragments can be seen under the arches of the next chapel of the Angelic Lady: under the first arch, mid-16C Renaissance painted decoration, and under the second, a mural (1616) depicting ten Apostles (two have been destroyed). The **Chapel of the Holy Trinity** was rebuilt in the 16C by di Quadro of Lugano (see p. 493), and contains the valuable sandstone and marble tomb of bishop Adam Konarski made by Canavesi in 1576. Another Italian, Bartolomeo Berrecci, famous for his work on the Wawel Hill in Kraków, designed the memorial slab of Jan Lubrański (d. 1520), the founder of the Academy (see below), which is in the Chapel of St John of Cantinus. Finally, past the south porch with 16C late Gothic sculptures and a 17C Crucifix, is the last chapel, that of St Stanisław. At the altar is Marcello Bacciarelli's painting of *SS John the Baptist and Stanisław.*

West of the cathedral is the best-preserved Gothic church in Poznań—the **Church of St Mary**. In 1431–48, this short, brick aisled hall replaced the former stone castle chapel, built c 965 after the arrival in Poznań of Mieszko's Christian wife, Dobrava. Despite much subsequent renovation, it has largely retained the form given it by Poznań masons. Its tall pinnacled west gable divided by long narrow blank arches looks curiously incomplete (no entrance—the moulded portal is on the south side instead). In the southeast corner is the so-called **Devil's Stone**, with notches allegedly made by knights who believed that striking the stone with their sword would give it magical powers. Inside, the star vaults are covered with post-war painted decoration by Wacław Taranczewski; the same artist designed the stained-glass and the high altar.

West of St Mary's is the late Gothic **Psalter**, with a pretty gable decorated with blank ogee arches. It was funded by Bishop Lubrański in 1520 for 12 cathedral cantors. His coat of arms can be seen on the east wall.

On the square west of the cathedral stands an **obelisk** commemorating **Jan Kochanowski,** the provost of Poznań Cathedral and the greatest Polish poet before Adam Mickiewicz (see p. 81). Originally erected in 1884 to celebrate the tricentenary of Kochanowski's birth, the obelisk was destroyed by the Nazis and not reconstructed until 1984. Walking east along ul. Mieszka I, with the Cathedral to your left, you pass several canons' houses, the parish offices, the Curia—all 18C–19C—and the Archbishop's Palace, originally 14C–15C, but rebuilt many times, with Neo-classical and Baroque elements. From a bench under the chestnut trees east of the cathedral, you can contemplate the Golden Chapel's exterior, the sculptures, the three lantern-towers and the west towers rising behind.

Continue around the cathedral on its north side and turn right into UL. LUBRAŃSKIEGO.

At the corner of ul. Ks. Posadzego stands the former vicarage (1850), which has recently been converted into the **Diocesan Museum** (open 09.00–15.00 except Sun). In addition to various liturgical items and church vestments, the museum has fine collections of sketches by Leon Wyczółkowski, wooden religious sculptures, including the Romanesque/Gothic *Madonna of Ołobok* (1310), and a 'Beautiful Madonna' (1410) from Wielkopolska. Among the paintings on display, the most notable are van Dyck's *Mourning* (mid-17C), canvases by Teodor Axentowicz, a *Homage of the Magi* attributed to Dolabella, and a few dozen coffin portraits (see p. 69).

A radically different tone and mood is introduced by an assortment of *fin-de-siècle* knick-knacks and *objets d'art* that take you to the world of 19C bourgeois high society. Of particular interest is the unusual 'iron jewellery', worn by women who had donated their diamonds and rubies to the national cause and who in this way mourned the crushed January Uprising of 1863–4. The entire collection was donated to the museum by Wiesława Cichowicz (d. 1976), a renowned opera-singer whose image you can see in two portraits, one by Leon Wyczółkowski, the other by Teodor Axentowicz, both of whom were her friends.

West of the museum, on the opposite side of ul. Lubrańskiego, is the **Lubrański Academy**, or Collegium Lubranscianum. Founded in 1518, it was the first institution of higher education in Poznań, and the second in Poland (after Kraków). However, it was soon eclipsed by the Jesuit College, with which it was merged in 1780. The building was erected in 1518–30 and much altered in the 18C–19C.

Leave Ostrów Tumski by the Mieszko I Bridge over the river Cybina, which links Lake Malta with the river Warta, and enter **Śródka**.

> Śródka was the property of the Wielkopolska dukes until 1288, when Przemysł II gave it to the bishop in return for land on the left bank of the Warta river. It was founded as a separate town, with its own council, mayor and town hall, and eventually incorporated into Poznań by the Prussians in 1800.

Go left to the Śródka Market Square with its **Church of St Margaret**, one of the few reasonably well-preserved Gothic buildings in Poznań, having gabled chapels on the south and north, a stepped west gable and the remains of the tower in front.

> St Margaret's was mentioned for the first time c 1231, when the Dominican order was brought to the city. The existing main church building dates from the 14C, with the Chapel of St Barbara and tower following a century later. Though much damaged by the Swedes, the church was faithfully reconstructed in the mid-17C by the parish priest, who also brought the Philippine Order to Śródka, which he himself then joined.
>
> The monastic building stands on the other side of ul. Filipińska. This L-shaped house, with pilasters topped by ornate capitals, has a small gable on

the inside corner of the L and two curly gables at both ends. Badly in need of renovation, it is now occupied by a local clinic.

The nearby **Reformed Franciscans' Church**, which stands on a hill, is accessible from ul. Bydgoska, at right angles to ul. Filipińska. The Baroque church and monastery were built at the turn of the 17C, the complex later becoming a military hospital (19C) and finally a school for the deaf (which still occupies the monastic building). Often closed, the church has 18C Baroque and Rococo furniture.

Church of St John of Jerusalem

Walk south along UL. BYDGOSKA to UL. WYSZYŃSKIEGO and cross the Śródka roundabout. By the busy UL. WARSZAWSKA stands the Church of St John of Jerusalem.

The first church on this site—dedicated to St Michael—was mentioned as early as 1146. In 1170 Mieszko the Old established a hospice for pilgrims and the sick here. This was soon turned over to the Knights Hospitallers of St John of Jerusalem, otherwise known as the Knights of Malta. The suburb in the vicinity of the church and the lake (southeast) is thus known as Malta. The wooden church of St Michael was replaced with a brick structure (in fact, one of the oldest brick churches in Poland) at the turn of the 12C, and Gothicised some 300 years later. Alterations made in the 18C gave it a Baroque character, but in post-war rebuilding the original Romanesque/Gothic style was largely restored, except for the Baroque Chapel of the Holy Cross (1736).

The building is a patchwork of contrasting elements and styles: the brick Gothic body, rendered asymmetrical by the north aisle; an incongruous plastered and domed Baroque chapel clinging to the south wall; and in the northwest corner the stub of a former tower. The west **façade** consists of a gable with a brick spiked circle above a portal with Romanesque sandstone columns (the one on the right is a reconstruction).

From the church of St John of Jerusalem walk south, passing a ship's anchor—a monument to the *SS Poznań*, 1926–72—and terminus of the children's railway line, which runs east to the zoo. Then cross back over the Cybina river, with a view from the bridge of Ostrów Tumski and its cathedral towers.

Walk Three ~ The New Town

This walk leads west of the Market Square to the commercial centre of Poznań. The highlight is the National Museum with an excellent exhibition of European and Polish art.

Walk up UL. PADEREWSKIEGO from the southwest corner of the Main Market Square to the elongated PL. WOLNOŚCI, which becomes ul. 27 Grudnia further on. Until the 18C the area was covered by gardens and known as the Hill of Flies. It was later renamed Napoleon Square, Wilhelmsplatz (in honour of the Prussian monarch) and, finally, Freedom Square, in memory of the successful Wielkopolska Uprising and the oath taken here in 1919 by the insurgents.

Looking in the direction of the Old Market Square you will see two buildings of note on ul. Paderewskiego: the Bazaar and the National Museum. On the right is the famous 19C '**Bazaar**', now freshly renovated. Its construction was initiated by Dr Karol Marcinkowski, an eminent physician and philanthropist. His aim was to promote the cultural and economic growth of the Polish population of Poznań, and especially—Marcinkowski's *idée fixe*—the 'brotherhood' of landowners and bourgeoisie. Construction began in 1839 and was financed mainly by the Mielżyńskis, a wealthy landowning family. Upon completion in 1841, the Bazaar immediately became the centre of social life: a hotel, trading hall, crafts centre and bookshop, a place where the most fashionable balls took place, where concerts, dinners and meetings were held. There was even a casino, with a share of the proceeds going to the Society for Educational Assistance, also founded by Marcinkowski, which gave scholarships to poor students. The main façade of the large Neo-classical 'Bazaar' faces ul. Paderewskiego; the part visible from pl. Wolności was added in 1899.

The National Museum
At the opposite corner of ul. Paderewskiego is the Neo-Renaissance ***National Museum**, designed in 1900 as the Prussian Friedrich Museum, and handsomely decorated with mosaics (the best of which face ul. Paderewskiego). The museum has one of the best collections of Polish painting in the country.

■ **Open** Tues 12.00–18.00, Wed, Fri, Sat 10.00–16.00, Thur 10.00–17.00, Sun 10.00–15.00

Ground floor
This is devoted to medieval art, modern Polish art and temporary exhibitions. The medieval section traces the evolution of religious art from early Romanesque to the 'broken' style. The most precious items are perhaps a limestone sculpture of the Madonna (c 1400) by the 'Master of Beautiful Madonnas', one of the finest examples of this style found in Europe, and a late 15C sculpture of *Jesus Riding a Donkey*.

First floor
The first floor includes 15C–17C Dutch and Flemish painting, 14C–18C Italian and Spanish painting and 18C–20C Polish art.

A collection of coffin portraits (see p. 69) precedes a room of works by Jacek Malczewski (1854–1929). The next room (right) has 18C paintings by Bacciarelli, Canaletto and Norblin. This is followed by 19C Polish art: Michałowski, Matejko, Siemiradzki, Gerson, J. Kossak, Chełmoński, Axentowicz, Fałat and V. Hofmann. Jugendstil is represented by Wyspiański, Mehoffer and Weiss; post-Impressionism by Stanisławski, Pankiewicz, Ślewiński and Boznańska, and Naturalism by Podkowiński, Gierymski, Wyczółkowski and Stanisławski. Your circular tour round the first floor finally brings you to a room of European art with 16C–18C Italian works, Spanish works of all the major schools, and 15C–17C Flemish canvases, including the celebrated *Madonna with Child and Lamb* by Quentin Massys (1465–1530).

By the north side of PL. WOLNOŚCI and at right angles to AL. MARCINKOWSKIEGO stands the **Raczyński Library** (currently a public library), the oldest building on the square, recognisable by its broad, lightweight colonnade of 12 pairs of slender cast-iron columns, modest pediment and balustrade along the roof edge. Designed by an unknown Italian architect and erected in 1822–29, it was funded by Count Edward Raczyński, who also donated some 30,000 volumes to the library. A large portion of its original collection of old books and manuscripts luckily survived the Second World War, hidden in one of Raczyński's country estates. In front of the building is a statue of *Hygeia*, the Greek goddess of health.

Walk up pl. Wolności, passing the '*Arcadia*', built in 1878–79 on the site of a former Prussian theatre. Behind it is an uncommonly pretty tenement house designed in the early 20C by the renowned Poznań architect, Roger Sławski. Further along is the **Polish Theatre** with the inscription '*The Nation to Itself*'. The building, erected in 1873–5 despite resistance by the Prussian authorities, was funded entirely from voluntary contributions by Poznań's Polish population. Finally, at the end of the elongated promenade (an extension of pl. Wolności) is the 'Okrąglak' shopping centre—a functionalist cylindrical structure of glass and reinforced concrete designed by Marek Leykam in 1955. Continue along UL. FREDRY, passing on your right the Neo-Gothic Protestant Church of Our Saviour (1866–69). On the same side of the street, past UL. KOŚCIUSZKI, is **Collegium Maius**, now owned by the University. This large three-storey Neo-Baroque building was originally built in 1908 for the Prussian Colonisation Commission, established in 1886 by Bismarck.

The aim of the Commission was to counteract the *Ostflucht*—a sudden impulse that spread like wildfire among Germans in the eastern provinces, causing some three million to move west during the two decades preceding the First World War—as well as to help German settlers acquire land. The Commission was a spectacular failure, and the most enduring trace of its activity might well be the fame of the popular hero, **Michał Drzymała**.

After Drzymała, a Polish peasant from Wielkopolska, had purchased a piece of land, he discovered that a regulation of the Commission forbade him as a Pole to build a permanent residence. So as not to be out-done by bureaucracy, he acquired a Gypsy caravan instead, and for more than a decade tenaciously held onto his land. His case, which even managed to attract international media interest, is a striking illustration of the differences between life in the Russian and Prussian zones. While equally oppressive, the Prussian regime always adhered strictly to previously established rules and regulations and never succumbed to the whimsical arbitrariness of Czarist despotism.

Finally, you come to the imposing **Opera** building (1910) with Pegasus crowning the pediment, which rests on heavy Ionic columns. Flanking the stairs are two lions: a young woman sits astride one of them, and a youth stands frozen in mid-step by the other. Turn left (south) and walk past the pond to PL. MICKIEWICZA, where there is a **statue** of the Romantic poet, Adam Mickiewicz. Close by is another **monument**: two asymmetrical crosses and an eagle's head (1981) commemorating the events of June 1956, when nearly 200 defenceless demonstrators were killed by police and troops.

The 1956 Uprising

In June 1956, the workers of the Cegielski factory (then, like so many others, named after Józef Stalin) went on strike. They were soon joined by workers from other factories in the city. A rally took place on pl. Wolności, at which demands were raised for political liberalisation and higher standards of living. When the protesters realised that the authorities were not going to heed their demands, they stormed the prison, setting the inmates free, and burned down the local jamming station. (Like censorship or shortages of toilet paper, the jamming of Western short-wave radio broadcasts was a characteristic feature of life under communism. The Polish government spent more on jamming Radio Free Europe than it cost the US Congress to finance the station; other stations that were jammed included the BBC and the Voice of America).

The local Communist Party HQ and the regional State Security Police buildings were surrounded. Those inside responded with machine-gun fire, killing scores of defenceless civilians, including women and children. Barricades were erected and weapons captured from the prison guards were put to use, first against the Citizens' Militia, and then against the army units sent in to restore order. The uneven battle lasted two days, leaving some 200 dead and over 1000 wounded. Edward Gierek (see p. 60) and Józef Cyrankiewicz rushed from Warsaw to try to allay the situation. The latter made a remarkable radio speech, in which he threatened that anyone who dared to raise an arm against the People's Government 'would have it chopped off'.

To the right (west) is the pretty Neo-Renaissance **Collegium Minus**, with a triangular pinnacled gable between two angular towers. Inside is the University Auditorium, where, owing to the excellent acoustics, the **International Wieniawski Violin Competition** is held every five years. A plaque in the hall commemorates several mathematicians from the University of Poznań who made a truly monumental contribution to Allied success during the Second World War by breaking the Enigma Code used by the Germans for encrypting top-secret military messages.

Monument to June 1956

On the opposite side of pl. Mickiewicza is the Neo-Romanesque **Castle of Wilhelm II** with a square tower at its south end. Built in 1905–10 as a summer residence for the monarch, it is decorated with motifs illustrating German mythology and the Prussian *Drang nach Osten* (eastward drive). The inner courtyard (entered from ul. Kościuszki) has a copy of the famous Alhambra Fountain, looking rather incongruous in these surroundings. The castle now houses a puppet theatre, cinema and art workshops.

Go back towards the city centre

along ul. Św. Marcin to the **Church of St Martin**. After the Swedish invasion in the early 18C it was rebuilt in Baroque style, but after the Second World War the original 16C Gothic appearance was restored. Over the main portal is a fine image of *St Martin* (E. Haupt, 1953). The plain nave and aisles are star-vaulted; the chancel walls are covered with impressive painted decoration by W. Taranczewski (1957). The apse contains a Late Gothic Silesian triptych (1498), and a Gothic sculpture from Wielkopolska—*Madonna with Child* (c 1510)—stands in the south aisle.

East of the church is a low pedestal, on which a monument to Mickiewicz once stood. It was destroyed by the Nazis and never restored; instead a new one was made and placed on pl. Mickiewicza (see above).

From the church of St Martin walk east along ul. Św. Marcin and then ul. Podgórna towards the towers of the **Bernardine Church**, visible in the distance.

> The church, badly damaged during the last war, was restored in the Baroque form it received after destruction by the Swedes in 1655 and by fire in 1668. The façade and towers are a later addition (1730–37). The first, wooden church on this spot was built in the mid-15C by Franciscan monks. A brick Gothic replacement went up after 1473, to which the Renaissance chapel of Our Lady of Loreto was added in 1609.

Entering the church you climb several stairs, as there is a high crypt underneath. The interior is long and narrow: the aisles could almost be taken for passages leading through the inner buttresses. In contrast, the cornice is broad and conspicuous, supported on pillars decorated with double pilasters and sculptures. The furniture is modern, except for an 18C Passion group on the rood beam.

To the left of the church is the former Polish **lycée** of St Mary Magdalene, which played an important role in resisting Germanisation during the partitions.

A short detour beyond a small park with a fountain takes you to the **Ethnographical Museum** (away from the centre along ul. Bohaterów, then left into ul. Mostowa). The museum (**open** Tues, Wed, Fri, Sat 10.00–16.00; Sun 10.00–15.00) is housed in a 19C classical building formerly belonging to a Masonic lodge.

The **first floor** contains wooden pillars with sculptures of saints—once a common sight in Wielkopolska—as well as other religious sculptures and paintings, some of them modern. Pictures of women in Bamberg dress (see p. 498) are displayed along the staircase; you can see a real example of this attire, complete with gaudy headgear, on the **second floor**, among dresses from the Wielkopolska region, folk instruments, paintings on glass, pottery and iron objects.

Turn left into ul. Garbary and continue past the Bernardine church, turning right into ul. Strzelecka. You will finally come to the **Corpus Christi Church** on ul. Krakowska.

> This large Gothic structure was erected in the second half of the 15C for the Carmelites. After a fire in 1657, it was rebuilt partly in Baroque style (the gable). The Reformed Franciscans moved in after the dissolution of the Carmelite order in 1823, saving it from total destruction. Badly damaged in

1945, it was restored a few years later. The church was often flooded by the Warta—small plaques on the wall indicate the dates and the water level on each occasion.

Rich moulding and glazed brick decorate the elongated windows and the deep, pointed-arch portals. Inside, these Gothic elements are echoed in the aisles' pointed-arch arcades and star vaults. Otherwise, the tone of the interior is pure Baroque, dominated by the splendid **high altar**, the work of Pompeo Ferrari, with a painting of the *Last Supper* by an unknown artist of the same period. Ferrari also designed the St Mary Chapel, entered by a staircase from the chancel. The paintings in the chancel depict the founders of the church: Władysław Jagiełło and Queen Jadwiga.

Walk Four ~ The Citadel

This walk, featuring military and memorial sights, takes you north of the Market Square to a verdant hill once covered with vineyards, later transformed into a mighty fortress, and then into a war cemetery and mausoleum.

From the Market Square walk north, crossing pl. Wielkopolski with its Socialist Realist architecture, to UL. WOLNICA. From here ascend UL. ŚW. WOJCIECH, which begins a short distance to the right. The Baroque façade of the Discalced Carmelites' **Church of St Joseph** soon comes to view on the left.

St Joseph's was built in the 17C by Cristoforo Bonadura the Elder and Giorgio Catenaci on the site of a Protestant church of the Czech Brethren, which had burned down some years previously. After using it as a warehouse and military hospital, the Prussian authorities turned it over to the Protestant community; thus it became a garrison church, at first Protestant and then, after the First World War, Roman Catholic.

Most impressive is the broad, three-tiered **façade**. The aisled interior contains bland, modern furniture. Adjacent to the church and monastery is the oldest **cemetery** in Poznań. Established in the early 19C, it was made into a cemetery for the deserving after the last war. Restored and remodelled in 1980–81, it is now a pleasant hilly park with many old trees and criss-crossing paths, ideal for a relaxed walk on a sunny afternoon.

A short way back, on the opposite side of the street, is the **Church of St Adalbert** (c 1220), which stands on a hillock. In front of its west façade is a reconstructed 18C wooden belfry.

The church was expanded several times, most importantly in the 16C, when the late Gothic aisles were added, and in the 17C, when it acquired the pretty Renaissance gables at the east and west ends, and the Chapel of St Anthony to the south. Unfortunately, the church suffered badly during the battle for the Citadel in 1945 (see below); the excellent stained-glass windows, as well as other precious items, were destroyed.

The dark, star-vaulted **interior** with Secessionist painted decoration throws into contrast the stained-glass window in the apse and the gilded triptych serving as a high altar, which has a 16C relief depicting the *Ascension*. The late Renaissance altar in the north aisle contains a painting by the celebrated Wielkopolska artist, Krzysztof Aleksander Boguszewski (?–1635). The south aisle also contains a late Renaissance altar (with a 16C Italian painting—*Lament* *for Christ*), as well as 17C coffin portraits of the Naramowski family and the marble tomb of Karol Marcinkowski. The underground crypt contains the ashes of Józef Wybicki (1747–1822, author of the Polish anthem), and the composer Feliks Nowowiejski (1877–1946).

Down the hill, opposite the old cemetery, is the **Monument to the 'Poznań' Army**, erected in 1982. In a rather obvious allegory, several shiny spikes represent the heroic resistance of the Polish army to the German onslaught, shown as four grey threatening slabs.

The Citadel

Walk down the hill past the monument to PL. NIEPODLEGŁOŚCI. Then turn right at the green sign in English ('Poznań Old Garrison Cemetery, Commonwealth Section') into al. Niepodległości and pass under the rail bridge. Two German cannons guard the entrance to what is known as the **Citadel**.

The hill was originally covered with idyllic vineyards until Napoleon remarked upon its defensive capabilities. He did not have enough time to implement this brilliant idea, but the Prussians did: in 1828–39 they built a formidable stronghold, 100 hectares in area, with 3km of embankment supplemented by a brick-reinforced dry moat. It was one of the largest such structures in Europe at that time. And yet, when the Wielkopolska Uprising broke out in 1919, the Prussian troops surrendered the Citadel without a fight.

Likewise, the Polish army abandoned it in 1939. Only the Nazis took it seriously and had some 20,000 troops defend it for nearly a month against Soviet attack in 1945. Air raids and artillery bombardment almost completely levelled the buildings. Nearly all were dismantled after the war and the huge quantities of brick were used for housing construction. After 1962 the site was declared a 'Monument to Polish-Soviet Friendship', the few remnants of fortifications were restored, and a park, the largest in Poznań, was laid out.

Ascend the long flight of stairs towards the obelisk in memory of Red Army soldiers. On both sides of the stairway are innumerable graves of the 10,000 Soviet soldiers who died during the battle of Poznań in 1945. Pass the 23m-high obelisk at the top and continue to the **Museum of the Liberation of Poznań** (**open** Tues–Sat 09.00–16.00; Sun 10.00–16.00), housed in the former munitions depot. In front of the museum stand several tanks from the last war, while other armoured vehicles, cars, cannons and fighter planes are put on the roof of the museum building. Inside is a collection of photographs and other objects connected with the history of the Citadel, the liberation of Poznań by the Red Army, examples of Second World War weaponry, Red Army and Wehrmacht badges, and urns with earth brought from various battlefields in Russia.

Turn back towards the obelisk. To the left of it is a monument to the Polish victims of 1939–56. Steps lead down the hill, passing on the left the British Soldiers' Cemetery, with graves from both the First and Second World Wars. The cemetery was established in 1920 for British POWs who had died in German camps. After the Second World War the graves of captured British servicemen and pilots shot down over Poland were added (15 of them were Poles who had served in the RAF).

Walk down to al. Armii Poznań and turn left. A small alleyway (left) brings you to the former sluice, now the **Museum of the 'Poznań' Army** (**open** Tues–Sat 09.00–16.00; Sun 10.00–16.00). The long and damp corridor

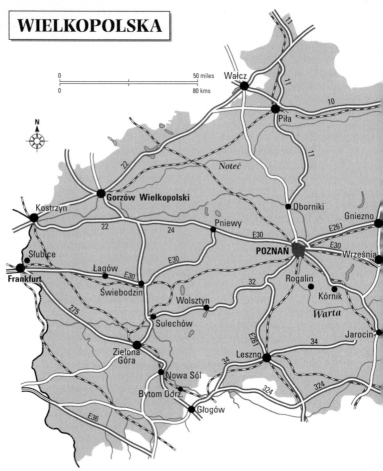

contains sundry objects illustrating the military history of Wielkopolska from 1918 to 1945, focusing on the participation of the 'Poznań' Army in the September 1939 campaign (the Battle of Bzura) and the resistance movement during the Second World War.

Kórnik and Rogalin

❖ Kórnik • Rogalin • Poznań

To the south of Poznań, in close proximity to each other, lie the exquisite Kórnik Castle with an excellent museum, and the somewhat neglected, though still impressive, former residence of the Raczyński family in Rogalin.

Leave Poznań southeast along road 42 in the direction of Wrocław and Łódź;

turn off at the white signpost marked 'Kórnik' (22km); then right again onto road 434 marked 'Mosina, Rawicz, Kórnik'.

As you reach Kórnik market square, the **parish church** comes to view on the left. Originally Gothic, founded in the 15C by the Górkas, it was rebuilt in 1838 in Romantic style, to the design of F. M. Lanci. Its west façade, with a broad frieze, a large brick rosette and a stepped gable with turrets, is flanked by two squat towers with false machicolations. Arched passages separate them from the church. The entrance to the **Zamoyski crypt** is in the north chapel; the **Działyński tombs** are contained within a large stone box of a chapel south of the church.

Kórnik Castle

Further on is the **castle (open Tues–Sun 09.00–17.30) set in spacious grounds and encircled by a moat.

The two families that left an indelible mark on Kórnik were the **Górkas and the Działyńskis**. The former became politically influential, particularly in Wielkopolska, during the 15C, and continued to prosper throughout the 16C (it was then that Andrzej Górka built the Górka Palace in Poznań (see p. 501). The brick and stone foundations of the castle in Kórnik, which are still visible in the cellars, must have been laid in the early 15C at the latest. A century later, Stanisław Górka expanded the castle, replacing the timber structure with brick and stone and surrounding it with fortifications—a task made easier by the terrain: marshland with an island protected by a broad moat. With Stanisław Górka's death in 1592, the last scion of the powerful family had perished; the castle changed hands several times, and finally came into the possession of the Działyński clan.

The Działyńskis founded the park, now the arboretum, and rebuilt the castle in Baroque style (18C). Tytus Działyński, one of the wealthiest magnates in Wielkopolska, had the castle rebuilt in Neo-Gothic 'English' style (19C), to the design of Karl Friedrich Schinkel. This grand undertaking was continued after his death by his son, Jan Działyński. The latter was forced by his over-ambitious father to marry princess Izabela Czartoryska, herself not too keen on the marriage, and died childless in 1880. In a symbolic ceremony, the Działyński coat of arms was broken over his coffin, and a knight in black armour rode on horseback into the church in Kórnik, where the burial took place.

The castle, with all its precious art and a rich collection of manuscripts, maps and rare prints which Tytus had assembled, was left to Jan's nephew Władysław Zamoyski. This atypical count, who spurned all luxury, ate potatoes with cabbage, travelled fourth class on trains, and helped village women returning home from Poznań to carry their heavy baskets, established the **Kórnik Foundation** in 1925, with the aim of turning the property over to the nation. Zamoyski's fortune amounted to some 20,250ha of land, real estate and valuable collections of art. The property was confiscated first by the Nazis, then by the Communists, and the Foundation ceased to exist in 1953. Kórnik castle was given to the Polish Academy of Sciences, which financed large-scale renovation work and continued to develop the arboretum, where some 2500 species of trees and shrubs are now grown.

Enter the castle, and from the vestibule, covered with a coffered ceiling bearing the Działyński and Czartoryski coats of arms go right, through the portal leading to the **study**. This was used in turn by Tytus Działyński, his son, and Władysław Zamoyski. In a niche is a rare Baroque Gdańsk wardrobe. The early 19C mahogany desk with bronze fittings is the only item of furniture in the room that stood here in former times. Above a map rack is the centrepiece of a 16C Renaissance triptych showing the kneeling figure of Łukasz Górka, Palatine of Poznań, and one-time owner of Kórnik. The parquet floor is exquisitely decorated with geometrical and floral patterns in birch, mahogany and walnut.

Pass to the **Chamber of the General's Wife**, its walls adorned with paintings: the *Passing of the Constitution of 3 May, 1791*, by Jean Pierre Norblin (1745–1830), two works by Artur Grottger (1837–67), and sketches by Marcello Bacciarelli (1731–1818). Miniatures, photographs, drawings and memorabilia of the Działyński family are distributed around the furniture, which is mostly Baroque, originating from Denmark, England and Gdańsk.

Next along is the **Drawing Room**, with gilded stuccos on the ceiling and ornate wooden portals in North Renaissance style. Tytus Działyński sternly surveys the room from a gilt-framed portrait above the fireplace. In addition to other family portraits there are two copies of miniatures by the outstanding painter Stanisław Samostrzelnik (1485–1541; see p. 236); the originals are in the Kórnik library. The grand piano is reputed to have been played by Chopin. Adjoining the drawing room is a small parlour in the southwest corner tower. Opposite the entrance hangs a 16C portrait of the eight-year-old Galeazzin, son of Duke Bonaventure. To the left is a 17C *Death of St Sebastian*, reputedly from the Rubens workshop. The portrait of Frederick III, on the right-hand wall, originates from the workshop of Lucas Cranach the Elder. Above the marble fireplace hangs a Saxony mirror; most of the remaining furniture is 18C, Baroque and Neo-classical. Pass through the drawing room to the marble-floored **Black Hall**, with a small collection of coins, medals and paintings.

From the Black Hall, continue to the east wing: first you come to the **Dining Room** with a coffered ceiling bearing 15C Polish coats of arms, and portraits of Działyński family members on the walls. Two Baroque wardrobes stand by the door, one Dutch, the other from Gdańsk. The small adjacent room in the southeast angle tower, behind a door with Renaissance inlaid decoration, has Rococo furnishing and a watercolour portrait by Juliusz Kossak of *Władysław Zamoyski*. Passing through the dining room you enter the chamber once occupied by Jan Działyński's wife and then by Zamoyski's sister. The ceiling is covered with oriental stuccowork, and bears an Arabic inscription: 'There is no God above Allah'— Tytus Działyński's tribute to the Ottoman Empire, which refused to acknowledge the partitioning of Poland. The Zamoyskis are represented in several portraits on the walls. Next, in the tower, comes the round, diamond-vaulted **Hunter's Lodge**. In addition to the usual

Kórnik Castle

hunting trophies, there is a collection gathered by Zamoyski during his expeditions to Australia, New Caledonia, New Zealand and Oceania in 1879–81. A particularly treasured item is a bamboo pipe which the count received from Australian Aborigines.

Ascend the stairs to the **Moresque Hall**, with oriental decoration reminiscent of the Alhambra. The hall contains a display of military paraphernalia, including Polish hussars' armour. Among the historical paintings depicting kings and Polish field commanders, there is one in which Duke Beauharnais, Napoleon's stepson, is rescuing general Stanisław Klicki (see p. 159). Napoleon himself is represented in a miniature painted on ivory by Jean Baptiste Isabey. Occupying the middle section of the hall is a display of medals and badges, as well as goldwork, silverware and porcelain, including a plate from the huge Meissen 'Swan' set made for count Brühl. In the last section of the hall there is a collection of religious items, including a valuable **17C triptych** with sixteen silver reliefs representing the *Mysteries of the Rosary*, and a French ivory **14C diptych** showing the *Coronation of the Virgin* and the *Adoration of the Magi*. Also of interest is the memorial to Jan Borek from Wiślica, made in Kraków in 1520–30. Leaving the hall you enter the vaulted second floor vestibule with several 17C–18C portraits of Polish kings. It terminates in a room with a large window overlooking the courtyard. Among the paintings here is the portrait of Stanisław August Poniatowski by Marcello Bacciarelli (1790).

After visiting the castle, a stroll in the arboretum is pleasant.

The Raczyński Palace

Return along the Poznań road for a short distance, turn left marked 'Mosina' (road 431), and drive on to **ROGALIN** (11km).

Set among pleasant woodland, close to the Warta river, is the outwardly impressive *Raczyński Palace (**open** Tues–Sun 10.00–16.00; until 18.00 on Sun in high season). It is possible to rent a room with a bath (☎ 061 813-8030).

The origins of Rogalin reach back to the 13C. The Raczyński family bought it for the first time in 1511, losing it soon afterwards. It was recovered in

1768 by Kazimierz Raczyński and thereafter remained in the family's possession until the Second World War. Raczyński also replaced the modest estate, typical of the Polish gentry, with a magnificent residence befitting his position as Palatine of Wielkopolska and Grand Marshal of the Crown. He also funded the Guardhouse on Poznań's Main Market Square, and restored the castle on Przemysław Hill. Construction in Rogalin began soon after the estate was purchased. The original architect is unknown, but later such excellent architects as Domenico Merlini and Jan Chrystian Kamsetzer, famous for their creations in Warsaw, were enlisted.

Rococo with a dash of classicism manifests itself not only in the façade and decoration, but also in the layout of the entire estate, ruled just as much by strict symmetry, as by fanciful imagination. Crossing the moat over a stone bridge and passing through a grand gate, carriages would enter an alleyway lined with chestnut trees and ending in a *cour d'honneur* (entrance courtyard). Stepping out of the carriage, the visitor would be immediately struck—as one is today—by the imposing, broad **façade**, 17 windows wide and two-storeys high, with a mezzanine, pediment and pilasters. The ends of the façade merge with gently curving colonnades, providing a convenient link from the main building to the stable (right) and the coach house (left).

Today's **interior**, converted into a museum, attempts to capture something of each epoch in Raczyńskis' illustrious history, but in so doing fails to be true to any. There are plans to open more rooms (particularly on the first floor, the *piano nobile*), but at the moment you can only inspect the south colonnade and the chilly cellar of the south wing, where some miscellaneous paintings and pieces of furniture have been gathered to simulate a Rococo parlour, a Venetian boudoir, a traditional dining room, Count Raczyński's study, and an Empire-style lady's dressing room. Of greater interest is the **art gallery** situated behind a wall adjacent to the former coach house. Inside are 19C–20C Polish paintings by such artists as Jan Matejko, Jacek Malczewski, Leon Wyczółkowski and Olga Boznańska, as well as a few foreign works, notably by Claude Monet, Arnold Böcklin and Friedrich Overbeck.

The work commenced by Kazimierz Raczyński was continued after his death by his cousin and son-in-law, Filip, and then by his grandson, Edward, to whom Poznań owes the Raczyński library. The statue of *Hygeia* in front of the library was modelled on Edward's beloved wife Konstancja, the widow of Jan Potocki (author of *Manuscrit trouvé à Saragosse*, see p. 82). The statue is a copy; the original was placed on Edward's grave in Zaniemyśl, where he committed suicide by shooting himself with a small cannon. His great-grandson (also Edward), born in 1891, a diplomat and a man of letters, witnessed the rebirth of the Polish state in 1918, served it as Ambassador to Great Britain, saw it trampled by the Soviets and Nazis (who converted his Rogalin estate into a training centre for the *Hitlerjugend*), went into exile and held the office of President-in-Exile of the Republic of Poland for more than 40 years, in defiance of the Yalta agreements. Yet, this quixotic Count, whose gaunt figure could sometimes be seen strolling the streets of London before old age finally confined him to a wheelchair, became a symbol of Poland's resistance to Soviet occupation. He died at the age of 102, four years after the collapse of communism.

The splendour of the palace erected by Kazimierz Raczyński had to be matched by an exquisite formal, **landscaped park** at the back (**open** 10.00–17.00). In spite of all the practice shooting and goose-stepping it had to suffer during the Second World War, the park still preserves some of its former grandeur. Its wonderful oak trees (*quercus sessilis*), forming one of the largest preserves of ancient oaks in Europe, emanate an aura of unquestioned nobility. Three of them have even been given the names of the legendary brother-princes, the founders of the Slav nations: Lech, Czech and Rus.

Walk back along the chestnut alley and through the gate. On both sides are some former peasant dwellings. In one on the right (south) a **coach house** has been set up, with a display of carriages, most of which were actually used by the owners of Rogalin. Still further on along the east-west axis of the estate, standing on a hillock, is the **Chapel-Mausoleum**, erected in the 19C by Edward Raczyński, as he wanted to convert the palace chapel into a Neo-Gothic armoury. The exterior is Neo-classical, modelled on the Maison Carrée in Nîmes. Inside is a Neo-Romanesque aisled and vaulted hall, with stuccos on the ceiling (1830) and geometric designs on the floor. It contains the **tombs of Roger Raczyński**, his **wife Konstancja**, and **Count Edward Raczyński**, whose remains were brought to Rogalin from Britain in 1993.

Return to Poznań the way you came (33km), or continue for 8km to Mosina (road 431), and then head north on the 430 (16km).

Toruń to Poznań ~ The Piast Route

❖ Kruszwica • Strzelno • Mogilno • Trzemeszno • Gniezno • (detour: Biskupin) • Dziekanowice (Ostrów Lednicki) • Poznań

This trip passes through several places associated with the earliest period in Polish history and the country's first royal dynasty—the Piasts. The highlights are Gniezno, with its famous cathedral, and the (reconstructed) prehistoric settlement in Biskupin.

Leave Toruń south on road 52, joining the 25 in Inowrocław, marked 'Konin'. At Tupadły, turn left onto road 265. Despite its industry, **KRUSZWICA** (53km from Toruń) is one of the oldest towns in Poland, with traces of prehistoric settlement dating back to 5200 BC. It is associated with King Popiel, the ruler of the Goplanie tribe,

Collegiate church of St Mary, Kruszwica

who, according to legend, took refuge in a tower on Lake Gopło, and was eaten alive by mice. During the 10C–12C, Kruszwica was an important centre of the Piast state. Kazimierz the Great erected a brick castle in the mid-14C, which survived until the Swedish invasions of the mid-17C (see p. 49).

Today, the town's main attractions, apart from lake Gopło and the nature reserve, are the collegiate church and the picturesque **Mouse Tower** (32m), east of the Market Square (follow the signs to 'Mysia Wieża'). The name of the tower obviously refers to the unfortunate Popiel, though it was actually built in the 14C, as part of the castle. Inside folk costumes from the Kujawy region are displayed, and from the top there is a good view of the lake. The nearby **Collegiate Church of St Mary**, a Romanesque stone basilica of 1120–40, was initially settled by the Benedictines from Cluny, and some of its architectural elements still hark back to their famous abbey. Remodelled in 1586 (when the late Gothic west tower was added), and 1856–9, the church regained its pure Romanesque character after the war. The sparsely furnished **interior**, entered through an arched and columned portal in the south side, has a wooden beam ceiling, and contains a stone font to the left of the chancel, a stoop in the south-west corner of the nave, and a reliefed mensa at the high altar, all Romanesque.

Column fragment (Strzelno)

Backtrack towards Ino-wrocław, turning left onto road 257 at Kobylniki. **STRZELNO** (15km) is famous for its ***Premonstratensian Nuns' Abbey**, which has dominated the town for centuries. It is located on St Adalbert's Hill east of the Main Square. The church, a Romanesque stone basilica with a transept and twin towers, was erected after 1175, receiving its fine late Gothic star vault during remodelling in the 15C. The Baroque accretions, such as the gabled west façade with sculptures, and the chapels on the south side, date from the mid-18C. Of greatest interest, however, are the remarkable **Romanesque pillars** (c 1170) supporting the aisle arches. Restored after the war, two of the pillars bear rich figural bas-reliefs framed by three tiers of miniature arcades. The bases of the pillars are partly concealed by the floor, and the capitals are disproportionately large in relation to the slender shafts. Romanesque fragments also survive in the vaulted chapel to the south of the chancel.

Entering the church through the doorway to the left (north) of the main porch, you will find a Romanesque stone portal, discovered after the Second World War, with a carved tympanum showing Christ surrounded by saints and angels. Another roughly contemporaneous portal is found at the west end of the south aisle. Here, the tympanum shows the founders of the church presenting a model of it to the Virgin and St Anne.

Close by stands the **Rotunda of St Procopius**, built of ashlars in c 1160, with a brick, partly reconstructed superstructure of the 15C–16C.

The Benedictine Abbey at Mogilno

Eighteen kilometres from Strzelno is the town of **MOGILNO**. Head west along road 256, turning right onto the 254 for Mogilno. This otherwise unassuming town is noted for its **Benedictine Abbey**, set on the shores of Lake Mogileńskie.

According to the medieval historian Jan Długosz, the abbey was founded in 1065 by **Kazimierz the Restorer**. Situated on the borders of the Piast realm, it initially served as a fortress protecting Wielkopolska from the pagan tribes to the north—evidence of this is provided by the huge masonry retrenchment erected in the 13C in place of the wooden palisade. Closed by the Prussian authorities in 1833, the convent later served as a hospital, and, during the Second World War, as a camp for British POWs.

The abbey (now parish) **Church of St John the Evangelist**, a large Romanesque basilica with two crypts, was erected in the late 11C, and rebuilt in brick after 1550. It originally had a unique two-tiered chancel, but this was disfigured by later remodelling. Romanesque granite blocks are still discernible in the stairs, pillars, and fragments of the walls and windows (consult the ground plan displayed in the west porch, and the billboard map by the entrance to the church grounds). The nave is covered with Gothic star vaults and the aisles with rare cellular vaults. Below the preserved Romanesque apse to the east are the vaulted crypts with a display of archaeological finds (1970–80) from the region. The twin-towered west façade and most of the church furnishings are late Baroque (18C).

Regain road 256 and continue 16km west to **TRZEMESZNO**, one of the earliest settlements in Wielkopolska. Head straight for the **church** on PL. KOSMOWSKIEGO.

The history of the church dates from the 10C, when, according to legend, **St Adalbert** (see p. 44) founded a monastery for the Benedictines—the first in Poland. In 997, St Adalbert's body was temporarily stored here before being taken to Gniezno for burial (see below). The first pre-Romanesque church was destroyed during an invasion by the Czech prince Bretislav in 1038. A century later, Bolesław the Wry-mouthed founded a new monastery and Romanesque basilica for the Canons Lateran, who remained the owners until their expulsion by the Prussian authorities in 1793.

Viewed from the outside, the church is a conglomeration of domes. Its present form dates primarily from the 18C, when it was expanded and remodelled according to late Baroque paradigms. The interior is largely the result of reconstruction carried out after war damage. The central dome, with a lantern, Corinthian pilasters, and 12 windows around, is decorated with frescoes attributed to Franciszek Smuglewicz (18C). More frescoes, depicting the life of St Adalbert, adorn the nave vault. The crossing, directly under the dome, is the focal point of eight axes: the transepts, nave, chancel, and four side chapels. Slightly off-centre stands the altar of St Adalbert, with a sculpture depicting the martyr-missionary. Fine 18C bas-reliefs line the nave, crossing and chancel. The blank arcades at the back of the nave, together with the porch vault, constitute the only Gothic remnants inside the church.

Gniezno

Further west on road 256 lies Gniezno (17km), today a mere provincial town, but one that will forever be associated with the origins of the Polish state.

According to legend, Gniezno was founded by **Lech**, ruler of the pagan Polanie tribe, who, hunting in the forest, discovered a white eagle's nest (*gniazdo*), and chose it as the site of a new settlement—the white eagle has to this day remained **Poland's national emblem**. Lech's successor, **Mieszko I**, is credited with bringing Christianity to Poland, when he was baptised in Gniezno in 966, becoming ruler of the Duchy of Polonia, now formally a part of Christendom. Archaeological excavations confirm the existence of a pre-Romanesque church of 970–77 raised by Mieszko on Lech Hill, where the present cathedral (see below) now stands.

Gniezno acquired still greater significance in 1000, when it played host to a historic meeting between **Emperor Otto III** and Mieszko's son, **Bolesław the Brave** (Chrobry). Urged by the Pope, the Emperor came to Gniezno to establish a metropolitan see—the first Polish archbishopric—and to celebrate the canonisation of the monk Adalbert (Wojciech in Polish), a Bohemian missionary cruelly murdered and mutilated by the pagan Prussians.

Recovered by the Poles 'for his weight in gold', and buried in Gniezno, the martyr soon became one of the most revered Polish saints. The Emperor rewarded Bolesław by calling him a friend and ally of the Empire; in 1025 he was crowned King of Poland in Gniezno cathedral. Gniezno's association with Polish statehood has endured over the centuries. Today it remains the country's official ecclesiastical seat, with the Primate of Poland holding the title of Archbishop of Gniezno.

The Cathedral

The pre-Romanesque church in which St Adalbert was buried no longer exists, nor does its Romanesque successor, destroyed by the Teutonic Knights in 1331. The present ****cathedral**, founded by Archbishop J. Bogoria Skotnicki, dates from 1342–1602, but it suffered several fires, notably in 1613 and 1760. The Neo-classical form it received after that (Ephraim Schröger, 1761–90) was largely lost in 1945 and during subsequent renovation, when the original Gothic appearance was restored. Two original 15C portals have been preserved, and there are remnants of the two earlier churches in the underground **crypt**.

- **cathedral open** to visitors Mon–Sat 10.00–17.00, Sun 13.30–17.30. For a guided tour, ask at the sacristy, Tues–Sat 10.00–12.00, 13.00–14.00.

- **crypt open** 10.00–12.00, 13.00–14.00 and 15.00–16.00 for groups of more than 10; entrance in the northwest corner).

The cathedral is a large basilica with a nave and chancel of equal height and width, and an ambulatory behind seven narrow, pointed arches. At the west end of the south aisle is the showpiece monument—the famous ***GNIEZNO DOORS**. Cast in bronze in c 1175, probably in Magdeburg, the doors are one of the finest examples of European Romanesque art. Inscribed on them is a cycle of eighteen exquisite reliefs, framed in animal and plant motifs, telling the story of St Adalbert. Reading clockwise from the bottom, the LEFT DOOR shows the life of the Saint from his birth in Libice (now in the Czech Republic) in 956 until his arrival in Poland; the theme of the RIGHT DOOR is his missionary work, death, martyrdom, and burial in the cathedral. Enclosing the doors is one of the Gothic portals, with a scene of *Christ in Majesty* in the tympanum. A slightly later scene of the *Crucifixion* is found above the north portal. Beside it is the chapter library, with a collection of medieval illuminated manuscripts.

Detail from the Gniezno doors

At the entrance to the chancel, under the 15C rood, stands the tomb slab of St Adalbert, with an alabaster figure of the saint, carved in c 1480 by Hans Brandt from Gdańsk. Two scenes from the saint's life are found on the sandstone base. In the middle of the monastic choir is the more impressive silver repoussé reliquary of St Adalbert, made in 1662 by Pieter van der Rennen, author of the similar shrine of St Stanisław in Kraków's Wawel cathedral (see p. 213). Scenes from the life of St Adalbert adorn the coffin, which is supported by six eagles. The reclining figure was stolen in 1986, when it was damaged quite badly. It was later recovered and reconstructed.

Among the many **chapels** and **epitaph slabs** in the cathedral, there are several that deserve a special mention. Embedded in the west wall is the red marble slab of Archbishop Oleśnicki (d. 1493), carved by Veit Stoss in 1495, and, to the right of it, the Flemish bronze tomb slab of Archbishop Jakub of Sienna (d. 1480). Going east along the north aisle you pass a sandstone relief sponsored by Archbishop Sprowski in 1460, and a carved wooden door that used to lead to the library, bearing images of eminent Poles (Nicholas Copernicus among them).

The door is followed by the Baroque **Potocki chapel**, built by Pompeo Ferrari in 1728–30. The adjacent **Sprowski chapel** contains (against its north wall) an altar with a wooden tabernacle by Ephraim Schröger (c 1781). Next to the entrance to the **Doctors' chapel**, in the north ambulatory, is the Renaissance red marble memorial slab of Archbishop Jan Łaski, one of four he commissioned from Giovanni Fiorentino; the remaining three are further east, past the entrance to the prelates' sacristy, built by Ephraim Schröger in 1780 in Baroque/classical style. A Renaissance sandstone epitaph is followed by the entrance to the chapel of Jesus, with an altar by Giacopo Fontana (1740–6), and *a trompe l'oeil* dome. The easternmost chapel, closed off with a Renaissance grille, contains several noteworthy sculptures, among them the memorial to Archbishop Gembicki by Sebastiano Sala (1636–42). Next come the early Baroque **Kołudzki chapel** (1647), and the **Olszowski chapel**, whose entrance still bears original Gothic decoration of human and animal forms on the underside of the arch. The 14C **Bogoria chapel**, named after the founder of the cathedral, was extensively rebuilt in subsequent centuries, and is now dedicated to Our Lady of Częstochowa. Last in the ambulatory is the Renaissance **Dzierzgowski chapel** (1554), with two fine Renaissance tomb slabs; above that of Archbishop Dzierzgowski is a tondo with the Virgin supported by putti, a work attributed to Gian-Maria Padovano. West of the south entrance is one more Baroque/classical **chapel** (c 1778), and the New Chapter House, closed off with an excellent late Renaissance grille made in Gdańsk (17C).

The collections from the cathedral treasury have been moved to the Archdiocesan museum (see below). More Gothic sculpture, including a triptych of c 1400, can be found in the Old Chapter House, usually locked, by the nave's west wall.

Close to the cathedral stands the stone **Collegiate Church of St George**, originally 12C, but rebuilt and furnished entirely in Baroque style in 1782. Behind it, at No. 2 ul. Kolegiaty, is the **Archdiocesan Museum** (open Tues–Sat 09.00–16.00), which occupies a Baroque canonry building of 1738. The exceptionally rich display includes medieval religious art, liturgical items and vestments, coffin portraits, and a copy of the famous Gniezno doors.

Walking down the hill along UL. TUMSKA you reach the Market Square, where you can turn back for a good view of the cathedral. At the end of UL. FARNA, south of the square, stands the Gothic **Parish Church of the Holy Trinity** which acquired its Baroque elements during remodelling in 1687 and 1787.

The Franciscans, brought to Gniezno by Bolesław the Pious and the Blessed Jolanta in c 1259, built their monastery north of the square. There you can visit the **Church of the Ascension and of St Anthony**, originally early Gothic, but much altered in the 18C–20C. One of the Gothic remnants is the slender brick tower which stands to the left (north) of the Baroque west façade. The odd, asymmetrical interior, with only the south aisle preserved, was partly regothicised in the 1930s.

Further north, standing on a hill, is the **Church of St John the Baptist**, formerly belonging to the Canons Regular of the Holy Sepulchre (also known as the Knights Hospitallers). The oldest hospital in Gniezno, erected in the 13C, once stood on this site. The Knights Hospitallers, whose emblem—the Maltese cross—is visible over the entrance to the church, came from Miechów near Kraków in 1234. In 1916–20, original 14C Gothic frescoes of great artistic and historical value were discovered on the chancel vaults under a layer of plaster. These paintings, executed al secco, depict 17 heads of Old Testament kings and prophets, with scenes from the life of Jesus, SS Mary, John the Baptist, and other saints. Notice, also, the bosses and corbels of the Gothic ribbed vaults, decorated with crests, mascarons and allegorical scenes. The holes in the external south wall of the nave were drilled in the Middle Ages and used to kindle ritual fire.

On the other side of Lake Jelonek, at ul. Kostrzewskiego 1, is the **Museum of the Origins of the Polish State** (open Tues–Sat 10.00–17.00), contained in an ugly modern building by a park. The poor display, covering the pre-history of Wielkopolska and the culture of the Piasts, comprises paintings, documents, and archaeological finds from the region.

The Prehistoric Settlement at Biskupin

From Gniezno you could make a long but very worthwhile **detour** (78km) to Biskupin. To get there, head north along road 5, turning right onto a minor road about 5km before you reach Żnin. The discovery of a fortified *Prehistoric Settlement in BISKUPIN, one of the best-preserved in Europe, was a happy coincidence. A teacher picnicking with his students in 1933 on the bank of Lake Biskupin noticed some curious stakes sticking out of the water; later they proved to be part of a ring-shaped wooden palisade built thousands of years ago. The oldest finds reach back to the Paleolithic era, while some of the larger houses found beneath the mud and silt date from the Neolithic period. Most of the objects, however, originate from the early Iron Age, the period of Lusatian culture, which began around 1200 BC and lasted almost 1000 years. During its heyday, the settlement comprised about 100 houses, providing shelter to nearly a thousand people. It was abandoned around 400 BC for unknown reasons.

Archaeological work began in Biskupin in the 1930s and was resumed after the Second World War. The settlement has been partially reconstructed on the basis of the excavations. On the peninsula (originally an island), you can examine the palisade, rampart, gate, and houses with reconstructed interiors. Originally, the gate was reached from the mainland by a 120m causeway. The **museum** (open 10.00–17.00) has an exhibition on the history of the settlement and the life of its inhabitants from earliest times until the Piast period. In addition, archaeological experiments are being carried out on the peninsula, aiming to reconstruct the prehistoric techniques used by the protoslavic people in agriculture, construction, pottery and bronze production.

Apart from the archaeological park and museum, Biskupin's other attractions include a **cruise** on the lake on board the *Devil of Venice* (09.00–17.00; departures every half-hour from the jetty), and a ride on the narrow-gauge railway to nearby Wenecja (five times a day), where you can visit a **Museum of Narrow Gauge Rail** (open 09.00–18.00). On display are engines, signals, fully-equipped carriages, railway uniforms, an antique ticket puncher, and lots of other railway paraphernalia. There is even a waiting room with timetables—long out of date. Close to the museum grounds are the ruins of a 14C **castle** built by the notorious Mikołaj Nałęcz, dubbed 'the Devil of Venice'. In contrition for his wrongdoings, the castle was given by his grandson to the Gniezno diocese; it was expanded and equipped with bastions—one of the first such systems in Europe—in 1435–36. However, it fell into decline after the defeat of the Teutonic Order, when it lost its military significance.

To reach the island of Ostrów Lednicki return to Gniezno and continue west along road 5 towards Poznań. Turn right, signposted 'Komorowo' (there is also a white sign marked 'Skansen Legnicki'), to the **skansen** in Dziekanowice (open Tues–Sun 09.00–17.00). Scenically set on the shores of **Lake Lednickie**, the site is still only half finished. The plan is to recreate a typical 19C village of the Wielkopolska region, complete with a manor house, church, school, inn, and peasant farmsteads.

Drive for a further 2km towards Komorowo to the **Museum of the First Piasts** (open Apr–Oct 09.00–18.00). The first section, on the lakeside, comprises an 18C granary with a display of 10C skeletons dug up from the Lednicki cemetery, an old trestle-type windmill of 1585, and a church with a display of 10C–11C archaeological finds, notably a wooden canoe hewn from a single tree trunk. All the remaining sites are located on the island of **Ostrów Lednicki**, to which you cross by boat. Archaeological excavations indicate that the island was already inhabited in the 9C, and in the 10C became an important centre of the nascent Piast state. Its defensive potential and location—midway between Poznań and Gniezno—must have tempted the Polanian rulers to erect first the fortified stronghold, and then the stone palatium and chapel, whose foundations are still visible. In 1988, archaeologists discovered what some claim to be the baptismal font in which Mieszko I was christened. Whether this is true or not, Ostrów Lednicki was undoubtedly an important settlement and burial site of the early Piasts. The main Poznań-Gniezno road crossed lake and island over a long wooden bridge (400m). Though the palatium was destroyed by the Czech prince Bretislav in 1038, the chapel continued to be used as a parish church, and the island became a vast cemetery, one of the largest in central Europe from that period (12C–15C), with over 2000 graves.

Return to road 5 and continue west to Poznań (28km).

Poznań to Warsaw

❖ Ciążeń • Ląd

Leave Poznań on the dual carriageway (E30), which becomes a motorway after Września. Come off at the junction just before Kąty and head south (road 466).

For centuries CIĄŻEŃ was the property of the bishops of Poznań. Giuseppe Sacco began work on their summer residence in 1760, and the late Baroque **palace** was completed in 1794–1806. In 1818, it passed into private hands, after the last war becoming a school, and finally a library. Much more ornamental than the front is the back façade, with pediments and sculptures. The palace, pleasantly set by an 18C–19C park, is mainly used by Poznań University library, but also accommodates a conference centre and hotel.

The Cistercian Monastery at Ląd

Road 467 follows the Warta river east to the village of Ląd, which is dominated by the *Cistercian Monastery, a magnificent building, though relatively undiscovered by tourists, perhaps on account of its out-of-the-way location.

> Founded in c 1175 at the initiative of King Mieszko III, the monastery remained in the hands of the Cistercians until 1819. Their original Gothic church was pulled down after the Swedish Deluge (see p. 49), and replaced with a late Baroque one in 1680–1740. The main architect was **Pompeo Ferrari**, an Italian brought to Poland by the Leszczyńskis. Many changes were introduced by the Capuchins from Warsaw, who owned the monastery after 1850.
>
> In 1863, however, the monks were ousted for supporting the January Uprising (see p. 52); one of them was hanged on the market square in Konin, the rest were banished to Siberia. As the monastery had originally been run by German Cistercians, the Nazis spared it physical destruction during the Second World War.

The octagonal nave is covered with a huge, lanterned dome, a superb work by Pompeo Ferrari. In the corners of the nave stand four confessionals surmounted with sculptures representing penitent sinners (SS Peter, Magdalene, David and King Bolesław the Bold). The iron slab in the floor marks the entrance to the former crypts—now an underground theatre, with seating for 350 people, where **Nativity and Mystery Plays** are held at Christmas and Easter, respectively. Above the carved oak stalls (c 1700) hang early 18C paintings by Adam

Swach, a Franciscan monk from Poznań. Many more of his works are found in the church and monastery, notably in the 14C cloisters, and in the **Abbot's Hall** (1772), where he covered the ceiling with a huge mural, a feat which took him only 33 days (look for his self-portrait in the lower left-hand corner). The **Chapter House**, with vaults arising from a single pillar, is decorated with fanciful bosses (mascarons, roses, leaves). Cistercian monks are shown in the 16C paintings on the stalls either side of the Baroque altar.

Regain the E-30 and continue to Warsaw (230km).

Kalisz

Kalisz (250km from Warsaw and 130km from Poznań) a provincial capital, can with some justification lay claim to being the oldest city in Poland, with a history reaching back to the 2C, when it was first mentioned by Ptolemy. *Calisia*, as he called it, lay on the **Amber Route**, which linked the Empire to the Baltic sea, a source of the precious yellow resin, believed by the Romans to possess magical properties. Indeed, post-war excavations led to the discovery of many relics from those ancient times, including Roman coins. Kalisz suffered badly during the First World War, when a barrage of artillery fire from the invading German army virtually levelled the town, leaving only the churches standing.

■ **Practical information**
Hotel. ★★★★*Orbis-Prosna*. Ul. Górnośląska 53, ☎ 764-49-74. Modern and well-run. Car park, business services. 108 rooms.
Tourist information (PAPT). Ul. Garbarska 2, ☎ 764-2184.
ORBIS. Ul. Śródmiejska 26, ☎ 57-7522.
Main post office. Ul. Zamkowa.
Telephone code. (0–62).

The city centre

What remains of the historic town centre occupies the north bank of the Prosna river. In the Main Square sits the ponderous, four-winged **Town Hall** of 1920–25, its front pediment bearing the city crest. You can climb to the top of the building for a bird's eye view of the town. South of the Square, on PL. ŚW. STANISŁAWA, stands the Franciscan monastery and **church**. The early Gothic brick basilica was built during the second half of the 13C, and transformed into an aisled hall during the mid-14C. It was remodelled again in Renaissance and Mannerist style in 1599–1632 by Albin Fontana, who added elegant stucco decoration to the vaults.

Walk west along ul. Św. Stanisława, turning left into UL. ŚRÓDMIEJSKA, which crosses the Prosna river by a Neo-classical stone **bridge** (1825), adorned with the city crest. Turning right into UL. KOŚCIUSZKI you reach the **Regional Museum** (open Tues–Thur, Sat–Sun 10.00–15.00, Wed, Fri 12.00–18.00) at No. 12, with a mediocre archaeological and ethnographical display. Return to ul. Śródmiejska and continue south to see Kalisz's only surviving tollgate: the **Wrocław Toll-gate**, built in 1822. At the opposite corner of the junction stands the **Reformed Franciscan Church** (Baroque, 1665–73, rebuilt in 1919–36), with curly gables and saints in niches. Unpainted wooden Rococo furniture lends the interior a peculiar mellow charm. The shallow chancel uncomfortably houses a wooden altar, which looks as if its upward growth has been thwarted by the low vaults.

The five side altars, on the other hand, have managed to break out of their cramped niches, and crawl up towards the large lunettes under the ceiling.

Cross to the north bank of the river and skirt the edge of the **municipal park** to UL. ŁAZIENNA, on which stands the early 19C building of the **Cultural Centre**. Next to it are buildings belonging to the former Jesuit monastery, which house a **Museum** (open Wed, Fri–Sun 10.00–15.00, Thur 12.00–18.00) devoted to the Polish artist **Tadeusz Kulisiewicz**, a native of Kalisz.

Two churches stand on PL. ŚW. JÓZEFA, around the corner. The more interesting **Collegiate Church of the Ascension** has retained its Gothic chancel (1353–54) despite thorough remodelling in late Baroque style in 1790. Inside, the highlights are the Kalisz Polyptych (late Gothic, c 1500) at the end of the north aisle, and, in the treasury, a Romanesque **silver paten** (12C). Behind the church, bordering the municipal park, is a fragment of the medieval town fortifications, of which the best-preserved part is the Gothic **Dorotka Tower** (rebuilt in the 17C and later).

UL. GRODZKA ends at the **Church of St Nicholas**, the oldest church in Kalisz. The medieval brick chancel (c 1275) sports a late Gothic vault (16C); the pseudo-basilican body proper dates from the mid-14C, and was rebuilt with the addition of late Renaissance stucco decoration in 1612 by Albin Fontana. In 1869–76 the church was partly regothicised. A fire in 1973 destroyed the painting of the *Deposition* (c 1620, workshop of Peter Paul Rubens), which used to hang at the Baroque high altar (the present one is a copy). In the Polish chapel, note the modern murals by W. Tetmajer (1861–1923).

Around Kalisz

The Castle in Gołuchów

From Kalisz, road 42 takes you directly to GOŁUCHÓW (16km), the site of a picturesque *fortress-château*. It was erected in stages by the Leszczyńskis from the mid-16C to the 17C, and its two angle towers of c 1560 are the most conspicuous surviving part. The château was bought by the Działyńskis in 1856 and remodelled in 1872–85 in French Renaissance style by **Izabela Działyńska** née Czartoryska, the sister of Władysław, founder of the Czartoryski museum in Kraków (see p. 226), and wife of Jan Działyński (see p. 515). She employed Zygmunt Gorgolewski and **Maurice-Auguste Ouradou** to implement the ideas of the fashionable French architect Eugène Viollet-le-Duc, bringing in many gifted artists and craftsmen from France and from Kórnik near Poznań, the Działyńskis' family seat (see p. 514). Izabela Działyńska was also an avid art collector and connoisseur; she founded a **museum** in Gołuchów, which she bequeathed to the Polish nation, and which survived until the Second World War. Its rich collections, however, were looted first by the Nazis, then by the Russians. Most of the exhibits you see today were brought in from other places, though some were recovered from the Soviet Union in 1956 (the museum is **open** Tues–Sun 10.00–15.00, with guided tours beginning every half hour).

You enter through the peaceful arcaded courtyard, which still preserves 17C arcades in the upper section of the south wing. A long series of rooms and corridors contains furniture, busts and statues, weaponry, paintings, earthenware and porcelain, family portraits, clocks and candleholders, reliefs and murals.

Especially valuable is the surviving part of Działyńska's collection of **ancient Greek vases**, 1C–2C Roman busts, Spanish furniture, paintings by Alonso Coello (*Monarch's Feast*), Breughel, and Marcello Bacciarelli (coronation portrait of Stanisław August Poniatowski), Brussels tapestries, a staircase designed by Maurice Ouradou, and an ornate French fireplace.

Part of the château, including the former stable to the north and outbuilding to the south (**open** Tues–Fri 10.00–15.00, Sat, Sun 11.00–16.00), is devoted to the subjects of forestry and Polish bisons (*żubry*). On display is a good selection of forestry equipment and machinery, items relating to the history of forestry and environmental protection, and contemporary art, again connected with forestry. Refreshments are available in the café at the back of the outbuilding.

The château is set in a large landscaped park (1876–99), ideal for a stroll after a visit to the museum. Here you will find over 600 varieties of trees and shrubs, ponds and canals spanned by delightful bridges, a lime-tree alley, an apiary, and even a Baroque mausoleum with an artificial cave beneath it (situated on a hillock close to the outbuilding). In the forest to the west of the park you can visit a 22ha bison reserve.

Antonin ~ Prince Radziwiłł's hunting lodge

Antonin is 40km from Kalisz. Leave Kalisz on road 25 and at Ostrów Wielkopolski continue south along road 43 to Antonin, where in 1822–24 the Berlin architect **Karl Friedrich Schinkel** built a wooden hunting lodge for Prince Antoni Radziwiłł. It is a rather unusual construction—a huge octagonal space, surrounded by galleries, with a central pillar-cum-chimney in the main hall. Yet, Antonin is noted less for Radziwiłł's Romantic residence, than for the fact that Fryderyk Chopin stayed here at least twice as Radziwiłł's guest, giving concerts, and composing his *Introduction* and *Polonaise* op. 3. There is the inevitable 'Chopin room', and regular **concerts** are organised, particularly in mid-September, during the 'Chopin in the Colours of Autumn' festival. Guest rooms are available (☎ 0-62 734-81-16/736-16-51).

Zielona Góra

For centuries, Zielona Góra (119km from Poznań and 62km from the German border) was known as a producer of wine—its medieval grape plantations were the northernmost in Europe, and the wine was sour and pungent because of the cold climate. Today, you can see a vestige of the once-abundant plantations by the Orangery in Park Winny, at the corner of ul. Wrocławska and ul. Podgórna. Every September, the **Grape Harvest Festival** is celebrated as a reminder of the town's wine-making traditions.

Zielona Góra was founded in 1323 by the Duke of Głogów and Żagań, and, except for a brief interlude under the Jagiellons, it belonged to the Czech crown. The Thirty Years War and a disastrous fire in 1651 brought to an end the prosperity of the 15C–16C. The town fell into Prussian hands in 1742, and continued under German influence until 1945. It avoided significant war damage, and today much of the pre-war architecture has been preserved.

■ **Practical information**

Hotel. ★★★★*Orbis-Polan*. Ul. Staszica 9a, ☎ 327-0091. Car park, business services, wheelchair access. 78 rooms.

Tourist information. Ul. Pod Filarami 1, ☎ 324–4636.
ORBIS. Ul. Kupiecka 23, ☎ 320–2311.
Main post office. Ul. Bohaterów Westerplatte 21.
Telephone code. (0–68).

The city centre

The centre of the Market Square is dominated by the **Town Hall**, with its tall, octagonal tower (54m). Originally built in the 15C, it was damaged by fires several times, and remodelled in Neo-classical style in 1801, obliterating all Gothic elements. The tower superstructure and its three-tiered crowning date from 1678.

On UL. MICKIEWICZA, north of the square, is the former Protestant, now Catholic **Church of Our Lady of Częstochowa**, a half-timbered structure built in 1746–48, and given a Neo-classical façade and tower in 1821–8. The interior, surrounded by two-tiered galleries and covered with a flat wooden ceiling, is furnished in Rococo style.

Continue along AL. NIEPODLEGŁOŚCI, Zielona Góra's main pedestrian zone. At No. 15 is the **Regional Museum** (open Wed–Fri 11.00–17.00, Sat 10.00–15.00, Sun 10.00–16.00), with a permanent exhibition entitled 'Wine-Making: Art, Craft, Tradition', as well as contemporary art. There is a commendable art gallery next door.

Return to the Square and head east along UL. KOŚCIELNA to the **Parish Church of St Jadwiga**. This brick aisled hall was erected in the 14C, and rebuilt several times following fires. The cross vaults arising from octagonal pillars went up in the 17C–18C, replacing the Gothic ones, which have been preserved only in the south vestibule. After the original tower collapsed in 1776, it was replaced by a Neo-classical one, surmounted with a balcony and a dome. The organ loft has preserved its Baroque paintings of saints.

On PL. POCZTOWY, south of the Market Square, stands the late Gothic **Bath Tower** (also known as the Starvation Tower). It was built in 1487 as part of the town fortifications, but also served as a prison. Initially it was a gate tower with an arched passage underneath, but after cracks appeared in the walls, the passage had to be bricked up. The Baroque copper crowning was added in 1717.

Around Zielona Góra

The Skansen in Ochla

Seven kilometres south of Zielona Góra, in the village of OCHLA, is a **Skansen of Folk Architecture** (open Wed–Thur 10.00–16.00, Fri–Sun 10.00–17.00; during off-season months 10.00–14.00), a potentially good museum, marred only by the musical accompaniment played on various folk instruments and amplified by powerful loudspeakers. The buildings consist mainly of 18C–19C thatched cottages from the region, some with furnished interiors. The highlights are a hut from 1675, a barn of 1808 with a corn-grinding machine, and a wine tower with a balcony you can walk around.

Wolsztyn, and the Cistercian Monastery in Obra

Head north from Zielona Góra on road 3. In Sulechów (see p. 532), join the 32 for **WOLSZTYN**, an incongruously prosperous little town 60km from Zielona

Góra, with boutiques, fashion shops and clean streets. On UL. 5 STYCZNIA, the main thoroughfare connecting the roads to Zielona Góra and Poznań, a columned building at No. 34 houses the **Marcin Rożek Museum** (open Tues–Fri 09.00–16.00, Sat–Sun 10.00–14.00). Rożek was an outstanding sculptor and painter who perished at Auschwitz in 1944. Another famous personage connected with Wolsztyn is Robert Koch, the German bacteriologist, known for his pioneering research on tuberculosis. A **museum** devoted to him is found at No. 12 ul. Roberta Kocha.

Back in ul. 5 Stycznia, if you continue in the direction of Zielona Góra, you will pass a **Red Army Cemetery** on the left, with immaculate rows of graves, all with Soviet five stars and hammer-and-sickles in lieu of crosses. In the centre stands a monument: a bronze statue of an anonymous Red Army soldier crushing an eagle and a swastika under foot. The inscription in Russian reads: 'Eternal glory to the heroes who perished fighting for the freedom and independence of our motherland'.

Turn left just before the railway lines and follow them for about 500m. Some old steam engines and a round-house will come into view. These are part of a unique **Rail Museum**, which is also the only active steam engine shop left in Poland. The museum offers spartan accommodation ('not for ladies', in the director's own words), and pleasure trips on board old trains to any place in Poland or abroad accessible by normal rail (for information on renting a train, write to Parowozownia Wolsztyn, ul. Fabryczna 1, 64–200 Wolsztyn, ☎ Wolsztyn 20–08 ext. 393, 368 or 381).

Return to ul. 5 Stycznia and cross the tracks. Continue straight, turning right at the sign to Chorzenna, after the bridge. Soon, several thatched cottages will come into view. These belong to a small **skansen** (open Tues–Fri 10.00–16.00, Sat 10.00–14.00, Sun 12.00–16.00) with a display of regional folk architecture, tools, household items, dress, etc., including a cottage of 1706 with original interiors.

As you leave Wolsztyn on the Poznań road (32), you will pass a Neo-classical **Palace** of 1845 set on the shores of a lake. It is now a hotel.

To reach the Cistercian monastery in **OBRA**, head south from Wolsztyn on road 315. The Cistercians from Cologne founded a monastery here as early as 1231, but the present Baroque **Church of St James** dates from 1722–1756. Roughly contemporaneous are the organist's house, farm buildings, figure of St John Nepomuk, and most of the furniture and decoration, including the fine *trompe l'oeil* painting on the vaults.

Łagów Castle and its environs

❖ Sulechów • Świebodzin • Łagów • Gościkowo • Kaława

This trips takes you north of Zielona Góra through the most picturesque part of Wielkopolska—the Lubusz Lake District. The highlight is the town of Łagów with its Teutonic castle, beautifully set between two lakes.

Leave Zielona Góra on road 3 marked 'Szczecin', which crosses the massive flood plain of the Odra river—once much broader than it is now. To get to the centre of **SULECHÓW** (21km from Zielona Góra), turn off the main road following signs to Poznań (road 32), and head for the Main Square.

A plaque (1958) on the **Town Hall** tower commemorates the 130th anniversary of Chopin's sojourn in the town.

> Chopin was travelling from Berlin to Warsaw, and the carriage happened to stop in Sulechów to change horses. Bored with waiting, he began trying out a piano he found in the postmaster's office, but ended up giving a full-scale, unplanned concert. Meanwhile, the carriage was ready to go; the passengers, captivated by the virtuoso's masterly improvisation, made no complaints about the extra delay.

The inn, unfortunately, has not been preserved, but Sulechów still cultivates its association with Chopin by hosting the **November Chopin Festival** and the **Polish Competition for Young Pianists**.

The **Parish Church of St Mary**, just off the square, is a late Gothic brick aisled hall of 1499, with an earlier chancel (14C), and galleries flanking the nave. Its impressive thick-ribbed star vaults supported on octagonal pillars were constructed in 1557–62, as were the tower on the south side and the triangular west gable above the exceptionally large porch. The church bears the clear marks of Neo-Gothic restoration in the late 19C.

South of the church, at the end of UL. PIASTOWSKA, stands the late Baroque **Piast Gate**, also known as the Krosno Gate (1704). The remains of the former **castle** (16C), off the square, consist of a squat stone tower and a bricked up wing, rebuilt in Baroque style in 1750 and expanded in Neo-classical style a century later.

Regain road 3, following signs to Gorzów and continue north. In **ŚWIEBODZIN** (24km from Sulechów), begin at the **parish church** in the northeast corner of the Main Square. It was founded in 1379 by Henryk IV, Duke of Wrocław, receiving chapels and a north aisle during the 15C. Its broad west façade, bristling with pinnacles and triangular shapes, consists of five gables, corresponding to the four aisles and the nave. The east end is likewise a complex mass consisting of the apse, corner towers and gables. During reconstruction after a fire in 1640 the nave was lowered by 3m, producing a very unusual interior, broader than it is long, covered with extremely dense and intricate net vaults resting on fat pillars. The vaults may indeed bring to mind the net cast by St Peter, which they are meant to symbolise. Between the easternmost pair of pillars stands the high altar, of which the most valuable part is a late Gothic triptych (1556) containing a sculpture depicting *The Last Supper* (15C, school of Veit Stoss).

The Renaissance **Town Hall** (1547), with a battlemented tower, occupies the centre of the charming paved Market Square. The building, currently used by the municipal authorities, also houses a café (in the cellars) and a **Regional Museum** (**open** Tues–Thur 09.00–15.00, Fri–Sat 10.00–16.00, Sun 10.00–14.00). More impressive than the display itself are the vaulted rooms on the ground floor. Best of all is the tiny vaulted cell at the end, with a few objects of religious art behind a 15C–16C wrought-iron door.

Łagów Castle

Łagów is about 21km west of Świebodzin. Leave Świebodzin on road 2, following signs to Świecko. Turn right for Łagów, and watch out for the easy-to-miss sign marked 'Hotel Zamek'; the road skirts the edge of a lake.

The Knights Hospitallers of St John of Jerusalem purchased land in **Łagów** at the turn of the 13C, and raised a *castle there soon afterwards, of which the oldest surviving parts are the tower (35m; now a viewpoint) and the west wing. The castle's location—wedged between two lakes atop an artificial hill—was dictated by defence needs. Its ability to resist attack was further enhanced with the construction of a double ring of walls, of which the two late Gothic gate towers—Marchian (first half of the 16C) and Polish (15C)—form a part. Their timber superstructures are a 17C accretion. Also of later date are the arcades around the castle courtyard. The oldest preserved room is the cross-vaulted café.

Today, the castle is used as a small hotel (for 26 guests in double rooms; ☎ 0-68 341-2010/341-2119; ul. Kościuszki 3). The unusually clean lakes, three nature reserves, and beautiful beech and oak forests in the vicinity make Łagów one of the major attractions of the region.

Even before the war, when it was part of Germany, the place was much frequented by tourists from Berlin and Frankfurt, and was advertised as the smallest town in Europe—indeed, it consisted of only a single street within the outer ring of walls, with eight or nine houses. Nowadays, it is art students who seem to be the most regular visitors, contributing to the pleasantly bohemian atmosphere of the place. If you arrive in June/July, be sure not to miss the **film festival** held in the amphitheatre by the castle.

The minor roads to the east of Łagów are hazardous, at times degenerating into dirt track. To continue the tour of the area, it is better to return to Świebodzin and head north for 28km to Gościkowo on road 3.

The ***Cistercian Abbey** in Paradyż was founded in 1230 by Bonisius, the Palatine of Poznań. Having no heir, he donated all his property to the Church, including land in what is now the village of **Gościkowo**. Soon, five Cistercian monks led by abbot Henry were brought from Brandenburg to establish a monastery here. A 17C Baroque painting in the south aisle of the church, close to its east end, shows the monks receiving the foundation act from the hands of the palatine. The lower part of the painting depicts the *Battle of Legnica* (see p. 468), the Polish knights dressed in anachronistic Baroque armour.

The early Gothic brick basilica, begun in 1234, was rebuilt in late Baroque style in c 1750–88 by the royal architect Karl Martin Frantz, and extensively renovated after the Second World War. Its twin-towered west **façade** contains a sculpture of St Martin, patron of the poor, in the niche over the portal. The austere Gothic cross vaults in the nave and aisles contrast nicely with opulent Baroque decoration, particularly exuberant in the two-tiered high altar, carved from lime wood in 1739. Its two paintings—the *Ascension* and *St Martin* are by Felix Anton Scheffler. Three chapels devoted to the founders of the Cistercian order are entered from the ambulatory. The chapel of Our Lady of Paradyż at the east end of the south aisle contains a copy of a Byzantine icon; after an attempted robbery, the valuable original is now kept in a safe. In the north aisle you will find a memorial slab—unusual because Death is personified as male rather than female.

In **KAŁAWA**, 4km further north, turn left at the sign marked 'Międzyrzecki Zespół Umocnień' (the Międzyrzecz Defence Line). In a **barrack** on the left is a small display devoted entirely to bats (**open** 10.00–16.00). Some 30,000 of them, belonging to 12 different species—one of the largest populations in the world—live in the complex of underground corridors and bunkers nearby. This largely undamaged **labyrinth** stretches for more than 30km, but only a tiny section is accessible to tourists; even that takes over 2 hours to see (**open** daily during season 10.00–18.00; during off-season months on weekends; English-speaking guides available; good walking shoes and warm clothes are a must).

The corridors are part of a system of fortifications extending from the Baltic sea to the Carpathians, begun in 1934 and never completed. Despite being one of the largest and best-fortified defence lines in history, the Germans surrendered it without a fight to the Red Army in 1945. Equipped with electric power, a ventilation system, running water and sewage, it consisted of about 50 bunkers (*panzenwerks*) capable of withstanding shelling and bombing, connected by a 50km stretch of underground corridors, along which sped electric trains supplying soldiers and munitions.

Glossary

Aedicule an opening framed by two columns supporting an entablature and pediment, originally used in Classical architecture

Altarpiece an ornamental carving or painting above and behind an altar

Ambulatory a semicircular or polygonal aisle enclosing an apse or the rear of a chancel

Antependium a decorative covering for the front of an altar

Apse the semicircular or polygonal rear wall of a chancel or chapel

Architrave the lowest part of an entablature, or the horizontal frame above a door

Archivolt the underside of an arch or the ornamental moulding on the face of an arch

Art Nouveau a style in decorative arts and architecture that emerged in the late 19C as a reaction to Historicism (see below), and characterised by undulating designs styled from nature

Ashlar (ashler) a building stone with square edges and even faces

Atlantes columns, in the form of carved male figures, supporting an entablature

Attic a low wall or storey above the entablature of a building

Baldachin (baldacchino) a canopy, usually supported on columns, over an altar, tomb or pulpit

Baroque a style in European architecture that lasted approximately from the early 17C to the mid-18C, characterised by elaborate, opulent decoration, highly dramatic effects, and an emphasis on symmetry and illusion.

Basilica church with aisles lower than the nave, a clerestory, apse and no transepts. Also, in the Roman Catholic tradition, a church granted special rights of ceremony

Bema an elevated pulpit in synagogues, from which the Scripture is read

Black Madonna an icon depicting the Virgin with Child, the most revered religious painting in Poland, kept at the Paulite monastery in Częstochowa (see p. 267)

Blind arcades a range of arches attached to a wall

Boss an ornamental knob placed at the intersection of ribs in a vault

Calvary an outdoor representation of the Way of the Cross, often in the form of chapels spread out over a hillside

Capital an element crowning a column

Carillon a set of (church) bells, each producing a different tone

Cartouche an ornamental panel in the form of a scroll, often inscribed with a coat of arms (armourial cartouche)

Caryatids female atlantes (see above)

Castellan regional administrator, higher in rank than a starost

Cavalier a raised earth-platform used in military architecture

Chancel the east part of a church where the high altar is located; reserved for the clergy and choir, and sometimes separated from the nave by means of a rood screen (see below)

Chapter house a meeting place for members of a monastery where chapters of the monastic rule are read

Chełmno law a system of municipal administration modelled on Magdeburg Law, first accorded to **Chełmno** and later used in many other towns, especially in Prussia, Pomerania and Mazovia (see also p. 371)

Choir a part of the chancel reserved for singers of the divine service

Ciborium a casket or tabernacle containing the host, or a columned stone/wood canopy over the high altar

Classicism a style in art and architecture–particularly its late 18C manifestation–inspired by classical Greek and Roman models and characterised by balance, simplicity and restraint

Clerestory the upper parts of the walls of a church above the aisles, containing windows

Coffering vault, ceiling or dome decoration consisting of sunken ornamental panels

Collegiate church a church served by resident canons

Composite a column that is a combination of the Ionic and Corinthian orders

Console an ornamental bracket used to support a bust, cornice etc.

Corbel a projecting block, usually of stone, supporting a cornice, arch etc.

Cordovan a coloured leather, originally manufactured by Arab craftsmen in Cordoba, Spain

Corinthian a column with a fluted shaft and elaborately sculpted capital

Cornice the uppermost part of an entablature, or a horizontal, decorative moulding along the top of a wall

Corpus the main body of a church

Corvée obligatory labour services which in feudal society a peasant had to render to his lord in exchange for a hereditary right of use of his farm

Cour d'Honneur the front court of a palace

Crenellation a battlement

Crossing the space in a church where the nave, chancel and transepts intersect, sometimes covered by a dome

Crowning the uppermost part of a wall, façade, tower etc.

Cupola a small dome

Dansker a medieval latrine tower, often found in Teutonic castles

Dietines local assemblies

Doric a column with fluted shaft and an unadorned capital

Drum a circular or polygonal wall supporting a dome or cupola

Eclectic a mixture of various historical styles, common in the design of buildings in the late 19C

Empire a version of classicism that originated in France during Napoleon's Empire (1804–15) and characterised by

grandness, rich ornamentation and motifs of antiquity

Entablature the band at top of a column, comprising an achitrave, frieze and cornice

Finial the decorative tip of a gable, pinnacle or spire

Fresco a painting executed on wet plaster

Frieze an ornamental band along the upper part of a wall, or the middle part of an entablature between the architrave and cornice

Galilee a vestibule or chapel between the porch and nave of a church; also also known as a narthex

Gothic a style in European art and architecture that lasted approximately from the 12C to the early 16C, characterised by rib vaults, buttresses, pointed arches and large windows

Greek Cross a cross with the arms of equal length

Hall church a church with the nave and aisles of equal height and with no transepts or distinct chancel

Hansa (Hanse) another term for the Hanseatic League

Hanseatic League a medieval union of Baltic towns, established to protect their economic interests

Hetman royal field commander

Historicism the revival of historical (period) styles in architecture in the late 19C

Icon in the Eastern Orthodox tradition, a religious picture or image revered as sacred

Iconostatis in Eastern Orthodox churches, a partition, usually covered with icons, separating the nave from the sanctuary

Ionic a column with a fluted shaft and a capital adorned with volutes

Jamb the vertical frame of an arch, door or window

Jugendstil a Germanic term for Secession or Art Nouveau

Keystone the central, uppermost stone of an arch

Lantern a polygonal, windowed turret

crowning a tower, dome or the crossing of a church

Loggia a covered gallery, open on one side

Lunette a semicircular space in a vault or ceiling, or above a door or window, often decorated with a painting or relief

Machicolation a narrow gallery projecting from the walls of a castle, with openings in the floor through which boiling tar or oil could be dropped onto besieging troops

Magdeburg Law a system of municipal administration originally developed in Magdeburg in the 13C, and later adopted by other towns in Central Europe

Mannerism a late variety of the Renaissance style in architecture, originally developed in Florence and Rome and common in Europe during the 16C

Mansard roof a roof with a double slope on each of its four sides; the lower slope is steeper and longer than the upper

Mascaron a grotesque head sculpted in stone, used as decoration

Mensa a part of the altar in a Christian church (literally: table)

Monstrance a receptacle for the consecrated host

Narthex another term for galilee (see above)

Nave the main part of a church, extending from the west entrance to the chancel and often enclosed by aisles to the north and south

Ogee arch a pointed arch with an S-shaped curve on each side

Order the type of column (shaft, capital, entablature and sometimes base)

Oriel a bay (projecting) window on an upper storey of a building

Palatinate territory ruled by a palatine, equivalent to a modern voivodship

Palatine royal officer

Parapet a low wall along the edge of a roof, balcony etc., sometimes battlemented; the 'Polish parapet', as on Kraków's Cloth Hall, has a decorative cresting in place of battlements and

completely conceals the roof

Parterre a garden space with flower beds laid out in formal patterns

Paten a metal plate for holding the bread at the Eucharist

Pediment a low-pitched triangular gable above a doorway or portico; a broken pediment is one that has a gap at the apex or base

Piano Nobile the main floor of a palace or mansion, where the reception rooms are located

Pier a heavy, usually square pillar, used to reinforce masonry

Pietà a sculpture of the Virgin mourning the dead Christ

Pilaster a shallow pier or column projecting slightly from a wall

Pinnacle a small ornamented turret terminating a spire, buttress, pier etc.

Plafond a decorated ceiling or ceiling painting

Polychrome multicoloured, used to describe painted religious scenes

Polyptych a set of four or more hinged and painted panels, used as an altarpiece

Portico covered colonnade forming the main entrance of a classical building; if the columns recede into the building, the portico is called *in antis*

Predella a small painting or panel, usually in sections, attached below an altarpiece, illustrating the story of a Saint, the Life of the Virgin etc.

Putto (pl. putti) a sculpted or painted figure, usually nude, of a young male angel or cupid

Quadriga a horse-drawn, two-wheeled chariot; a sculpted representation of this often crowns the facades of buildings, as in Warsaw's Krasiński Palace

Quatrefoil a four-lobed design often found in Gothic tracery

Regency a style found in decorative arts predominant during the regency of George, Prince of Wales, and his reign as King George IV, characterised by a return to Classical Greek and Roman models

Renaissance a style in art and architecture that originated in Italy in the mid-15C, marked by the frequent use of domes and arcades, and by delicate, Roman-inspired decoration. The most original indigenous contribution to the style was the 'Polish parapet' (see above).

Retable an ornamental shelf at the back of an altar, often with carved central figures and painted wings

Rococo a late form of the Baroque style in art and architecture that originated in Paris in the early 18C, marked by profuse ornamentation, lightness and grace

Romanesque a style in European art and architecture that preceded the Gothic and derived its main impetus from the activity of monastic orders; typically, churches in this style are low, built of stone and characterised by round arches, thick walls and small windows

Rondelle a small round structure used in military architecture

Rood screen a screen below the rood, or crucifix, dividing the nave from the chancel of a church

Rotunda a small, usually domed building on a circular plan

Rustication large masonry blocks separated by prominent joints, used to give a rustic appearance to an exterior wall

Secession the Central European version of Art Nouveau

Sejm the Polish-Lithuanian (now Polish) parliament

Sgraffito a method of producing designs on plaster by incising the top coat to reveal a differently coloured one beneath

Skansen an open-air museum, usually displaying rural architecture

Socialist realism the official art and architecture doctrine of the Soviet Union and other communist countries, mainly during 1946–53, characterised by grandiose, monumental forms

Spandrel the surface between two arches in an arcade or the triangular space on either side of an arch

Starost district administrator

Stoup a vessel for holy water, usually situated near the west entrance of a church

Stucco a fine plaster used for surfacing walls or for moulding architectural decoration

Tabernacle an ornamental receptacle containing the consecrated host, usually placed at the high altar of a church

Tondo (pl. tondi) a round painting or relief

Tracery ornamental masonry forming intersecting lines in a window or blind arch, common in Gothic architecture

Transept the part of a cross-shaped church between, and at right angles to, the nave and chancel

Trefoil a three-lobed design often found in Gothic tracery

Triptych a set of three hinged and painted panels, used as an altarpiece

Trompe l'oeil literally, a deception of the eye; used to describe illusionist decoration, painted architectural perspectives, etc.

Tuscan a column with a plain (non-fluted) shaft and capital

Tympanum the recessed triangular space enclosed by a pediment (see above), often containing sculptural decoration; also, a similar space above a window or at the top of a building

Vault an arched roof or ceiling

Vistulian Gothic a version of the Gothic style found in Poland; its characteristic features include inner buttresses and low aisles, and a preponderance of brick over stone

Voivodship administrative unit, equivalent to an English county

Volute a spiral scroll found on Ionic and Corinthian capitals

Voussoir any of the wedge-shaped stones forming the curve of an arch

Index

Ł

M